Cases on Teaching Critical Thinking through Visual Representation Strategies

Leonard J. Shedletsky
University of Southern Maine, USA

Jeffrey S. Beaudry
University of Southern Maine, USA

A volume in the Advances
in Educational Technologies
and Instructional Design
(AETID) Book Series

Information Science
REFERENCE
An Imprint of IGI Global

Managing Director:	Lindsay Johnston
Production Editor:	Jennifer Yoder
Development Editor:	Allison McGinniss
Acquisitions Editor:	Kayla Wolfe
Typesetter:	Christina Henning
Cover Design:	Jason Mull

Published in the United States of America by
Information Science Reference (an imprint of IGI Global)
701 E. Chocolate Avenue
Hershey PA 17033
Tel: 717-533-8845
Fax: 717-533-8661
E-mail: cust@igi-global.com
Web site: http://www.igi-global.com

Library of Congress Cataloging-in-Publication Data

Cases on teaching critical thinking through visual representation strategies / Leonard J. Shedletsky and Jeffrey S. Beaudry, editors.
    pages cm
 Includes bibliographical references and index.
  ISBN 978-1-4666-5816-5 (hardcover) -- ISBN 978-1-4666-5817-2 (ebook) -- ISBN 978-1-4666-5819-6 (print & perpetual access) 1. Critical thinking--Study and teaching. 2. Visual aids. I. Shedletsky, Leonard, 1944-, editor of compilation.
 LB1590.3.C374 2014
 370.15'2--dc23
                                        2014005464

This book is published in the IGI Global book series Advances in Educational Technologies and Instructional Design (AETID) (ISSN: 2326-8905; eISSN: 2326-8913)

British Cataloguing in Publication Data
A Cataloguing in Publication record for this book is available from the British Library.

All work contributed to this book is new, previously-unpublished material. The views expressed in this book are those of the authors, but not necessarily of the publisher.

Advances in Educational Technologies and Instructional Design (AETID) Book Series

ISSN: 2326-8905
EISSN: 2326-8913

MISSION

Education has undergone, and continues to undergo, immense changes in the way it is enacted and distributed to both child and adult learners. From distance education, Massive-Open-Online-Courses (MOOCs), and electronic tablets in the classroom, technology is now an integral part of the educational experience and is also affecting the way educators communicate information to students.

The **Advances in Educational Technologies & Instructional Design (AETID) Book Series** is a resource where researchers, students, administrators, and educators alike can find the most updated research and theories regarding technology's integration within education and its effect on teaching as a practice.

COVERAGE

- Adaptive Learning
- Collaboration Tools
- Curriculum Development
- Digital Divide in Education
- E-Learning
- Game-Based Learning
- Hybrid Learning
- Instructional Design
- Social Media Effects on Education
- Web 2.0 and Education

IGI Global is currently accepting manuscripts for publication within this series. To submit a proposal for a volume in this series, please contact our Acquisition Editors at Acquisitions@igi-global.com or visit: http://www.igi-global.com/publish/.

Titles in this Series

For a list of additional titles in this series, please visit: www.igi-global.com

Handbook of Research on Education and Technology in a Changing Society
Victor C.X. Wang (Florida Atlantic University, USA)
Information Science Reference • copyright 2014 • 1350pp • H/C (ISBN: 9781466660465)
• US $495.00 (our price)

Educational Technology Use and Design for Improved Learning Opportunities
Mehdi Khosrow-Pour (Information Resources Management Association, USA)
Information Science Reference • copyright 2014 • 359pp • H/C (ISBN: 9781466661028)
• US $215.00 (our price)

Handbook of Research on Digital Tools for Writing Instruction in K-12 Settings
Rebecca S. Anderson (University of Memphis, USA) and Clif Mims (University of Memphis, USA)
Information Science Reference • copyright 2014 • 684pp • H/C (ISBN: 9781466659827)
• US $325.00 (our price)

Cases on Teaching Critical Thinking through Visual Representation Strategies
Leonard J. Shedletsky (University of Southern Maine, USA) and Jeffrey S. Beaudry (University of Southern Maine, USA)
Information Science Reference • copyright 2014 • 325pp • H/C (ISBN: 9781466658165)
• US $195.00 (our price)

Online Tutor 2.0 Methodologies and Case Studies for Successful Learning
Francisco José García-Peñalvo (University of Salamanca, Spain) and Antonio Miguel Seoane Pardo (University of Salamanca, Spain)
Information Science Reference • copyright 2014 • 384pp • H/C (ISBN: 9781466658325)
• US $195.00 (our price)

Andragogical and Pedagogical Methods for Curriculum and Program Development
Victor C. X. Wang (Florida Atlantic University, USA) and Valerie C. Bryan (Florida Atlantic University, USA)
Information Science Reference • copyright 2014 • 350pp • H/C (ISBN: 9781466658721)
• US $195.00 (our price)

www.igi-global.com

701 E. Chocolate Ave., Hershey, PA 17033
Order online at www.igi-global.com or call 717-533-8845 x100
To place a standing order for titles released in this series,
contact: cust@igi-global.com
Mon-Fri 8:00 am - 5:00 pm (est) or fax 24 hours a day 717-533-8661

Table of Contents

Section 1
Teaching, Learning and Assessment

Section 2
Visual Representations for Design and Collaboration

Detailed Table of Contents

Section 1
Teaching, Learning and Assessment

Chapter 1
The Nature of Third Grade Student Experiences with Concept Maps to
Support Learning of Science Concepts 1
Margaret L. Merrill, Educational Consultant, USA

To support effective science teaching, educators need methods to reveal student understandings and misconceptions of science concepts and to offer all students an opportunity to reflect on their own knowledge construction and organization. Students can benefit by engaging in scientific activities in which they build personal connections between what they learn and their own experiences. Integrating student-constructed concept mapping into the science curriculum can reveal to both students and teachers the conceptual organization and understanding of science content, which can assist in building connections between concepts and personal experiences. This chapter describes how a class of third grade students used concept maps to understand science concepts (specifically, "watershed systems"). During class discussions and interviews, students revised concept map content and structure as their ideas developed. The study's results demonstrate how students' critical thinking (self-reflection and revision) was supported as misconceptions were revealed through their construction of concept maps over time.

Robin M. Bright, University of Lethbridge, Canada
Bev Smith, Jennie Emery Elementary School, Canada

In this chapter, the authors present a case study that explores grade three students' work with informational text over a month-long unit in order to document the students' developing thinking skills about text structures and features. Students were introduced to informational mentor texts to discover insight into expository text structures and create their own "All About…" books using their own background knowledge and interests. In writing their own informational texts, the students were encouraged to use a variety of visual representation formats such as lists, checklists, and diagrams. They also used common expository text structures found in informational trade books including description, sequence, and comparison. These structures provided an overall framework for students to organize their writing and use the skills of conceptualizing, applying, synthesizing, and evaluating their knowledge. One of the primary successes of the unit for developing students' critical thinking was the opportunity to teach others about an area of expertise. Scaffolding for student success in a variety of ways throughout the writing process was also important for student learning. Choosing mentor texts with text features and visuals that were desired in the students' finished pieces provided concrete examples for the class. Overall, the reading and writing of informational text was successful in promoting the development of important thinking skills that support students' need to critically evaluate information from a variety of sources.

Cristine G. Goldberg, University of West Georgia, USA

Through discussions with colleagues at several different institutions and teachers from all levels in my home state, it became apparent that classroom teachers have little or no exposure to good concept mapping practices. Background information about why concept mapping should be a primary tool in everyone's "toolbox" for learning and performance success is not common knowledge. Secondly, practicing teachers need concrete ideas for using concept mapping by and with students. After a couple of years of conversations at conferences and informally surveying my own undergraduate and graduate students, I decided to make an attempt to fill in this void. In this chapter I have presented relevant information about where, when, and how to use concept mapping as well as critical "how-to" tips for implementation by interested parties.

This study began with the question: Can mapping improve the quality of critical thinking in essay writing in an introductory level, core curriculum class? Two sections of the course, Introduction to Communication, were compared, without mapping and with mapping. Dependent measures were: (1) the word count for summarizing the critical incident to be analyzed; (2) the number of concepts/theories employed to analyze the critical incident; (3) the number of times a connection was made between the analytical concepts/theories and the critical incident; (4) the number of words used in summarizing the essay as a whole; and (5) the total number of words in the essay. In addition, the data were analyzed for practice since there were three attempts at essay writing. Practice at writing the paper had an especial effect on writing and mapping had an especial effect on laying out the problem and applying analytical concepts to it.

Chapter 5

This chapter is based on the classroom work of a course on critical thinking designed as part of a pre-service teacher education program in English language teaching at a large-size Turkish state university. With its dual focus on both modernist and postmodern approaches to critical thinking, the course offers scope for classwork that concentrates on the skills to identify the parts and structure of arguments. To this end, argument mapping has been utilized to enhance understanding of the components of arguments and to facilitate the analysis of arguments. This chapter seeks to illustrate the materials and activities used when argument maps have been constructed during the class sessions. Furthermore, drawing from the data gathered from students' journal entries, I argue for a high interplay of the perceived efficacy of argument mapping with the content, length, and complexity of arguments as well as the anxiety evoked by these factors.

The goal of this pilot study was to develop a learner-centered teaching tool that would promote meaningful learning and enable higher education instructors to model critical thinking through concept mapping. Learner-centered approaches emphasize not only content, but the context, purpose, and process of learning. They also focus on the need for students to take responsibility for their own learning. However, students may not possess the foundational critical thinking skills necessary to be independent learners. Concept mapping allows university instructors to demonstrate basic critical thinking processes and provides students with the opportunity to practice the critical thinking that is essential to their success inside and outside the classroom. It can also facilitate meaningful learning by encouraging students to integrate new knowledge into prior knowledge structures.

Chapter 7

This chapter presents a visual sense-making activity in the field of intercultural communication. The activity is rooted in the literature that treats learning as a process of constructing meaning. The premise for this activity is that critical thinking depends on learning beyond memorizing discrete items. This perspective views learning for critical thinking as a process of integrating new knowledge into existing mental frameworks, which are then re-shaped in the learning process. The discussion begins with foundations in learning theory and their application to teaching intercultural communication. The description of the activity begins with the classroom setting and concludes with an appraisal of the activity in practice. Considerations of technology, curriculum design, and combining pedagogical strategies are included.

Chapter 8

In this chapter, the authors discuss ways in which pedagogical considerations involved in using a theoretical framework for self-inquiry and socially constructed knowledge led to the selection and implementation of mapping as a tool to (1) activate prior knowledge and scaffold content and process for pre-service educators working with students and families who are at risk and (2) assist adult learners in organizing multiple perspectives during small and large group discussion, while developing critical thinking and shared leadership skills through meaningful connections and action. A case study on how the utilization of a multidisciplinary approach informed the type of curriculum decisions to engage learners is provided. The case study also illustrates when and why instructional techniques and strategies were introduced and embedded to encourage both interactions and discussions focusing on modeling the ongoing use of skills for critical thinking and how each mapping strategy/tool served as a formative and summative assessment plan to improve verbal and written communication.

Chapter 9

Amina Sadik, Touro University Nevada, USA

Helping students learn the basic sciences and demonstrating their importance in the practice of medicine presents a challenge for the majority of medical science educators. A curriculum change of medical biochemistry was implemented to include concept mapping as a visual strategy to enhance the analytical and critical thinking skills during clinical case-based workshops. A rubric was used to give detailed feedback and provide guidance to students. A number of clinical cases were judiciously selected to illustrate specific topics. Students meet with a faculty member to discuss the concept map prior to the workshop. During such meetings, all members are asked to participate in explaining their reasoning and decision-making and to thereby justify the flow of the concept map. This activity gives students the opportunity to demonstrate their capacity to visualize their knowledge using the concept map construction.

Chapter 10

Gloria Gomez, University of Southern Denmark, Denmark
Robin Griffiths, University of Otago, New Zealand
Pooshan Navathe, University of Otago, New Zealand

Marking efficiency and timely student feedback are two aspects of assessment that may be greatly improved with concept maps (cmaps), if student learning style preference for more traditional approaches can be overcome. A semester-long exploratory case study was designed and performed in a distance aviation medicine course. This involved participant observations, interviews, and task analysis to investigate cmaps' claimed advantages for meaningful learning. The results showed that cmaps could be suitable replacements of written essays in the assessment of complex medical conceptual knowledge. Both present similar strengths and weaknesses; however, cmaps are faster to mark, and quickly reveal student understanding of a particular topic. The discussion of results is informed by relevant literature on concept mapping (cmapping) in medical education, assessment for deep understanding, and learning styles. This research can benefit online postgraduate education programmes searching for alternatives to improve the assessment process.

The Talmud, as the basic source of Jewish law and thought, continues to receive the attention of scholars and students from a wide age group. Study of the Talmud is complicated by its complex and involved legal arguments. Talmud Diagrams are designed to be easy to read graphical representations of the logic of the Talmud that aid its comprehension and retention. In particular, Talmud Diagrams are maps of legal opinions that consist of rulings on a set of related cases. Passages in the Talmud are represented by a series of Talmud Diagrams that portray the evolution of the legal opinions, challenges, and resolutions. The principle of a fortiori is embedded within the structure and formation rules of Talmud Diagrams, allowing the use of Talmud Diagrams to be extended to other legal systems where a fortiori applies.

Section 2
Visual Representations for Design and Collaboration

In this case, the authors propose a pathway of visual mapping through which the science education system from professional educators who produce representations of national and state standards to curriculum coordinators at the school district level to individual teachers and students in the classroom could be aligned in order to promote meaningful learning of a connected set of concepts. Conceptual mapping is demonstrated to be a tool that promotes critical thinking, cohesion, and meaningful learning in opposition to the learning of arbitrary facts and rote memorization. The authors offer many examples of conceptual maps that have been produced to externalize thinking at each level. This chapter provides a "synthesis case" demonstrating that not only does it require critical thinking to create conceptual maps, but, equally salient, these visual representations of our thinking catalyze further critical thinking and coherence within the science education system.

Chapter 13

Richard C. Emanuel, Alabama State University, USA
Siu Challons-Lipton, Queens University of Charlotte, USA

Critical thinking involves the comprehension and expression of the meaning or
significance of a wide variety of experiences, situations, data, events, judgments,
conventions, beliefs, rules, procedures, and criteria. One important aspect of critical thinking is the analysis, interpretation, and understanding of images. This is
generally known as visual literacy. Visual literacy may be initially demonstrated at
the basic levels of recognition and understanding – recognizing an image, telling
what a symbol means, indicating the name of a painting and/or its artist. As one
becomes more skilled at analyzing and interpreting the meaning of visuals, they
are maturing toward visual fluency. Studying a cultural artifact provides students
an opportunity to put things in context and to practice critical thinking. Two works
of art—the Coffee Cup print and The Death of Marat painting—are provided along
with example analysis.

Chapter 14

Roxanne M. O'Connell, Roger Williams University, USA

Mind mapping is a visual technique that exploits the way we actually think—
through synaptic connections and non-linear associations. Because mind mapping
gives practitioners, be they professional or student, access to subconscious observations and connections, it is a powerful thinking tool, useful in a variety of situations in business and in education. This chapter focuses on how mind mapping
fosters the kind of flexible and organic thinking vital to critical thinking and the
creative problem-solving process. It explains what is at work in the brain as we
create new knowledge and how mind mapping exploits these processes to gain
intuitive and concrete understanding in situations requiring critical thinking. A
step-by-step outline of how to mind map in both individual and group settings is
followed by examples of mind maps from both business and education.

Chapter 15

Kristen M. Snyder, Mid Sweden University, Sweden

The context of this chapter has its roots in an educational movement that recognizes the importance of preparing youth for living and working in a global community. Central to this is a belief in 1) engaging students in collaborative learning,

2) developing cultural sensitivity, 3) using digital media for communication and creativity, and 4) transforming pedagogical practice to foster reflection, divergent thinking, and creativity. The question addressed in this chapter is how teachers can use digital media and visual images to spawn divergent thinking and dialogue in a global learning context. This chapter presents a case analysis to examine evidence of inquiry-based collaborative learning and three-dimensional thinking among students when using digital images and collaborative software in a global partnership project.

    Amnon Glassner, The Kaye Academic College of Education, Israel
    Baruch B. Schwarz, The Hebrew University of Jerusalem, Israel

Several computerized representation tools have been developed to enhance collective argumentation in schools. The authors describe Digalo, a graphical synchronous e-discussion tool (Schwarz & Glassner, 2007). They focus on how Digalo was used in a program (the Kishurim program) dedicated to foster dialogic and dialectic thinking among students in lessons centered on scientific and social issues. The studies undertaken on the use of Digalo suggest important lessons that moderators of e-discussions should keep in mind while designing, moderating, and evaluating small-group e-discussions.

    Camille B. Kandiko Howson, King's College London, UK
    Ian Kinchin, University of Surrey, UK

This chapter reports on the results of a four-year longitudinal study of PhD students and their supervisors, from which the evidence gained suggests that the students tend to focus on the PhD in terms of a product to be completed (in terms of writing a thesis and peer-reviewed journals), whilst the supervisors tend to concentrate more on the process of learning and scientific development, placing the student's contribution into the wider disciplinary discourse. The structural observations from the concept maps generated within this research are that the students perceive the PhD as a linear structure, whereas the supervisors are more likely to generate a cyclic structure to illustrate the dynamic, iterative processes of research more generally. Further structural elements emerge from the analysis of the maps, indicating the need for holistic understanding of the content, structure, and meanings in concept maps and their relationship with safe spaces for the development of critical thinking.

Chapter 18

Annette deCharon, University of Maine, USA

Funded by the Centers for Ocean Sciences Education Excellence (COSEE) program of the National Science Foundation (NSF), COSEE-Ocean Systems (OS) has employed concept mapping to facilitate collaboration and communication between oceans scientists and educators. Based on iterative feedback from and interaction with its participants, COSEE-OS has developed online concept mapping software linked to an ever-growing database with thousands of scientist-vetted resources, known as the Concept-Linked Integrated Media Builder (CLIMB; cosee.umaine. edu/climb). Concomitant with the evolution of its CLIMB software functionality, COSEE-OS has transitioned from exclusively holding in-person concept mapping workshops to predominantly preparing for and delivering concept map-based Webinar events, featuring ocean science researchers. This transition to Webinars has greatly increased the number of participants and expanded the geographic reach from local to global. This chapter focuses on three key areas in which COSEE-OS has supported critical thinking: (1) the collaborative process of making meaningful learning by creating, analyzing, and improving concept maps with others; (2) facilitating subject-matter experts in the formulation of concept map-based presentations, which audiences can use to evaluate the validity of their connections and conclusions; and (3) the training of scientists to use concept mapping as a technique to more clearly delineate and explain how their research is tied to societally relevant issues. Three case descriptions on how COSEE-OS concept mapping facilitation and infrastructure have been applied to ocean sciences education efforts—both within the COSEE Network and beyond to the National Aeronautics and Space Administration (NASA)—are also presented.

Chapter 19

Patrícia Lupion Torres, Pontifical Catholic University of Paraná (PUCPr),
Brazil

Marcus Vinicius Santos Kucharski, Federal University of Technology – Paraná
(UTFPr), Brazil

Rita de Cássia Veiga Marriott, Federal University of Technology – Paraná
(UTFPr), Brazil

The act of doing research, reviewing recent literature, checking data, and articulating results and meanings are important but not enough when working with scientific publications in graduate schools. A vital part of the work is authoring an informative text that can be clear enough as to communicate findings of the study and, at the same time, reinforce chosen arguments. This chapter focuses on an experiment at a renowned Brazilian graduate school of education, which uses concept mapping and collective assessment of such maps as fundamental pre-writing stages to guide the authorship of well-thought, well-knit scientific/argumentative texts. Results indicate that the experiment was successful in making students negotiate meanings, clarify ideas and purposes, and write in an academically acceptable style. All this was conducted from a methodological standpoint that makes meaningful knowledge, collective construction, and the reflective, critical work of the author from the first draft to the final collectively written version given the foundations to perform a better job at communicating the processes and results of the investigative work.

Foreword

Most educators agree today that the teaching of critical thinking must be a primary goal for education at any age level and in every discipline. Lenny Shedletsky and Jeff Beaudry have gathered together 19 studies and reports, all of which deal with practices that use some form of graphic representation to facilitate acquisition of critical thinking skills. The scope and variety of the reports presented make this book useful to teachers at all levels of education and in all disciplines.

When I first began the study of education in the early 1950s, North American psychology was overwhelmingly dominated by behavioral psychology, and one must not speculate on the hidden workings of the brain. Only manifest behavior was to be a data source for making inferences about animal or human learning. While this psychology was sufficient for the study of learning of rats, pigeons, and cats, I failed to see any significant value in behavioral psychology for understanding human learning. My first 10 years in the study of education was marked by a frustrating search for a learning theory that could help me become a better educator. While there was Jean Piaget's work with children's reasoning in the 1920s and Frederick Bartlett's cognitive psychology in the 1930s, none of this was taught in the psychology courses I took at the University of Minnesota in the 1950s. However, when I later learned of this work, I still saw this of limited value for understanding how people acquire and use concepts in building understanding of any discipline. It was not until David Ausubel's *Psychology of Meaningful Verbal Learning* was published in 1963 that my graduate students and I finally found a theory of learning we thought could inform our work. Ausubel's theory deals with how learners acquire and use new concepts and propositions to think. More recently psychologists and educators have discovered the important work of Lev Vygotsky, done in the 1920s and '30s, showing the important role that social discourse plays in learning, and hence, the importance for using collaborative groups for new learning.

Ausubel makes the clear and important distinction between *rote learning* and *meaningful learning*. When the learner makes no effort to integrate new concepts and propositions into existing, relevant concepts in their cognitive structure, she/he is engaged in rote learning. Meaningful learning occurs when the learner actively seeks to relate new concepts and propositions to existing, relevant concepts and propositions into the learner's cognitive structure. Since learners vary in the degree to which their relevant concepts are developed, and in the amount of effort they make to achieve integration, there is a continuum from very rote learning to highly meaningful learning, not just a simple dichotomy. To achieve a high level of critical thinking in any domain of knowledge, a person must have developed highly differentiated concepts and propositions in that domain through meaningful learning.

In the early 1970s, our research group at Cornell University sought to teach 1st and 2nd grade children important basic concepts of science using audio-tutorial instruction. We had designed a series of science lessons involving a of variety hands-on activities guided by audiotape, 8mm loop films, and various illustrations. The lessons were well liked by the students and their teachers. Interviews with children after instruction showed they had made progress in learning the concepts taught, but it was difficult to show exactly what new ideas they had mastered or partially mastered. Building on Ausubelian theory, we decided to transform interview transcripts into a hierarchical arrangement of the concepts and propositions the students gave our interviewers. Thus was born the knowledge representation tool we call *concept map*. There are other similar tools, but they lack one or more of the following characteristics: all concepts are connected to other concepts with lines that include "linking words" that form a *proposition* or a clear statement of the relationship between the two concepts. Mind Maps™, for example, have no linking words and no propositions, and therefore, they cannot show explicit concept meanings. Second, concepts are arranged hierarchically from most general, most inclusive, to least general, most specific, moving from the top of the map to lower sections. This is in accordance with Ausubel's ideas of learning and cognitive structure formation. In the 1980s, I worked with the Florida Institute for Human and Machine Cognition (IHMC) to develop computer software to make it easy to make our kind of concept maps. This CmapTools software is available to anyone at no cost at: http://cmap. ihmc.us. Thousands of copies of this software are downloaded from IHMC servers every month from virtually all over the world. CmapTools also contain powerful assistance for collaborative learning and for attaching any kind of digital resource to concepts in the map.

In the chapters of this book, you will see a variety of knowledge representation tools utilized, including our form of concept maps. In every case, the goal has been to use these knowledge representation tools to help foster critical thinking. The book should be a rich resource for developing your own methods for teaching and appraising critical thinking. Moreover, helping students to become better critical thinkers also helps them to become better learners of any subject matter domain.

Moreover, students who become better learners also become more creative in applying the knowledge they have learned to new problems and situations. This is the goal every educator should seek to achieve.

Joseph D. Novak
Cornell University, USA & Florida Institute for Human and Machine
Cognition, USA

Joseph D. Novak *is currently Professor Emeritus, Cornell University, and Senior Research Scientist at IHMC. He is author or coauthor of 29 books and more than 140 book chapters and papers in professional books and journals. His Learning How to Learn (with Gowin) published in 1984 is now in 8 other languages and is widely read. He has consulted with more than 400 schools, universities, and corporations, including recent work with Procter and Gamble, NASA, Dept. of Navy, and EPRI. His recent book, Learning, Creating, and Using Knowledge: Concept Maps as Facilitative Tools in Schools and Corporations (Routledge, 2010) is currently being translated into 3 foreign languages.*

Preface

This book is about how the visual representation of ideas helps us think critically. The central idea behind the book is simple: Here are cases of how visual representation (mapping) was used to facilitate critical thinking and how it worked out. If you are new to mapping, this book will give you a very good idea of what mapping is and why visual representation is effective. You will see this "simple" mapping strategy and tool in action and how it worked out for practitioners. If you have used mapping, then you do not need us to persuade you to read on. You will be surprised to see the range of uses, the theoretical underpinning, and the effectiveness of the tool across ages and uses. It may help to hear about what motivates a teacher to give mapping a serious close look.

Some years ago, some of the faculty on our campus gathered to show one another how they were using technology in their teaching. At that gathering, Professor Jeffrey Beaudry talked about mapping and a course designer, Barbara Stebbins, at our university's Center for Technology Enhanced Learning who I had worked with closely, strongly encouraged me to get to know Jeff and to learn more about mapping. I didn't take mapping too seriously. I had looked at a brief display of mapping some years earlier and it seemed too simple, and I thought it was not likely to add much to my teaching.

A few more years went by. I continued to develop my interest in discussion, both in classroom discussion and online discussion. That interest led to a 2010 IGI Global book, *Cases on Online Discussion and Interaction: Experiences and Outcomes*, in which teachers talked about how they facilitated discussion in their classes. It became clear that a major problem in discussion was finding ways to bring about critical thinking. The more we explored critical thinking, the more it became clear that it is a real puzzle to understand what it is, how it works, and what we can do to facilitate it. Most scholarly attempts to increase critical thinking were bumping into a dead end. Researchers found that many students were only minimally improving their skills in critical thinking in college.

What this book demonstrates is that teachers using mapping techniques of various kinds, at various grade levels, with various assignments and levels of difficulty, find that mapping aids thought and writing. It facilitates critical thinking.

What began as a focus on discussion and critical thinking turned into questions about writing essays and critical thinking. A review of the scholarly literature did not offer much encouragement. However, work by a philosopher in Australia suggested that we could aid students to improve their critical thinking. Tim van Gelder had written a number of papers on his attempts to increase critical thinking in his students. He even gathered empirical evidence and showed in several papers that mapping had a real effect on critical thinking. Tim van Gelder's work strongly suggested that mapping could help. He wrote:

For the suitably skilled person, mapping a complex argument promotes clarity and insight, more rigorous and complete articulation, and more judicious evaluation. Teachers use argument mapping to help students acquire basic concepts, better understand how arguments are constructed, and enhance their reasoning skills. Argument mapping can be an effective way to improve general critical thinking skills. In the workplace, argument mapping can promote rational resolution in complex, fractious debates; improved communication of important arguments; and better decision-making. (van Gelder, 2013)

Finally, I talked to Professor Jeff Beaudry about mapping. Happily, Jeff, being a scholar and teacher, mentored me. At that time, I began to design a field study of my students' essay writing in an introductory communication course. I compared students who mapped to students who did not map on a series of analytical essays they wrote for the course. That work is presented in this book. Mapping worked. And little did I know as I did my research and as I experimented with my students' use of mapping that scholars all over the globe were using mapping, often in more intricate ways compared to my approach and with more depth of understanding of the cognitive forces operating than I had. I came to know that only after Jeff and I put out a call to teachers to write about how they used visual representation (often in the form of mapping) to facilitate critical thinking. We were thrilled with what teachers submitted for this book. The manuscripts came from many distant places, with a variety of locations on the globe, from a variety of cultures and languages, with a range of ages of participants, doing a great variety of tasks with visual representation, but the work converged on a demonstration that mapping and visual representation more generally do aid in a number of cognitive outcomes including critical thinking. A theme that weaves through all of the chapters is meaningful learning. Meaningful learning has been the passion of our teaching careers and is based in the research literature on cognition as well as personal experience as learners and teachers. Meaningful learning is echoed throughout the book, from the foreword by Joseph Novak to the very last chapter. Meaningful learning is all the more important as a central concept in this book, since we did not plan for this theme to emerge. As you read these chapters, our hope is that you will deepen your understanding of the use of mapping and visual representation, and the huge potential to improve critical thinking.

CHAPTERS

In this, I present a brief summary of each chapter. Overall, 13 out of 19 chapters focus on teachers and classrooms, and the remaining chapters treat the topics more generally or talk about critical thinking and visual representation in terms of collaboration and new social identities. What follows are executive summaries of each chapter, ranging from third grade to higher education, undergraduate and postgraduate education, from classrooms in 8 countries. Visual representations like concept maps, mind maps, and argument maps are used as displays of understanding and, most importantly, as a medium for productive collaboration.

Introduction: Thinking Critically about Visual Representations: A Visual Journey to Understand Critical Thinking (Beaudry)

Teachers are searching for ways to solve the perennial problem of how they can improve their craft and improve the quality of the learning and achievement of their students. This chapter reviews past research and discusses themes that represent all 19 case studies in this book and does this by exploring the connections of visual representations to improve critical thinking.

Chapter 1: The Nature of Third Grade Student Experiences with Concept Maps to Support Learning of Science Concepts (Merrill)

The chapter by Merrill provides an in-depth view of teaching and learning in a third grade science classroom with concept maps. Concept mapping was introduced as a strategy to increase students' understanding of watersheds, and students were asked to use the iPad app, *InspireMaps*, to do their mapping. Merrill used a modified version of the Hay and Kinchin assessment tool to score the concept maps, and conducted interviews with a sample of students throughout the unit.

Chapter 2: Critical Thinking and Writing Informational Texts in a Grade Three Classroom (Bright and Smith)

The authors examine grade three students' work with informational texts over a month-long unit to analyze students' thinking skills about text structures and features. Students were introduced to informational mentor texts to discover insight into expository text structures and create their own "All About…" using a variety of visual representation formats such as lists, checklists, and diagrams. In addition, students were taught to use common expository text structures such as description, sequence, and comparison. These structures were visual scaffolding for students to organize their writing and use the skills of conceptualizing, applying, synthesizing, and evaluating their knowledge.

Chapter 3: Examples of Concept Mapping in a School Setting: A Look at Practical Uses (Goldberg)

The chapter presents a variety of strategies for the use of mind mapping and concept mapping. It is one of the few chapter in which the mind maps are done entirely by hand. Goldberg offers a series of applications for mapping, which include reading comprehension, brainstorming, pre-writing for essays and research papers, "big picture" thinking, and others that go into the everyone's "toolbox" for learning, and performance success is not common knowledge. This chapter presents relevant information about where, when, and how to use concept mapping as well as critical "how-to" tips for implementation by interested parties.

Chapter 4: Can Mapping Improve the Quality of Critical Thinking in Essay Writing in an Introductory Level, Core Curriculum Class? (Shedletsky)

This chapter began with the question: Can mapping improve the quality of critical thinking in essay writing in an introductory level, core curriculum class? Two sections of the course, Introduction to Communication, were compared, without mapping and with mapping. Dependent measures were: (1) the word count for summarizing the critical incident to be analyzed, (2) the number of concepts/theories employed to analyze the critical incident, (3) the number of times a connection was made between the analytical concepts/theories and the critical incident, (4) the number of words used in summarizing the essay as a whole, and (5) the total number of words in the essay. In addition, the data were analyzed for practice since there were three attempts at essay writing.

Chapter 5: A Case on Teaching Critical Thinking and Argument Mapping in a Teacher Education Context (Oral)

This chapter is based on the classroom work of a course on critical thinking designed as part of a pre-service teacher education program in English language teaching at a large-size Turkish state university. With its dual focus on both modernist and postmodern approaches to critical thinking, the course offers scope for class work that concentrates on the skills to identify the parts and structure of arguments. To this end, argument mapping has been utilized to enhance understanding of the components of arguments and to facilitate the analysis of arguments.

Chapter 6: Confronting Critical Thinking Challenges "in" the College Classroom (Utah and Waters)

The chapter brings together the two key concepts of the book, critical thinking and concept mapping. The goal of this pilot study was to develop a learner-centered teaching tool that would promote meaningful learning and enable higher education instructors to model critical thinking through concept mapping. Concept mapping allows university instructors to demonstrate basic critical thinking processes and provides students with the opportunity to practice the critical thinking that is essential to their success as self-regulated learners. It can also facilitate meaningful learning by encouraging students to integrate new knowledge into prior knowledge structures.

Chapter 7: Making Sense of Intercultural Interaction (Dunsmore)

The chapter by Dunsmore on inter-cultural interaction builds on the assumption that critical thinking goes well beyond memorization, and that learners should be able to self-assess as well as assess and incorporate multiple cultural perspectives. Critical thinking means that we make judgments based on criteria, communicate the meaning of the judgment, the process, and the evidence for making it. The use of concept mapping and visualization is as important as text-based learning, lectures, and studying because it supports deep learning by incorporating prior knowledge. Visual representation of new knowledge supports the active role of the learner in the construction and co-construction of knowledge.

Chapter 8: Self-Inquiry and Group Dynamics: A Multidisciplinary Framework for Critical Thinking (Gonzalez, Frumkin, and Montgomery)

This chapter focuses on critical thinking and combines several models for visuals, concept mapping, consideration of multiple perspectives in van Gelder's visual deliberation, and illustrates how they can be used primarily for formative assessment of speaking and writing. These strategies were used to enhance shared critical reflection between faculty and students in a graduate-level capstone course. In this culminating educational experience, teachers created a supportive learning environment for students to develop the highest possible levels of critical thinking by embedding mapping in self-inquiry and collaborative group work.

Chapter 9: Teaching Critical Thinking to First-Year Medical Students through Concept Mapping (Sadik)

Sadik examined the use of concept mapping to improve knowledge of medical biochemistry and support a shift in curriculum from traditional lectures to clinical case-based problem solving. Clinical cases required clear objectives and outcomes, guiding questions for the case. In this approach, students used critical thinking for the construction of concept maps, and over a semester, students and faculty co-constructed nine concept maps in a series of small group discussions. The primary purpose for concept maps was formative assessment, although a rubric was used for scoring concept maps.

Chapter 10: Concept Maps as Replacements of Written Essays in Efficient Assessment of Complex Medical Knowledge (Gomez, Griffiths, and Navathe)

In the chapter by Gomez, Griffiths, and Navathe, concept mapping is examined as a key strategy for more efficient assessment of medical knowledge in a distance aviation medicine course. This case study examines the teacher-student interactions around concept maps in an online course setting. The authors conclude that concept maps could be suitable replacements of written essays in the assessment of complex medical conceptual knowledge; because of the efficiency and timesaving of concept maps, they are faster to read and grade, and can quickly reveal student understanding.

Chapter 11: Talmud Diagrams (Ury)

The Talmud Diagrams are unique additions to these papers about critical thinking and visual representations. The diagrams have formal rules for construction, analogous to cartographic maps that "guide students through the complex terrain of logic that characterizes passages in the Talmud." The use of diagrams reduced the cognitive load of students; since they did not need to figure out the structure of the discussion or argument, they were allowed to focus on learning the principles of the legal discussion. According to Ury, diagrams and forms of arguments are easier to remember than the specific words and text of an argument.

Chapter 12: Conceptual Mapping Facilitates Coherence and Critical Thinking in the Science Education System (Gorman and Heinze-Fry)

In this case, the authors propose a pathway of visual mapping through which the science education system from professional educators who produce representations of national and state standards to curriculum coordinators at the school district level to individual teachers and students in the classroom could be aligned in order to promote meaningful learning of a connected set of concepts. Conceptual mapping is demonstrated to be a tool that promotes critical thinking, cohesion, and meaningful learning in opposition to the learning of arbitrary facts and rote memorization. The authors offer many examples of conceptual maps that have been produced to externalize thinking at each level, and a "synthesis case" to show how students demonstrate critical thinking to create conceptual maps.

Chapter 13: Critical Thinking, Critical Looking: Key Characteristics of an Educated Person (Emanuel and Challons-Upton)

Critical thinking involves the comprehension and expression of the meaning or significance of a wide variety of experiences, situations, data, events, judgments, conventions, beliefs, rules, procedures, and criteria. One important aspect of critical thinking is the analysis, interpretation, and understanding of images. This is generally known as visual literacy. Visual literacy may be initially demonstrated at the basic levels of recognition and understanding – recognizing an image, telling what a symbol means, indicating the name of a painting and/or its artist. As one becomes more skilled at analyzing and interpreting the meaning of visuals, they are maturing toward visual fluency. In this chapter, two works of art—the "Coffee Cup" print and "The Death of Marat" painting—are provided along with example analysis.

Chapter 14: Mind Mapping for Critical Thinking (O'Connell)

Mind mapping is a visual technique that exploits the way we actually think—through synaptic connections and non-linear associations. Because mind mapping gives practitioners, be they professional or student, access to subconscious observations and connections, it is a powerful thinking tool, useful in a variety of situations in business and in education. This chapter focuses on how mind mapping fosters the kind of flexible and organic thinking vital to critical thinking and the creative problem-solving process. A step-by-step outline of how to mind map in both individual and group settings is followed by examples of mind maps from both business and education.

Chapter 15: Concept Maps, VoiceThread, and Visual Images: Helping Teachers Spawn Divergent Thinking and Dialogic Learning (Snyder)

The context of this chapter has its roots in an educational movement that recognizes the importance of preparing youth for living and working in a global community. Central to this is a belief in 1) engaging students in collaborative learning, 2) developing cultural sensitivity, 3) using digital media for communication and creativity, and 4) transforming pedagogical practice to foster reflection, divergent thinking, and creativity. The question addressed in this chapter is how teachers can use digital media and visual images to spawn divergent thinking and dialogue in a global learning context. This chapter presents a case analysis to examine evidence of inquiry-based collaborative learning and three-dimensional thinking among students when using digital images and collaborative software in a global partnership project.

Chapter 16: Learning Argumentation Practices in School with a Graphical Synchronous Discussion Tool (Glassner and Schwarz)

Several computerized representation tools have been developed to enhance collective argumentation in schools. The authors describe Digalo, a graphical synchronous e-discussion tool. They focus on how Digalo was used in a program dedicated to foster dialogic and dialectic thinking among students in lessons centered on scientific and social issues. The studies undertaken on the use of Digalo suggest important lessons that moderators of e-discussions should keep in mind while designing, moderating, and evaluating small-group e-discussions.

Chapter 17: Mapping the Doctorate: A Longitudinal Study of PhD Students and their Supervisors (Howson and Kinchin)

This chapter reports on the results of a four-year longitudinal study of PhD students and their supervisors, from which the evidence gained suggests that the students tend to focus on the PhD in terms of a product to be completed (in terms of writing a thesis and peer-reviewed journals), whilst the supervisors tend to concentrate more on the process of learning and scientific development, placing the student's contribution into the wider disciplinary discourse. The structural observations from the concept maps generated within this research are that the students perceive the PhD as a linear structure, whereas the supervisors are more likely to generate a cyclic structure to illustrate the dynamic, iterative processes of research more generally.

Chapter 18: Evolution of the Concept-Linked Integrated Media Builder (CLIMB) for Centers for Ocean Sciences Education Excellence (COSEE) Network (deCharon)

Funded by the Centers for Ocean Sciences Education Excellence (COSEE) program of the National Science Foundation (NSF), COSEE-Ocean Systems (OS) has employed concept mapping to facilitate collaboration and communication between ocean scientists and educators. This chapter focuses on three key areas in which COSEE-OS has supported critical thinking: (1) the collaborative process of making meaningful learning by creating, analyzing, and improving concept maps with others; (2) facilitating subject-matter experts in the formulation of concept map-based presentations, which audiences can use to evaluate the validity of their connections and conclusions; and (3) the training of scientists to use concept mapping as a technique to more clearly delineate and explain how their research is tied to societally relevant issues. Three case descriptions on how COSEE-OS concept mapping facilitation and infrastructure have been applied to ocean sciences education efforts—both within the COSEE Network and beyond to the National Aeronautics and Space Administration (NASA)—are also presented.

Chapter 19: Concept Maps and the Sytematization of Knowledge (Torres, Kucharski, and Marriott)

The act of doing research, reviewing recent literature, checking data, articulating results and meanings are important but not enough when working with scientific publications in graduate schools. A vital part of the work is authoring an informative text that can be clear enough as to communicate findings of the study and, at the same time, reinforce chosen arguments. This chapter focuses on an experiment at a renowned Brazilian graduate school of Education that uses Concept Mapping and collective assessment of such maps as fundamental pre-writing stages to guide the authorship of well-thought, well-knit scientific/argumentative texts. Results indicate that the experiment was successful in making students negotiate meanings, clarify ideas and purposes, and write in an academically acceptable style. All this was conducted from a methodological standpoint that makes meaningful knowledge, collective construction, and the reflective, critical work of the author from the first draft to the final collectively written version the foundation to perform a better job at communicating the processes and results of the investigative thought, well-knit scientific/argumentative texts.

OUR INVITATION FOR YOU TO READ ON

As we have collaborated over the past three years, we have maintained a level of interest and engagement about this project that goes beyond the academic; we are teachers continuing the search for a better classroom. We have come to a firm agreement, validated by these fellow teacher-practitioners, that visual representations and mapping and critical thinking are linked together and will be valuable tools to assist us in the pursuit of excellence in teaching, learning, and assessment. The case studies we have gathered in this book will provide us with resources for future collaborative, critical thinking, and visual representations. We hope they inspire teachers at all levels.

Leonard J. Shedletsky
University of Southern Maine, USA

Jeffrey S. Beaudry
University of Southern Maine, USA

Acknowledgment

We thank IGI Global for its patience with us as we put this book together. We appreciate the help from IGI, particularly our editorial staff of Christine Smith, Vince D'Imperio, and Allison McGinnis. We thank the many scholars who were willing to review manuscripts for this book.

Lenny especially wants to acknowledge and thank two University of Southern Maine professors. One is his co-editor, Jeff Beaudry, who is the original "map guy" at USM, who brought the idea of mapping to us. Jeff has been steady and patient and resilient in the face of those of us who did not catch on quickly to the merits of mapping. He must also thank Professor John Broida, a Professor of Psychology at USM, who made it possible for Lenny to analyze the data in the study. They are two generous gems amongst us.

Jeff wants to thank Lenny for his scholarly pursuit of effective and engaging pedagogy, his collaborative spirit, and his endless appetite for discussion. He has offered many versions of workshops about concept mapping over the years, but realized that for the work to go forward he needed to collaborate. From what he can see, we are mapping out a bright future. Most of all Jeff thanks his wife Judy; she has been the silent writing partner throughout the formation and production of this book.

Leonard J. Shedletsky
University of Southern Maine, USA

Jeffrey S. Beaudry
University of Southern Maine, USA

Introduction

THINKING CRITICALLY ABOUT VISUAL REPRESENTATIONS: A VISUAL JOURNEY TO UNDERSTAND CRITICAL THINKING

EXECUTIVE SUMMARY

Teachers are searching for ways to solve the perennial problem, how can they improve their craft and improve the quality of the learning and achievement of their students. These case studies present a variety of approaches to the use of visual representations to improve critical thinking; ranging from third grade to higher education, undergraduate and postgraduate education; from classrooms in eight countries. Visual representations like concept maps, mind maps and argument maps are used as displays of understanding, and, most importantly, as a medium for productive collaboration.

INTRODUCTION

Visual representations occupy a very essential, but uneasy place in the toolbox of instructional strategies. Increased access to multimedia environments supports claims that media users see more images, photos, and graphics than ever. Successful participation in a visually saturated environment requires teachers and learners to possess a thorough appreciation of how to use, interpret, and create visual and graphic information. Teachers in these case studies are grappling with the connections between visual representations, in the broadest sense, and critical thinking. The case studies that are in this book are organized into two broad sections, 1) teaching, learning and assessment (Chapters 1 – 11), and 2) visual representations for design and collaboration (Chapters 12 – 19). The first section focuses more directly on classroom teaching experiences, and the second section presents examples of how visual representations are used to promote growth of communities, to assist in the design and development of multimedia, and to provide a more in-depth understanding of visual literacy. Each of the case studies is followed by a brief list of key terms and definitions and resources for further professional development.

In addition there are several themes that characterize these scholarly contributions: 1) a deeper understanding of the connection between visual representations and critical thinking, 2) practical applications of visual representations, 3) development of map-making skills, 4) formative and summative assessment, and 5) cross-cultural communications, critical thinking and collaboration.

CRITICAL THINKING AND VISUAL REPRESENTATION

Critical thinking is identified as an essential component of 21st century skills, along with communication, collaboration and creativity (Shute, Dennen, Kim, Donmez, & Wang, 2010). What we found out in this book is that visual representation becomes an integral part of critical thinking for teachers and learners in a way that expands the types of products, feedback and efficiency for teaching, learning and assessing.

Lenny and I read these papers kept meeting and talking about the topics and our ongoing professional practice of visual representation several themes emerged. First of all, we thought that visual representation indeed has a great deal to contribute to critical thinking. In a surprising way it opened up and expanded the definition and understanding of critical thinking to fit in a wider variety of contexts than we anticipated.

We chose to concentrate on critical thinking as a highly valued competency, an amalgam of thought processes, understanding, analysis, evaluation, and creativity, which can be represented in visuals, graphic organizers, and concept map products. We also chose to use the broad term visual representation to capture the variety of practices used to illuminate and illustrate critical thinking. The authors in this book help us demonstrate the range of strategies being used, from specific argument mapping (van Gelder, 2013) and expressive mind mapping (Buzan, 1996) with illustrations and icons to structured and refined concept mapping (Novak & Gowin, 1984; Novak & Canas, 2006). The *Handbook of Research on Collaborative Learning Using Concept Mapping* (Torres & Marriott, 2010) focused on concept mapping and included topics like distance learning, e-learning, inquiry maps, online learning, online portfolios, shared concept maps and virtual teams. The book was a collection of primary research on collaborative learning and concept mapping establishing the connection between these group process and visual representations. I co-authored a paper for this book with Polly Wilson in which we examined the concept of visual literacy and formative assessment.

Our express purpose for this book was to provide a forum for teachers who would share practitioner research in the form of case studies, more interpretive and reflective, with more empirical research methods as well. We want to see examples, to know more about how teachers and researchers use visual representations to teach critical thinking, and how critical thinking is affected by visual representations.

In our textbook (Beaudry & Miller, 2014) on research literacy we depict visual representation as a literacy strategy that operates with other literacies to form the construct of research literacy. (See Figure 1) Visual representation as a field is all around us, but has not received enough attention to identify the emerging practices of visual representation and critical thinking, across educational levels and in an international and cross-cultural context. This opening chapter provides a summary of the chapters in the book, in text and visual representations of the key concepts in the field.

As Lenny and I talked and read, and mapped, and talked more about the submitted manuscripts a number of themes emerged for the book. The use of visual representations contributed to: 1) the development and clarity of critical thinking and visual representation, 2) an improved ability to analyze and evaluate complex ideas in speech and writing, 3) the progression of visual representation skills from novice to expert, 4) the improved use of formative and summative assessment, and 5) unique support for cross-cultural communications and collaboration (See Figure 2).

CRITICAL THINKING IS A COMPLEX REASONING OR THINKING SKILL MADE BETTER WITH VISUAL REPRESENTATIONS

Critical thinking and visual representations is a combination of cognitive processes and communication skills. This book explores the use of visual representations, primarily concept maps, as the tangible medium and cognitive catalyst for teach-

Figure 1. Visual representation of research literacy (Beaudry & Miller, 2014)

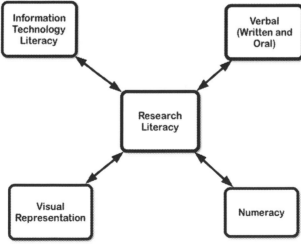

Figure 2. Themes from our book about critical thinking and visual representations

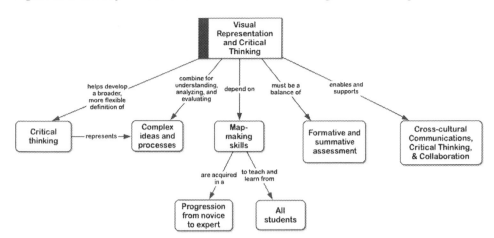

ers and students to collaborate on the acquisition and consolidation of knowledge for meaningful learning, argumentation, and problem solving. Cognitive student outcomes range from conceptual knowledge to problem solving, and skills include self-regulated learning and meta-cognition, group process and individual and collaborative construction of concept maps, and group leadership. Case studies refer to work by Facione (1995) and the new taxonomy of cognitive objectives by Anderson and Krathwohl (2001), Paul and Elder (2002), and the milestone definition of critical thinking derived from a Delphi process of 46 published experts: it "is the process of purposeful, self-regulatory judgment. This process gives reasoned consideration to evidence, contexts, conceptualizations, methods and criteria" (American Philosophical Association, 1990, p. 2). To that I would add the skill of communications, and visual representations (mind maps, concept maps and argument maps). The mapping tools provide a concrete process and product that allow learners to learn and communicate critical thinking. In their case study Gorman and Heinze-Frey write about the "emerging synergy" of critical thinking and concept mapping" in understanding and using the science education standards "as advance organizers for each succeeding level of the [education] system" (p. 5). I have more to say about these learning progressions in the following sections, learning progressions and concept mapping.

Many teachers prefaced their chapter with the observation that students were having difficulty with critical thinking tasks. As teachers do, there was a search for strategies to engage students in critical thinking and to produce tangible products as evidence. This book presents visual representations as a robust strategy to solve this problem; complementary to oral communications, group processes and written essays and capable of adding unique value to the process of critical thinking.

Critical thinking for teachers consisted of matching student learning targets to the assessment afforded by visual representations and concept maps, constructing exemplars and models of expert visual representations, learning how to read and provide formative and summative assessment of students' products, and designing technological environments based on the effective use of visual representations. In the paper by Torres et al, critical thinking goes beyond the classroom and prompts us to be critical of our society, as well.

Visual representations are flexible and can be quickly read and revised, creating a new choice for efficient assessment of critical thinking as described by Gomez et al; Shedletsky; and Merrill. A comparison of the time it took an instructor to read and evaluate (mark) visual representations and concept maps to the time it took to read and evaluate an essay for aviation medicine indicated a substantial time-saving for the instructor, not to mention the added value of the concept map as it is transferred to other tasks like group discussion, writing and assimilation of knowledge. A more efficient way to provide feedback sounds great, but needs to be validated with more research.

MAPPING SKILLS AND A LEARNING PROGRESSION

Looking at the nineteen chapters in this book overall, critical thinking is an essential goal for life-long learning, and visual representations are a gateway strategy as well as a product to demonstrate this complex reasoning target. The essays in this book extend from early elementary education (Merrill; Bright, & Smith; Goldberg) to adult, professional endeavors (Gomez et al.; Sadik). While this book is a survey of case studies critical thinking and visual representations there are several chapters that provide vivid classroom examples of visual representations, concept maps and mind maps, for grades 3 and above. While we don't have any papers from early childhood, pre-school up to second grade, this is the stage of development when drawings and marks become letters and words; until that happens pictures (doodlings and sketches) are the primary conveyors of meaning. I would argue that 5-year old children are thinking critically when they are in these transition stages. One of the messages with this book – we need to take drawing and mapping as skills to nurture throughout the progression of learning, both as artistic renderings and visual literacy tools. Goldberg's case study summarizes her teaching experiences with mind maps and concept maps across the grades, and includes a description of whole school adoption of mapping. Her suggestions are students embed drawing, clip art and graphics in their mind maps and concept maps. Teachers model the creation of mind maps and concept maps but students are constructing their own maps from the earliest grades. Goldberg's sense of critical thinking includes students' focus on details, short- and long-term memory, big picture understanding, essay writing, project planning and reading difficult text. Merrill's case study relies on the formal structure of concept maps, the node-and-link with verbs as the visual representation strategy in a science unit on watershed systems for third graders. Novak and Gowin's concept maps are words in shapes, linking lines or arrows, hierarchies (from big concept to supporting details) and cross-links. Evidence from Merrill's case study suggests that students are ready to move on a mapping progression and acquire mapping skills, which in turn support deeper understanding of complex science concepts.

Looking at the papers in this book it is remarkable to see how many teacher/authors (Shedletsky; Gonzalez & Frumkin; Gomez et al.; Sadik) discovered visual representations in their own quest for improvement, and decided to incorporate visual representations to improve critical thinking with students who had little prior knowledge or skills in visual representations. These structures are natural for some and for others may take getting used to, but the essential feature is that those structures depend on language and spatial thinking. Our sample of papers shows the relevance, impact and synergy of visual representations and critical thinking, but there are scant references to a framework for the development of visual representations, even concept maps, as a coherent, continuous developmental standard. If visual representation is such a powerful tool for critical thinking how do we proceed?

One paper is about science standards, learning progressions and expert concept maps, Gorman and Heinze-Fry use "strand maps" to represent continuity of learning from pre-K to high school level. They use the strand maps to identify 1) unsupported standards, 2) gaps in standards, 3) and patterns of divergence, convergence and cross-linking. In their artful self-assessment Gorman and Heinze-Fry stated: "It certainly took a considerable amount of critical thinking to produce these maps (note the transition of an outline style to a learning progressions style with linkages among concepts" (p. 6). This paper presents expert skeleton concept maps developed by the teachers, but there is no mention of what a learning progression for concept mapping itself would look like.

If visual representations just pop up at different points in the career of teachers and learners is there value to more explicit development of these skills from early childhood to postgraduate and professional education? Just looking at the case studies in the book the answer is YES! That said, it will take a concerted effort to accomplish this task, but it will be critical thinking for and of visual representation. We already mentioned that our case studies provide in-depth examples from grade 3 to adult learning.

We wanted to use the idea of visual representations as the overarching concept since we did not want to limit the forms of visual representations to a single category. Looking across the 19 case studies the predominant category is concept maps (Novak & Gowin, 1984), followed by argument maps (van Gelder, 2013), mind maps

(Buzan and Buzan, 2006), and Talmudic Diagrams (Ury). This book represents a convergence of these forms of visual representations, and supports speculation that visual representations represent the larger organizing category. Davies (2011) writes from an adult, higher education perspective and contends that the differences among concept mapping, mind mapping and argument mapping reflect the purposes. We agree and add that pictures and structured diagrams are complementary and synergistic with oral and written forms of communication.

So, if you are interested in adopting visual representation strategies to improve critical thinking what should you do? As teachers there should be more explicit acknowledgement of the value of visual representations in teaching standards, and deliberate exposure to all of these forms as young learners and as adults. The case studies provide numerous examples of how teachers introduced new learning strategies based on visual representations: Merrill's study of third grade science, Shedletsky's study of undergraduates, Sadik's study of first-year medical education, Gomez et al. examination of aviation medicine, Gorman and Heinze-Fry's discussion of learning progressions with high school physics classroom examples, and De Charon's development of collaborative concept maps.

Depending on the complexity of the content and the skills, training in the characteristics and construction of visual representations by individual students requires at least 4-5 opportunities for students to learn and demonstrate competence. In all these cases a variety of techniques were used to train students to understand the purpose of and to construct visual representations, including teacher modeling, brainstorming and mapping topics as a group, parking lot examples (Novak & Canas, 2006), and expert map templates. While learners may adopt this strategy quickly these case studies show the value for learners of very deliberate, repeated practice of these visual representation techniques, especially if there is an expectation to evaluate the maps with marks and scores. Even if the visual representations are used to support group dialogue and writing visual representation require feedback from teachers and self-reflection and are likely to benefit from collaborative dialogue with student peers.

BALANCING FORMATIVE AND SUMMATIVE ASSESSMENT

Most of the case studies present examples of visual representations as formative assessment products embedded in group process, self-reflection, and teachers' feedback. The purpose of formative assessment is to keep students focused on self-regulated learning and meta-cognition, especially through peer- and self-assessment. The visual representation products supported frequent self-assessment within lengthy assignments and, as a result were more likely to produce positive effects than instruction focusing only on grading or performance and summative assessment. There are seven strategies associated with formative assessment suggested by Stiggins, Arter, Chappuis, and Chappuis, (2007) that help students and teachers with formative assessment strategies.

- Where am I going?
  - Provide a clear and understandable version of the learning target.
  - Use examples and models of strong and weak work.
- Where am I now?
  - Offer regular, descriptive feedback.
  - Teach students to self-assess and set goals.
- What do I need to do to get there? How can I close the gap?
  - Design lessons to focus on one aspect of the quality at a time.
  - Teach students focused revision.
  - Engage students in self-reflection, and let them keep track of and share their learning. (p. 42)

One of the key findings in research reviews by Black and Wiliam (1998a) and Hattie (2011) is that the quality of feedback from teachers and/or other students can be a very positive component to student learning. In addition Hattie noted that concept mapping is considered to be a teaching strategy which yields a high impact on learning, if done right. These case studies provide examples of visual representations from the first, most novice stage to the end of learning in that unit or course of study, when the students can be considered "accomplished novices" (Sadik). As mentioned, Gomez et al. found that concept maps were superior to essays in formative assessment, instructor feedback to students, and improved summative assessment, more efficient understanding and grading or "marking" of student work.

Mapping and self-assessment is another formative assessment example in many case studies. There are examples of rubrics and scoring guides that use a model (Kinchin, Hay, & Adam, 2000) to differentiate types and qualities of concept maps. Their rubric provides a low score for a chain or list, a mid-level score for a spoke-and-wheel map, and the highest score for a network map with multiple levels, linking words, cross-links and a systems view. In these case studies Sadik developed a scoring guide, as did Gomez et al., but in some cases maps did not receive marks and were not scored; visual representations were used only for formative assessment. Novak and Gowin validated a scoring system for concept maps (1986) and showed how to achieve reliable scores as well. Additional research by Kinchin, Hay, and Adam (2000) developed a model for summative assessment of conceptual development using visual representations with high level of validity and reliability. The model of assessment and the accompanying rubric are incorporated in numerous case studies, e.g., for third grade science (Merrill), and by Gorman and Heinze-Fry for high school science. Concept maps, mind maps and argument maps can be incorporated into the summative assessments and grading of units and courses. However, the press to use visual representations for summative assessment cautions teachers to insure the opportunity to learn and formative assessment. These case studies showcase the dedication that teachers have to improve their craft, and the care taken to balance the development and improvement of students' knowledge and skills with the teachers' need to demonstrate empirical measures of achievement.

CROSS-CULTURAL COMMUNICATIONS AND COLLABORATION

The more I look at these case studies and the visual representations in them the more I understand the essential role of collaboration to elicit the full potential of visual representations to improve critical thinking. Moreover, there is an international, cross-cultural component to collaboration. This book has papers submitted from at least eight different countries; an international sampling of papers signifying a cross-cultural base of case studies. Our case studies recount a similar international response to *The Handbook of Research on Collaborative Learning and Concept Mapping* (Marriott & Torres, 2010). The handbook was dedicated to the exploration of collaboration and there is more in these case studies that secures the role of social as well as individual learning; the papers represented an international array as well.

The case study by Dunsmore described improvements to an undergraduate course in intercultural communication. The instructor wanted to improve the course by making a more appropriate match of the learning target, critical thinking, with the assessment method the learning target. The assessment method of selected response was insufficient to assess the collaborative problem solving in the course.

Snyder wrote her case about an international partnership of elementary and middle school teachers from China and Florida, USA. The purpose of the Gulf Oil Spill Crisis project was to support pedagogical innovation with international collaboration. The concept mapping program, *Webspiration*, and the interactive video program, *VoiceThread*, were used to engage students in collaborative learning to develop cultural sensitivity, self-reflection, divergent thinking and creativity. There is the other evidence that concept maps effective tools for cross-cultural collaboration. Gomez et al. discuss the potential for concept maps to be used in a distance-learning, online course across cultures. While it is a small case study they looked at the potential of concept maps to replace essays, and the results indicated that maps were culture-neutral and much more efficient for teachers to read and score than essays. Dunsmore presented a case for "visual sense-making" approach to intercultural communication supported by "the literature on surface and deep learning, formation of mental models, visualization, peer learning and on concept mapping" (Dunsmore, p. 3). The emphasis was on the synergy of collaboration and concept mapping to enhance intercultural communication.

CONCLUSION

The visual representations in this collection of case studies provide a fresh perspective on critical thinking, and they provide insights into collaboration and communication. As we assembled this book, reading each new paper Lenny and I were struck by the diversity of contexts, the drive to learn, and the new source of evidence, the visual representations. In our meetings we would often share new maps with each other, some of them our own and some from our students, to answer the essential question, how do visual representations improve critical thinking.

Understanding and mastery of visual representations like concept maps, mind maps and argument maps are essential graphic competencies for educators who seek to utilize and strengthen choices and strategies for learning critical thinking skills. The need is especially important in the elementary school years as learners make the transition from viewing and speaking to formal language acquisition and incorporate the rules of speaking and writing. The key message show an expanded role for visual representations throughout the elementary learning experiences and into upper grades and higher education where visual representations are effective tools for engaged, high-quality critical thinking and products that mark the progression of knowledge for teachers and learners.

The future is a challenge, create and sustain collaborative professional development for teachers in visual representations and critical thinking. The case studies in this book represent new resources, the volume represents a new collaboration, and the visual representations reveal new understandings of critical thinking. We will share our work on our website as we progress https://sites.google.com/a/maine.edu/visualliteracy20/. With this collection of case studies Lenny and I have begun to map out the next steps for our collaboration.

Jeffrey S. Beaudry
University of Southern Maine, USA

REFERENCES

American Philosophical Association. (1990). Critical thinking: A statement of expert consensus for purpose of educational assessment and instruction. Columbus, OH Center on Education and Training for Employment. College of Education. The Ohio State University (ERIC) Document Reproduction No. ED 315-423.

Anderson, L. (Ed.) and Krathwohl, D. (Ed.). A taxonomy for learning, teaching and assessing: A revision of Bloom's taxonomy of educational objectives (complete edition). New York: Longman.

Beaudry, J., & Miller, L. (forthcoming). *Research literacy: Combining method with meaning*. Los Angeles, CA: Guilford Publications.

Beaudry, J., & Wilson, P. (2010). Concept mapping and formative assessment: Elements supporting literacy and learning. In *Handbook of research on collaborative learning using concept mapping*. Hershey, PA: IGI Global Publications.

Black, P., & Wiliam, D. (1998a). Inside the black box. *Phi Delta Kappan, 80*(2), 9–21.

Black, P., & Wiliam, D. (1998b). Assessment and classroom learning. *Assessment in Education, 5*(1), 7–85. doi:10.1080/0969595980050102

Buzan, T., & Buzan, B. (2006). *The mind map book: How to use radiant thinking to maximize your brain's untapped potential*. Upper Saddle River, NJ: Pearson Education.

Davies, M. (2011). Concept mapping, mind mapping, and argument mapping: What are the differences and do they matter? *Higher Education, 62*(279), 279–301. doi:10.1007/s10734-010-9387-6

Facione, P. (1990). *Critical thinking: A statement of expert consensus for purposes of educational assessment and instruction*. Milbrae, CA: The California Academic Press.

Hattie, J. (2009). *Visible teaching*. Academic Press.

Hyerle, D. (2009). *Visual tools for transforming information into knowledge*. Thousand Oaks, CA: Corwin Press.

Novak, J., & Canas, A. (2006). *The theory underlying concept maps and how to construct them (Technical Report IHMC CmapTools 2006-01)*. Florida Institute for Human and Machine Cognition.

Novak, J., & Gowin, D. (1984). *Learning how to learn*. New York: Cambridge University Press. doi:10.1017/CBO9781139173469

Paul, R., & Elder, L. (2002). *Critical thinking: Tools for taking charge of your professional and personal life*. Upper Saddle River, NJ: Prentice Hall.

Sinatra, R., Beaudry, J., Pizzo, J., & Geisert, G. (1994). Using computer-based semantic mapping, reading, and writing approach with at-risk fourth graders. *Journal of Computing in Childhood Education, 5*(11), 93–112.

Stiggins, R., Arter, J., Chappuis, J., & Chappuis, S. (2007). *Classroom assessment for student learning*. Portland, OR: Assessment Training Institute.

Van Gelder, T. (2013). Argument mapping. In H. Pashler (Ed.), *Encyclopedia of the mind*. Thousand Oaks, CA: Sage. doi:10.4135/9781452257044.n19

ADDITIONAL READING

Beaudry, J. (2014). Visual representations and critical thinking: A repository of resources and collaborative opportunities. https://sites.google.com/a/maine.edu/visualliteracy20/

Shute, V., Dennen, V. P., Kim, Y. J., Donmez, Y., & Wang, C. Y. (2010). *21st century assessment to promote 21st century learning: The benefits of blinking*. Academic Press.

KEY TERMS AND DEFINITIONS

Argument Map: A visual representation of the structure and flow of an argument; an example of how to improve critical thinking.

Collaboration: working and learning together in a group; visual representations are effective tools to engage collaborative learning.

Concept Map: A very effective type of visual representation developed by Novak and Gowin (1984); a visual arrangement with a focus question, showing nodes (concepts) and links (verbs or connecting words) arranged in a hierarchy with cross-links to show relationships; effective as a tool for oral and written communication and collaboration.

Critical Thinking: Critical thinking is an amalgam of traits and outcomes from conceptual knowledge to problem solving; critical thinking skills include self-regulated learning and meta-cognition, group process and individual and collaborative construction of concept maps, and group leadership. Critical thinking "is the process of purposeful, self-regulatory judgment. This process gives reasoned consideration to evidence, contexts, conceptualizations, methods and criteria" (American Philosophical Association, 1990, p. 2). To that I would add the skill of communications, and visual representations (mind maps, concept maps and argument maps).

Mind Map: A very effective type of visual representation developed by Tony Buzan with a central idea and supporting ideas radiating outward to assist memorization, recall and concept organization; usually drawn by hand with accompanying graphic images.

Visual Representations: Visual graphic organizers like concept maps, mind maps, and argument maps constructed or co-constructed by teachers and learners to understand and communicate concepts, sub-concepts and details, and the relationships of concept.

Section 1
Teaching, Learning and Assessment

Chapter 1

The Nature of Third Grade Student Experiences with Concept Maps to Support Learning of Science Concepts

Margaret L. Merrill
Educational Consultant, USA

EXECUTIVE SUMMARY

To support effective science teaching, educators need methods to reveal student understandings and misconceptions of science concepts and to offer all students an opportunity to reflect on their own knowledge construction and organization. Students can benefit by engaging in scientific activities in which they build personal connections between what they learn and their own experiences. Integrating student-constructed concept mapping into the science curriculum can reveal to both students and teachers the conceptual organization and understanding of science content, which can assist in building connections between concepts and personal experiences. This chapter describes how a class of third grade students used concept maps to understand science concepts (specifically, "watershed systems"). During class discussions and interviews, students revised concept map content and structure as their ideas developed. The study's results demonstrate how students' critical thinking (self-reflection and revision) was supported as misconceptions were revealed through their construction of concept maps over time.

DOI: 10.4018/978-1-4666-5816-5.ch001

INTRODUCTION

This chapter details the benefits of using concept mapping to support students in their investigations into the study of watershed systems and the local watershed's natural history. Watershed systems were a concept the students in this study had yet to encounter in their science investigations. Improvement in critical thinking, which is foundational for the growth and development of higher thinking skills, revealed itself over time as students became more involved in the process of self-reflection while questioning their prior assumptions about science content. Additionally, this teaching approach presented a way to increase discourse between teacher and students enriching the learning experience for all. Participating students reported a growth in awareness of personal and content-focused connections leading to a strong sense of ownership over both the process and outcomes of learning.

A concept map is a hierarchical diagram made up of concepts that demonstrate the builder's understanding. The concepts are related by linking words which are placed on connecting lines between concept boxes. Linking words reveal the learner's knowledge and label the connecting lines while explaining the learner's understanding of the main concept in the concept map.

Ownership over learning can lead to increased motivation within the classroom. Motivation, which can lead to increased effort, trumps intelligence in academic achievement and is fundamental to success in school (Dweck, 2008). Student understanding of science concepts was complex as their concept maps' content and structure revealed. In the study referenced in this chapter, connections between science concepts and personal knowledge within the individual concept maps were developed as students enhanced each newly revised concept map with additional concepts. Establishing connections between content and personal experiences contributes to building student investment in learning.

Student-constructed concept maps can support cognitive change leading to meaningful learning within the domain of the natural sciences (Jonassen, Howland, Mara, & Crismond, 1999; Hay, Kinchin, & Lygo-Baker, 2008; Novak, 2002) from which the learner is then able to construct new understanding (Ausubel, Novak, & Hanesian, 1978; Novak, 2002). Through reflection on individual concept map content and structure, each student critiques his own work and is then able to construct new understanding through revision of the map by adding, deleting or rearranging concepts.

Constructivism, where all experience filters through the existing lens (perspective) of the learner, supports knowledge modification over replacement, a process which guides the learner in restructuring understandings (Smith, diSessa, & Roschelle, 1993). Gains in proficiency have more to do with cognitive restructuring, which is supported by the process of concept map construction, than with the accumulation of discrete facts. The class teacher was of the concluding opinion that student thinking shifted from isolated knowledge bits to a more global perspective supported by the interconnectedness of their science studies.

To achieve a comprehensive perspective on the science topic, students were required to engage in a process of thinking about their accumulated knowledge and then apply that information in a manner that made sense to each student. As students were able to reflect on their own journey of learning, their awareness of how their understanding contributed to outcomes progressed and was revealed through their concept maps.

Through becoming aware of how students construct understanding of science concepts, teachers are able to intercede where misconceptions override content. Using information made available from a student's concept map, a teacher may intervene so conceptual knowledge can be grounded in scientifically valid understanding, which can lead to meaningful learning.

BACKGROUND

Constructivism and the Nature of Science

Constructivism is the idea whereby each learner's prior knowledge provides the lens through which all new learning occurs (is constructed), including classroom instruction (Smith, diSessa, & Roschelle, 1993). Students (and all humans) actively construct an understanding of the world around them, reflecting that individual's unique perspective, strongly influenced by prior knowledge (Lederman, Lederman, and Bell, 2004). People interpret the world that they experience and give it meaning grounded in their prior experience. Meaning is embedded in and categorized by experience. Students are always constructing knowledge regardless of whether the context (learning situation) supports a constructivist perspective or not. Therefore, in order to support students in building meaning, gaining a perspective on their prior understandings is a key aspect of constructing knowledge.

That all students come with individualized conceptions of science, and that those understandings are not necessarily correct, are important instructional perspectives for all teachers of science. Ascertaining students' conceptions of science is necessary by the teacher in order to craft learning activities that will engage and challenge a learner's understandings of the nature of science. The identification and clarification of those existing concepts will provide a useful scaffold on which additional learning can be built. A comprehensive teaching and learning experience in the sciences cannot occur without acquiring foundational knowledge in the nature of science (Hammerich, 1998). Determining students' perceptions of the nature of science, how they understand the process and its application, helps provide a framework within which prior conceptions (misconceptions) can be revised and then modified.

Meaningful Learning

Meaningful learning refers to the quality of knowledge-building that humans experience beginning at birth. Research into meaningful learning and retention is typically focused on how meanings are constructed and then incorporated into existing cognitive structure (Ausubel, 1963). Meaningful learning has been proposed as necessary in order for cognitive growth and change to occur. According to Ausubel's learning theory, cognitive structure is organized hierarchically. The most inclusive and general concepts are positioned at the apex in the hierarchical structure of knowledge, while the less inclusive and more specific ideas and subconcepts are incorporated or subsumed within the more inclusive ones. Meaningful learning occurs when new ideas are able to be subsumed under already existing or anchoring ideas. Through subsumption, ideas that were initally dissociable from established knowledge units in the hierarchical knowledge structure are able to be retained and assimilated into the existing knowledge units. The desired outcome is for the learner to gain meaningful and useful knowledge from which to construct new understanding (Ausubel, Novak & Hanesian, 1978; Novak, 2002).

The single most important factor influencing learning (*learning* is defined within this context as acquisition, retention and transferability of knowledge) is the learner's prior knowledge, meaning what he or she already knows or thinks to be valid (Ausubel, 2000, Novak & Gowin, 1984). Using student-created concept maps, this information can be made available to the teacher.

Student Misconceptions

The study of student misconceptions in science has been the topic of discourse and investigation by the National Research Council (NRC) (2007), and others in the fields of education and social sciences (Novak & Cañas, 2008; Smith, diSessa, & Roschelle, 1993). Smith et al. (1993) uses the term misconception "to designate a student conception that produces a systematic pattern of errors" (p.119). However, children's misconceptions can present a roadmap for guiding a student from a series of misconceptions to a more authentic understanding of that particular domain (NRC, 2007). The assumptions about the natural world that young children bring to the classroom can provide jumping off points for science instructors as they create and leverage a bridge to new knowledge from established understandings (Lederman, Lederman, & Bell, 2004).

Children are likely to bring preconceived ideas to their school experiences about how the world around them works. These understandings can conflict with scientific teachings at times. It is not always easy for the teacher to discern student misconceptions. Children might appear to understand and accept a new explanation for an observed event while maintaining their original mental model of the phenomenon. An example of a concept about which students in this study were unclear was the 'water table'. The water table is the uppermost level of ground water separating the saturated zone (ground water) from the unsaturated zone (Caduto, 1985). This concept, within the context of the watershed study, came up many times. However, it existed in an abstract nature to most children; the phrase 'water table' represents an idea and is that idea. Young children do not have prior experience or personal knowledge of a 'water table'. However, they may have personal experience of drought and flooding and how those phenomena affect the level of observable and non-observable water in a system. The teacher worked at tying those ideas together for students to make the connection between classroom content and personal experience.

Children's conceptual knowledge builds on prior experiences, personal knowledge and understandings, a process that provides foundational platforms upon which subsequent knowledge is constructed. New information is acquired through direct experiences and classroom teachings. Children then endeavor to create coherent explanations reflecting earlier ontological understandings of the mechanisms and classification of things. Misconceptions arise as children work to conflate earlier conceptual understanding with scientific knowledge that is not always intuitive.

For children to learn a new concept that appears to conflict with their own scheme of understanding, conceptual restructuring is necessary. This is difficult because it asks the learner to let go of familiar and seemingly sensible explanations and restructure their body of knowledge (Smith, deSessa, & Roschelle, 1993). Experiences that confront children's naïve conceptions must be provided in the science classroom. It is through the process (guided and supported by the teacher) of confrontation and cognitive conflict, followed by resolution, that pathways to conceptual change may be achieved. An approach known as *conceptual change model* (CCM, Stepans, 2003) identifies the following four conditions to be met in order for students to be able to effect conceptual change (Stepans, 2003):

- Students must be dissatisfied with their existing views
- The new conception must appear somewhat plausible
- The new conception must be more attractive
- The new conception must have explanatory and predictive powers

The CCM is a way for students to achieve expertise within the sciences through cognitive change. A 2007 study of the National Research Council concludes, "When all students develop a coherent understanding of the organizing principles of science, they are more likely to be able to apply their knowledge appropriately and will learn new, related material more effectively" (NRC 2007, p.120).

As students work to construct new knowledge from prior knowledge, a window of opportunity presents itself for engaging the learner in thoughtful reflection on his knowledge building and organization. The learner is presented with an opportunity to direct and correct his own understanding, promoting the attributes of a critical thinker.

Concept Maps and the Facilitation of Meaningful Learning

Results from a study by Novak and Musonda (1991) demonstrate the "value of concept maps as a representational tool for cognitive developmental changes" (p. 117). Concept mapping as an evaluative tool and knowledge organizer, had its origin in a study conducted at Cornell University under the auspices of Novak and his research team. The study examined cognitive changes in students' conceptual understandings of science topics over a 12-year span of schooling (Horton, McConney, Gallo, Woods, Senn, & Hamelin, 1993; Novak, 1990; Novak & Gowin, 1984; Novak & Musonda, 1991). The study results suggests the worth of using concept maps as a tool to represent cognitive structure and change and that concept maps can support and enhance the learning and teaching continuum by creating transparency in all students' knowledge structure (Novak & Musonda).

In rote learning the pupil is presented with new knowledge unanchorable onto prior knowledge due to the manner of instruction and content. The content is memorized without subsuming the arbitrary and verbatim information into an already existing knowledge structure. When new knowledge is presented in rote fashion, the learner is challenged to make connections between what is already known and what is new. Without subsumption, new knowledge is not retained for long periods, nor is the transferability of new knowledge easily attained (Ausubel, 1963; Novak, 2002).

Concept maps are representational models of knowledge structures which can be constructed either with paper and pencil, or through the use of a computer-based software or online program. Included in these maps are *nodes* or *bubbles* housing concepts (ideas); connecting lines indicating a relationship between concepts; and linking words or phrases placed on connecting lines describing a connection between the two concepts, creating a propositional statement (Novak, 2002; Novak & Cañas, 2008). *Propositions*, also known as semantic units or units of meaning (Novak, 2002; Novak & Cañas, 2008), are made up of at least two linked concepts, along with linking words which create a complete or meaningful thought. The hierarchical levels of concept map structures can be created as *spokes* (one main idea, or hierarchical level with all sub-concepts radiating off of the central bubble), *chains* (multiple main ideas, many hierarchical levels with bubbles lined up in a chain structure), or *networks* (at least two or more main ideas, or multiple hierarchical levels with many sub-concepts connecting and interconnecting with the main ideas) (Hay, Kinchin, & Lyogo-Baker, 2008). Learning becomes increasingly visible through the use of student-created concept maps, as each concept map shape can reveal conceptual understanding of the learner.

Student-created concept maps are tools for learners to observe and reflect on how they are understanding information from classroom-based lessons. All students can organize, arrange, and make connections using either paper and pencil concept maps or computer-based concept maps.

Used within learning contexts, concept maps can provide a mode for all students to organize ideas revealing conceptual understanding through the transparent nature of concept maps (Hay, Kinchin, & Lygo-Baker, 2008) or to represent their current ideas.

RESEARCH APPROACH AND DESIGN

This chapter references a qualitative case study that was conducted in one third-grade classroom in a small rural Maine elementary school (K-8). The study lasted for six months of the school year (November – April). The participating classroom teacher ('the teacher') taught all the science units over the course of the school year. All students received training on the construction of concept maps using paper and pencil first, then the software. The teacher received instruction before the beginning of the study on the use of the software technology and constructing concept maps, and was given a brief introduction to the theoretic framework underpinning the study. Participants in the study were the classroom teacher and 10 out of a total of 15 students in the class. All classroom students created concept maps, however only participating students were interviewed.

Data were collected from three different sources: science class observations, student and teacher interviews (occurring three times) and artifacts. Artifacts comprised all science work sheets, concept maps, assessments, K-W-L charts, and the Concept Map Evaluative Rubric (CMER). The study incorporated a What I **K**now, What I **W**ant to Know, What I **L**earned (K-W-L) chart as a tool to access student prior knowledge; a pre- and post-science unit assessment comprised of a collection of selected responses and short answers; and a concept map evaluative rubric.

The students' first encounter with building concept maps was with paper and pencil, followed by the use of a concept mapping software program on classroom laptops. Student ideas were included in their concept maps, and the structural organization of the map displayed how information was organized hierarchically and connected to other concepts.

Using information made available from students' maps, the teacher intervened so concepts based in scientifically valid understanding occurred. This in turn contributed to a more grounded foundation of understanding, as evaluated through techniques described in the following section, and represented a process which provided additional support to students' learning as science concepts build upon prior understanding.

Concept Map Evaluative Rubric (CMER)

The Concept Map Evaluative Rubric (CMER) was a tool used to record changes over time on student-constructed concept maps (see Table 1). The author developed this tool with input from the participating teacher. The CMER used the conceptual work of Kinchin and Hay (2008) as a guide in its construction and organization. The resulting rubric was, however, the work of the author. The CMER displayed changes in structure, content and scientific conceptions for each participating student. The CMER captured snapshots of each student's perceptions of science content by recording frequencies of concepts, lines, and linking words (valid linking words and clearly stated propositions). The rubric also noted hierarchical structure for each concept map. Three raters evaluated each concept map. One of the raters was a science content expert who evaluated each map for science content validity. The other two raters, a non-participating teacher within the school, and the author, scored each concept map for structure by recording frequency of concepts (boxes), connecting lines, arrows on connecting lines, and linking words in addition to changes in hierarchical levels and concept validity. This included valid linking words creating a complete thought or clearly stated propositions (concept - linking word – concept). Students created a total of seven concept maps over course of the study. Each concept map was evaluated using the CMER.

The CMER was used as a road map, charting each child's journey in the building of concept maps over time. It provided a window into changes in both structure and content of each map so that the learner's progress with content could be observed and compared to other indicators of each particular student, such as the assessment, in-class discussions, and interviews where participating students, using their concept maps as guides, responded to questions focusing on content and connections. Concept maps were compared within each student's file, not student to student.

Table 1. Concept Map Evaluative Rubric (CMER)

Student:					
Date:					
Spoke		**Absent**	**Partially Present (1 – 3)**	**Present (4 – 8)**	**Abundantly Present (8+)**
	Nodes (Bubbles)				
	Connecting Lines				
	Arrows: Single Direction 2 - Way				
	Linking Words				
	Valid Linking Words				
	Clearly Stated Propositions (Concept – Link – Concept)				
		1 Low	**2**	**3**	**4 High**
	Science Content Validity				
		Not Present	**Emerging**	**Developing**	**Proficient**
	Hierarchical Levels				
	Concept Validity				
Chain		**Absent**	**Partially Present (1 – 3)**	**Present (4 – 8)**	**Abundantly Present (8+)**
	Nodes (Bubbles)				
	Connecting Lines				
	Arrows: Single Direction 2 - Way				
	Linking Words				

continued on following page

Table 1. Continued

	Valid Linking Words				
	Clearly Stated Propositions (Concept-Link-Concept)				
		1 **Low**	**2**	**3**	**4** **High**
	Science Content Validity				
		Not Present	**Emerging**	**Developing**	**Proficient**
	Hierarchical Levels				
	Concept Validity				
Network		**Absent**	**Partially Present (1 – 3)**	**Present (4 – 8)**	**Abundantly Present (8+)**
	Nodes (Bubbles)				
	Connecting Lines				
	Arrows: Single Direction 2 - Way				
	Linking Words				
	Valid Linking Words				
	Clearly Stated Propositions (Concept-Link-Concept)				
		1 **Low**	**2**	**3**	**4** **High**
	Science Content Validity				
		Not Present	**Emerging**	**Developing**	**Proficient**
	Hierarchical Levels				
	Concept Validity				

Accessing Prior Knowledge

The *What I Know, What I Want to Learn, What I Learned* (K-W-L) chart developed by Ogle (1986) is a simple approach to gain access to students' prior knowledge. Other variations on this chart have been created but the idea behind them (to generate and record students' prior knowledge before a study commences) is similar (PRC$_2$: Partner Reading and Content, Too [Ogle, 2009]; KLEW: what I Know, what I want to Learn, Evidence all students gather, Wonderings [McCloud, 2007]). During or immediately following the study of a specific science unit all students record what they learned in a K-W-L chart. This is a straightforward method of documenting what learners know or believe they know about certain topics; and is a popular method used among many elementary teachers (personal experience).

This method is a window into students' belief systems about a specific content topic over time. It does not analyze, determine, nor predict students' cognitive scheme of understanding but rather represents one approach to gaining access to students' prior knowledge (see Table 2). Table 2 is a compilation of student information entered into personal K-W-L charts over the six month study period. The dates indicate when watershed concepts were entered into K-W-L charts.

*Table 2. What I **K**now, What I **W**ant to Know, What I **L**earned chart*

KWL: A Watershed		
What I Know (November 2010) (Whole class discussion)	**What I Want to Know (April 2011)**	**What I Learned (February & April 2011)**
It has something to do with water A shed with water inside A windmill A shed with things we use on the water The name of a boat Shedding water Like a greenhouse with barrels of water	What would happen if one of the steps of the water cycle was taken out? Why doesn't the ocean overflow? What percent of water is saltwater? Why do lakes and rivers connect? I want to know why they named it the watershed? Why do people dirty up our watershed?	I learned about biomagnification And precipitation, evaporation, condensation, H$_2$O, and water cycle, and zones (Feb. 2011) I learned that what we thought it [watershed] was, was not true. That a watershed is mostly ridgelines (April 2011) I learned that where ever [*sic*] you are, you are in a watershed (April 2011) I know about pollution, oil, water, sun, food, people, life in the ocean, ponds, lakes, rivers, fish, animals, estuaries, anadromous, and catadromous fish (April 2011) Biodiversity, eutrophication, ecology, nonpoint pollution and point-source pollution (April 2011)

Assessment

The assessment protocol used throughout the study referenced in this chapter was a set of questions on general watershed concepts. Some questions named specific bodies of water in the region, while others were of a more general nature. The children took the assessment four times during the science unit (September, December, and twice in April). Questions were constructed to test student knowledge, comprehension, application, and analysis of watershed concepts. Types of questions included short answers, true/false, multiple choice, and interpretive exercise. The assessment was a way to gauge application of learned concepts in a more formalized context while applying test-taking skills.

STUDY MODEL

All learners bring to science class an epistemology personal to the individual. This knowledge represents idiosyncratic approaches, based on constructivist perspectives, to making sense of empirical events in students' lives that are not necessarily apparent to the teacher. Students develop their individual understanding of new science concepts in relation to concepts already anchored in their cognitive scheme. This may potentially lead, at times, to misconceptions on the student's part where new information is mismatched or incompatible with a preconceived notion of observable events. If the teacher guides the learner to reconstruct naïve knowledge already established within his/her hierarchical scheme of understanding, it can lead to the modification of embedded concepts resulting in valid scientific knowledge (Smith, deSessa, & Roschelle, 1993). Accessing a student's prior knowledge that he or she brings to the classroom contributes to the teacher's ability to guide learning into channels whereby new concepts can be assimilated into the existing scheme of knowledge. The benefit of using concept mapping to support and scaffold student learning provides a window for the teacher into the learner's way of thinking.

The purpose of the study referenced in this chapter was to reveal student understandings and misconceptions of science concepts through their construction of concept maps over time. The study also investigated the ways students used concept maps to understand watershed system concepts through revision of content and structure as ideas developed during class discussions and interviews. Using this approach of self-critiquing concept maps, students were encouraged to question their own perceptions and to develop an open mind receptive to possible alterations in their thinking and understanding of certain concepts. Self-critiquing by questioning prior assumptions is an integral aspect of developing critical thinking in learners.

The central research focus revealed that the nature of students' experiences with concept maps helped them and their teacher to see how the science content they were learning could be arranged, organized, connected, and hierarchically structured to represent a map of their own thoughts. Exposure to concept maps, as many students expressed in interviews and class discussion, enabled them to express the ways by which they comprehend the known information taught in class and how to relate that understanding to old and new knowledge. Some of the changes observed by the teacher throughout the study were in students' understanding of science concepts as misconceptions. Hierarchical awareness of content began to make sense as students reviewed and then reflected on their concept maps. They then correlated their map's content and structure to science class curriculum, self-correcting as a result of the evaluating process students engaged in with their concept maps. Perceiving how one idea builds onto another idea began to emerge in students' thinking. Connections between science concepts and personal links became stronger as students gained in confidence and understanding of content.

Science Study

Spreading the third-grade class study of the watershed unit over six months built flexibility into the science unit, which provided time for developing the students' areas of interest, expertise, and personal connections. Because the students had the opportunity to build understanding over time with content and through the experience of concept maps, they could experience a non-linear mode of instruction and learning. Certain science concepts were presented in multiple contexts and moved among those contexts giving students numerous exposures to similar ideas but housed in different settings. For example, the theme of *pollution* was everpresent in all the contexts of the watershed study, whether the term was embedded in a book (*The Watershed Journey of Linus the Loon,* J. Atwood), in a discussion with a representative from the state Department of Environmental Protection (DEP) or in a natural history slide show of the local watershed system. The issue of pollution was explored through causes and effects, along with long- and short-term outcomes. In other words, the students experienced many aspects of the concept of pollution within a watershed system.

This fundamental idea of pollution within the watershed system presented in a nonlinear context, challenged students' thinking about the nature of pollution and its impact on the ecosystems found within the different parts of the watershed they studied. Another theme brought up in a variety of contexts was the *water cycle*. Students learned the key phases (evaporation, condensation, transpiration and precipitation) through a game with the DEP representative during her fall visit and included it in their concept maps. The phases were displayed on one of the classroom bulletin boards. The water cycle's impact on the watershed was discussed with the students as each new element of the watershed system was introduced, such as new bodies of water, key features of a watershed, and the different plants and animals found in the varied environments within a watershed. The variability of water availability, as it connects to the different phases of the water cycle and different geologic locations, began to emerge as the topic of the water cycle. Over time the students began to see the connections between the different phases of the water cycle and different aspects of watershed-related issues. One student asked why the ocean never overflows such as a pond or river might with water spilling over its banks. The concept of overflowing was distinct from flooding in the student's mind. As the student began to understand the water cycle better, a theory developed about evaporation which helped the student in understanding that particular phase of the water cycle.

Ecology, as a study that examines the relationships between organisms and their environment, was another integral aspect of the science unit. Students experienced concepts of ecology as they learned about the interconnectedness of the different parts of the watershed and how environmental changes could effect both plants and animals. Sources and types of pollution was an important ecological concept. The students became 'pollution detectives' on the alert for sources of pollution from run-off of lawn fertilizer into the nearest body of water, or from garbage in and around watershed areas.

The overarching curricular goal of the watershed unit was for students to understand the interconnectedness within watershed systems of its many constituent parts and the impact human activities can have on the watershed. Through questioning the assumptions they held about watersheds, uncovering their individual prior knowledge, and then addressing misconceptions, students were able to develop a deeper awareness of their own knowledge construction of the watershed and its processes. The insights students provided during class discussions and interviews, in the pre and post test data, along with the key factors seen within their concept maps, attested to their heightened awareness of the sensitivity of the watershed and the interconnectedness among the different aspects of all watershed sytems.

Connections: Prior Knowledge, Science Content, and Misconceptions

The student experience of creating connections among already established concepts (prior knowledge), recognizing new connections among science concepts, and then building additional connections within concept maps provided the means for the teacher to observe and identify student misconceptions. Additionally, the structure of each map, *spoke, chain, or network*, presented to the teacher the organizational perception of main ideas and sub-concepts. On an individual student basis concept map content and structure would evolve from map to map as science topics expanded, new ones were added, and student perception of the organization of watershed issues housed within concept map bubbles grew. How students individually perceived their personal connections to science content became apparent during class discussions and interviews. Subsequently these perceptions were displayed in concept map structure and content through the inclusion of individual experience and the unique perspective each student brings to the learning experience. Once misconceptions were identified by the teacher via concept map structure, content, and student discussion she re-taught and re-contextualized the science concepts. Re-contextualizing the concept involved embedding the idea within a learning situation connected to the student's personal experience and prior knowledge.

The key, according to Lederman et al. (2004) is to make use of students' prior knowledge in order to create an anchor for embedding new information into already established concepts. Relating what they had just heard to something they were familiar with motivated students to connect actively with classroom discussions and the science content. As students engaged with the science content on a personal level, concept map content and structure evolved revealing growth in valid science conceptions growing out of misconceptions.

Through class discussion and probing questions, the teacher was able to determine whether knowledge modification had occurred in the student's understanding of the misconception. However, ascertaining whether prior knowledge and personal experience contained valid understandings of the science concept or not was necessary. Once the teacher had made that determination, she would proceed and then monitor the outcomes through discussion and concept map content. The teacher's precept for teaching science content to her students rested upon this approach. As she explained, "I think I have to bring it [content or events] back to what the kids can connect to with the most ease. Whatever is the center with that little ripple, it has to be connected to *self* and once they can connect it to *self*, they can then expand their understanding of it…" (Interview excerpt, 1/6/11).

Concept Maps: The Process of Creating Connections

The tools of the concept-mapping software provided the affordances students needed to create content and structure. Students were accustomed to the classroom laptops having used them in second grade. All students were familiar with the process for accessing the software. Additionally, students were versed in the rudimentary aspects of word-processing, such as spell check, delete, copy and paste, caps function, etc. Therefore, when the concept mapping software was introduced, students could focus on the new tools without being distracted with learning basic word processing skills.

With these new concept-mapping program tools, students were able to experiment with creating and revising their connections among watershed concepts and their personal knowledge by placing connecting lines and (sometimes) arrows at the end of some connecting lines between their science concepts. Students discussed among themselves, with the teacher, and in interviews, their intent behind the connections they had created with their connecting lines and arrows. This process provided a window of opportunity for both student and teacher to view the hierarchical organization as best representing each child's knowledge structure. The concept-mapping software tools allowed changes to be made easily within each map so students, as they were discussing content and structure, and could alter, edit, remove or add elements if they deemed it necessary and appropriate. Some students understood the process as a means of putting their ideas down on paper in a way that provided easy access to them. Others saw the process as building a comprehensive whole from bits and pieces that when put together created an understandable representation of their thoughts and ideas.

The teacher moved the students through the process of constructing concept maps in science class in a slow, methodical manner. With few exceptions this allowed software tools to be mastered, and their effectiveness to be determined and applied in a meaningful way for each student. In other words, students had the time to experiment with each software tool and learn its applications since they were using only a few new tools at a time. However, one student encountered challenges using the software tools. This student would have benefited from creating concept maps using paper and pencils. He had trouble hitting the laptop keys with accuracy, which at times led to frustration on his part. This held him up so he was not able to achieve the concept map structure with the science content he had in mind. These issues arose during interviews as he explained that the map did not look like he wanted it to look and that he had run out of time to work on it.

An interview with Student #1 on the first concept map (see Figure 1), focused on the content and connections, which highlighted the process underwent as the map was constructed and then the student explained the map. Student #1's understanding of watersheds at this point in the study was revealed through comments on the map content and structure. The map was a *spoke* shape, with most of the ideas radiating out from or into the central theme of watersheds. This map structure shows the student's centralized perception of the information being learned. The student was in the process of organizing all the watershed ideas as they connected to the main idea. Student #1 included everything that had been learned so far about watersheds in the first map. Hierarchical structure was simple (one level) while organization of concepts was not apparent in the initial map. The connections created and then explained in this interview show how Student #1's understanding of watershed-related ideas, as they connected and related to the watershed, had not evolved

Figure 1. Student #1 concept map 1

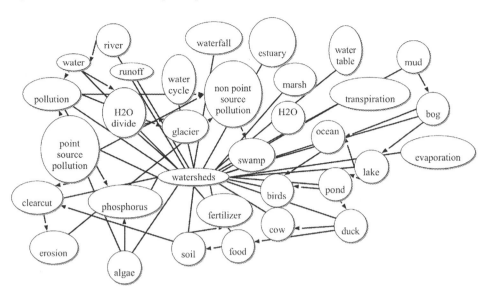

beyond the conviction that all the concepts were connected to the watershed with equal importance and validity. Student #1 was in the emergent phase of creating connections between sub-concepts.

Interview Excerpt with Student #1 (1/25/11):

Student #1: *I knew that everything would connect to watershed and then I had to think what would they be connected to [sub-concepts], so I thought of all these different things and when I thought about them, I had to add new ones too [ideas]. I thought of new ones too, its like, um well the fertilizer would go with food 'cause fertilizer is food for the soil so those three would go together and then the cows would go with the food 'cause cows eat food and the cow…*

Researcher: *Explain connections between ponds and oceans.*

Student #1: *They are both bodies of waters and so is lakes so those three connect and so does that too 'cause a bog is a part of a water [bog and watershed].*

Researcher: *Line to mud from watershed, what's that connection?*

Student #1: *Well, if there is dirt and it rains it can make mud so that has to do with water*

and then I have the evaporation that goes with watershed because that is part of the water cycle. I though the water table would probably go with evaporation because um, it just sort of … that it would go.

Researcher: *What is the water table?*

Student #1: *It's like a um, sort of like, um... the water table is sort of like, I can picture it in my head I just don't know.*

Student #4 described the process she experienced as she created her concept maps in the following interview excerpt (see Figure 2). This student was actively engaged in reflective thinking about the building process and understanding watersheds and connections as she percieved them.

Interview Excerpt with Student #4 (4/29/11):

Student #4: *...it's kind of like a puzzle of figuring what goes with what and all that.*
Researcher: *How did you figure or what process did you use when you were putting your puzzle together?*
Student #4: *I just put one [bubble] on there and thought about it and put another one on there [bubble] and I thought about that one and then, well, just put some on that that I really thought were interesting and then I would see if they [ideas] would go together.*

Figure 2. Student #4 concept map 7

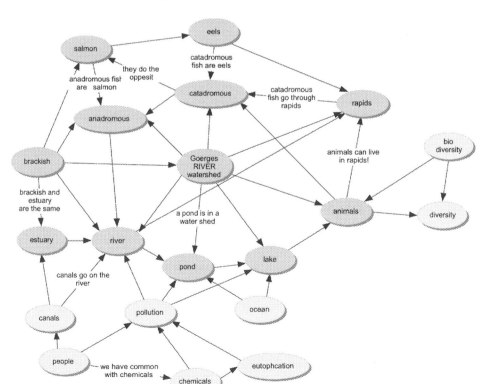

Researcher: *How did you decide what goes with something?*
Student #4: *I was thinking 'cause I had chemicals and biomagnification and then I thought about it and yeah, that would be kinda [sic] the same so I put that there.*

Of the ten participating students, eight students' concept maps evolved from basic *spoke* shape arrangements with everything they had learned about watershed systems radiating out from or into the central theme of watersheds, to complex structures. These complex structures contained science content carefully chosen to highlight each student's main idea along with sub-concepts arranged in such a way as to convey to themselves and others their understanding of their central theme. The process students experienced as they built and revised concept maps helped them make sense of their newly acquired knowledge on watersheds. Experimenting with ideas and the connections to other ideas allowed for comparisons among concepts, which in turn helped students develop an awareness of the attributes of each idea, the similarities and differences, and how one thing connects to another thing.

Using Concept Maps

Students' responses to interview questions regarding the use of concept maps in science class to help their understanding and thinking indicated the experience had been positive and helpful. Students organized information in a way that made sense to them and underscored their perception of a concept map as a learning tool (see Table 3).

The concept maps provided a way for seeing how ideas flowed and to see connections. In addition, the use of their concept maps to self-reflect on the organization and structure of important ideas was key to most of the participating students' benefits stemming from those maps. Gaining access to watershed information was essential to many; students perceived that concept maps provided this access. The following is an interview excerpt (4/28/11) with Student #3 explaining what a concept map is and what they can be used for.

Researcher: *How would you explain what a concept map is?*
Student #3: *It's sort of like a spider web one thread connecting to the other thing to pull those two ideas together.*
Researcher: *What do you use them for?*
Student #3: *I think you use them to help us improve our knowledge like our thought.*

Table 3. Types of student experiences creating and using concept map

Types of Student Experiences Creating Concept Maps	Types of Student Experiences Using Concept Maps	Categories of Experiences
"We have a main idea; I would say some stuff about [it] in other little bubbles around it and I could color code them. I would draw lines to those… I drew some bubbles around that and I would connect them with one connector [connecting line]."	"These [concept maps] were helpful because I could look back to my information about watersheds to find out, like, do watersheds have streams, do streams make waterfalls, do head waters flow to rivers..."	Memory Aid, Organizational Aid Reflection
"At first I did not understand these [concept maps] but when I got into it, I realized what I was supposed to do. I could see other people's [concept maps] and I understood everything about the watershed goes into that bubble and linking words like that would connect to that and that would connect to that…"	"…you basically got to put every one of your ideas down that you found in your head." "It probably did because if I didn't use them [concept maps] I would probably lose a bunch of stuff in my memory cause if I put it down on paper and I keep learning more and more, I kinda [sic] um, I kinda [sic] keep putting it down [in concept maps], and it kinda [sic] helps so I don't lose [forget] any of it."	Memory Aid, Organizational Aid
"I wanted to go back and forth, like I wanted to make it a shape like a circle. I can put bubbles everywhere so I can connect them to the watershed."	"…I have it all right there in front of me and I can just take ideas off of this map and throw them onto my new map that I'm making." "…I know more, I learn more and more everyday so I can put this stuff I learned again in, then the stuff that's old that I have in my other map."	Memory Aid, Organizational Aid
"I went through the process of creating the main idea, which would be watersheds, and then creating all of these little words about things that are created by a watershed, and this information that creates another piece of information."	"…It was pretty cool to figure out what a Web could do, could tell people what a watershed is."	Make Learning Visible
"I just put one [bubble] on there and thought about it and put another one on there [bubble] and I thought about that one and then, well, just put some on that that I really thought were interesting and then I would see if they [ideas] would go together."	" I used to think it was just all land and that everything was connected, but it's actually different land [different bodies of water flow into different watersheds]. Like in one place it's a different watershed so, now I know that some places we go I used to think were in the [local] watershed, but no." "I can see everything I've learned when I look at all of mine [all of his concept maps]. When the first one only had four bubbles, and I can see like with watershed map1 and was concept map 2, I can see how I developed it because I can see the same 4 [bubbles with ideas] but with more connections."	Content Clarification/ Make Learning Visible Memory Aid Reflection

Cognitive Tools for Building Concept Maps: Notes and Color-Coding

As well as the key structural components of the concept maps described in previous sections, additional tools used in the building of students' maps were *notes* and *color-coding* (see Figure 3). These cognitive tools, which are collectively defined as "instruments that can enhance the cognitive powers of learners during their thinking, problem-solving and learning" (Jonassen, Reeves, Hong, Harvey, & Peters, 1997, p. 293), supported student learners in becoming successful problem solvers as they worked over their concept map content and structure. *Notes* (a nesting text box which could be closed and opened from the bubble or node with which it was associated) provided text boxes, which could be nested within the larger concept node or bubble for students to further develop their thoughts without cluttering up their concept map organization. This aspect for many of the students was important. Students choosing to use this tool would hide, or nest these notes until called upon to talk about their map or share it with someone else, such as the teacher or the rest of the class.

Student-identified color-coding of themes was another cognitive tool for students to use in creating structure and personal coherence out of content. Boundaries regarding the use of the color-coding tool were delineated for the students before

Figure 3. Student #3 concept map 5

color-coding was integrated into the process of creating concept maps. From prior experience with these students, it had been observed that color-coding without clear guidelines resulted in artistic applications of colors often reflecting the student's preference for pattern and arrangement. Thus, the teacher waited a few weeks before introducing the color-coding application. Students were encouraged to think how certain parts of their concept maps might share similar traits, or conversely, students were asked to think about how certain ideas might be different from other watershed ideas. In order to determine color-coding of different concepts for each map, students needed to question assumptions they held about the different attributes of ideas and then to test through application of color-coding whether the assumption would apply and then pertain.

Student #3 applied color-coding and notes to Concept Map 5 (see Figure 3). The distinctions among concepts as he applied his color scheme underscored his classification system and made visible how certain connections and shared attributes are organized cognitively. Instead of color-coding all bodies of water blue, which he did for one group, he separated them into specific categories of location and quality of water (large body of water with movement: rivers, waterfalls, streams, head waters) to bodies of water with abundant vegetative growth relative to other bodies of water (marshes, bogs, and swamps).

Culture of Teaching

The learning environment fostered by the teacher provided a safe context in which her students could test, tryout, and otherwise experiment with their prior knowledge and personal connections, while working to create new connections to the science content. Providing a learning environment where students felt safe enough to test out their ideas was created through the types of interactions and relationships promoted by the teacher and responded to by the students. Giving each child opportunities to ask questions, in a learning context of respect and interest, encouraged further investigations into watershed -related topics on the students' part. Discovering students' areas of expertise and interest guided the teacher as she crafted the science content for the study of the watershed. Using different pedagogical styles with her students whereby instruction moved between an informational format to whole class discussions encouraged students to engage with new information over time in a variety of ways. This format gave the students an opportunity to reflect on their own personal knowledge and connection to what was transpiring in class, to access their prior knowledge and then to add it to the mix of ideas being shared among classmates and teacher. Asking her students, "What did you uncover today?" framed their experiences within the context of their own learning and knowledge scheme.

Within this learning environment, students' naïve knowledge on watershed systems and associated science topics, such as energy from water, notions about pollution, the impact humans (including the students) have on the quality of watershed environments for the plants and animals, and an understanding of ways to effectively preserve the natural world for subsequent generations became visible through classroom discussion, and the concept maps. The characteristics of watershed systems presented challeges for students. Many concrete examples were used before students grasped the idea that a ridgeline created the boundary differentiating one watershed from another. Students knew about many of the different bodies of water making up parts of the local watershed; they often swam in the lakes and ponds in the summer and skated on them in the winter. However their ability to differentiate characteristics between a pond and a lake or a bog and a swamp was not developed. Students were able to describe similarities, but were challenged when it came to differences. These examples provided the teacher with opportunities to re-teach and re-introduce the topics for additional class discussions.

Concept Map Evaluative Rubric

As previously mentioned, a Concept Map Evaluative Rubric (CMER) was used to record changes in students' concept map structure and science content validity and to capture qualitative changes in hierarchical structure and science content over time (see Table 1). Hierarchical and content validity were determined as 'emerging', 'developing', or 'proficient'. Changes in concept map structures were recorded as frequencies. The structures counted were the number of nodes (concept bubbles), connecting lines, arrows, linking words (valid linking words) and clearly stated propositions (concept-linking word-concept). Changes in hierarchical levels and concept validity were assessed by using qualitative parameters with *Not Present* and *Exemplary* anchoring opposite ends of the spectrum.

Frequency and qualitative trends within the CMER were observable as students progressed in determining science content validity, and as facility with the software increased. Each student constructed 7 concept maps. Concept maps 1, 2, 4, and 5 built upon the previous map in the sequence. Concept map 3 introduced a new main idea and was a stand-alone. The content of concept maps 6 and 7 featured the local watershed located within the school's community. A trend towards an increase in specific structures over time and within the same themed concept map occurred within most students' CMER. Specific structures included *nodes, connecting lines, arrows*, and *linking words*. Students perceived linking words as challenging. Over time and within the same themed concept map, the use of *linking words* and *valid linking words* also increased. Science content validity dipped with the introduction of a new theme, but then would increase in the next iteration of that same theme.

Student maps displayed the same trajectory of conceptual growth as they experienced in class. Simple maps reflecting a novice's appreciation of the new concepts were built until a more complex understanding of science content was achieved and then map structured evolved and developed. Concept maps made student thinking visible which was supported by evidence captured in each student's CMER.

Three participating students' concept maps shifted from *spoke* to *network* by concept map 7, the final one. One student ended up with a *chain structure*, while the remaining six concept maps were *spokes*. The trend in hierarchical and content validity, once again, shifted between *emerging* and *developing* for most participating students. Some students' growth with concept maps reached *proficient* levels. The *emerging* distinction indicated that signs of concept validity and hierarchical levels were discernible without the clarity of *developing* levels. *Developing* was a transitional phase between *emerging* and *proficient*. Most students were located in that phase, shifting at times between *emerging* and *developing* depending on concept map.

Presented here are two concept maps (first and fifth in the series) and accompanying CMER graphs on these particular maps from Student #9. The CMER recording for Concept Map 1 (Table 4 and Figure 4) notes a Spoke shape with 7/10 *Clearly Stated Propositions/Total # Propostions* (there was a total of 10 with 7 as Clearly

Table 4. CMER student #9 concept map 1

Concept Map 1				
#9				
Spoke	**Absent**	**Partially Present (1 - 3)**	**Present (4 - 8)**	**Abundantly Present (8+)**	
Nodes				x	
Connecting Lines				x	
Arrows: Single				x	
Arrows: 2-Way	x				
Linking Words				x	
Valid Linking Words			x		
Clearly Stated Propositions/ Total #Propositions	7/10				
	1 Low	**2**	**3**	**4 High**	
Science Content Validity			3		
	Not Present	**Emerging**	**Developing**	**Proficient**	**Exemplary**
Hierarchical Levels		x			
Concept Validity		x			

Figure 4. Student #9 concept map 1

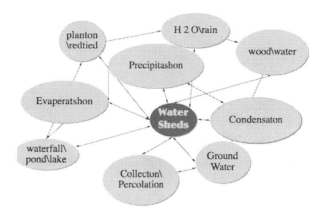

Stated Propostions). Science Content Validity ranks as a *3* and Hierarchical Levels and Concept Validity are described as *Emerging*. By the fifth concept map (Table 5 and Figure 5), the *Clearly Stated Propositions/Total # Propostions* increased to 27/28. Hierarchical Level and Concept Validity progressed to *Developing*.

Table 5. CMER student #9 concept map 5

Concept Map 5				
#9				
Spoke	**Absent**	**Partially Present (1 - 3)**	**Present (4 - 8)**	**Abundantly Present (8+)**	
Nodes				x	
Connecting Lines				x	
Arrows: Single				x	
Arrows: 2-Way	x				
Linking Words				x	
Valid Linking Words				x	
Clearly Stated Propositions/Total #Propositions	27/28				
	1 Low	**2**	**3**	**4 High**	
Science Content Validity			3		
	Not Present	**Emerging**	**Developing**	**Proficient**	**Exemplary**
Hierarchical Levels			x		
Concept Validity			x		

Figure 5. Student #9 concept map 5

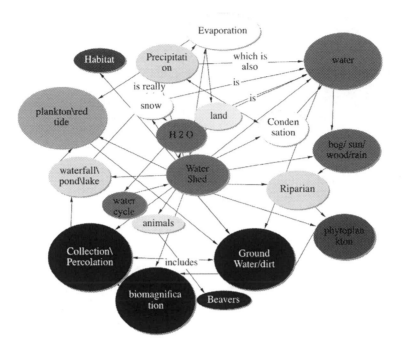

Both maps are spokes which denotes a single hierarchical level. A single hierarchical level suggests, as the CMER records, that understanding is on a continuum of development as content is introduced, discussed and connections built. Connections created between concepts chart the path of knowledge as conceptualized at that time by the student. Concept Map 1 is a brief description of a watershed. By Concept Map 5, the content has increased and the spoke structure is more detailed even though the map remains primarily a description of a watershed. The connections between concepts are conceptualizations of the student's undertstanding of watersheds. The fifth map is color-coded reflecting the student's perception of similarities among concepts (the CMER did not evaluate color-coding). Color-coding of concepts by the student reveals a type of classification system specific to that particular student's organization of concepts.

The Concept Map Evaluative Rubric caught and recorded snapshots of change between each student's concept map over time. Comparisons were specific to each student's collection of concept maps and not student-to-student. This case study explored the use and applicability of a CMER to gauge change in content knowledge over time and to assess whether concept maps did indeed affect overall learning and cognititive growth within a content area. Used in conjunction with the additional assessment protocols, the author determined the integration of concept maps positively affected student learning outcomes.

In this case study, the CMER was used for the purposes of the author's research and for the teacher's use as a means to gauge student concept map change over time as it correlated with accompanying content assessment protocols. Students did not see the CMER, as the assessments were conducted at the conclusion of the study. However, students were able to see all their maps during their exit interviews with the author and at that time appreciated the changes and growth within each series of maps.

Assessment

The students received an assessment from the teacher four times over the course of the watershed study. Questions were constructed to test student knowledge, comprehension, application, and analysis of watershed concepts. The types of questions asked included short answers, true/false, multiple choice, and interpretive exercise. The assessment was a way to gauge application of learned concepts in a more formalized context while applying test-taking skills. All students' scores increased from the lowest score of 3.25/12 at the beginning of the study (number correct over total possible correct) to the highest score of 12/12 by the end of the science study.

The assessment was used by the teacher before the science unit began in the early fall and then following significant teaching sessions. She administered the assessment in mid-December after the DEP representative had visited the class. Also during the month of December the students were introduced to key watershed system concepts. The class took the assessment again in the spring. The assessment occurred twice, during and after the local expert on the geology and history of the local watershed showed his slide show to the class. The teacher wanted a gauge of what her students took away from the content rich slide show sessions, which lasted three days. In addition, a representative from the local land trust paid a visit during that time to the class to talk about land and watershed conservation.

The frequencies in the comprehension and application sections of the assessment rose steadily over time. Students were in possession of a lot of information. Their sorting through their fund of watershed information in order to respond to this assessment required the ability to discriminate among the questions and the concepts they were familiar with and then, deciding if and what matched both in their own minds and on the assessment.

The teacher's primary choice of assessment in her class revolved around hands-on projects and formative assessments. The teacher rarely administered summative or formal tests with the exception of spelling and math tests. It is noteworthy that student scores reflected a positive trend in the analysis section of the assessment.

This reflected the teacher's unit goals of having students develop an understanding of the interconnectedness of watershed systems and human activities. The children's concept maps and the assessment collectively demonstrated their understanding of the sensitivity of the ecology of the watersheds, both on a global and local level.

A Reflection on One Student's Journey with Concept Maps

Student #2's journey of learning about watershed systems became accessible to both the student and the teacher through the inclusion of his concept maps. His concept maps reflected his approach to integrating directions with his own decisions on how to accomplish a task. However, as was detailed with many of his maps, the student was able to develop and explain his conceptions (and misconceptions), progression of thoughts, and how different concepts connected and affected others on his maps. The student's interest in science engaged him in class discussions providing him with a forum for sharing his background knowledge and personal connections to current topics under discussion. Pollution of his local watershed was an important discussion point for Student #2 both in class and during interviews. During interviews, this student often shared that his concept maps were not complete (or the way he wanted them) because there had not been enough time to work on them. However, the lack of completeness did not deter him from fully discussing watershed concepts he brought up in response to questions during interviews.

The overall progression of structure and content throughout this student's concept maps reveals a development of ideas through the process of self-reflection and then revision. Also, Student #2's use of the concept map to organize the watershed topics he chose to include along with growth in appreciation of the interconnectedness of watershed systems about which he was learning, especially his local watershed was made visible. He was able to acknowledge his assumptions (prior knowledge) about watershed systems and then self-correct through concept map revision. His sensitivity and awareness of that interconnectivity among the watershed systems was revealed in his complex array of connecting (linking) lines and arrows. His system of connections also displayed his conceptions (and misconceptions) of watershed concepts.

In Figure 6, Student #2 has included many watershed concepts from the class word list. Concept Map 1 is a spoke shape, but with some variation in bubble and connecting line arrangement. He has included arrows on the connecting lines and made connections between phases of the water cycle. There is a connection between collection/percolation and groundwater. All his concepts connect to the central watershed bubble.

Figure 6. Student #2 concept map 1

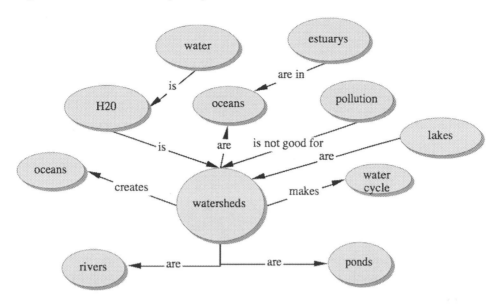

Interview Excerpt with Student #2 on Concept Map 1 (1/24/11):

Researcher: *What is precipitation?*

Student #2: *Rain, and then water goes down a mountain, this is one of the ways, water goes down a mountain and then when it gets to a good spot and goes into the soil and that's sometimes pretty bad because water can bring soil.*

Researcher: *What's bad about that?*

Student #2: *The soil has bugs, sometimes, tiny, tiny bugs, not even the eye can see, it also can include germs and then there is dirt.*

Researcher: *What is wrong with dirt?*

Student #2: *Well, its dirty and uh, sometimes it well, say you had a pond in the back of your yard, and you put some water on the dirt and you will see a little water piece on the dirt. How about I just do this; pretend I had sand which is kind of like dirt and I put it in the water and the water turned a little brownish and so well if you put enough dirt or sand into the water it can actually turn brown.*

Researcher: *Is that a problem for water to turn a different color?*

Student #2: *Um, well, sometimes, yes.*

Researcher: *Why?*

Student #2: *In a book that you know, um, A River Ran Wild (Cherry, 1992) you, basically they [people living near the Nashua River in MA] basically would go into the river and sometimes they would come out like blue or green or brown or something like that, and that is one way, and after a little while it gets kind of smelly [this was due to the dyes and chemicals used in the textile and paper factories on the Nashua River at one time].*

Concept Map 5 of Student #2 includes new concepts (see Figure 7). His structure continues to evolve while it remains basically a spoke shape with a single hierarchical level. Color-coding has been introduced in this map along with linking words. Student #2's use of color-coding suggests specific connections he perceives based on his own assumptions about the watershed systems and its sub-concepts. An important concept included in this map is *Biomagnification* (the process in an ecosystem whereby substances become more concentrated in organisms higher in the food chain usually through predator-prey interactions). His interview comments reveal a complex understanding of the process. The student continued to use his concept map as a guide as he discussed watershed concepts during the interview. He also engaged in self-revisions within his map as he reflected on the interview questions and his responses. The student felt it was hard to come up with linking words for use in his maps, which accounted for the few entries of linking words.

Figure 7. Student #2 concept map 5

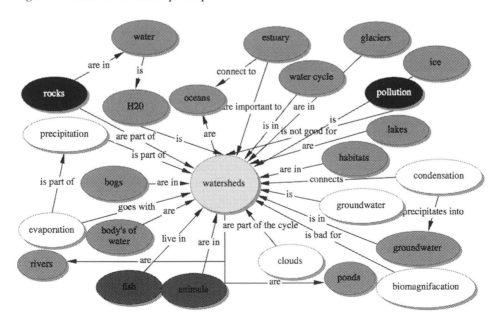

Interview Excerpt with Student #2 on Concept Map 5 (3/4/11):

Student #2: *Basically a watershed is a circle and it isn't a circle because sometimes it goes winding and sometimes it goes straight but it still goes back to where it began.*

Researcher: *In what way does it go back to where it begins?*

Student #2: *Like, if it went from precipitation coming down from the mountain, it would come down the mountain, and then it would go to the closest possible stream or river, pond, or it would just keep on going down to the water - ground water and then it might, it might collect some pollution, it would basically collect in biomagnification, kind of.*

Researcher: *What is biomagnification?*

Student #2: *The stuff that is biomagnification is basically, plankton or red tide. Basically it is plankton, some of it. Well, anyway, plankton would become the dirt that would, the water would find and go to the ocean and then this is a matter of eating - small fish eat at least - five small fish eat at least about 50 or less plankton, then one big fish eats about five small fish and then some bigger or a bird would eat that bigger fish and would get the plankton and then we would probably eat the bird by shooting it and eat the bird, and then we got the biomagnification.*

Researcher: *So....,whoever is eating the animal that has been part of the cycle you were just explaining, are they eating biomagnification?*

Student #2: *Soon it will become the results of biomagnification.*

His discussion of this environmental process during this interview revealed a complex level of understanding including both conceptual accuracy (pollution travels within the food chain and accumulates as it travels up the chain) and naïve epistemology of biomagnification (biomagnification as the outcome of certain events and not a process). Biomagnification was introduced in his concept map 2 (CM2) and he kept it in CM4 and 5.

Student #2's assessment scores are an indicator of his conceptual growth in understanding of the science topics (Scores: 6/12; 7.75/12; 10/12; 10/12). The CMER tracked content, structure, and science content validity. Student #2's science content validity (scored by the DEP rater) hovered around 3 out of 4. His hierarchical levels and concept validity were both mostly scored at an *Emerging* level of development. His focus while working on his concept maps was on science concepts and how he understood their connections to each other and to his map's main idea. That he did not develop a more complex system within the structure (hierarchical level) was more a reflection on his classroom learning style than on his understanding.

Student #2 liked using concept maps in science class. He claimed they helped him as he learned the science content. He commented during our final interview (4/28/11) that they helped him remember the concepts so he could then talk about them, which was exactly what he did.

SUMMARY

The theoretical premise of this chapter's study (that student-constructed concept maps, when used in science class for the duration of a science unit, support student learning while providing a window into student cognitive organization and understanding) is primarily founded upon the work of Novak (2002), Ausubel (1963, 2000), and Kinchin (2000), and is supported by the empirical outcomes of the study.

The benefits of this teaching approach were apparent as students responded enthusiastically and with strong motivation to the inclusion of concept maps in their studies. Following the conclusion of the research project, students requested the use of concept maps for other content areas. They were willing to spend additional time working through science lessons with the use of concept maps. Motivation plays an important part in the learning environment. When students are motivated to achieve a goal, their investment in the learning activities reflects that energy. Concept maps added to the element of motivation throughout the watershed study.

Bridging the gap between how students learn, what they are learning, and how they are taught is the goal of thoughtful and meaningful science instruction (Carey & Smith, 1993; Lederman, Lederman, & Bell, 2004; NRC, 2007). Discerning the process of how students transition from what they know (prior knowledge) to experiencing the nature of science as a way of knowing facilitates a constructivist approach to learning. Guiding students towards conceptual change as a process may foster a greater ability to succeed with the scientific undertaking of misconception modification as the learner restructures his understandings.

From this platform of scientific endeavor, the process of knowledge modification and conceptual growth can occur and develop within each student. Constructing advanced understandings of science topics, and processes, along with gaining an appreciation for what knowledge is available within each student's repository of accumulated information advances through the process of cognitive conflict, whereby the learner works to conflate what he knows with what he is learning. The integration of student-constructed concept maps in science class over time supports and enhances the process whereby students self-reflect on their own knowledge organization while providing the teacher with a pedagogical tool displaying student misconceptions within the content and structure of each student's concept map.

A watershed as a system comprised of many distinct (visible to the students) and non-distinct (not immediately apparent to the students) parts that are interconnected and interdependent with each other was a concept third grade students in this study had not previously encountered, as the science curriculum K – 2 embraced different topics and focus. Taking the students to a place of understanding whereby they could envision how so many individual parts could add up to a system was a long process. It was not until the class undertook to construct 3-D models of their local watershed system that the concept of one system made up of many parts, such as lakes, streams, ponds, bogs, and other elements of the water cycle, could be simultaneously seen and understood as one thing, and as many things.

Evidence from the study suggests there are many advantages to integrating this teaching approach across the curriculum. A growth in critical thinking, which forms the foundation of analytical skills necessary for higher order thinking, was apparent as students worked to create and revise their concept maps. Part of the value of this model can be found in making misconceptions explicit and in identifying emerging and complex connections between concepts and personal knowledge. This teaching model also offers a means for increased communication between student and teacher enhancing classroom engagement.

Recommendations for Teachers

The study referenced in this chapter clearly demonstrated that integrating and using concept maps and concept mapping techniques supports student learning in the sciences by making explicit misconceptions and student understandings. However, the successful implementation of this learning strategy would necessitate certain changes within the classroom for both the student and the teacher. Using concept maps as they were used in this research requires a greater amount of time, and the science study will progress at a slower pace. Additionally, carving out time for student conferences on their concept maps was a key aspect of using maps successfully according to this project's model. The learning outcomes from incorporating this model into the science curriculum can provide the learner with a thoughtful perspective on the science topics covered through digging down into the science content while allowing for reflection and revision of ideas. Additionally, this model allows students to bring and then integrate their personal experiences and prior knowledge into the classroom study, a process that validates students as learners. These are all strong and compelling reasons to bring the use of concept maps into the science and other curriculum areas.

Researching and experimenting with different concept mapping models, whether they are pencil and paper, an online program, or a software program necessitates extra time on the teacher's part. There are free online concept mapping programs. However, some concept mapping software can be expensive, but could be purchased through grants from the PTO or other organization supportive of educational technology.

Extra time is not always available to the teacher, but with administrative support, should be made available to interested teachers. Allowing for teachers who are using concept maps to share experiences with their teaching colleagues, to brainstorm, and to problem solve also needs to be incorporated into the experience of using concept maps in science class. Enlisting administrative and collegial support is a key element to creating a successful experience for both teachers and students interested in and willing to experiment with using concept maps in science class.

Recommendations for Further Research

To build on this research model of using student-created concept maps over time in science class, a pursuit of additional areas for studies in the early elementary grades of K – 5 would be beneficial. For instance, a comparison between two groups of students within one class where one group uses concept maps and the other group does not might show how students use concept maps to support their understanding and to reveal misconceptions. In addition, such a comparison could aid in determining if there is a difference between groups in measurable conceptual understanding and growth.

Tracking student use and development of concept maps in science class as students advance through the elementary grades would also offer an interesting topic for investigation of both short- and longer-term benefits.

Integrating concept maps in content areas other than science in the different elementary grades would be an important focus for research. Using the research model from this study of student-led teacher-modeled concept mapping in social studies, reading, or writing would provide additional data for how students use concept maps to support their own learning and knowledge building. Those content areas would provide a rich resource for students to integrate their personal experiences and prior knowledge as they develop expertise in reading and writing.

Developing the sensitivity of the Concept Map Evaluative Rubric (CMER) to include student-identified themes and the use of *Notes* would provide an additional venue for further research in the field of concept maps in the early elementary grades. The research model suggested student motivation for learning science and building and using concept maps increased resulting from a sense of ownership over the concept map process. An additional scoring device could be created within the CMER to make student motivation visible during a science study.

REFERENCES

Ausubel, D. P. (1963). *The psychology of meaningful verbal learning*. New York: Grune & Stratton.

Ausubel, D. P. (2000). *The acquisition and retention of knowledge*. Dordrecht, The Netherlands: Kluwer. doi:10.1007/978-94-015-9454-7

Ausubel, D. P., Novak, J. D., & Hanesian, H. (1978). *Educational psychology: A cognitive view*. New York: Holt, Rinehart, & Winston.

Caduto, M. J. (1985). *Pond and brook*. Englewood Cliffs, NJ: Prentice-Hall, Inc.

Carey, S., & Smith, C. (1993). On understanding the nature of scientific knowledge. *Educational Psychologist*, *28*(3), 235–251. doi:10.1207/s15326985ep2803_4

Dweck, C. S. (2007/2008). The secret to raising smart kids. *Scientific American Mind*, *18*(6), 36–43. doi:10.1038/scientificamericanmind1207-36

Hammerich, P. (1998). Confronting students' conceptions of the nature of science with cooperative controversy. In *The nature of science in science education ratio-nales and strategies* (pp. 127–136). Dordrecht, The Netherlands: Kluwer Academic Publishers.

Hay, D., & Kinchin, I. (2008). Using concept mapping to measure learning quality. *Education + Training*, *50*, 167–182. doi:10.1108/00400910810862146

Hay, D., Kinchin, I., & Lygo-Baker, S. (2008). Making learning visible: The role of concept mapping in higher education. *Studies in Higher Education*, *33*, 295–311. doi:10.1080/03075070802049251

Horton, P. B., McConney, A. A., Gallo, M., Woods, A. L., Senn, G. J., & Hamelin, D. (1993). An investigation of the effectiveness of concept mapping as an instructional tool. *Science Education*, *77*, 95–111. doi:10.1002/sce.3730770107

Jonassen, D. H., Howland, J., Marra, R. M., & Crismond, D. (1999). *Meaningful learning with technology* (3rd ed.). Columbus, OH: Pearson.

Jonassen, D. H., Reeves, T. C., Hong, N., Harvey, D., & Peters, K. (1997). Concept mapping as cognitive learning and assessment tools. *Journal of Interactive Learning Research*, *8*, 289–308.

Kinchin, I. M. (2000). Using concept maps to reveal understanding: A two-tier analysis. *The School Science Review*, *81*, 41–46.

Lederman, N., Lederman, J., & Bell, R. (2004). *Constructing science in elementary classrooms*. Boston: Pearson.

McCloud, C. (2007). *Enhance comprehension in the science classroom*. Comments from CRISS.

National Research Council. (2007). *Taking science to school: Learning and teaching science in grades K - 8*. Washington, DC: National Academies Press.

Novak, J. D. (1990). Concept mapping: A useful tool for science education. *Journal of Research in Science Teaching, 27*, 937–949. doi:10.1002/tea.3660271003

Novak, J. D. (2002). Meaningful learning: The essential factor for conceptual change in limited or inappropriate propositional hierarchies leading to empowerment of learners. *Science Education, 86*, 548–571. doi:10.1002/sce.10032

Novak, J. D., & Cañas, A. J. (2006). *The theory underlying concept maps and how to construct them (Technical Report IHMC CmapTools 2006-01 Rev 01-2008)*. Florida Institute for Human and Machine Cognition.

Novak, J. D., & Gowin, D. B. (1984). *Learning how to learn* (21st ed.). New York: Cambridge University Press. doi:10.1017/CBO9781139173469

Novak, J. D., & Musonda, D. (1991). A twelve-year longitudinal study of science concept learning. *American Educational Research Journal, 28*, 117–153. doi:10.3102/00028312028001117

Ogle, D. (1986). A teaching model that develops active reading of expository text. *The Reading Teacher, 39*(6), 564–570. doi:10.1598/RT.39.6.11

Ogle, D. (2009). Creating contexts for inquiry: From KWL to PRC2. *Knowedge Quest, 38*(1), 57–61.

Smith, J., diSessa, & Roschelle, J. (1993). Misconceptions reconceived: A constructivist analysis of knowledge in transition. *Journal of the Learning Sciences, 3*, 115–163. doi:10.1207/s15327809jls0302_1

Stepans, J. (2003). *Targeting students' science misconceptions*. Tampa, FL: Showboard, Inc.

KEY TERMS AND DEFINITIONS

Critical Thinking: A process of self-reflection leading to a questioning of prior assumptions with an outcome of revision.

Concept Map: Representational model of knowledge structures.

Connection: An association perceived by the learner between content and personal knowledge.

Constructivism: Where all new learning occurs through the lens of the learner's prior knowledge.

Knowledge: Organization of information into a conceptual pattern.

Meaningful Learning: Quality of knowledge building that humans experience beginning at birth.

Misconception: Preliminary naïve theory about the observed physical world.

Prior Knowledge: A belief system about a specific content topic.

Reflection: Thoughtful consideration of the self in both deed and thought.

Watershed: A region of land where all underlying and surface water drains off into the same place.

Chapter 2
Critical Thinking and Writing Informational Texts in a Grade Three Classroom

Robin M. Bright
University of Lethbridge, Canada

Bev Smith
Jennie Emery Elementary School, Canada

EXECUTIVE SUMMARY

In this chapter, the authors present a case study that explores grade three students' work with informational text over a month-long unit in order to document the students' developing thinking skills about text structures and features. Students were introduced to informational mentor texts to discover insight into expository text structures and create their own "All About..." books using their own background knowledge and interests. In writing their own informational texts, the students were encouraged to use a variety of visual representation formats such as lists, checklists, and diagrams. They also used common expository text structures found in informational trade books including description, sequence, and comparison. These structures provided an overall framework for students to organize their writing and use the skills of conceptualizing, applying, synthesizing, and evaluating their knowledge. One of the primary successes of the unit for developing students' critical thinking was the opportunity to teach others about an area of expertise. Scaffolding for student success in a variety of ways throughout the writing process was also important

DOI: 10.4018/978-1-4666-5816-5.ch002

for student learning. Choosing mentor texts with text features and visuals that were desired in the students' finished pieces provided concrete examples for the class. Overall, the reading and writing of informational text was successful in promoting the development of important thinking skills that support students' need to critically evaluate information from a variety of sources.

INTRODUCTION

Bev (co-author and grade three teacher), while completing work for her Master's Degree in Education, focused her course work and research on literacy and content-area writing. After attending the Teachers' College Reading and Writing Project (TCRWP) Summer Writing Institute and engaging in a graduate-level independent study with Robin (co-author and supervisor), she began transforming the way she taught writing informational text in her grade three classroom. This chapter documents Bev's and her supervisor's research of the students' month-long unit of study of informational writing. We share the background research into critical thinking and informational writing, the visual instructional procedures followed, the children's thinking and writing, and the teacher's reflections, to show how students can become effective learners of nonfiction content.

In the primary grades, teachers focus the majority of instructional time available to them on helping students learn to read and write. Acquiring these early literacy skills consists of developing knowledge of phonics, phonemic awareness, and vocabulary (Adams, 1990). Once students become proficient readers and writers, they are encouraged to use their literacy skills to learn and focus on comprehension and fluency. That is, once students in the elementary grades *learn to read and write*, they quickly shift their attention to *reading and writing to learn.* This area is known as content area literacy and "has to do with the ways teachers meld effective reading and writing strategies into core subject instruction…" (Cooter & Perkins, 2011, p. 565).

In school and beyond, children read and write informational (expository) or nonfiction texts in the disciplines of school, for instance, in science, social studies, mathematics, and other curriculum areas, in order to apply their literacy skills to other areas of learning. Young and Noss (2006) indicate that when teachers provide access to nonfiction trade books, they are giving them experience to a genre that will comprise most of the reading they will do throughout their schooling and into adulthood. Students continue to read fiction, but are introduced more and more to nonfiction texts in order to become academically literate. While fiction allows the reader to take an "aesthetic" stance towards the text for the purpose of enjoying it, nonfiction often requires an "efferent" stance in which information is presented and considered critically by the reader (Rosenblatt, 1978). According to Cooter and

Perkins (2011), the demand to read and write nonfiction text is critical to achieving higher levels of communication, and its decline has been linked to "plummeting graduation rates." It is, therefore, important to discover insight into pedagogical practices that motivate children to engage with informational texts and the critical thinking that accompanies it (Thompson, 2011).

As adults, the writing that is done in daily life tends to be informational, yet, in many of today's classrooms, instruction focuses on narrative writing, particularly personal narrative writing. Today's' students need writing skills for their lives in the future and by neglecting to incorporate informational writing into the curriculum, there can be a huge instructional gap in their education. Daniels (1990) contends:

The writing curriculum experienced by many students as they go up through the grades is essentially: story, story, story, story, story, story, story, story, story, story, story, story, term paper. This collision with the dreaded term paper assignment is the most dramatic, most worried over and perhaps the most dramatic demonstration of the "expository gap" in the curriculum. (p. 107, as cited in Read, 2005, p. 36)

Researcher and teacher, Stead (2002) examined the interactions with text that he and his young son shared together. He discovered that 80 to 90 percent of their interactions with text were outside the narrative genre. This finding is congruent with the observation that, in the daily lives of people, the writing of lists, emails, and letters dominate over the need and frequency to write narrative text. In order for students to be successful in navigating the reading and writing of informational genres, teachers must provide direct instruction in how to do so. Furthermore, Read (2005) contends that, "…for some children, interacting with non-narrative text may be the best path to overall literacy, particularly for boys and struggling readers and writers" (p. 36). Moss (2005) also indicates that motivation for reading increases with students in the primary grades who are able to access and read informational texts in their classrooms.

It is clear that learning to read, write and think critically about content is becoming even more important and necessary in elementary classrooms (Miller & Veatch, 2010). The sheer amount of information visible to children on a daily basis is increasing, through exposure to the media, on TV, computers, tablets and cell phones. This calls for students to be able to know how to contrast fact and fiction, how to evaluate realism, how to detect bias, and finally, how to develop their understanding of perspective. That is, they need to learn how to think critically about the information that surrounds them. This chapter describes one grade three teacher's work over a month-long unit to develop and implement a writing strategy called "All About…" books. By reading and writing informational texts and developing an awareness of their visual and print features, these young students learned to use the critical thinking skills of conceptualizing, applying, synthesizing, and evaluating information.

CRITICAL THINKING, WRITING AND VISUAL REPRESENTATION

While a definition of critical thinking may be somewhat elusive, this area of study is supported by the work of educational psychologists (Halpern, 1995), social constructivists (Vygotsky, 1962) and brain-based learning theorists (Sylwester, 1995) who agree that to foster critical thinking skills, students need learning environments that let them try out their understanding of the world in different ways. This is a shift away from thinking about learning as repetition and recall, and instead focuses the learner's attention on *how* to think rather than *what* to think (Baddeley, 2007). It requires a view of knowledge, not as discrete units of content, but rather as information that is created alongside of what is already known (Bean, 2011). In order to help students develop their critical thinking skills, the teacher's approach, therefore, focuses on student-centered learning, process and think-aloud strategies. Using this type of approach helps students engage in recognizing patterns and relationships; applying knowledge to solve problems; synthesizing ideas; and evaluating the accuracy of information (Sylwester, 1995). In this way, a learner creates a model, map or story about the world. One of the most effective ways to develop critical thinking is to provide children with learning experiences and opportunities to share their developing understanding through visual representations that expand their mental models of the world (Renate & Caine, 1991).

A definition of critical thinking needs to encompass "the intellectually disciplined process of actively and skillfully conceptualizing, applying, analyzing, synthesizing, and/or evaluating information gathered from, or generated by observation, experience, reflection, reasoning, or communication as a rubric to belief and action" (Scriven & Paul, 2003, p. 3). These researchers have identified seven key areas of critical thinking as follows:

- Identification of a problem or issue
- Establishment of a clear perspective on the issue
- Recognition of alternative perspectives
- Location of the issue within an appropriate context(s)
- Identification and evaluation of evidence

- Recognition of fundamental assumptions implicit or stated by the representation of an issue
- Assessment of implications and potential conclusions

They suggest that the relationship between writing and critical thinking needs to be a conscious one and requires explicit instruction. For our work with grade three students, we define critical thinking as the ability to conceptualize, apply, synthesize and evaluate information and content.

There is a well-established link between writing and the development of thinking skills through initiatives such as write-to-learn, academic literacy, and writing across the curriculum (Bazerman, Little, Chavkin, Fouquette, & Garfus, 2005; Cooter & Perkins, 2011). In the past, it has been generally accepted by teachers and researchers that writing is the tool of thinking and research supports using writing to support thinking skills in children and adults (Condon & Kelly-Riley, 2004). However, studies of post-secondary students found that writing could meet acceptable levels of achievement without demonstrating higher order thinking. While writing is a vehicle for critical thinking, it does not, in and of itself, translate into the development of higher-level thinking. It is, therefore, important to consider how writing assignments might be developed that will integrate expectations for critical thinking into instruction.

Bean (2011) asserts that, "the most intensive and demanding tool for eliciting sustained critical thought is a well-designed writing assignment..." (p. xvi). Specifically, he explains that the writing assignment should link to either the students' background or previously existing knowledge or their personal experiences. In addition, a well-designed writing assignment should allow students to explain their knowledge to others; this permits them to take on the role of teacher in helping others understand their research and content. Others suggest that the use of drawing and visual representation will assist young students in their attempts to verbalize experiences that can then be written and read (Kane, 1982).

In the past 25 years, researchers have been paying attention to children's ways of constructing meaning through visual representation (Dyson, 1989; Kress, 1997; Pantaleo, 2005). Their studies demonstrate that visual modes of representation are not temporary forms of literacy but rather alternative ways to communicate knowledge meaningfully. While visual aspects of early literacy may be "under-valued, under-researched, and under-represented," (Anning, 2003, p. 5), they are valued by educators as ways to activate meaning-making in children. To illustrate, Kendrik and Mckay (2004) documented how drawing and other forms of writing, such as using labels and lists, allowed young children to show their understanding of complex topics in ways that traditional print did not. They concluded that different forms of representation "challenge the politics of classroom practices that privilege language-dependent modes of representation" (p. 9). Furthermore, combining visual and verbal skills encourages the asking of deep and meaningful questions among 3 to 5 year olds and the early development of critical literacy skills (Vaquez, 2008).

WRITING INFORMATIONAL TEXTS

Informational texts are used extensively in elementary classrooms to support reading and thinking skills (Dreher & Voelker, 2004; Smolken & Donovan, 2004). In the past, teachers have had students read informational text for the purpose of answering questions but this has not necessarily lead to growth in thinking or writing skills (Thompson, 2011). Rather, the teaching of critical thinking in schools requires "a philosophical shift from output to process, learning to thinking and subject isolation to subject integration" (p. 1). Stead encourages teachers to understand that students need to be introduced to nonfiction texts, as readers and writers, early in their educational careers but perhaps in a different manner than has been used in the past. He writes, "What we as teachers must do is help children discover what the types of nonfiction writing look like and the structures and features that competent writers use for specific purposes" (2002, p. 11). Providing students with the opportunity to write informational text gives insight into what they know and think about the genre and what they can do as writers.

Teachers find that helping students write informational texts improves their abilities to comprehend this type of genre on their own and begins the process of helping them to read to learn across the curriculum. Calkins (1994) states, "Out of what comes to school in children's pockets and backpacks, out of what they see and wonder about and poke into, their nonfiction writing emerges" (p. 432). When we draw upon our students' own areas of expertise, we are able to focus on the instruction of writing informational text as opposed to research which is an entirely different set of skills to develop. Calkins also suggests that, "When children's interests and observations are invited into the classroom, the writing workshop will contain information writing and children will move easily between nonfiction and all other genres" (p. 434). Writing instruction of informational genres must begin early so that children have the opportunity to develop the skills necessary for informational writing with growing complexity as they progress through the grades.

It is universally accepted that critical thinking is necessary to educating students. "Thinking is a fundamental human characteristic, an activity in which we all engage, from the moment we are born and even before" (Robson, 2006, p. 1). We propose that learning about and writing nonfiction text is an essential way to develop those critical thinking skills. Specifically, we are interested in developing a teaching strategy to introduce informational text to grade three students that encourages them to read, write, visually represent, and use critical thinking skills to understand and create expository text.

MENTOR TEXTS

A mentor text is a trade book with specific features and structures that can be used as a model for students to use in their own writing. Others have characterized mentor texts as having curriculum potential and as being particularly useful to students and teachers in learning how authors practice their craft. Dorfman and Cappelli (2007) suggest that, "Mentor texts help writers notice things about an author's work that is not like anything they have done before, and empower them to try something new (p. 3). Calkins and her colleagues from the Reading and Writing Project (2011) stress that, "The fundamental thing to remember about informational writing is that the writer aims to teach readers about a topic" and a good mentor text can help to illustrate this (p. 74).

In the context of the classroom, mentor texts are examined and used for the qualities they demonstrate of good nonfiction writing. Then, students can work together to determine what they notice about informational text. Some of the qualities the teacher brings to their attention include: how background is presented, how like-information is chunked together, how text features are included, and how expert language is used. The page layout is often different from that of narrative text. Authors may compare and contrast their topic with other topics; the readers may be asked a question; visuals such as photographs, diagrams, and figures communicate additional information; and colours, shapes and fonts are used to draw the attention of the reader to the text. Students notice that informational text may include narrative woven into the overall design-a story may appear, for instance-so that the students can relate what they have learned in previous units focusing on narrative writing to this type of writing.

Over the past decade, informational texts have gained popularity in elementary classrooms, but research shows that many students are not able to use them effectively or understand them in order to think deeply and critically about the concepts explained therein. McTigue and Flowers (2011) indicate "students are not explicitly taught how to grapple with science diagrams and other visuals…" (p. 581). They suggest that teachers take time to guide students through visuals used in informational texts, not only pointing at them, but by going into detail and thinking about how they present information and what they mean to the reader.

Kristo and Bamford (2004) encourage the use of mentor texts to help students develop as readers, writers, and inquirers of specialized content-rich material, noting that this is the kind of reading they are asked to do as they continue through the grades. They define nonfiction text as books that deliver information, explain, argue and or demonstrate. Other researchers suggest that students who are exposed to informational writing learn to read and understand it better (Duke & Bennett-Armistead, 2003). As adults, most of the reading and writing we do is with informational text, so helping children develop their skills in this area could have long term effects. Stead (2000) further asserts that it is important for teachers to harness their students' natural curiosity about the world around them and to involve them in meaningful reading and writing activities and tasks.

Students in this particular grade three classroom were taught a writing strategy using mentor texts for informational writing. These texts model exemplary samples of this kind of writing (Dorfman & Cappelli, 2009). For instance, mentor texts demonstrate an overarching topic, offer supporting information for the big ideas presented, link related information together; and display interesting text features and page layout that capture the readers' attention. Given previous research on informational and mentor texts and using writing to teach critical thinking, we believe that young students can be taught to use higher order thinking skills in their writing of informational texts.

OVERVIEW OF THE INSTRUCTIONAL PROCEDURE: "ALL ABOUT..." BOOKS

We describe a project conducted in a third grade classroom over a month-long unit on informational writing. The teaching strategy called "All About..." books was used to help students write informational text using their own background knowledge and interests as a starting point in order to develop critical thinking skills about text structures and features. "The need to connect to students' backgrounds, interests, and cultures goes without saying, but determining the level at which it should occur is subjective. Although not always cited as an effective teacher characteristic, many effective teachers know what television shows students are watching, what movies are their favorites, and the video games they are mastering" (Flynt & Brozo, 2009, p. 537).

There were several stages in the instructional process including: reading mentor texts, brainstorming, researching and note-taking; trying on the topic and subtopics (using a "tent" metaphor); considering topical or sequential structure possibilities; creating a table of contents; and using visual representations within chapters, such as using boxes and/or bullets, diagrams, compare and contrast information, how-to descriptions, narrative information, and suggesting pros and cons.

The writing process of prewriting, drafting, revising, editing and publishing (Calkins, 2012) was very important to teaching this strategy. The teacher encouraged prewriting through brainstorming where students considered a number of different topics they might like to write about from an expert's point of view. She then encouraged the students to engage in drafting or elaborating the ideas gathered. Next, the stage of revision was introduced and practiced (both reading aloud and asking questions were encouraged by the teacher) and finally students were involved in publishing their writing as "All About…" books.

Throughout this process, there were pitfalls and challenges identified by the teacher and the students and these became apparent throughout the process. For instance, some of the students wrote about only one aspect of the topic and needed to be encouraged to add new information. It was also discovered that some children appeared afraid to write in case they would be wrong, and so they moved back to their old ways of writing, which was copying down information from other texts. Since this did not have the desired effect of encouraged critical thinking skills, the teacher modified her lessons to address the importance of putting information "into their own words" and modeled how to do this throughout the unit. The teacher also reviewed note-taking strategies to help her students develop more background information about the topic and by viewing videos, reading, and talking with others.

Lastly, the project focused on the question: how did this group of grade three students engage in critical thinking? To demonstrate students' thinking skills, examples of their work at different times throughout the process of reading and writing informational texts and their own "All About…" books was examined. Students' comments throughout the writing process accompanied their writing samples. The teacher also documented her thinking about the process through a reflective journal and shares her comments, thoughts and ideas. Our conclusions show that while writing achievement varied, as might be expected in a grade three classroom, the majority of students showed attention to developing critical thinking skills by conceptualizing (gathering), applying (organizing), synthesizing, evaluating, and presenting information they wanted to share with an audience of their peers. We conclude that teachers play an important role in helping students enhance their ability to think critically. This was particularly true when introducing nonfiction text to young students.

STARTING REFLECTIONS

Like many teachers in elementary school, Bev shared her ideas about when and how she used informational writing in the curriculum in ways that conformed to producing a school report. " Nonfiction used to be saved for the genre studies in which young writers created a set of directions or engaged in crafting a report about animals" (Stead & Hoyt, 2011, p. 1). In her journal, she indicated that she would link the writing of nonfiction to the Social Studies curriculum by having the students select an animal from the region they were learning about and then "research" it through books and on the Internet. The students' research usually consisted of choosing a book that interested them; if they could read it independently, they often copied the required information into the appropriate spot on their graphic organizer word-for-word, despite the discussion of copyright and the importance of "putting things into your own words." If they could not read their research source independently, an adult would assist them and lead them through paraphrasing what had been read and then they would enter the information on the graphic organizer. It occurred to Bev that the students might be learning new information about their chosen animal, but she was not seeing an improvement in the students' abilities to think about information in new and creative ways and then write their own informational texts. Her observations indicated that the students were repeating the author's writing and were not using the writing process effectively to become better writers themselves. If the teacher's goal was simply that the students learn about an animal, then this process was fine, but Bev's goal was to help students think about the information in new ways and then write about it. She wanted to help her students become better writers of informational text but felt that her instruction was not reflective of the process approach to writing.

In the summer of 2011, Bev attended the Teachers' College Reading and Writing Project (TCRWP) Summer Writing Institute and completed a graduate-level independent study course with Robin and wrote about transforming the way she taught writing in her grade three classroom. Specifically, she attended sessions at the Institute that focused on informational writing. After reflecting upon what had and had not worked in her writing curriculum over the course of the previous year, she decided to return to the ideas from the Writing Institute in hopes that her instruction in the area of informational writing could become as effective as it was in narrative writing.

Rationale: Why Use "All About..." Books

The key to the success of the unit of study in informational writing in Bev's classroom was that students began to write informational texts, referred to as "All About..." books; the texts emerged from students' areas of personal expertise. It was based on the belief that educators need to embrace the curiosities and passions children have as a means to further their literacy development. Bev was encouraged, both by the literature she was reading and by the leaders of the Writing Institute, to draw upon her students' own areas of expertise in order to focus on the instruction of writing informational text. This approach is contrasted with that of having the students engage in their own research and report-writing which would require the development of an entirely different set of reading and writing skills.

In Bev's grade three class, students had been writing personal narratives, and so it was a natural extension to include their expertise on topics of personal interest to further their writing abilities. In the beginning, the struggle to generate ideas for writing was alleviated because the students were able to use their own lives and interests in writing informational text and this provided an emotional connection to the learning and contributed to student engagement (J. Parsons, October 8, 2011). Her students began with a list of ideas for writing that was based on topics they felt they were experts on, and included: semi-trucks (also known as a semi-trailer trucks), toddlers, annoying little brothers, shoes, Pokemon, scrap-booking, making macaroni, camping, hunting and building snow-forts, to name a few.

Scaffolding

Donovan and Smolkin (2011) indicate that it is the teacher's role to scaffold the students' learning through the developmental continuum. Vgotsky (1978) maintains that adult support is necessary so that learners can close the gap between their current skill set and one within their "zone of proximal development." This can be achieved by first identifying the level a student is functioning at and then modeling, providing exemplars, and coaching the child into the next level. Trade books were available that were used as mentor texts at each student's level, as well, Bev modeled writing at a slightly higher level for the students and then worked with them to try new structures and visual representations in their own writing. The mentor texts and Bev's own writing provided visual representations to guide the students' own work. In scaffolding, the teacher gradually removes support as the student demonstrates more independence. Read (2005) found that, "Given appropriate instruction in the skills of writing and a topic that they've chosen and find interesting, young students are fully capable of dealing with the complex problems that occur when reading and writing informational text" (p. 44).

Once Bev determined what her students were interested in and what they needed to know, she used that information in planning the unit on informational writing. As others have suggested, it is important for the teacher to ask him or herself, "What are my kids doing well? What are they not doing that I think is important and need to teach?" Stead (2002) identified eight factors that contribute to successful instruction of informational writing. He said that:

Children best learn how to write nonfiction when they:

- See a purpose for the writing and have an audience in mind.

- See many models of different types of nonfiction writing for a variety of purposes.
- See demonstrations of how to write different text types for different purposes.
- Are given time and opportunity to engage in working with nonfiction texts.
- Are allowed to take on responsibility for their learning.
- Are given opportunities to learn from each other.
- Are expected to learn.
- Feel comfortable in having a try. (p. 15)

Students need to be engaged in their attempts at informational writing and Stead's advice provided guidelines for this unit of study. Providing students with visual models and demonstrations, as Stead recommends, allows them to conceptualize and analyze their thinking about informational writing.

THE TEACHING STRATEGY

Step 1: Examining Non-Fiction through Mentor Texts

Throughout the early part of the year, students in Bev's classroom had exposure to nonfiction reading materials with the integration of content area subject topics into the reading instruction in the classroom. She helped students examine and talk about text features and the structure of informational books in support of reading comprehension. Then, to provide writing instruction, she had the students re-examine the "All About…" books written by published authors for organization and features with an eye towards thinking how they could use these texts as models for their own writing. This was one way in which exemplars were shared. In addition, Bev used scaffolding to support student learning and discussed mentor texts as visual models to support their writing.

The students in Bev's classroom examined mentor texts in groups of three looking for characteristics they discovered that were unique and distinguishable from narrative texts. Some of the qualities that students noted or that Bev brought to their attention included: the type and amount of background information presented, how like-information was chunked together, the kinds of text features that were included, and the way that expert language was used. She demonstrated that the page layout in nonfiction text is often different from that of narrative text. In addition, she showed examples of how some authors used compare and contrast to show how their topics related to other topics. Students noticed, from the mentor texts shared, that informational text can include narrative text and this was discussed as a potential way that students could think about their own writing.

Bev identified several exemplary mentor texts that appealed to a variety of reading levels and used these in her lessons. For instance, The National Geographic Readers provides excellent examples upon which students can model their writing. *Cats vs. Dogs,* provides an exemplar for the compare and contrast structure that can be used in informational writing (Carney, 2011). Carney uses questions as a lead for beginning subtopics. This is a strategy young writers can emulate as a way to create good beginnings in informational text. An illustrated glossary and top ten "cool" facts are also included. In *Deadliest Animals*, Melissa Stewart uses many informational text features such as text boxes and captioned photographs effectively (Stewart, 2011). Stewart includes text boxes for differing purposes such as offering the reader interesting trivia and word definitions. She further divides her subtopics within each section of the book, a strategy to encourage students at higher levels of ability. Like Carney, Stewart also includes a glossary and a top ten section within her book. DK Readers are another source for informational text to use as mentor texts at a variety of levels. In *Shark Attack*, Cathy East Dubowski includes a narrative about a survivor of a shark attack (Dubowski, 2009). Students in Bev's class could see how they might include a story within an informational text using this text as an example. Dubowski incorporates other features such as maps indicating where shark attacks have occurred and a labeled diagram that provides additional information to the reader. At this point, Bev encouraged her students to visually represent the ideas found in the mentor texts that they thought were important to include in their own writing. Most of the students chose to make lists of those features they deemed important in informational writing (See Figure 1).

Step 2: Generating Topics

Research supports offering children opportunities for planning writing, which promotes the development of thinking skills particularly as they learn to conceptualize a topic to explore (Epstein, 2003). Strategies to encourage planning include: 1) mapping ideas on paper, 2) asking children questions, and 3) encouraging children to elaborate on their plans. Fostering the development of critical thinking skills through planning and writing was the focus of the teaching strategy used in this grade three classroom. Specifically, students were provided with an opportunity to engage with and understand non-fiction text by reading it, analyzing its features, and planning and writing their own non-fiction texts.

The students began the unit of study by generating lists of topics that they believed they were experts on. These lists were broad and varied topics about which the students felt they had excellent knowledge. The range of topics included everything from cooking, Halloween, Jesus, and video games, to shoes, and annoying brothers, and were entirely based upon students' interests and background knowledge. Jared's

Figure 1. Student's observations about informational text

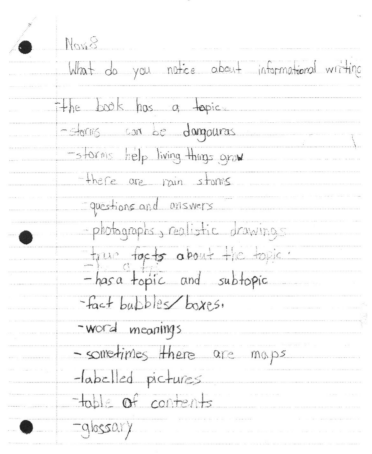

Nov.8

What do you notice about informational writing

-the book has a topic

-storms can be dangouras

-storms help living things grow

-there are rain storms

-questions and answers

-photographs, realistic drawings

-true facts about the topic

-has a topic and subtopic

-fact bubbles/boxes.

-word meanings

-sometimes there are maps

-labelled pictures

-table of contents

-glossary

list of possible writing topics included sixteen items, ten of which he starred and one which received five stars from him-the topic he eventually wrote about, "shoes." (See Figure 2 for Jared's list of topics).

Ashley listed ten possible topics, starred six of them and circled one to write about. This process of starting out with as many different topics that one is knowledgeable about and then narrowing down choices helped the students conceptualize their topics. Stronger or older writers were coached to choose more focused topics. For example, rather than writing an "All About…" book on "sisters," Paige narrowed her topic to "annoying brothers" in order to include specific details that she was not able to articulate for her original topic. When the students placed a star beside those topics they felt they could teach others about by writing an "All About…" book, they evaluated their own background knowledge as either sufficient or deficient for the writing task. These needed to be the topics they felt they had the most informa-

Figure 2. Student's list of potential topics for writing

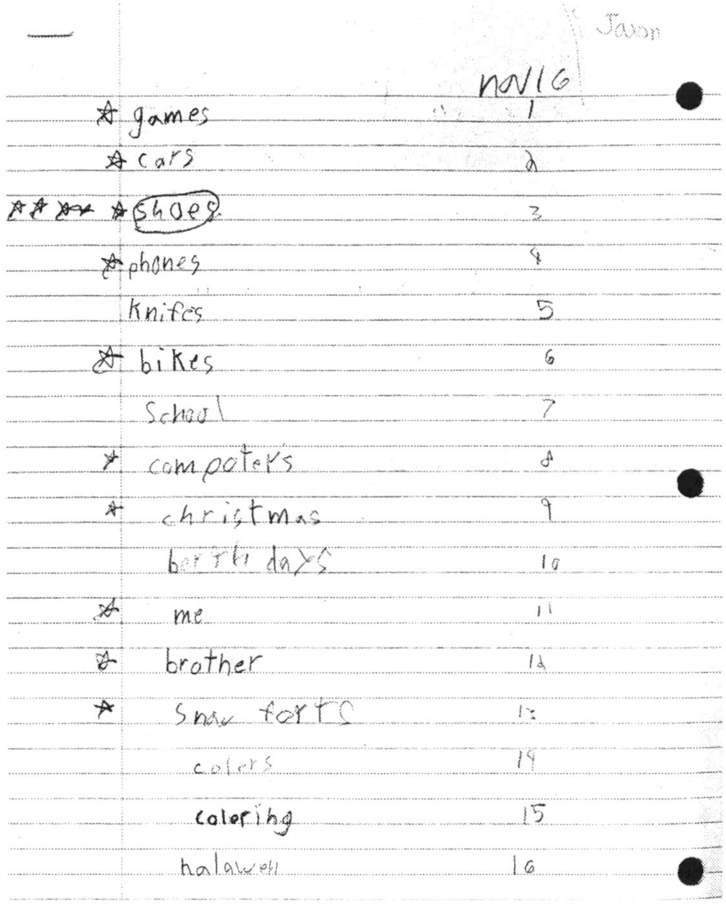

tion about which to share and could write about at some length. The students' initial brainstorming lists and pictures illustrate they were learning to conceptualize knowledge regarding the nonfiction genre.

Next, Bev had the students do some pre-writing, to generate thinking about their tentatively chosen topics (See Figure 3). During this time, Bev encouraged them to answer one or more of the following questions: why does this subject matter? How is this connected to something else? How is it different or similar to another subject? These conversations served to stimulate the students to think in different ways about their topic. For instance, William wrote about several aspects of Pokemon that a reader would want to know: Pokemon matters because it can keep you entertained; Pokemon are like hockey cards; I used to hate Pokemon but now I know that I love it. Jared contrasted his topic of shoes in the following manner: Shoes are differ-

Figure 3. Prewriting to generate thinking about potential topics

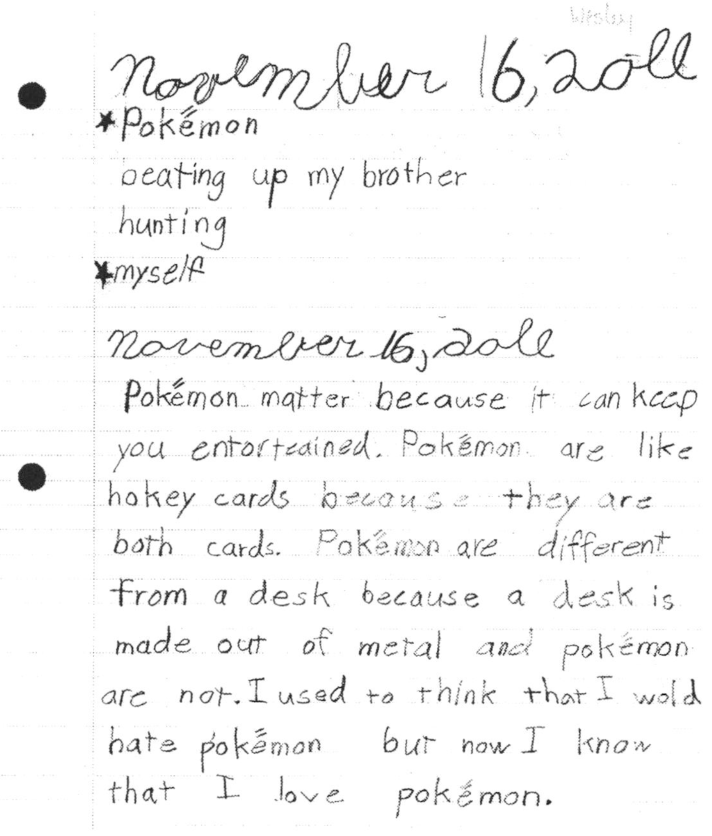

Wesley

November 16, 2011
*Pokémon
beating up my brother
hunting
*myself

November 16, 2011
Pokémon matter because it can keep
you entorteained. Pokémon are like
hokey cards because they are
both cards. Pokémon are different
from a desk because a desk is
made out of metal and pokémon
are not. I used to think that I wold
hate pokémon but now I know
that I love pokémon.

ent from skateboards because skateboards have wheels and shoes don't. Andrew was a very reluctant writer but the opportunity to write an informational text on a topic of great interest to him, semi-trucks, engaged him in the writing process. In the prewriting phase, Bev conferred with Andrew and generated thinking about semi-trucks in unusual ways. At first Andrew could not identify why he wanted to write about semi-trucks or why his topic was important to share with others, other than to say he liked them. The conversation with Bev was the vehicle to begin to help him think more deeply about his topic and reflect on the fact that his expertise with semi-trucks was a result of his personal experiences with his own father in his semi-truck trailer. Some of these prewriting experiences were incorporated into the students' drafts, but at the very least, they were used to support and encourage thinking. The questions stimulated the students to think in different ways about their topic. For example, Annette's prewriting on the topic of "toddlers" looked like this:

Toddlers matter because they can be helpful and silly. Toddlers are like cubs because cubs are toddlers but they are animals. Toddlers are different from an animal because toddlers have a heated home and a comfy bed. I used to think toddlers were useless but now I know that they are very helpful.

Step 3: The "Tent" Visual

The students used the mentor texts to notice how informational books were organized. In a minilesson, Bev related the organization of texts to the analogy of a "tent." Figure 4 shows the anchor chart of the visual representation for the "tent" that Bev created and shared with the students. She described the topic of the book as being the cover for the tent, that is, what it is all about. She showed the students that the tent needs to be supported by tent poles—the subtopics (C. Cruz, August 15, 2011). The anchor chart was on display throughout the unit for students to refer to in order to structure and organize their writing.

The students needed to be able to imagine many possibilities for their tent. To do this, they selected their topics and then began to imagine possibilities for subtopics which were called the tent poles or chapters for their "All About..." books. For example, Andrew chose to write about semi-trucks. He envisioned the chapters of his book to include: semi-parts, what semis can do, types of semis, semis vs. trucks,

Figure 4. Class anchor chart for the "tent" analogy

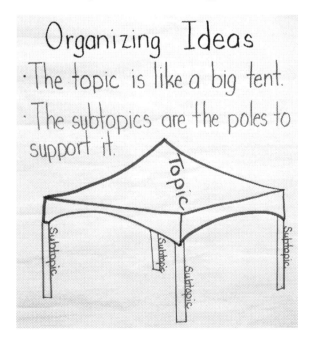

and what not to do when you fix a semi. William decided to organize his tent poles into a table of contents. He included chapters on: Pokemon™ groups, double types, advantages in the groups, evolving three, big but weak, and how to play Pokemon™. The table of contents provided the students with a sequential visual aid to help them organize their thinking and writing.

The students then tried out their structures by rehearsing them orally with another student. The students were encouraged to, "…list points across their fingers, use gestures and drama to re-enact, refer to diagrams, and use an explaining voice" in order to teach another child about their topic (Calkins, 2011, p. 77). Once they were comfortable with the structure for their piece they began to draft the chapters of their text.

Step 4: Drafting

When children are writing about topics that they do not have experience and expertise with, their drafting turns into an exercise in paraphrasing what others have said about their topic. Calkins (1994) says:

If they are writing about topics they've experienced as well as studied, if they've gathered pages and pages of entries about their topic, if they've chosen a specific form and voice and angle after trying other possibilities, we probably will not have to worry about our children writing "in their own words" (p. 445).

Students also need to remember who their audience is when they begin to draft and use their voice to draw the reader in. They need to keep in mind their purpose for writing the book. Calkins contends that the goal of first drafts is, "…fluency, voice and an organizing image" (p. 447).

Bev felt that in drafting the chapters of their books, students did not need to begin with chapter one, in fact many children chose to begin with another chapter. Their process was a recursive one in the same way that the writing process is not linear. If there was a chapter that was particularly exciting for a student to write or that he or she had a lot to say about, it was felt that this was the best starting place for that student. Students were also provided with a variety of types of organizational features on paper to match the type of information they were drafting. This provided visual and physical support to their writing. For instance, if the student included diagrams, he or she required paper with boxes for these. If the writer was comparing and contrasting information, then he or she needed paper with, "…side by side picture boxes with lines underneath" (Calkins, 2011, p. 79). Students were developing an understanding that the visual structures they used were choices to be made and that there were many ways to present their information.

Paige's page entitled, How to Tell the Difference, included two side-by-side pictures in which she compared and contrasted "non-annoying" with "annoying little brothers" (See Figure 5). William used pages that featured 4 boxes along the left-hand side of the page, and numbers and lines on the right-hand side, so he could draw and write the sequence of instructions for playing Pokemon. For him, it was important to present these in the correct order for the reader to follow (See Figure 6). This same page structure was used by Annette but she chose to use the boxes as a way to check off the information she was sharing both in the pictures she drew and in the descriptions of them (See Figure 7).

Step 5: Elaborating

Once the students had established a structure for their informational writing and drafting has begun, they required strategies to help them elaborate their ideas. Cruz said, "Informational writing is built with information—with specifics. It is important

Figure 5. Student's comparison text structure

Figure 6. Student's sequence text structure

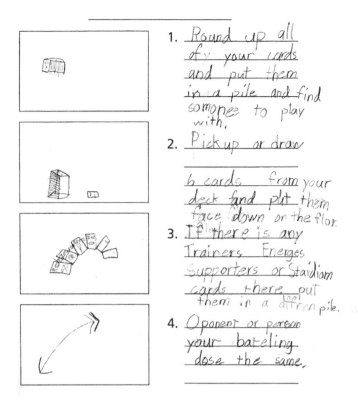

1. Round up all of your cards and put them in a pile and find somonee to play with.

2. Pick up or draw 6 cards from your deck and put them face down on the flor.

3. If there is any Trainers Energes Supporters or Staidiam cards there put them in a diffren pile.

4. Oponent or person your bateling dose the same.

for a writer to draw on a wealth of specific information" (personal communication, August 15, 2011). It is the specific information the writer has included that provides the means to elaborate. Elaboration can be accomplished in one of two ways. First, writers can weave narrative elements into the informational piece in order to add meaning and context. Second, students can be taught to utilize the strategy of twin sentences (Calkins, 2011, p. 79). This strategy has the writer write a second sentence elaborating on the first sentence. Bev modeled how to writing twin sentences in a number of ways. She demonstrated how to relate the student's written information to something readers already know, and how to add a sentence that ensured the text was technically accurate. She assisted the students in looking for gaps in information that needed to be added and lastly, she encouraged them to add a twin sentence that evaluated the information or offered an opinion. In talking with Paige about this strategy, the student wrote in her "Annoying Brothers" book, "He can make the most annoying sounds! For example, he would say: 'Blah! Blah! Blah!'"

Another strategy for elaboration is that of, "moving up and down levels of abstraction" (p. 80). The writer relates what he or she has said to something the reader

Figure 7. Student's illustrations and checklist

may already know or by giving a fact and then an example. In Andrew's chapter on Semi Parts he wrote, "Workers replace an engine. Semi engines are usually the size of a pickup's cab. Semis are like a home on wheels." By relating the semi cab to a home on wheels, Andrew applies relevant or pertinent information to the text with which the reader can connect. Alternatively, the author can give an opinion and the reasons for their opinion. In this step, the students develop critical thinking skills that let them practice application, synthesis and evaluation.

Step 6: Revising and Editing

Throughout the cycle of writing informational text, the students needed to revise their work. Sometimes this revision led to increased elaboration, other times it refined what they had already written. Other times they started over. In addition to the repertoire of revision strategies these writers learned for narrative text, they needed to learn to revise their informational pieces for the specifics of the genre.

As the teacher, Bev modeled this for the students through her own piece throughout the writing process. The creation of a chart specifically with revision strategies for informational writing was beneficial for students so that they had a visual reminder to assist them as they worked to revise their writing. They needed to ensure that "like information" was grouped together and focused on the topic or subtopic.

She encouraged students to use precise language that was domain specific to their topic. It is this detail that lent authority to their writing and helped keep the readers' interest when sharing their writing with others. Students were encouraged, when they edited, to make sure that vocabulary words were spelled correctly to further the appearance of their authority on the subject matter. The inclusion of diagrams and drawings were also included in revision and throughout the writing process. For instance, in Andrew's writing on semi-trucks, he included a detailed drawing with labels to demonstrate his understanding of the value of a visual representation in conveying information and demonstrating his knowledge (see Andrew's diagram in Figure 8).

Figure 8. Student's labeled diagram

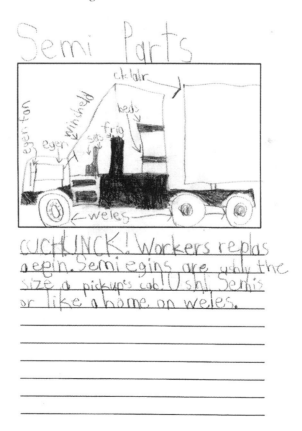

Step 7: Publishing, Sharing, and Reflecting

These grade three students spent a month learning about and creating their own informational texts. They had opportunities during and at the end of the unit to share their writing with others, in pairs, small groups and to the whole class. The teacher made a decision not to have her students re-copy or word-process their work into a final copy, given the time, hard work and perseverance they had already demonstrated in their writing. Instead, the students created a title page for their informational texts, which fulfilled their desire to complete their writing in a final, published form. In addition, the work they had done in the prewriting stage and in response to conferences with the teacher, were kept and given to the students and their families at the end of the unit.

Reflecting upon the unit of study, Bev identified successes and considerations for teaching the unit in the future. One of the primary strengths of the unit for developing students' critical thinking was the opportunity to teach others about an area of expertise each had. The students were able to analyze and synthesize their own knowledge on a selected topic. They needed to critically evaluate which information would be important to their topic to share with others and which information to exclude. This is consistent with the constructs identified by Scriven and Paul (2003) for critical thinking. Bev felt that the use of the visual representation of the tent served as way to help students conceptualize and organize their topics. Scaffolding for student success in a variety of ways throughout the writing process was important for student learning. Choosing mentor texts with text features and visuals that were desired in the students' finished pieces provided concrete examples for the class. For example, Andrew was able to incorporate labeled diagrams like those he had seen in *Shark Attack* into his writing. Bev also thought that providing students with a variety of paper choices helped to visually organize and present their writing. This focused their thinking and writing in a way that she had not observed when teaching informational writing in previous years. She noted this, in particular, in William's writing when he created a procedural page for playing Pokemon™.

Some students realized when they were well into the writing process that they had not evaluated their level of expertise in some areas accurately. This led to some frustration on their parts. Bev needed to spend additional time with these students assisting them in reevaluating their chapters and generating new chapters. This was somewhat time-consuming, however, the students learned that they needed to think more deeply when choosing their topics. Bev realized that the next time this unit of study was taught she would have to be more vigilant and perhaps monitor students' choices more carefully.

Many teachers would like their students to take their writing through to a final "good copy." Bev did not have her students complete a clean copy. This is an area of which she still has some uncertainty. While a final version that was free of errors in spelling and conventions and was without editing and revision markings would have been more visually pleasing and would have taken the students fully through the writing processes, Bev struggled with the logistics of the students duplicating the visuals they had created to support their drafts. She also notes that many of her students continue to make the same mechanical errors in their final pieces that they do in the original drafts, leading her to believe that corrections are made to please the teacher more so than because they understand what the error is. She feels that the final copy would have looked more visually appealing had she taken the time to have students complete another copy of their work. Bev is considering modifying the publishing stage in future years, by asking students to cut out their illustrations and glue these onto a final copy to create a more finished looking piece.

INSTRUCTIONAL IMPLICATIONS

The most effective way to develop critical thinking skills in students is to provide them with learning experiences that expand their mental models of the world (Renate & Caine, 1991). Learning experiences that focus on informational text is increasingly important in the lives of students. "They need to be able to not just read informational texts but read them critically, evaluating their "truth value" and relevance. Furthermore, they need to be able to compare and contrast information across a variety of sources, see the relationships among the information they find, and synthesize those findings" (Moss, 2005).

Assisting primary students as they examine a variety of informational mentor texts, come up with their own ideas for writing information texts and learn to gather, organize, synthesize, evaluate and present their own non-fiction writing is one way for teachers to encourage critical thinking and is strongly supported by visual representations in the classroom. Once the students have had the opportunity to focus on learning the skills and processes of informational writing, they can use this genre to show what they know across the curriculum. Moss (2005) and others suggest the importance of integrating reading and writing instruction with content instruction in the elementary grades. Students need to be able to transfer their literacy skills to the content areas. In reading, they are taught how to read; in content areas they are reading to learn. In writing, students are taught the process of writing; in the content areas they write to know and show what they have learned (Cruz, 2011).

When the process of informational writing is internalized students can begin to create, not only research reports, but almanacs, fact books, biographies, autobiographies and other content-related writing. Note-taking skills allow children to record information from a source that may be new to them, or important to the topic of their research that may be used in an informational report created by the student. They must be taught how to take notes so that this does not revert to paraphrasing what others have said, but so that the content becomes their own. One suggestion for this transfer of skills would be after learning about cultural celebrations in other countries such as Peru, India, Tunisia and the Ukraine in a Social Studies unit, students could choose another country of interest to them and write an informational book about the celebrations that take place in that country. This incorporates learning from the curriculum, but also requires that the child fill in the gaps with outside research, "Because I teach, I learn" (Calkins, 1994, p. 450). Alternatively the students might choose to compare and contrast celebrations in each country with a celebration from their home country. This is an opportunity for the children to demonstrate their concept development.

Learners who participate in informational writing are allowed to share knowledge that matters to them, which Dunleavy and Milton (2009) found to be significant in their synthesis of student responses. "If today's students are to meet the literacy demands of the future, they need authentic experiences with expository texts from the beginning of their school careers" (Moss, 2005, p. 50). Informational writing gives learners a format for making connections between writing and expressing prior learning that is of personal importance or relevance. Antonetti (2008) describes this authenticity as meaningful for learner engagement. After students have undertaken an initial study of how to write informational text using a variety of visual supports, this could be capitalized on in other subject areas such as Social Studies and Science, in which students share their learning through the creation of a chapter book highlighting important concepts they have learned. This could be undertaken individually or as a shared responsibility with their peers, which would provide the learner with the chance to co-operate and build knowledge with others. In doing so, teachers have the opportunity to help students develop the critical thinking skills needed to conceptualize, apply, synthesize, and evaluate the ever-increasing expanse of information in their lives.

REFERENCES

Adams, M. (1990). *Beginning to read: Thinking and learning about print*. New York: Bradford Books.

Anning, A. (2003). Pathways to the graphicacy club: The crossroad of home and pre-school. *Journal of Early Childhood Literacy*, *4*(1), 109–128.

Antonetti, J. (2008). *Using writing as a measure and model of thinking*. Phoenix, AZ: Flying Monkeys Press.

Baddeley, A. D. (2007). *Working memory, thought and action.* Oxford, UK: Oxford University Press. doi:10.1093/acprof:oso/9780198528012.001.0001

Bazerman, C., Little, J., Bethel, L., Chavkin, T., Fouquette, D., & Garfus, J. (2005). *Reference guide to writing across the curriculum (WAC).* West Lafayette, IN: Parlor Press and WAC Clearinghouse.

Bean, J. (2011). *Engaging ideas: The professor's guide to integrating writing, critical thinking, and active learning in the classroom* (2nd ed.). San Francisco, CA: John Wiley & Sons, Inc.

Caine, R., & Caine, G. (1991). *Making connections: Teaching and the human brain.* Association for Supervision and Curriculum Development.

Calkins, L. (1994). *The art of teaching writing.* Portsmouth, NH: Heinemann.

Calkins, L. (2011). *A curricular plan for the writing workshop grade 3.* Portsmouth, NH: Heinemann.

Calkins, L., Ehrenworth, M., & Lehman, C. (2012). *Pathways to the common core: Accelerating achievement.* Portsmouth, NH: Heinemann.

Carney, E. (2011). *Cats vs. dogs.* Washington, DC: National Geographic Society.

Condon, W., & Kelly-Riley, D. (2004). Assessing and teaching what we value: The relationship between college level writing and critical thinking abilities. *Assessing Writing, 9*, 56–75. doi:10.1016/j.asw.2004.01.003

Cooter, B., & Perkins, H. (2011). Much done, much yet to do. *The Reading Teacher, 64*(8), 563–566.

Daniels, H. A. (1990). Developing a sense of audience. In T. Shanahan (Ed.), *Reading and writing together: New per-spectives for the classroom* (pp. 99–125). Norwood, MA: Christopher-Gordon.

Donovan, C., & Smolkin, L. (2011). Supporting informational writing in the elementary grades. *The Reading Teacher,* 406–416. doi:10.1598/RT.64.6.2

Dorfman, L., & Cappelli, R. (2009). *Mentor texts: Teaching informational writing through children's literature K-8.* Portland, ME: Stenhouse.

Dubowski, C. (2009). *Shark attack.* New York, NY: DK Publishing.

Duke, N., & Bennett-Armistead, S. (2003). *Reading and writing informational text in the primary grades.* New York: Scholastic.

Dunleavy, J., & Milton, P. (2009). *What did you do in school today? Exploring the concept of student engagement and its implications for teaching and learning in Canada*. Toronto, Canada: Canadian Education Association.

Dyson, A. (1989). *Multiple worlds of childwriters: Friends learning to write*. New York: Teachers College Press.

Epstein, A. (2003). Me, you, us: Social-emotional learning in preschool. *Young Children, 58*(5), 28–36.

Flynt, E., & Brozo, W. (2011). It's all about the teacher. *The Reading Teacher, 62*(6), 536–538. doi: doi:10.1598/RT.62.6

Kane, F. (1982). Thinking, drawing-writing, reading. *Childhood Education, 58*(5), 292–297. doi:10.1080/00094056.1982.10520534

Kendrick, M., & McKay, R. (2004). Drawings as an alternative way of understanding young children's constructions of literacy. *Journal of Early Childhood Literacy, 4*(1), 109–128. doi:10.1177/1468798404041458

Kletzien, S. B., & Dreher, M. J. (2004). *Informational text in K-3 classrooms: Helping children read and write*. Newark, DE: International Reading Association.

Kress, G. (1997). *Before writing: Rethinking the paths to literacy*. London: Routledge.

Kristo, J., & Bamford, R. (2004). *Non-fiction in focus: A comprehensive framework for helping students become independent readers and writers of non-fiction*. New York: Scholastic.

McTigue, E., & Flowers, A. (2011). Science visual literacy: Learners' perceptions and knowledge of diagrams. *The Reading Teacher, 64*(8), 578–589. doi:10.1598/RT.64.8.3

Miller, M., & Veatch, N. (2010). Teaching literacy in context: Choosing and using instructional strategies. *The Reading Teacher, 64*(3), 154–165. doi:10.1598/RT.64.3.1

Moss, B. (2005). Making a case and a place for effective content area literacy instruction in the elementary grades. *The Reading Teacher, 59*(1), 46–55. doi:10.1598/RT.59.1.5

Nummedal, S., & Halpern, D. (1995). Making the case for psychologists teach critical thinking. *Teaching of Psychology, 22*(1), 4–5.

Pantaleo, S. (2005). Reading young children's visual texts. *Early Childhood Research and Practice, 7* (1). doi: http://ecrp.uiuc.edu/v7n1/pantaleo.html

Read, S. (2005). First and second graders writing informational text. *The Reading Teacher*, 36–44. doi:10.1598/RT.59.1.4

Robson, S. (2006). *Developing thinking and understanding in young children*. New York, NY: Routledge.

Rosenblatt, L. (1978). *The reader, the poem, the text: The transactional theory of the literary work*. Carbondale, IL: Southern Illinois University Press.

Scriven, M., & Paul, R. (2003). *Defining critical thinking*. Retrieved from http://www.criticalthinking.org/University/univclass/Defining.html

Smolken & Donovan. (2004). Improving science instruction with information books: Understanding multimodal presentations. In E. W. Saul (Ed.), *Crossing borders in literacy and science education: Perspectives on theory and science instruction* (pp. 190–208). Newark, DE: International Reading Association.

Stead, T. (2000). *Should there be zoos? A persuasive text*. New York, NY: Mondo Publishing.

Stead, T. (2002). *Is that a fact? Teaching non-fiction writing K-3*. Portland, ME: Stenhouse.

Stead, T., & Hoyt, L. (2011). A guide to teaching nonfiction writing, K-2: Explorations in nonfiction writing. Portsmouth, NH: firsthand.

Stewart, M. (2011). *Deadliest animals*. Washington, DC: National Geographic Society.

Sylwester, R. (1995). *A celebration of neurons: An educator's guide to the human brain*. Andrewandria, VA: ASCD.

Thompson, C. (2011). Critical thinking across the curriculum. *International Journal of Humanities and Social Sciences*, *1*(9), 1–7.

Vasquez, V. (2008). *Negotiating critical literacies with young children*. Mahwah, NJ: Lawrence Erlbaum Associates, Inc.

Vygotsky, L. (1962). *Thought and language*. Boston, MA: The MIT Press. doi:10.1037/11193-000

Vygotsky, L. (1978). *Mind and society*. Cambridge, MA: Harvard University Press.

Young, T., & Moss, B. (2006). Nonfiction in the classroom library: A literacy necessity. *Childhood Education*, *82*(4), 207–212. doi:10.1080/00094056.2006.10522824

KEY TERMS AND DEFINITIONS

Critical Thinking: The ability to conceptualize, apply, synthesize and evaluate information.

Expository Text: A type of text in which the author's purpose is to inform, explain, describe, or define a particular subject to the reader.

Informational Text: A kind of non-fiction writing designed to convey information.

Mentor Texts: Books that show good examples of writing for students to learn from and emulate.

Text Structures: The manner in which an informational text is organized, for instance, can show description, sequence, comparison, cause and effect, or problem and solution.

Visual Representation: A drawing or map that communicates meaning.

The Writing Process: A recursive set of steps that writers use to produce a piece of text that include: prewriting, drafting, revising, editing, and publishing.

Chapter 3

Examples of Concept Mapping in a School Setting:
A Look at Practical Uses

Cristine G. Goldberg
University of West Georgia, USA

EXECUTIVE SUMMARY

Through discussions with colleagues at several different institutions and teachers from all levels in my home state, it became apparent that classroom teachers have little or no exposure to good concept mapping practices. Background information about why concept mapping should be a primary tool in everyone's "toolbox" for learning and performance success is not common knowledge. Secondly, practicing teachers need concrete ideas for using concept mapping by and with students. After a couple of years of conversations at conferences and informally surveying my own undergraduate and graduate students, I decided to make an attempt to fill in this void. In this chapter I have presented relevant information about where, when, and how to use concept mapping as well as critical "how-to" tips for implementation by interested parties.

DOI: 10.4018/978-1-4666-5816-5.ch003

INTRODUCTION

Most schools and colleges of education do not expose pre-candidates to the use of concept mapping with students to any measurable extent. This means that teachers arrive in the classroom with virtually no training in the best practices of concept mapping. Without formal training in the process and without theoretical information as to how and why mapping can work well for a wide variety of students, an educator is not likely to instinctively know how helpful concept mapping with students can be. Concept mapping is also called idea mapping, mental mapping or mind mapping. According to Chan (2009), a concept map is a hierarchical form of structure diagram that illustrates conceptual knowledge and relationships within a specific topic from general to specific concepts. Another way to put it could be this: "Concept mapping is a method for representing knowledge graphically" (Hilbert & Renkl, 2008, p. 53).

My utilization of concept maps throughout many years adheres to principles developed and changed over time by Buzan (1996), Mukerjea (2004) and Nast (2006 and personal communications 2006, 2007, 2010), as well as North (personal communications 1999, 2000, 2001, 2003, 2006, 2010). A synthesis of the meaning of concept mapping, to me, is a visualization of some type of knowledge that allows for relationships to be readily seen; new ideas added or changed and also may be used as an effective planning and/or presentation tool for many tasks. The technique is powerful for brainstorming, representing complex structures or ideas, helping others to understand those complex structures and ideas, as well as a quick assessment of knowledge of subject matter and promoting group understanding, learning and collaboration.

As a faculty member who regularly teaches a technology integration course to pre-teacher candidates in a university's college of education, I often informally survey students with open-ended questions about strategies learned and applied in their student teaching opportunities. Four terms of this informal survey approach and anecdotal notation during face-to-face conversations and online class meetings have provided me the information that concept mapping is either a big void in the curriculum or dismissed as a useful technique by their instructors. The informal results and discussions with colleagues at several other institutions have all led me to two conclusions 1.) Graduates leave our institutions with little or no knowledge of the large role that concept mapping can play in the development of learning in a classroom; 2.) Students in the classrooms of our graduates are being denied more successful learning outcomes and the opportunities to be more productive and engaged.

I believe that professionals who are looking to improve student understanding of content, context and connections will better comprehend the possibilities for classroom use through the presentation of concrete examples and various uses in this chapter. Pre-service teachers are generally exposed to theories or strategies of learning for implementation into the classroom setting during their undergraduate courses. Concept mapping as a strategy is an exception to the previous statement. Even when there has been some exposure to the idea of concept mapping, precious little information has been passed along about how and why visual emphasis helps the brain with learning, how a concept map is a complete visual prompt that allows users to make connections quickly and, just as importantly, what is missing from the scene are examples of how seasoned practitioners have utilized concept maps in specific content areas and other learning situations.

This is a compilation of many years of my own practice as a concept mapper and mentor of others who are interested in concept mapping. The stories and examples shared in this book chapter are not a case study in the traditional sense, these are summaries that are organized to illustrate various aspects of concept mapping aspects of concept mapping that are important to someone who may want to learn more about it. Further, it will help those individuals no matter what age or level in the educational field, apply and implement this tool or strategy in their own setting. A brief overview of each of the ten sections follows.

1. General information from a variety of sources that provides the reader with more background as to why a person might want to include concept mapping as an excellent tool for students to employ.
2. The attention moves to information about sequencing and short term memory.
3. Increased understanding and examples of how a map presented by the teacher to the class can assist with increased student understanding.
4. Long term memory is very important in the current climate of high stakes testing. This section describes ideas of how to promote long term memory through mapping and the sharing of maps.
5. As critical thinking skills repeatedly appear in standards lists, skills lists and employers lists of required skills, it is important for teacher to address this area. Therefore, the ability to see, understand or get the big picture is necessary. Here the reader will find ideas and other food for thought in your own practice.
6. All students must conduct research, write essays, produce a product of some type or complete a project throughout their K-12 journey. In this section I provide activities and ideas for inclusion into classrooms.
7. The section on textbooks, lectures and documentaries explains how to incorporate concept mapping into the process for increased student success.
8. A brief overview of digital mapping will broaden the conversation about including Web 2.0 tools in the mix of mapping for and with students.

9. As with any new skill, teachers need tips for modeling the skill and assisting student with their own skills development. Included in this section are a few miscellaneous ideas for use that might not normally come to mind.
10. The last section is an overview from a whole school implementation in Australia that includes observations and comments from the principal and teachers in that school.

1. CONCEPT MAPPING: SELECTED INFORMATION

One might ask why learn and use concept mapping? The answer is because it supports student learning across every level of instruction from early childhood to the university and beyond.

In their detailed descriptions of the learning process, Joyce, Calhoun and Hopkins (2000) include in their findings that students create their own meaning (schemas) from stimuli provided by teachers and that students learn best in an atmosphere of support and collaboration in the classrooms where these practices are developed and encouraged. Have you ever thought that your students were not following or getting what you were saying? Maybe it is because, as you are speaking, they are accessing their own patterns of thought or pre-conceived models of meanings and theirs are not the same as yours. Concept mapping is the key to bridging the aforementioned gap.

Concept mapping provides learners a way to understand their own cognitive processes that the traditional lecture mode and linear note-taking does not do. When teachers move to concept mapping as the method of presenting the content, learning becomes more constructive and expansive and offers the stimuli described above in the format of maps to students (Buzan, 1996; Dexter & Hughes, 2011; Mukerjea, 2004). As students become involved in constructing and building their mental models of understanding, their own concept maps are the vehicle that accomplishes this task. Each of us arrives at school daily and then leaves with his or her mental models, known as schemas, that have been modified, enlarged or developed in some ways.

It is a relevant fact that when we and our students make the maps we create visible to others, it then becomes easier for us to question, share with others and reflect upon them (Seabrook report, 2004). Taking that sentence further, the process of being "up front" or "on stage" generally promotes an increase in the levels of communication, collaboration and cooperation in paired and group work that promotes an environment for lasting changes in how classrooms foster and achieve real learning. Often, students are impacted positively in how they view themselves and behaviors that are unwelcome either lessen significantly or disappear (Buzan, 1996; Seabrook report, 2004).

Examples of Concept Mapping in a School Setting

Riding and Rayner (1998) looked at all the learning styles from the 1940s to the nineties and their research revealed how individuals organize information and how they represent it. One of the things their research found is that information is represented verbally and visually but that most people seem to remember or recall pictures rather than words. Words, of course, are not separated completely from the pictures as they help to explain the pictures. When the concept map is drawn, the student sees both the whole and the parts at the same time. This visual is also verbal because key words clarify images and vice versa. In its total form a map is a visual image. The fact that visuals are processed and remembered more than text, 60,000 times faster according to Burmark (2002), should encourage teachers more than ever to acquire and model concept mapping. Other images within the total map will increase the chances for longer term memory.

Teachers can utilize Riding and Rayner's research by presenting the big picture to students. Students are helped when they see the big picture before learning, before an event, before a project. The teacher can think of the process as a flower development. You have the bud or inner core – the main idea. That would be putting the main topic or subject front and center. As the teachers moves from the center and out to the branches of the units, more layers of petals are added – that would be the next level. The sub-branches are the rest of the flowers or cluster of flowers and that could be considered all of the details, facts, or findings that add to the main idea. When approached in this manner, the teacher is making learning intentions clear at the start of each lesson and provides the student with a global context where the narrower or specific data reside (Smith, 2001). Students can actually see the big picture as maps are presented and developed across a week or unit of study. If the big picture maps are also large, they become useful for class reviews, additions are made as learning blooms and maps can be put up and down easily as longer reviews are needed. The entire class sees the large map daily as well as their own maps.

Figure 1 (Chinese New Year Unit) is an example of a large class map (approximately 7 foot by 7 foot). It was started in the classroom and then moved into the hallway outside the classroom for parents and others coming into the school to see what students had learned during the unit study of Chinese New Year. Students were observed eagerly explaining their learning to their parents during the class celebration of the holiday. Figure 2 (Chinese New Year Branch Detail) shows the details of a branch from the large wall map and provides an idea of the scope of instruction during the unit. Students had their personal maps of the unit on the walls in the classroom for parental review.

Figure 1. Chinese New Year unit

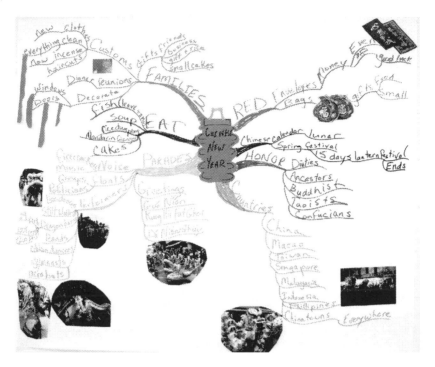

Figure 2. Chinese New Year branch detail

2. CONCEPT MAPPING RELATED TO SEQUENCE AND SHORT TERM MEMORY

Most elementary schools in the state of Georgia participate in the annual Georgia Picture Storybook awards contest (Georgia Children's Book Awards, http://gcba. com). Media specialists and classroom teachers read the books to students over a period of approximately four months and then each student votes on his/her favorite. All votes are submitted to the sponsoring group and the winner and runner-up are announced. Several years ago, I decided to conduct an informal pilot study to determine if mapping some of the stories read in the media center to a group of students would help them remember the stories better when voting time arrived. It should be noted here that the first through third grade teachers had expressed that the children were having difficulty with sequencing and remembering even over short time frames. Therefore, the decision to map story lines was also an opportunity to work on sequencing and short term memory from the standpoint of the larger picture within that grade level.

Three of the four third grade classrooms participated. Each of the books was read to the students in the media center the same as a normal story-time session. Next, the maps were drawn by hand on a large flip chart as no whiteboard was available for use with these groups. The final map was briefly reviewed and the students were told to take a good look at it, then close their eyes and picture it. In hindsight, this use of flipcharts proved to be a great strategy. The next week the first thing that was completed was to redraw the map of the prior week's story from recall. Students were prompted to recall the sequence of events with a few details added by those students who remembered more of the book. The originals were so close to the map drawn this second week that it was a verification of the process. Figure 3 (*Bubba, The Cowboy Prince*) is the map drawn following the reading of the story. Figure 4 (*Bubba, The Cowboy Prince*) is the map drawn by the students one week later at story-time. When both maps are examined, it is very clear that the students' recall was excellent. Neither myself nor the teachers of each group prompted students to get responses for the redrawing of the maps. Each group's maps were extremely similar on both the original drawings and the subsequent redraws.

The process was completed for each of the eight books that had been chosen to read in the media center. When it came time to vote, the maps were brought out and hung up in the media center so the third graders would see them as they entered the media center. The students were quickly drawn to the maps and talked about the stories with each other. The teachers mentioned several other books that they had read but not mapped with students. The students did not have the same level of recall for the unmapped books as the books that had been group mapped. The fourth

Figure 3. Bubba, The Cowboy Prince

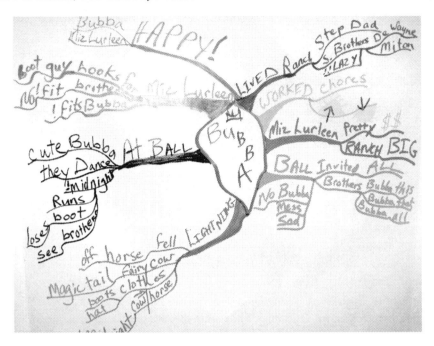

Figure 4. Bubba, The Cowboy Prince, one week later

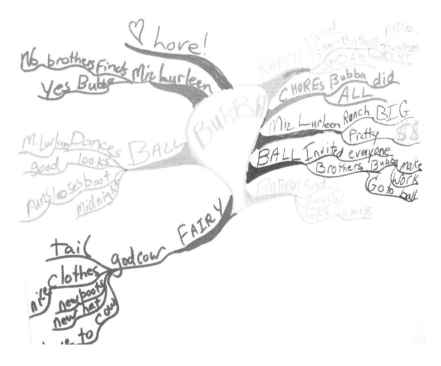

class, which was not part of the mapping at story-time, had little to no recall of any of the books that had been read to them.

The following year, third grade teachers and I worked together to teach sequencing to second grade students as well as continuing the book awards with third graders. The first two second grade projects were to re-read well-known children's stories in small groups and have the students draw a map of the flow of the story (sequence). Then each group presented their findings to another group and they compared maps. Several books were chosen and students could map whichever book they chose. A map of *The Three Little Pigs* completed by a rising second grader can be seen in Figure 5 (*Three Little Pigs*). This particular group learned mapping mechanics before the book awards even began and the results of mapping the stories in the media center were, once more, excellent. Figure 6 (*Three Little Pigs*, Special Needs) was the very first attempt at mapping as the particular child was new to the school. The teacher was very pleased because both she and the paraprofessional in the classroom were having a difficult time getting the student to put anything down on paper.

With their own third graders one of the first tasks the third grade teachers gave to students for language arts was to take the familiar stories or take-offs of familiar stories and begin mapping instruction. Figure 7 (*The True Story Of The Three Little Pigs*) was the book chosen by a student with real difficulty in following directions. The task was to draw the map using character, setting, main events and outcome or

Figure 5. Three Little Pigs

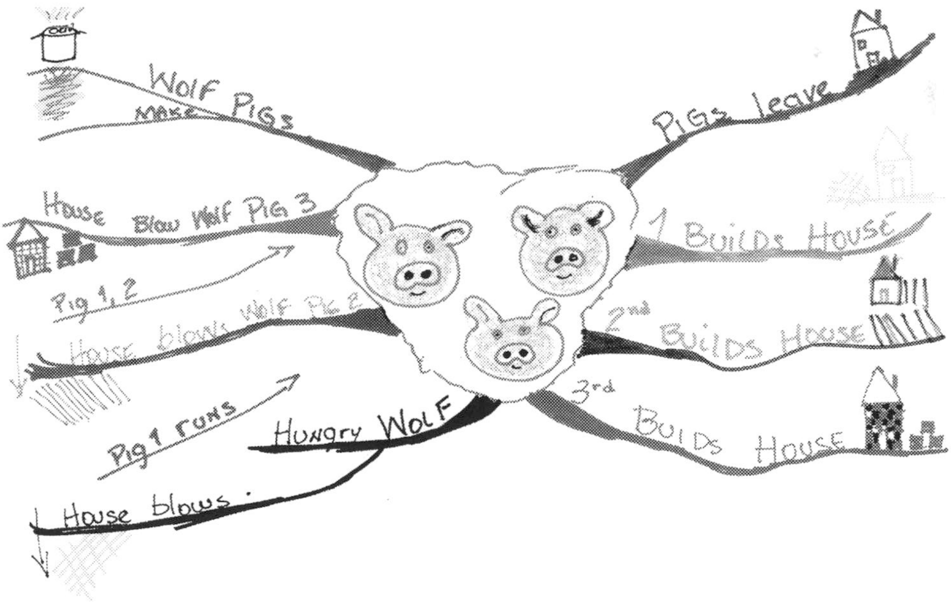

Figure 6. Three Little Pigs, special needs

Figure 7. The True Story of The Three Little Pigs

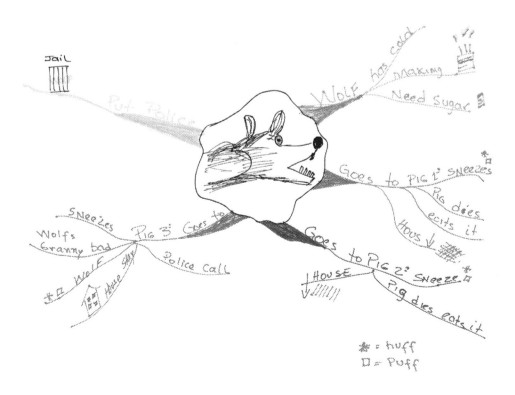

end of story. Although the student did not specifically name the branches as such, it was clear that his map was close to that story. A few branches placed in a slightly different spot were all it would have taken for this student to have been very close to the assignment's expectations.

While the third grade was mapping some books from the book award list, the fifth grade was attempting to learn more about the Caldecott Medal award winners. Two of the teachers firmly believed that more questions on the Caldecott books would be on the annual testing of students at this grade level. The teachers looked at the list and chose 20 books to read. I would read ten of these in the media center and map them with our students and the teachers would read the other ten in their own classrooms. The same process of mapping the book following the reading was used with a redrawing of the map the following week when they came to the media center. Figure 8 (Partial Map Of *Snowflake Bentley*) is what the initial map looked like with only a few branches drawn. It clearly displays that the children, when asked immediately after reading the book, could come up with items read to them quite easily. Figure 9 (*Snowflake Bentley*) shows the map as it looked when finished with the major elements that the children could provide from the book reading. The students were asked again to take a good look at the map, to close their eyes and think about the map, and then to open their eyes and look at the map again before leaving the media center. When you look at Figure 10 (*Snowflake Bentley* Redrawn), it becomes apparent that the students remembered well the original map.

Sequencing was also reinforced in a collaborative effort with the music teacher, the media center and several first grade classes. The students came to the media center during their music time several weeks in a row the same years that the upper

Figure 8. Partial map of Snowflake Bentley

Figure 9. Snowflake Bentley

Figure 10. Snowflake Bentley redrawn

grades were completing the above-mentioned projects. The music teacher would arrive and a new song was sung that was progressive in nature. The music teacher would teach a verse and the hand or motions for a song and the children would follow along. As each verse was completed, a para-professional from the class drew a branch on the map that represented the verse. Figure 11 (Bear Hunt) is the map that was made of the children's song, Going on a Bear Hunt or, in some quarters, known as We're Going on a Bear Hunt. The week after this song was taught, one group of the children filed in and the music teacher had sent notice that she would be about five minutes late. The classroom teacher pulled out the chart with the map and the students started to sing it by themselves. They needed very little direction to get through the song. That was a very pleasant surprise to every adult in the room, myself included. This pattern of being able to easily sing along using the map continued throughout the rest of the project.

3. INCREASING UNDERSTANDING THROUGH CONCEPT MAPPING

When students are younger, it is a good idea to draw a class map when introducing concepts. Not only is this good modeling, it immediately aligns related items as the teacher is giving them to students. It is easier for students to make their own maps

Figure 11. Bear Hunt

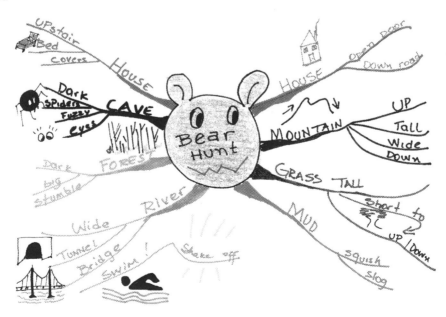

instead of figuring out exactly what are the key words and relationships from a lecture. Figure 12 (*Cendrillon*) is an example of a map drawn for a fifth grade class that was being asked to make their stories more complex. The book, *Cendrillon*, was read to the students, discussed through questioning by the teacher and then a map was drawn of the story. In this particular map the students felt the middle had two distinct sections and that the ending also was a double meaning conceptually. Both of these are clearly shown on the map. Students copied this map and then added more details to it for an activity in the evening. The next day students read their own books that they had checked out from the media center and drew their maps. As the teacher reviewed them, it was very evident to her that the students clearly had understood the point of complexity related to characters and plot line. From that point students then developed a map for writing their own story based upon any of four ideas supplied by the teacher or an original idea that the student wished to develop. Figure 13 (Planning A Story) is one student's rendering of the initial planning for the opening and main characters. This student map was drawn by a male who rarely had written entire stories with this much information. Resulting stories from all students except two were more complex.

An example, adapted from a map by Dilip Mukerjea (2004), was built upon the opening lecture by a teacher of a unit about animals. She challenged the students to

Figure 12. Cendrillon

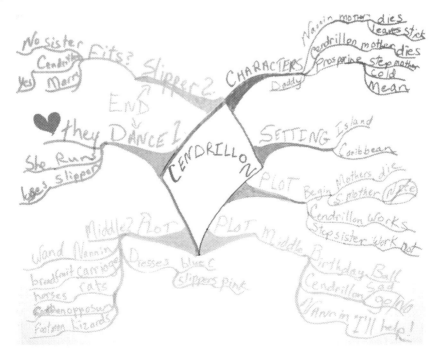

Figure 13. Planning a story

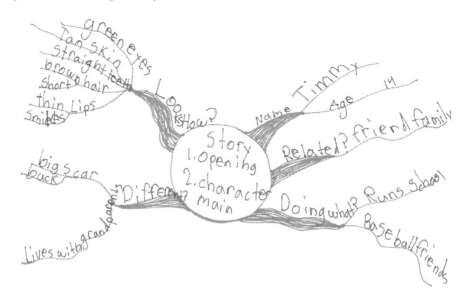

draw as many of the animals discussed as they could rather than writing them. Figure 14 (Animals) was drawn by a student who looked at the Mukerjea map for ideas and drew the map as the teacher talked. At the end, the student quickly added some names of the animals that he did not feel confident enough to draw without a picture to look at. Following the opening lecture, each student was to look at the teacher's master map and to pick two animals from different branches, research the animals, and draw a quick map to help them present to the class. The teacher later stated that the exercise would have worked better if she had told the students to draw a map on the class whiteboard for each animal as they presented. I agree with her assessment, however, because she had them draw a map of their presentation, it still was helpful and helped to ground the student presentations.

Another example of modeling mapping for students to understand the principles of mapping can be seen in Figure 15 (Research Country). This particular map was drawn with the teacher completing it on the whiteboard as the mini lecture on "How I want your country map to look like" was given. Again, the idea was taken from the Mukerjea (2004) book, *Unleashing Genius*, as the master guide. It is worth noting here that the teacher had no formal training in concept mapping and was self-teaching through reading and then emulating this book. As the teacher became more confident with the skill of mapping, there was movement from using the ideas of others to individual ownership. The point of the lecture was to model concept mapping with students being allowed to check details of the branches and offer input on those specifics, such as land mass, popular animals, products of the coun-

Figure 14. Animals

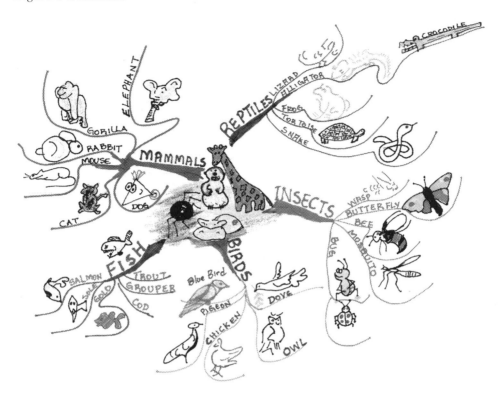

try, and so forth. Students would then draw a map for their own country and it would contain many more specifics. Figure 15 was completed in a short time frame of approximately 20 minutes and the students were cautioned about the expectations for a much more detailed map for their own countries. When I interviewed the teacher, she relayed to me that the students actually enjoyed the project and wanted to do more projects this way. Several times throughout the two remaining months of the school year, students were allowed to choose to produce a map and "read the map back" to the teacher or use one of two other options given to them. She stated that approximately eighty percent (80%) of the students chose to do a map versus the other options.

A middle grades teacher who utilized mapping when presenting lecture information to students told me that her students always said they could grasp the concepts and ideas because she "drew" them out for them and other teachers did not. Just because students are in grades 6-8 and are supposed to be more mature, does not mean that they have had enough practice in finding key words and phrases and can automatically make connections and relationships to other ideas or concepts. When they can see them up front, the understanding of such concepts is easier for them.

Examples of Concept Mapping in a School Setting

Figure 15. Research country

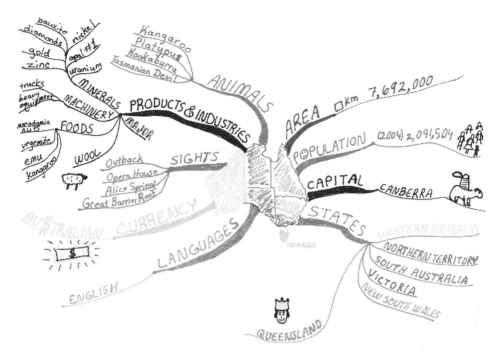

Again, the modeling aspect is present when the teacher draws a map. Student drawn maps are most helpful for long term retention and work in the future, but many students need the map from a teacher, too, when introducing new or complex topics.

New Common Core Standards in the United States have changed the base information that many students learn. The intent of the establishment of these standards was so all states would be teaching the same content to students and there would be consistency, higher expectations and the knowledge and skills expected of students would be more relevant to the real world (http://www.corestandards.org/). Genre information is an example of an area that has changed drastically. There is more information for students to absorb. Students, who had been exposed to similar information prior to these Common Core Standards, may have a different idea of what that information is. One instructor decided to give three different lectures about genres and the second of those lectures provided the student map discussed. Figure 16 (Genre Overview One) is the student drawn map. It is only completed enough to be used for the second part of the genre lesson that came later. The teacher wanted students to draw an initial map while she briefly lectured. Each genre only received two or three sentences of information from the teacher. Then each student was to write down names of books that he/she had read or been exposed to and that they felt met the brief information given. When the genres covered were finished, the

Figure 16. Genre overview one

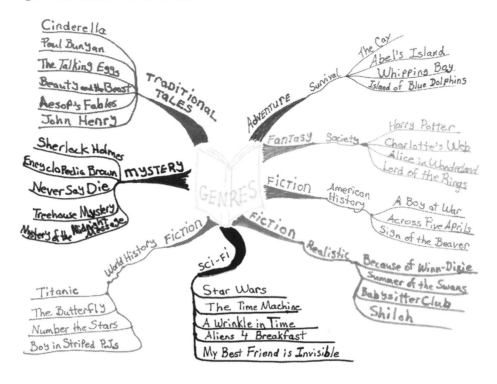

teacher asked students to share the names of individual books that they had written down. The assignment for homework was to go home, redraw the map, and add one detail from each book that would help them to remember why it was in that particular genre.

4. CONCEPT MAPPING AS RELATED TO LONG TERM MEMORY

With the rise of End Of Course Tests (EOCT) and the heavy emphasis on state and national testing, students need to remember and recall what they have learned. Students in higher grades are expected to take and pass exams about the entire course term of a semester in content areas. The real goal should be that students need to be able not to do this just for tests, but for everyday situations. Concept mapping helps with connections because of the big picture and the overall visual the student has in his or her brain. Test preparation can be through the use of partners or groups and it works. This works best when the students have become experienced with mapping through their own efforts and prior group work.

Examples of Concept Mapping in a School Setting

If the teacher produces maps of the content in the subject area and revises them as learning occurs throughout the unit, then students are already being assisted in the process. Students take a cue from the teacher and they will have also revised their own maps (the process becomes automatic after a short time frame). If the teacher also uses pairs and groups to explain their maps to each other, it is another opportunity for the content to take hold. The task of explaining to another student and questioning and being questioned by each other as to what is what on a map or to clarify a point is another point of retention. Pictures and diagrams on each others' maps serve to increase awareness of the material. The best part is that students may, and will, add to maps during this process as connections become apparent. The process of explaining and studying is known as "reading the map" back. During paired, group or individual study, the student literally reads a map back to others or to him/herself by stating everything into complete sentences. Again, this process helps with clarification, retention and the ability to communicate the information either to others or on a test.

Assuming that the teacher allows enough time for pairs to present back and forth and then to meet with small groups, this process can be very effective. When the process is finished, the teacher should have students take a break. A bit later, if time permits, the students can redraw the map from memory as a self-mental task. If time is not available, the teacher can suggest that students redraw a map from memory as soon as they arrive home. It usually does not take long even for young students to realize that this exercise is helpful. Older students, once they have figured out how effective this activity of reviewing together is, will willingly engage in the process. Short reviews of maps when there are five to ten minute segments of time that unexpectedly come available during class time are perfect uses of such time and will eliminate the useless time spent on cramming for unit or the previously mentioned EOCT tests at the last minute.

Another technique that may prove particularly effective with older students, especially those with dyslexia or organizational difficulties, might be the utilization of course content maps in the child's own room at home. A very large piece of paper, perhaps a small flip chart size, is used for each course. Each week, whatever maps that have been created for each course at school, are added to this master map in the appropriate places. Then the student uses the "read the map back" technique as a weekly review. This has powerful potential for all students as it provides a constant review. As the time for EOCT or other testing nears, all the student needs to do is to read the map back a few times and that is all that will be required because the student has maintained familiarity with the course all along. Lana Israel, a mapper since age 13, provides a video segment of this technique in her DVD, *Get Ahead and Ace Your Exams*. If put into practice, this study strategy should produce no cramming, no all-nighters attempting to study and much less anxiety on the part of your students. If your are reluctant or unsure about trying this, pilot the idea with a small group of students from one class for a term or two and you should be able to determine if this course content map is helpful to your students. I would especially recommend that you include a few students with special learning needs in that first group of students. You could have them take pictures of their large home maps and show them to you each week so you can check the implementation of this method by your students.

Nesbit and Adesope (2006) examined 55 studies involving the use of concept mapping with students that ranged from grade 4 to post-secondary. What they were attempting to determine was if the use of mapping increased knowledge and/or retention of various concepts. A thorough examination suggested that, when compared to merely listening to lectures, participating in class and reading texts, concept mappers retained more knowledge and, thus, mapping was effective in student success. This was found to be true across curriculum and content areas. This examination of concept mapping by Nesbit and Adesope (2006) supports the information provided in this section on long term memory and use.

5. CRITICAL THINKING AND BIG PICTURE UNDERSTANDING PRACTICED THROUGH CONCEPT MAPPING

Concept mapping can help with critical thinking and the "big picture" for understanding. When the visual is in full view, it helps to eliminate or lessen disconnections because of the simple fact that the whole topic, concept, idea, project, or whatever is in front of you, the group, and/or the class. When students conduct science experiments, if they draw a map as the experiment proceeds, it will be an easier task for them to either write up the experiment or discuss it in group or whole class time. An example might be the common experiment in elementary science that involves the floating and sinking of various objects in water. In times past, the teacher would have a transparent water container in the front and put various items into it. The students would fill out a two-columned chart as the items either floated or sank. The problem with this method is that students were not actively engaged. Nowadays students usually work in pairs on this task and then a group meeting takes place where students can share their observations of which items floated and which items sank. The physical process of doing the activity yourself creates more engagement on the part of students. If students use a two-branched concept map to record, it provides one visual picture for the brain to absorb. The group meeting offers opportunities for students to participate in the speaking process. Figure 17 (Float Or Sink) is an example of one pair's results.

Figure 17. Float or Sink

Sometimes the task is to evaluate information, another of those critical thinking skills. In those situations a simple two branch "yes or no" map is easy to draw out. The information is in full view of everyone. After all the yes and no reasons are listed, the participants could attach points determined by importance to each of the sub-branches and add each side up. The critical thinking is applied both in the yes or no listing of the reasons but also in how many points to attach to each item. At other times the task is more complex but the general idea is the same. If the information is put forth in front of everyone involved, the bigger picture is easier to determine.

Quick assessment is not that easy for teachers. If a teacher asks a student or students to draw a map about whatever the content is, the maps will show you what your students know and how they know it. For example, in the case of the floating and sinking experiment above, the teacher had each pair of students read their map to her and asked them to give ideas as to why certain items sank and others floated. Every pair figured out that the items that floated weighed less. The next year the teacher had more items and some of them weighed the same to start with but were so porous that they absorbed a lot more water and then sank. This made the task rise to a higher thinking level. The process of working with the students and discussing why the items sank caused the teacher to realize that the standard experiment needed an improvement of higher level thinking skills.

Typical elementary field trips can be improved by following some of these steps:

1. Map what they know, or think they know, just before students leave for home the day before the trip.
2. Leave that map up on the board.
3. Revisit the map upon return and add or change information based upon the trip.

4.   Ask students to talk with parents about the field trip for grades K-1.
5.   Do research in pairs or groups on something from the trip and revise again for grades 2-5.
6.   Double check the map depending upon the grade level and add, change and talk about the trip again.

This method really helps students with both facts and long term memory of the trip. This field trip routine helps students to pay attention to details while on a trip and to think more critically about the trip upon return and can also be placed in the scaffolding for learning category.

The following weather event can be used across many grade levels to work with critical thinking skills. There is an ice storm that took place in Versoix, Switzerland in 2005. You can find this readily via an Internet search from several sources. Play this for your students and then use any of the following or choices of the following for student projects:

1.   Journal entry of a day living in this environment,
2.   Write a persuasive essay to get someone to move to this town,
3.   Prepare a news broadcast of this event,
4.   Research and report on frostbite,
5.   Plan an emergency kit appropriate for this type of weather event,
6.   Develop a presentation about the effects this event will have on, people, animals, transportation, schools, businesses, and so forth,
7.   What will happen when all the water melts
8.   Design a utility vehicle that can be used in these conditions,
9.   What types of careers are needed for this event – who will help?

This short listing is offered to make you think more broadly on how concept mapping can be applied. Every item above can use a map as the major planning tool. If you want something else, how about the tsunami and nuclear energy plant disaster at Fukushima, Japan (Spring 2011) or Hurricane Sandy in the United States during the Fall of 2012 for starters? Opportunities abound for thinking about how to incorporate real life into learning content for students. Map a plan for a parents' night; map age appropriate TED lectures (http://www.ted.com/); map the "5 W's" (Who, What, Where, Why or How, When) for any journalistic project; or map a business start-up.

6. THE ROLE OF CONCEPT MAPPING WITH PAPERS, ESSAYS, RESEARCH AND PROJECTS

The use of concept mapping to organize essays, conduct research and complete projects is one of the most useful roles for students, as well as one of the easiest to implement, once students have completed several maps with and without the teacher. In planning for writing, the teacher is always hopeful that students will produce good work. In most cases, students hope so, also. However, writing is not every student's favorite activity. We ask students to write in a variety of styles but for many it is a chore, or worse, a nightmare. Often students who struggle do not know what it is that prevents them from being a successful writer.

Teachers who teach their students to map out their essays, reports and other tasks such as these, frequently discover that even boys are willing to complete redrafts of their work. It is easy and quick to revise a map. If the teacher purposely makes the first couple of exercises easy, the students will gain confidence with the process and with their own writing. Furthermore, the teacher should use partners for questioning and thinking and this can act as a peer evaluation. In addition students should feel free to use pictures, symbols, or an individual code in order to promote more thinking before the actual task begins. The teacher can easily call the map a first draft, thus, giving the perception that round one is in progress or over on the writing task. At this point the student can move from branch to branch, writing as they go. For the most part, they will soon be checking for small revisions and grammar and spelling. Through the partnership of supporting each other, students will probably lose most of their anxieties about writing assignments over a short time period. Those students who do not struggle as much with writing tasks will become quicker at completing their own writing tasks and reluctant writers will gain confidence. Dexter and Hughes (2011) described concept maps as graphic organizers that are used to organize concepts or information for writing and reading content which supports the above-mentioned information.

Former students of mine, Heather Davidson and Jeff McNeish (personal communications, 2006, 2007, 2013) of Grove City Schools in Pennsylvania, have shared a few ideas that may help readers expand their own thinking on offering students more opportunities for mapping application.

- **Third Grade:** Group maps for holidays other than Chinese New Year such as, Cinco de Mayo and St. Patrick's Day; individual and then class maps for important events in your own city or town's history for a community unit; individual map of the characteristics of a fable; individual maps of groups of Spanish words learned by category (or another language).

- **Fourth Grade:** Individual map of characteristics of a tall tale; group map steps to an archaeological dig from a unit on archeology; individual map of a timeline of famous state people for state history; map the parts of speech, what they do and then examples of each part of speech.
- **Fifth Grade:** Individual map of the characteristics of a career in Forensic Science that they chose to research; individual map of the setting, plot, characters for their own mystery story; individual and then class map of the different species found in the streams of the area.
- **Sixth Grade:** Individual map of the characteristics of their own mythology figure; group maps comparing and contrasting mythology figures; individual map of research for President's reports; individual maps of the important features of roller coasters for their own design and features of any machines.
- **Older Grades:** Usually teach propaganda in one of their social studies courses and this was also offered by Jeff McNeish: Individual maps and then class maps for each propaganda technique; individual maps and group maps of examples of propaganda from advertisements and commercials; individual map for an advertising campaign promoting their own product.

7. TACKLING TEXTBOOKS, LECTURES AND DOCUMENTARIES THROUGH CONCEPT MAPPING

Students do not like textbooks; just ask them and they will be honest about it. However, even with all of the resources available to teachers via the Internet and state purchased databases available in the K-12 environment, most school systems still utilize textbooks or e-textbooks for general instruction and administrators expect that teachers will cover the textbook during the term. There is a process for mapping textbooks that works very well. Initially, the teacher will have to show students the process. The teacher should point out and discuss what are the main sections, what are the chapters under those sections, and then what are the points of each chapter as being the best way to look at the larger picture to detail aspects of a textbook. There are always certain figures or graphs that are important and the students should be guided as to how to note them or how to draw enough information to spark memory. Many students need help with identifying key words and key concepts, especially if they are not familiar with the mapping process. In general, it is safe to say that that 90% of the text or lecture is not needed by the student in order to understand the concepts. Once students, through guided practice, understand how to determine the key words and concepts, they will end up with only one or two maps per chapter instead of a sheath of notes that are difficult to interpret, thus making it next to impossible to find the important concepts, let alone being able to study effectively from these notes.

Teachers might consider using the group method here, also. Instead of completing research on a topic and then presenting it to the class, students could be divided into groups for chapter purposes. The teacher could take a unit and chapter or a part of a chapter could be given to a group to study and present using a concept map to the class as a whole. The students make a map of their own based upon each group's presentation. Dilip Mukerjea, who has perfected and utilized this process for many years, describes the group study process in detail in his book, *Unleashing Genius* (2004). The teacher could interrupt for important points, to add additional information, to correct anything that needed correcting and so forth, but the speed of getting through a pile of required information with reliable recall, would allow more class time for other more engaging or meaningful projects or extended learning on specific topics. This textbook taming technique is especially applicable from late middle school through high school. Students will have more ownership of the subject matter and more responsibility to pay attention to each group as they present when they are involved in constructing their own maps.

News programs on television and documentaries on television are great for older students to develop skills with concept mapping when they have little or no prior experience. After initial exposure and practice with several maps on content as you lecture or they read short articles, the teacher can try the following activities. The first step for broadening mapping skills would be to have each student map the nightly news (as much as possible, students should try to use the same station). Students would bring their maps in and discuss them in groups. The teacher would spend a few minutes with each group in order to gain an overview of student progress with the skill. In the second step, the teacher would have a class watch the same program one night and bring in their maps the next day and then make a class master map of that topic utilizing the individual maps. At the same time each student would have the opportunity to correct and add to his/her individual map. This will also reinforce the process for when they are working in their groups in the classroom. An example from one of these class exercises is Figure 18 (Levee Documentary). This map was made by a student while viewing a television documentary about levees that was broadcast several years ago.

In preparation for a research project in the field of medicine, students were given detailed articles on several topics to read. A student interested in Methicillin-resistant Staphylococcus aureus (MRSA) took notes from the article, scanned it into a computer paint program and added the little images to the map. The student wanted to draw images but did not feel competent enough to draw the more difficult ones and, thus, made a quick scan and was able to add images in a short time frame. Although this was the student's first attempt at mapping an article, Figure 19. (MRSA

Figure 18. Levee documentary

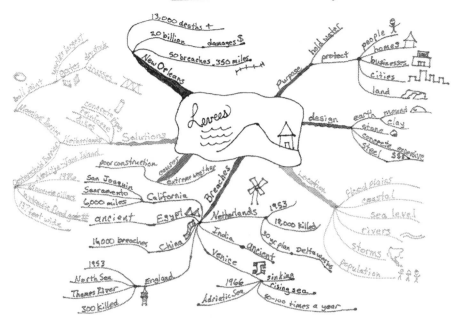

Figure 19. MRSA article

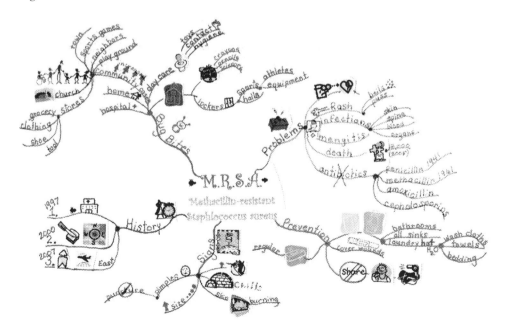

Article) clearly shows that the student was able to extract the main points from the article. The teacher pointed out to the student that in the future it would be wise to write all the bibliographic information on the back of the map for easy entry to a reference list and to note page numbers where appropriate on the map where an excellent quote might be extracted later in the writing process.

8. DIGITAL: THE NEW KID ON THE BLOCK

The tools available to teachers and students in Web 2.0 format are numerous. Concept mapping is no exception to this phenomenon. Several are available for use and it is recommended that users try out several to determine which tools best serve the users' particular need. Tools such as bubbl.us, wisemapper.com and spiderscribe. net are easy to learn and access is not a question as the tools are all residing in the cloud, so to speak. An excellent use of concept mapping tools is a class brainstorming activity on the electronic whiteboard. The teacher only has to have an active account in order to quickly pull-up a new map and the brainstorming could begin. The resulting map could be saved for later review and eliminated later if not needed. Students with access to smartphones, tablets and other devices with Internet access could use one of these tools to record quick thinking maps that may assist them later with ongoing work on essays or presentations.

The downside with the sole use of digital is that it lacks the kinesthetic element. The VAK learning styles (Visual, Auditory, Kinesthetic) encourages the use of all three for thorough learning experiences. Typing items into a Web 2.0 concept mapping application is not the same thing is actually drawing and redrawing something. For long term memory, making connections, and adding images and symbols that are meaningful to the student, it is the physical act of making the concept map that is important. An example of the difference between digital and hand-drawn maps might be the large wall Chinese New Year map described above. A teacher could have used a Web 2.0 tool to make a version of the big map and simply projected it on a wall for parents to see. However, the children contributed to this large map and it developed over the time spent on this unit. When it was hung up outside the classroom, the children had pride of being a part of the development of this unit. Ask yourself, would a parent want to this class map and then his/her child's individual maps or would they like to see a computer map instead? This does not mean that digital applications should be eschewed; it only means that both types of concept mapping serve various needs of the learner. Best practices for hand-drawn maps examples may include the following; note-taking, study and review, planning papers and presentations, chapters of textbooks and impromptu situations (known as drawing on the back of the napkin). Best practices for digital use may include the following; presenting to a group, images in publications, checking prior knowledge either group or individual, the above-mentioned brainstorming and pre-planned meetings (hand-out the printed map to all and they make notes) while the pre-made map is projected on an electronic whiteboard. These lists, are not complete, however, they may be used as starting examples for those new to the concept mapping strategy.

9. SOME HOW-TO TIPS TO BUILD MAPPING SKILLS AND MISCELLANEOUS USES OF CONCEPT MAPPING

The tips provided here are ones that may make the transition to a concept mapping classroom a lot easier for both the teacher and students. They are based upon my experiences, observations of others when utilizing or introducing concept mapping and conversations with other mappers over many years. If you are looking for the basics of "how-to" start a concept map and the construction of maps, please look at various sources from the resource list for this chapter.

- Practice is essential. This is a skill just like any other skill. I like to say that ten maps made upon simple ideas or concepts will get you moving. Twenty maps with some variety and the process is more than on your radar. By the time a person has made forty maps across content areas or types of uses, the process is ingrained. Ninety-eight percent of the people I know that have made it to that point in skill practice do not go back to old ways. Map what you know or something that is easy to start with but then move to what you do not know. Map what you are reading. Have your students map what they are reading. This is all great practice. Create maps of any talk, seminar or training session you attend. This will increase your skills and your students' skills rapidly.

- Sometimes the teacher starts with branches and then adds more and, especially with abstract concepts, the teacher may want to have main branches ready to go and then talk about a concept while the class is deciding where to put it. This is a good process of sharing, works at any level and can train students to use higher level thinking skills.

- Graphics are important and students can use easy to draw symbols or images. Images also engage students in the constructing of a map. It has generally been discovered that uppercase lettering, especially in the first level of branches, is the easiest to read. Sometimes lower case use also can quickly degenerate into our ordinary "scribbling" with the end result that it is not readable in the long term. However, what works for each individual student is the most important element in the whole process. Over the years I have come to use uppercase on the main branches and usually (but not always) a capital first letter on sub-branches.

- Generally, the center and the first branch are the largest printing with the details getting smaller. This also helps with the hierarchical view. You can make the most important key words thicker or circle them or highlight them.

- When doing initial or rough planning, color is not necessary for most students. However, it may help ADD, ADHD, LD and ESL learners to use color whenever they are mapping. I suggest that the teacher always use color in classroom maps or large maps on the wall outside of the classroom. Test preparation and recall are increased with the use of color. Color is also useful with difficult or abstract subjects.

- If you or your students are doing this for long term memory and recall, you should definitely use color and the central image should have at least three colors – there is something about the three colors that seems to be a memory trigger. One does not have to use color when the task is just trying to capture the essence of something or do a quick planning. The writer starts with a central image and puts a label on it for long term work. Color enhances but you still need the underlying thought patterns for the map to be effective.

- No matter the level of instruction, students need to practice with familiar items before working with the unfamiliar. As students build confidence, the instructor should move to the unfamiliar and to more complex mapping tasks.

- Some students may need to work around clusters of words or small ideas at first and then merge them into a map. That is okay. Eventually they will be able to skip this and work at a higher level.

- Sometimes students are not sure of a central image or idea of the map. The teacher can just have the students put down ideas and then go back and categorize or group them before they actually complete a map. Remind students that they can add branches as they go along. Fixing something they do not like or have changed their mind about is a simple thing to take care of in the redrawing of any map.

If the teacher is a club sponsor (a very common requirement of teachers in schools in the United States), try running the meetings with a map of the basic items to be discussed. Better yet, have the student who is president of the club do it. The meetings will run smoother and everyone will leave with a copy of the map with notes in their own hand. This process can be utilized by the teacher when working with other groups of teachers on a project or presentation. One is less likely to get off topic when the meeting starts with a map of the main branches. Tasks can be assigned and everyone knows upon leaving the meeting who is responsible for it because initials are quickly added of the person who will do it or head the task up.

Most teachers have to speak to the full faculty at meetings and this would be an opportune time for presenting with a map. If the teacher utilized a hand-drawn map on a whiteboard, it would allow for additions to be made easily, however, a digital map could also prove powerful. With more and more districts turning inward to provide professional learning opportunities, this would be an excellent opportunity for recruitment of new teachers to the strategy of concept mapping. If the professional learning sessions are full of concept maps, the participants in those sessions will be attracted to it in a subtle manner. I call this the "Relax with a latte while eating your peas" strategy. If the teacher is modeling to other teachers without being overly pushy of the strategy, there may well be enough inquiry for the presenter to offer a testimonial to the benefits of concept mapping.

Another great opportunity for concept mapping application is in the creation of a course or the heavy remodeling of an existing course. I have utilized concept mapping for many years when faced with this task (more than twenty-five courses). Concept mapping proved particularly helpful when moving entire courses from face-to-face mode to a completely online delivery mode. Which assignments transfer easily; which assignments are no longer relevant or do not transfer to the new environment well and must be completely replaced; how do you want the course to flow; and how will you assess are some of the multitude of questions that must be carefully considered. Hand drawn maps can be adjusted quickly and relationships marked easily with arrows when thinking the new courses through. Draw a beginning map for each course and put it on the wall by your desk. As flashes of genius fly through the mind, the map can be accessed quickly and changes noted or additions made with ease. In the course of a few days the incubation or rumination in the mind and a few nights of sleep will help the process of refinement to occur naturally.

10. OBSERVATIONS FROM A WHOLE SCHOOL IMPLEMENTATION

Seabrook Elementary School, Melbourne, Australia is an example of a school that implemented a whole school effort to promote concept mapping. Over a period of several years the school staff had been trained in a wide variety of programs such as, Multiple Intelligences, Teaching and Learning Styles, De Bono's Thinking About Thinking and Six Hats, Brain Gym, Herrmann Brain Dominance, Habits of Mind and others specific to Australia and the Pacific area. In 2002 they sent three people for intensive training in Mind Mapping and it did not take long for them to realize that this was what they were looking for to pull everything together for students. The following quotes, mostly from the school principal, Lyn Jobson, are all taken from the 2004 revised Seabrook report on this effort.

Examples of Concept Mapping in a School Setting

From a guided reading group's comprehension questions on a specific book in a concept map:

Emily, a child who usually has difficulty answering comprehension questions in linear form, happily did it in the form of a mind map – and did it well. When I asked her, does all this make sense to you? She answered: It makes perfect sense! (Grade 4 teacher, p. 5)

On the quickness of adopting concept mapping at the school arising from the students:

So, the impetus to Mind Map came from the students, which then encouraged the teachers to continue applying it in the classroom. (Lyn Jobson, p. 9)

Student perceptions of self:

For the first time some of the students' work had a quality about it that they felt reflected who they thought they were..... It help put their learning difference in the proper little place it should be, which is a small place. (Lyn Jobson, p. 11)

About successes with students with learning difficulties:

What we found was that the successes weren't at the top end necessarily – the most empowering thing was the instant successes were with the most difficult students. (Lyn Jobson, p. 12)

Discussing the impact with autistic children and restless children:

Four students in particular, Huang, Jess, Sam and Jackson, have all found a way to communicate through Mind Maps whereas previously they didn't. They couldn't! (Lyn Jobson, p. 16)

For Huang, Mind Maps are a reflection of the order he has in his mind, how he is thinking, and how his mind is working. (p. 17)

Mind Mapping is good for restless students because …. Is about changing pens, fiddling is ok, doodling with images and flicking that pen around. (Jeanette Finegan, p. 20)

The final comment from Lyn Jobson was made about the increased results on tests of students that required more literacy support:

We have been telling these students for years 'trust me, I can make a difference for you' and most of those techniques we have given students don't really move them and so they become disengaged, they don't believe you. They just think you are telling them another hoodwink story to get them to do some more work. However, this time we could prove that this was working for them, and the students actually moved from being disengaged learners to being really co-operative. (pp. 14-15)

To my mind, it seems that it is probably safe to say that concept mapping is the glue they were looking for to bring as much success in learning as possible for their students. The dedication of the staff to implement many types of strategies from their professional trainings and then to wrap all of it around concept mapping with students is a true success story that can be replicated anywhere.

CONCLUSION, SUMMARY, AND A CALL TO ACTION

In summary, I first offer a vignette of one person's journey with concept mapping in the classroom that, to me, says it all. Several years ago, a friend of mine decided to instruct her middle school language arts students in the making and applications of concept maps. Her long term goal was that the students would produce better essays and score higher on subject matter tests. Although spreadsheet data was not maintained, in the space of only one term she discovered the following:

- Note taking and planning activities for essays and speeches were completed more rapidly and without complaint.
- Essays that were completed tended to be more clearly organized and more detailed with paragraphs developed more thoroughly.
- Grades received on writing assignments improved by a minimum of two letter grades for students who were in the middle tier academically.
- Summarizing skills appeared to be offered up more readily and rapidly during class content time. The ability to summarize learning is generally considered a best practice technique and follows Robert Marzano's work on key skills and essential instructional strategies with which many teachers are already familiar (https://ncwlearningwithtechnology.wikispaces.com/file/view/Marzano's+Nine.pdf). The redrawing of a map for summarization also served as the essential first review (Buzan, 1996; Mukerjea, 2004).

- Students, for the most part, got away from the five paragraph essay format and wrote whatever amount the content, report, research called for in order to complete the task.
- Test preparation was done utilizing maps from notes and done in pairs or small groups without student complaints.
- Students began to exhibit more self-confidence and absenteeism decreased when compared to the prior two years (approximately an average of six less days per year).
- Grades improved not only in her course but in a few other courses where teachers allowed the students to utilize what she had taught them.

The teacher instructed her students each year for a period of four more years until her retirement. She continued to have higher scores from her students on annual statewide tests in the content area than others teaching the same content at her grade level. Her comment at a retirement reception with fellow faculty was, "I wish y'all would apply what I've been telling you for the past five years with your students." If a teacher who taught for thirty-six years could radically change her strategies for instruction the last five years of her career and be excited about it, then those entering the field may find it more than worthwhile professionally to cultivate mapping skills and instruct their own students in the process.

Here are the kernels of mapping in a nutshell that are directly related to positive student outcome:

- Students will ultimately understand more fully how they process information.
- Students will know that this works well when done collaboratively in pairs, groups and whole class situations.
- Students will understand the benefits of making their thinking (schemas) visible to themselves and others in their classroom environment when they personally experience improved scores and less difficulty with studying in courses and more success with personal learning projects.
- Students will sense that although we are all different with varying strengths and weaknesses and represent a variety of learning styles, that concept mapping is a fantastic multiple use tool and that it will help them to make meaning or to organize whatever content or task is presented to them.

Finally, the main reason to be a good role model for concept mapping is that you are the model, guide or "important other" in many students' lives. You will teach thousands of students by the end of your career. When students see you modeling how to map, they will want to do it too. I encourage all of you to think of the dissemination of the skill as a moral imperative. The words, "if not now, when," spring to mind. Those in the field, who understand the enormous effect visual learning can yield for student learning, are the ones who can lead the way. Share with others who ask about what you are doing. Mentor other teachers, especially those who are entering the field. Critical mass of users is what will be the tipping point to move concept mapping to the forefront as a great strategy. Bolder and wiser must be the alternative to "drill and kill" education; it is the ability to understand connections and learn and work smarter that will make a difference classroom to classroom. As students become more proficient in the mechanics of mapping across content areas and different purposes, it will make the value of concept mapping apparent to them. Eventually it will become their modus operandi and they will not return to the old linear method of note taking, organizing, studying or presenting.

REFERENCES

Burmark, L. (2002). *Visual literacy: Learn to see, see to learn.* Alexandria, VA: Association for Supervision and Curriculum Development.

Buzan, T. (1996). *The mind map book, How to use radiant thinking to maximize your brain's untapped potential.* New York, NY: Penguin Books.

Chan, C. (2009). *Assessment: Concept map, assessment resources@HKU.* University of Hong Kong. Retrieved from http://ar.cetl.hku.hk

Dexter, D. D., & Hughes, C. A. (2011). Graphic organizers and students with learning disabilities: A meta-analysis. *Learning Disability Quarterly, 34*(1), 51–72.

Hilbert, T., & Renkl, A. (2006). *Concept mapping as a follow-up strategy to learning from texts: What characterizes good and poor mappers.* Freiburg, Germany: Department of Psychology, University of Freiburg.

Israel, L. (2005). *Get ahead and ace your grades.* [DVD]. London, UK: Aulis Publishers.

Joyce, B., Calhoun, E., & Hopkins, D. (2000). *Models of learning, Tools for teaching.* Berkshire, UK: McGraw-Hill Education.

Mukerjea, D. (2004). *Unleashing genius: With the world's most powerful learning systems.* Singapore: The Brainware Press.

Nast, J. (2006). *Idea mapping, How to access your hidden brain power, learn faster, remember more and achieve success in business.* Hoboken, NJ: John Wiley & Sons, Inc.

Nesbit, J. C., & Adesope, O. O. (2006). Learning with concept and knowledge maps: A meta-analysis. *Review of Educational Research*, *76*(3), 413–448. doi:10.3102/00346543076003413

Riding, R., & Raynor, S. (1998). *Cognitive styles and learning strategies*. London: David Fulton Publishers, Ltd.

Seabrook Primary School. (2004). *Seabrook report: Mind mapping the learning platform at Seabrook Primary School*. Melbourne, Australia: Seabrook Primary School.

Smith, A. (2001). *The brain's behind it*. Stafford, UK: Network Educational Press Ltd.

KEY TERMS AND DEFINITIONS

Concept Map: A visualization of some/any type of knowledge that allows for relationships to be readily seen; new ideas added or changed and also may be used as an effective planning and/or presentation tool for many tasks (Author's Definition).

Concept Map: A concept map is a hierarchical form of structure diagram that illustrates conceptual knowledge and relationships within a specific topic from general to specific concepts (Chan, 2009). Another take is "Concept mapping is a method for representing knowledge graphically" (Hilbert & Renkl, 2008, p.53).

Critical Thinking Skills: Moving students up the ladder of Revised Bloom's Taxonomy in their reasoning abilities (Author's Definition for purposes of this chapter). According to Dictionary.com, the term is defined as "the mental process of actively and skillfully conceptualizing, applying, analyzing, synthesizing and evaluating information to reach an answer or conclusion" (http://dictionary.reference.com. Accessed: March 6, 2014).

Long Term Memory: Information that remains in our brains for a very long time or indefinitely that we can access and bring into use as needed or required by the situation at hand.

Chapter 4

Can Mapping Improve the Quality of Critical Thinking in Essay Writing in an Introductory Level, Core Curriculum Class?

Leonard Shedletsky
University of Southern Maine, USA

EXECUTIVE SUMMARY

This study began with the question: Can mapping improve the quality of critical thinking in essay writing in an introductory level, core curriculum class? Two sections of the course, Introduction to Communication, were compared, without mapping and with mapping. Dependent measures were: (1) the word count for summarizing the critical incident to be analyzed; (2) the number of concepts/theories employed to analyze the critical incident; (3) the number of times a connection was made between the analytical concepts/theories and the critical incident; (4) the number of words used in summarizing the essay as a whole; and (5) the total number of words in the essay. In addition, the data were analyzed for practice since there were three attempts at essay writing. Practice at writing the paper had an especial effect on writing and mapping had an especial effect on laying out the problem and applying analytical concepts to it.

DOI: 10.4018/978-1-4666-5816-5.ch004

INTRODUCTION

For the suitably skilled person, mapping a complex argument promotes clarity and insight, more rigorous and complete articulation, and more judicious evaluation. Teachers use argument mapping to help students acquire basic concepts, better understand how arguments are constructed, and enhance their reasoning skills. Argument mapping can be an effective way to improve general critical thinking skills. In the workplace, argument mapping can promote rational resolution in complex, fractious debates; improved communication of important arguments; and better decision making (Tim Van Gelder, 2013).

In recent years, with the onset and dramatic growth of online education, a great deal of research interest has been given over to discussion and critical thinking. After all, one of the key arguments made for online education is its ability to offer discussion as a primary way in which learning takes place. Most educators seem to agree that critical thinking is a worthy goal of higher education. It has long been known that most online courses use discussion (Berge, 1997). Time and again we are presented with the idea—the claim-- that discussion is especially well suited for online environments, that students inter-act with one another and the teacher. We are told that they debate, they collaborate and offer constructive feedback and engage one another in ideas. We are reminded that online students get more time to think about what is said; they get more time to construct their responses. They write their thoughts which some tell us increases the opportunity to be mindful. Much of the reason for discussion is the belief that discussion exercises and helps to develop critical thinking. Derek Bok has written that faculties generally agree that "teaching students to think critically is the principal aim of undergraduate education" (Bok, 2006, p. 109).

Unfortunately, research does not find real support for the contention that online education produces higher levels of critical thinking. In fact, research into critical thinking online and in the classroom finds a real dearth of critical thinking in discussion. Based on a number of reviews of the literature, it appears that the amount and the quality of online discussion are quite poor (Garrison, Anderson, & Archer, 2001; 2003; Hunt, Simonds, & Simonds, 2007; Meyer, 2003; Rourke & Kanuka, 2007). We have encountered few individual teachers or students who take real issue with this claim. Moreover, as we explore further, we begin to see that this claim holds true for much of discussion in the classroom as well. As you might expect, the low level of critical thinking evidenced in discussion is also present in students' writing (http://wsuctproject.wsu.edu/; Van Gelder, 2005). Arum and Roksa (2011) wrote: ". . . many students are only minimally improving their skills in critical thinking, complex reasoning, and writing during their journeys through higher education" (p. 35).

Research does support the claim that students learn more when they are actively engaged with the material, their instructor, and their classmates (Howard & Baird, 2000; Ambrose, Bridges, DiPietro, Lovett, & Norman, 2010). Some research suggests that critical thinking is fostered by students' active participation in learning (Garside, 1996; Smith, 1977). We hasten to add that our own research on critical thinking has generally found that it is extremely difficult to increase the amount of critical thinking (Shedletsky, 2010). Other researchers have reported that it is difficult to improve students' argumentation and critical thinking skills through short-term instructional methods (Terenzini, 1995; McMillan, 1987) McMillan (1987), reviewed 27 studies on specific instructional methods, and no single instructional method was found to consistently enhance critical thinking in college students. Mc-Millan reasoned that a semester is simply too brief and isolated to have an impact on critical thinking. McMillan concluded that " . . . it appears from these studies that college students' critical thinking improves while attending college, but it is not clear what factors affect this change" (p.15). On the other hand, McKeachie, Pintrich, Lin, and Smith (1986) claimed that stressing student discussion and placing emphasis on problem-solving procedures and methods may enhance critical thinking. Similarly, Kelly-Riley, Brown, Condon and Law (2007) reported that using a seven point critical thinking rubric integrated into teaching, produces significantly elevated " . . . higher order thinking abilities over the course of the semester" (p. 8), though when the same student work is scored for writing there was an inverse relationship to critical thinking scores. In other words, they found that writing could be assessed as adequate while critical thinking was low. Jenson (2011) found that combining three instructional strategies helped to improve critical reflection in her first year students' writing. She had students respond to a questionnaire that had students think about how they went about writing, when and where and how; classroom discussion designed to make explicit the purpose of the writing assignment, the skills involved and how they related to other courses and at work; and third, she had students write in an ePortfolio to reflect on the writing, e.g., what they learned and how they might make changes in a next paper. Jenson concluded that these three strategies dramatically increased the depth of thinking. It appears then that there is some reason to believe that focusing on critical thinking in various ways, being explicit about the processes of reflecting and writing can improve critical thinking.

Most educators seem to agree that critical thinking is a worthy goal of higher education and yet it is difficult to define and it is difficult to determine what we can do to improve it. One scholar of critical thinking (Ennis, 1985, p. 45) defined critical thinking as reflective and reasonable thinking about what to believe and or do. With this sort of broad definition, it is no wonder that it is difficult to measure critical thinking and difficult to determine what can improve critical thinking. Nevertheless, the growth in online education has made it important to return to questions about critical thinking and discussion. Online courses are growing in number and discussion in these courses substitutes for classroom interaction. In case you are wondering why we do not simply digitize lectures and make them available online, we should note that the lecture method has not been found to facilitate higher order thinking (http://www.brookes.ac.uk/services/ocsld/resources/20reasons.html; Gibbs, 1981; London & Draper, 2008).

With the aid of computer technology, scholars have turned to software to aid in diagramming the structure of argument. Research is showing that Argument Mapping is producing increased levels of critical thinking in students, above and beyond what they get from a semester long course without argument mapping (Van Gelder, 2006). For instance, here is a link to slides showing the progression of my students' map making over a semester http://media.usm.maine.edu/~lenny/new_mappers_F_11.ppt

This research focuses on the question of whether or not mapping can improve the quality of critical thinking in essay writing in a freshman level course. At the same time, it follows up on the finding by Kelly-Riley, Brown, Condon and Law (available online at: http://wsuctproject.wsu.edu/) that students' high scores on critical thinking do not necessarily predict high scores on their writing.

METHOD

Data were gathered from two sections of the researcher's Introduction to Communication course. In both iterations of the course, students analyzed and wrote essays about three communication incidents. In one section (fall, 2011), students were introduced to mapping techniques and mapped the communication incidents and their analyses before writing each of three essays. This class was given the following instructions:

WEBSPIRATIONPRO EXERCISES

There are 3 critical incidents to analyze for this course. For each one of them, you are asked to use WebspirationPro to map and work on your analysis of the incident. By mapping the incident, what is meant is that you lay out the components of the incident. By analyze the incident, what is meant is that you insert concepts and theories from the course into your map of the incident in places where it makes sense and in that way you build your essays.

In the other section (fall, 2010), there was no mapping. For each class, with and without mapping, we used three essays from the first, second and third analyses. The randomly selected essays were coded, so that we would know which essays were first, second and third essays and which were done with and without mapping but the rater did not know any of this.

RESULTS

This study began with the question: Can Mapping Improve the Quality of Critical Thinking in Essay Writing in an Introductory Level, Core Curriculum Class? We compared two sections of the course, Introduction to Communication, without mapping (Fall, 2010) and with mapping (Fall, 2011), taught by this researcher. We took as our dependent measures (1) the word count for summarizing the critical incident to be analyzed; (2) the number of concepts/theories employed to analyze the critical incident; (3) the number of times a connection was made between the analytical concepts/theories and the critical incident; (4) the number of words used in summarizing the essay as a whole; and (5) the total number of words in the essay.

A repeated measures ANOVA was used to assess the impact of mapping. Because one class was not exposed to the mapping technique, all students in that class were placed in a "no mapping" group. Additional students, from the class where mapping was discussed, were also included in that no mapping group when it was determined that they had not used this technique (Table 1).

Table 1. The effect of course on five dependent measures

Dependent Variables	Independent Variables: Course (with PAPER the repeated measure)	Means	Significance
Summary of CI	No Mapping	139.233	not sig.
	Mapping Required	159.938	
Concepts	No Mapping	3.182	sig.
	Mapping Required	5.729	
Connections	No Mapping	2.303	sig.
	Mapping Required	4.854	
Essay Summary	No Mapping	95.182	not sig.
	Mapping Required	93.667	
Total Words	No Mapping	763.788	not sig.
	Mapping Required	847.167	

It turns out that many of the students in the section of the course instructed to map (Mapping Required), did not map. Students had three opportunities to map (in the Fall, 2011 class) and to show their map on our course Web site. If they mapped at least one time that we could verify, we counted them as mapping. One class had no mapping opportunity, but another class did. However, not all in the latter class took advantage of mapping. It was therefore necessary to directly compare students who mapped with those who did not. When we look at the dependent variables by those individuals who mapped (N =33) and those who did not (N = 76), we get the results shown in Table 2.

The results from students who did use mapping shows effects for the number of words used to summarize the critical incident, for the number of concepts they referred to from the course in writing their analyses, and for the number of connections they made between concepts and the critical incident (Figure 1 and Figure 2).

Since the students wrote three essays for each of the courses, we performed a repeated measures ANOVA to test the effects of Course on the five dependent measures, with papers 1, 2 & 3 as repeated measures (Figure 3).

The variable Course, i.e., the section of the course with mapping versus the section without mapping, did not produce an effect on the number of words used to summarize the critical incident (F = .838, df = 1, 24, p > .05). Course showed an effect on the number of concepts used to analyze the critical incident (F = 10.377, df = 1, 25. P < .004). Course produced an effect on the number of connections made between the concepts and the critical incident (F = 15.730, df = 1, 25. P < .001).

Figure 1. Mean number of concepts used to analyze the CI showing a statistically significant difference between non-mapping and mapping

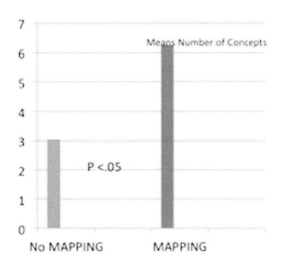

Table 2. The effect of the individual mapping on five dependent measures

Dependent Variable	Mapped vs. Did not Map	Mean	Significance
Summary of CI	no mapping	128.194	sig.
	mapping	179.861	
Concepts	no mapping	3.051	sig.
	mapping	6.250	
Connections	no mapping	2.282	sig.
	mapping	5.278	
Essay Summary	no mapping	90.615	not sig.
	mapping	96.056	
Total Words	no mapping	748.795	not sig.
	mapping	872.639	

Figure 2. Mean number of connections made between concepts and the CI showing a statistically significant difference between non-mappers and mappers

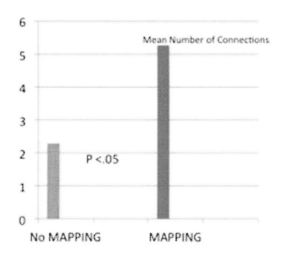

Course did not show an effect on the number of words used to summarize the essays (F = .014, df = 1, 25. P > .05). Course did not produce an effect on the total number of words used to write the essay papers (F = .747, df = 1, 25. P > .05).

Paper (essay 1, 2 or 3) did produce an effect on the number of words used to summarize the CI (F = 8.659, df =2, 44, p < .001). The mean number of words for paper 1 = 115.542; paper 2 = 175.208; and paper 3 = 171.333. Paper did have an effect on the number of concepts that students referred to in analyzing the Critical Incident (F = 10.300, df = 2, 46, p < .000) (Figure 4).

Figure 3. Mean number of words to summarize the CI by paper and by course (without and with mapping instructions)

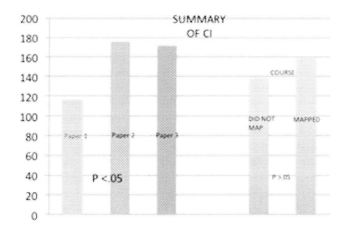

Paper did have an effect on the number of connections students made between concepts and the Critical Incident in analyzing the CI (F = 10.944, df = 2, 46, p < .000) (Figure 5).

Paper did have an effect on the number of words students used to summarize their essays as a whole (F = 4.992, df = 2, 46, p < .000) (Figure 6).

Paper did have an effect on the number of total words students used in analyzing the CI (F = 51.441, df = 2, 46, p < .000) (Figure 7).

Figure 4. Mean number of concepts by paper

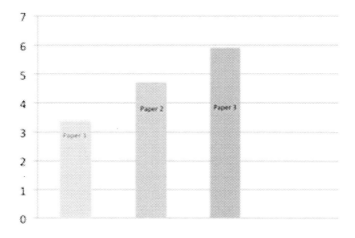

Figure 5. Mean number of connections between concepts and the critical incident

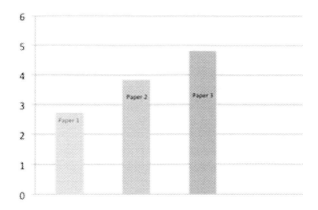

Whether the student mapped or not (again, some in the class required to map did not follow instructions and did not show a map) had an effect on the number of words used to summarize the CI, (F = 5.793, df = 1, 22, p < .025); the number of concepts used, (F = 19.211, df = 1, 23, p < .000); the number of connections made between concepts and the CI, (F = 25.346, df = 1, 23, p < .000); but no effect on the number of words used to summarize the essay, (F = .159, df = 1, 23, p > .05); or the total words in the essay, (F = 1.513, df = 1, 23, p > .05).

Figure 6. Mean number of words used to summarize the essay by paper and by mapping

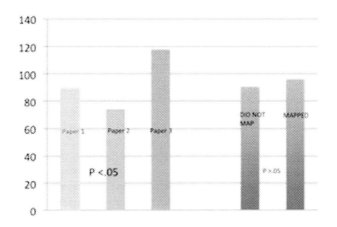

Figure 7. Mean number of total words used to write the paper by paper and by whether or not the individual mapped

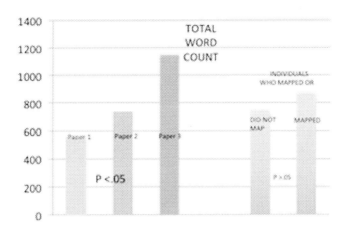

The interaction for mapping and paper did not show a statistically significant effect (F= .934, df = 2, 46, p > .05). These two independent variables operated independently of one another.

Both mapping and writing multiple papers appear to result in an increased number of words used to summarize the CI, an increased number of concepts used to analyze the CI, and an increased number of connections made between concepts and the critical incident. In addition, with writing more papers, the student also showed an increase in the number of words used to summarize the essay and the total number of words used in the essay. One possible way to interpret these findings is to say that practice at writing the paper had an especial effect on writing and mapping had an especial effect on laying out the problem and applying analytical concepts to it. The effect of mapping on writing versus critical thinking is discussed later.

We wanted to learn whether or not a faculty member would recognize a qualitative difference in the essays written by students who mapped versus students who did not map. Two tenured college faculty members were asked to grade 18 essays, 9 from each of the two sections, mapping vs. non-mapping, randomly chosen from each section. They were given the following instructions:

There are 18 essays to be graded. We are interested in the numerical grade taking into account the quality of the writing, e.g., structure of the essay, and also the quality of the content in terms of things like elaborating on ideas and offering support for ideas presented (reference to the text), critical thinking.

Please grade each paper with a numeric grade, using the following scale:

Grading Scale:

- A 93-100%
- 90-92%
- B+ 87-89%
- B 83-86%
- B- 80-82%
- C+ 77-79%
- C 73-76%
- C- 70-72%
- D 60-69%
- F less than 60%

Please place your grade on the top of each essay. And finally, please read these essays in the order from the first in the pile to the last.

The two raters produced grades that were quite consistent across the two sections of the course, showing little difference in grades for mappers versus non-mappers and little difference between the two raters (see Table 3).

A paired samples t-test was performed to test for differences in ratings between the two raters, finding no significant difference between the two raters, t (17) = .474, p > .05.

DISCUSSION

Can mapping aid the student in critical thinking and essay writing? This study suggests a qualified "yes." Mapping produced an effect on the number of words in the summary of the critical incident, the number of concepts used to analyze the critical incident, the number of connections made between the concepts and the critical incident but not on the summary of the essay or the total number of words used to

Table 3. Mean ratings by mapping

	Mapping 1 = no mapping 2 = mapping	N	Mean	Std. Deviation
Rater 1	1	9	80.11	12.160
	2	9	80.78	6.572
Rater 2	1	9	80.33	3.742
	2	9	82.56	2.028

write the essay. These results suggest that mapping has its greatest effect on critical thinking rather than on writing *per se*. With mapping, it appears that the student goes deeper, offers a more detailed accounting of the incident to be analyzed, then refers to a larger number of concepts to apply to the analysis, and makes more connections between the theoretical notions named and the data to be analyzed. At the same time, the summary of the essay and the total words used to write the essay do not differ from the non-mappers.

Also, it is of note that the two professors grading a sample of these essays did not discriminate between mappers and non-mappers in their grading. We originally thought that the mappers would receive higher grades on their essays. One way to account for this failure to grade mapper papers higher is to speculate that teachers are not grading for critical thinking as much as for some other variable(s), possibly writing style. We must note that several other researchers have pointed to a disconnect between critical thinking in essays and grades on essays (Kelly-Riley, D., Brown, G., Condon, B., & Law, R. (2007; Grabau, 2007). Moon (2005) draws a distinction between the provision of evidence in critical thinking and the written representation of the evidence, between clarity and precision in critical thinking and in writing. She wrote: "Clarity and precision are similarly qualities of critical thinking that apply both to the quality of thinking itself and separately, to the manner in which the critical thinking is represented" (p. 32).

For instance Kelly-Riley, D., Brown, G., Condon, B., & Law, R. (2007) found that student writing was regarded as generally excellent, while an independent assessment of critical thinking skills shown in student writing revealed relatively little development, even by the junior year. Grabau (2007) reported that "Tsui (2002) found that a strong writing (and re-writing) orientation and class discussions across the entire curriculum were associated with enhanced critical thinking skills. Tsui (2002) emphasized that while individual instructors could engage their students in more extensive writing assignments (particularly of an analytical rather than a descriptive nature), an institutional commitment to such activities is necessary for optimal student growth in critical thinking skills" (p. 7). There is a relationship between writing and critical thinking but it is not a simple one.

Another way of understanding these findings is to consider Hyerle's discussion of persistence. Hyerle (2008) wrote that maps help students to generate ideas, to persist with a problem, to strive for accuracy and precision as opposed to an impulsive reaction to a task. Expanding on the idea of sticking with a problem, Hyerle wrote this about 1st graders using mapping:

By the time students had returned to their desks and mapped out their thinking for a piece of writing, they had expanded and clarified their thinking. When we take into account short-term memory capacity, having a visual record along with a verbal explanation gives students and teachers a way of adding more information in a structured way. The visual form allows for clarity of expression because students can clearly see the reasoning that they are doing and present this to classmates and their teacher as a clear view of how they have put information together (p. 167).

It would make sense that the same cognitive habits affect the college student trying to analyze a story. And it is proposed that that is precisely what made for the differences in the mapping and non-mapping groups in this study. Because the mappers in this study produced longer summaries of the incident to be analyzed, referred to more concepts with which to analyze and made more connections between these concepts and the incident than for non-mappers, we can say that the mappers persisted with the problem, elaborated on it, analyzed it more extensively and with greater support. This is what we are calling indications of critical thinking. With regard to cognitive load, Ambrose, Bridges, DiPietro, Lovett & Norman put it this way: "Research has shown that removing extraneous load—that is, aspects of a task that make it difficult to complete but that are unrelated to what students need to learn—is helpful" (p. 106). They go on to point out that reducing cognitive load is especially helpful when students are performing a complex task and they are new at the task. In this study, with the cognitive load lightened by producing the map, students were able to focus on the parts of the task requiring learning, that is, applying theoretical concepts to an incident. Doing the assignment three times over the semester, with or without mapping, influenced all five dependent measures, suggesting that practice alone aided the quality of the essays and the writing *per se*. Since paper (essay 1, 2 & 3) and mapping did not interact, practice and mapping appear to function in ways that distinguish them from one another. We speculate, as we have said, that paper or practice has a greater effect on writing, and mapping has a greater effect on critical thinking.

REFERENCES

Ambrose, S. A., Bridges, M. W., DiPietro, M., Lovett, C., & Norman, M. (2010). *How learning works: Seven research-based principles for smart teaching.* San Francisco, CA: Josey-Bass.

Anderson, L. W., & Krathwohl, D. R. (Eds.). (2001). *A taxonomy for learning, teaching, and assessing: A revision of Bloom's taxonomy of educational objectives.* New York: Longman.

Arum, R., & Roksa, J. (2011). *Academically adrift: Limited learning on college campuses.* Chicago: University of Chicago Press.

Beaudry, J., & Wilson, P. (2010). Concept mapping and formative assessment: Elements supporting literacy and learning. In *Handbook of research on collaborative learning using concept mapping*. Hershey, PA: IGI Publishing.

Berge, Z. L. (1997). Characteristics of online teaching in post-secondary, formal education. *Educational Technology, 37*(3), 35–47.

Bok, D. (2006). *Our underachieving colleges: A candid look at how much students learn and why they should be learning more*. Princeton, NJ: Princeton University Press.

Davies, M. (2010). Concept mapping, mind mapping and argument mapping: What are the differences and do they matter? *Higher Education, 62*(3), 279–301. doi:10.1007/s10734-010-9387-6

Ennis, R. H. (1985). A logical basis for measuring critical thinking skills. *Educational Leadership, 43*(2), 44–48.

Garrison, D. R., Anderson, T., & Archer, W. (2001). Critical thinking, cognitive presence, and computer conferencing in distance education. *American Journal of Distance Education, 15*(1), 7–23. doi:10.1080/08923640109527071

Garrison, D. R., Anderson, T., & Archer, W. (2003). Critical thinking, cognitive presence, and computer conferencing in distance education. *American Journal of Distance Education, 15*(1), 7–23. doi:10.1080/08923640109527071

Garside, C. (1996). Look who's talking: A comparison of lecture and group discussion teaching strategies in developing critical thinking skills. *Communication Education, 45*, 212–227. doi:10.1080/03634529609379050

Gibbs, G. (1981, December). *Twenty terrible reasons for lecturing* (SCEDSIP Occasional Paper No.8). Birmingham, UK: SCED Publications.

Grabau, L. J. (2007). Effective teaching and learning strategies for critical thinking to foster cognitive development and transformational learning. *Kentucky Journal for Excellence in College Teaching and Learning, 5*, 123–156.

Howard, J. R., & Baird, R. (2000). The consolidation of responsibility and students' definitions of the college classroom. *The Journal of Higher Education, 71*, 700–721. doi:10.2307/2649159

Hunt, S., Simonds, C., & Simonds, B. (2007, November). Uniquely qualified, distinctively competent: Delivering 21st century skills in the basic course. In *Proceedings of 93rd Annual Convention*. National Communication Association.

Hyerle, D. (1996). *Visual tools for constructing knowledge*. Alexandria, VA: Association for Supervision and Curriculum Development.

Hyerle, D. (2008). Thinking maps: Visual tools for activating habits of mind. In *Learning and leading with habits of mind: 16 essential characteristics for success* (pp. 149–176). Academic Press.

Hyerle, D. (2009). *Visual tools for transforming information into knowledge* (2nd ed.). Thousand Oaks, CA: Sage.

Hyerle, D., & Williams, K. (2010). Bifocal assessment in the cognitive age: Thinking maps for assessing content learning and cognitive processes. *The New Hampshire Journal of Education*, 32-38. Retrieved from http://thinkingfoundation.org/research/journal_articles/journal_articles.html

Jenson, J. D. (2011). Promoting self-regulation and critical reflection through writing students' use of electronic portfolio. *International Journal of ePortfolio, 1*(1), 49-60.

Kelly-Riley, D., Brown, G., Condon, B., & Law, R. (2007). *Washington State University critical thinking project*. Retrieved April 27, 2007 from http://wsuctproject.ctlt.wsu.edu/ctm.htm

Korb, K., & van Gelder, T. (2010). Editorial and interview with Tim van Gelder. *The Reasoner, 4*(2), 18–21.

London, H., & Draper, M. (2008). The silent revolution in higher education. *Academic Questions, 21*(2), 221–225. doi:10.1007/s12129-008-9052-z

McKeachie, W., Pintrich, P., Lin, Y., & Smith, D. (1986). *Teaching and learning in the college classroom: A review of the research literature*. Ann Arbor, MI: University of Michigan, National Center for Research to Improve Post-Secondary Teaching and Learning.

McMillan, J. H. (1987). Enhancing college students' critical thinking: A review of studies. *Research in Higher Education, 26*(1), 3–29. doi:10.1007/BF00991931

Meyer, K. (2003). Face-to-face versus threaded discussion: The role of time and higher-order thinking. *JALN, 7*(3), 55–65.

Moon, J. (2005). *We seek it here…a new perspective on the elusive activity of critical thinking: A theoretical and practical approach*. ESCalate Discussion Series. Retrieved November 29, 2012 from http://escalate.ac.uk/downloads/2041.pdf

Nesbit, J., & Adesope, O. (2006). Learning with concept and knowledge maps: A meta-analysis. *Review of Educational Research, 76*(3), 413–448. doi:10.3102/00346543076003413

Novak, J. (1998). *Learning, creating, and using knowledge: Concept maps as facilitative tools in schools and corporations.* Hoboken, NJ: Lawrence Erlbaum Associates.

Novak, J., & Gowin, D. (1984). *Learning how to learn.* New York: Cambridge University Press. doi:10.1017/CBO9781139173469

Novak, J. D. (2005). Results and implications of a 12-year longitudinal study of science concept learning. *Research in Science Education, 35*(1), 23–40. doi:10.1007/s11165-004-3431-4

Rourke, L., & Kanuka, H. (2007). Computer conferencing and distance learning. In *The handbook of computer networks* (Vol. 3, pp. 831–842). Hoboken, NJ: John Wiley & Sons.

Shedletsky, L. (2010). Does online discussion produce increased interaction and critical thinking? In L. Shedletsky, & J. Aitken (Eds.), *Cases on online discussion and interaction: Experiences and outcomes.* Hershey, PA: IGI Global. doi:10.4018/978-1-61520-863-0.ch001

Shedletsky, L. (2010). Critical thinking in discussion: Online versus face-to-face. In D. Russell (Ed.), *Cases on collaboration in virtual environments: Processes and interactions.* Hershey, PA: Information Science Reference.

Shedletsky, L., & Aitken, J. (Eds.). (2010). *Cases on online discussion and interaction: Experiences and outcomes.* Hershey, PA: IGI Global. doi:10.4018/978-1-61520-863-0

Sinatra, R. (1986). *Visual literacy connections to thinking, reading, and writing.* Springfield, IL: Charles Thomas Press.

Smith, D. G. (1977). College classroom interactions and critical thinking. *Journal of Educational Psychology, 69,* 180–190. doi:10.1037/0022-0663.69.2.180

Terenzini, P. T., Springer, L., Pascarella, E. T., & Nora, A. (1995). Influences affecting the development of students' critical thinking skills. *Research in Higher Education, 36*(1), 23–39. doi:10.1007/BF02207765

Tsui, L. (2002). Fostering critical thinking through effective pedagogy: Evidence from four institutional case studies. *The Journal of Higher Education, 73,* 740–763. doi:10.1353/jhe.2002.0056 van Gelder, T. J. (2005). Teaching critical thinking: some lessons from cognitive science. *College Teaching*, *53*, 41–46. doi:10.3200/CTCH.53.1.41-48

van Gelder, T. J. (2006). Vertical thinking. *Leadership Excellence*, *23*(7), 20.

van Gelder, T. J. (2013). Argument mapping. In H. Pashler (Ed.), *Encyclopedia of the mind*. Thousand Oaks, CA: Sage. doi:10.4135/9781452257044.n19

WSU Critical Thinking Project. (n.d.). Retrieved from http://wsuctproject.wsu.edu/

WSU Critical Thinking Rubric. (n.d.). Retrieved from http://wsuctproject.wsu.edu/fa-1.htm

KEY TERMS AND DEFINITIONS

Active Participation in Learning: Teaching approaches that create opportunities for students to engage new material, while teachers serve as guides to help them understand and apply information. Students clarify, question, apply, and consolidate new knowledge.

Argument Mapping: Argument mapping is diagramming the structure of argument. It involves reasoning, drawing inferences, debating, and analyzing cases.

Cognitive Load: Cognitive aspects of a task that make it difficult to complete but that are unrelated to what students need to learn.

Critical Thinking: The process of actively and skillfully thinking, applying, analyzing, synthesizing, and/or evaluating information. The critical thinker may gather information through observation, experience, reflection, reasoning, or communication. Critical thinking becomes a guide to belief and action. The following criteria are closely associated with critical thinking: clarity, accuracy, precision, consistency, relevance, sound evidence, good reasons, depth, breadth, and fairness.

Discussion: Discussion is used here not to mean talking either to win or to vent one's feelings (informed or uninformed). In stead, discussion is used to mean talking to deliberate, to apply knowledge, to resolve questions.

Persistence: To persist with a problem, to strive for accuracy and precision as opposed to an impulsive reaction to a task.

Chapter 5

A Case on Teaching Critical Thinking and Argument Mapping in a Teacher Education Context

Yasemin Oral
İstanbul University, Turkey

EXECUTIVE SUMMARY

This chapter is based on the classroom work of a course on critical thinking designed as part of a pre-service teacher education program in English language teaching at a large-size Turkish state university. With its dual focus on both modernist and postmodern approaches to critical thinking, the course offers scope for classwork that concentrates on the skills to identify the parts and structure of arguments. To this end, argument mapping has been utilized to enhance understanding of the components of arguments and to facilitate the analysis of arguments. This chapter seeks to illustrate the materials and activities used when argument maps have been constructed during the class sessions. Furthermore, drawing from the data gathered from students' journal entries, I argue for a high interplay of the perceived efficacy of argument mapping with the content, length, and complexity of arguments as well as the anxiety evoked by these factors.

DOI: 10.4018/978-1-4666-5816-5.ch005

INTRODUCTION

Few would disagree about the centrality of critical work in educational settings. Although "critical thinking has been central to higher education as a desirable attribute of graduates since at least the beginning of the twentieth century" (Davies, 2011, p. 255), it has taken on a special role in the twenty first century not only in general education but also in teacher education due to the sociopolitical circumstances of the age (Williams, 2005). The need to integrate critical thinking into all facets of education has now come to be widely recognized. One key question for educators is thus how they can best promote students' critical thinking. One of the major emergent themes in this regard is the use of visual representation strategies such as concept mapping and argument mapping. Although the idea of displaying complex information visually is quite old, the beginning of the twenty first century marked a new turn in the teaching of critical thinking with the advent of computer-aided tools to help visualize elements of thinking (Davies, 2010; Davies, 2011).

In this perspective, there is an emerging body of empirical evidence from the cognitive sciences which shows that visual displays and concept/argument mapping enhance learning (Davies, 2010). In a quantitative study, which investigated the influence of concept mapping as a post-reading strategy on EFL learners' critical thinking by utilizing a pre-test post-test control and experimental group design, for instance, Khodaday and Ghanizadeh (2011) concludes that "concept mapping positively and significantly influenced critical thinking" (p. 53). In another experimental study, Harrell (2008) reports that while on average all of the students improved their critical thinking abilities the most dramatic improvements were made by the students who were able to construct argument maps. Twardy (2004) also found that critical thinking classes taught with argument-mapping-based approaches displayed substantial improvement in critical thinking while critical thinking classes taught with other methods did not. However, one major shortcoming of these quantitative experimental studies is that they are often inadequate to capture the complexity and richness of the issues under study despite their recognized contributions. Given that the continuing ascendancy of the quantitative studies bears significant limitations that hinder an in-depth understanding of these issues, more qualitative research is needed into the lived learning experiences of the students taking critical thinking courses.

Driven by the overall question if and how students can improve their critical thinking when given practice in argument mapping and diagramming, this chapter thus sets out to provide a qualitative perspective on the classroom uses of argument mapping in a teacher education context in an attempt to address such gap. Nevertheless, a thorough understanding of the case first necessitates a brief introduction to field which is marked by different lines of thought as each of them has distinctive implications for teaching critical thinking. In this regard, I will start out by discussing the prospects and possibilities that the current focus on critical work in educational contexts can offer as well as the controversies and challenges faced today. Then, in the following sections, I will first briefly address the increasing scope for critical thinking in teacher education, which accounts for the recent offer of such a course in a pre-service teacher education program in English language teaching at a Turkish state university, in order to provide a comprehensive background to the case presented, as well as an overview of the critical thinking course taught. Subsequently, I will present a detailed description of the case on teaching critical thinking together with argument mapping alongside the obstacles and problems encountered during the implementation of the course and a set of recommendations to overcome them.

TEACHING CRITICAL THINKING: CHALLENGES AND PROSPECTS

Much has been written over the years about the centrality of critical work in education in academic circles, but opinions and positions are diverse in how such work is to be conceptualized and translated into pedagogic practices. It is not even possible to speak of a monolithic perception of the notion of what it means to be critical or to do critical work. While Benesch (1993), for instance, defines criticality as a search for the social, historical, and political roots of conventional knowledge with an orientation to transform society, Paul (1982) describes it as the ability to think critically about one's own and others' positions, arguments, assumptions and worldview. The field seems to be marked by competing views, at both conceptual and pedagogical levels, within and between competing discourses. To sketch a crude picture of the territory around the term, rather than survey the large literature on different takes on critical work, drawing from Pennycook (2001), I will distinguish between the modernist and postmodern takes on criticality, while acknowledging that there might be many viewpoints in between. The modernist view of criticality focuses on the 'objective' analysis and evaluation of texts and arguments by remaining isolated from issues of power, politics and ideology, whereas the postmodern view emphasizes the political and ideological meanings embedded in them. In the pedagogical realm, the modernist perspectives are fleshed out in the critical thinking movement while the postmodern perspectives in critical pedagogy and critical reading. Yet, just like in the definition of criticality, as Burbules and Berk (1999) note, neither critical thinking nor critical pedagogy is monolithic or homogeneous. Among the vigorously debated views within the critical thinking movement in education are some challenging- albeit crucial, issues such as the subject-specificity and transfer-ability of critical thinking and the feasibility of teaching critical thinking (Lai, 2011).

To start with, one major area of contestation within different academic strands of critical thinking is the subject-specificity of critical thinking. On the one hand, some researchers argue that critical thinking skills can be generalized across different subjects and can thus be taught in a generic way, while, on the other hand, some others argue that critical thinking skills can only be taught in the context of a specific subject domain (Lai, 2011). Another issue that is closely related to the subject-specificity of critical thinking is the transferability of critical thinking skills to new contexts and domains (Lai, 2011). Ennis (1992, cited in Mason, 2008: 3), for instance, claims that the skills associated with critical thinking can be learned independently of specific disciplines, and can thus be transferred from one domain to another, while acknowledging that a certain minimum competence in a particular discipline is essential before one can apply the skills of critical thought to that domain. Unlike Ennis, McPeck (1981, cited in Mason, 2008, p. 3) argues that critical thinking cannot be taught independently of a particular subject domain as, for him, it depends on a thorough knowledge and understanding of the content and epistemology of the discipline. Holding a rather middle position, Siegel (1990, cited in Mason, 2008, p. 4) asserts that both subject-neutral and subject-specific principles and skills are relevant to critical thinking. As for the empirical evidence on the transferability of critical thinking skills, studies seem to document both successes and failures (Lai, 2011; Reece, 2002).

As for the feasibility of teaching critical thinking, it is widely maintained that critical thinking skills and abilities can be taught (Kennedy et al., 1991; Lai, 2011). In this regard, the key questions seem to mount up about the effects of different instructional designs. One widely-used typology of instructional approaches is that of Ennis (1989) which classifies four types: The 'general approach' involves teaching generalized critical thinking skills in a critical thinking course without specific subject-matter content, the 'infusion approach' requires explicit teaching of critical thinking skills from within a subject course, the 'immersion approach' assumes that students will acquire the subject-specific critical thinking skills implicitly and indirectly through taking the subject course, and the 'mixed- model approach' combines a general course with either an infusion or immersion approach. Among several reviews of the studies investigating the efficacy of the instructional interventions, one recent study that has summarized the available empirical evidence to date on the development of critical thinking skills in educational contexts concludes that the data suggests (a) a generally positive effect of instruction on students' critical thinking skills despite some evidence of negative effects and (b) that mixed-model approach significantly outperforms all other approaches while immersion approach underperforms them (Abrami et al., 2008). Yet, many of the books on critical thinking seem to adopt a general approach. In the preface to his book on critical thinking, Fisher (2001), for instance, states that the book aims to *teach* critical thinking skills *explicitly* and *directly* so that they can be *transfer*red to other studies and everyday life (emphasis mine). Likewise, Thomson (2002) adopts a general approach which, as she puts it, "does not require any specialist knowledge" and focuses on some widely-shared critical thinking skills which she argues are transferable (p. 4).

However, the issue of teaching critical thinking is not free from controversy either. Atkinson (1997), for instance, argues that critical thinking is acquired through an unconscious process of socialization and that it cannot thus be taught at schools. Atkinson (1997) further argues that "[c]ritical thinking is cultural thinking" (p. 89, emphasis original) and then makes a case that critical thinking is harder for English-as-a-second-language learners because of their lack of socialization in critical thinking while it is easier for native-English-speaking students as they have already been socialized as critical thinkers. In this way, the students from 'non-Western' countries are portrayed as lacking critical thinking skills due to their cultural backgrounds. This culturist position, which has long dominated at least the field of English language education in many different ways, however, has attracted severe criticism lately on the grounds that it is essentialist, reductive and bound with otherization (Holliday, 2005). Floyd's (2011) research on the effects that thinking in a second language have on critical thinking performance also challenges the assumption that any perceived lack of critical thinking skills is solely attributable to the influence of cultural factors. Moreover, drawing from the distinction between monological and dialogical critical thinking, Benesch (1999) convincingly maintains that opposition to the teaching of critical thinking is a political and ideological position in that it excludes students from examining their thinking and questioning and possibly challenging status quo.

ORGANIZATION BACKGROUND

In debates about critical thinking, as is implied above, perhaps the only single point on which there is a good deal of consensus is the desirability of promoting criticality as an educational goal. Critical thinking is a crucial component of the curricula, either as a separate course or as an underlying principle, in many educational settings all around the world. Although the two literatures do not discuss one another with very few exceptions, as Burbules and Berk (1999) have noted, both modernist and post-modern approaches share a sense of urgency to help students become more skeptical toward commonly accepted truisms and have more critically oriented classrooms in their own ways. In much the same vein, critical thinking skills is now viewed as a major qualification to be acquired in teacher education programs since, as Williams (2005) has noted, unless teacher trainees become skilled in critical thinking, they are unlikely to teach and model those skills to their students.

This growing interest in critical thinking is also mirrored in the official educational policy documents in Turkey. The elementary school curriculum reform of 2005 emphasized analytic and critical thinking, problem solving skills and enquiry skills (Cappelle et al., 2010; Koç et al., 2007) and identified the instructional objectives that would contribute to the improvement of these skills (Koç et al., 2007). In line with these developments, as an important stage of the education reform, generic teacher competencies were prepared to support the new developments in the curriculum (Ministry of National Education, 2006). One of the sub-competencies highlighted is that teachers should be able develop and effectively use their critical thinking skills (Ministry of National Education, 2006). Similarly, teacher education curriculum was changed as well to respond to the new content and methodology of primary education in 2006 (Tarman, 2010). The Turkish teacher education curriculum, which had long been highly centralized in course offerings, was revised in a way that allowed the faculties of education to determine 30% of the components of the program they offer, which in turn created the opportunity to offer elective courses (Tarman, 2010).

It was within such a climate of concern over criticality that a specific elective course named *Critical Thinking Skills in Foreign Language Education* started for the first time in the English Language Teaching Department of a Turkish state university in spring 2010 in order to provide teacher trainees with extensive practice opportunities in critical thinking and critical language study and to introduce ways of promoting critical thinking in their classes. Thus, the provision of such a course on critical thinking can be viewed as a response to the increasing emphasis on criticality in teacher education at both national and international levels. In this way, critical thinking, which was prior rather an underlying orientation reflected in all the courses, gained a further status of a separate subject.

Despite its increasing importance, "the literature on critical thinking in teacher education is not extensive," notes Williams (2005, p. 172). As far as the research on critical thinking in teacher education in Turkey is concerned, over the last few years, a rather large body of research has emerged exploring critical thinking dispositions and levels of teacher trainees of different programs (Beşoluk & Önder, 2010; Çubukcu, 2006; Demirhan et al., 2011; Yenice, 2011; Yücel & Koçak, 2010); qualitative studies that describe and document instructional experiences designed to teach and foster critical thinking skills of teacher trainees are still scarce though, which makes the reporting of such cases timely.

SETTING THE STAGE

This chapter derives from the classroom work of a course on critical thinking offered as part of a pre-service teacher education program in English language teaching at a large-size state university in Turkey. In what follows, I shall provide a brief overview of the course including the course description, teaching methodology and the assessment and of the use of dialogue journals.

Overview of the Course

The two-credit course named *Critical Thinking Skills in Foreign Language Education* is an elective one offered to the senior students of the program in the spring semester. The course aims to provide the students with a comprehensive understanding of critical thinking, develop their skills in critical thinking and critical language study, and introduce ways of incorporating critical thinking into English language classes. Following Wallace (2003), the modernist view of criticality is seen as a staging post in the pursuit to engage with issues of power and ideology and to attend to wider implications which relate to the circulation of dominant discourses within texts. Therefore, with its dual focus on both approaches to critical thinking, the course, with 12 weeks of instruction, offers scope for both promoting skills in reasoning and analyzing and evaluating arguments and fostering critical language awareness to uncover values, beliefs and ideologies embedded in texts.

In the spring semester of the 2010-2011 academic year, all senior students, 69 students in total, were enrolled in the course as there was no other alternative elective course available then. The course started with an introduction to different perspectives in the field of critical thinking while the remainder of the course had two main parts: the first included a series of lectures and class discussions that addressed both the fundamentals of critical thinking skills and how to apply them to actual arguments in academic texts primarily on foreign language education, and the second part focused on the postmodern view of 'critical', which is concerned with issues of power and cultural politics, working on primarily different types of media texts. In addition, perspectives for fostering critical thinking and critical language awareness in EFL classes were explored in order to expand and diversify the pedagogical repertoire and instructional resources of the trainees in this regard.

Building on the premise that the best way to develop critical thinking is to use and practice it (van Gelder, 2005), the teaching methodology of the course emphasized making connections between theory and practice; it thus involved students in learning by doing through in-class activities and exercises, accompanied by lectures, presentations and demonstrations by the instructor. In addition, having recognized the significance of a non-threatening, nurturing classroom atmosphere in the fostering of critical thinking (Moon, 2005), a classroom environment where students could express themselves freely and risk-taking was tolerated was tried to be generated as much as possible. As for the assessment, it took the form of one mid-term exam, one final exam and an assignment requiring the students to write an argumentative response paper to an assigned article.

Dialogue Journals as a Means of Reflection

During the first part of the course where the focus was on the skills associated with critical thinking, the students were invited to write dialogue journals in order to provide a space for one-on-one conversation between the author/instructor and the students on the issues relevant to the course and to promote further reflection, which is often considered to be a crucial component of critical thinking (Moon, 2005). Dialogue journals are defined as journals "in which a student carries on a private written conversation with the teacher for an extended period of time" (Staton, 1988, p. 198). Among the reported benefits of dialogue journals are facilitating learning of course material, promoting self-reflection and self-understanding, providing opportunity to express ideas and concerns, receiving feedback on ideas and questions, improving the teacher-student relationship, personalizing learning (Garmon, 2001; Lee, 2004). From her research, Hoover (1994) particularly suggests the use of dialogue journals with prospective teachers as a means of challenging them to think more critically.

In line with the benefits documented in the literature, the primary motive for the use of dialogue journals was basically to encourage students to reflect on the readings and classroom practices and to relate the course content to ideas and personal experiences of their own. Thus, each week journal entries were scheduled to be sent by the volunteered students via e-mail and responded by the instructor before the following class meeting. In responding to the trainees' journal entries, a positive encouraging tone of voice was adopted by the instructor by avoiding negative evaluative feedback, giving thorough answers to their questions, showing consideration for their comments about the course and classes, and the like. The dialogue journal entries written by the trainees have been utilized for the purposes of this chapter as a source of data to discuss the efficacy of argument mapping as perceived by them. To ensure the anonymity and confidentiality of the trainees, their names will not be given in the subsequent discussion.

CASE DESCRIPTION

This section sets out to present a detailed description of the case, where argument mapping was used as a supplementary pedagogical tool in the teaching of critical thinking, including the classroom activities and materials as well as a discussion of the effectiveness of argument mapping with reference to the written reflective work of the trainees on argument analysis and mapping.

Classroom Uses of Argument Mapping

Despite the lack of generally agreed set of skills that constitutes critical thinking, there seems to be a fair agreement on argument analysis, that is, the ability to understand, reconstruct and evaluate arguments, as an essential component among the educators (Harrell, 2011). Accordingly, in line with the first focus of the course on critical thinking skills in its modernist sense, a series of class sessions that concentrate on the skills to identify the parts and structure of arguments were carried out. To this end, argument mapping was used as rather a supplementary aid to enhance understanding of the components and structure of arguments and thus to facilitate the analysis work since it generally proves to be helpful in discovering the elements of arguments and explicating how an argument is structured and thus contributes to the development of critical thinking skills (Harrell, 2008; Harrell, 2011; van Gelder, 2005).

Becoming an increasingly popular pedagogical tool, an argument map is "a visualization of an argument that makes explicit which statement is the conclusion and which statements are the premises, as well as the inferential connections between the premises and the conclusion" (Harrell, 2008, p. 12). Argument mapping concerns with explicating the inferential structure of arguments; that is, inferences between the propositions (Davies, 2010). Therefore, argument maps clarify which statements are premises and which one is the conclusion and how they are connected (Harrell, 2008). Despite the grounds that the computer-aided argument mapping has been gaining, in our course, pen and paper and/or board and slides were used as a medium of building argument maps on the grounds that, as Harrell (2008) highlighted, "there has been no research to determine whether the crucial factor is the mere ability to construct argument maps, or the aid of a computer platform and tutor, or possibly both" (p. 6).

Over a five-week period, which comprised ten-hour classroom work, out of twelve weeks, students were provided with extensive practice in argument analysis, including identifying arguments, distinguishing arguments from non-arguments, identifying the structure and parts of an argument including premises (joint and independent), conclusions (intermediate and main) and logical connections, and evaluating arguments. Throughout, argument mapping was mainly utilized as a supplementary resource for assistance in the analysis and evaluation of arguments presented in given texts. At the start of the semester, the basics of argument mapping were introduced implicitly through demonstration, rather than through explicit instruction, by the instructor/author. That is to say, the students were taken through the process of analyzing arguments and creating argument maps step by step, starting from reading a text for an argument, singling out the statements and claims, using logical indicators and context to determine the inferential connections among these statements, removing extraneous verbiage to finally identifying the overall logical structure of an argument and reflecting it in a diagram. The students were shown how to construct maps to reflect the arguments studied accurately by putting the claims into boxes and representing the inferential connections by arrows. Then, they were given various passages to practice argument analysis and mapping and received oral feedback on their work during the classes.

Initially, in the introductory classes, a certain amount of time was devoted to build up a shared sense of terminology. Although the course was not intended to be one on primarily the theory of critical thinking, given that "the all-important practice is more effective when supplemented by appropriate levels of theoretical understanding" (van Gelder, 2005, p. 44), particular emphasis was placed on the integration of certain amount of theoretical and terminological knowledge into the practical class-work. Figure 1 is a sample task used to this end.

With the use of such tasks, the class work was geared towards structured discussions in which a guided inductive instructional approach was adopted to introduce the key terms such as position, argument, premise and conclusion together with scaffolded practice in identifying the parts and structure of arguments. At the following stages, relatively simple and short arguments with a main conclusion and a few premises, which were then represented in simple maps, were introduced in order to familiarize the students with the components of arguments as well as the inferential connections among them. An argument map constructed in an argument mapping task, which required the trainees to work on a simple argument with a focus on the workings of the premises, is given in Figure 2.

This map served to clarify the structure of the argument by visually representing how the premises work independently to support the conclusion. Given the quite simple nature of the argument with no extraneous material and sufficient signposting, it further allowed us to proceed in evaluating the argument by focusing on the strength and relevance of the premises in the boxes. Then, more complex and extended arguments extracted from academic texts of their field of study were used for argument analysis and construction of argument maps. An example map of a

Figure 1. A sample task

> ➢ **Read the following extract and (1) identify the main point which the author is trying to get us accept or believe. (2) Does the author give any extra information which tells why we should believe it?**

Due to the fact that English has now turned into an international language and thus most of the communication carried out in English is between people who are themselves the so-called non-native speakers of English with a distinct cultural identity of their own, there is little need for the teaching of Anglo-American culture in EFL settings. In addition, in most communication settings, what people want to express is not the target culture but their own culture and cultural identity. (Akbari, 2008)

> ➢ **Do you agree with the author's position? Put a cross on the line below to show where you stand on this issue.**

1	2	3	4	5
Completely agree				Completely disagree

> ➢ **Now write down a sentence which expresses your position on the issue.**

....

....

> ➢ **Now write down one or two reasons in support of your position.**

I think ....

....

because ....

....

more extended argument from Akbari (2008) concerning the use of students' first language as a resource in the second/ foreign language classrooms is given in Figure 3.

The argument map shows a contention at the top, followed by two two-tier premises. The second premise, which entails a rebuttal of the common state of practice, is joined with the first premise, which is supported by two independent reasons, in giving space for the claim presented in the first premise. Furthermore, the two premises with their own reasons can be regarded as intermediate conclusions, which in turn become reasons to support the main conclusion. When the premises of the argument had been analyzed, for instance, by producing a list, it

Figure 2. Argument map representing a simple argument from Marinova-Todd et al. (2000)

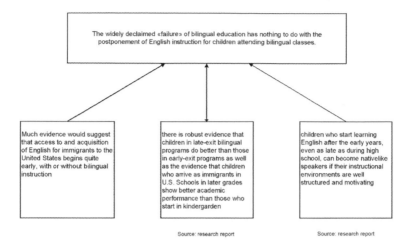

Figure 3. Argument map representing an extended argument from Akbari (2008)

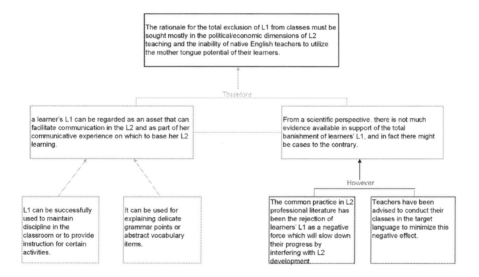

could have been much more difficult to show the way the premises work to support the main conclusion.

Overall, a substantial amount of time was devoted to the reading of arguments, ranging in length from a few sentences to one page and the analysis of the components and structure of arguments on the board, slides or handouts, followed by a discussion of the truth of the premises and how well they support the conclusion and in-class tasks where the trainees worked on various arguments to analyze and map them. Throughout, argument mapping was integrated as a supplementary pedagogical tool into the class sessions whereby the main aim was to help students develop certain critical thinking skills, that is, the skills to understand, analyze and evaluate arguments, in order to further facilitate the comprehension of arguments and increase the accuracy of argument analysis.

Effectiveness of Argument Mapping

Over the course of the semester, there was no particular purpose of testing the efficacy of argument mapping; however, the analysis of the qualitative data that emerged from trainees' dialogue journal entries has provided insights into how the trainees perceived argument mapping. Particular themes that recurrently occurred in the trainees' entries were identified; the issue of the effectiveness of arguments was one of the emergent themes that deemed to be relevant to a discussion on trainees' perceptions of the issue. To start with, although they were not asked to comment on it particularly, the majority of the trainees brought up the benefits of mapping in argument analysis. Right after the first introduction of argument mapping, as the following extracts illustrate, the trainees reflected on the issue despite their inability to use the appropriate terminology at that stage:

To be honest, I couldn't find the premises in the first lesson. However, I could find the independent and joint premises this week. I understand the subject clearly. So, the last lesson was very useful. The skeleton of the sentences that you drew on the board was very beneficial for me.

The lesson was good for me because I wasn't good at making skeletons of arguments but you gave importance to it and I learned how to make a skeleton. I think that will be helpful to me.

Diagramming helped us to identify the main and intermediate conclusions and joint and independent premises. Diagramming is obviously one way of tidying up the arguments.

Showing premises, intermediate and main conclusions using boxes is really helpful because if I want to add or change some of them it will be easier.

This result adds qualitatively to the above-mentioned positive quantitative evidence in the literature on the benefits of argument mapping and diagramming. Yet, another common theme revolved around the issue of the effectiveness of mapping in argument analysis is the complexity and length of arguments, which in turn complicates a straightforward reading of the issue. Among the common reflections of the trainees on that matter are:

For the last lesson, I can say that I have enjoyed creating diagrams and analysing structures of arguments. We have dwelled on the extracts that included some logical indicators, joint or independent premises, intermediate conclusions and main conclusion. Analysing the components of a typical argument is really and relatively easy, underlining somehow explanatory sentences as premises or else reasons isn't challenging but if we do it on a more complicated passage, I fear that I'm going to get confused. However, I still think that firstly understanding the text and then searching for statements, conclusions, premises etc. is a good way of avoding mistakes while making analysis throughout passages.

In the previous week, I wrote that it was hard for me to identify which one is a premise or which one is a conclusion...The things that we did this week really helped me to understand premises and conclusions more clearly...Especially, diagramming really make them more clear in my mind...But when we worked on the long extract, it was hard for me to identify the parts of the argument.

It is really easy to work with simple arguments, needless to say that. Actually, the text was not difficult to understand at all but the length made me a bit worried when I just saw it. Although it was easy to get the point from the text, working on the argument and finding the premises were not that easy. I mean, I found the reasons but I couldn't relate them at once.

Apparently, the shift from simple arguments to more complex, extended arguments obscured the trainees' positive perceptions about the uses of mapping. Their responses seem to suggest that argument analysis and mapping were not carried out simultaneously but rather successively when dealing with extended and longer arguments; argument mapping was rather used to check or clarify their understanding once they were able to correctly recognize the premises and the conclusion(s) and to decide how they are connected to each other. That is to say, according to the trainees, building up a correct argument map seemed to be very difficult without correctly identifying the parts of the arguments and the ways they are related in longer and more complex texts. Despite the ungeneralizable nature of the findings, this point seems to contradict with the widely-held supposition that the more complex the reasoning in an argument becomes the more argument mapping helps (van Gelder, 2005; Harrell, 2011) and, thus, might add to the discussions on "what the effect of teaching argument diagramming would be on a student's ability to analyze longer and more complex arguments" (Harrell, 2011, p. 384) by implying negative evidence.

Another significant issue emerged from the trainees' reflective work is related to the content or subject-matter of the arguments. Surprisingly to the instructor/author, there were a few instances, as the following extract exemplifies, in which the trainees found the arguments the subject-matter of which are from their own field of study more difficult to understand:

Actually, at the beginning of this week's lesson, I was so glad to realise that I could really understand and find conclusions and premises of an argument. But, when you gave us the long extract, I realised that I am not good enough at finding conclusion, intermediate conclusion and premises in a long extract. Because, the passage was about ELT and so the subject was not concrete like Sherlock Holmes example. This is also a factor for me in being insufficient for finding conclusions and premises. Furthermore, in the exam for instance, because of the anxiety and excitement, I wonder whether I could concentrate the passage or not.

The above-given statement indicates that the subject-matter of the arguments alongside their lengths might be a crucial factor as well in the analysis and in turn mapping process. This finding resonates with the work of Davies (2010) who highlights the disadvantage that "argument mapping exercises can assume that students have a sufficiently clear understanding of a topic or issue" (p. 23). Furthermore, all these factors, when combined, seem to lend themselves easily into anxiety on the part of the learners. A similar attitude has been observed in the majority of the journal entries, which is evidenced in the use of such descriptive adjectives as "intimidating," "scary" and "hard to do" by the trainees while reflecting on their in-class experiences.

On the whole, while there is a certain set of positive evidence on the efficacy of mapping in argument analysis, the data gathered from the trainees have rather put forward the complexity of the relationship between the use of argument maps and their effectiveness. The findings deny a straightforward correlation between an ability to construct argument maps and an improvement in understanding the structure and components of arguments. What emerged is rather a high interplay of the perceived efficacy of argument mapping with the content, length, and complexity of arguments as well as such psychological factors as anxiety which seems to be evoked by the above-listed factors involved.

CURRENT CHALLENGES FACING THE ORGANIZATION

While one major challenge which was directly related to argument mapping emerged as a result of the shift from simple arguments to complex arguments for study as is discussed above, other obstacles and problems that were encountered in the implementation of the course including the perceived difficulty of the course activities and materials, widely-expressed need for far more in-class practice, large number of students and associated time limitations, and influence of the formal requirements for the successful completion of the course can be construed as indirectly influencing the effectiveness of argument mapping. The first, and perhaps most important, challenge was the difficulty of the course activities and materials as perceived by the trainees although most of them expressed and displayed their recognition of the importance of critical thinking. It is exigent to reckon the sources of this perception due to the insufficiency of the data at hand; it might be well related to motivation and achievement factors but the appearance of such discernments is not puzzling at all since, as van Gelder (2005) put it simply, critical thinking itself is hard.

A second major issue, which is in fact intertwined with the difficulty problem, was the trainees' need for more practice opportunities in argument analysis, mapping and evaluation. When this concern arrived on the scene in their journal entries, an immediate action was taken to provide the trainees with additional tasks and exercises which they could carry out outside the class and which were not to be assessed or graded. While this sort of extra practice opportunities, which offered them specific and individual feedback, were appreciated at first, the trainees eventually expressed that in-class practice, which was guided and scaffolded by the instructor, was far more beneficial. However, it was not a viable option at the time given the course content and materials to be covered throughout the semester. A further challenge entangled with the difficulty and additional practice issues was the large number of students, who displayed considerable differences in pace and timing during task completion as well as in learning approaches and styles, which in turn required more time and effort on the part of the instructor to cater for the individual needs as much as possible while attending to the common expectations and exigencies.

A final and overarching issue connected with all the problems mentioned above is the effects of the formal requirements for the successful completion of the course, especially the exams and the assignments. Despite their increasing improvement as reflected in their in-class activities and conceded by themselves in their journal entries, most of the trainees expressed concern, both orally and in writing, for failure in the exams and assignments, which were to be graded due to the formal requirements. When juxtaposed with their often-stated motivation, this state of affairs might be interpreted as a clash between their "deep motive" to understand and make sense of the course material, in the words of Scouller (1998, p. 453), and their "surface motive" to reproduce them in the exams and pass the course. It should be acknowledged at this stage that this conflict might have been reinforced by the assessment method chosen. That is to say, while in the classroom and dialogue journals their mistakes were welcomed, their trial-and-error processes tolerated, and various lines of thinking encouraged, in the exams and assignments, due to their very nature, the trainees were expected to apply the skills and knowledge they learned accurately.

SOLUTIONS AND RECOMMENDATIONS

In order to address the obstacles and challenges reported above and to offer solutions, it first needs be noted that what is specific to the course is the particular needs of the program which aims to train *language teachers*. Despite the fact that the content of the course is amenable to criticism due to its alleged overload, the multiple foci points of the course, including the modernist sense of critical thinking, which allows for the study of argument analysis, mapping and evaluation, and critical language study in a more postmodern sense alongside a focus on the perspectives for promoting criticality in teaching contexts, is justified on that basis. Furthermore, not only does the time period devoted to each focus represent a well-balanced ratio but also the accompanying emphasis placed on critical thinking as an underlying principle of the program is meant to reinforce the educational attainments of the course.

The perceived difficulty of the course in general and of the argument analysis and evaluation in particular can be considered together with the need for more in-class practice opportunities. It is of particular significance in this regard to underline that the course was designed to make the trainees engage in the skills themselves rather than merely learn about the theory of critical thinking with the use of activities and materials graded from simple to more complex under the guidance and supervision of the instructor, which would provide them with sufficient know-how and tools to apply whatever was done in the class outside the class on their own. Ultimately, as van Gelder (2005) implies, the quantity of deliberate practice required to achieve high levels of excellence in critical thinking is not attainable in a single-semester course. Therefore, while one obvious solution is still to increase practice opportunities, especially on complex and longer arguments, as much as possible, another possible solution could be to include awareness-raising activities to encourage a perspective that "critical thinking is of more a life-long journey" (van Gelder, 2005, p. 42) than something that can be picked up in a weeks-long course, and that this sort of courses serve to found a sound informed ground for this journey. Likewise, we, as instructors, should hold realistic expectations from our students with an understanding that they will not just happen to be perfect critical thinkers overnight.

The problems emerged as a result of the large number of students and the associated time pressures are in fact temporary and circumstantial. If such a course is compulsory, the course could be sectionized in a way that would admit a manageable and affordable number of students into each section; alternately, if the course is an elective one, just like in our case, the number of the students to be accepted should be decided by considering the above-mentioned issues that might hinder the successful implementation of the course. Finally, in order to minimize the negative effects of the exams and assignments, the mismatch between the teaching methods and the assessment methods should be minimized as well.

REFERENCES

Abrami, P. C., Bernard, R. M., Borokhovski, E., Wade, A., Surkes, M. A., Tamim, R., & Zhang, D. (2008). Instructional interventions affecting critical thinking skills and dispositions: A stage 1 meta-analysis. *Review of Educational Research*, *78*(4), 1102–1134. doi:10.3102/0034654308326084

Akbari, R. (2008). Transforming lives: Introducing critical pedagogy into ELT classroom. *ELT Journal*, *62*(3), 276–283. doi:10.1093/elt/ccn025

Atkinson, D. (1997). A critical approach to critical thinking in TESOL. *TESOL Quarterly*, *31*(1), 71–94. doi:10.2307/3587975

Benesch, S. (1993). Critical thinking: A learning process for democracy. *TESOL Quarterly*, *27*(3), 545–548. doi:10.2307/3587485

Benesch, S. (1999). Thinking critically, thinking dialogically. *TESOL Quarterly*, *33*(3), 573–580. doi:10.2307/3587682

Beşoluk, Ş., & Önder, İ. (2010). Investigation of teacher candidates' learning approaches, learning styles and critical thinking dispositions. *Elementary Education Online*, *9*(2), 679–693.

Burbules, N. C., & Berk, R. (1999). Critical thinking and critical pedagogy: Relations, differences, and limits. In T. S. Popkewitz, & L. Fendler (Eds.), *Critical theories in education*. New York: Routledge.

Cappelle, G., Crippin, G., & Lundgren, U. (2010). *Emerging global dimensions in education*. London, UK: CiCe Network Working Group.

Çubukcu, Z. (2006). Critical thinking dispositions of the Turkish teacher candidates. *The Turkish Online Journal of Educational Technology*, *5*(4), 22–36.

Davies, M. (2010). Concept mapping, mind mapping and argument mapping: What are the differences and do they matter? *Higher Education*. doi: doi:10.1007/s10734-010-9387-6

Davies, M. (2011). Introduction to the special issue on critical thinking in higher education. *Higher Education Research & Development*, *30*(3), 255–260. doi:10.1080/07294360.2011.562145

Demirhan, E., Beşoluk, Ş., & Önder, İ. (2011). The change in academic achievement and critical thinking disposition scores of pre-service science teachers over time. *Western Anatolia Journal of Educational Science*, 403-406.

Ennis, R. H. (1989). Critical thinking and subject specificity: Clarification and needed research. *Educational Researcher*, *18*(3), 4–10. doi:10.3102/0013189X018003004

Fisher, A. (2001). *Critical thinking: An introduction*. Cambridge, UK: Cambridge University Press.

Floyd, C. B. (2011). Critical thinking in a second language. *Higher Education Research & Development*, *30*(3), 289–302. doi:10.1080/07294360.2010.501076

Garmon, M. A. (2001, Fall). The benefits of dialogue journals: What prospective teachers say. *Teacher Education Quarterly*, 37–50.

Harrell, M. (2008). *No computer program required: Even pencil-and-paper argument mapping improves critical thinking skills.* Department of Philosophy, Paper 350. Retrieved May 15, 2012 from http://repository.cmu.edu/philosophy/350

Harrell, M. (2011). Argument diagramming and critical thinking in introductory philosophy. *Higher Education Research & Development*, *30*(3), 371–385. doi:10.1080/07294360.2010.502559

Holliday, A. (2005). *The struggle to teach English as an international language*. Oxford, UK: Oxford University Press.

Hoover, L. A. (1994). Reflective writing as a window on preservice teachers' thought processes. *Teaching and Teacher Education*, *10*(1), 83–93. doi:10.1016/0742-051X(94)90042-6

Kennedy, M., Fisher, M. B., & Ennis, R. H. (1991). Critical thinking: Literature review and needed research. In L. Idol, & B. F. Jones (Eds.), *Educational values and cognitive instruction: Implications for reform* (pp. 11–40). Hillsdale, NJ: Lawrence Erlbaum & Associates.

Khodadady, E., & Ghanizadeh, A. (2011). The impact of concept mapping on EFL learners' critical thinking ability. *English Language Teaching, 4*(4), 49–60. doi:10.5539/elt.v4n4p49

Koç, Y., Isiksal, M., & Bulut, S. (2007). Elementary school curriculum reform in Turkey. *International Education Journal, 8*(1), 30–39.

Lai, E. R. (2011). *Critical thinking: A literature review* (Research Report). Retrieved May 10, 2012 from http://www.pearsonassessments.com/hai/images/tmrs/Critical-ThinkingReviewFINAL

Lee, I. (2004, Summer). Using dialogue journals as a multi-purpose tool for preservice teacher preparation: How effective is it? *Teacher Education Quarterly*, 73–97.

Marinova-Todd, S. H., Marshall, D. B., & Snow, C. E. (2000). Three misconceptions about age and L2 learning. *TESOL Quarterly, 34*(1), 9–34. doi:10.2307/3588095

Mason, M. (2008). Critical thinking and learning. In M. Mason (Ed.), *Critical thinking and learning*. Malden, MA: Blackwell Publishing. doi:10.1002/9781444306774.ch1

Ministry of National Education. (2006). *Support to basic education project teacher training component: Generic teacher competencies*. Ankara, Turkey: Author.

Moon, J. (2005). *We seek it here...a new perspective on the elusive activity of critical thinking: A theoretical and practical approach*. ESCalate Discussion Series. Retrieved April 22, 2011 from http://escalate.ac.uk/downloads/2041.pdf

Paul, R. (1982). Teaching critical thinking in the 'strong sense': A focus on self-deception, world views, and a dialectical mode of analysis. *Informal Logic Newsletter, 4*(2).

Pennycook, A. (2001). *Critical applied linguistics: A critical introduction*. Mahwah, NJ: Erlbaum Associates.

Reece, G. (2002). *Critical thinking and transferability: A review of the literature*. American University Library. Retrieved May 15, 2012 from http://www.library.american.edu/Help/research/lit_review/critical_thinking.pdf

Scouller, K. (1998). The influence of assessment method on students' learning approaches: Multiple choice question examination versus assignment essay. *Higher Education, 35*, 453–472. doi:10.1023/A:1003196224280

Staton, J. (1988). ERIC/RCS report: Dialogue journals. *Language Arts, 65*, 198–201.

Tarman, B. (2010). Global perspectives and challenges on teacher education in Turkey. *International Journal of Arts and Sciences, 3*(17), 78–96.

Thomson, A. (2002). *Critical reasoning: A practical introduction.* London: Routledge.

Twardy, C. R. (2004). Argument maps improve critical thinking. *Teaching Philosophy*, *27*(2). doi:10.5840/teachphil200427213

van Gelder, T. (2005). Teaching critical thinking: Some lessons from cognitive science. *College Teaching*, *53*(1), 41–46. doi:10.3200/CTCH.53.1.41-48

Wallace, C. (2003). *Critical reading in language education.* New York: Palgrave Macmillan. doi:10.1057/9780230514447

Williams, R. L. (2005). Targeting critical thinking within teacher education: The potential impact on society. *Teacher Educator*, *40*(3), 163–187. doi:10.1080/08878730509555359

Yenice, N. (2011). Investigating pre-service teachers' critical thinking disposition in terms of different variables. *European Journal of Soil Science*, *20*(4), 593–603.

Yücel, A. S. Ö., & Koçak, C. (2010). Determining the critical thinking levels of the student teachers and evaluating through some variables. *International Online Journal of Educational Sciences*, *2*(3), 865–882.

KEY TERMS AND DEFINITIONS

Argument: It is a set of reasons/evidence in support of a given claim/point of view, usually presented to persuade audiences to agree with.

Argument Map: It is a visual representation of the structure and components of an argument, outlining the logical and inferential connections among them.

Critical Thinking: It is a set of higher-order cognitive skills aimed at analyzing and evaluating one's own and others' positions, actions and beliefs, by applying objective critical standards.

Dialogue Journal: It is a journal in which a student carries on a one-on-one, private conversation with the teacher regarding course content and material in order to improve self-reflection and self-understanding.

Modernist View of Criticality: It refers to the objective analysis and evaluation of the reasoning embedded in texts of all kinds in order to improve rationality and logic.

Postmodern View of Criticality: It is primarily concerned with the issues of politics, power and ideology embedded in texts of all kinds in order the unveil and challenge the wider implications related to the (re)production and circulation of dominant discourses within them.

Chapter 6
Confronting Critical Thinking Challenges "in" the College Classroom

Chigozirim Ifedapo Utah
University of Nebraska – Lincoln, USA

Alexis Waters
University of Nebraska – Lincoln, USA

EXECUTIVE SUMMARY

The goal of this pilot study was to develop a learner-centered teaching tool that would promote meaningful learning and enable higher education instructors to model critical thinking through concept mapping. Learner-centered approaches emphasize not only content, but the context, purpose, and process of learning. They also focus on the need for students to take responsibility for their own learning. However, students may not possess the foundational critical thinking skills necessary to be independent learners. Concept mapping allows university instructors to demonstrate basic critical thinking processes and provides students with the opportunity to practice the critical thinking that is essential to their success inside and outside the classroom. It can also facilitate meaningful learning by encouraging students to integrate new knowledge into prior knowledge structures.

DOI: 10.4018/978-1-4666-5816-5.ch006

INTRODUCTION

Chigozirim

One of my students approached me after class to explain why she was not contributing to discussions. Though she had studied the assigned readings in detail, she was still at a loss as to how to relevantly connect this information to discussions. I offered some sage words of advice and left the conversation feeling a bit too pleased with my performance. A few weeks later, she dropped the class. I have often operated under the assumption that setting a positive climate, asking the right questions, playing the role of lively facilitator, and giving students ample opportunity to voice their opinions would be enough to support my "progressive" learner-centered approach to teaching. In fits of frustration (laced with a little arrogance), I have often said to colleagues, "This is college and I am not going to spoon-feed adults. Students need to take responsibility for their learning." In the course of this project, I have learned that while it is important for undergraduates to play a more active role in the learning process, it is unrealistic to shove students into a new learning environment or paradigm without a compass and expect them not to get lost. However, translating this realization into every day practice is easier said than done.

Alexis

My students often come to office hours to discuss issues they have with assignments. When I ask them about their concerns, many are unable to formulate clear questions. This pattern of uncertainty has raised red flags in my mind concerning undergraduate education. Good students are not working to their fullest potential, and those who are struggling with their classes must make the life-changing decision of whether or not to remain in school. At the macro level, many universities are taking action to increase retention rates, but there must also be an increased emphasis on meaningful learning. On the micro scale, university faculty and instructors must strive to help students manage information and analyze it critically. It is the job of educators not only to help students "get through" college, but to acquire the life-long learning skills that are necessary inside and outside the classroom. Therefore, our goal here was to provide our students with a basic critical thinking tool to enhance their learning capabilities. My hope is that I will be able to have productive conversations with my students about their work in the future.

Purpose

As neophyte educators, we were plagued with the same question at the end of each semester: *did our students really learn anything?* Was there a qualitative change in their way of seeing, experiencing, understanding, conceptualizing something in the real world (Marton & Ramsden, 1988)? If the central purpose of education is to empower learners to take charge of their own meaning making (Novak, 2010, p. 13), then it was painfully clear that we were missing the mark. Hence, we turned to learner-centered approaches in our teaching.

Learner-centered pedagogy has emerged in higher education settings partly as an antidote to information transfer models of education. Barr and Tagg (1995) describe this as a shift from providing information (i.e. an instruction paradigm) to producing learning (i.e. a learning paradigm). Weimer (2002) states:

The learner-centered approach focuses squarely on learning: what the student is learning, how the student is learning, the conditions under which the student is learning, whether the student is retaining and applying the learning, and how current learning positions the student for future learning. (p. xvi)

When instruction is learner-centered, the action focuses on what students (not teachers) are doing; because the instructional action now features students, this learner-centered orientation accepts, cultivates, and builds on the ultimate responsibility students have for learning (Weimer, 2002, p. xvi). While learning can only be the responsibility of the learner (Hay, Kinchin, & Lygo-Baker, 2008, p. 304), such a stance does not negate the responsibilities of the teacher; teachers can (and should) teach in ways that encourage student meaning making (p. 304). Unfortunately, we assumed that the learning and critical thinking skills our students needed to take charge of their own learning would "develop by osmosis" (Weimer, 2002, p. 50). As Chigozirim's narrative illustrates, some students do not have the foundational critical thinking skills they need to be independent learners.

In reality, even upper-level undergraduates might still be novice learners; i.e. they perceive the information received in each course as isolated individual sets of data. On the other hand, students who are more expert learners are able to link new data to organized bodies of prior knowledge and experience, providing them an advantage in the classroom. Since they know "how" to learn, they are in a better position to self-educate, and flourish in learner-centered environments. Therefore, our challenge was figuring out ways to incorporate critical thinking instruction into our daily teaching in order to facilitate meaningful learning.

We posit that by utilizing concept mapping in a learner-centered environment, instructors can model the basic process of critical thinking in everyday pedagogical practice, and create opportunities for students to practice vital critical thinking skills in the classroom. This in turn can facilitate more meaningful learning as it allows students to integrate new knowledge into prior knowledge structures and participate in meaning making. It is not our intention to characterize students as helpless and powerless individuals who are completely unable to solve problems. However, this project is our attempt to take responsibility for our role in facilitating the learning process. We hope to inspire other instructors to self-reflect and do the same.

BACKGROUND

One of our major concerns is that many of our students seemed to have great difficulty in recalling, articulating and drawing out insights from course content. While it is easy to chalk this up to poor study habits, laziness, and a lack of student motivation, educators must also evaluate their teaching approaches. According to Kinchin, Lygo-Baker, and Hay (2008):

Where experts (teachers) only disclose unanchored fragments of their understanding (as chains of knowledge) the student is excluded from meaningful discourse, except as a passive observer; as a result, the student will adopt surface learning strategies that result in non-learning outcomes (p. 89).

When the student is excluded from meaning-making, the result is rote learning, i.e. when the learner memorizes information without relating it to prior knowledge or when learning information that has no relationship to prior knowledge (Novak, 2010, p. 24). Knowledge gained by intensive rehearsing and rote learning such as "cramming" is not applicable in the real world, and is easily lost, leading to feelings of being a "fraudulent learner" (Novak, 1990a, p. 942). On the other hand, meaningful learning occurs when a learner consciously chooses to relate new information to prior knowledge (Novak, 2010). Conventional teaching and lectures can promote rote learning because instructors translate their rich, complex networks of knowledge into linear chains without disclosing the underlying understanding from which they were derived to their students; this can impede meaningful learning (Hay et al., 2008).

Also, higher education institutions increasingly resemble the marketplace (Newman, Couturier, & Scully, 2004). The decision to obtain a college education is largely economically motivated, therefore students are less likely to love learning for its own sake (Bok, 2005). Lewis (2006) posits that universities have lost sight of the essential purpose of undergraduate education. He states, "There is little reward in today's universities for equipping students with the knowledge and habits of the mind that will make them wise and productive citizens (p. xi). In our own classes, we find that many students are so intensely focused on gaining just enough information to get an A that they think less about the problem solving capabilities, ethics and good character required to excel and progress in their chosen careers. Course content that does not have an obvious correlation to their anticipated career field may automatically be deemed "irrelevant." While a critical concern of post-secondary education is to prepare students for their professional lives, meeting this purpose requires supporting students in developing deep understandings of their disciplines *and* in honing critical thinking abilities (Thompson, Licklider, & Jungst, 2003, p. 133).

Critical Thinking

The literature on critical thinking is vast and multidisciplinary (Case, 2005; Ennis 1985; Facione, 1990; Halpern, 1998; Lewis & Smith 1993; Paul 1992; Paul, Sternberg, 1986; Willingham, 2008). Confusion about the definition of critical thinking instigated the Delphi Project in 1990 which included a cross-disciplinary panel of critical thinking theoreticians. The consensus achieved is stated in the Delphi report (Facione, 1990):

We understand critical thinking to be purposeful, self-regulatory judgment which results in interpretation, analysis, evaluation and inference as well as explanation of the evidential conceptual, methodological, criteriological or contextual considerations upon which that judgment was based. Critical thinking is essential as a tool of inquiry. Critical thinking is a pervasive and self-rectifying human phenomenon. The ideal critical thinker is habitually inquisitive, well-informed, honest in facing personal biases, prudent in making judgments, willing to consider, clear about issues, orderly in complex matters, diligent in seeking relevant information, reasonable in selection of criteria, focused in inquiry and persistent in seeking results which are as precise as the subject and the circumstances of inquiry permit. Thus, educating good critical thinkers means working toward this ideal. It combines developing CT skills with nurturing those dispositions which consistently yield useful insights and which are the basis of a rational and democratic society (p. 2).

Thus, critical thinking involves developing *cognitive* capabilities in interpretation, analysis, evaluation, inference, explanation and self-regulation (p. 5) as well as the *disposition* to critically think, i.e. a *consistent internal* motivation to engage problems and make decisions by using critical thinking (Facione, 2000, p. 65).

In the classroom, a certain mystique surrounds students who are more skillful critical thinkers. Their seemingly natural ability to analyze problems and the clarity with which they express their thoughts and ideas makes them appear more sophisticated, competent and intelligent. During group projects, other students look to them for leadership because they just seem to "get it." Their contributions during class discussions come across as "deep" and profound, sending insecure students further into a spiral of silence. Thus, critical thinking can begin to look like a natural ability or skill that is attainable by especially sharp people. However, all humans are capable of being critical thinkers (Lewis & Smith, 1993). Through practice, and with guidance from a good instructor, we can develop our thinking skills (like our artistic, athletic, or leadership skills) to the extent our natural abilities allow (Facione, 2000, p. 62). Therefore, our goal was to incorporate critical thinking instruction into our already tight teaching schedules in order to facilitate more meaningful learning on a daily basis. Concept mapping has been used successfully in medical and science education for decades and has been shown to improve critical thinking and promote meaningful learning (Abel & Freeze, 2006; Daley & Torre, 2010; Hicks-Moore, 2005; Hsuh & Hsieh, 2005, Novak, 1990a; Roop, 2002; Wandersee, 1990; Wheeler & Collins, 2003).

Concept Mapping

A concept is a perceived regularity in events or objects or in records of events or objects, designated by a label (Novak, 1990b, p. 29). Concept mapping requires learners to plot concepts and their interrelations in a meaningful organizational network (Hay et al., 2008, p. 218). Other popular mapping methods are mind mapping (Buzan & Buzan, 2000) and spider diagramming (Trowbridge & Wandersee 1998). Concept mapping offers several pedagogical benefits.

Most obviously, concept maps enable students to see their thoughts and ideas emerge in a non-linear visual format. In a classroom with multiple learning objectives, visual maps can be especially helpful in clarifying ideas (Novak & Gowin, 1984) and helping students keep track of new information. If used repeatedly over a semester for instance, students can see their knowledge and understanding change and expand (Hay et al., 2008). In one of our classes for instances, mapping is used at different points in the semester when large amounts of information have been covered to gauge understanding and enhance memory. Secondly, mapping methods enable teachers to assist in the development of their students by providing a general guide to understand information (Baugh & Mellott 1998; All & Havens, 1997). Instructors can map their understanding of topic to give students access to the complexity and richness of their knowledge (Hay et al., 2008). Thirdly, concept mapping can be taught in 10 to 20 minutes (Hay et al., 2008, p. 302); since it does not require whole class periods, it can be integrated into a variety of learning approaches and objectives such as group work, brainstorming and project conceptualization. It is already being used in many different ways such as lesson planning, measurement of change, organization of group work, knowledge sharing, etc. (Hay et al., 2008). Fourthly, concept mapping is a powerful meta-cognitive tool which allows students to evaluate and take charge of their own meaning making (Novak & Gowin, 1984). Overtime, concept maps can help students "learn how to learn" (Novak, 1990a; 1990b).

In summary, a focus on meaningful learning and the learner must be accompanied by the teaching of the foundation critical thinking skills needed to self-educate. We propose concept mapping as a way for instructors to model the learning and critical thinking process. We also propose practicing this is a collaborative environment where teachers and students learn together. Some challenges to implementation however must be noted. Many institutions of higher education are still using 40 year old teaching practices for their undergraduates (Forstd & Taylor, 2001). These approaches are familiar and comfortable; therefore, student (and even faculty) resistance to learner-centered approaches can be expected (Weimer, 2002). Another challenge is that in our experience, some students may not see the value in insightful, critical thinking in lower level, required college courses. As noted above, economic rationales for education dominate. As a result, students might not see the utility of any activity that does not explicitly relate to their career path. Teaching evaluations for required classes are notoriously harsh and innovative instructors might be met with resistance in the form of unfavorable evaluations, complaints about workload and "busy work" and sometimes the refusal to participate in class. Thirdly, instructors should be careful about sending confusing and contradictory messages. For instance, it is not uncommon to announce at the beginning of the semester that buying the textbook is important because the quizzes are straight from the book. Inadvertently, teachers might be communicating that there is no point in going "beyond the book."

IMPLEMENTATION

Pilot Study

The study was conducted in four lower level communication courses at both group and individual levels, based on class time restrictions and the learning objectives set forth during the study week. The two larger classes contained 40 students each, and the smaller classes contained 24 students each. The two larger classes were different sections of the same course (COMM 111a and COMM 111b) and the two smaller classes were separate courses (COMM 222 and COMM 333).

In COMM 111a and COMM 111b, mapping was conducted on a class workshop day focused on formulating, organizing, and outlining an informative speech in which students were responsible for selecting their own topic and performing supporting research. In COMM 222, mapping took place on day set aside for reviewing course material. In COMM 333, students used maps to develop their arguments for a persuasive speaking assignment.

Method

Our method includes three easy steps: orientation, mapping and debrief. The *orientation stage* consists of giving students a brief preview of the learning objectives and key concepts of the day. We also recommend clarifying the purpose of the mapping activity. As stated above, the *disposition* to critically think is vital. Therefore, it is important to take time to motivate students by explaining how concept mapping can enhance their learning, and inviting them to join in the process of meaning-making. This step is especially important in a collaborative learner-centered environment where the role of the instructor is facilitator, as opposed to "sage on the stage" (King, 1993). In COMM 111a and COMM 333, sample maps were shown to students in the orientation phase and the mapping steps were explained while in COMM 111b and 222, a step-by-step method was utilized, i.e. drawing each level of the map with the students and explaining the significance of each level.

The *mapping phase* is based on the mapping model laid out in the mapping literature (Novak, 1990a, 1990b; Okebukola, 1992,;Wandersee, 1990). Our modification includes three foundational levels: the main idea, sub-ideas, and support (course concepts, research, and prior experience). The goal in this phase is to stimulate the cognitive skills necessary for critical thinking through deliberate facilitation. We presented the mapping activity as a task; for instance, in COMM 222, groups of four to five students were asked to synthesize a sub-section of the text that was centered on the concept of identity. Based on their readings and class discussions, the students then had to *interpret*, i.e. ascertain the meaning or significance of whatever data they are supposed to map (Facione, 1990). In order to figure out sub-ideas and support, they were required to *analyze*, i.e. identify intended and actual inferential relationships among statements, questions, concepts, descriptions or other forms of representation intended to express beliefs, judgments, experiences, reasons, information, or opinions (p. 7). The whole mapping process is one of continuous *evaluation*, i.e. assessing the credibility of statements or other representations which are accounts or descriptions of a person's perception, experience, situation, judgment, belief, or opinion; and to assess the logical strength of the actual or intend inferential relationships among statements, descriptions, questions or other forms of representation (p. 8). *Inference* is also important, i.e. to identify and secure elements needed to draw reasonable conclusions (p. 9). At this stage, we will often ask the students, "so what"? This question is aimed at moving students towards

Figure 1. COMM 222 student group mapping

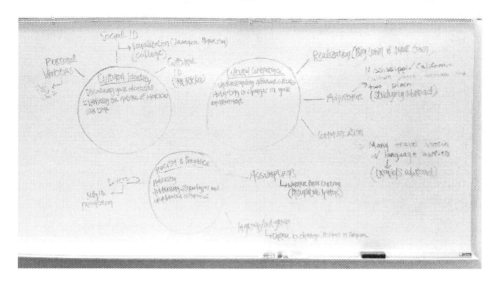

drawing out insights and implications from the data they are mapping. Students are then required to give *explanations* for their maps, i.e. to state the results of one's reasoning (p. 10) not only to the instructor but to other members of a small group or the class. In COMM 111a, 111b and 333, students worked individually, while COMM 222 students worked in groups of four to five, making large scale maps on white boards. An example is shown in Figure 1.

Finally, *self-regulation* governs the whole process, i.e. self-consciously to monitor one's cognitive activities (p. 10). During the activity, we recommend friendly questioning, discussion and comparison of student maps. It is also important to supervise, facilitate and give feedback without "taking over." Throughout the mapping phase, we actively facilitated by asking and answering questions, walking around the room to look at maps, encouraged those working in groups to collaborate, and providing instant feedback. With the different cognitive skills in mind, we asked the students questions and encouraged them to clarify different ideas that were vague.

The debrief phase consists of discussing the implications of the exercise with the students. Here we ask students to reflect on what they have learned (or still have difficulty grasping). We also emphasize the cross-applicability of this method to different assignments, problem-solving tasks, group work and classes. Obviously, this phase should be compatible with the particular learning requirements of the day. For instance, in COMM 222, the class discussed the similarities and differences between group maps and the significance of these differences to their perceptions of course material.

Findings

Consistent with the literature, concept maps proved to be a great tool for organizing information (Novak, 1990a). In COMM 111a and b, we collected finished maps from students, provided feedback, and returned maps to students during another class period. Several students asked for their maps to be returned early so that they could use it to prepare their speech outlines. This was an indicator to us that they found the maps useful as an organizing tool. Secondly, concept mapping facilitated the process of feedback (Daley & Torre, 2010). We were able to observe areas of strength and weakness for individual students and provide speedy feedback on the spot. Students were also forced to confront gaps in their own learning. Holistically, we were able to quickly recognize areas that most students were having trouble understanding. We were then able to focus on knowledge and understanding gaps in the debriefing phase, correct misunderstandings and expand on relevant course concepts for the remainder of the class. The time spent in evaluating student work was thus significantly reduced.

Another advantage of concept mapping observed in our study was that it stimulated student-teacher dialogue and collaboration. As Novak and Gowin (1984) state, concept maps can foster cooperation between student and teacher in a battle in which the "monster" to be conquered is meaninglessness of information and the victory is shared meaning (p. 23). We believe this is partly because concept mapping can validate the meanings that students bring to the classroom (i.e. their prior knowledge and experience). In our method, students include their prior knowledge under "support"; as such they were able to see that what they already know is not insignificant, but connected to a larger Web of knowledge. Empowering students to use the knowledge they already possess gives them a solid starting place for learning (McPeck, 1990). At the classroom level, educators must think of tasks that will enable students to link concepts taught in their course to personal experience and prior knowledge (Bean, 2011).

Surprisingly, the implementation of the tool during the pilot study was met with very little resistance on the part of the students. Most of our students took the process seriously and maintained a positive attitude. However, as we have continued to incorporate concept mapping into our regular course work, a few observations are important to note. Firstly, the change has to first occur in the instructor. We are both products of instructional paradigms; therefore, the "information exchange mode" was our default. Let the students do it themselves! Resist the urge to give them the answers. One way to avoid this trap is to respond to questions with questions. For instance if a student asks, "Do you think this makes sense?," consider the student's map and take them through each step asking questions such as, "Do *you* think your thesis is clear and distinct?" and "Do your main points answer the question the thesis poses?." This places the responsibility for reasoning back in the hands of the student. Guiding them through the process by questioning provides them with just enough support to achieve learning goals.

Secondly, as mentioned in our background section, students come into the classroom with varying levels of prior experience and critical thinking ability. Therefore, some students are able to complete the process much quicker and effectively than others. In order to keep those students occupied, providing back-up tasks such as working on a related assignment might be helpful. Thirdly, in our study, we did not use technological mapping tools. This does not mean we have anything against these tools. However, it is important not to assume that technology is automatically better because it is "current." While technology is becoming more common in classroom settings, and more people have access than ever before, the digital divide is still a reality and there are still students who do not have the access they need (Selwyn & Facer, 2007). We believe it is important to consider factors such as learning objectives, the student demographics, possible disparities in access, technological proficiency and class size before deciding to use technological mapping tools. While we acknowledge the rapid growth of technology use we were more focused on fostering engagement and interaction in the classroom.

CONCLUSION

In our research, we are moving towards developing learning toolkits (that include methods such as concept mapping) that instructors can use in a variety of courses. We would like to extend testing of concept mapping to a broader range of classes, learning objectives, etc. and provide concrete, empirical and classroom tested applications for other instructors. We would also like to include students as consultants in the process. Finally, we aim to develop ways to make concept mapping more applicable to the technologies that students use on a regular basis. In the right environment and with the right tools, students can improve their critical thinking. Firstly there must be a shift from information-centered perspectives to learner-centered approaches that emphasize meaningful learning. Secondly, critical thinking must be viewed not as a separate skill to be honed, but as a regular component of college education. Students' minds should be constantly challenged in class. There is a wealth of research on critical thinking, mapping, meaningful learning and learner-centered approaches that remains sadly under-utilized. While we have emphasized student responsibility throughout this essay, we conclude by saying that college teachers must not allow the stress and politics of higher education make us forgetful of our responsibility to our students.

REFERENCES

Abel, W. M., & Freeze, M. (2006). Evaluation of concept mapping in an associate degree nursing program. *The Journal of Nursing Education, 45*(9), 356–365. PMID:17002082

All, A. C., & Havens, R. L. (1997). Cognitive/concept mapping: A teaching strategy for nursing. *Journal of Advanced Nursing, 25,* 1210–1219. doi:10.1046/j.1365-2648.1997.19970251210.x PMID:9181419

Barr, R. B., & Tagg, J. (1995). From teaching to learning: A new paradigm for undergraduate education. *Change, 27*(6), 13–25. doi:10.1080/00091383.1995.10544672

Baugh, N., & Mellott, K. (1998). Clinical concept mapping as preparation for student nurses' clinical experiences. *The Journal of Nursing Education, 37,* 253–256. PMID:9749811

Bean, J. (2011). *Engaging ideas: The professor's guide to integrating writing, critical thinking, and active learning in the classroom.* San Francisco, CA: Jossey Bass.

Bok, D. (2005). *Our underachieving colleges: A candid look at how much students learn and why they should be learning more.* Princeton, NJ: Princeton University Press.

Buzan, T., & Buzan, B. (2006). *The mind map book: How to use radiant thinking to maximize your brain's untapped potential.* Upper Saddle River, NJ: Pearson Education.

Case, R. (2005). Moving critical thinking to the main stage. *Education Canada, 45*(2), 45–49.

Daley, B. J., & Torre, D. M. (2010). Concept maps in medical education: An analytical literature review. *Medical Education, 44*(5), 440–448. doi:10.1111/j.1365-2923.2010.03628.x PMID:20374475

Ennis, R. H. (1985). A logical basis for measuring critical thinking skills. *Educational Leadership, 43*(2), 44–48.

Facione, P. A. (1990). *Critical thinking: A statement of expert consensus for purposes of educational assessment and instruction.* Millbrae, CA: The California Academic Press.

Facione, P. A. (2000). The disposition toward critical thinking: Its character, measurement, and relationship to critical thinking skill. *Informal Logic, 20*(1), 61–84.

Forstd, N., & Taylor, R. (2001). Patterns of change in the university: The impact of "lifelong learning" and the "world of work". *Studies in the Education of Adults, 33*(1), 49–60.

Halpern, D. F. (1998). Teaching critical thinking for transfer across domains: Dispositions, skills, structure training, and metacognitive monitoring. *The American Psychologist, 53*(4), 449–455. doi:10.1037/0003-066X.53.4.449 PMID:9572008

Hay, D., Kinchin, I., & Lygo-Baker, S. (2008). Making learning visible: the role of concept mapping in higher education. *Studies in Higher Education, 33*(3), 295–311. doi:10.1080/03075070802049251

Hicks-Moore, S. L. (2005). Clinical concept maps in nursing education: An effective way to link theory and practice. *Nurse Education in Practice, 5*(6), 348–352. doi:10.1016/j.nepr.2005.05.003 PMID:19040844

Hsu, L., & Hsieh, S. I. (2005). Concept maps as an assessment tool in a nursing course. *Journal of Professional Nursing, 21*(3), 141–149. doi:10.1016/j.profnurs.2005.04.006 PMID:16021557

Kinchin, I. M., Lygo-Baker, & Hay. (2008). Universities as centers of non-learning. *Studies in Higher Education, 33*(1), 89–103. doi:10.1080/03075070701794858

King, A. (1993). From sage on the stage to guide on the side. *College Teaching, 41*(1), 30–35. doi:10.1080/87567555.1993.9926781

Lewis, A., & Smith, D. (1993). Defining higher order thinking. *Theory into Practice, 32*(3), 131–137. doi:10.1080/00405849309543588

Lewis, H. (2006). *Excellence without a soul: How a great university forgot education*. New York, NY: Public Affairs.

Marton, F., & Ramsden, P. (1988). What does it take to improve learning? In P. Ramsden (Ed.), *Improving learning: New perspectives* (pp. 268–286). London: Kogan Page.

McPeck, J. E. (1990). Critical thinking and subject specificity: A reply to Ennis. *Educational Researcher, 19*(4), 10–12. doi:10.3102/0013189X019004010

Newman, F., Couturier, L., & Scurry, J. (2004). *The future of higher education: Rhetoric, reality the risks of the market*. San Francisco, CA: Jossey-Bass.

Novak, J., & Gowin, D. (1984). *Learning how to learn*. New York: Cambridge University Press. doi:10.1017/CBO9781139173469

Novak, J. D. (1990). Concept mapping: A useful tool for science education. *Journal of Research in Science Teaching*, *27*(10), 937–949. doi:10.1002/tea.3660271003

Novak, J. D. (1990). Concept maps and Vee diagrams: Two metacognitive tools to facilitate meaningful learning. *Instructional Science*, *19*(1), 29–52. doi:10.1007/BF00377984

Novak, J. D. (2010). *Learning, creating and using knowledge: Concept maps as facilitative tools in schools and corporations* (2nd ed.). New York, NY: Routledge.

Okebukola, P. A. (1992). Concept mapping with a cooperative learning flavor. *The American Biology Teacher*, 218–221.

Paul, R. W. (1992). Critical thinking: What, why, and how? *New Directions for Community Colleges*, (77): 3–24. doi:10.1002/cc.36819927703

Roop, K. M. (2002). *Effect of concept mapping as a learning strategy on certificate practical nursing students' academic achievement and critical thinking development.* (Doctoral dissertation). Wilmington College, Wilmington, DE.

Selwyn, N., & Facer, K. (2007). *Beyond the digital divide: Rethinking digital inclusion for the 21st.* Retrieved from http://www.futurelab.org.uk/resources/documents/opening_education/Digital_Divide.pdf

Sternberg, R. J. (1986). *Critical thinking: Its nature, measurement, and improvement.* National Institute of Education. Retrieved from http://eric.ed.gov/PDFS/ED272882.pdf

Thompson, J., Licklider, B., & Jungst, S. (2003). Learner-centered teaching: Post-secondary strategies that promote thinking like a professional. *Theory into Practice*, *42*(2), 133–141.

Trowbridge, J. E., & Wandersee, J. H. (1998). Theory-driven graphic organizers. In J. J. Mintzes, J. H. Wandersee, & J. D. Novak (Eds.), *Assessing science understanding: A human constructivist view* (pp. 15–40). San Diego, CA: Academic Press.

Wandersee, J. H. (1990). Concept mapping and the cartography of cognition. *Journal of Research in Science Teaching*, *27*(10), 923–936. doi:10.1002/tea.3660271002

Weimer, M. (2002). *Learner-centered teaching: Five key changes to practice.* San Francisco: Jossey-Bass.

Wheeler, L. A., & Collins, S. K. (2003). The influence of concept mapping on critical thinking in baccalaureate nursing students. *Journal of Professional Nursing*, *19*(6), 339–346. doi:10.1016/S8755-7223(03)00134-0 PMID:14689390

Willingham, D. T. (2008). Critical thinking: Why is it so hard to teach? *Arts Education Policy Review*, *109*(4), 21–32. doi:10.3200/AEPR.109.4.21-32

ADDITIONAL READING

Allen, M., & Berkowitz, S. (1999). A meta-analysis of the impact of forensics and communication education on critical thinking. *Communication Education*, *48*(1), 18. doi:10.1080/03634529909379149

Ausbel, D., Novak, J., & Hanesian, H. (1978). *Educational psychology: A cognitive view* (2nd ed.). New York: Werbel and Peck.

Bailin, S. (2002). Critical thinking and science education. *Science & Education*, *11*(4), 361–375. doi:10.1023/A:1016042608621

Bailin, S., Case, R., Coombs, J. R., & Daniels, L. B. (1999). Conceptualizing critical thinking. *Journal of Curriculum Studies*, *31*(3), 285–302. doi:10.1080/002202799183133

Blumberg, P., & Pontiggia, L. (2011). Benchmarking the Degree of Implementation of Learner Centered Approaches. *Innovative Higher Education*, *36*(3), 189–202. doi:10.1007/s10755-010-9168-2

Bosch, W., Hester, J., MacEntee, V., MacKenzie, J., Morey, T. T., Nichols, J., & Young, R. (2008). Beyond Lip-service: An Operational Definition of Learning-centered College. *Innovative Higher Education*, *33*(2), 83–98. doi:10.1007/s10755-008-9072-1

Boyer, E. (1987). *College: The undergraduate experience in America*. New York, NY: Harper and Row.

Brown, A. L. (1990). Domain specific principles affect learning and transfer in children. *Cognitive Science*, *14*, 107–133.

Clayton, L. H. (2006). Concept mapping: An effective, active teaching-learning method. *Nursing Education Perspectives*, *27*(4), 197–203. PMID:16921805

Daley, B. J., Shaw, C. R., Balistrieri, T., Glasenapp, K., & Placentine, L. (1999). Concept maps: A strategy to teach and evaluate critical thinking. *The Journal of Nursing Education*, *38*(1), 42–47. PMID:9921788

Ennis, R. H. (1989). Critical thinking and subject specificity: Clarification and needed research. *Educational Researcher*, *18*(3), 4–10. doi:10.3102/0013189X018003004

Fear, F. A., Doberneck, D. M., Robinson, C. F., Fear, K. L., Barr, R. B., Van Den Berg, H., & Petrulis, R. (2003). Meaning Making and The Learning Paradigm: A Provocative Idea in Practice. *Innovative Higher Education*, *27*(3), 151. doi:10.1023/A:1022351126015

Fisher, K. M. (1990). Computer-Based Concept Mapping. *Journal of College Science Teaching*, *19*(6), 347–352.

Fullan, M. (2007). The NEW meaning of educational change (4th ed.). NewYork: Teachers' College Press.

Garrison, D. R., Anderson, T., & Archer, W. (2004). Critical thinking, cognitive presence, and computer conferencing in distance education. *American Journal of Distance Education*, *15*(1), 7–23. doi:10.1080/08923640109527071

Halpern, D. F. (2001). Assessing the effectiveness of critical thinking instruction. *The Journal of General Education*, *50*(4), 270–286. doi:10.1353/jge.2001.0024

Hicks-Moore, S. L., & Pastirik, P. J. (2006). Evaluating critical thinking in clinical concept maps: A pilot study. *International Journal of Nursing Education Scholarship*, *3*(1). doi:10.2202/1548-923X.1314 PMID:17140395

Mayer, R. E. (2002). Rote versus meaningful learning. *Theory into Practice*, *41*(4), 226–232. doi:10.1207/s15430421tip4104_4

Nesbit, J. C., & Adesope, O. O. (2006). Learning with concept and knowledge maps: A meta-analysis. *Review of Educational Research*, *76*(3), 413–448. doi:10.3102/00346543076003413

Novak, J. D. (2002). Meaningful learning: The essential factor for conceptual change in limited or inappropriate propositional hierarchies leading to empowerment of learners. *Science Education*, *86*(4), 548–571. doi:10.1002/sce.10032

Okebukola, P. A., & Jegede, O. J. (1988). Cognitive preference and learning mode as determinants of meaningful learning through concept mapping. *Science Education*, *72*(4), 489–500. doi:10.1002/sce.3730720408

Robertson, D. R. (2003). *Making time, making change: Avoiding overload in college teaching*. Stillwater, OK: New Forums.

Splitter, L., & Sharp, A. M. (1995). *Teaching for better thinking: The classroom community of inquiry*. Melbourne: Australian Council for Educational Research.

Taylor, E. W. (2003). The relationship between the prior school lives of adult educators and their beliefs about teaching adults. *International Journal of Lifelong Education, 22*(1), 59–77. doi:10.1080/02601370304828

Weinstein, C. S. (1989). Teacher education students' preconceptions of teaching. *Journal of Teacher Education, 40*(2), 53–60. doi:10.1177/002248718904000210

KEY TERMS AND DEFINITIONS

Concept Mapping: A visual organizational network that represents past, present and emerging structures of meaning.

Critical Thinking: A purposeful, reflective and self-regulatory mode of thinking or judgment.

Critical Thinking "Disposition": Habits of the mind such as inquisitiveness, open-mindedness and flexibility that incline an individual towards critical thinking.

Learner-Centered Pedagogy: An approach to teaching that places the teacher in the role of facilitator and the responsibility for learning in the hands of the student.

Meaningful Learning: Learning in which the learner consciously integrates new knowledge into prior knowledge structures.

Meaning Making: The construction of frameworks of understanding.

Rote Learning: Memorization of new information without linkage to prior knowledge structures.

Chapter 7
Making Sense of Intercultural Interaction

Kate Dunsmore
Fairleigh Dickinson University, USA

EXECUTIVE SUMMARY

This chapter presents a visual sense-making activity in the field of intercultural communication. The activity is rooted in the literature that treats learning as a process of constructing meaning. The premise for this activity is that critical thinking depends on learning beyond memorizing discrete items. This perspective views learning for critical thinking as a process of integrating new knowledge into existing mental frameworks, which are then re-shaped in the learning process. The discussion begins with foundations in learning theory and their application to teaching intercultural communication. The description of the activity begins with the classroom setting and concludes with an appraisal of the activity in practice. Considerations of technology, curriculum design, and combining pedagogical strategies are included.

KEY IDEAS FROM LEARNING THEORY

This book explores the role of visual representation in fostering critical thinking. Halx and Reybold (2005) review the definitions of critical thinking that a range of researchers have investigated, concluding that there is broad agreement that critical thinking involves "purposeful, reasoned and goal-directed" engagement with a

DOI: 10.4018/978-1-4666-5816-5.ch007

topic (p. 294). Consideration of multiple perspectives and "an evaluation of one's own thought processes" are also widely agreed upon constituents of critical thinking (pp. 294-5).

The American Philosophical Association assembled a cross-disciplinary panel in 1990 to develop by consensus a definition of critical thinking. The definition below is taken from the *Executive Summary of the Delphi Report* (Facione, 1990):

We understand critical thinking to be purposeful, self-regulatory judgment which results in interpretation, analysis, evaluation, and inference, as well as explanation of the evidential, conceptual, methodological, criteriological, or contextual considerations upon which that judgment is based (p. 2).

Thus agreement seems strong that critical thinking involves judgment and the ability to articulate reasoning. In this regard, concept mapping and other forms of visual representation would be likely to foster critical thinking because they support the process of students making sense of a conceptual framework (Novak, 2007). This emphasis on the process of students constructing meaning and understanding rather than on how information is delivered is promoted in constructivist learning environments. Constructivist approaches tend toward collaborative and sense-making activities and away from traditional lectures (Wilson, 1996). For more on the constructivist theories of Piaget and Vygotsky, please see the Support Material, which is available on request.

Boghossian (2012) sounds a note of caution regarding constructivist or constructionist approaches that have insufficient opportunities for correction of student conceptions. However, I would argue that approaches tied to deep or meaningful learning (defined below) provide such opportunities without sacrificing the advantages constructivist approaches offer in developing the self-regulatory aspect of critical thinking. Much of the literature on concept mapping and other forms of visual deliberation expresses the advantage of these techniques in terms of fostering deep learning or meaningful learning. There is considerable overlap in the ways researchers define and use these terms, as well as those who discuss learning in terms of mental models. I turn now to a review of these areas of overlap.

The integration of new concepts into existing understandings has been characterized as meaningful learning (Novak & Cañas, 2008; Windschitl, 2002, p. 136) or deep learning (Tagg, 2003; Lau, Liem, & Nie, 2008). Deep learning involves integrating knowledge across multiple contexts (Nelson Laird & Garver, 2009) and is thought to foster greater retention in contrast with rote memorization (Tagg, 2003; Windschitl, 2002).

The process of integrating multiple frameworks has also been discussed as replacing mental models (Oliver & Hannafin, 2001) and as connecting schemas (Nishida,

2005). A useful definition of mental models is "representations that are active while solving a particular problem and that provide the workspace for inference and mental operations"(Halford, 1993, p. 23). Schemas have been understood as "special cases of procedures for constructing mental models" (Johnson-Laird, 1983, pp. 397-98) and as a representation of "constraints between variables" (Halford, 1993, p. 34).

While cognitive scientists continue refining an understanding of the processes involved, at the least we can see that models and schemas are involved in meaning construction and thus in meaningful learning. Glynn and Duit (1995) describe students learning by constructing models as "making sense of their experiences – they are making meaning" (p. 4). As Glynn and Duit (1995) describe the process of meaningful learning, students "activate their existing knowledge, relate it to educational experiences, and construct new knowledge in the form of conceptual models" (pp. 4-5).

Novak and Cañas (2008) argue that meaningful learning requires that "the material to be learned must be conceptually clear and presented with language and examples relatable to the learner's prior knowledge," that "the learner must possess relevant prior knowledge," and that "the learner must choose to learn meaningfully…." Meaningful learning, then, occurs when "students choose to learn by attempting to incorporate new meanings into their prior knowledge, rather than simply memorizing concept definitions or propositional statements or computational procedures" (pp. 3-4).

The definition Hay (2007) – drawing on Novak – offers for deep learning is:

- That the learner has prior knowledge that is relevant to the new learning to be done;
- That what is to be learnt is presented in ways that have meaning;
- That the learner must choose to learn meaningfully (p. 41).

So, although Hay uses the term "deep learning," we see that he is referencing substantially the same phenomenon known as "meaningful learning."

An examination of these definitions shows that the distinctions between deep learning, meaningful learning and critical thinking are less important for the present purpose than the considerable overlap between these concepts. The distinction between deep (or meaningful) learning and surface (or rote) learning is highly pertinent to the topic of this chapter, as the activity described here leverages these different approaches to learning. For the purpose of this chapter, the discussion will reference deep learning and meaningful learning interchangeably with the understanding that students engaging in these processes are indeed engaging in critical thinking as it has been most consistently defined. The Support Material (available on request) includes sources discussing the closely related concept of authentic learning and supportive approaches such as problem-based inquiry.

For the purpose of this chapter, the power of concept mapping and visual representation activities is the impact they have on activating schemas and mental models and bringing new and old schemas/mental models into coherence in the newly constructed schema/model represented in the concept map or representation.

Educational researchers have striven to identify which student activities result in deep learning. The expectation is that "deep learning approaches seek meanings, search for relationships among the concepts, and integrate the newly learned knowledge into existing knowledge structures and prior experiences" (Chang & Chang, 2008). Tagg (2003) describes deep learning approaches as focused on the meaning of the material, self-conscious, mindful and reinforcing incremental processes such as rereading and taking different approaches.

Novak and Cañas (2008) argue that meaningful learning occurs when students correctly apply concepts from one context to another and that concept mapping is a creative act that helps students organize concepts meaningfully. Clayton (2006) reviewed seven studies of the effectiveness of concept mapping in nursing education, concluding that there is evidence it does improve critical thinking, while also noting that the study designs did not permit broad generalization. Hay and Kinchin (2008) discuss a method of scoring concept maps at intervals to demonstrate increased knowledge and integration of knowledge from previous to new frameworks. They conclude that even in large classes, concept mapping facilitates articulation of mental models. This sense-making is one constituent of critical thinking.

Research on concept mapping indicates that it facilitates awareness of already-held conceptions and their relation to new concepts (van Boxtel, van der Linden, Roelofs, & Erkens, 2002). This quality of connection across contexts is also a hallmark of meaningful (or deep) learning. Maneval, Filburn, Deringer and Lum (2011) found experimentally that teaching with concept mapping resulted in practical nursing students passed credentialing tests as well as with conventional teaching methods and "performed better in the areas of health promotion, client education, and safety, issues extending to a deeper understanding of patients beyond the experience of acute illness" (p. 232). This finding relates to the significance of mindfulness and self-conscious engagement with the issue as Tagg (2003) discusses.

Halpern and Hakel (2003) argue that the key to deep learning is providing varied opportunities to practice retrieving content knowledge. In particular they argue that repeated opportunities presented over time are more effective. Asking students to retrieve knowledge and re-present it in different formats is also more effective (p. 38-39). The implication is that surface learning must be achieved as a foundation in order for deep learning approaches to be effective (Halpern & Hakel, 2003, p. 39).

This suggests that deep learning approaches, such as concept mapping, be combined with surface learning activities.

STRUCTURING CONCEPT MAPPING AND VISUALIZATION

Researchers have investigated a number of approaches to structuring activities involving concept mapping and visual representation. Concerns that have been investigated include complexity of the process, use of mapping programs, effect of online environments, and impact of peer learning (Wang, Peng, Cheng, Zhou, & Liu, 2011; Spanjers, van Gog, & van Merriënboer, 2010; Villalon & Calvo, 2011; Chang & Chang, 2008; Novak & Cañas, 2008).

Including a collaborative element to concept mapping activities in face-to-face classes also yielded learning gains (van Boxtel et al., 2002). Collaborative concept mapping required negotiating shared meaning, fostered surfacing of knowledge gaps, and sponsored articulation of mental models. The collaborative element necessitated reflection on the conceptual framework and the relations between concepts. It is this necessity to articulate to peers that especially facilitates deep learning and critical thinking.

Studies have demonstrated positive results from complex concept mapping activities and from a simpler, online approach involving peer learning (Chang & Chang, 2008). The approach described here is a simpler form, utilizing peer learning, adapted to a face-to-face classroom situation. It is also appropriate for classrooms and populations with limited technology resources.

APPLICABILITY OF MAPPING/VISUALIZATION ACTIVITIES TO LEARNING INTERCULTURAL COMMUNICATION

Being able to view the world from a cultural perspective different from one's own requires an objective standpoint on culture generally, but also skills for communicating across cultural boundaries. Thus, in addition to shifting mental models of the nature of culture, students must also shift models of communication practices.

Synthesis of new mental models and the deep learning this entails is key both to learning a theoretical framework for intercultural interaction and to practicing the performance of intercultural interaction. This chapter discusses a multi-step mapping activity to help students integrate a conceptual model of intercultural interaction with their own models of interaction. The structure of the activity is supported by the literature on surface and deep learning, formation of mental models, visualization, peer learning, and on concept mapping itself as discussed above. Further comments related to learning theory will follow the activity description. Further references on learning theory are provided in the Support Material, which is available upon request.

COURSE SETTING

The course in which this activity was used is an upper division required course covering communication across cultural boundaries. Students learning to step outside their own set of filters experience a kind of culture shock which increases the difficulty of learning new communication strategies. While there is some evidence that conventional memorization and drill is most effective in surface learning (Larson, Butler, & Roediger, 2009; Swaminatham, 2006), the goal of integrating a framework into one's repertoire of communicative responses goes beyond basic acquisition of content knowledge. Because students needed to master a framework and then demonstrate intercultural awareness in applying it, integrating the framework into their existing mental models was essential for success.

THE NATURE OF INTERCULTURAL COMMUNICATION

Understanding intercultural interaction from a social scientific standpoint involves learning a model of human interaction which, for most people, differs significantly from the understanding they were raised with. For example, most people do not think of their own culture as "a culture." It is simply the way they see the world. Nor do most people look at their culture analytically or as a system which may be objectively compared to other systems of equal validity (Gudykunst & Kim, 1997; Nishida, 2005). Rather, their concern is distinguishing strangers from fellow members in an effort to advance their own life concerns. The field of intercultural communication arose in large part to develop neutral ways to characterize cultures (Rogers & Steinfatt, 1999).

Our understanding of ourselves and strangers is shaped by a web of cultural orientations that constitute a filter through which we interact with people from other cultures (Varner & Beamer, 2011). This web, which has been theorized as cultural schemas which are activated in interactions (Nishida, 2005), constitutes a mental model. It is "our theory of the game being played in interacting with the other people we encounter" (Gudykunst & Kim, 1997, p. 17).

Becoming aware of the nature of this web of perceptions is key, then, to effective intercultural interaction. Varner and Beamer (2011) describe rigid adherence to one's starting conceptions as stereotypical thinking and contrast this with prototypical thinking which is subject to change in the face of new information (pp.

99-100). Lustig and Koester (2010) present a tool specifically to assist people to recognize their own attribution of meaning to the verbal and non-verbal behavior of others (pp. 78-77). The act of recognition is presented as a first, necessary step to altering our own schemas.

Achieving this more neutral way of describing and interpreting the behavior of others involves a reflective process which may be learned; that is, practicing the process reduces the tendency to reductive characterization (stereotyping) and enhances our capacity to change our view of others (Varner & Beamer, 2011). The process of intercultural communication has also been theorized as adaption requiring unlearning existing conceptual frameworks in the process of acquiring new ones (Kim, 2005, pp. 382-383). These processes are consonant with the descriptions of deep learning of a complex form, involving personal identity as well as cognitive, perceptual and communicative frameworks.

In addition to understanding the nature of culture cognitively, it is beneficial to learn a framework for managing communicative acts in an intercultural situation to help in overcoming psychological factors in dealing with those we consider foreign (Gudykunst, 2004). The framework students were to master in the course included concepts capturing both cognitive and communicative categories of cultural difference. The cognitive categories related to cultural orientations include preferences for soft data or hard data, for direct or indirect approaches to communication, and for ends-based or means-based decision-making (Varner & Beamer, 2011). Communicative categories include approach to managing conflict, communication style and strategies such as expressing agreement where one can (Varner & Beamer, 2011).

The activity described here was a bridge between surface learning of an analytical framework and full application of the framework to a problem rooted in real intercultural conflict. The full set of concepts making up the framework was presented to the students in the form of a study guide (see Appendix) along with a series of memorization drills. The first part of the concept mapping activity took place three class sessions after the test of content knowledge. The second part of the activity took place two weeks later, after students had completed an assignment where they had to use the framework to develop a plan for a specific intercultural interaction.

RELATION OF ACTIVITY TO OTHER COURSEWORK

Across the semester, students progressed from conventional testing to simple application to problem-based learning.

Students first encountered the framework at the level of knowledge and comprehension. They were tested in conventional ways asking them to define and explain the terms of the framework. This was primarily a test of rote memorization. They next had to apply the framework by labeling elements of scenarios from the text-book and from news accounts of intercultural interaction. The mapping activity followed several days of this labeling practice and tasked them with synthesizing the framework as a whole, not just in discrete pieces as was the case with the labeling.

The mapping activity prepared them for their final assignment which took the form of problem-based learning. (For more on the nature of problem-based learning, see the Resources for Further Study.) Their final assignment required them to develop a recommendation for resolving an intercultural conflict, demonstrating the kind of self-awareness necessary for effective intercultural communication. The final assignment, which to a significant extent required students to define the problem to be investigated, provided the means for authentic learning; that is, a learning environment that authentically engages with real life situations (Meyers & Nulty, 2009). This final assignment was based on two earlier papers written before the introduction of the framework covered by the mapping activity.

They had first written a conventional research paper about a conflict in a single country. This was followed by practice in inferring values from statements by stake-holders in the issue. This skill is related to the nature of culture as ranking priorities, shaping attitudes and influencing behavior, which is a foundational conception in intercultural communication.

The final exam presented scenarios of intercultural interaction and asked them to infer the values and attitudes of the participants from the behavior described. Other questions asked them to infer what cultural orientations could explain the behavior in the scenario provided. In this way students were presented with mini-problems in which to apply the framework. Successful answers required inferring values and attitudes from stated behaviors and explaining the behavior in terms of the framework. The inferences and explanations were based on appreciating how the concepts in the framework fit together within a given cultural context.

TECHNOLOGY CONSIDERATIONS

This activity did not require technology beyond paper, pens, pencils, crayons, pastels, markers and tape. Providing students with materials to produce collages would be another possible approach if the preference were more toward visualization other than conventional node-link concept maps. Providing some drawing media opened up the range of visualizations without clearly moving away from node-link mapping.

Researchers have argued for the advantages of computer-assisted concept mapping. Maps may be altered easily to include additional concepts (Plotnick, 2001) and mapping programs can speed the process. However, many students are not familiar with these programs, and many classrooms are not equipped with computers. Students who are entirely at home with computer-based drawing programs may prefer to use them. A limitation of computer-based mapping is being able to display the concept maps for the entire class to see simultaneously. I also found that integrating more drawing materials lightened the feeling in the class and led to deeper engagement with the mapping task. However, using a program could also be highly engaging, based on results reported in published studies.

ACTIVITY DESCRIPTION

Part 1: First Concept Mapping/Visualization

Students were given 8 ½ x 14-inch sheets of paper. This size provides sufficient space while still being manageable on stand-alone desks. Rooms with tables could accommodate larger sheets.

Students were allowed to choose from a range of drawing media including pens and pencils in a range of colors, crayons, and markers. In previous iterations of this activity, students used only the drawing media they happened to have with them.

The directions given were minimal. Students were reminded of the concept handout they had previously received and were allowed to refer to their notes. They were instructed to visually represent the framework of the concepts. Students sought confirmation about the nature of the visual representation they were expected to produce. I assured them that it was their choice and that any form of representation was acceptable. I explained that representation could be anything from simple flow charts to graphic novels and repeated that the choice was theirs so long as they represented the entire framework. They were given about 45 minutes to work. Then all the pages were put on display around the room for a gallery walk interaction.

The students were instructed to view all the pages and to consider how their approach differed from the approaches of others. Some students were asked to discuss their maps.

Student maps were produced with a variety of drawing media. The structure of the student maps has been rendered here in line form.

Flow charts were fairly common, as in the example rendering in Figure 2.

Many students chose to depict the conceptual framework in narrative form, illustrating a story as in the example rendering in Figure 3.

Some students produced conventional node-link concept maps. However, even with the conventional concept maps, students included personalization, such as a variety of node shapes. Rather than use the conventional oval, students might use a cloud, heart, flower or other shape as in the example rendering in Figure 4.

Figure 1. Flow of the activity

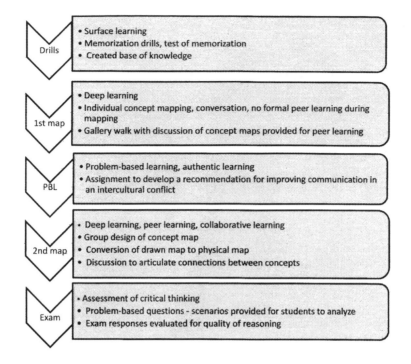

Figure 2. Rendering of flow chart example

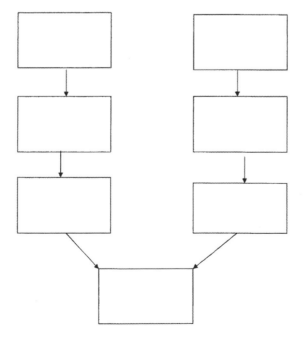

Figure 3. Rendering of a narrative example. Some students pursued a strategy of combining a narrative cartoon with nodes. The linkage between concepts was accomplished through the narrative in these cases. In some cases elements of node-link-node and/or flow charts were incorporated.

Figure 4. Rendering of multiform mapping. Some students combined node-link-node visual forms with other shapes conveying emotional aspects of an interaction. When asked about the depictions, students would say this was for emphasis or that they just liked the shape.

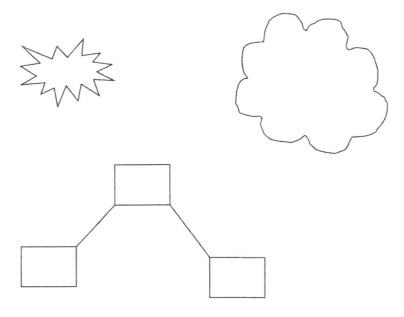

Part 2: Group Mapping/Visualization

This portion of the activity took place after students had applied the concept framework to a specific situation. Approximately two weeks separated the first mapping activity from this portion of the activity. This second concept mapping focused more on peer learning and creating a generalized integration of the concept framework.

Students were put in small groups and told to draw a model of the concepts. They were working on chalkboards and could easily alter their maps. They were given about five minutes to brainstorm, at which point there was a check-in. They were given a few minutes more to complete their map and to develop a presentation of their map. Each group then presented their map.

Part 3: Negotiating a Physical Representation

This part of the activity immediately followed the group mapping activity. Each group elected one person to be a facilitator for the full class mapping.

Students were given a card that had one concept from the full set of concepts. The facilitators were given the responsibility of placing cards with arrows to indicate flows between concepts.

Students then arranged themselves (according to the concept card each held) into a representation of the full integration of the concepts. This process required discussion and achieving consensus.

After 10-15 minutes, students were asked to stop and look around at the map they were creating. They were prompted to consider the questions in Table 1, which led to discussion and revision of the map.

APPRAISAL OF ACTIVITY

The activity discussed here builds on a surface learning process, but takes advantage of concept mapping to stimulate deep learning. The activity discussed here is

Table 1. Class discussion questions

What does your position in the model say to you about the impact your concept has on communication in the interaction?
Are there feedback loops that are not represented in the map as it exists right now?
(As students identified feedback loops, they were given lengths of ribbon to connect the feedback loops.)
How would you change the map to reflect the impact of cultural orientations such as high/low context or collectivist/individualist?
(This question would be adapted to the concepts in the particular framework being learned.)

rooted in the literature as described earlier and is easy to implement in a range of classroom environments.

This appraisal is based on practical experience using the components of the activity in classes over time. Conducting these activities in a research setting would result in more exact observations and results than is possible from the present practice-based discussion.

Each step in the activity described here was incorporated singly into multiple course offerings. The activity described here is based on course offerings that incorporated all three steps. While there had been an opportunity for peer learning with the individual concept mapping activity alone, this came at the end of the activity and was only a single opportunity for peer learning. This multi-step activity built in collaboration beyond summative discussion. The complexity of student responses with the present activity suggests that repeating the visualization activity and enhancing it supports student success in integrating a new model into their existing model of intercultural interaction.

Research suggests that deep learning requires a base of prior knowledge (Novak & Cañas, 2008), and that objective testing of surface learning (verbatim recall) "may be impeded by meaningful learning where new knowledge is assimilated into existing frameworks, making it difficult to recall specific, verbatim definitions or descriptions" (p. 4). Performing the surface learning prior to the concept mapping and visual representation provides both the required prior knowledge and the opportunity to move to deep learning. The surface learning assessed through conventional testing limited cognitive load enabling students to more efficiently acquire knowledge (Vogel-Walcutt, Gebrim, Bowers, Carper, & Nicholson, 2011). The labeling practice and the visualization activity each advanced what Vygotsky termed the zone of proximal development (Daniels, 1996) from knowledge acquisition to application to synthesis.

Villalon and Calvo (2011) advocate visual representation to enable students "to reflect on their own knowledge and also to help students see their writing from a different perspective," but acknowledge the limitations imposed by the complexity of strict concept-mapping (p. 16). They developed and tested an automated form of concept mapping tool for writing courses, demonstrating that concept mapping could be successful as a less complex proceeding. Many of the most meaningful outcomes for social science courses involve forming new perspectives on social interactions, which necessitates managing emotional and psychological reactions to shifting one's own cultural schemas. The activity discussed here accomplishes reflection on intercultural interaction simply and relatively quickly without greatly increasing instructor grading load. Using drawing media and physical movement make the process more enjoyable and reduce the anxiety that comes with shifting cultural schemas.

Rather than requiring strict node-link forms of concept mapping, the activity permitted students to use a range of visual representations including node-link concept maps, flow charts, cartoons, and iconography. The freedom to choose a form of visual representation reduced the need for instruction in a specific form of mapping. It also expanded the range of finished representation, providing a rich basis for the subsequent comparison and discussion.

Allowing students to represent connections between concepts in various ways did not place the form of representation as an obstacle in itself. In listening to student questions and conversation with each other, anxiety about not correctly drawing the map was a common topic. Explicitly assuring them that it was expected that they would use different forms of representation resulted in all the students moving forward to the actual drawing process. In a few cases students needed an additional suggestion to begin by representing just one aspect of the conceptual framework and then add in other aspects.

Opening up the form of the mapping allows students to access their own preferred form of representation. This demotion of concern about correctness makes it possible for students to place primary focus on considering how they themselves understand the conceptual framework could be mapped. This adds the valuable element of meaningful reflection on the learning process.

For many students, a narrative form of representation was preferred. Students drew cartoons, employing even the convention of successive frames enclosing successive stages of the story. When asked to explain the cartoon they produced, they responded with fully elaborated stories including biographies of characters, imagined conversations, reasoning about motivations of characters, and predictions about effects of the exchange on the imagined futures of characters. Students were given the opportunity to own the framework, which Vygotsky and more recent constructionists argue promotes deep learning (Daniels, 1996).

These narrative responses indicated integration of the conceptual framework into lived experience. The stories were not abstract, but rather, drawn from their own social environments. The visualization activity gave them an opportunity to articulate how the conceptual framework would apply in a situation familiar to them. This articulation is evidence of the process of integrating a new conceptual framework into an existing conceptual framework. This engagement with concepts through meaningful, realistic contexts has been associated with enhanced critical thinking skills and improved transfer of skills to multiple environments beyond the classroom (Dunlap & Grabinger, 1996). Opening up the concept mapping to include narrative sense-making enriches the range of contexts students may associate with the target conceptual system.

In the earliest course offerings, students used pens or pencils they happened to bring to class. Providing a range of drawing media to students greatly improved engagement with the activity. Students exchanged or shared different drawing media which led to conversations about the drawing process and the maps or drawings themselves. Students explicitly compared how they and others were using the various drawing media. Providing a range of drawing media provided an additional opportunity for peer learning as they reflected on the drawing process itself. Thus, in several ways the social exchange needed for constructionist learning environments was provided.

The second concept mapping stage of the activity (part 2 described above) was fully collaborative. Students needed to articulate and negotiate connections between concepts in order to create the group mapping. These maps were node-link forms primarily. In a few cases, additional symbols were incorporated adjacent to the central node-link map. These maps were drawn on chalkboard, making them easy to revise and to compare to each other when completed.

The final stage of the activity (part 3 described above) involved physical movement and students adopting positions relative to each other to represent the relationships between the concepts. In the several times this form of visualization exercise was incorporated into a course, students were always able to develop a physical depiction of the relationships between the concepts. By having to create a physical map, students surfaced assumptions about where the framework "begins." This surfacing led to discussion of how interactions are entered into and how the conceptual framework applies to actual interactions. It provided a way to embed the student in the situation of the interaction, which is a deeper engagement than visually representing the conceptual framework as a separate two-dimensional object.

In the discussion of the physical mapping (part 3 described above), students were expressing the connections between concepts using full sentences of their own composition, rather than single word or brief phrase responses to questions. The complexity of the construction of their responses is evidence of deeper learning. The capacity to express these connections in more complex ways can also be understood as demonstrating "emergent understanding" (Scardamalia & Bereiter, 2006). Rather than describe single elements of the framework, students could connect the elements that previously they had only understood at a surface level.

The questions for discussion did not explicitly request rationales. Yet, students included rationales for their assertions of connections. That students would volunteer rationales in support of their descriptions of connections was not expected. Volunteering rationales provides good evidence of deeper learning not only of the connections between concepts, but also of the nature of reasoning. In other assignments and on exams, students had been asked to explicitly provide rationales for their analyses of factors in specific intercultural interactions. In part 1 of the concept-mapping activity, students were asked to explain what their drawings meant (although not to give rationales for their choices). Volunteering rationales for their argument that concepts were related to each other in a particular way was a transferring of skills from other assignments and exams. This bridging across different domains is a hallmark of deep learning and critical thinking.

CONCLUSION

The enhanced activity described here resulted in students making statements about the *nature* of the connections between concepts. Previous versions of the activity did not provide the range of opportunities for students to express this level of reflection. Expanding the extent of the peer learning and including multiple rounds of model-making provided more opportunity for students to discuss the model-making itself. Reflection on the learning process has been linked with higher-level thinking (McGregor, 1994), making opportunities for reflection a valuable component of concept mapping and visual representation activities.

The classroom experience suggests that providing separate surface learning opportunities, enriching the visual representation tools, repeating the concept mapping, and enhancing the peer learning component leads to better synthesis of the conceptual framework. Testing of each of these aspects could lead to more exact understanding of their relationship to each other and to student learning. The simplicity and accessibility of the activity described here may make it feasible for instructors in a range of settings to attempt even without formal research of these specific components.

REFERENCES

Boghossian, P. (2012). Critical thinking and constructivism: Mambo dog fish to the banana patch. *Journal of Philosophy of Education, 46*(1), 73–84. doi:10.1111/j.1467-9752.2011.00832.x

Chang, S., & Chang, Y. (2008). Using online concept mapping with peer learning to enhance concept application. *Quarterly Review of Distance Education, 9*(1), 17–27.

Clayton, L. H. (2006). Concept mapping: An effective teaching-learning method. *Nursing Education Perspectives, 27*(4), 197–203. PMID:16921805

Daniels, H. (1996). *An introduction to Vygotsky*. New York: Routledge.

Dunlap, J. C., & Grabinger, R. S. (1996). Rich environments for active learning in the higher education classroom. In B. G. Wilson (Ed.), *Constructivist learning environments: Case studies in instructional design* (pp. 65–82). Englewood Cliffs, NJ: Educational Technology Publications.

Facione, P. W. (1990). *Critical thinking: A statement of expert consensus for purposes of educational assessment and instruction, executive summary.* Millbrae, CA: California Academic Press. Retrieved from http://assessment.aas.duke.edu/documents/Delphi_Report.pdf

Glynn, S. M., & Duit, R. (1995). Learning science meaningfully: Constructing conceptual models. In S. Glynn, & R. Duit (Eds.), *Learning science in the schools: Research reforming practice* (pp. 3–33). Mahwah, NJ: Lawrence Erlbaum Associates.

Gudykunst, W. B. (2004). *Bridging differences: Effective intergroup communication* (4th ed.). Thousand Oaks, CA: Sage Publications.

Gudykunst, W. B., & Kim, Y. Y. (1997). *Communicating with strangers* (3rd ed.). New York: McGraw-Hill.

Halford, G. S. (1993). *Children's understanding: The development of mental models.* Hillsdale, NJ: Lawrence Erlbaum Associates.

Halpern, D. F., & Hakel, M. D. (2003). Applying the science of learning to the university and beyond. *Change, 35*(4), 36–41. doi:10.1080/00091380309604109

Halx, M. D., & Reybold, L. E. (2005). A pedagogy of force: Faculty perspectives of critical thinking capacity in undergraduate students. *The Journal of General Education, 54*(4), 293–315. doi:10.1353/jge.2006.0009

Hay, D. B. (2007). Using concept mapping to measure deep, surface and non-learning outcomes. *Studies in Higher Education, 32*(1), 39–57. doi:10.1080/03075070601099432

Hay, D. B., & Kinchin, I. (2008). Using concept mapping to measure learning quality. *Education + Training, 50*(2), 167-182. DOI 10.1108/00400910810862146

Johnson-Laird, P. N. (1983). *Mental models.* Cambridge, MA: Harvard University Press.

Kim, Y. Y. (2005). Adapting to a new culture: An integrative communication theory. In W. B. Gudykunst (Ed.), *Theorizing about intercultural communication* (pp. 375–400). Thousand Oaks, CA: Sage Publications.

Larson, D. P., Butler, A. C., & Roediger, H. L. (2009). Repeated testing improves long-term retention relative to repeated study: A randomised controlled trial. *Medical Education*, *43*(12), 1174–1181. doi:10.1111/j.1365-2923.2009.03518.x PMID:19930508

Lau, S., Liem, A. D., & Nie, Y. (2008). Task- and self-related pathways to deep learning: The mediating role of achievement goals, classroom attentiveness, and group participation. *The British Journal of Educational Psychology*, *78*, 639–662. doi:10.1348/000709907X270261 PMID:18166143

Lustig, M. W., & Koester, J. (2010). *Intercultural competence: Interpersonal communication across cultures* (6th ed.). New York: Allyn & Bacon.

Maneval, R., Filburn, M., Deringer, S., & Lum, G. (2011). Concept mapping: Does it improve critical thinking ability in practical nursing students? *Nursing Education Perspectives*, *32*(4), 229–233. doi:10.5480/1536-5026-32.4.229 PMID:21923002

McGregor, J. H. (1994). Information seeking and use, students and their mental models. *Journal of Youth Services in Libraries*, *8*(1), 69–76.

Meyers, N. M., & Nulty, D. D. (2009). How to use (five) curriculum design principles to align authentic learning environments, assessment, students' approaches to thinking and learning outcomes. *Assessment & Evaluation in Higher Education*, *34*(5), 565–577. doi:10.1080/02602930802226502

Nelson Laird, T. F., & Garver, A. K. (2010). The effect of teaching general education courses on deep approaches to learning: How disciplinary context matters. *Research in Higher Education*, *51*(3), 248–265. doi:10.1007/s11162-009-9154-7

Nishida, H. (2005). Cultural schema theory. In W. B. Gudykunst (Ed.), *Theorizing about intercultural communication* (pp. 401–418). Thousand Oaks, CA: Sage Publications.

Novak, J. D. (2007). *The theory underlying concept maps and how to construct them.* Retrieved from http://cmap.ihmc.us/Publications/ResearchPapers/TheoryUnderlyingConceptMaps.pdf

Novak, J. D., & Cañas. (2008). *The theory underlying concept maps and how to construct and use them, technical report IHMC Cmaptools 2006-01 Rev 01-2008.* Florida Institute for Human and Machine Cognition. Retrieved from http://cmap.ihmc.us/Publications/ResearchPapers/TheoryUnderlyingConceptMaps.pdf

Oliver, K., & Hannafin, M. (2001). Developing and refining mental models in open-ended learning environments: A case study. *Educational Technology Research and Development*, *49*(4), 5–32. doi:10.1007/BF02504945

Plotnick, E. (2001). A graphical system for understanding the relationship between concepts. *Teacher Librarian*, *28*(4), 42–45.

Rogers, E. M., & Steinfatt, T. M. (1999). *Intercultural communication*. Long Grove, IL: Waveland Press.

Scardamalia, M., & Bereiter, C. (2006). Knowledge building: Theory, pedagogy and technology. In R. K. Sawyer (Ed.), *The Cambridge handbook of the learning sciences* (pp. 97–118). New York: Cambridge University Press.

Spanjers, I. E., van Gog, T., & van Merriënboer, J. G. (2010). A theoretical analysis of how segmentation of dynamic visualizations optimizes students' learning. *Educational Psychology Review*, *22*(4), 411–423. doi:10.1007/s10648-010-9135-6

Swaminatham, N. (2006). Testing improves retention--Even of material not on exam. *Scientific American*, *295*(5).

Tagg, J. (2003). *The learning paradigm college*. San Francisco, CA: Anker Publishing.

van Boxtel, C., van der Linden, J., Roelofs, E., & Erkens, G. (2002). Collaborative concept mapping: Provoking and supporting meaningful discourse. *Theory into Practice*, *41*(1), 40–46. doi:10.1207/s15430421tip4101_7

Varner, I., & Beamer, L. (2010). *Intercultural communication in the global workplace* (5th ed.). New York: McGraw-Hill.

Villalon, J., & Calvo, R. A. (2011). Concept maps as cognitive visualizations of writing assignments. *Journal of Educational Technology & Society*, *14*(3), 16–27.

Vogel-Walcutt, J.J., Gebrim, J.B., Bowers, C., & Carper, T.M., & Nicholson. (2011). Cognitive load theory vs. constructivist approaches: Which best leads to efficient, deep learning? *Journal of Computer Assisted Learning*, *27*, 133–145. doi:10.1111/j.1365-2729.2010.00381.x

Wang, M., Peng, J., Cheng, B., Zhou, H., & Liu, J. (2011). Knowledge visualization for self-regulated learning. *Journal of Educational Technology & Society*, *14*(3), 28–42.

Wilson, B. G. (1996). What is a constructivist learning environment? In B. G. Wilson (Ed.), *Constructivist learning environments: Case studies in instructional design* (pp. 3–8). Englewood Cliffs, NJ: Educational Technology Publications.

Windschitl, M. (2002). Framing constructivism in practice as the negotiation of dilemmas: An analysis of the conceptual, pedagogical, cultural and political challenges facing teachers. *Review of Educational Research*, 72(2), 131–175. doi:10.3102/00346543072002131

KEY TERMS AND DEFINITIONS

Collaborative Learning: A teaching strategy that involves active participation of students in sense-making activities as compared with simply witnessing a lecture.

Concept Mapping: A range of activities requiring students to explicitly "map" their associations between concepts they have learned. Mapping may be conducted in several ways.

Constructionist: The perspective on communication that holds that meaning is not pre-set, but co-constructed by participants in a communicative interaction.

Deep Learning: Learning beyond simple memorization and recall. Such learning is associated with critical thinking.

Intercultural Communication: The process of communicating across a cultural boundary. Such boundaries can include ethnicity, gender, race, religion, and nationality.

Mental Models: Sense-making notions that assign causal relationships and other associations between elements in our surroundings.

Peer Learning: The process of learning from peers as opposed to authority figures such as instructors.

Sense-Making: A perspective on communication that holds that communication is a result of our quest to make sense of our world.

Teaching Strategies: Approaches to teaching. This idea assumes that there are multiple ways to approach teaching that may be strategically employed.

APPENDIX

Table 2.

Form of Information	Type of Culture
Hard data	Low context
Soft data	High context
Formal	Low context
Informal	High context
Source of Information	**Type of Culture**
Formal	Low context
Informal	High context
Basis of Decisions	**Type of Culture**
Ends	Low context
Means	High context
Definition of Problem	**Type of Culture**
Externalized, objectified, something to be eliminated	Individualist
Part of context, focus on problem-solving process	Collectivist
Conflict Management Mode	**Communication Style**
Competing	Dominating (emotion-expressing)
Collaboration	Integrating
Compromising (bargaining, mediation, arbitration)	Bargaining
Avoiding	Avoiding
Accommodating	Obliging

Communication Strategies

1. Listen sincerely
2. Express agreement where you can
3. Identify common goals
4. Explain your position
5. Identify resolutions that accommodate cultural priorities

This appendix was designed as a study guide for chapter 8 of *Intercultural Communication in the Global Workplace*, by Iris Varner and Linda Beamer, the textbook used in the course.

Chapter 8
Self–Inquiry and Group Dynamics:
A Multidisciplinary Framework for Critical Thinking

Katia Gonzalez
Wagner College, USA

Rhoda Frumkin
Wagner College, USA

John Montgomery
SUNY, New Paltz, USA

EXECUTIVE SUMMARY

In this chapter, the authors discuss ways in which pedagogical considerations involved in using a theoretical framework for self-inquiry and socially constructed knowledge led to the selection and implementation of mapping as a tool to (1) activate prior knowledge and scaffold content and process for pre-service educators working with students and families who are at risk and (2) assist adult learners in organizing multiple perspectives during small and large group discussion, while developing critical thinking and shared leadership skills through meaningful connections and action. A case study on how the utilization of a multidisciplinary approach informed the type of curriculum decisions to engage learners is provided. The case study also illustrates when and why instructional techniques and strategies were introduced and embedded to encourage both interactions and discussions focusing on modeling the ongoing use of skills for critical thinking and how each mapping strategy/ tool served as a formative and summative assessment plan to improve verbal and written communication.

DOI: 10.4018/978-1-4666-5816-5.ch008

ORGANIZATION BACKGROUND

This case study showcases a framework for learning used in the capstone course in the graduate education program of a private, coeducational, non-sectarian, 80% residential, liberal arts college of approximately 1850 traditional aged undergraduates and about 300 graduate students in selected professional programs. The College, with a student-faculty ratio of 16:1, has been widely recognized for its innovative curriculum that integrates a core curriculum, required learning communities, experiential learning, and civic education.

The graduate education program prepares students for teaching positions in grades pre-kindergarten through high school in local public and charter schools. Graduate education students enroll in this capstone course in conjunction with full-time supervised student teaching experiences.

SETTING THE STAGE

Critical Thinking and Knowledge Construction: Prior Experiences and Pedagogical Considerations with Adult Learners

In higher education, we often discuss and promote concepts related to shared knowledge as a way to encourage and empower learners to engage in collaborative practices leading to individual and group goals. "...Central to the goal of adult education in democratic societies is the process of helping learners become more aware of the context of their problematic understandings and beliefs, more critically reflective on their assumptions and those of others, more fully and freely engaged in discourse, and more effective in taking action on their reflective judgments" (Mezirow, 2000, p. 31). Sharing multiple perspectives often provides opportunities for learners to experience the responsibility of being active members of democratic learning environments in which everyone has a role in the process of knowledge creation. As learners share knowledge, they take on "collective cognitive responsibility: the responsibility for knowing what needs to be known and for insuring that others know what needs to be known" (Scardamalia, 2002, p. 2). Empowering learners individually and collectively to use a critical lense in order to participate in .".. the art of analyzing and evaluating thinking with a view to improving it" (Eider & Paul, 2008, p. 2) is important; however, " ...studies of student learning in higher education often point to the lack of skills for solving complex problems or ill-defined questions" (Muukkonen & Lakkala, 2009, p. 188). Faculty members interested in tackling this challenge must select and embed the right tools and techniques within their courses to facilitate learners' critical thinking processes for knowledge construction leading to meaningful learning, carefully considering the role of learner engagement in this process.

When prior knowledge, skills, and dispositions are diverse, learners must reexamine prior experiences related to discussion topics that may be inaccurate, limited, or altogether non-existent. Reexamination of prior knowledge is important since prior knowledge ."..can provide a basis for new learning (consistent with a constructivist theory) and ...also serve as a source of misconceptions and erroneous ideas that can undermine accurate understanding" (Thompson & Zamboaga, 2004. p. 779). According to Dochy (1992) it is essential to keep in mind the influence prior knowledge may have in knowledge creation since misleading or incomplete information as part of a learner's repertoire could significantly affect the process of critical reflection for the individual learner as well as the students participating in the collaborative process of shared knowledge. Paul and Elder (2008) explained how as humans ."..we do not naturally recognize our egocentric assumptions, the egocentric way we use information, the egocentric way we interpret data, the source of our egocentric concepts and ideas, the implications of our egocentric thought" (p.21). We often "believe in intuitive perceptions" not always utilizing skills related to an "intellectual standards in thinking" to construct knowledge. These "intellectual standards must be taught explicitly...since the ...ultimate goal...is for these standards to become infused in the thinking of students, forming part of their inner voice, guiding them to reason better" (Paul & Elder, 2008, p. 8).

Facilitating opportunities for learners and faculty members to be able to identify and determine the sources and criteria used for reasoning and decision-making becomes a necessary function for any classroom seeking to enhance critical thinking skills leading to meaningful learning. Faculty members should "examine teaching practices through the use of a critical thinking stance... to consider closely how decisions about groupings and tools shape the learning environment for collaboration. Those "pedagogical" decisions can either create barriers for students, which inhibit learning, or they can provide opportunities for all stakeholders to learn from different perspectives while promoting higher order thinking skills" (Gonzalez & Preskill, 2011, p.159). "Critical thinking is... self-directed, self-disciplined, self-monitored, and self-corrective thinking... it requires rigorous standards of excellence and mindful command of their use... with skills such as... effective communication, problem solving abilities, and a commitment to overcoming ...native egocentrism and socio-centrism" (Paul and Elder, 2008, p. 2). Learners participating in experiences in which critical thinking is practiced and modeled through self- inquiry, healthy collaborations, and the sharing of multiple perspectives can feel empowered to share information and target " ...influential assumptions..." (Brookfield, 1995, p. 29) that may affect knowledge construction.

Consciously Connecting to the Self and Others: Self-Inquiry and Critical Thinking

Empowering students with opportunities to reflect critically on topics by using pedagogical approaches framed under the theoretical umbrella of self-inquiry and social constructivism allows for the process of inquiry to take place individually and in groups. The use of small and large group discussions, a pedagogical strategy and technique popular in higher education, is often the norm as a way to increase students' active engagement with the process of inquiry. During discussions the ongoing application and facilitation of higher order thinking skills and questions leading to the use of "Universal Intellectual Standards" must include 1) Clarity, 2) Accuracy, 3) Depth, 4) Breadth, 5) Significance, and 6) Fairness (Paul & Elder, 2008, p. 10). Brookfield and Preskill (2005) explained how helping learners with the process and skills needed for democratic discussion takes considerable time and effort by facilitators and how ."..asking questions that stimulate and provoke students to examine their own and other's experiences ...is essential in order...to establish an atmosphere for critical thinking" (p. 100). The need to consider variables that may impact the process of establishing an environment that is optimal for critical thinking to take place often relates to the way faculty members model and reinforce dispositions related to making connections with peers leading to collaboration. Careful consideration of the quality of helping students reach higher order thinking is essential since in order ."..to think at the highest level of quality, we need not only intellectual skills, but intellectual traits as well" (Paul & Elder, 2008, p.7).

To help learners develop the necessary intellectual traits for critical thinking, we must teach and model these within a safe, nurturing, and intellectual environment that fosters connections and collaboration among peers.

The greatest need for any person is to "connect" at various levels: specifically, to align thought and behavior patterns with various elements of the self – such as authentic feelings or emotions, true goals and aspirations, and deeply-held core values – and then, through this healthy connection to the self, to connect with the broader environment, and to "attach" to, or connect with, others (Montgomery & Ritchey, 2008). When connection occurs at all of these levels, a person will tend to be in a state of physiological, emotional, and cognitive equilibrium, or "homeostasis," that is optimal for learning and critical thinking (Montgomery & Ritchey, 2010). But when people's thought and behavior patterns are *not* aligned with emotions, goals, and core values, their brains are far more likely to be repeatedly triggered into stressful states of "survival-mode," in which survival is consciously or unconsciously perceived to be at risk. While low amounts of stress may help focus and energize thought in some instances, any strong survival-mode state, such as fear or anxiety, will release large amounts of stress hormones into the brain, creating activity patterns and states of hyper-vigilance that tend to make learning and critical thinking far more difficult (Yuen et al., 2012). Furthermore, negative moods or emotional states in general have been shown to lead to high levels of distractibility, and a greater frequency of task-irrelevant thoughts (Smallwood et al., 2009). A key goal is to create states of homeostasis in prospective learners to optimize their learning capacities and critical thinking skills.

This is accomplished in three complementary ways. First, we minimize the risk of "triggering" students into negative emotional states. Such triggers may involve, for example, a student being led to feel socially excluded, unfavorably "judged" by the faculty member or other students, or less important or worthy than other students. In general, creating an environment that encourages feelings of physical, emotional, and social safety enables the highest levels of interpersonal and group connection. Second, through group discussions and specific interactive and organized exercises, we help students to discover or come to terms with previous personal experiences that, when reactivated, may interfere with learning and healthy group dynamics. Third, we encourage each individual to align his or her understandings, assumptions, beliefs, and behavior with his or her core values. Essential to any learning environment seeking to promote critical thinking is the careful consideration of pedagogical practices that may hinder or promote successful interactions for knowledge construction and transformative learning.

Knowledge Construction and Transformative Learning

Knowledge construction is a process of integrating prior knowledge with acquired knowledge to produce new learning. "Where knowledge change is a consequence of the integration of new material and the prior-knowledge structure, this satisfies the criteria of meaningful learning" (Hay, Kinchin, & Lygo-Baker, 2008, p. 300). When learning is meaningful, learners actively connect new ideas to their prior knowledge (Jonassen, 2003), engaging in a "...process of using a prior interpretation to construe a new or revised interpretation of the meaning of one's experience as a guide to future action" (Mezirow, 2000, p. 5). Learners consider new input in relation to their particular fund of background knowledge, and then connect prior and new knowledge to create a revised understanding of an experience. This active process results in varied versions of understanding, as learners draw on a unique fund of experiences and envision new learning in unique ways. According to Mezirow

(2002), we all seek to understand the meaning of our experience. Adults draw from their body of experience – the associations, values, concepts, feelings, conditioned responses: the frames of reference through which they define their world. In our contemporary society, adults want to make their own individual interpretations and construct their own knowledge rather than depend on the purposes, judgments, beliefs, and feelings of others. A key goal of adult education is to facilitate this understanding with the goal of reaching a transformative learning experience. "Transformative learning develops autonomous thinking" (Mezirow, 1997, p. 5) and adults can change "taken for-granted" (2000, p. 7) frames of reference – our assumptions and expectations – to make them more "inclusive, discriminating, open, emotionally capable of change, and reflective" (pp.7 - 8). Such frames of reference enable adults to create opinions and beliefs that will "prove more true" (Mezirow, 2003, p. 59) or justified in guiding action. Often, this revised understanding of an experience is framed by the context of the situation in which new information is learned. When knowledge is acquired through group discussion, and with a focus on higher order thinking skills, individual learning may be influenced and expanded upon by others' ideas, perceptions, and perspectives. These discussions can contribute to transforming our learning. Mezirow (2000) suggested that transformative learning includes participation in "constructive discourse" (p. 8) This allows learners to consider the experiences of others when evaluating reasons for justifying assumptions. Then they use the resulting insights as the basis for an "action decision" (p. 8) which is often the end goal of any critical thinking experience. For "constructive discourse" (Mezirow, 2000, p. 8) to become part of a learner's skill set, pedagogical considerations must be carefully structured in order to provide opportunities for decision-making. These pedagogical considerations should focus on learners' knowledge, attitudes, and efficacy beliefs which are often defined by previous experiences. Adult learners must think critically as they consider multiple perspectives in the course of discussion, and begin to integrate these new perspectives with their background knowledge while considering how it impacts a current need. Critical thinkers consider questions and problems within alternative systems of thought with an open mind, recognizing and assessing assumptions, implications, and practical consequences as needed. They engage in effective communication with others to figure out conclusions to complex problems. As faculty members work with adult learners to facilitate the activation of prior knowledge and assist them in organizing multiple perspectives while expanding or learning skills sets to assist with the process of critical thinking, learners are engaged in deliberation, and new experiences are created.

Faculty members facilitating higher order thinking exercises for learners need to consider how intellectual traits and skills are modeled, taught, reinforced, or expanded upon, and how assessments for evaluating the process of reasoning are considered to make ongoing pedagogical adaptations to impact a learner's experience.

CASE DESCRIPTION

Curriculum Decisions to Organize the Process of Critical Thinking in a Graduate Course: Selection of Pedagogical Techniques and Tools

The capstone course in our graduate education program served as the practical application of our theoretical perspectives. This course, which was paired with student teaching, highlighted issues related to school, diversity and society and focused on course topics related to many of the challenging situations that the graduate students would encounter during student teaching. We emphasized learning through discussion, and wanted to create an environment in which students felt empowered to engage in the process of critical thinking while exchanging multiple perspectives and constructing shared knowledge through self-inquiry and social-constructivism. Additionally, we wanted to establish a classroom dynamic for critical reflection leading to action that would impact the learning of both the student teachers and their young students. Most of the graduate students lacked prior encounters with current school challenges and, as a result, lacked the prior knowledge needed as a reference for decision-making. Accordingly, we needed to consider how experiences were connected to course goals and objectives and then scaffold information leading to constructive reasoning. Facilitating collaborative work and in-depth critical reflection about challenging topics that were being discussed as well as experienced during their student teaching placements required our clear understanding of the implications of assumptions and of the role of previous experiences and skill sets that influence knowledge construction leading to a transformational experience. The use of higher order thinking skills as the standard for facilitating experiences and skills sets learners will encounter was critical. However, when "prior knowledge inevitably forms a scaffold for new learning, but where it comprises significant misconceptions then new knowledge acquisition is impeded" (Hay, Kinchin, & Lygo-Baker, 2008, p.301), and tools to serve as medium for critical reflection needed to be considered.

Mapping: Higher Order Discourse and Knowledge Construction

Discussion as a strategy can provide opportunities for hearing multiple perspectives while targeting key concepts and skills development through carefully design curriculum plans. The use of mapping to assist with the process of higher order levels of discourse and knowledge construction helps learners with the process of knowledge construction based on critical reflection. Mapping to assist students in developing meaning through integrating their prior knowledge with others' multiple perspectives as they engaged in ongoing dialogue can be a great medium to organize and scaffold reasoning. Further, mapping tools can help students enhance, retain, and improve knowledge (Davies, 2010) in several ways. First, through mapping, students are able to use a diagram to represent or manipulate a complex set of relationships. This increases the likelihood that students will understand and remember these relationships as well as their ability to analyze component parts. Next, some kinds of maps may be easier to follow than written or verbal directions, and last, the process of mapping increases active engagement, leading to greater learning (Davies, 2010). Mapping may also increase learning by incorporating multiple modalities. Constructing maps allows for the separate encoding of information in visual and propositional form, thus enabling learners to process information both verbally and pictorially (Davies, 2010). Using visual deliberation during mapping to provide "meaning making" experiences for knowledge construction based on "rhetorical renderings" (Trenton, 2012) creates opportunities to use varied mediums for facilitating the process of knowledge construction when real life experiences with challenging topics or concepts may not possible or readily available.

We can make a decision about where we stand through deliberation focused on determining one's own attitude. Often, deliberation is a collective activity of multiple voices, and involves both argumentation and reasoning (Van Gelder, 2010). ."..During an argumentative or deliberative event, the visual makes meaning making—the actual construction of reality (or a reality)—possible" (Teston, 2012, p.189).

Backward Design and Assessment: Ingredients for the Development of Successful Critical Thinking Experiences

It was important for us as faculty to be able to start with a curriculum design that could provide a "blueprint" for course development. Key to the process of enhancing critical thinking in students is to provide a flexible structure to model the necessary skills and knowledge development. Although many of the topics discussed during class expanded and evolved based on individual concept maps students developed in response to the development of their own graphic organizers, we identified enduring understandings – the big ideas at the heart of a discipline that have lasting value outside the classroom - ahead of time in order to provide a focus during the visual deliberation that happened during each class session. These visual deliberations became a focus for each class discussion as the professor teaching the course facilitated through questioning how to model higher order thinking skills, reasoning, and action- oriented approaches based on theory and experiences. In their research, Haynes and Bailey (2003) emphasized the importance of asking the right questions to stimulate students' critical thinking skills. Other researchers (Brown & Kelley, 1986; Hemming, 2000) also focused on integrating questioning techniques into class discussions to support an educational environment where students can demonstrate and practice critical thinking skills. Brown and Kelley's book, *Asking the Right Questions: A Guide to Critical Thinking*, documented the premise that students' critical thinking is best supported when instructors use critical questioning techniques to engage students actively in the learning process.

Sample questions include the following:

- What do you think about this?
- Why do you think that?
- What is your knowledge based upon?
- What does it imply and presuppose?
- What explains it, connects to it, leads from it?
- How are you viewing it?
- Should it be viewed differently?

These questions require students to evaluate the clarity and accuracy of their thinking as well as the depth and breadth of their thinking. Have they considered all the alternatives? Do they know why they think the way they do? Students need to determine whether the content they are using is relevant and if their thinking process is logical. By questioning their thought process, students can begin thinking about their thinking and graphic organizers serving as concept maps can aid in this process.

The utilization of a backward design approach (Wiggins & McTighe, 1998) proved to be essential in organizing our pedagogical practices based on course content and goals since it allowed us to consider three key areas: "1) What is worthy and requiring of understanding? 2) What is evidence of understanding? 3) What learning experiences and teaching promote understanding, interest and excellence?" (Wiggins & McTighe, 1998, p. 342). Using a backward design approach to establish priorities in terms of knowledge and skills development needed from all learners, as well as to identify "essential questions serving as guiding/focus questions for deliberation" helped us select tools to embed during visual deliberation. This provided opportunities for reasoning and the sharing of a variety of perspectives needed for critical reflection to take place. Although the selection of a design approach was helpful in terms of overall structure and organization, the use of formative assessments to inform our practice as faculty members was essential in order to make necessary adaptations before the course ended. Brookfield's (1995) Critical Incident Questionnaire (CIQ) in which students are asked to respond to five questions can be a useful tool for faculty interested in receiving students' input regarding pedagogical practices being implemented during their courses. The questions are:

1.   At what moment in class this week did you feel most engaged with what was happening?
2.   At what moment in class this week did you feel most distanced from what was happening?
3.   What action that anyone (teacher or student) took in class this week did you find most affirming or helpful?
4.   What action that anyone (teacher or student) took in class this week did you find most puzzling or confusing?
5.   What about the class this week surprised you the most? (This could be something about your own reactions to what went on, or something that someone did, or anything else that occurs to you) (p. 115).

We believe this process can be particularly helpful for courses in which critical thinking is a focus since it provides faculty with the opportunity to ask for individual feedback about specific experiences in relation to the course goal and objectives and types of activities, tools and techniques learners are utilizing or experiencing. In this way, students feel empowered to participate in a democratic classroom environment in which their input is valued and taken into consideration. As faculty, we have incorporated CIQs in the past (Gonzalez & Preskill, 2011) in order to receive anonymous weekly feedback from students while also adding at the end of the CIQs a section with questions related to the benefits of specific tools and techniques being utilized in our class to assess students' perceptions of their benefits. Ongoing feedback from students can be a valuable way to let them know that their input is important while also providing faculty with the opportunity to have an ongoing conversation with students about the CIQ received and why certain pedagogical decisions are being made (when changes/adaptations may or may not occur and why). These conversations are another way to model and reinforce intellectual skills and traits. CIQs can be done in person at the end of a class or a link can be sent online, always keeping in mind that the option of a student providing feedback anonymously is key to the process.

Engaging Students: An Example of Strategies for Critical Thinking Leading to Action

The utilization of a framework to serve as a graphic organizer (Table 1) based on a social constructivist and inquiry-based model was a way to assist students with the organization of multiple perspectives while the scaffolding of information provided opportunities for self and group inquiry with guidance from the professor. Students, working individually and in groups, completed a framework. After reading newly assigned text and thinking about it in relation to background knowledge, each student

Table 1. Framework for discussion and shared leadership

1 – Theory Research/Author's Perspective • Select three key words related to the main message of the reading. • Explain why those words were selected providing examples from the text. **SHARED LEADERSHIP MOMENT:**	4 – Pedagogical Goal · Identify a need and develop a pedagogical goal. · Seek and try out three different experiences related to goal. · Seek out three different resources that may help you achieve your goal. **SHARED LEADERSHIP MOMENT:**
2 – Theory & Practice Connecting Theory to Individual Experience · Select one word from Step 1 (theory) and explain why you selected that word **SHARED LEADERSHIP MOMENT:**	5 – Assessment: Individual/Peer · How did you assess the experiences and resources utilized to help you achieve your pedagogical goal? · Which action and resources you considered most helpful? Please explain why. **SHARED LEADERSHIP MOMENT:**
3 – Multiple Perspectives Small and Large Group Discussion · Gather a small group of peers and discuss steps 1 and 2 paying close attention to the focus question of the day. · Write down your thoughts about the small group discussions. · Identify one speaker from the small group to report to the larger group key items discussed. · Write down your thoughts about the large group discussion. **SHARED LEADERSHIP MOMENT:**	6 – Next Steps: Action Oriented · New/Expanded-Revised Pedagogical Goal. · Explain why you selected this goal and if you incorporated any of the ideas provided by the peers. **SHARED LEADERSHIP MOMENT:**
7 – Impact on Student Learning · Explain how/if your pedagogical goal impacted the learning of your student and your development as a professional. Please make sure to provide specific examples. **SHARED LEADERSHIP MOMENT:**	

(Gonzalez & Frumkin, 2012)

submitted a framework as a written project. The framework served as a formative assessment to evaluate students' growth related to critical thinking skills. We required students to include a "shared leadership moment" in all sections of the framework. This addition was the result of our belief that each step, with national, international and regional theory/perspectives from the readings framing the discussion, provided learners with a particular focus on action-oriented problem solving examples prior to their own development of action-oriented pedagogical decisions based on the identified problem during visual deliberation.

Students began to identify their own knowledge, skills, and dispositions related to the discussion topics. This resulted from their participation in class discussions, framed by essential questions, about the theoretical perspectives from the course readings. Students then utilized the framework for discussion, usually structured around a problem or challenge focusing on "enduring understandings," to critically reflect upon theory, organize input from multiple perspectives, and think about and assess their experiences in the field and current/future actions as professionals which lead to the identification of their own topic-related knowledge, skills, and dispositions.

We encouraged students' engagement in these experiences and provided them with opportunities to focus on their impact as action-oriented teachers/leaders. The framework, a written tool that is completed individually with scaffolding inherent in each step, also helped students concentrate on specific areas they wanted to further develop or seek out as additional opportunities, since the multiple perspectives from the discussion often opened up additional viewpoints. The professor provided additional scaffolding to individualize feedback for each student.

Visual Deliberation: Skills and Knowledge Set for Engaged and Critical Discussions

In working with graduate students participating in their student teaching during the day, we used visual deliberation as a way to help with reasoning about theoretical knowledge and practical experiences while providing opportunities to share multiple perspectives as assumptions about challenging topics in a nurturing environment in which all perspectives were heard (Figure 1). The goal was to assist all learners in developing and expanding their ability to critically reflect by communicating effectively with the language and skills required of the profession while also making sure learners had the opportunity to realize that "good critical thinking involves making accurate judgments" (Cottrell, 2005, p. 6). Keeping in mind that " the distinction between a good student and an average one is the degree to which they can reason and communicate in a clear and systematic manner" (Patterson, 2007, p. 79), we selected visual deliberation as a way to help students with the process of reasoning while everyone in the class had the opportunity to participate. We introduced visual deliberation, which happened during whole class discussion, after students had the opportunity to work individually and in small groups on steps 1, 2, and part of step 3 of their graphic organizer (Table 1). For sections of the graphic organizers, application of "universal intellectual standards: and questions that can be used to apply them" (Paul & Elder, 2009, p. 8) were modeled and encouraged. Using a framework for discussion helped learners break down, examine, and analyze ideas from multiple sources while considering a variety of viewpoints and applications

Figure 1. Example of a map created by a student during our visual deliberation exercise based on topics and concepts written on the board during the sharing of multiple perspectives

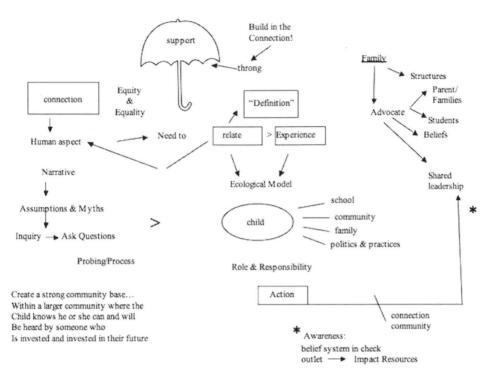

to their experiences in schools. The framework served as a graphic organizer and assisted learners in reasoning and generating dialogue during visual deliberation. Learners were engaged with the readings and weekly class discussions and also had opportunities to develop skills and knowledge needed to enhance verbal and written communication for critical reflection.

During the small group discussions, learners gathered a small group of peers and began a conversation aimed at sharing their reasoning behind the selection of specific concepts/words from the readings and experiences (steps 1 and 2 of table 1), their rationale for selecting one particular word, and the relationship of the word to the focus question supplied by the professor. The large group during step 3 (table 1) reconvened to begin a discussion aimed at sharing ideas that emerged from the small group discussions outlining a relationship among these ideas (Davies, 2010). We used mapping to capture the key points from the discussions as a way to make students' thinking visible for ongoing consideration. To facilitate the discussion, the professor elicited ideas from each group spokesperson, using prompts based on higher order thinking skills to encourage and model intellectual skills and traits for critical thinking and the identification of connections and reasoning among ideas. We used the deliberation process for decision-making from the start to the end of the class, and continued with specific action-oriented exercises to encourage development of efficacy skills in a facilitated environment. The professor recorded these ideas on the board and added lines and arrows indicating suggested relationships between ideas and the direction of these relationships. Learners helped make the connections through the process of reasoning facilitated by the professor. The process of using discussion combined with visual representation of the ideas that emerged from the discussion was similar to Van Gelder's process of visual deliberation. According to Van Gelder (2003), visual deliberation is "a process of deciding whether some claim ought to be believed by considering the relevant arguments" (p.93). Because the course discussion was often focused on controversial topics (for example, single sex schools), students engaged in thinking through which they determined their own attitudes about the controversy. They determined "where they stand" by considering relevant perspectives of multiple voices (including those of colleagues, authors of articles, guest speakers, clips, Websites). The deliberation was a collaborative activity and involved presenting and justifying opinions based on prior knowledge, experiences, and others' points of view.

SOLUTIONS AND RECOMMENDATIONS

This chapter highlights the use of mapping as a tool to activate prior knowledge and scaffold content and process for student teachers, and to assist them in organizing multiple perspectives during small and large group discussion while developing critical thinking and shared leadership skills through meaningful connections and action. We review the research that informed our decision to use visual deliberation as a process for integrating students' background knowledge with multiple perspectives emerging during large group discussions. The case study serves as an example of the ways in which a scaffolded discussion through visual deliberation facilitated students' ability to construct relationships among key ideas related to a focus topic about school, diversity, and society. The purposeful identification of relationships and the opportunities to view, consider, and refine these relationships based on new perspectives – both those of others and students' own revised perspectives – requires critical thinking. Students needed to weigh their own (perhaps developing and/or changing) perspectives and those of others against their store of background knowledge to construct and justify new understandings. This can be a challenging process as students re-examine long-held beliefs and reconsider their position in light of new knowledge and experience.

We often observed students' willingness to consider, accept and, at times, own a new perspective brought to their attention through the intersection of experiences, background knowledge, and newly introduced or acquired perspectives, all scrutinized through the lens of critical reflection. We believe that the process of organized discussion and, as used in this capstone course, visual deliberation, is a powerful tool for looking at the "why" of beliefs, knowledge, and practice: Why do we believe all children can learn? What knowledge do we need to make this happen? How can I structure my classroom environment and instructional practices to create learning opportunities for all? Questions about beliefs, knowledge, and practice often had divergent answers. We believe that by scaffolding self-inquiry and dynamic group interactions, we can promote the critical thinking students need to generate and answer their own questions.

Our exploration of the impact of visual deliberation on students' critical thinking led us to consider further exploration of this topic for future research. As we work with our students, we wonder if students' use of visual deliberation during small group discussions would increase critical thinking. This change requires students to develop independent ability to identify and map relationships between the important concepts emerging from small group discussions. We plan to incorporate this interaction into future capstone courses. Accordingly, we are engaged in discussions about best ways in which to foster students' independence in visual deliberation by using teacher modeling and scaffolded practice and application. We are also investigating ways to assess any changes in students' critical thinking abilities focusing on the use of simulations for knowledge construction. For us, the exploration of relationships of self-inquiry and group dynamics for critical thinking continues.

REFERENCES

Brookfield, S. (1995). *Becoming a critically reflective teacher*. San Francisco, CA: Jossey Bass.

Brookfield, S., & Preskill, S. (2005). *Discussion as a way of teaching: Tools and techniques for democratic classrooms* (2nd ed.). San Francisco, CA: Josey Bass.

Brown, M. N., & Kelley, S. M. (1986). *Asking the right questions: A guide to critical thinking* (7th ed.). Englewood Cliffs, NJ: Prentice Hall.

Cottrell, S. (2005). *Critical thinking skills: Developing effective analysis and argument*. London: Palgrave Macmillan.

Davies, M. (2010). Concept mapping, mind mapping and argument mapping: What are the differences and do they matter? *Higher Education, 62*(3), 279–301. doi:10.1007/s10734-010-9387-6

Dochy, F. J. R. C. (1992). *Assessment of prior knowledge or expertise as a determinant for future learning: The use of prior knowledge state tests and knowledge profiles*. London: Jessica Kingsley.

Donaldson, G. (2007). What do teachers bring to leadership? *Educational Leadership, 65*(1), 26–29.

Gonzalez, K., Frumkin, R., & Lauria, J. (2012). Study groups and service learning: A framework for discussion to engage pre-service teachers. In T. Murphy, & J. Tan (Eds.), *Service learning and educating in challenging contexts: International perspectives. Location*. Continuum Publishers.

Gonzalez-Acquaro, K., & Preskill, S. (2011). Using the four lenses of critical reflection to promote collaboration and support creative adaptations of web 2.0 tools in an online environment. In F. Pozzi, & D. Persico (Eds.), *Techniques for fostering collaboration in online learning communities: Theoretical and practical perspectives*. Hershey, PA: IGI Global.

Gurlitt, J., & Renkl, A. (2008). Are high-coherent concept maps better for prior knowledge activation? Differential effects of concept mapping tasks on high school vs. university students. *Journal of Computer Assisted Learning, 24*(5), 407–419. doi:10.1111/j.1365-2729.2008.00277.x

Hay, D., Kinchin, I., & Lygo-Baker, S. (2008). Making learning visible: The role of concept mapping in higher education. *Studies in Higher Education, 33*(3), 295–311. doi:10.1080/03075070802049251

Haynes, T., & Bailey, G. (2003). Are you and your basic business students asking the right questions? *Business Education Forum, 57*(3), 33–37.

Hemming, H. E. (2000). Encouraging critical thinking: But...what does that mean? *Journal of Education, 35*(2), 173–186.

Irvine, L. C. (1995). Can concept mapping be used to promote meaningful learning in nurse education? *Journal of Advanced Nursing, 21*(6), 1175–1179. doi:10.1046/j.1365-2648.1995.21061175.x PMID:7665784

Jonassen, D. H. (1996). *Computers in the classroom: Mindtools for critical thinking*. Columbus, OH: Merrill/Prentice-Hall.

Jonassen, D. H. (2000). Toward a design theory of problem solving. *Educational Technology Research and Development, 48*(4), 63–63. doi:10.1007/BF02300500

Kesteren, M. T. R., & Fernández, G. (2011). Stress-related noradrenergic activity prompts large-scale neural network reconfiguration. *Science, 334,* 1151–1153. doi:10.1126/science.1209603 PMID:22116887

Kinchin, I., & Hay, D. (2000). How a qualitative approach to concept map analysis can be used to aid learning by illustrating patterns of conceptual development. *Educational Research, 42*(1), 43–57. doi:10.1080/001318800363908

Mayer, R. E., & Moreno, R. (2003). Nine ways to reduce cognitive load in multimedia learning. *Educational Psychologist, 38*(1), 43–52. doi:10.1207/S15326985EP3801_6

McAleese, R. (1994). A theoretical view on concept mapping. *Research in Learning Technology, 2* (1).

Mezirow, J. (2000). Learning to think like an adult. In J. Mezirow & X. Associates (Eds.), *Learning as transformation: Critical perspectives on a theory in progress* (pp. 3–34). San Francisco, CA: Jossey-Bass.

Mezirow, J. (2003). Transforming learning as discourse. *Journal of Transformative Education, 1*(1), 58–63. doi:10.1177/1541344603252172

Mezirow, J. (1997). Transformation theory: Theory to practice. *New Directions for Adult and Continuing Education, 74,* 5-12.

Miller, K. J. (2009). Concept mappping as a research tool to evaluate conceptual change related to instructional methods. *Teacher Education and Special Education: The Journal of the Teacher Education Division of the Council for Exceptional Children, 32*(4), 365–378. doi:10.1177/0888406409346149

Montgomery, J., & Ritchey, T. (2008). *The answer model theory*. Santa Monica, CA: TAM Books.

Montgomery, J. M., & Ritchey, T. (2010). *The answer model: A new path to healing*. Santa Monica, CA: TAM Books.

Muukkonen, H., & Lakkala, M. (2009). Exploring metaskills of knowledge-creating inquiry in higher education. *International Journal of Computer-Supported Collaborative Learning, 4*(2), 187–211. doi:10.1007/s11412-009-9063-y

Novak, J. D., & Cañas, A. J. (2006). The origins of the concept mapping tool and the continuing evolution of the tool. *Information Visualization, 5*(3), 175–175. doi:10.1057/palgrave.ivs.9500126

Novak, J. D., & Gowin, D. B. (1984). *Learning how to learn*. New York: Cambridge University Press. doi:10.1017/CBO9781139173469

Patterson, F. (2007). *Provoking students into thinking*. Retrieved from http://images. austhink.com/pdf/Compak_Critical_Thinking_in_Legal_Studies_March_07.pdf

Paul, R., & Elder, L. (2008). *Critical thinking*. Dillon Beach, CA: Foundation for Critical Thinking.

Scardamalia, M. (2002). Collective cognitive responsibility for the advancement of knowledge. In B. Smith (Ed.), *Liberal education in a knowledge society* (pp. 67–98). Chicago, IL: Open Court.

Schreiber, J. B., Verdi, M. P., Patock-Peckham, J., Johnson, J. T., & Kealy, W. A. (2002). Differing map construction and text organization and their effects on retention. *Journal of Experimental Education*, *70*(2), 114–130. doi:10.1080/00220970209599502

Snyder, M. J. (2008). Teaching critical thinking and problem solving skills. *Delta Pi Epsilon Journal*, *50*(2), 90–99.

Thompson, R., & Zamboanga, B. (2004). Academic aptitude and prior knowledge as predictors of student achievement in introduction to psychology. *Journal of Educational Psychology*, *96*, 778–784. doi:10.1037/0022-0663.96.4.778

Van Gelder, T. (2003). Enhancing deliberation through computer supported argument visualization. In *Visualizing argumentation: Software tools for collaborative and educational sense-making* (pp. 97–115). Academic Press. doi:10.1007/978-1-4471-0037-9_5

Van Gelder, T. (n.d.). *What is visual deliberation?* Retrieved from http://timvangelder. com/2010/09/27/what-is-visual-deliberation/

Wiggins, G. P., & McTighe, J. (1998). *Understanding by design*. Alexandria, VA: Association for Supervision and Curriculum Development.

Wilgis, M., & McConnell, J. (2008). Concept mapping: An educational strategy to improve graduate nurses' critical thinking skills during a hospital orientation program. *Journal of Continuing Education in Nursing*, *39*(3), 119–126. doi:10.3928/00220124-20080301-12 PMID:18386699

Yuen, E. Y., Wei, J., Liu, W., Zhong, P., Li, X., & Yan, Z. (2012). Repeated stress causes cognitive impairment by suppressing glutamate receptor expression and function in prefrontal cortex. *Neuron*, *73*, 962–977. doi:10.1016/j.neuron.2011.12.033 PMID:22405206

KEY TERMS AND DEFINITIONS

Critical Thinking: The process of carefully considering different perspectives and experiences, through the use of higher order thinking skills, to construct or expand meaningful knowledge.

Curriculum: Blueprint for course organization.

Discussion: Sharing of multiple perspectives between individuals through the use of higher order thinking skills.

Mapping: Graphic representation of information and relationship between information.

Chapter 9
Teaching Critical Thinking to First-Year Medical Students through Concept Mapping

Amina Sadik
Touro University Nevada, USA

EXECUTIVE SUMMARY

Helping students learn the basic sciences and demonstrating their importance in the practice of medicine presents a challenge for the majority of medical science educators. A curriculum change of medical biochemistry was implemented to include concept mapping as a visual strategy to enhance the analytical and critical thinking skills during clinical case-based workshops. A rubric was used to give detailed feedback and provide guidance to students. A number of clinical cases were judiciously selected to illustrate specific topics. Students meet with a faculty member to discuss the concept map prior to the workshop. During such meetings, all members are asked to participate in explaining their reasoning and decision-making and to thereby justify the flow of the concept map. This activity gives students the opportunity to demonstrate their capacity to visualize their knowledge using the concept map construction.

DOI: 10.4018/978-1-4666-5816-5.ch009

INTRODUCTION

Teaching basic sciences in medical school can be challenging because some concepts are not easily connected to the practice of medicine and because formative assessments are not made central to learning. One of the major difficulties for a basic science educator is to make the connection between the sciences taught and their relevance to the functioning of the human body in health and disease. Students frequently perceive basic science as useful only for passing exams and allowing them to move into their clinical years. A recent study by the National Board of Medical Examiners demonstrated that by the STEP 2 clinical exam, students shed a significant portion of their basic science knowledge, including medical biochemistry (Haist, Swanson, Holtzman, & Grande, 2010). This trend is alarming, especially because basic sciences provide the foundation for one of the core competencies of a physician: practicing evidence-based medicine (Bierer, Dannefer, Taylor, Hall, & Hull, 2008). Research in cognitive psychology has shown that retention of basic science knowledge is dramatically improved when the connections between biomedical science and its clinical relevance are made (Woods, 2007; Woods, Brooks, & Norman, 2007a, 2007b). Consequently, it is the medical educator's responsibility to make these connections for learners early on in order to engage them in doing more than just memorizing and practicing pattern recognition.

The formative and summative evaluations of our students over the first five years have left us with a sense of urgency for changing our existing teaching methods. A needs assessment was conducted to discover the students' perception of the current learning environment. It assisted us in shaping the new curriculum by engaging students who otherwise would not have expressed their needs, either because (a) they lacked motivation to learn, (b) they might not have wanted to be identified as lacking knowledge, or (c) they were simply not given the opportunity to express their needs in the past.

This chapter describes the steps that have been taken to shift from an exclusively lecture-based biochemistry curriculum to a more scenario-based curriculum that incorporates team-based workshops of clinical cases where concept mapping was used as a means to visualize knowledge and make logical connections between biochemical concepts and the expression of a disease.

CONCEPT MAPPING A POWERFUL TOOL FOR TEACHING CRITICAL THINKING

The goal of using concept mapping as a teaching tool is to demonstrate to students that there is a way to visualize knowledge and to think critically through a medical problem using principles acquired in the classroom. It trains students from the start to be responsible for their learning and enables them to become self-motivated, good team players and lifelong learners as medical knowledge and practice continue to evolve.

We chose concept mapping as a method to teach critical thinking in biochemistry because we believe in learning by doing. Concept maps foster understanding of the biochemical background of disease because their construction requires logical reasoning and critical thinking. In clinical case-based workshops, students are expected to construct a logical map, with "linking words" between concepts and "notes" that explain how altered biochemical pathways were responsible for a patient's physical symptoms and abnormal lab results. Building a successful concept map requires (a) knowledge of the relevant biochemical concepts and (b) identification of correct hierarchical relationships among these concepts as well as between the concepts and the pathophysiological changes of the patient. Now that one of the core competencies in medicine education is reinforcing the teaching of evidence-based medicine, this concept mapping exercise introduces students to the physician thought process early in the curriculum.

Before the implementation of the change in the curriculum that included concept mapping as one of its major components, the instruction of basic sciences curriculum (including the medical biochemistry course) was primarily based on Microsoft PowerPoint lectures. This approach tended to lead to a dry delivery of the material without soliciting the participation of students, due to the fact that there is an enormous wealth of material to be covered in a short time. The problem with this "exhaustive" lecturing is further compounded by the fact that there were no workshops or small group activities that would assist students to clearly understand and master the concepts through a clinical scenario. In this transmission type curriculum, students tend to memorize pages of pathways and disease names without trying to understand the mechanism by which the dysfunction of one organ or another occurs as a result of a specific metabolic disorder. When faced with a vignette type question on a summative assessment such as a board exam, the majority of students confessed to not being able to solve a medical problem. Therefore, it became evident that there was a need to implement changes in the medical biochemistry curriculum and to expose our students to the clinical relevance of basic science concepts early in the curriculum. Studies have previously shown that early exposure to any clinical teaching reaps positive results and is beneficial in the long run (Bowen, 2006).

According to Novak and Caňas (2006), concept maps represent knowledge geographically by enclosing important concepts in shapes and connecting them to show relationships and the logical flow of a given process. Ambrose et al. (2010) cite concept mapping as one strategy to reveal and enhance knowledge organization. They define concept mapping as "a technique that helps people represent their knowledge organization visually" (p. 59).

A typical concept map showing an example of knowledge and understanding of a first- year student in medical biochemistry is depicted in Figure 1. Students utilize the Inspiration 9.0 ™ software to build concept maps. As an initiation to this visualization tool, they are given a one- hour presentation on successful concept map creation using the software. Additional reading on the theory behind concept mapping is also provided (Beaudry & Wilson, 2009; Novak & Cañas, 2006).

The majority of small group-based activities tend to present students with clinical scenarios that may require some degree of critical thinking but fail to teach critical thinking as a skill. Increasing the number of opportunities for students to apply a skill they have not mastered does not necessarily help them master the skill. In the clinical years of medical education, clinical cases are used to teach pattern recognition void of any clinical reasoning. Being able to master pattern recognition through practice does not teach critical thinking and may lead to false conclusions when decisions are based on memorization rather than logical deduction. Although every educator strives to foster an environment that is inclusive of all students during small group activity to teach critical thinking, activities that are limited to presenting scenarios that may require critical thinking allow students who lack critical thinking to gain credit based on the effort of students who possessed the skill before the activity began. Including concept mapping as an activity that requires individual participation forces each student to develop the mechanics of critical thinking, and because students will be assessed individually on their mastery of the skill, their dependence on peers is greatly diminished through the activity.

One could approach teaching critical thinking by trying to define to students how critical thinking should happen and why it is important if one is to acquire a deep understanding of concepts behind any basic science discipline. However, designing a group activity to teach students how to visualize their knowledge using concepts learned during lecture and through assigned reading and finding the logical flow of disease processes proved to be a more effective method to engage students and teach critical thinking without being philosophical. Using concept mapping in medical biochemistry is not only a tool for visual learners to retain difficult content, but also a powerful self-assessment tool that leads any given student to deeply understand and irrevocably retain the basic concepts using logical and deductive reasoning. This process is facilitated by the fact that it is grounded by the use of clinical case scenarios discussed in a small group setting. Learning to think critically seems to be a social learning process (Brookfield, 2012).

Figure 1. A concept map explaining a genetically based disease, glucose-6-phosphatase or Von Gierke, process based on medical biochemistry concepts. A few "Notes" were opened to show their use

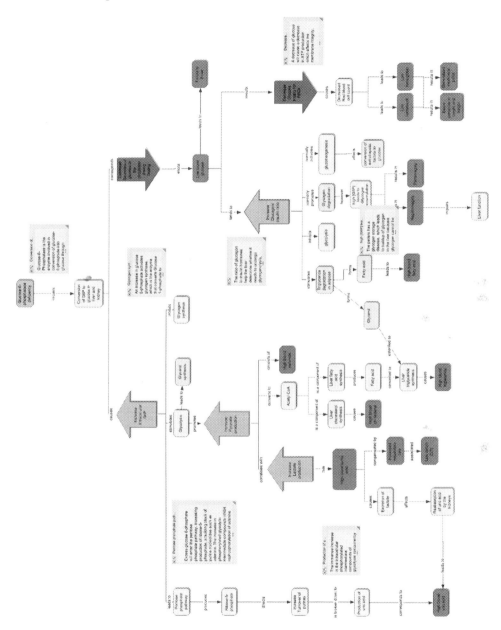

CLINICAL-CASE- BASED WORKSHOPS

The first step toward teaching critical thinking through concept mapping is finding clinical cases that will illustrate the material at hand. Clinical case- based workshops were introduced into the curriculum of the entering class of fall 2009. The nine workshops that currently span the fall semester are organized into quasi-Team Based Learning™ sessions that also incorporate concept mapping as a tool to teach how to visualize knowledge and to apply biochemical concepts to physiological/ pathological processes (Beaudry & Wilson, 2009; Novak & Canas, 2006). This approach enforces reasoning and critical thinking skills, both of which are required in the construction of a concept map with complete "Notes" and in a careful selection of "Linking Words." Figure 2 is an example showing open "Notes" and "Linking Words." One can choose to close all the "Notes" in order to have a better idea of the flow of the concept map as it can be seen on Figure 1. By the end of the course and after completing nine concept maps, students become almost expert in this process as we will discuss later in the chapter.

The workshops are based on clinical cases that are posted at least 4 days before the workshop date. Students are grouped into teams of five to seven students. On the day of the workshop, after taking a readiness assurance quiz individually and as a team, students are given time to finalize their concept maps within their groups. Feedback provided by faculty members during meetings prior to the workshop, during the workshop, and after the concept map is submitted assists students in

Figure 2. A section of a concept map illustrating Thalassemia where "Linking Words" and "Note" are shown

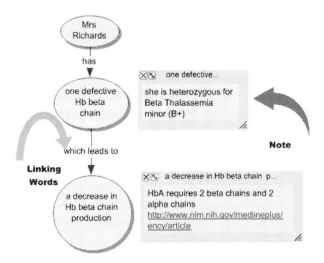

identifying the gaps in their knowledge. Students are encouraged to use adequate "Linking Words" that tell the story. Although they may not provide complete sentences or full assays, students are required to explain the flow of their concept maps in a "Note."

It is very interesting to observe the evolution of the construction of the concept maps as the course progresses. At first, students are taken aback by the idea of visualizing their knowledge using concept mapping. Eventually they start using concept mapping to make connections in other disciplines such gross anatomy and physiology. One second- year student said "I [hand-write] concept maps of the information I am studying to keep things logical and use the visual presentation of the flow of the information to review the material in a concise manner."

Figure 1 shows the end product of a concept map explaining a metabolic disease caused by genetic inheritance, Von Gierke disease. As one can see from the flow of the bubbles and the notes, students were able to explain the different symptoms and laboratory findings based on medical biochemistry principles and not based on physical diagnosis and/or pattern recognition. This method contributes the most in teaching basic sciences in the practice of medicine as required in a competency-based curriculum (Bierer et al., 2008; Litzelman & Cottingham, 2007; Smith, Dollase, & Boss, 2003).

Acquiring Clinical Cases

The workshops of our medical biochemistry curriculum are designed to make needed connections between basic science concepts and their clinical relevance. Consequently, each case study illustrates a topic in medical biochemistry. For example, the first case is about a pregnant woman without prenatal care with a history of alcoholism. She presents with vomiting, which cannot be stopped by antiemetic drugs, hyperventilation and acidosis. This case illustrates the need for vitamins as cofactors to enzymes. We want students to realize that excessive alcohol consumption interferes with the absorption and therefore storage of certain vitamins (such as thiamine), that the absence of vitamin-derived coenzymes prevents enzymatic activities such as that of pyruvate dehydrogenase, thereby leading to other metabolic pathways modifications inside the cell. Consequently, the absence of cofactors leads to the medical condition called "lactic acidosis" which results in a blood pH decrease that can be rectified by buffering mechanisms such as vomiting through which protons (H+) are eliminated from the body resulting in a pH increase (Figure 3).

The study cases we use are published clinical scenarios (Anderson, 2007, 2008, 2009; Anderson & Kirkish, 2007; Toy, Seifert, Strobel, & Harms, 2005). We modify some cases such that they more accurately illustrate the concepts at hand.

Figure 3. A concept map showing the flow of events in lactic acidosis to illustrate the importance of vitamins as cofactors necessary for enzymatic activity

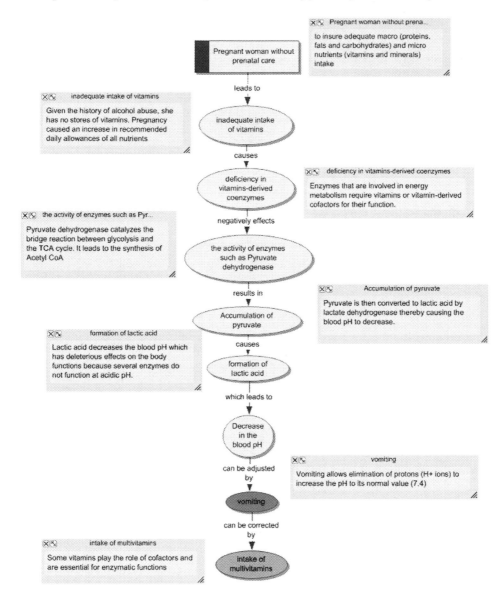

A typical case contains a two page description of the history, symptoms and lab data of the patient. This information is supplemented with "guiding questions" in order to assist students in their readiness for the workshop and for the construction of the concept map.

Although the presence of the questions could seem "too guiding" to some, they are designed to direct students' focus in the right direction and to better use their time. Because the body has a limited number of symptoms to show its malfunction, several diseases have more than one symptom in common and very few specific characteristics. The guiding questions allow students to find these characteristics as they are usually covered in that week's lecture material and assigned reading. In this way, students are free to think critically in order to find the correct flow of events in the body function that led to the final symptoms without the risk of wasting time by pursuing irrelevant lines of thought. Additional information (such as further lab tests or biochemically and/or nutritionally relevant treatments) is provided two days before the workshop via Blackboard Learning Management System™.

Modifying the Case Material

Although we downloaded the case material from MedPortal, modifications were made to better illustrate the concepts as to the importance of a combination of medicinal drugs, nutritional changes, and exercise for a successful recovery. We then decide what will be included in the first post in order to introduce the case and give enough information without giving away the final diagnosis. For example students analyze the case of *Familial hypercholesterolemia* (shown in Appendix 1) during the fourteenth week of the course. This case of myocardial infarction was chosen because it beautifully illustrates lipid metabolism and focuses students' attention on a major health problem linked to the diet. It makes the function of lipoproteins seem more concrete and introduces the importance of knowing a key enzyme in the synthesis of cholesterol and how drugs target this enzyme specifically.

Components of the First Post

Objectives

Outcome-based curriculum designs are rapidly gaining popularity in medical education (Harden, Crosby, Davis, & Friedman, 1999; Smith & Dollase, 1999). One of the reasons for this popularity is the tremendous expansion of medical knowledge in the last few decades, which has made traditional transmission-type curriculum impractical. Teaching in the medical field is becoming more and more assessment-driven to emphasize clinically relevant basic science information that a medical student must possess to become a competent physician. In order to adhere to this trend in medical biochemistry curricula, every faculty member is required to provide a clear "learning outcomes and performance indicators" section at the start of every lecture. This section generally summarizes the most important biochemical concepts and their relevance to medical applications while providing guidance to students as to their preparedness for success in any type of assessment (Azila, Tan, & Tan, 2006; Boudreau, Jagosh, Slee, Macdonald, & Steinert, 2008; Callahan, 1998; Carraccio, Benson, Nixon, & Derstine, 2008; Hamilton, 1999; Hawke, 2002). Knowing what a medical student should know is the first step to being a skilled educational planner and one of the essential competencies any teacher should possess (McTighe & O'Connor, 2005). In addition, we provide objectives for each clinical case's material in the first post (see Appendix 2). These objectives are usually very carefully formulated to orient students' focus to the most relevant material and assist them in being well prepared for their formative and summative assessments. Care is taken to use the cognitive words indicated in the article by Leslie Owen Wilson (2006), which allow us to adhere to one of the core competencies requiring that a learning objective must start with a word indicating assessable knowledge or a skill.

Guiding Questions

Guiding questions are designed to be specific to the clinical case at hand. Answers to the guiding questions will lead students to ideas that they will include in the concept map and the appropriate order of these concepts. The questions are randomized so that students are forced to think critically and to make decisions at the individual and team levels to determine the most logical flow of events in order to explain the disease process based on the biochemical concepts.

Introduction to Medical Vocabulary

We provide a list of vocabulary words that are necessary to tell the story on the concept map. These words are tools that are meant to trigger the thinking process that leads to choosing orderly logical reasoning. Students that succeed in using all the vocabulary words in the bubbles of their concept map and/or in the "notes" to explain the reasoning behind their depiction of the flow of events show the extent of their learning and the depth of their knowledge of that specific process.

Each group is encouraged to meet with a faculty member prior to the workshop in order to assess the progress of the concept map. During this meeting, one can orchestrate the discussion among team members and elicit the participation of each individual in demonstrating the logic of choices made to tell the story through the visualization of their understanding of the lecture material and therefore of the clinical case. Moreover, the discussion among team members, as facilitated by the faculty member, can allow him or her to observe the dynamic within the learning team.

Bubble Words

Providing bubble words instead of medical vocabulary can decrease the time students spend on creating the right combinations of words. Students then have to place the words in their concept map in a way that will visualize their understanding of the topic and the clinical case at hand. Again, they still have to provide their reasoning by adding a "Note" for most concepts included in the bubbles. The real learning occurs when students choose words to link concepts in the bubbles and select modifiers such as *increased*, *decreased*, *accumulation*, or *deficiency* to include in the bubble that will indicate that they understand the relationships between bubble words as they pertain to key concepts in the biochemical basis of medicine. As the course progresses, students learn that the flow of the story depends on correct choices of linking words and modifiers. These choices constitute progress toward acquiring critical thinking skills for those who lack such skills, and they hone the abilities of those who are already critical thinkers.

The Concept Map

The climax of the workshop is the construction of the concept map. This is the sole assignment in this course for which students come together to answer questions, help each other understand concepts or clarify material that may have skipped their attention during the lecture and/or the assigned reading, and receive feedback from a faculty member. Each team member has to assume leadership of the team at least once during the semester. The workshop leader usually assigns each team member the task of answering specific guiding questions and mapping a section of the case. An hour is assigned in the schedule for the first meeting among the team members. At the meeting, students are expected to discuss and verify their answers to the guiding questions using the course material and/or reference material provided with the case. We will discuss the importance of this formative assessment and its role in preparing students to do well on their summative assessments in the following sections.

The Beginners and Almost Experts

As in every aspect of learning, applying acquired knowledge to a new skill takes practice and requires feedback. Although students are given examples of successfully completed concept maps and guidance on how they should construct their concept maps, students rarely submit a perfect draft on their first try. However, as the semester progresses and even as early as the third concept map, students start to prepare complete, well connected, well justified concept maps. By the end of course, they are almost experts in constructing maps, and their concept maps reflect not only the mastery of the software used to construct the concept map but also the sophistication they reach in communicating their knowledge and understanding visually. Some students take pleasure in using icons to show the increase or the decrease of a metabolite and which organ and/or tissue is affected by the changes thereby making their concept maps more visually appealing and/or easier to read (Figure 4).

THE ROLE OF CONCEPT MAPPING IN TEACHING CRITICAL THINKING AND THE RETENTION OF MATERIAL

As indicated by Westberg and Jason in their *Fostering Learning in Small Groups: A Practical Guide* (2004), any activity that allows students to interact and discuss what they are learning fosters learning. Using concept mapping as formative assessment provides learners an environment where they can build their knowledge, visualize it, make decisions, and receive feedback. Feedback is given using a very descriptive rubric (Appendix 3). The combination of two methods of teaching (lectures and clinical case-based workshops) as well as two methods of assessment (summative in the form of multiple-choice vignette questions and formative in the form of concept mapping) has contributed to increased scores on board exams. Indeed, the school's average biochemistry board exam scores (COMLEX step 1) went from below the national average before the change of the curriculum to above the national average after the change was implemented (Table 1). We firmly believe, as indicated in other studies, that having included a formative assessment using concept mapping has helped increase students' deep understanding of the major concepts of medical biochemistry and equipped all students with critical thinking skills (Bierer, et al., 2008; Rushton, 2005).

It is noteworthy that working within a team of classmates that have the same purpose plays an important role in students' appreciation of the importance of working with concept mapping. This setting provides the opportunity for students to build leadership and communication skills as well as professionalism. Before receiving feedback from faculty, students are encouraged to give feedback to each other on the answers to the "guiding questions" and to be prepared to receive feedback from others. They are also required to provide references for every question they answer and to be ready to explain the choices they make. Although students do not have to answer guiding questions in full sentences or paragraphs, the process of critical reasoning to complete the concept map using "Notes" and adequate "Linking Words" is crucial. Additionally, the feedback provided by faculty members helps students identify the gaps in their knowledge as the semester progresses. Moreover,

Figure 4. A student concept map with additional icons showing the organs affected by the disease as wells as the possible foods that initiated the disease process

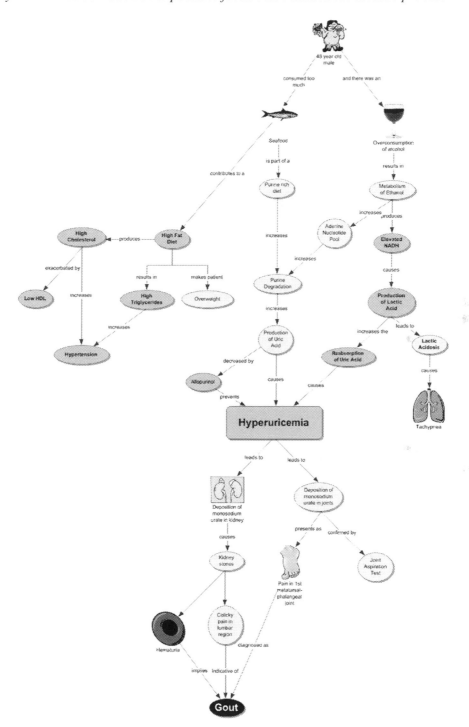

Table 1. Using concept mapping to teach critical thinking and the organization of knowledge and understanding visually allowed an increase in the board exam scores

COMLEX Date	Total COMLEX	Biochem TUN Mean	Biochem Natl Mean	TUN SD	Natl SD	n
5/08-4/09	470	481.27	518.68	110.06	120.86	131
5/09-4/10	503	520.69	523.96	106.14	121.79	117
5/10-4/11	509	516.87	515.92	131.03	143.71	134
5/11-4/12	524	546.73	541.77	154.81	153.51	121

the majority (90%) of student evaluations reflected their satisfaction with the new course design. We read student comments very closely and try to address their concerns. For example when group leaders indicated that they found themselves carrying most of the responsibility of organizing the meeting and finalizing the concept maps throughout the semester, we made the leadership rotational. Now, every student in the team is required to lead the team at least once during the semester. Here are some of the students' comments:

…concepts were clinically related (which enhanced my understanding/made subject more interesting and relevant), and professors did a great job teaching the complex topics…

I enjoyed the concept maps because I felt that they helped me to understand the material better.

…The concept map exercises, although at times seemed like extra work, were very effective for me to learn that material…

…The cases were definitely very interesting. I enjoyed having the clinical scenarios…

Workshops were a very effective use of our time…

Constructing a concept map in a group setting allows for peer learning and teaching and provides a means for checks and balances. It is humbling to observe the interactions among team members, which illustrate the capacity students have to explain difficult concepts to each other more simply than a specialist may. We all know that our knowledge can prove irrelevant if one does not have the skill to share it in a clear and concise manner.

REFERENCES

Anderson, M. (2007). What about Bob? *MedEdPORTAL*. Retrieved from http://services.aamc.org/30/mededportal/servlet/s/segment/mededportal/?subid=684

Anderson, M. (2008). Fred and Wilma's lucky day. *MedEdPORTAL*. Retrieved from http://services.aamc.org/30/mededportal/servlet/s/segment/mededportal/?subid=1675

Anderson, M. (2009). Rachel Jacobson's painful hip. *MedEdPORTAL*. Retrieved from http://services.aamc.org/30/mededportal/servlet/s/segment/mededportal/?subid=7702

Anderson, M., & Kirkish, M. (2007). Sophie Claiborne's upset stomach - An ornithine transcarbamolyase deficiency problem-based learning case. *MedEdPORTAL*. Retrieved from http://services.aamc.org/30/mededportal/servlet/s/segment/mededportal/?subid=642

Azila, N. M., Tan, N. H., & Tan, C. P. L. (2006). Inducing curricular change: Initial evaluation of outcomes. *Medical Education, 40*, 123–1147. doi:10.1111/j.1365-2929.2006.02574.x PMID:17054624

Beaudry, J., & Wilson, P. (2009). *Concept mapping and formative assessment: Elements supporting literacy and learning*. Retrieved from https://blackboard.une.edu/Webct/RelativeResourceManager/Template/Session5/ConceptMappingand-FormativeAssessment.pdf

Bierer, S. B., Dannefer, E. F., Taylor, C., Hall, P., & Hull, A. (2008). Methods to assess students' acquisition, application and integration of basic science knowledge in an innovative competency-based curriculum. *Medical Teacher, 30*(7), e171–e177. doi:10.1080/01421590802139740 PMID:18777415

Boudreau, J. D., Jagosh, J., Slee, R., Macdonald, M. E., & Steinert, Y. (2008). Patients' perspectives on physicians' roles: Implications for curricular reform. *Academic Medicine, 83*(8), 744–753. doi:10.1097/ACM.0b013e31817eb4c0 PMID:18667888

Bowen, J. L. (2006). Medical education: Educational strategies to promote clinical diagnostic reasoning. *The New England Journal of Medicine, 355*, 2217–2225. doi:10.1056/NEJMra054782 PMID:17124019

Brookfield, S. D. (2012). *Teaching for critical thinking: Tools and techniques to help students question their assumptions*. San Francisco, CA: Jossey-Bass.

Callahan, D. (1998). Medical education and the goals of medicine. *Medical Teacher, 20*, 85–86. doi:10.1080/01421599881147

Carraccio, C. L., Benson, B. J., Nixon, L. J., & Derstine, P. L. (2008). From the educational bench to the clinical bedside: Translating the Dreyfus developmental model to the learning of clinical skills. *Academic Medicine, 83*(8), 761–767. doi:10.1097/ACM.0b013e31817eb632 PMID:18667892

Haist, S. A., Swanson, D. B., Holtzman, K. Z., & Grande, J. P. (2010). *The scientific foundations of medicine: Going beyond the first two years of medical school.* Paper presented at the Fourteenth Annual Meeting of the International Association of Medical Science Educators. New Orleans, LA. Retrieved from http://iamse.org/conf/conf14/3fs5.html

Hamilton, J. D. (1999). Outcomes in medical education must be wide, long and deep. *Medical Teacher, 21*, 125–126. doi:10.1080/01421599979725 PMID:21275724

Harden, R. M., Crosby, J. R., Davis, M. H., & Friedman, M. (1999). AMEE guide no.14: Outcome-based education: Part 5--from competency to meta-competency: A model for the specification of learning outcomes. *Medical Teacher, 21*(6), 546–553. doi:10.1080/01421599978951 PMID:21281173

Hawke, G. (2002). *Keeping curriculum relevant in a changing world.* Paper presented at the SENAI International Seminar. Belo Horizante, Brasil.

Litzelman, D. K., & Cottingham, A. H. (2007). The new formal competency-based curriculum and informal curriculum at Indiana University School of Medicine: Overview and five-year analysis. *Academic Medicine, 82*(4), 410–421. doi:10.1097/ACM.0b013e31803327f3 PMID:17414200

McTighe, J., & O'Connor, K. (2005). Seven practices for effective learning. *Educational Leadership, 63*, 10–17.

Novak, J. D., & Canas, A. (2006). *The theory underlying concept maps and how to construct and use them (Technical Report IHMC CmapTools Rev 2008-01).* IHMC.

Rushton, A. (2005). Formative assessment: a key to deep learning? *Medical Teacher, 27*(6), 509–513. doi:10.1080/01421590500129159 PMID:16199357

Smith, S. R., & Dollase, R. (1999). An introduction to outcome-based education. *Medical Teacher, 21*(1), 15–22. doi:10.1080/01421599979978

Smith, S. R., Dollase, R. H., & Boss, J. A. (2003). Assessing students' performances in a competency-based curriculum. *Academic Medicine, 78*(1), 97–107. doi:10.1097/00001888-200301000-00019 PMID:12525418

Toy, E. C., Seifert, W. E., Strobel, H. W., & Harms, K. P. (2005). *Case files biochemistry.* New York: McGraw-Hill, Medical Publishing Division.

Woods, N. N. (2007). Science is fundamental: The role of biomedical knowledge in clinical reasoning. *Medical Education*, *41*(12), 1173–1177. doi:10.1111/j.1365-2923.2007.02911.x PMID:18045369

Woods, N. N., Brooks, L. R., & Norman, G. R. (2007a). It all make sense: Biomedical knowledge, causal connections and memory in the novice diagnostician. *Advances in Health Sciences Education: Theory and Practice*, *12*, 405–415. doi:10.1007/s10459-006-9055-x PMID:17318360

Woods, N. N., Brooks, L. R., & Norman, G. R. (2007b). The role of biomedical knowledge in diagnosis of difficult clinical cases. *Advances in Health Sciences Education : Theory and Practice*, *12*(4), 417–426. doi:10.1007/s10459-006-9054-y PMID:17206465

KEY TERMS AND DEFINITIONS

Basic Sciences: Disciplines such physiology, biochemistry, immunology and microbiology that are at the root of understanding the functions of the human body.

Clinical Scenario: A sequence of signs and symptoms, real or imagined, used to illustrate a concept in medical biochemistry or any other basic science discipline that uses clinical cases.

COMLEX: National board of osteopathic medical examiners licensure exam, usually taken after the two first years or the preclinical years of medical education.

Concept Mapping: A visual representation of knowledge in a geographical manner showing a logical flow of events to justify or explain a phenomenon.

Familial Hypercholesterolemia: An inherited disease leading to the accumulation of cholesterol in the bloodstream.

Guiding Questions: Questions meant to force students to read the material for understanding. If answered correctly, they lead to solving the case and constructing the concept map with relative ease.

Hyperventilation: Rapid breathing leading to the elimination of carbon dioxide from the body.

Inspiration: Software allowing for the construction of a concept map using templates.

Linking Words: Selected words from a list provided by the software or created by the user to make a logical connection between two events on the concept map.

Metabolic Acidosis: A decrease in the blood pH caused by the accumulation of a chemical compound, such as lactate or a ketone body, as a consequence of an enzymatic malfunction or an ingestion of a xenobiotic such as alcohol.

APPENDIX 1

Preparing to Teach Concept Mapping via Faculty Development

Designing a small group activity to teach critical thinking to medical students, especially surrounding a challenging task such as making the connection between a basic science discipline and the practice of medicine, requires a commitment to excellence in medical education. Medical students can detect very quickly the interest a faculty member has in what he or she is trying to teach as well as the degree of cohesiveness between faculty members. Students can become frustrated if faculty members fail to model the behavior they expect from students. If we are to teach students how to behave professionally while working in a group and to instill responsibility, we must show them how a group of seemingly different individuals can transform into a cohesive team. We have to model our expectations for the students. First, regardless of who is the major contributor to the lecture is, we work as a team on each clinical case that will be used to illustrate the major topic of the week. Then, each of us constructs the concept map that we think should be used as a template showing all the concepts of medical biochemistry that should be used to explain the disease processes covered in the clinical case (Figure 5). Though we are all experts in the discipline of medical biochemistry, not every faculty member uses the same method to communicate his or her knowledge on the concept map. In the beginning, it took the team a few hours to make each other understand how knowledge should be organized in the model concept map and communicated to students. With time and experience and even when new clinical case is used or new information comes to light about an existing case, the team reaches consensus relatively quickly. Each faculty member contributes actively to construction of the model concept map and to the modifications of the case to accurately illustrate the topic at hand. Again, these meetings take preparation before the material is posted on Blackboard Learning Management System™. Each faculty member attends faculty development sessions in order to reach a stage where all the participating faculty members are able to model preparedness and effective teamwork for students. It is not an easy task to teach concept mapping to students if one is not aware of how he or she would organize his or her own knowledge. To echo Ambrose et al. (2010), "It can be difficult for experts to recognize how they organize their own knowledge, and thus difficult for them to communicate this organization to students. One way to make your own knowledge organization apparent to yourself is to create your own concept map" (p. 59). In addition to creating a model concept maps based on our existing knowledge, we strive to acquire new knowledge and experience in teaching medical students — especially those who are not naturally interested in knowing the minutia of our respective research interests. The teaching experience of the faculty members in our team of biochemistry experts ranges from five to 23 years. All three faculty members completed (a) the Essential Skills in Medical Education (ESME) course, (b) a Team Based Learning™ workshop, (c) Test question writing, and d) the "How to be an Efficient Course Director" workshop, all of which were offered at the International Association of Medical Science Educators conference (IAMSE). It is rare indeed to make a group of faculty teaching the same discipline evolve to form a team, administer a curriculum that is student oriented, be willing to leave their comfort zone, and use a new and challenging method to teach critical thinking. Critical thinking can be learned when (a) the goals are focused, (b) the assessments are limited and yet they are of quantity and frequency that allow for skill development and academic progress, and (c) the feedback is behavioral and specific so that the students know what they do well in order to continue do it and what they do not do well so they may improve.

Figure 5. A template of the familial hypercholesterolemia as constructed by the three faculty members before posting the case

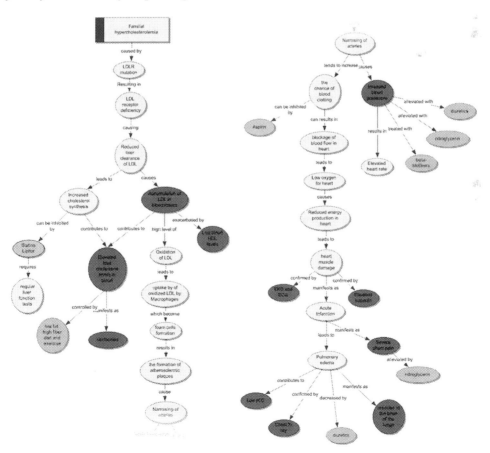

APPENDIX 2

First Post of the Case Material

The Biochemical Basis of Medicine

John Dorsey's Severe Chest Pains
By: *Marshall Anderson, Ph.D. Modified by Amina Sadik, Ph.D.*

Objectives

1.   Identify the roles of the various lipoproteins in lipid transport and metabolism.
2.   Name the lipoproteins necessary for chylomicron maturation
     a.   Indicate their source, and
     b.   provide their function (s)
3.   Name the enzymes that interact with lipoproteins.
4.   Describe the synthesis of LDL and diagram its path of delivery of cholesterol to cells
5.   Explain the role of the LDL receptor in the regulation of cholesterol concentration in the hepatocytes
6.   Explain the role(s) of each apoprotein in lipoprotein function(s)
7.   Discuss the mechanism by which atherosclerotic plaques form
8.   List the manageable and none manageable risk factors in coronary artery disease
9.   List the lipoproteins the level of which is directly proportional to CHD
10.   List the proteins and enzymes used in the diagnosis of myocardial infarction, and explain how the diagnosis is made on the basis of these values
11.   List the functions of cholesterol in the body
12.   List the sources of cholesterol found in the body

John Dorsey's Severe Chest Pains

John Dorsey is a 39-year-old black male who is admitted to the hospital with a three-hour history of severe chest pain. He describes similar but less severe pain in the chest during heavy exertion over the last year, but he thought that it was due to pain in the chest muscles. Mr. Dorsey describes himself as an insomniac and associates the beginning of his sleep problems with his first experiences of chest pain. This present pain is the worst he has ever experienced, and it is felt in both arms, his neck, and back. He reports feeling sick to his stomach and having some trouble breathing.

Mr. Dorsey had no significant medical problems until three years ago when he began to have chest pains and noticed small growths on his hands. Mr. Dorsey is a real sports fan and eats a lot of fast foods, and enjoys potato chips and beer while watching the Sox, Bears, Hawks, and Bulls on TV.

Dr. Sigh, the emergency room physician, treats Mr. Dorsey with aspirin (325 mg orally) followed by nitroglycerin to relieve the acute pain, and she performs a quick physical exam.

Significant findings on the physical exam are the following:

- Blood pressure:160/100
- Heart rate: 110/min
- Respirations are 20/min
- No fever
- Crackles in the bases of the lungs
- Systolic bulge at the left of the sternum
- S4 gallop is heard over the ventricle and a systolic murmur is present
- Abdominal exam: normal
- Extremities: xanthomas over the tendons of the hands
- Electrocardiogram (EKG) shows evidence of acute infarction of the left anterior wall of the heart.
- The nitroglycerin is controlling the acute pain, so morphine was not administered.
- Blood was drawn for analysis, a beta blocker and a chest X-ray was ordered, and Mr. Dorsey was transferred to the coronary care unit or CCU.

Lab Result for John Dorsey

Mr. Dorsey is treated with oxygen by mask and is given a dose of diuretic to reduce fluid accumulation in the lungs. An echocardiogram shows that the anterior wall of the left ventricle contracts poorly. Mr. Dorsey receives the necessary care that allowed for normal contractions the following day.

Mr. Dorsey comes from a large family with three brothers and four sisters. His father died of a massive heart attack at the age of 42 and two brothers and one sister have had heart attacks in their mid-thirties. Mr. Dorsey had a normal childhood, with the normal array of childhood illnesses, including chicken pox and measles. He smoked one pack a day for six years in his twenties, but hasn't smoked since then. He was hospitalized once, at the age of 31 for injuries from a traffic accident, but otherwise has had no significant medical problems, until the chest pains began three years ago. He has never been overweight. Mr. Dorsey is a mailman, so he gets some

Table 2. Lab Result for John Dorsey

	John	Normal Reference Range
Electrolytes	normal	
Blood count	normal	
Troponin T	positive	(negative)
Troponin I	positive	(negative)
Arterial Blood Gas		
pH	7.46	7.36-7.45
pO_2	65	90
pCO_2	35	35-45
Chest X-Ray		
pulmonary edema, normal heart size		
Lipid Profile		
Cholesterol	510 mg/dl	(< 200 mg/dl)
HDL cholesterol	27 mg/dl	(35-55 mg/dl)
LDL cholesterol	483 mg/dl	(65-190 mg/dl)
Triglycerides	100 mg/dl	(30-200 mg/dl)

exercise every day walking from house to house, except Sunday. His wife has urged him to have his cholesterol checked, but he hasn't found time to get around to it.

Given Mr. Dorsey's family history of cardiovascular diseases, Dr. Sigh ordered a genetic test.

Guiding Questions

1. What would cause such severe chest pains in this patient?
2. What is the nature of the growths on the patient's hands?
3. What is the significance of the patient liking "junk food"?
4. What is the significance of the elevated blood pressure?
5. What do aspirin and nitroglycerin do?
6. Why was the patient given a diuretic?
7. What are xanthomas?
8. What does a positive Troponin T and I signify when found in the blood sample of this patient?
9. Why is the pO_2 decreased?

10. Why is it necessary to reduce fluid accumulations in the lungs in this patient?
11. Would the patient's previous history of smoking contribute to his condition?
12. What are the risk factors for coronary artery disease?

Bubble Words

1. HDL levels
2. Xanthomas
3. LDL levels
4. EKG and ECG
5. Total cholesterol in the blood
6. Cholesterol synthesis
7. LDL receptor
8. Chest X-ray
9. LDL oxidation
10. Macrophages
11. Foam cells
12. Atherosclerotic plaques
13. Levels of Troponin T and I
14. Severe chest pains
15. Liver clearance of LDL
16. Aspirin
17. Narrowing of arteries
18. Blood pressure
19. Heart rate
20. Heart muscle damage
21. Crackles in the bases of the lungs
22. Low O_2 in arterial blood
23. Blood clotting
24. Diuretics
25. Energy production in heart
26. Pulmonary edema
27. Acute infarction
28. Nitroglycerine
29. Beta blocker
30. Blockage of blood flow in heart
31. Oxygen for heart muscle

References

Thompson and Thompson Genetics In Medicine, 7th ed, Authors: R.L. Nussbaum, R. R. McInnes, and H.F. Willard ISBN-978-1-4160-3080-5 pp 260-261

Marks' Basic Medical Biochemistry, A Clinical Approach by M. Lieberman and A. Marks, 2013, 4th ed. ISBN: 13: 978-1-60831-572-7

Biochemistry, Molecular Biology and Genetics, BRS Board Review Series, by T.A. Swanson, S. I. Kim, and M.J. Glucksman, 5th ed. ISBN-13:9780781798754

Schaefer, E. J. (2002) Lipoproteins, nutrition, and heart disease Am. J. Clin. Nutr., 75 (2):191-212.

World Wide Web Resources

Hypercholesterolemia: http://ghr.nlm.nih.gov/condition/hypercholesterolemia

Primary Disorders of LDL-Cholesterol Metabolism: http://www.uptodate.com/contents/primary-disorders-of-ldl-cholesterol-metabolism(accessedSeptember16,2011)

Hyperlipidemia: http://www.heart.org/HEARTORG/Conditions/Cholesterol/AboutCholesterol/Hyperlipidemia_UCM_434965_Article.jsp (sccessed October 25, 2012)

Statin Drugs: http://www.nlm.nih.gov/medlineplus/statins.html (accessed October 25, 2012)

Lipitor: http://www.lipitor.com/aboutLipitor/benefitsOfLipitor.aspx?source=google&HBX_PK=s_+lipitor+benefits&HBX_OU=50&o=23127370|166376222|0&skwid=43700003061901690 (accessed October 25, 2012)

Second Post of the Case Material

Additional Information

Mr. Dorsey is diagnosed as a heterozygous familial hypercholesterolemia with a mutation of the LDLR common in Afrikaners. This defective gene is located on chromosome 19 p. He has a few risk factors for coronary artery disease, yet, has abnormally high total cholesterol and high LDL values and the presence of xanthomas on the tendons of his hands. Following his hospital stay of ten days, he is put on a low fat, high fiber diet, with no eggs or organ meats, and given 20 mg Lipitor® orally once a day to control his blood cholesterol and to continue on the beta blocker until a re-evaluation at his next check-up in one month. He is enrolled in the cardiac patient exercise program at the hospital to increase his exercise level, and is told to cut out potato chips and beer while watching sports on TV. His liver function will be monitored at regular intervals.

Guiding Questions

1.   What is hypercholesterolemia and what are its causes?
2.   What is the role of LDL receptor in cholesterol regulation?
3.   What are the differences in disease management between a homozygous and a heterozygous case?
4.   Why is the patient advised to eat a low fat, high fiber diet?
5.   Why is the patient advised to have liver function tests done at regular intervals?

Additional Bubble Words

1.   Genetic mutation in LDLR
2.   Familial hypercholesterolemia
3.   Lipitor®
4.   Low fat, high fiber diet and exercise
5.   Regular liver function tests

References

Rader DJ, Cohen J, Hobbs HH. 2003. Monogenic hypercholesterolemia: new insights in pathogenesis and treatment. *J. Clin. Invest.* 111: 1795–1803

APPENDIX 3

Table 3. Rubric for the concept map assignment

Total point possible = 10 Points					
BMS 680/BSCI 609					
Names:					
The Instructor's Comments:					
Criteria	Excellent 2.5	Very Good 2.0	Good 1.5	Fair 1	Poor 0.5
Completeness (Bubbles)	90+ % of the concepts are mapped	80-90% of the concepts are mapped	70-80% of the concepts are mapped	60-70% of the concepts are mapped	less than 60% of the concepts are mapped
Relationship (Arrows and their connecting words)	90+% of the relationships are mapped correctly	80-90% of the relationships are mapped correctly	70-80% of the relationships are mapped correctly	60-70% of the relationships are mapped correctly	less than 60% of the relationships are mapped correctly
Communication (Structure and clarity of explanations included in the "Note")	90+ % of the information is presented clearly and allows for a high level of understanding	80-90% of the information is presented clearly and allows for a good level of understanding	70-80% or f the information is presented clearly and allows for a basic level of understanding	60 -70% of the information is presented clearly and some understanding can be gained	less than 60% of the information is clear, very difficult to understand
Timeliness	CM completed and submitted on time				

- **NB:** Completeness of concepts means that important pathways, metabolites, enzymes, symptoms, tissues involved, genetic background (if applicable), etc are placed in the bubbles on the map.
- **Relationship:** Means the placement of arrows connecting bubbles (pointing to the correct direction) with appropriate short text (connecting words) placed by the arrows.
- **Communication:** Covers, the structure of the non-linear map (tree) that is easily understandable with no crossovers, as well as the clarity of explanations placed at the right side of the bubble using the "Note" icon.
- **Assessment of Medical Biochemistry Concept Mapping:** There is a total of four criteria yielding a possible *10 points*. Each of the criteria is defined in the rubric. The criteria are weighted differently.

Chapter 10
Concept Maps as Replacements of Written Essays in Efficient Assessment of Complex Medical Knowledge

Gloria Gomez
University of Southern Denmark, Denmark

Robin Griffiths
University of Otago, New Zealand

Pooshan Navathe
University of Otago, New Zealand

EXECUTIVE SUMMARY

Marking efficiency and timely student feedback are two aspects of assessment that may be greatly improved with concept maps (cmaps), if student learning style preference for more traditional approaches can be overcome. A semester-long exploratory case study was designed and performed in a distance aviation medicine course. This involved participant observations, interviews, and task analysis to investigate cmaps' claimed advantages for meaningful learning. The results showed that cmaps could be suitable replacements of written essays in the assessment of complex medical conceptual knowledge. Both present similar strengths and weaknesses; however, cmaps are faster to mark, and quickly reveal student understanding of a particular

DOI: 10.4018/978-1-4666-5816-5.ch010

topic. The discussion of results is informed by relevant literature on concept mapping (cmapping) in medical education, assessment for deep understanding, and learning styles. This research can benefit online postgraduate education programmes searching for alternatives to improve the assessment process.

INTRODUCTION

This chapter discusses outcomes of a pilot exploratory case study related to the use of Joseph Novak's concept map template (concept → linking phrase → concept; see Figure 1) in a distance postgraduate course, and its suitability as a replacement for written essays in efficient assessment of medical knowledge. Specifically, the aim was to investigate if cmaps could be used as an alternative method to evaluate students' individual conceptual understanding in "clinical aviation medicine." Before a more in depth description, some information about the study's origins is introduced.

As part of the expansion of the Occupational and Aviation Medicine Department, preliminary discussions have been undertaken on offering aviation medicine courses in Asia through the University of Otago's distance learning programme, potentially multiplying enrollments to several hundred students. Development of an alternative assessment system that is operationally feasible at a distance might address the assessment issues generated by educational programmes taught in high volumes, and to students with very different cultural and linguistic backgrounds.

This research into university teaching was undertaken in 408 hours with the support of the 2007 E-learning Enhancement Grant, awarded by the Committee for the Advancement of Learning and Teaching (CALT). Its overarching goal was to investigate how cmaps could be used in the courses run by the Department, since previous research demonstrates that they have been applied as an effective learning strategy for enhancing understanding and assessment tool in various educational areas including medicine. The project had four aims:

1. Review of the cmapping literature as it pertains to distance education, medical education, formative and summative evaluation
2. Development of master cmaps for subject areas
3. Trial cmaps in an existing aviation medicine course
4. Assess the use of cmapping as a part of a strategy to assist in the internationalisation of aviation medicine course content

While Gomez (2008) reports on every aim of the project, this chapter limits its scope to present only outcomes that impact aims 3 and 4. It uses the literature review gathered for aim 1 to inform the discussion and answer the research questions formulated by two lecturers teaching the course that was used in the study.

The distance aviation medicine programme is run via synchronous and asynchronous technologies, and caters to the educational needs of extremely busy and highly skilled professionals (medical doctors) distributed worldwide, with limited time for new learning, but who need to update their knowledge for professional or career advancement reasons.

This pilot study was designed to explore how cmapping could be best incorporated into existing courses, and if its use could lead to assessment of learning for understanding of graduate students. At the time it was undertaken, exploratory or formal research studies within a distance postgraduate medical course had not yet been reported. In the majority of the 24 reports on cmapping in medical education that were reviewed, cmaps were chosen as a learning strategy for promoting meaningful learning. The educators were interested in the development of cognitive skills that have an impact in medical processes requiring reasoning, such as diagnosis, analysis of patient data, or understanding the impact of a condition. Since its completion in late 2008, studies with similar characteristics, but in undergraduate education, have been published. See for example Passmore, Owen, and Prabakaran (2011). In online postgraduate medical education, the "Portal for Postgraduates in Medicine" has been launched, and strongly encourages through examples, background literature, and related references the use of concept maps as a formative assessment tool (Walsh, 2010).

A caveat. The study reported here does not aim to demonstrate that cmaps are better than essays. Instead, it presents early evidence that they may be as efficient as written essays in representing individual medical complex thinking, with the advantage of being faster to mark, and therefore, have the potential to improve student feedback. However, student and lecturer acceptability may prevent the successful incorporation of this strategy as a formative assessment tool.

The chapter is comprised of five sections. The "background" section presents Joseph Novak's concept maps. Its benefits for critical thinking, transferring theory into practice, and educational planning are briefly explained, in support of the claim that these tools facilitate easy visualization and attentive interpretation of complex medical concepts. Faster adoption in postgraduate medical courses is dependent upon three conditions: learning how to build "good" cmaps, students' overcoming preferences for traditional study styles, and valid and reliable measuring methods. The section closes with similarities and differences between cmaps and written essays as an assessment tool.

The "case study approach" section describes the methodologies and methods that informed the research design. A conversation with the two lecturers in charge of the course informed the formulation of the guiding research questions, how the students should be engaged as participants within the study. The cmapping instruction was designed for online engagement at the start of the academic semester, around the constraints dictated by the course, and the suggestions given by the lecturer (third author). Participatory observation, unstructured interviews, formal and informal email communication were the methods chosen to learn about this community of people in their natural setting. Diverse data gathering methods were used including synchronous and asynchronous Web technologies for sharing, communicating, and exchanging study materials. The section ends with a detailed explanation as to how the data was used during the analysis for answering the research questions.

The results are presented in three separate sections. First result; a step-by step review of the process the lecturer followed in marking the students' cmap assignment provides evidence that it is possible to evaluate deep understanding with this alternative tool in an aviation medical course, if the students have mastered the skills of building "good" cmaps. The assessed cmaps with low, good, and higher scores provided supporting evidence. Second result; doing a time-analysis of the audio-recording of the session in which the lecturer and instructor evaluated the assignments, revealed that these cmaps were faster to mark than written essays. The lecturer could assess six cmaps on varied aeromedical decision topics in approximately 15.5 minutes. Third result; all students but one mastered the technique, the software, and therefore, were able to effectively represent complex medical concepts for an assessment task. The attitudinal responses of three students, who responded to a questionnaire, and the lecturer's opinion on the pilot's outcomes, provide evidence on how easily, or not, it would be for cmap assignments to be adopted for regular use in a course.

Supported by the literature review, the "discussion" section uses the results to argue several claims. First, that Novak's cmaps facilitate the representation and evaluation of complex medical concepts. Second, that they present two advantages over written essays that might improve staff marking efficiency and student feedback. Third, effective and systematic implementation of this alternative in the aviation courses should be preceded by suitable cmapping instruction, not only to overcome student and lecturer preference for using traditional assessment tools, such as written assignments, but also to support those who show a natural inclination for using alternative assignments with a greater visual component.

This chapter concludes with a brief discussion of what the outcomes of this small exploratory study may mean for future research in the area of evaluating medical knowledge of large numbers of students with diverse language backgrounds, and in distributed online distance medical courses.

BACKGROUND

Definition, Structure, and Characteristics

Concept maps are tools or templates for organising and representing knowledge. They have been proven to be effective for the promotion of meaningful learning, as they facilitate knowledge retention, preservation and sharing. A person who learns how to use the template's structural design and its basic application rules can represent and manipulate conceptual ideas held in their head or cognitive structure (Cañas & Novak, 2006; Cañas, Novak, & González, 2004; Mintzes, Wandersee, & Novak, 2005; Novak, 1998; Novak & Gowin, 1984; Novak & Wandersee, 1990; Torres & Marriott, c2010).

A cmap is usually employed to represent the response, analysis or solution to a particular question, situation, or event that the knowledge producer (e.g. a postgraduate medical student) is trying to understand. It is a semi-hierarchical structure comprised of concepts and linking phrases where the most inclusive, most general concept sits at the top, and the more specific, less general concepts are arranged hierarchically below in order of relevance. Within the structure, the concepts are usually enclosed in a box or circle of some type. Two or more concepts connected by a line, and with a linking phrase in between, form a conceptual relationship (also known as proposition or semantic unit of meaning). The linking phrase describes the type of relationship between the connected concepts. Concepts within the structure can be labelled with words or symbols such as % or + (Novak, 1998; Novak & Cañas, 2006b; Novak & Gowin, 1984).

Figure 1 illustrates a cmap and its key elements (See full map in Figure 4). For example, concepts are "Meniere's Disease," "evidence" and "stage two." Linking phrases are "must take into account" and "consists of." Propositions are "stage three consists of severe hearing loss" and "Meniere's Disease" must take into account stage of illness.

Cross-links make evident the creative leaps in the thinking of a learner and represent the relationship between two or more concepts in opposite domains of the cmap. In Figure 2 "side effects may be influenced by flight stresses" and in Figure 6 "ATC information also via visual communication forms" are not only propositions but also "cross-links."

According to Novak and Gowin (1984), cmaps are "so powerful" in the facilitation of meaningful learning because they:

1. Serve as a kind of template to help organize and structure knowledge. When utilised in learning, the learner constructs new knowledge by the observation of events or objects using concepts they already possess; in order to do so they have to identify and select the knowledge to be learned.

227

Figure 1. A snapshot of a cmap built by a study participant. It represents the focus question "How would we make an aeromedical decision in a case of Meniere's disease?"

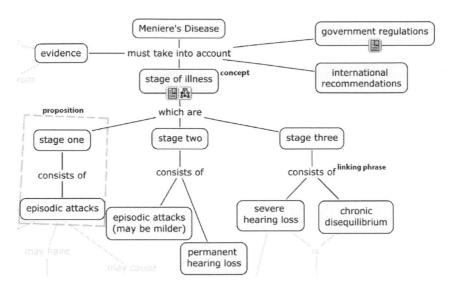

Figure 2. Cross-links

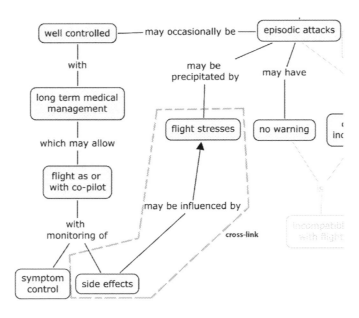

2. Facilitate a creative activity resulting in the process of concept assimilation, a type of learning, which is typically characterized by an active process of relation to, differentiation from, and integration with, existing relevant concepts (Novak, 1998). People who follow the procedure for building a map are actually putting in practice this process that leads to understanding a piece of information (Novak, 2004; Novak & Cañas, 2006b).

3. Help people explicitly see the nature and role of concepts and the relationships between them in a particular piece of knowledge. They take advantage of our learning capacity for using written and spoken symbols to communicate perceived regularities in events or objects around us, as well as our capacity to recognize patterns in images, facilitating learning and recall. Humans have the unique ability to invent and to use language or symbols to label and communicate concepts. People think with concepts and propositions: language allows us to translate concepts into words and/or symbols, to describe thoughts, feelings, events and actions (see Figure 1 and Figure 2).

In the case of this study, the students organised and structured knowledge using cmaps on the course topic "clinical aviation medicine." The students were taught the procedure that is illustrated in a concept map/flowchart hybrid published in the CmapTools software Website (2007). The cmaps built for assignments have enabled the lecturer, the students themselves, and the readers for this chapter to see the nature and role of the concepts and the relationships between them in relation to six questions on clinical aeromedical decisions. For example:

-   How would we make an aeromedical decision in a case of Meniere's disease? Figure 4 and Figure 5
-   How would we make an aeromedical decision in case of a hearing loss? Figure 6
-   How do we make an aeromedical decision in the case of multifocal contact lenses? Figure 7

Easy Visualization and Attentive Interpretation of Complex Medical Concepts

For more than a decade, medical educators have been willing to consider the incorporation of teaching and learning strategies that "… [help] students 'learn to learn' rather than teaching them to memorise by rote or how to arbitrarily store vast amounts of useless knowledge" (Watson, 1998, p. 266) and that enable them to develop strong critical thinking and clinical problem-solving skills "…for remaining competent in such evolving medical environment" (Daley et al., 2006, p. 24).

Cmaps and cmapping software tools have proved highly effective at organising knowledge, and have become widely used within educational and business settings. Elementary and high school teachers, university professors, business people, all make use of cmapping for varied knowledge acquisition purposes (Novak, 1998; Novak & Cañas, 2006b). Research shows it is a useful strategy in identifying a learner's current understanding, misconceptions and conceptual change; as a formal assessment tool; in collaboration and cooperative learning; in organizing and presenting information; as an advance organizer; as a navigational aid in hypermedia; among many other uses (Coffey et al., 2003). Literature reviews on the use of cmaps in varied fields can be consulted (Cañas & Novak, 2006; Cañas, Novak, et al., 2004; Institute for Human and Machine Cognition, 2008; Mintzes et al., 2005; Novak & Wandersee, 1990; Torres & Marriott, c2010).

Research studies, some quantitative, others qualitative, have been performed to investigate particular changes in the cognitive (or knowledge) structure, learning styles, motivation, and student attitudes towards Novak's concept mapping and to other strategies that are aimed to promote meaningful learning such as problem-based learning (Kinchin, Hay, & Adams, 2000; Kostovich, Poradzisz, Wood, & O'Brien, 2007; Laight, 2004, 2006; Rendas, Fonseca, & Pinto, 2006; Schmidt, 2004; West, Park, Pomeroy, & Sandoval, 2002).

This strategy has been mainly applied in biological sciences (Mintzes et al., 2005). Within medical education, most reporting has occurred in nursing. Other fields, such as veterinary, pharmacology and biomedical sciences, have published a lot less, but have applied it in a similar fashion. Reported areas covered topics such as the development of problem-solving skills, reporting clinical patient data, investigating student learning styles, and assessing knowledge acquisition. The activity of building cmaps promotes lifelong learning skills (Williams, 2004) and independent learning (Wilkes, Cooper, Lewin, & Batts, 1999) in medical students, and has positive implications for critical thinking, instruction, and easy visualization and interpretation of clinical data (Beitz, 1998; Schuster, 2000). Some of the benefits reported by medical educators mainly in nursing are now presented and later are discussed in relation to the pilot study.

Benefit One: The Advantage to Critical Analysis and Creative Thinking

All, Huycke, and Fisher (2003) summarized other experts' work to say, "…The experience of viewing and creating concept maps assist students in remaining attentive and on task when critically analysing new information (17, 18)" (p. 312). Beitz (1998) reported on a clear benefit; they may reduce the challenge of grasping critical learning issues, as they increase learning efficiency and decrease anxiety. Schuster (2000) and Hinck et al. (2006) have reported similar outcomes of employing cmaps instead of nursing plans in their courses. The former said that they were shown to enhance critical thinking skills and reasoning because students and faculty could clearly and succinctly visualise priorities and relationships of clinical patient data. While the latter said that they improved students' abilities to see patterns and relationships in the planning and evaluation of nursing care.

Benefit Two: Facilitating the Process of Transferring Theory into Practice

Cmaps facilitate the interpretation of patient instruction (L. H. Hill, 2006; Wilkes et al., 1999) or the process of synthesizing clinical experience to show knowledge gain (C. M. Hill, 2006). They have also been used to support nursing research and nursing research education, for identifying data collection, writing research proposals, clarify differing concepts and philosophies, and synthetising literature reviews (Beitz, 1998, p. 40).

Benefit Three: Planning Instruction, Examination, and Curriculum

Cmaps are often used for formative assessment (Beitz, 1998; Hinck et al., 2006; Williams, 2004). In an empirical study testing learning and satisfaction, Beitz (1998) has reported on using them in the process of formulating questions for quizzes during examination preparation and curriculum planning. In the latter, teachers find that they facilitate the representation of 1) cross-course integration of a nursing curriculum by drawing together major concepts, themes and relationships, and 2) theory-driven curriculum development or curricular revision: "We used concept mapping to track the use of systems theory as a thread pervading courses" (p. 40).

The three benefits for cmapping just described are revisited later in relation to the study results, which can be summarised in two aspects: the students learning to build cmaps to show knowledge acquisition, and putting clinical aviation theory into practice, by showing skills in making an aeromedical decision in the form of a cmap assignment.

Three Conditions for Faster Adoption in Medical Courses

Novak's concept mapping has yet to become mainstream as an evaluation method despite being recommended in several books on educational psychology (Gage & Berliner, 1992; Thornburg, 1984) and classroom assessment (Ainsworth & Viegut,

2006; Phye, 1997; Shermis & DiVesta, 2011). In relation to nursing education, Williams (2004) explains,

Since higher and nurse education became more modular, the predominant assessment strategy has been essay writing. While there have been innovations in teaching methods, assessment strategies have been slower to adopt student-centred approaches that make assessment part of the learning process (p. 33).

The following three conditions appear to be required for a faster adoption of cmaps as an assessment tool into a medical education course taught online and at a distance.

Condition One: Learning How to Build Good Concept Maps

In order to evaluate knowledge acquisition, the structural features of a cmap need to be incorporated into the thinking frameworks of resident doctors (West et al., 2002). Instructional design developed towards understanding its building rules (Novak & Cañas, 2006b) may only be successful if these fit within the pressing schedule under which the medical community teaches and studies.

Condition Two: Overcoming Preference for Traditional Study Styles

Novak (1998) and colleagues noticed in their studies that medical students displayed great resistance to the use of cmaps "… Their previous successes with rote-learning approaches [e.g. reciting, memory aids, clustering, and passive highlighting of notes/readings] make them very insecure in moving into meaningful learning strategies" (p. 195). Novak and Cañas (2006b, p. 9) continue to say that "learning style" differences are to a large extent derivative from differences in the patterns of learning that have been employed, varying from high commitment to rote-mode learning to almost exclusive commitment to meaningful mode learning. They add; it is not easy to help students in the former mode to move to patterns of learning of the latter mode. Some medical educators provide support for these claims about learning styles issues (Eitel & Steiner, 1999; Kostovich et al., 2007; Laight, 2006), while others show that with practice medical students can overcome limitations in representing knowledge with graphic organisers such as cmaps (Beitz, 1998; C. M. Hill, 2006; Wilkes et al., 1999; Williams, 2004). Hick and colleagues (2006) explain that this strategy requires people to use a set of patterns for learning that is different from the one used with more traditional assessment tools such as essay writing.

Condition Three: Development of Valid and Reliable Measuring Methods

One explanation for the paucity of research regarding the use of cmaps in summative assessment may arise from the concerns that its application is not primarily focused on final testing, but enhancing learning for understanding (Beitz, 1998; Hinck et al., 2006; Schuster, 2000; West et al., 2002; Williams, 2004). Schmidt (2004) says, "to advance this field of research [in medical education] it is critical to further explore the construct validity of concept maps generated by both direct and indirect methods as measures of knowledge structure" (p. 254). Some medical authors agree with Schmidt to a large extent (Daley et al., 2006, p. 27; Eitel & Steiner, 1999; Laight, 2004; West et al., 2002). However, it is important to note that these are reporting work performed in undergraduate courses where there is great emphasis in summative assessment of formative concepts, and in which cmaps have been used to replace exams of the multiple-choice variety.

On the other hand, the study reported in the coming sections took place in a postgraduate medical course, seeking to evaluate deep understanding of complex medical concepts in the form of essays or cmaps, and therefore, reliability and validity are achieved through different kinds of measures than the ones used in assessment of formative concepts.

Similarities and Differences between Concept Maps and Written Essays

Cmaps and written essays appear to have some similarities during assessment. Both approaches can be used to evaluate complex medical knowledge, are prone to marker bias, and have low validity and reliability.

Watson (1998) says cmaps can be counted among those tools that enhance understanding of a constantly increasing and complex body of medical knowledge. His claim is representative of other medical authors cited in the section reporting on benefits. In a similar fashion, written essays are used in online and off-line postgraduate and undergraduate courses seeking to evaluate complex thinking. Gage and Berliner (1992) explain that an essay question is useful when evaluating a student's ability to organise and carry out an attack on a fairly complex problem. The writing activity may demand all the cognitive processes of Bloom's taxonomy: knowing, comprehending, applying, analysing, synthesising, and evaluating.

O'Neil and Klein (1997) have reported that "on the same topic, concept maps and essays correlate about 0.7, which indicates reasonable evidence that they are measuring similar things" (p. 3). Through a study performed for the National Center for Evaluation, Standards and Student Testing (CRESST), they investigated the development and testing of a computerised system for automated evaluation of cmaps, created with paper-and-pencil, by thousands of students in American schools. Their overall aim was to look for a replacement to multiple-choice questions.

In terms of being prone to marker bias, written essays and cmaps require knowledge expert input for judging the validity and importance of their content. These quotes further explain:

Because answers are so complex, [essay questions] are hard to score reliably. Here reliability means agreement among teachers scoring the same test (Gage & Berliner, 1992, p. 633).

[the focus on reliability] should be on inter-rater reliability (do people scoring the maps agree), and the internal reliability of the measure (Coffey et al., 2003, p. 27).

The similarities just described are only logical if it is remembered that cmaps were invented as a visual tool " to translate [hundreds of written] interview transcripts into a hierarchical structure of concepts, and relationships between concepts, i.e., propositions." Underpinned by three aspects of Ausubel's (1978) Assimilation Theory, the template's structural design facilitated researchers to observe 1) patterns in how children's cognitive structures of science concepts were changing over time, and 2) that propositions used by children would usually improve in relevance, number, and quality with instruction (Novak & Cañas, 2006a, p. 177).

The difference between both strategies lies in the following activity. A cmap visual structure is easier to interpret than an essay word-based structure because the human capacity to quickly recognize patterns in images may help people (in this case lecturer and students) to explicitly see the nature and role of concepts and the relationship between them in a particular piece of knowledge (e.g. risk management in clinical aviation medicine). This is one of the three reasons, presented near the start of this section, as to why cmaps are considered "so powerful" in the facilitation of meaningful learning (Novak & Gowin, 1984).

In this "background" section, Novak's cmaps have been defined, and the structural components, and characteristics illustrated. Three benefits leading to easy visualisation and attentive representation of complex medical concepts were briefly introduced, and followed by the conditions that might facilitate its faster adoption in a medical study programme. Similarities and differences between cmaps and essays were also established. These topics are revisited in the "discussion" section in relation to the study outcomes. But first, the qualitative research methodology used for this pilot study is described.

CASE STUDY APPROACH

As far as we are aware, this pilot may be the first in medical education to incorporate cmaps for assessment in an online medical postgraduate course. The literature reporting on its application in other medical teaching was quite informative on asserting its benefits for evaluating learning for understanding (Beitz, 1998; Eitel & Steiner, 1999; C. M. Hill, 2006; L. H. Hill, 2006; Hinck et al., 2006; Schmidt, 2004; Schuster, 2000; Wilkes et al., 1999; Williams, 2004). Like this pilot, those projects' instructional design were implemented according to specific student group characteristics and supported by established foundational literature (Mintzes et al., 2005; Novak, 1998, 2004; Novak & Gowin, 1984). However, they were of limited use in the sense that the projects reported were carried out face to face with undergraduate students. This pilot differs in that it explores ways to implement cmapping in a course that is performed via online delivery, using e-learning technologies, and for mature students who are full-time employed medical professionals.

Since there were not previous studies to consult, the case study approach was chosen because it is often used in many fields, including education, for knowing about an issue that has not yet been systematically researched. Paraphrasing Stake (1995, p. 8), the real business of the case study is particularization, not generalization. A particular case is taken and the primary objective is to know it well, not how different it is from others, but what it is and what it does. The emphasis is on understanding the case itself.

Edwards (2001), Rolfe (2001), and Siraj-Blatchford and Siraj-Blatchford (2001) say that this approach is for investigating research questions in depth through the observation of people in their own context and with the purpose of building an understanding about their interactions and behaviours in relation to a problem or situation being investigated. They continue to say that mixed data collection methods and instruments increase the value and the insights obtained in case study research.

Flyvbjerg (2006) says, through intense observation and participation in the activities of the social world enabled by the case study method, a researcher can cast off preconceived notions and theories. Intense observation is an activity, a central element in learning and in achieving new insights.

...the proximity to reality, which the case study entails, and the learning processes that it generates for the researcher will often constitute a prerequisite for advanced understanding... More simple forms of understanding must yield to more complex ones as one moves from beginner to expert' (pp. 236-237).

Research Questions

The case study approach was found appropriate for exploring four aims for the pilot that emerged from conversations with the two lecturers who taught the "clinical aviation medicine" subject (or AVMX 714 paper, a term used in New Zealand universities to mean course). The aims were to study and explore the suitability of cmaps as an alternative assessment tool to written essays, which shaped the research questions (RQ) discussed later in the relevant section:

RQ1: How effective can cmaps be as a learning tool?
RQ2: How easily might students embrace cmaps?
RQ3: Can potential problems using cmaps in our courses be identified?
RQ4: Determine whether cmaps may likely be something we can use regularly in AVMX courses

Research Design

With a time investment (TI) of 378 hours, the pilot was undertaken in three stages during semester II of 2007 and 2008:

1. A literature review was performed on Novak's cmapping, cmapping in medical education, and automated assessment with cmaps (TI: 54 hours).
2. An instructional design was implemented for teaching concept mapping via online resources and within a 10-day period (TI: 50 hours).
3. A demonstration pilot based on a semester-long case study was performed where students learned to build cmaps, and employed them to represent acquired technical knowledge as part of assignments (TI: 274 hours).

Organising Participation and Establishing Roles within the Study

In a two-hour workshop early in February 2008, the instructor taught the two lecturers how to read and build cmaps using paper with magnetic backings and a marker on a whiteboard. Due to tight work schedules, it was not possible to work with the related software technologies. After this activity, they agreed to run the pilot study in the second semester of 2008 and; once the following requirements were fulfilled:

[The] students [have become] familiar with the demands and style of an [Aviation Medicine] paper, and therefore, [are] more likely to be open-minded toward something different

Concept mapping relied on computer technology [e.g. CmapTools software], and those students who were technophobes would have had a semester getting used to Oceanbrowser [the conferencing system and forum service] etc (personal email communication, February 18, 2008).

The study participants comprised: the lecturer teaching the subject (the third author), a cmapping instructor (from now on called instructor), and six students situated in New Zealand, Australia, and the United Kingdom. The lecturer carried out the main study programme, decided at which points the students should engage with cmapping, and also assessed the cmaps produced for assignments. The instructor developed the instructional design, worked with the students, the lecturer, and aviation programme coordinator (second author), and collected and analysed the data gathered during the course. Pseudonyms have been used to protect the students' identities. They are referred to as Jim, Seth, Samuel, Nancy, Danielle, and Timothy.

The Concept Mapping Instruction

The lecturer allocated 10-hours in weeks 2 and 3 of the semester (from a total of 16 weeks) for the students to practice and learn to build "good" cmaps, so they could apply the skills acquired in the first assignment in week 10. The instruction was designed to meet his teaching plan.

The first objective was twofold and involved teaching students 1) the steps in building a cmap by using the eight procedures published on the CmapTools software Website (2007), and 2) to self-evaluate their cmaps according to the approach reported by Kinchin et al. (2000). These authors' classification of spoke, net, and chain structures may quickly and easily help a student self-evaluate and identify structural issues within a cmap.

The second objective was learning to build cmaps with the CmapTools software, which incorporates features to attach resources (e.g. videos, images, and PDF documents), record map-building steps, and publish them online for sharing via the CmapServer (Cañas, Hill, et al., 2004). Figure 3 shows a cmap with images, videos, and other documents attached.

The instructor provided feedback on the ease of building cmaps during the instructional period and before the first assignment was due (week 10). Virtual interactions with the students were mainly asynchronous via email and synchronous via two teleconferences. One-to-one synchronous instruction was available at an individual's request. An online forum monitored by the instructor and a Website (see Figure 3) which included video tutorials (http://bit.ly/ZwMaUL), examples of medical cmaps, and other resources were set up. Around week 5, the initial 10-hour instruction developed was further refined to fit within a 4-hour instruction, to ac-

Figure 3. Welcome page of the online training on concept maps. By clicking on the icons below the boxed-concepts, students opened menus for accessing study resources. (Zoom in for details or access at http://www.gloriagomez.com/cmaptraining)

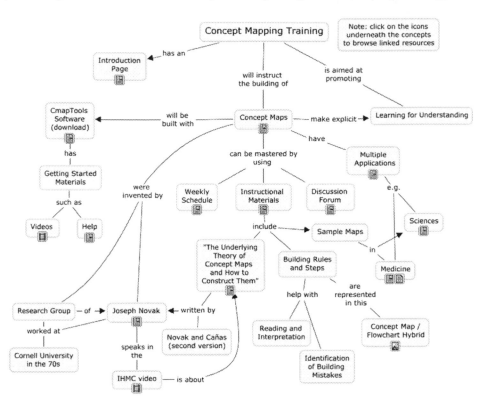

commodate those beginning the course late. The shorter instruction included access to a recorded teleconference of week 2 and a summary document explaining (with examples) each step for building a "good" cmap.

Methods and Instruments for Data Gathering

Participant observation was the method chosen for learning and achieving new insights about this community. The researchers were the instructor (first author and principal researcher) and the lecturer (third author). The first author immersed herself in the world of the lecturer and students of this distance medical course, and from there gathered information and elaborated a meaningful (or well-substantiated) story to support and/or challenge the research questions. The lecturer made space in his class for cmapping activities to happen, at key moments motivated the students to persevere, and provided insights on the relevance (or not) of the activities performed.

The data were gathered using observations, unstructured interviews, and open-ended questionnaires. The software CmapTools, GotoMeeting, and the Ocean-browser's conferencing system were used and all have recording features. Therefore, the cmapping process of each student, the sessions in which the lecturer and the instructor evaluated the student cmaps, and teleconferences could all be recorded for later task analysis.

The qualitative data analysis was informed by rich unstructured data (e.g. email communication, cmap assignments, transcripts of conversations during assessment, and video-recorded activities) organised into three main themes.

Theme One: the cmap assignments revealed (or not) student understanding of the course topics. At the lecturer's request, each student built a cmap for assignment-1 that answered a focus question related to technical knowledge in "clinical aviation medicine." For example, "how would we make an aeromedical decision in a case of Meniere's disease?" (Figure 4 and Figure 5). Students were to submit an essay for assignment-2 and offered a choice of submitting a cmap for assignment-3.

Theme Two: marking-related activities during cmap assessment were evaluated to establish (or not) efficiency and relevance. The lecturer, together with the instructor, performed synchronous on-screen marking of the cmap-assignments submitted on time and asynchronous on-screen marking of the late submissions. The evaluative comments were audio-recorded using the GoToMeeting software.

Theme Three: student and teacher opinion provided evidence (or not) on the use, relevance, and acceptability of concept maps as an alternative assessment tool in the course. The evidence was given in the form of answered unstructured questionnaires and email communication sustained during the course. The students showed their preference or dislike in conversations with the instructor, with the lecturer and instructor together.

How the Data Collected was used in the Analysis

Table 1 presents each research question (left column), and what data excerpts were employed to argue it (middle column). Finally, the excerpts were associated with the theoretical aspects introduced in the "background" section (right column) to answer the respective question.

This section has introduced the methodology and methods used in this pilot. The case study approach was chosen to inform the research design, as there are no prec-

Table 1. Data excerpts and background literature used in the research analysis

Research Questions	Relevant Data Excerpts	Relation to Background Literature

How effective can cmaps be as a learning tool?	• Students' marks obtained for assignments 1, 2, and 3
	• Marking guidelines for written essays and concept maps (Table 2)
	• Transcript excerpts from the audio-recorded session in which the lecturer and instructor evaluated and marked the cmaps and student performance
		• Cmaps can facilitate the representation and evaluation of complex medical concepts; three benefits
		• Three conditions for faster incorporation in medical courses:
		  o Learning how to build "good" concept maps
		  o Overcoming preference for traditional learning styles
		  o Development of valid and reliable measuring methods

How easily might students embrace cmaps? Identify potential problems using cmaps in our courses	• Excerpts from email communication that state benefits, or potential problems, or possible ways for adoption of cmaps • Questionnaire responses stating individual students' perception of the use of cmaps • Transcript excerpts from the audio-recorded session "marking a concept map assignment" in which the lecturer provided his opinion on the benefits and potential issues that could emerge from using this assessment tool in the courses	
Determine whether cmaps may likely be something we can use regularly in AVMX courses	• Time analysis of tasks (activities) associated with "the process of marking a concept-map assignment" • Email communication between the instructor and the lecture in which the latter talks about the time, he thinks that he spends on the evaluation of individual 3000-word written assignments	• Might improve staff marking efficiency, and therefore, timely student feedback • Cmaps and written essays present similar strengths and weaknesses during assessment for deep understanding • Easy visualisation and attentive representation of complex medical concepts

edents of research with distance postgraduate medical education and Novak's cmaps. The lecturers teaching the course formulated the research questions, when and how the study participants should be engaged. The concept mapping instruction, and underpinning theoretical literature, was briefly described, as this aspect is pivotal for enabling students to correctly author cmaps to be submitted for assessment. Several data gathering methods and instruments were employed to capture diverse study activities, undertaken synchronously and asynchronously, in this distance course with mature medical professionals. In the next sections, three research outcomes are presented:

- The process of marking a cmap assignment
- Student and teacher acceptability of cmap assignments
- Determining cmaps are faster to mark than written essays

RESULT: THE PROCESS OF MARKING A CONCEPT-MAP ASSIGNMENT

The lecturer evaluated the cmap assignments from a content perspective, and together with the instructor, from a structural perspective.

Table 2 shows assignment assessment guidelines that we designed based on the scoring system the lecturer usually employs for written essays. In both cases, the assignments were evaluated based on their technical medical content; logical argument, approach and reasoning; research and referencing, as well as presentation and layout. Only additional comments for the cmap assignment were provided since the students were familiar with doing written assignments in the master programme. For example, guideline "… appropriate hierarchy in the defining of the concepts" should be achieved through a "well- designed hierarchical organisation of concepts [that] reveals the logic of the argument and reasoning" (see left column, second cell). The descriptions and examples given during instruction were to be followed for obtaining these five marks.

Table 2. The assignment assessment guidelines were used in the evaluation of essays and concept maps. Students were advised to follow them during the preparation of their individual assignments.

Lecturer's Guidelines for Written Essays	Lecturer and Instructor's Guidelines for Concept Maps
8 marks for technical medical content	8 marks for technical medical content Make sure that relevant technical [medical] concepts are included in the map
5 marks for logical argument, approach and reasoning	5 marks for appropriate hierarchy in the defining of the concepts Well-designed hierarchical organisation of concepts reveals the logic of the argument and reasoning
4 marks for research and referencing	4 marks for research and referencing You can link references, Websites, and text documents to your map. To learn how to do this, please see video tutorial
3 marks for presentation and layout	3 marks for presentation and layout Make sure your map is easy to read, if the map has become too big for printing on an A4 page, place some of that content in sub-maps and link them back to the main map. Use the alignment and the curve line features [of CmapTools] to help readability (again, see video tutorial of last teleconference on concept mapping)
20 marks in total	20 marks in total

Note: 3 marks for submission on or before due date. These are applied by reducing 3 marks for those who do NOT submit in time

The traditional scoring (or marking) systems for cmapping focusing on the evaluation of a cmap's structural aspects (Hinck et al., 2006; Novak & Gowin, 1984; Trowbridge & Wandersee, 2005) were not applied. The lecturer and instructor never discussed this decision. In retrospect, however, it would not have been possible to apply those scoring systems for two reasons. First, the lecturer's assessment was focused on the right answer to an aeromedical decision during risk assessment; his interest was not associated with weighting and assigning points for valid propositions, levels of hierarchy, number of branchings, cross links, and specific examples. Second, this study's main purpose was to find ways to incorporate this new tool into his existing assessment approaches.

Table 3 shows that Jim, Nancy, and Samuel obtained similar marks with either assignment (the marks of Jim and Nancy's cmap assignment are slightly higher and Samuel's slightly lower). Nancy obtained higher marks for the cmap assignments than for the written assignment. Seth and Timothy obtained higher marks for the written assignments than for the cmap assignment. Danielle obtained high marks for the cmap assignment, but there are no written assignment marks to compare with because she decided to complete her studies in a later year.

In the next three subsections, the cmap assignments of Nancy, Samuel and Seth are analysed to illustrate the logic behind marking a cmap with highest scores, good scores, or low scores by the lecturer and the instructor with the support of the guidelines (Table 2). The analysis of Jim's, Danielle's, and Timothy's cmaps are referred to when appropriate in the reporting of these results, but due to space limitations, figures have not been included. A summary of all the marks awarded to students grouped by their performance is presented. However, the main focus of this section is on the activities demonstrating that the lecturer was able to assess technical medical content.

Table 3. Students' marks obtained for three assignments during the semester pilot

Student Name	Concept Map		Written Essay	
	Assignment 1	Assignment 3	Assignment 2	Assignment 3
Jim	19 marks		17 marks	16 marks
Seth	10 marks		16 marks	17 marks
Samuel	15 marks		17 marks	16 marks
Nancy	20 marks	18 marks	17 marks	
*Danielle	18 marks		no marks	no marks
Timothy	13 marks		14 marks	16 marks

* Applied for Terms Carried Over (TCO). This means she will take the exam in a later year

Cmaps with Highest Scores

Nancy obtained a full mark of 19 (see Table 3), comprised as follows:

- 8 marks for technical medical content
- 5 marks for appropriate hierarchy in the defining of concepts
- 3 marks for presentation and layout
- 3 marks for submission on or before the due date

Top scores, 8 out of 8 marks, were obtained for the representation of technical medical content in assignment-1. Her two cmaps (Figure 4 and Figure 5) answered the focus question "How would we make an aeromedical decision in a case of Meniere's disease?" The lecturer explained:

[Nancy] talked about all the possible options... etiology,... pathogenesis,... diagnosis,... lifestyle management, surgery, other means of dealing with it. So, it is really very complete. If you read this concept map [see Figure 5], you'll get a complete idea about what Meniere's disease is and how to decide whether or not the person is able to get back into aviation...

The cmaps also obtained good marks for appropriate hierarchical representation, referencing and layout. Concept representation was concise and the ideas were organised in a semi-hierarchical manner that revealed the logic behind the argument, further enhanced by a clean layout and the choice of presenting information in two cmaps. The linked resources (e.g. see icons below concept "stage of illness") took to references in the form of Websites or journal articles. Each cmap had only four minor mistakes related to linking phrase misrepresentation, which did not prevent the lecturer from assessing the content.

Students Jim and Danielle not only obtained top marks, 7 out of 8, for technical medical content in their respective cmap assignments, but also for appropriate hierarchical representation in concept definition, research and referencing, presentation and layout. When asked why these students obtained one mark less than Nancy, the lecturer explained:

You give someone 8 [marks] when [the student]'s got absolutely everything that you can think of... to someone... absolutely outstanding, ... [Nancy]'s come up with something which nobody thought of...

Figure 4. Concept map assignment with high scores by Nancy, answering the focus question "How would we make an aeromedical decision in a case of Meniere's disease?" Cmap 1 of 2 that the lecturer read and evaluated in 1.87 minutes. He said that it introduces the stages of the illness, the type of evidence and recommendations to be taken into account during the decision-making process. Minor building mistakes, misconstrued linking phrases, are highlighted within dashed circle. (Zoom in to see details or access online at http://bit.ly/TpbJDO)

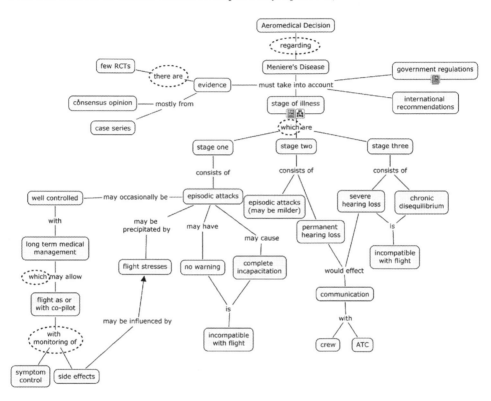

Cmaps with Good Scores

Samuel obtained a full mark of 15 (Table 3), comprised as follows:

- 6 marks for technical medical content
- 3 marks for appropriate hierarchy in the defining of concepts
- 4 marks for research and referencing
- 2 marks for presentation and layout

Figure 5. Concept map assignment with high scores by Nancy. Cmap 2 of 2 that the lecturer read and evaluated in 1.37 minutes. He said "If you read this concept map, you'll get a complete idea about what Meniere's disease is and how to decide whether or not the person is able to get back into aviation…" because it talks about all the possible options: etiology, pathogenesis, diagnosis, lifestyle management, surgery, other means of dealing with it. Minor building mistakes, misconstrued linking phrases, are highlighted with dash circles. (Zoom in for details or access at http://bit.ly/RN1MRT)

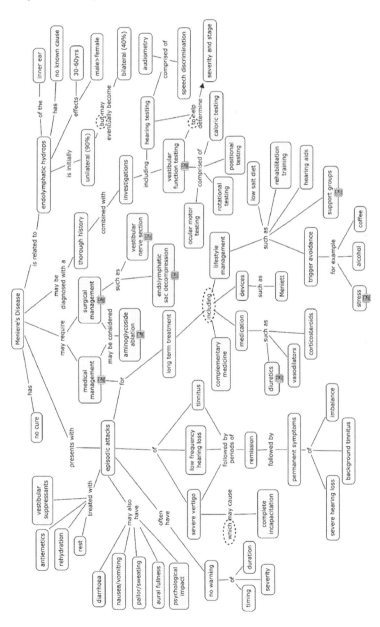

Good scores, 6 out of 8 marks, were obtained on the representation of technical medical content in assignment-1. The cmap (Figure 6) was incomplete and did not fully answer the question "How would we make an aeromedical decision in a case of hearing loss?" It does not represent concepts explaining the basis of a decision made. The lecturer explained:

[Samuel] got lot of information there, and I think that it's well ordered... [T]alks about how the decisions would be made and that decision ends abruptly. ... You see "Pure tone testing" and "in-flight noise simulation"... The "DME" is done, the "Audiometry" is done... [Samuel] looked at that and then a decision has been made. But there is no explanation as to what is the basis of that decision. This part of the screen [meaning left side of the cmap] needs to be linked in some way to the right side of the screen [again referring to the cmap] that talks about if there is adequate functional hearing for the person to communicate properly or not. So that is not there and that's why I won't give him 7 marks [a high score] for this. I give him 6 [marks]

(The concepts mentioned in the quote above "Pure tone testing," "in-flight" noise simulation" and "audiometry" have been marked with * in the cmap.)

In addition, the cmap lost 3 marks for inappropriate hierarchical organisation in concept definition and 2 marks for presentation and layout. Some linking phrases were erroneously built. The concepts were placed too close together, without space in between, which made it hard to read. Another building iteration was probably needed for obtaining a clean look that enhanced readability.

Similarly to Samuel's cmap, Timothy obtained 5 out of 8 marks for technical medical content because of a conceptual misunderstanding in relation to the focus question. Timothy's low overall mark of 13 out of 20 was due to late submission and for not including the references. He obtained 3 marks for hierarchical organisation of concepts and lost 1 mark for poor representation of four linking phrases and poor hierarchical arrangement of a cmap's section.

Cmaps with Low Scores

Seth obtained a full mark of 10 (see Table 3), comprised as follows:

- 4 marks for technical content
- 3 marks for appropriate hierarchy in the defining of the concepts
- 1 mark for research and referencing
- 2 marks for presentation and layout

Figure 6. Concept map assignment with good scores by Samuel. The cmap answers the focus question "How would we make an aeromedical decision in case of a hearing loss?" The lecturer read and evaluated it in 2.84 minutes. He said, "there is no explanation as to what is the basis of that decision." The content of the left side needs to be linked to the right side "that talks about if there is adequate functional hearing for the person to communicate properly or not." Building mistakes, misconstrued linking phrases and concepts, are highlighted with dashed circles and rectangles. (Zoom in for details or access at http://bit.ly/Ruu0iO)

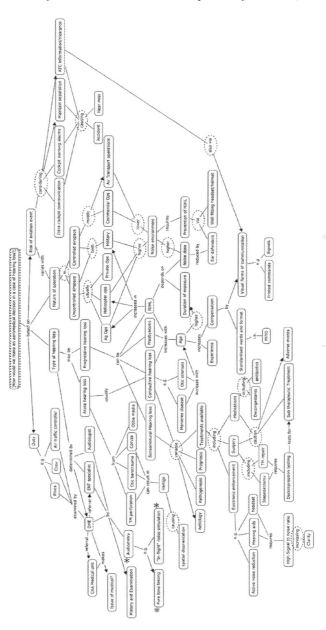

Figure 7. Concept map assignment receiving low scores by Seth. The cmap answered the focus question "How do we make an aeromedical decision in the case of multifocal contact lenses?" The lecturer read and evaluated it in 1.32. He said that it describes all the types of lenses, visual differences, a lot of other things. But, it does not describe the issues of multimodal focal lenses: "... bifocal glasses that you know, you can move your eyes to different parts whether multifocal contact lenses you cannot move your eyes..." Building mistakes and misconstrued linking phrases are highlighted with dashed circles. (Zoom in for details or access at http:// bit.ly/UvZMjQ)

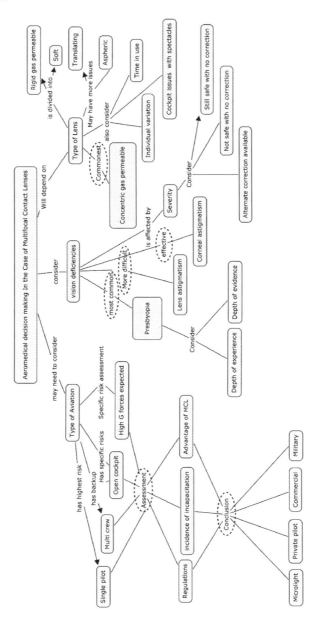

Low scores, 4 out of 8 marks, were obtained for representation of technical medical concepts in assignment-1. This cmap (Figure 7) does not address the focus question. Some relevant concepts dealing with contact lenses have been represented, but it is missing concepts related to multifocal lenses. The lecturer explained:

[Seth] has not provided information. The question is how to make... [an] aero-medical decision on multifocal contact lenses. What happens in multifocal contact lenses? [the lecturer is thinking aloud] It's that some parts are not clear... It's like using bifocal glasses, but the problem is [that] bifocal glasses that you know, you can move your eyes to different parts but with multifocal contact lenses you can not move your eyes. So your vision is degraded at some level for, I mean, some distances at all times. And that issue has not been described at all in this chart [meaning this cmap]. I mean [Seth] talks about all the types of lenses, [Seth] talks about visual differences, [Seth] talks about a lot of other things. Some of that is useful, but if this had been a written assignment, I would have marked [Seth] very low on content, because there's no mention of the issues of multifocal contact lenses.

Hierarchical representation of concepts is reasonable, but the student lost marks for cmap readability due to misconstruction of linking phrases, leading in turn, to preventing the process of making relationships among represented concepts. Seth's cmap obtained the lowest mark out of those submitted for assignments 1 and 3. Difficulties with computer technology and returning to academic study after 25 years might explain this student's poor performance during the activity. These topics are reported in more detailed in section "student and lecturer attitudes and acceptability."

In this section, the process of evaluating and marking three cmap assignments has been illustrated to show the decision making associated with awarding low, good or high scores. Five students out of six did well in the assignments with minor differences. The cmaps revealed students ability (or not) to relate clinical content to aviation situations. Gaps in knowledge were identified, for example (Figure 6) by pointing out what concepts are missing. Nancy's cmaps demonstrate that it is possible to represent understanding of medical knowledge with an alternative assessment tool. Her cmaps allowed the lecturer to assess that she had taken into account every aspect in the process of making an aeromedical decision: etiology, pathogenesis, diagnosis, lifestyle management, surgery, and other treatment and management (Figure 4 and Figure 5).

RESULT: FASTER TO MARK THAN WRITTEN ASSIGNMENTS

Table 4 presents the results of the time analysis performed on the marking-related tasks (activities). The process of marking 12 cmaps took approximately 15.5 minutes. While the process of marking a single written assignment of 2000-3000 words might take, as reported by the lecturer, 15 minutes (Table 5) or more.

Table 4. Analysis of the time spent by the lecturer reading 12 cmaps for assignments 1 and 3

Student Pseudonym	Time in Minutes Spent by Lecturer in Reading Concept Map (cmap) for an Assignment				
	Cmaps Built per Assignment	**Assignment 1**	**Minutes**	**Assignment 3**	**Minutes**
Jim	1	Cmap 1 – very big	**1.67 min**		
Seth	1	Cmap 1	**1.32 min**		
Samuel	1	Cmap 1 (big)	**2.84 min**		
Nancy	4	Cmap 1	**1.82 min**	Cmap 1*	**1.91 min**
		Cmap 2	**1. 37 min**	Cmap 2*	
Danielle	4	Main Cmap (big)	**1.06 min**		
		Cmap 2	**0.96 min**		
		Cmap 3 (small)			
		Cmap 4 (small)	**0.8 min**		
		5 assignments	**11.84 min**		
Timothy	1	Cmap 1*	**1. 66 min**		
Total	**12 cmaps**	**6 assignments**	**13.5 min**	**1 assignment**	**1.91 min**
Summary: 12 cmaps assignments equal 15.41 min					

* Late submissions

Table 5. Time spent by lecturer in assessing written assignments (a loose estimation)

Time Spent by Lecturer in Assessment of Written Essay Includes Note-Taking	
Assignments 2 and 3	
Task one	Lecturer reads through all assignments
Task two	Lecturer goes back and takes notes taking *15 minutes approx. each assignment*
7 assignments X 15 minutes = 105 minutes or 1.75hours (lecturer alone, time estimation)	

Time Spent in Assessment: The audiorecording of the assessment meeting was analysed to calculate the time spent reading, discussing, and marking each student's cmap(s). The meeting lasted 1h 22min 09sec (including resolution of technical mishaps and general conversation). Table 4 presents the exact time in minutes that the lecturer took to read and evaluate each cmap representing assignments 1 and 3. Within this period, he was able to determine why a student cmap(s) deserved 8, 7, 6 or 5 marks (see Table 2) for medical technical content. The following tasks were performed during the analysis:

- The instructor opened the cmap using CmapTools on her computer and used GotoMeeting to share the screen with the lecturer
- The lecturer read the cmap for evaluating technical medical content
- The instructor asked the lecturer to explain the reasons for awarding particular marks to a student cmap assignment
- The lecturer provided marks for technical content (either 8, 7, 6, 4 marks)
- The instructor provided comments from a building-rules perspective
- The instructor and lecturer discussed this perspective plus other issues in relation to the student performance
- The instructor and lecturer assigned full marks while the instructor took notes for the final report that would be given to the student

Cmaps marked with * were late submissions and were evaluated asynchronously in weeks 15 or 16. The lecturer evaluated them using a Web-version (created with CmapTools by the instructor) because it was not possible to meet synchronously due to clashing schedules. The lecturer timed himself during the evaluation of Timothy's cmap assignment-1 and Nancy's cmaps assignment-3, and emailed the details to the instructor.

Time Spent in Assessment of Written Essays: In an email, the lecturer described the tasks involved in this activity. "I take about 15 minutes to assess [each of] the assignments. I first read them all, and then go back and read one critically to assess it." Table 5 shows a hypothetical loose calculation of the total time, 105 minutes, that would take him to read seven student assignments.

The lecturer marked and assessed the validity of the technical medical content of 7 student cmap-assignments without reading them a second time in approximately 15.5 minutes (Table 4). The lecturer self-reported that marking and assessing the content validity of one written essay of 2,000 or 3,000 words takes him 15 minutes and requires him to go over it more than once. Therefore, it can be stated that he can assess conceptual validity faster with a cmap assignment (see Table 4) than with a written assignment (see Table 5). Nancy's cmap 2 was read in 1.37 minutes

(Figure 4), Samuel's cmap 1 in 2.84 minutes (Figure 6), and Seth's cmap 1 in 1.32 minutes (Figure 7). Finally, Danielle's small cmap 4 representing only a few related concepts was read in 0.8 minutes.

These results should not be generalised. A formal comparative study would need to be designed to investigate the claim that a lecturer with great expert knowledge in clinical aviation can read and evaluate 12 cmap assignments of varied sizes in the same 15-minute period that he can read and evaluate a single written assignment of 2000 to 3000 words.

RESULT: ACCEPTABILITY OF CONCEPT MAPS

The use of cmaps had variable student acceptability because of the effort and time investment required for students to achieve the cmapping skills, in addition to undertaking the "clinical aviation medicine" course. The lecturer found the cmap assignments quite useful in revealing knowledge acquisition, but he had difficulties judging the reasons for a mistake. Was this because of a lack of knowledge or an inability to build a "good" cmap?

Three students completed the questionnaire evaluating the cmapping training and assignments. Their responses present differing viewpoints and identify issues that should be considered before implementation in regular semesters. One student found cmaps useful for representing learning, while two did not. Table 6 shows the questions asked and transcripts of individual comments.

Jim, who obtained 7 marks (a high score), said that assimilating building rules was very hard, which in turn made the cmapping process undesirable, tedious, and irrelevant to his learning as well as demoralising and not enjoyable to the point where he considered quitting the course, or in his words the " whole study module." This total rejection and frustration did not affect his production of well-built cmaps and ability to represent what he learned with them. You can access a Web version of cmap 1 at http://bit.ly/14Necyq and cmap 2 at http://bit.ly/UhohLK.

Seth, who obtained 4 marks (a low score), said that difficulties with the under-lying principles and proficient use of the technology prevented him from building "good" cmaps. This student was familiar with mapping techniques stating, "I use White board work with flow charts, priorities, relationships etc." Struggling with the CmapTools software combined with this distance course being his first academic study in a long time might offer other explanations for the student's low performance in this assignment. He commented:

… This is the first study course I have undertaken in 25 years and my study techniques are rusty, plus my confidence is low.

Table 6. Attitudinal responses of three students show their acceptability (or not) of using cmaps as an alternative assessment tool

Question Asked via Email Communication	Jim	Seth	Samuel
Did you find concept mapping useful as tool for representing learning?	No	No	Yes
Was it useful to your learning process to prepare your assignment 1 in the form of a concept map?	I did not It is important to understand the process to ensure I am able to correctly interpret concept maps. I do not feel that my ability (or lack of ability) to constuct [sic] a concept map accurately reflects my understanding or depth of knowledge of the of [sic] the subject depicted by the concept map I personally find the process of constructing a map, slow, tedious and of minimal or no benefit to my learning. I found the concept mapping process demoralising and not enjoyable almost to the extent of deciding to abandon the whole study module	I was struggling to get the underlying principles as well as the technology together - due to that I felt I could not express my knowledge on the subject. I found this frustrating.	Yes it was useful. I found it refreshing to be able to represent information in a different way. I normally study by writing copious notes. It also helped me to realise how different topics are related to each other aiding my recall of the subject.

In reviewing his performance, Seth produced some poor practice cmaps and good practice cmaps during the training programme in weeks 1 and 2, and before assignment-1 was due in week 10. One practice cmap he built selected for blind-commentary, in the second teleconference on cmapping, demonstrated (to the lecturer and instructor) that he understood the building rules, even though there were important technical medical concepts missing. Therefore, the instructor assumed the student's issues were of content, and not of a structural cmapping, nature. This student never requested one-to-one help, which was available, nor did he let the teaching staff know about his lack of confidence regarding computer and study skills. For these reasons, the instructor failed to identify that he was struggling. However, this issue should have not been unexpected. The course lecturers know that students enrolling in the master studies need a period of adjustment to the technologies used for distance engagement. For this reason, they suggested the pilot be run in the second semester.

Samuel, who obtained 6 marks (a good score), found cmaps a "refreshing" alternative to taking written essays, and claimed that they aided him in the process of recalling the subject, and identifying how different topics relate to each other. As a consequence of these benefits, he decided to use cmaps to "study anatomy" which is another course within the master programme.

Jim and Seth, who expressed concerns at the start of the pilot, were contacted via personal emails. These were also addressed in the second teleconference on concept mapping by using some references and examples from Novak and Cañas (2006b). In this paper they say that a skillful cmapping instruction should include topics illustrating the obvious differences between individual's abilities in learning. The topics should cover how the brain mechanisms and knowledge organisation works during a learning process, and the broad ranges of differences in human abilities for various kinds of learnings and performance.

Explanations by the instructor and the lecturer were given on cmapping being a new language with its own set of rules for communicating and representing acquired knowledge. This visual language, its pattern concept → linking phrase → concept, could be quite different and hard for medical students like them, as proficient writers since primary school and now experts in representing knowledge with written assignments. The lecturer also offered to adjust the mark of the cmap assignment, if this was lower in comparison to those obtained with the written assignment. He added:

The important thing here, is NOT for all of us to become expert concept mappers... The aim is to get enough of the skill we need, so that if we decide we want to use this for something else, that we have the basics in place. Most importantly, the process of making the concept maps forces us to think about the subject content, and that thinking is what the whole process of learning is all about. So look past the frustration of the medium, and look at the content. Making a concept map about the use of SSRIs [selective serotonin reuptake inhibitors] or warfarin, or viagra ... will require us to think about the concepts and that is what is important! (Personal Communication, August 10, 2008).

In the above message the lecturer has stated his viewpoint as to the relevance of cmaps to the formative assessment process, which helped students to see the positive aspects of using the cmap template (pattern), and dismiss the frustrating amount of effort that is required to learn a new tool. The first reason is that it "forces" their thinking about the concepts underpinning an aeromedical decision. The second reason is that the process of learning is about making connections among relevant concepts in relation to a focus question. Samuel supports this comment when he writes that cmaps "…helped me to realise how different topics are related to each other aiding my recall of the subject."

During the cmap assessment meeting, the instructor and the lecturer had the following exchange that is quite telling of his position on the use of cmaps as an alternative assessment tool in his course:

Instructor: *Is it easier for you to analyse the students' knowledge with the map... in comparison to evaluating essays? What do you think about concept mapping? Do you think it's more efficient, faster?... Is there any advantage of doing it like this?*

Lecturer: *I think there are difficulties. If a person has made a mistake in a concept map, it would be difficult to know if there is a problem of understanding or if there is a problem of concept mapping knowledge. It could well be that a person made a mistake because of poor concept mapping understanding, rather than poor knowledge understanding. So when we do a written assignment everybody knows that you can read and write, have been doing it for 35 years or 40 years. So everybody knows how to do that. So there is no chance of that error being available there. So if a person wrote something wrongly you know that he not understood it rightly. So there is a clear, a clear link between what is written and the knowledge or the lack of it. Where in this concept mapping, there may be in an error, one or two [in] places...*

The study results regarding student and lecture acceptability show that cmap assignments could be as effective as written assignments in helping students show understanding of a complex piece of medical knowledge. However, a lecturer might only view these positive results as supporting a switch to cmaps, if it could be guaranteed that all the students in a course can build "good" cmaps before the formative assessment period.

GENERAL DISCUSSION

Outcomes of the cmapping instruction were:

- All students but one could build cmaps after an online instruction. A flexible instructional programme can be developed, as short as 10-hours and undertaken within a 2-week period, or as short as 4-hours and undertaken within a one-to-three day period. Cmaps were built with CmapTools software.
- Instruction should be accompanied of context-relevant educational resources. For instance, lecturers could present students with video tutorials and relatable examples showing how medical concepts can be visualised in the form of a cmap.

- Synchronous meetings such as audio-conferences, but most importantly, asynchronous communication through emails between students, lecturers, and cmapping instructor is pivotal for students as it relates to just-in-time feedback.
- Students must be trained in cmapping. While lecturers would benefit from the training, the study showed that it is sufficient if they could develop a good understanding of the building rules for cmaps – a two to three hour workshop can be enough.

Outcomes on the ability to make cmaps for assessment were:

- Five students out of six were able to complete a cmap-assignment for formative assessment on topics such as "How would we make an aeromedical decision in a case of Meniere's disease?" Two students obtained excellent marks, one obtained good marks, and one obtained low marks due to misrepresentation of technical content, and finally, one student under-performed due to issues with CmapTools. Effective training may only be possible if the students are reasonably computer proficient.
- The lecturer found cmapping useful as an assignment, but expressed concerns in relation to assessment. He thought that it was uncleared if a student obtaining low marks in an assignment was due to an ability to make cmaps, or a lack of understanding of the medical knowledge being taught.
- Three students who answered the questionnaire expressed diverse opinions about using cmaps for assessment. They resisted or liked them; found them relevant or irrelevant to their learning styles. One student found them time consuming, boring and tedious, while another found that they really aid his learning.

Outcomes on assessing complex medical knowledge with cmaps and written essays:

- Assessment with cmaps appears to be faster than with written essays. A lecturer can review the relevance of the content of a large cmap in less than three minutes, and of a small cmap in less than one minute. Marking efficiency and timely student feedback are two aspects of assessment that may be greatly improved with cmaps, if student learning style preference for more traditional approaches can be overcome.
- Cmapping can be as effective as written essays in helping students show medical knowledge understanding. However, these outcomes might only be viewed as positive by lecturers, if it could be guaranteed that all the students in a teaching programme can build "good" cmaps.

In summary, according to the results just described, only practice accompanied by effective instruction could help students achieve a level of cmapping competence and familiarity sufficient to switch from written to cmap assignments. The four research questions, formulated by the lecturers teaching the course, are discussed in relation to the claims that give title to the next three sections. In the "case study approach" section, Table 1 shows how the questions were linked to the claims and the relevant data excerpts to inform the research analysis.

Facilitating the Representation and Evaluation of Complex Medical Concepts

This section answers the first research question. Six of seven cmap assignments provide evidence that Novak's cmapping can be effective as an assessment tool in the "clinical aviation medicine" course. Students used them to visualise and interpret complex medical concepts with varied levels of easiness and attentiveness. Therefore, the three benefits for using cmaps emerged (see "background" section) and are substantiated with excerpts from conversation and email communication sustained with the lecturer.

When asked, the lecturer explained, "the objective ... is for [the students] to ably apply [a] diagnosis in making an aeromedical decision, which is a risk management decision." Nancy's, Samuel's and Seth's assignments (see first results section) demonstrate that cmaps, whether built well or with minor structural issues, can show a student's ability (or not) to visualise, organise, interpret and analyse a fairly complex aeromedical decision. These comments support "the advantage to critical analysis and creative thinking":

... Making a concept map about the use of SSRIs [selective serotonin reuptake inhibitors] or warfarin, or viagra ... will require us to think about the concepts and that is what is important! (Personal communication, August 10, 2008).

...from the two [cmaps with high scores of Jim and Danielle] I've seen I am absolutely delighted... The most important thing here... is that when people start thinking in hierarchy, causes and effects, that's one of the most important things, then they start learning... (Transcript of audiorecorded meeting)

The excerpt below may support benefit two "facilitating the process of transferring theory into practice." The semi-hierarchical structure of a cmap assignment appeared to facilitate the process of reading and understanding the existing or non-existing logic underpinning the representation of some medical content, and consequently, assess how students related new medical knowledge to prior medical knowledge. The lecturer explained:

... so much of its content [in reference to this being clinical] is already well known. What is really important is to develop an aviation orientation in the approach to the subject [course] and then to think with that approach"

The next three excerpts support the examination component of benefit three "planning instruction, examination, and curriculum":

... If you read this concept map... you'll get a complete idea about what Meniere's disease is and how to decide whether or not the person is able to get back into aviation... (Nancy's maps in Figure 4 and Figure 5)

... The DME is done, the Audiometry is done... [Samuel] looked at that and then a decision has been made. But there is no explanation as to what is the basis of that decision... (Samuel's map in Figure 6)

... What happens in multifocal contact lenses?... that issue has not been described at all in this chart [meaning this concept map]... (Seth's map in Figure 7)

Expressions such as "you'll get a complete idea... and how to decide if a person is able to get back to aviation," "there's no explanation," and "issues that have not been described" show that cmaps have enabled evaluation of content quality in a formal assessment activity by making explicit a learner's conceptions, misconceptions, knowledge gaps or missing concepts.

The excerpts just presented provide further support for the benefit-related claims of several medical educators. Beitz (1998) and Schuster (2000) reported on the subject of easy visualization and attentive representation of complex concepts. Watson (1998) reported on its ability to enhance understanding of a constantly increasing body of medical knowledge. Finally, Wilkes et al. (1999) and Williams (2004) reported on the activity of building cmaps promoting lifelong and independent learning in medical students.

Issues that Might Prevent Regular use in Aviation Medicine Courses

Overcoming preferences for traditional study styles is one of the three conditions identified for faster adoption of cmaps in a medical course (see "background" section"). This condition is still to be met for students to embrace or accept cmap assignments. The small number of study participants makes it difficult to clearly say how easily a student cohort would adopt this technique. However, several issues emerged during the pilot that might also occur in other aviation medicine courses.

Preferred Learning Styles

This section answers the second research question. The process of learning and doing the cmap assignments made visible how six medical students adopted, performed (or underperformed), and accepted (or not) to use this non-traditional tool, in a course taught online and to a distributed student cohort located in three countries and two continents. The results illustrate that appeal of written assignments for markers and preferred learning styles, did not prevent using cmap assignments for formative assessment.

Three out of six students completed the cmapping building instructions within the 10-hour instruction in weeks 2 and 3, and two students with the 4-hour instruction designed for those beginning the course late. The students built cmaps that the lecturer could use to evaluate knowledge acquisition and mark for assessments 1 and 3. Difficulties with the software technology and the cmapping underpinning principles prevented one student from completing a good assignment. Interestingly, only this student out of the whole group had used mapping techniques before.

The feedback given by three students (Table 6) is representative of the reactions that a lecturer might encounter when cmapping is implemented for the first time. Some students can build really "good" cmaps, but hate and become frustrated by the process, because it demands extra effort unrelated, to the main topic. Some students often use mapping techniques, but are challenged by the required software application. This student type is likely to be encountered in the course, which already factors in likelihood of students requiring time to master the technologies for distance study. Finally, students that can build "good" cmaps, find the technique useful to learning, and decide to use it in another study topic. In the future, implementation of cmap assignments during formative assessment would need to address these potential reactions with suitable instructions for learning the strategy and operating the required software technology.

While some studies report similar negative student and lecturer attitudes toward cmaps (Eitel & Steiner, 1999; Kostovich et al., 2007; Laight, 2006), others report with practice students can overcome anxiety and learn to appreciate its advantages (Beitz, 1998; C. M. Hill, 2006; Williams, 2004). For example, Wilkes et al. (1999) reported a similar experience with their students: "all students commented that they were frightened when they started the unit because it was different. However as they progressed in the semester, they began to enjoy it and learned "just so much" (p. 44). In this study one person, Samuel with good scores – 15 marks, expressed liking concept maps and used them in another aviation course (Table 6), and one person, student Nancy volunteered to perform assignment 3 with a cmap. In both assignments she had high scores, 20 marks and 18 marks respectively (Table 3).

Suitable Student Instruction for Effective use and Assessment

This section answers the fourth research question. If this alternative assessment tool were to be regularly used in aviation medicine courses, condition one "learning how to build concept maps" needs to be resolved.

As explained in the "case study approach" section, the lecturers teaching the course learned to read cmaps in a two-hour session. The results demonstrate that for implementing cmap assessment across the courses, it may be sufficient for lecturers to learn how to read cmaps that students create. Consequently, it can be said that it might be difficult to implement cmap assessment with software applications such as CmapTools and GoToMeeting across the courses without the support of one or more cmapping instructors. The lecturers in this course are full time medical professionals. They most likely would not have the time to learn and teach cmapping to students in addition to teaching the main course topic.

The lecturer's main concern about the use of cmap assignments over written assignments appeared to focus on the ability of a student to master the technique enough to accurately represent acquired medical knowledge. His concern differs from that reported by other medical educators. Schmidt (2004) is concerned with the construct validity of cmaps, as introduced in the "background" section. While Hinck et al. (2006) appear to seek for a gold standard or "universal" criterion for evaluating cmaps representing medical conceptual understanding. The aviation medicine master appears not to evaluate students by a gold or universal standard. Instead, the interest appears to lie, if the lecturers' opinions presented in this chapter are carefully considered, in the students being able to convey in written essays or short notes what they know in relation to the study material.

Might Improve Staff Marking Efficiency and Student Feedback

This section also answers the fourth research question. Despite the positive outcomes appearing to favour the adoption of cmap assignments, it is still to be determined whether this alternative assessment tool is likely to be used regularly in the Aviation Medicine courses. Improvement of staff marking efficiency and student feedback may be two advantages over written assignments that might persuade medical educators to consider adopting cmaps in their courses.

As seen in the first section reporting results, cmaps enabled the lecturer to assess if a student has achieved deep understanding in a clinical aviation topic. The assessment process was carried out with minimal disruption to his teaching philosophy and schedule, and his preferred approaches for marking and evaluation (Table 2). When the cmap was well-built (or containing minor mistakes), he could identify gaps in knowledge representation or creative leaps. For example, the latter situation was evident in comments related to Nancy's cmap: "…you'll get a complete idea about Meniere's disease is and how to decide whether or not a person is able to get back into aviation." Also "…[Nancy]'s come up with something which nobody thought of…"

By using the term "nobody thought of," the lecturer was referring to himself, to his own knowledge as a subject matter expert on risk management in clinical aviation. He has employed "expert knowledge comparison" during the marking. This lecturer is a highly experienced aviation and occupational medicine consultant, having spent over two decades in the military as a flight surgeon, and a decade in regulatory aviation medicine in New Zealand and Australia. He has a regulatory role in aeromedical decision making, and has been involved in setting up the paradigms for evidence based aeromedical decision making in New Zealand, and leads a team that is working towards this in Australia.

Cmaps could be adopted as replacements of essays in the aviation medicine courses. The activity of writing an essay to explain all the aspects of an aeromedical decision demands the use of some cognitive processes that are also used in the activity of building of a cmap. These processes are knowing, comprehending, applying, analysing, synthesising, and evaluating (Gage & Berliner, 1992) and appear to be the foundation for university study skills: elaboration, organisation, and rehearsal strategies. Hardie (2009) summarises the work of authors, calling these strategies university study skills. While Pintrich, Smith, Garcia, and McKeachie (1991) report them as cognitive and metacognitive strategies. Organising by mapping (visual tools, diagrams) is categorised under organisation strategies. While explaining concepts in the form of essays are categorised under elaboration strategies. Therefore, the activities of essay writing and cmapping appear to enable the representation and evaluation of deep understanding, are prone to marker bias (rely on the opinion of a subject matter expert), and have low validity and reliability.

As introduced in the "background" section, this study provides supporting evidence for what Novak and Gowin (1984) consider to be the reasons why cmapping is "so powerful" in the facilitation of meaningful learning.

1. The six students could use the cmap template to help organize and structure knowledge about aeromedical decisions. They used their individual understanding of the content and performed further research to explain their views with supporting resources such as links to Websites, journal articles, images, videos, and/or citations.

2. Some cmaps (Figure 4) show evidence of creative activity. By following the rules for building a cmap, the students put in practice a process that leads to deep understanding, and therefore, meaningful learning. The lecturer also recognised this.

3. All cmaps helped people (e.g. lecturer, cmapping instructor, the readers of this chapter, the students' themselves) explicitly see the nature and role of concepts and the relationships between them in relation to an aeromedical decision. Transcript excerpts evidence were provided in the previous section.
4. Finally, cmaps take advantage of the human learning capacity for using written and spoken symbols to perceive regularities in events or objects around us, as well as the capacity to recognize patterns in images, facilitating learning and recall (Novak & Gowin, 1984, p. 28). For this reason, the lecturer spent less time marking each student's maps than the written essays.

Cmap marking might reduce work for staff because a lecturer is not sidetracked by modes of expression or spelling. This aspect can make essay marking time-consuming. This claim is supported by Luckie, Harrison, and Ebert-May (2004) "… [G]rading a single concept map may be less time-consuming than grading a long essay or extended response" (p. 1).

Gage and Berliner (1992) say that the penmanship of the writer among other aspects can have some effect on marking. The following example illustrates their comment. The lecturer of the course "Airport and Travel Health," also part of the aviation medicine master, provides guidelines for writing what he called "the exam script." In the following excerpt, he suggests writing short answers instead of complete grammatical sentences that are harder for him to read.

The aim of the exam script is for you to demonstrate to me that you know the material. If you express it in nice complete grammatically sentences, that will NOT win you any more marks than if you express it as a list of dot points. What's more, the nice complete sentences are harder for me to read!

So my advice to you for the exam is to use: Headings, Capitals, Underlining, Dot points, Indenting, Coloured pens, Even highlighting… And any other techniques to make things clearer to the reader.

Another suggestion is that you leave lots of spaces in your script personally when I do exams I double space so that there is a spare line after each line for me to make corrections later… Doctors have bad writing, so more space makes it easier to read (Personal communication, June 10, 2007).

The lecturer asked the students to use a collection of visual aids, cues, or patterns to make the content clearer to read, and therefore, show that they know the study material. The cmap template was developed (as introduced earlier) to see patterns in children's science concepts (Novak & Cañas, 2006a). Once a student is able to build a "good" cmap, this has been shown to enable a lecturer to see what a student understands. Therefore, it could be more effectively used in the assessment of medical knowledge, as the distracting issues identified with written essays are lessened.

In relation to British university student marking, Bloxham (2009, p. 209) argues "… in developing rigorous moderation procedures, we have created a huge burden for markers which adds little to accuracy and reliability but creates additional work for staff, constrains assessment choices and slows down feedback to students." The student group studied in this pilot submitted their assignments late (or withdrew from the course like Danielle) due to clashing work schedules or family commitments. Due to late student feedback, marked essays might have not been useful for learning from mistakes for future assignments or to inform preparation of final exams. Research on student feedback points out to better use of a marker's time and the development of targeted rubrics and criteria to improve formative assessment with essays (Heinrich, Milne, Ramsay, & Morrison, 2009; Walker, 2009) and concept maps (Filiz, Trumpower, & Atas, 2012; Trumpower & Sarwar, 2010).

CONCLUSION

This pilot exploratory study shows early, but promising, results. It demonstrates that a small student group, upon instruction, could make a Novak's cmap assignment, that in turn, a lecturer could use for evaluating "clinical aviation medicine" concepts - thus they can be a suitable replacement for written essays.

A qualitative research methodology called "case study approach" was employed. It involved participatory observation and interviews (e.g. email communication, unstructured questionnaire, and audio recorded informal conversations) undertaken via synchronous and asynchronous technologies. The lecturer and students were located in Australia, the United Kingdom, and New Zealand. Therefore, it was also found that it could be incorporated in a distance postgraduate course taught completely online, as long as, all students learn to build "good" cmaps, with no or minor mistake, and to use the relevant software applications.

Cmaps can be a suitable and faster alternative to assess deep understanding of complex medical thinking, according to the analysis of the students' assignments, marking tasks, and documents communicating student and lecturer opinion. The process of marking a big cmap (e.g. Samuel's cmap, 2.84 minutes) or a small cmap (e.g. Danielle's cmap 4, 0.8 minutes) may take significantly less time than the process of marking a single written essay (Table 4). However, the introduction of cmapping as an alternative tool during formative assessment might need to balance the competing interests. These were:

- Lecturer and student acceptability due to preferring more traditional learning styles
- Development and implementation of a cmapping instruction that fits within the study culture of the aviation medicine master. For example, it is unlikely that the teaching staff would have time available to learn and teach the cmapping rules.

As stated in the "introduction" section, the outcomes reported here mainly address aim (iii) of the project funded by the CALT grant. The evidence about potential benefits, conditions needed, and issues encountered may inform the decision-making process to incorporate cmap assignments, as additional or replacement tools, in a master-level medical course. Due to the sample size and the exploratory approach taken, another case study with a larger student cohort and more courses would be beneficial to validate the results obtained.

However, the outcomes related to "cmaps being faster to mark" could be re-directed to explore the aim (iv) "assess the use of concept mapping as a part of a strategy to assist in the internationalisation of aviation medicine course content." Cmap assignments were found to be operationally feasible and culturally neutral. Once a lecturer learns how to read the pattern (concept → linking phrase → concept), he or she is not sidetracked by modes of expression or spelling. As illustrated throughout the chapter, its visual structure helps focusing in on how students organize and establish relationships among concepts, in a manner that understanding of the topics being taught can be assessed. Therefore, it is recommended that they are considered as an alternative assessment system in online courses with high enrolments and students with very different cultural and linguistic backgrounds.

ACKNOWLEDGMENT

We would like to thank the members of the Committee for the Advancement of Learning and Teaching (CALT) that granted us the 2007 E-learning Enhancement Grant. Without their support, this research project could not have been carried out. Our gratitude also goes to the study participants, AVMX714 class of semester II 2008, and to lecturer David Powell who allowed us to use his personal communication on marking student written assignments. We thank the technical team from OceanBrowser ltd., as without their support the resolution of multiple technical situations, including management of teleconferences, audioconferences, and uploading of study materials to servers, would not have been possible. Finally, our gratitude go to Dr Sarah Stein for providing helpful insights on an earlier version in 2010, and to Rodney Tamblyn and Iris Levitis for proofreading the versions leading to this publication.

REFERENCES

Ainsworth, L., & Viegut, D. (2006). *Common formative assessments: How to connect ctandards-based instruction and assessment*. Thousand Oaks, CA: Sage.

All, A. C., Huycke, L. I., & Fisher, M. J. (2003). Instructional tools for nursing education: Concept maps. *Nursing Education Perspectives, 24*(6), 311–317. PMID:14705401

Ausubel, D. P., Novak, J. D., & Hanesian, H. (1978). *Educational psychology: A cognitive view* (2nd ed.). New York: Holt, Rinehart and Winston.

Beitz, J. M. (1998). Concept mapping: Navigating the learning process. *Nurse Educator, 23*(5), 35–41. doi:10.1097/00006223-199809000-00015 PMID:9866562

Bloxham, S. (2009). Marking and moderation in the UK: False assumptions and wasted resources. *Assessment & Evaluation in Higher Education, 34*(2), 209–220. doi:10.1080/02602930801955978

Cañas, A. J., Hill, G., Carff, R., Suri, N., Lott, J., Eskridge, T., & Carvajal, R. (2004). CmapTools: A knowledge modeling and sharing environment. In A. J. Cañas, J. D. Novak & F. M. González (Eds.), *Proceedings of the First International Conference on Concept Mapping* (Vol. 1, pp. 125-133). Multibaja, Spain: Novatext.

Cañas, A. J., & Novak, J. D. (Eds.). (2006). Concept maps: Theory, methodology, technology. In *Proceedings from the Second International Conference on Concept Mapping*. San José, Costa Rica: Universidad de Costa Rica.

Cañas, A. J., Novak, J. D., & González, F. M. (Eds.). (2004). Concept maps: Theory, methodology, technology. In *Proceedings from the First International Conference on Concept Mapping*. Multibaja, Spain: Novatext.

Coffey, J. W., Carnot, M. J., Feltovich, P. J., Feltovich, J., Hoffman, R. R., Cañas, A. J., & Novak, J. D. (2003). A summary of literature pertaining to the use of concept mapping techniques and technologies for education and performance support (Technical Report for the Chief of Naval Education and Training). Pensacola, FL: IHMC - Institute for Human and Machine Cognition. Retrieved from http://www.ihmc.us/users/acanas/Publications/ConceptMapLitReview/IHMC Literature Review on Concept Mapping.pdf

Daley, B., Torre, D., Stark-Schweitzer, T., Siddartha, S., Ziebert, M., & Petkova, J. (2006). Advancing teaching and learning in medical education through the use of concept maps. In A. J. Cañas & J. D. Novak (Eds.), *Proceedings of the Second International Conference on Concept Mapping*. San José, Costa Rica: Universidad de Costa Rica.

Edwards, A. (2001). Qualitative designs and analysis. In G. MacNaughton, S. A. Rolfe, & I. Siraj-Blatchford (Eds.), *Doing early childhood research: International perspectives on theory and practice* (pp. 117–135). Crows Nest, Australia: Alen & Unwin.

Eitel, F., & Steiner, S. (1999). Evidence-based learning. *Medical Teacher, 25*(5), 506–513.

Filiz, M., Trumpower, D. L., & Atas, S. (2012). Analysis of how well a concept mapping website conforms to principles of effective assessment for learning. In A. J. Cañas, J. D. Novak & J. Vanhear (Eds.), *Proceedings of the Fifth International Conference on Concept Mapping* (Vol. 2). Malta: Veritas Press.

Flyvbjerg, B. (2006). Five misunderstandings about case-study research. *Qualitative Inquiry, 12*(2), 219–245. doi:10.1177/1077800405284363

Gage, N. L., & Berliner, D. C. (1992). *Educational psychology* (5th ed.). Boston, MA: Houghton Mifflin Company.

Gomez, G. (2008). *Use of concept maps for student assessment in an aviation medicine graduate programme (Research Report for the CALT Grant Committee)*. New Zealand: University of Otago.

Hardie, J. C. (2009). *New opportunities or difficult challenges? Self-regulation of learning of chinese students in a western university setting*. (Doctoral Dissertation). University of Canterbury, New Zealand. Retrieved from http://hdl.handle.net/10092/3392

Heinrich, E., Milne, J., Ramsay, A., & Morrison, D. (2009). Recommendations for the use of e-tools for improvements around assignment marking quality. *Assessment & Evaluation in Higher Education, 34*(4), 469–479. doi:10.1080/02602930802071122

Hill, C. M. (2006). Integrating clinical experiences into the concept mapping process. *Nurse Educator, 31*(1), 36–39. doi:10.1097/00006223-200601000-00010 PMID:16601605

Hill, L. H. (2006). Using visual concept mapping to communicate medication information to patients with low health literacy: A preliminary study In *Proceedings of the Second International Conference on Concept Mapping* (Vol. 1, pp. 621-628). San Jose, Costa Rica: Universidad de Costa Rica.

Hinck, S. M., Webb, P., Sims-Giddens, S., Helton, C., Hope, K. L., Utley, R., & Yarbrough, S. (2006). Student learning with concept mapping of care plans in community-based education. *Journal of Professional Nursing*, 22(1), 23–29. doi:10.1016/j.profnurs.2005.12.004 PMID:16459286

Institute for Human and Machine Cognition. (2007). *Hybrid concept map/procedure on building a concept map*. Retrieved September 1, 2007, from http://cmapskm.ihmc.us/servlet/SBReadResourceServlet?rid=1064009710027_279131382_2708 8&partName=htmltext

Institute for Human and Machine Cognition. (2008). *Publications*. Retrieved April 27, 2008, from http://cmap.ihmc.us/Publications/

Kinchin, I. M., Hay, D. B., & Adams, A. (2000). How a qualitative approach to concept map analysis can be used to aid learning by illustrating patterns of conceptual development. *Educational Research*, 42(1), 43–57. doi:10.1080/001318800363908

Kostovich, C. T., Poradzisz, M., Wood, K., & O'Brien, K. L. (2007). Learning style preference and student aptitude for concept maps. *The Journal of Nursing Education*, 46(5), 225–231. PMID:17547346

Laight, D. W. (2004). Attitudes to concept maps as a teaching/learning activity in undergraduate health professional education: Influence of preferred learning style. *Medical Teacher*, 26(3), 229–233. doi:10.1080/0142159042000192064 PMID:15203499

Laight, D. W. (2006). Attitudes to concept maps as a teaching/learning activity in undergraduate health professional education: Influence of preferred approach to learning. *Medical Teacher*, 28(2), e64–e67. doi:10.1080/01421590600617574 PMID:16707287

Luckie, D. B., Harrison, S. H., & Ebert-May, D. (2004). Introduction to c-tools: Concept mapping tools for online learning. In *Proceedings of the First International Conference on Concept Mapping* (Vol. 2, pp. 211-214). Multibaja, Spain: Novatext.

Mintzes, J. J., Wandersee, J. H., & Novak, J. D. (Eds.). (2005). *Teaching sciences for understanding: A human constructivist view*. New York: Elsevier Academic Press.

Novak, J. D. (1998). *Learning, creating and using knowledge: Concept maps as facilitative tools in schools and corporations*. Mahwah, NJ: Lawrence Earlbaum Associates.

Novak, J. D. (2004). *The theory underlying concept maps and how to construct them*. Retrieved from http://cmap.coginst.uwf.edu/info/printer.html

Novak, J. D., & Cañas, A. J. (2006a). The origins of the concept mapping tool and the continuing evolution of the tool. *Information and Visualization Journal, 5*(3), 175–184. doi:10.1057/palgrave.ivs.9500126

Novak, J. D., & Cañas, A. J. (2006b). *The theory underlying concept maps and how to construct them (Technical Report IHMC CmapTools 2006-01 Rev 01-2008)*. Pensacola, FL: Florida Institute for Human and Machine Cognition.

Novak, J. D., & Gowin, D. B. (1984). *Learning how to learn*. New York: Cambridge University Press. doi:10.1017/CBO9781139173469

Novak, J. D., & Wandersee, J. (1990). Perspectives on concept mapping [Special issue]. *Journal of Research in Science Teaching, 27*(10), 921–1074.

O'Neil, H. F., & Klein, D. C. D. (1997). *Feasibility of machine scoring of concept maps* (CSE Technical Report 460). Los Angeles, CA: National Center for Research on Evaluation, Standards, and Student Testing.

Passmore, G. G., Owen, M. A., & Prabakaran, K. (2011). Empirical evidence of the effectiveness of concept mapping as a learning intervention for nuclear medicine technology students in a distance learning raditation protection and biology course. *Journal of Nuclear Medicine Technology, 39*(4), 284–289. doi:10.2967/jnmt.111.093062 PMID:22080436

Phye, G. D. (1997). *Handbook of classroom assessment: Learning, achievement, and adjustment*. San Diego, CA: Academic Press.

Pintrich, P. R., Smith, D. A. F., Garcia, T., & McKeachie, W. J. (1991). *A manual for the use of the motivated strategies for learning questionnaire (MSLQ)* (Technical Report No. 91-B-004). Ann Arbor, MI: National Center for Research to Improve Postsecondary Teaching and Learning.

Rendas, A. B., Fonseca, M., & Pinto, P. R. (2006). Toward meaningful learning in undergraduate medical education using concept maps in a PBL pathophysiology course. *Advances in Physiology Education, 30*(1), 23–29. doi:10.1152/advan.00036.2005 PMID:16481605

Rolfe, S. A. (2001). Direct observation. In G. MacNaughton, S. A. Rolfe, & I. Siraj-Blatchford (Eds.), *Doing early childhood research: International perspectives on theory and practice* (pp. 224–239). Crows Nest, Australia: Alen & Unwin.

Schmidt, H. J. (2004). Alternative approaches to concept mapping and implications for medical education: Commentary on reliability, validity and future research directions. *Advances in Health Sciences Education : Theory and Practice, 9*(3), 251–256. doi:10.1023/B:AHSE.0000038309.92212.44 PMID:15316275

Schuster, P. M. (2000). Concept mapping: Reducing clinical care plan paperwork and increasing learning. *Nurse Educator, 25*(2), 76–81. doi:10.1097/00006223-200003000-00009 PMID:11052005

Shermis, M. D., & DiVesta, F. J. (2011). *Classroom assessment in action*. Plymouth, UK: Rowman & Littlefield Publishers.

Siraj-Blatchford, I., & Siraj-Blatchford, J. (2001). An ethnographic approach to researching young children's learning. In G. MacNaughton, S. A. Rolfe, & I. Siraj-Blatchford (Eds.), *Doing early childhood research: International perspectives on theory and practice* (pp. 193–207). Crows Nest, Australia: Alen & Unwin.

Stake, R. E. (1995). *The art of case study research*. Thousand Oaks, CA: SAGE Publications, Inc.

Thornburg, H. D. (1984). *Introduction to educational psychology*. St. Paul, MN: West Publishing Company.

Torres, P. L., & Marriott, R. C. V. (Eds.). (2010). *Handbook of research on collaborative learning using concept mapping*. Hershey, PA: Information Science Reference.

Trowbridge, J. E., & Wandersee, J. E. (2005). Theory-driven graphic organizers. In J. J. Mintzes, J. H. Wandersee, & J. D. Novak (Eds.), *Teaching sciences for understanding: A human constructivist view* (pp. 95–131). New York: Elsevier Academic Press. doi:10.1016/B978-012498360-1/50005-2

Trumpower, D. L., & Sarwar, G. S. (2010). Formative structural assessment: Using concept maps as assessment for learning. In J. Sanchez, A. J. Cañas & J. D. Novak (Eds.), *Proceedings of the Fourth International Conference on Concept Mapping* (Vol. 2, pp. 132-136). Santiago de Chile: Lom Ediciones S.A.

Walker, M. (2009). An investigation into written comments on assignments: Do students find them usable? *Assessment & Evaluation in Higher Education, 34*(1), 67–78. doi:10.1080/02602930801895752

Walsh, S. (2010). The portal for postgraduates in medicine. In J. Sanchez, A. J. Cañas & J. D. Novak (Eds.), *Proceedings of the Fourth International Conference on Concept Mapping* (Vol. 2, pp. 224-227). Santiago de Chile: Lom Ediciones S.A.

Watson, G. R. (1998). What is. concept maps? *Medical Teacher, 11*(3-4), 265–269. doi:10.3109/01421598909146411

West, D. C., Park, J. K., Pomeroy, J. R., & Sandoval, J. (2002). Concept mapping assessment in medical education: A comparison of two scoring systems. *Medical Education, 38*, 820–826. doi:10.1046/j.1365-2923.2002.01292.x PMID:12354244

Wilkes, L., Cooper, K., Lewin, J., & Batts, J. (1999). Concept mapping: Promoting science learning in BN learners in Australia. *Journal of Continuing Education in Nursing, 30*(1), 37–44. PMID:10036416

Williams, M. (2004). Concept mapping - A strategy for assessment. *Nursing Standard, 19*(9), 33–38. doi:10.7748/ns2004.11.19.9.33.c3754 PMID:15574052

KEY TERMS AND DEFINITIONS

Asynchronous Technology: Refers to technologies used for asynchronous communication and collaboration such as discussion forums (e.g. Vbulletin) or email.

Complex Medical Knowledge (or Complex Medical Concepts, or Complex Medical Thinking): The ability of a postgraduate medical student to enlist the cognitive processes of knowing, comprehending, applying, analyzing, synthesising, and evaluation, in the explanation of (in this case) an aeromedical decision, for example, in a case of Meniere's disease, or hearing loss, or multimodal focal lenses. The explanation can be delivered in the form of verbal, visual and/or written communication.

Efficient Assessment of Complex Thinking: Refers to the claim that concept map assignments may lead to the improvement of marking efficiency and timely student feedback.

"Good" Concept Map: Refers to a concept map that has been built according to the rules stated by Joseph D. Novak, in which the pattern concept → linking phrase → concept is complete. It presents a semi-hierarchical structure with the more general concept at the top and the more specific ones following in order of importance. Cross-links, representing creative leaps in thinking, become visible when the rules have been carefully attended.

Marking Efficiency: Refers to student marking and to argue that concept maps may reduce work to staff because its economical visual structure prevents teaching staff from being distracted by writing style and grammar.

Student Feedback: This term is used in association to the claim that if concept maps are faster to mark than written essays, then teaching staff might be able to provide timely feedback to students.

Synchronous Technology: Refers in this case to technologies used for delivering course teleconferences – tutor and students meet in real time in a distributed network of learning, using software applications such as Oceanbrowser's conferencing system or GotoMeeting.

Chapter 11
Talmud Diagrams

Israel Ury
Jewish Content Laboratories, Israel

EXECUTIVE SUMMARY

The Talmud, as the basic source of Jewish law and thought, continues to receive the attention of scholars and students from a wide age group. Study of the Talmud is complicated by its complex and involved legal arguments. Talmud Diagrams are designed to be easy to read graphical representations of the logic of the Talmud that aid its comprehension and retention. In particular, Talmud Diagrams are maps of legal opinions that consist of rulings on a set of related cases. Passages in the Talmud are represented by a series of Talmud Diagrams that portray the evolution of the legal opinions, challenges, and resolutions. The principle of a fortiori is embedded within the structure and formation rules of Talmud Diagrams, allowing the use of Talmud Diagrams to be extended to other legal systems where a fortiori applies.

INTRODUCTION

The Talmud is the authoritative classical source of Jewish law and thought. Orthodox Jewish schools begin their instruction in Talmud as early as Grade 4 and students are expected to adopt Talmud study as a lifelong pursuit.

The Talmud is written in a combination of Hebrew and Aramaic, forming a first barrier to understanding the text. In addition, the logic of the Talmud is arcane and often very complex. With all these barriers present, not every student becomes proficient in Talmud study, often leading the student to frustration and self doubt. Several

DOI: 10.4018/978-1-4666-5816-5.ch011

translations and elucidations of the Talmud exist (Malinowitz et al., 1990-2005; Steinzaltz, 2012) so the language barrier and the logical elements of the Talmud can now be readily accessed. The complexity of the Talmud remains irreducible however, so putting together all the pieces in an understandable way remains challenging. The method of Talmud Diagrams (Ury, 2011) addresses the complexity issue by means of a visual presentation of the Talmud's logic. In analogy to a cartographic map, Talmud Diagrams guide the student through the complex terrain of logic that characterizes passages in the Talmud.

The objective of this chapter is to introduce the reader to the formalism of Talmud Diagrams. The method of Talmud Diagrams is easily learned and four steps are described for generating them. The principle of *a fortiori* is natively embedded within Talmud Diagrams and is expressed by means of a graphical rule for manipulating Talmud Diagrams to extend legal rulings from one case to another.

This chapter includes a complete, worked example from a brief passage in the Talmud, including an analysis by one of its classic commentaries. By going through the example, the explanatory power of Talmud Diagrams becomes apparent.

Beyond the Talmud, any system of reasoning that incorporates the principle of *a fortiori* as an accepted element is a candidate for using Talmud Diagrams. In particular, other legal systems besides Jewish law that make use of *a fortiori* can use Talmud Diagrams to argue a legal point. Legal experts and juries can benefit from the clarity that Talmud Diagrams bring to complex legal arguments. An example derived from an actual legal case is presented and Talmud Diagrams are used to present arguments for and against the judge's ruling.

BACKGROUND

The Talmud is the written record of Jewish Oral Law and consists of two parts, Mishnah and Gemara. The Mishnah consists of legal rulings that reflect a complete set of all principles in Jewish law, and was first redacted in the third century CE. The Gemara presents the subsequent discussions and analyses of the Mishnah that were conducted in the academies of Israel and Babylonia. The earlier Jerusalem Talmud (Malinowitz, 2006-2012) was succeeded by the Babylonian Talmud which itself was finally redacted several hundred years after the redaction of the Mishnah. Being a later text, the Babylonian Talmud is the authoritative source for all subsequent developments of Jewish law.

The Talmud derives Jewish law from written passages in the Bible using a number of rules of exegesis. The most commonly quoted list of these principles is Rabbi Yishamael's Thirteen Hermeneutical Principles (Steinsalz, 1976). The first principle in the list is *kal vachomer* – the principle of *a fortiori*. By being one of the principles of Bible hermeneutics, the *kal vachomer* goes beyond being a tool of rhetoric but rather becomes a method for establishing concrete laws. The idea is that the entire corpus of Jewish Law is consistent with the (nearly) universal application of *kal vachomer* as a guiding principle for establishing new rulings. The method of Talmud Diagrams incorporates the principle of *a fortiori* in a native way and therefore has great utility in helping to understand Talmudic discussions.

The Talmud is the Jewish text that enjoys the investment of the most hours of study by Orthodox Jews. Study of the Mishnah usually begins in about Grade 4 and Gemara instruction generally begins no later than Grade 6. Orthodox Jewish high school age students and adults are expected to spend hours a day studying Talmud.

Talmud study among adults has been popularized by the Daf Yomi – 'one folio a day' – program introduced in 1923 by Rabbi Meir Shapiro of Lublin, Poland. This program has enjoyed tremendous growth, especially in recent years. All participants in the Daf Yomi program are literally 'on the same page', studying the folio prescribed for that day. The Babylonian Talmud, in its classic Vilna edition consists of 2,711 folios (double sided pages), so at a rate of one folio a day, it takes about seven and a half years to complete a cycle of study that encompasses the entire Babylonian Talmud. A recent celebration in the USA of the completion of the twelfth cycle of the Daf Yomi (Otterman, 2012) drew a crowd of roughly 90,000 people, a significant fraction of whom had completed the cycle of study at least once.

The present popularity of Daf Yomi study can partially be attributed to the appearance in print in recent years of translations and elucidations of the text of the Talmud. In addition, a number of books (e.g. Cohen, 2006), online resources, software programs and tablet apps have become available to aid Talmud study. Even with all the aids, the Talmud remains a highly complex and difficult text to master. This is partly due to the fact that multiple opinions are contained within a typical passage in the Talmud, and there are a multitude of interpretations of the text by later authorities. The cases themselves are often very complex and involve a number of legal principles. Because of these challenges, the student of the Talmud is implored to 'hold on to your head' when trying to analyze a Talmudic passage.

The existing aids to Talmud study largely provide verbal explanations of the Talmud passage and rarely employ any visual means to provide conceptual explanations. Those visual aids that do exist consist largely of written tables listing the various opinions, illustrations of the physical situation of a case, or family trees to explain the family relation between parties. What is missing is a visual means to express the concepts expressed or implicitly stated in the Talmud. Talmud Diagrams aim to fill the gap between verbal explanation and true understanding by means of conceptual mapping.

TALMUD DIAGRAMS: A VISUAL METHOD FOR UNDERSTANDING THE TALMUD

Constructing and Interpreting Talmud Diagrams

Talmud Diagrams are designed to be compatible with simple pencil and paper construction. Color is not ordinarily used in a Talmud Diagram although its use is not precluded. Pencil and paper (or equivalently a graphics tablet and stylus) offer the unique ability for the student to sketch, scribble, and erase, and thereby consider and analyze a number of theories very rapidly. Seeing why a proposed theory is incorrect can be just as instructive or perhaps more instructive than immediately arriving at the correct theory.

When attempting to analyze a passage in the Talmud, a great deal of trial and error is generally employed, no matter what method is used to decipher it. Multiple approaches and theories must be tried and tested to get the correct understanding of the passage. Many questions present themselves: What is the meaning of the passage? Why does the stated question constitute a question? How does the stated answer resolve the question? What underlying principles are at work? A system such as the method of Talmud Diagrams is extremely valuable for rapidly considering a number of possible interpretations and for identifying the likely correct interpretation of a passage. Using the method of Talmud Diagrams also forces the student to identify the underlying principles behind the rulings that form the opinions in the Talmud. Finally, a series of Talmud Diagrams can be assembled to portray the flow of the legal arguments contained in a passage of the Talmud. In this way the student can immediately grasp the overall logical structure of the passage and commit it to memory.

The structure of a Talmud Diagram consists of an ordered collection of boxes arranged into a one dimensional, two dimensional, or less commonly, a three dimensional array. Each box in a Talmud Diagram represents a specific legal case, and the shading of the box represents the presence or absence of a particular 'law' i.e. a specific legal ruling (see Figure 1).

Interpretation of a Talmud Diagram is very straightforward. For every case, the applicability of the 'law' is reflected by the presence or absence of shading in the box corresponding to that case. The cases and hence the boxes are arranged according to the degree of presence of factors that determine whether the law in question is likely to apply or not. The number of independent factors represented in a Talmud diagram determines its dimensionality. One dimensional and two dimensional Talmud Diagrams are the ones that are most commonly used, but occasionally a three dimensional representation is the best way to understand a particularly complex case (Ury, 2011).

Figure 1. Talmud Diagrams take on the dimensionality of the number of factors involved

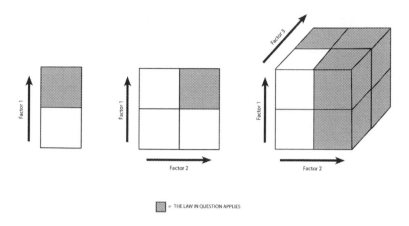

= THE LAW IN QUESTION APPLIES

Four Steps for Constructing Talmud Diagrams

The construction of Talmud Diagrams is a straightforward process but is best organized into four distinct steps. Following a formalized set of steps helps guide the student in the process of creating Talmud Diagrams on his own. The experienced user will not notice that four different steps are being performed when creating Talmud Diagrams, but those steps are nonetheless present. Here is a presentation and discussion of the four steps set in a language appropriate for two dimensional Talmud Diagrams, beginning with the first two steps.

Referring to Figure 2, we see a Talmud Diagram as it appears after performing the first two steps, those steps being defined below. The example here is a two dimensional Talmud Diagram covering a total of nine distinct cases represented by a three by three array of boxes. It is desired to know whether a certain legal ruling, or 'law', applies to each of the cases in question. The 'Key' defines the type of shading that is to be used in the Talmud Diagram to denote the applicability of the law. If the law applies, the box is shaded, if the law does not apply, the box is left blank. Here are statements of the first two steps in constructing a Talmud Diagram:

Step 1: Create a Talmud Diagram that contains all the relevant cases, arranged in order of likelihood that a particular law applies, with likelihood increasing up and to the right.

Step 2: Using the style of shading shown in the Key, shade the boxes corresponding to cases where the law applies. Leave boxes blank where the law does not apply. Mark all the other boxes with a question mark.

Figure 2. A Talmud Diagram after performing Steps 1 and 2 (©2011, TorahLab. Used with permission.)

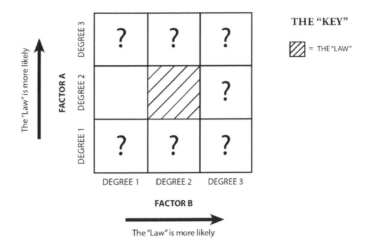

The cases and hence the boxes in a Talmud Diagram are arranged according to the likelihood that the law will apply to them. The arrows in Figure 2 indicate that the law is more likely to apply as you move up and to the right in the Talmud Diagram. In fact, this is always the case in a Talmud Diagram since it is constructed this way according to Step 1. The arrows also implicitly imply that there is a scalar factor at work behind the scenes causing the likelihood of the law applying to increase in the indicated directions. Each axis of a Talmud Diagram therefore represents a changing amount of a factor that affects the applicability of the law. The dimensionality of the Talmud Diagram indicates how many independent factors are being represented; a single factor demands a one dimensional Talmud Diagram, two factors require a two dimensional Talmud Diagram, etc.

In the example of Figure 2, two factors are at work and hence the Talmud Diagram is two-dimensional. The legal status of two of the nine cases is known. There is one shaded box indicating that the law applies to that case, and one box is blank indicating that the law definitely does not apply to that case. The next step is to use the argument *a fortiori* to determine the status of as many other boxes as possible.

The Talmud Diagram is tailor made for the argument *a fortiori*. In Talmudic Hermeneutics, the *a fortiori* argument is assumed to always yield correct results (with certain exceptions). A restatement of *a fortiori* in our context is: "If a law is more likely to apply in a second case than in a first case where it already applies, then the law applies in the second case as well; if a law is less likely to apply in a second case than in a first case where it already does not apply, then the law also does not apply in the second case." Since boxes representing cases where the law is more likely to apply are always above and to the right of a starting case, and boxes representing cases where the law is less likely to apply always lie to the left and below a starting case, we can restate the argument of *a fortiori* as the 'Shading Rule' as follows:

- **The Shading Rule:** "In a Talmud Diagram, if a box is shaded, all boxes above it and to its right are also shaded. If a box is blank, all boxes below it and to its left are also bank."

The third step in constructing a Talmud Diagram involves applying the Shading Rule to apply the principle of *a fortiori* to the cases where the legal rulings are not known or have not been explicitly stated. The third step can be stated as follows:

Step 3: Use the Shading Rule to determine the shading of as many of the remaining boxes as possible.

The Shading Rule provides an algorithm for completing Talmud Diagrams that possess unresolved cases. In the example of Figure 2, some of the question marks can be resolved using the Shading Rule. The arrows in Figure 3 show how this is done. The box that lies to the right of the center box must of necessity also be shaded because of its relative location on the right. A similar argument can be made for the box above the center box to prove that it must be shaded as well. The box at the top right must then also be shaded because it lies both above and to the right of other shaded boxes. The Shading Rule also dictates that the lower left box must be blank by virtue of the fact that the box above it is blank. In this way, four out of the seven boxes in question have been resolved. It is also instructive for the student to see that in this example, three of the boxes cannot be resolved by the *a fortiori*

Figure 3. The Shading Rule is used to resolve the status of boxes in a Talmud Diagram (©2011, TorahLab. Used with permission.)

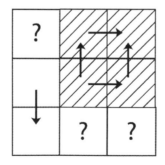

THE SHADING RULE

In a Diagram, if a box is shaded, all boxes above it and to its right are also shaded. If a box is blank, all boxes below it and to its left are also blank.

argument. Without further independent input, there can be no ruling made on the three remaining cases that still have question marks in their corresponding boxes.

The Shading Rule is very useful in identifying anomalous Talmud Diagrams. By virtue of the Shading Rule, all shaded boxes should be clumped into the upper corner of a Talmud Diagram. There can be no blank islands within a shaded region nor can there be shaded islands within blank regions. A cursory glance at a Talmud Diagram reveals in a straightforward visual way whether the principle of *a fortiori* is being obeyed or being violated. Any violations of the Shading Rule indicate either that there is some other hidden factor present, or that an error has been made and some rethinking of the passage is required.

The fourth and final step is a prescription for how to portray other opinions and evolving positions within a passage in the Talmud. It is also a warning not to fall into a common trap that leads to meaningless Talmud Diagrams. It is tempting to 'glue together' more than one opinion into a single Talmud Diagram, but this is a meaningless exercise. This type of diagram is motivated by the common use of charts where the columns or the rows are labeled by the authority expressing an opinion. In the context of Talmud Diagrams this form of organization is not allowed. If we were to label the first column 'Opinion 1' and the second column 'Opinion 2', would we conclude that if a box in the Opinion 1 column is shaded that the box in the Opinion 2 column must also be shaded by dint of Opinion 2 having been arbitrarily placed to the right of Opinion 2? This trap is avoided by following the prescription of the fourth step.

Step 4. Create separate Talmud Diagrams for separate opinions.

A Talmud Diagram therefore expresses a single opinion. An opinion in the context of Talmud Diagrams consists of a legal position taken on a collection of cases expressed by a Talmud Diagram. So far we have seen the legal opinion taking the form of applying a certain law to one case, represented by a shaded box, not applying the law to another case, represented by a blank box, and not resolving a case, represented by a box with a question mark. More than one law can also be represented on a Talmud Diagram by introducing additional shading patterns, for example a series of vertical or horizontal hash lines or the like. If more than one law applies to a particular case, the shading patterns can be superposed one on the other.

The real value of Talmud Diagrams becomes apparent when two or more Talmud Diagrams are compared. The two Talmud Diagrams may either represent two differing opinions by two authorities or the first might represent a question or challenge and the second an answer or a resolution. When the Talmud Diagrams from a complete passage are strung together, a picture emerges of the evolution of the passage. This technique is what Tufte (1990) calls 'Small Multiples'. These snapshots of the opinions held and the positions taken within a passage describe all that transpires within the passage in a concise and compact form that can be easily assimilated and recalled by the student. The representation of a passage by its associated Talmud Diagrams can perhaps be referred to as the 'meta-passage' because it is a mapping of the words of the passage into a visual explanatory form.

A Worked Example using Talmud Diagrams

In this section I present an example of a Talmudic discussion and its associated Talmud Diagrams. For more details see my book (Ury, 2011). The example is from the Babylonian Talmud, tractate Bava Metzia, page 21a (Malinowitz, 1992). This passage comes from the first page of Talmud ordinarily taught in the lower grades in Orthodox Jewish schools throughout the world. The material can be taught and understood at various levels. In this example we will explain the passage at first at a lower grade level and finally at a Grade 7 level.

Before diving into the details of the example, it is useful to consider a very common pattern in the use of Talmud Diagrams that will appear in the example. This pattern of reasoning is represented in the Talmud Diagram in Figure 4. What is portrayed in the figure is a very general Talmud Diagram without reference to the details of a particular case. There are no labels on the axes nor is there any explanation for the law indicating by shading a box, but we do assume that the Talmud Diagram is consistent with the four steps for generating a Talmud Diagram described earlier.

The four boxes in the Talmud Diagram of Figure 4 are labeled by the letter A through D for ease of referring to them. The status of the two boxes B and D is assumed to be given. In particular, the data we are given tell us that box B is shaded and that box D is blank. An application of the Shading Rule tells us that box C must be blank since it lies to the left of box D which itself is blank. We have no such luck with box A. We were given the status of boxes B and D, we were able to infer the status of box C, but the status of box A remains unresolvable. This means that the

Figure 4. An often encountered pattern in a two by two Talmud Diagram (©2011, TorahLab. Used with permission.)

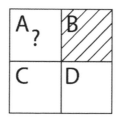

1. We know that B is shaded.

2. We know that D is blank.

3. We conclude that C must be blank.

4. We have no information on A.

case represented by box A cannot have its legal status determined by the application of the principle of *a fortiori* alone but can only be resolved using external information.

The chosen passage from the Talmud discusses the subject of the return of found objects. If an object is found in the public domain under conditions that indicate that the original owner has given up any hope for retrieval, the Talmud teaches us that the lost object may be kept by the finder. On the other hand, if it appears that the owner may have dropped it but would like to retrieve it if he can locate it, then the finder must publicly announce his find and cannot keep it for himself. So in a particular instance, the legal question at hand is whether the find must be announced or not.

Our particular case relates to a situation where a person is threshing his grain and discovers that the last person to use the threshing floor has left some grain scattered on the floor. The question is whether the owner of the scattered grain actually abandoned it, or will he make an effort to retrieve it. The Talmud quotes Rabbi Yitzchak who expresses an opinion which gives us the answer. According to Rabbi Yitzchak, if a measure of grain in the amount of a *kav* (a unit of volume) is scattered in an area of four by four *amos* ('*amos*' is the plural of '*amah*' = cubit) then the grain can be considered abandoned. Presumably, if more than a *kav* is scattered over that same area, or if a *kav* is spread over a smaller area, we must assume that the owner did not and will not abandon it and the find must be announced in an effort to locate the owner.

This ruling by Rabbi Yitzchak is expressed in the right hand column of Figure 5. The right hand column can be read in a straightforward manner to yield Rabbi Yitzchak's ruling. Starting with the lower right box, we see that it corresponds to an amount of grain equal to one *kav* spread over an area of four by four square *amos*. The key to the right of the Talmud Diagram tells us that shading indicates that the find must be announced, and that the lack of shading implies that the find may be kept. This then is exactly Rabbi Yitzchak's statement, namely that a *kav* of grain found to be scattered over an area of sixteen square *amos* may be kept. The top right box in Figure 5 corresponds to the case of one *kav* spread over an area of eight square *amos*, half the area of the case where Rabbi Yitzchak ruled that the find may be kept. We have presumed that for a case where a *kav* is spread over an area smaller than sixteen square *amos*, Rabbi Yitzchak rules that the find must be announced. The shading of the upper box and the lack of shading of the lower box therefore faithfully reflect Rabbi Yitzchak's position.

The Talmud continues its discussion with a query from a later scholar, Rabbi Yirmiyah, who ponders how we should rule in a case where half a *kav* of grain is found scattered in an area of two (by four) *amos*. Here the amount of grain is divided by two but so is the area. How would Rabbi Yitzchak rule in this case? Do we take into account the reduced area from which it is easier to gather the grain, or

Figure 5. Rabbi Yitzchak's statement and Rabbi Yirmiyah's query (©2011, TorahLab. Used with permission.)

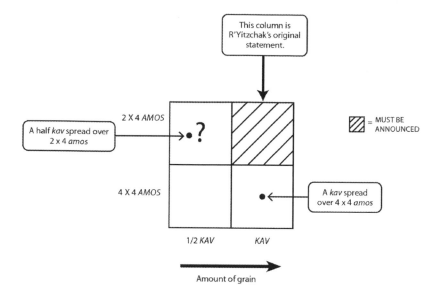

should we put more weight on the reduced value which is more likely to be abandoned by the owner? In the end the Talmud allows the query to stand and does not resolve it.

This is usually about as far as the explanation of the passage goes in a Grade 4 through Grade 6 lesson. For an adult, however, Rabbi Yirmiyah's query is a bit unsettling. What is the nature of his query? What point in the law is he addressing? How did he choose the details of the case about which he is inquiring? Why is his question unresolvable? These issues are not typically addressed in a Grade 4 through 6 lesson, and probably shouldn't. We can access the answers to these issues using Talmud Diagrams but it is questionable whether Talmud Diagrams are an appropriate tool for children below Grade 7. For the student in Grade 7 through adult however, the explanatory power of Talmud Diagrams is extremely helpful in analyzing Talmudic passages.

We can gain insight into Rabbi Yirmiyah's query by referring to the complete Talmud Diagram in Figure 5. Notice the similarity in structure between the Talmud Diagrams in Figures 4 and 5. The shading status of the top right and bottom right boxes is given, and using the Shading Rule, the blank status of the lower left box can be inferred from the fact that the lower right box is blank. In both situations a question mark has been placed in the box in the upper left corner since its status is indeterminate using the Shading Rule, meaning it cannot be inferred using the principle of *a fortiori*. This then is the background to Rabbi Yirmiyah's query. The case of a *kav* of grain scattered over an area of two by four square *amos* cannot be decided based on Rabbi Yitzchak's statement alone, even with the application of the principle of *a fortiori*. Upon examining the Talmud Diagram for this case, the student should be able to come up with Rabbi Yirmiyah's query even before becoming aware of it.

We have actually sidestepped a significant issue with our explanation of Rabbi Yirmiyah's query. This difficulty is dealt with by Tosafos - the medieval gloss on the Talmud that is found in the outer column of virtually every version of the Babylonian Talmud printed. The study of Tosafos does not usually begin before Grade 7 and is considered particularly challenging for the student. As in understanding the Talmud, understanding Tosafos can be aided by the method of Talmud Diagrams.

Referring first back to Figure 6, we see that we cheated somewhat by leaving off the vertical arrow and its explanatory label. The arrow's label and hence the ordering of the cases should have read "Area (decreasing)," but as we shall see there is a logical difficulty with taking this approach. Tosafos calls us on this, and his complaint can best be understood by referring to the Talmud Diagram in Figure 6. Notice that the horizontal arrow is labeled "Amount of grain" just as before, but the vertical axis is labeled "Concentration" and the rows of the Talmud Diagram are labeled with the actual concentrations of the amount of grain per square *amah* that are representative of the cases we have been considering. It makes sense to use concentration as one of the factors that affects the outcome of the cases since Rabbi Yitzchak's original statement seemed to depend on what side of the 'one *kav* per square *amah*' line the concentration lay. With this change in the structure of the Talmud Diagram, Rabbi Yirmiyah's query pertains to a case in the lower left corner rather than the upper left corner. We have already seen that there is no doubt (assuming

Figure 6. The difficulty with Rabbi Yirmiyah's query as posed by Tosafos (©2011, TorahLab. Used with permission.)

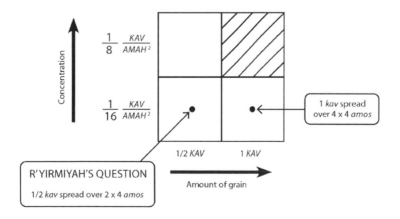

the validity of *a fortiori*) as to the ruling for the case in the lower left corner. After all, Rabbi Yitzchak has already ruled that if one *kav* is spread over sixteen square *amos* that the owner will definitely abandon his ownership, then a lesser value of grain, namely one half *kav,* found to be spread out at the same concentration, may surely be kept by the finder! Since there is no need to announce such a find, how could Rabbi Yirmiyah have any question as to what the ruling should be in the case of one half *kav* of grain spread over an area of two by four *amos*?

Tosafos supplies two solutions to the problem. The first solution portrayed in Figure 7(a) replaces the label on the vertical arrow with the words "Area (decreasing)." This has the effect of returning the Talmud Diagram to its original form as shown in Figure 5. The two factors that determine whether the find needs to be announced then become: 'amount of grain', and 'area' of the space in which it was found. As hinted to earlier, there is a logical problem with this portrayal that in fact originates outside the formalism of Talmud Diagrams and depends on aspects of human psychology. The issue is as follows: Rabbi Yirmiyah considers that there are two possible rulings for the case of one half *kav* spread over eight square *amos*. Let us consider for now the possibility that this type of find must be announced. At the same time we know that if a full *kav* is spread over sixteen square *amos*, no announcement is necessary. Now the half *kav* and the full *kav* cases both possess the same concentration of grain and the only difference is a factor of two in amount and in total area. So we can think of the one *kav* case as two contiguous patches of a half *kav* encountered in the half *kav* case.

To explain our point we can draw an analogy between the half *kav* case and the case of someone finding a single penny on the sidewalk. If the half *kav* case is analogous to finding a single penny on the sidewalk, then the full *kav* case is analogous to finding two pennies on the sidewalk. Here is the logical difficulty stemming from the assumptions we have made. We have assumed that a half *kav* spread over eight square *amos* must be announced and we know that a *kav* spread over sixteen square *amos* need not be announced. That means that the original owner does not abandon his ownership on a half *kav* spread over eight square *amos* but does abandon his ownership on a *kav* spread over sixteen square *amos.* Taking the penny analogy to its logical conclusion, does it make any sense to say that the original owner will come across his single penny that he lost and say, "There's my lost penny! I'll bend down and pick it up." yet the same person, had he lost two pennies and come across them would declare, "Picking up two pennies is too much work. I won't even bother to pick up even one of them." Why didn't the original owner even bother to pick up at least one of his two lost pennies if he would have bent down to pick up one penny had that been all he had lost?! This of course is the weakness in choosing 'area' as opposed to 'concentration' as one of the deciding factors.

Figure 7. Tosafos presents two solutions to the problem portrayed in Figure 6 (©2011, TorahLab. Used with permission.)

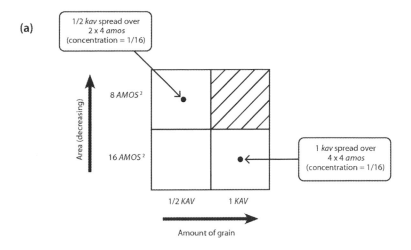

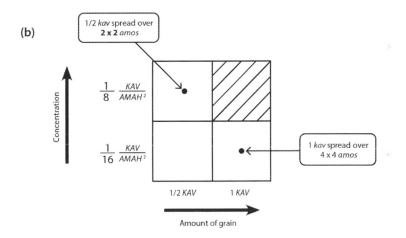

The answer to this objection is described explicitly by Tosafos but is a subtle point and hard to explain to a student in Grade 7. Tosafos argues that when a person is overwhelmed by a task he is liable to abort the entire task and not even attempt to start on even part of it. So for the case of the full *kav*, the owner might have abandoned his leftover grain because he felt that sweeping it up is just too much work, whereas had he left only half a *kav* he might undertake to gather it at a later time.

The second answer provided by Tosafos is portrayed in Figure 7(b). Tosafos alters our assumption about the conditions pertaining to Rabi Yirmiyah's query. When

Rabbi Yirmiyah inquired about the case of one half *kav* and referred to 'two *amos*', he in fact was referring to an area of two by two *amos* instead of two by four *amos* that we had previously assumed. This new assumption changes things drastically. As shown in Figure 7(b) the case corresponding to Rabbi Yirmiyah's query has migrated to the top left box whose shading status is indeed in question. The vertical axis remains 'Concentration' as it was in Tosafos' question (see Figure 6), but the case has moved to another box. In words we would say that Rabbi Yirmiyah's query boils down to the question whether increased concentration will motivate the owner to pick up his items or will the small value of one half *kav* dissuade him from retrieving the grain.

The use of Talmud Diagrams in this example demonstrates their utility and explanatory ability. In essence their use is a bookkeeping method to keep track of the cases including the factors that are present or absent in each case, the rulings that are known or unknown in each case, and the conclusions that can be drawn using the principle of *a fortiori*. Having all the facts straight and avoiding confusion allows the focus of the study session to shift to the truly interesting and exciting aspects of a Talmud passage. For example classroom discussions can focus on the interesting psychological reactions to large tasks that was mentioned earlier, or for a search for answers other than the two offered by Tosafos.

There is one more way in which Talmud Diagrams help the comprehension of a passage in the Talmud that was earlier alluded to briefly. In Figure 8 we have the entire progression of the discussion condensed into a small space. This simplifies the task for the student to comprehend and recall the unfolding of the discussion. The meta-passage represented by the multiple Talmud Diagrams is easier to remember than the words used in the original text. The meta-passage is more condensed because it uses symbols to represent complex cases and situations, the details of which are separate from the logical flow of the discussion. Because of this simplification, the discussion of the meta-passage can be carried out almost entirely divorced from the details of the situation being discussed. I refer to a discussion of the meta-passage as being carried out in the 'Language of Talmud Diagrams'. Here is the way we can read the four individual Talmud Diagrams in Figure 8 using the language of Talmud Diagrams.

1. Rabbi Yirmiyah inquires about the yet undetermined status of the box in the upper left corner.
2. Tosafos objects by pointing out that the query actually concerns a previously resolved box if one of the factors is taken to be 'concentration' as seems to be most reasonable.
3. Tosafos provides a first answer saying that Rabbi Yirmiyah's query makes sense if the factor 'concentration' is replaced by 'area'.

Figure 8. A condensed view of the passage using multiple Talmud Diagrams (©2011, TorahLab. Used with permission.)

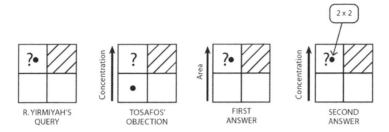

4. Tosafos provides a second answer saying that the case referred to by Rabbi Yirmiyah is different than first assumed and rightfully belongs in the top left box.

Once the student understands what the 'game plan' is for the passage it is much easier to engage in a conversation concerning its details and underlying logic. Too frequently the student is lost in the analysis of the basic kinematics of the passage and cannot participate in the discussion of the real legal issues at hand. Talmud Diagrams free the student from the challenge of discerning and retaining the structure of the discussion and enables learning the principles of the discussion.

Application of Talmud Diagrams to Other Legal Systems

Although created as an aid to the study of Talmud, Talmud Diagrams have application to legal systems other than Jewish Law. Goltzberg (2012) has suggested that Talmud Diagrams can be applied to the analysis of a specific legal case. Below is the analysis of an adaptation of that case, explained using Talmud Diagrams.

The statute contains the following rule: "An employer may not dismiss an employee for the only reason that he has been convicted of having broken the law if this breach is in no way related to his job." In an actual case an employer fired an employee who was accused of having broken a law that was not related to his job. At the time of the firing the employee was only suspected of having broken the law, not convicted of such. The employee charged that he was unlawfully terminated because the crime he committed was not related to his job. The judge in the case ended up siding with the employer based on the fact that the rule in the statute only prevented an employer from terminating an employee who was convicted of breaking the law, not someone who had only been accused of such. Use of a Talmud Diagram can help clarify the judge's somewhat surprising ruling.

Referring to the key in Figure 9, shading corresponds to the employer having broken the rule written in the statute. The judge's ruling and apparent analysis is shown in (a). The right hand column is just an expression of the rule. The employee has been dismissed. The bottom right box says that if the employee has been ter-

Figure 9. An employee files suit against his former employer. The judge's ruling is shown in (a). Tremblay questions the ruling based on his own analysis shown in (b). Goltzberg agrees with Tremblay's analysis but points out that a different analysis shown in (c) would have also led to a decision contrary to the judge's ruling.

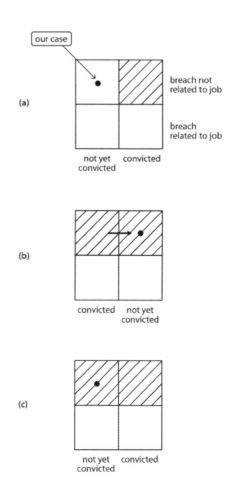

Rule: "An employer may not dismiss an employee for the only reason that he was convicted of having broken the law if this breach has nothing to do with his job."

= EMPLOYER HAS BROKEN THE RULE

minated for committing a crime that is related to his job, the employer has broken no rule by firing him. The top right box says that if the employee broke the law in a matter that is not related to his job, the employer has broken the rule by terminating him. Based on the judge's ruling, the judge apparently felt that the correct analysis for the case before him is represented by the Talmud Diagram in (a) with the case in question residing in the top left corner of the Talmud Diagram. He must have reasoned as follows. The law clearly states that the employer breaks the rule only if the employee was convicted at the time of the firing. Since the law specifies 'convicted' it must exclude 'not yet convicted' by the principle of 'argumentum a contrario'. Whatever the reason for demanding conviction, it clearly is absent if the employee was not convicted, so it is appropriate to place the 'not yet convicted' column to the left of the 'convicted' column where there is less reason for the law, and hence shading, to apply.

Tremblay (1999) criticized the judge's ruling, arguing that it is very hard to imagine that the statute would fault the employer for firing the employee after conviction more so than faulting the employer for firing prior to the employee's conviction. We can express Tremblay's argument using the Talmud Diagram in Figure 9 (b) where the column 'not yet convicted' is placed to the right of the other column. By this argument there is actually more reason to fault the employer if the firing was done when the employee was only suspected of committing a crime. Notice that our case, indicated by the dot, has now moved to the box in the upper right corner. Tremblay says that if the employer is at fault if the employee has already been convicted at the time of firing, then *a fortiori* the employer is at fault if the employee is only suspected. In the language of Talmud Diagrams we say that since the upper left box is shaded, then by the Shading Rule the upper right box must also be shaded.

Goltzberg (2012) agrees with Tremblay that the employer should have been found to have broken the rule by the argument of *a fortiori*. He disagrees however with Tremblay's implication that *a fortiori* was the only alternative to *a contrario* that would lead to a result opposite to the judge's ruling. It is in fact possible to disagree with the judge's ruling without having to go as far as invoking *a fortiori*. In other words, there are three possibilities when comparing the case of 'convicted', specified in the statute, with the case of 'not yet convicted'. Either the case not specified in the statute is: less likely, more likely, or just as likely to have the employer considered to have broken the rule. The judge invoked the principle of *a contrario* to say that the rule concerning the specified case is not broken in the unspecified case. Tremblay argued that the rule in the unspecified case is *a fortiori* broken in the unspecified case and Goltzberg agrees with this. Goltzberg points out however that the employer breaks the rule in the unspecified case even had the unspecified case been *a pari* (comparable) with the specified case. Goltzberg explains that the opposite of *a contrario* is in fact *a pari*, not *a fortiori*, so if the judge incorrectly excluded the unspecified case, either an argument of *a pari* or *a fortiori* would have led to an opposite ruling.

In the language of Talmud Diagrams and referring again to Figure 9, the judge ruled in accordance with Talmud Diagram (a) where the column labeled 'not yet convicted' lies to the left of the column labeled 'convicted'. Tremblay argues that the reverse order as shown in (b) is the correct order and that the judge should have found the employer to have broken the rule. Goltzberg agrees that this is indeed the case, but points out that there also exists a way to disagree with the judge without switching the order of the columns. It is possible to represent the situation by the Talmud Diagram shown in (c) which is the same as the one shown in (a) but with the top left box shaded, which results from considering the cases in the top right and top left corners as being comparable.

Once again we see how a meta-discussion of the legal issues using the language of Talmud Diagrams simplifies the comprehension and retention of the discussion. Three opinions on how to argue a case are summarized in a set of three drawings that present these opinions in a simple, graphical, easy to explain manner.

Challenges for the Acceptance of Talmud Diagrams in the Teaching of Talmud

As mentioned earlier, instruction in Talmud is done at a very diverse range of ages and skill levels. A certain amount of sophistication is required to understand a conceptual map such as a Talmud Diagram. This makes it less likely that Talmud Diagrams can be introduced to elementary school students, but perhaps can be appropriate as part of the curriculum for middle school students. The skills needed to read a conceptual map are becoming more common in younger students as the requisite skills, such as chart reading, are considered part of basic education.

There is also a slice of the population where individuals characterize themselves as not being 'visual learners'. Although validity of the theory of learning styles is a matter of some controversy, people who have convinced themselves that they are incapable of learning visually will naturally gravitate away from Talmud Diagrams and related visual methods.

Another barrier to adoption stems from an asymmetry in the use of Talmud Diagrams. It is fairly easy to read a Talmud Diagram but it can be quite difficult to generate one, especially for someone just starting out with the method. Several choices have to be made before even beginning to draw a Talmud Diagram, and the answers are not obvious, sometimes not until the passage is fully understood. For example, the dimensionality of the Talmud Diagram must be chosen. Will it be a one, two, or three-dimensional diagram? Other choices are equally hard or harder. What are the real factors involved? This is not always easy to ascertain without deep thought about the law and the cases involved. What are the 'laws' that needed to be represented by shading patterns? How many different shading patterns are needed to accurately represent the rulings being represented? How many rows or columns are needed for each factor?

The reality is that generating a Talmud Diagram is a trial and error process. Experience helps in the selection of a starting point for the dimensionality, factor selection, choosing the number of degrees and hence rows or columns for each factor, etc. The amount of work needed to create a Talmud Diagram however can be a worthwhile investment. The process of creating a Talmud Diagram is in itself a learning experience because one is forced to think deeply about the passage, and in fact to consider the appropriate rulings on each and every case at every stage of the discussion and for every opinion expressed. After all, no box can be ignored in a Talmud Diagram; it either has some kind of shading or not, or it may be officially indeterminate, but it cannot be ignored. For the experienced practitioner, taking the time to create the required Talmud Diagrams actually shortens the time needed to analyze a complex passage. The time wasted going over and over a passage without visual aids generally exceeds the investment in time needed to create Talmud Diagrams from the start.

The precision with which Talmud Diagrams represent a Talmudic discussion demands that the creator of a Talmud Diagram have a precise and accurate understanding of the Talmudic passage. The classic methods of determining the meaning of a Talmudic passage must still be employed in order to generate an accurate Talmud Diagram. Classically, the accepted meaning of a Talmudic passage is determined by reviewing the writings of the Rishonim – commentators who lived in roughly the eleventh through fifteenth centuries. The commentary of Tosafos mentioned earlier belongs in this category. A proper understanding of the Talmud with its commentaries is further obtained by studying all related passages in the Talmud. A misunderstanding of the correct interpretation of one passage is often revealed by apparent inconsistencies expressed in other related Talmudic passages. A further check on the correctness of analysis can be derived by examining later Rabbinic writings including works of Jewish law and responsa.

Since the method of Talmud Diagrams is still very new at the time of this writing, there is a very small inventory of Talmud Diagrams to share with others covering any significant number of passages. As mentioned earlier, it is easy to read a Talmud Diagram once it is created but without experience it is a non-trivial task to generate new ones. Most people will fall into the category of inexperienced content creators, so the widespread adoption of Talmud Diagrams awaits the creation of a critical mass of Talmud Diagrams to propel further interest. It may be that application of Talmud Diagrams to fields outside Talmud can lead to more rapid adoption of the approach. The monetary value of an improved legal argument, for example, could lead to the early adoption of Talmud Diagrams in the field of law.

As with any innovation, inertia is often the biggest obstacle. This may be particularly true in the case of Talmud study where the heritage in how it is studied is long and deep. There are certain advantages to doing things 'the old way' since these older methods have withstood the test of time. Nevertheless there is room for optimism in the adoption of visual techniques such as Talmud Diagrams in the realm of Talmud study. The study of the Talmud has an uncanny ability to adapt to the needs of the time and place. Just in the past decade we have witnessed a huge increase in the number of Talmud and Jewish law related works in the English language that are either entirely new or translations of earlier works. There is also the new phenomenon of computer based and online sites on Talmud related subjects including searchable databases of tens of thousands of books in Hebrew related to the Talmud. This bodes well for the adoption of other innovative techniques such as Talmud Diagrams in the study of the Talmud and Jewish law.

FUTURE DIRECTIONS

The method of Talmud Diagrams is very new and has not yet been tested in a classroom environment. Clearly this is something that is necessary to gauge the efficacy of Talmud Diagrams as a pedagogical tool. Proper testing of the method of Talmud Diagrams might involve a comparison of student performance on standardized tests with the inclusion of a control group for comparison.

As mentioned earlier, Talmud Diagrams are easy to read but comparatively hard to generate. Creation of Talmud Diagrams for the entire Babylonian Talmud is a formidable task and would require many person years of effort. Perhaps the most efficient way to generate this immense amount of information would be to employ 'crowd-sourcing' methods such as those used to create wikis.

The case for using Talmud Diagrams in the legal profession is compelling. The economic advantages of a convincing argument and the simplification of complex legal analyses are apparent. The adoption of the method of Talmud Diagrams by just a few in the legal profession may be enough to make the case for its more widespread adoption.

CONCLUSION

The method of Talmud Diagrams represents a powerful new tool for Talmud study. Talmud is studied by students of all ages and can be understood at various levels. The age appropriateness of Talmud Diagrams remains to be determined and indeed its efficacy as an explanatory tool needs to be verified experimentally. Talmud study has a very long history and introducing a concept mapping method such as Talmud Diagrams when none has been used before represents a challenge. Talmud Diagrams have been demonstrated to be applicable to other legal systems where they may prove useful in generating convincing legal arguments.

REFERENCES

Cohen, A. M. (2006). *Untangling the knot*. Southfield, MI: Targum Press.

Goltzberg, S. (2012). *Théorie bidimensionnelle de l'argumentation: Présomption et argument a fortiori*. Brussels: Bruylant.

Malinowitz, C., et al. (Eds.). (1990). Schottenstein Ed. Of the Talmud. New York, NY: Mesorah Publications.

Malinowitz, C., et al. (Eds.). (2006). Schottenstein ed. of Talmud Yerushalmi. New York, NY: Mesorah Publications.

Otterman, S. (2012, August 1). Orthodox Jews celebrate cycle of Talmudic study. *The New York Times*. Retrieved from http://www.nytimes.com

Steinsaltz, A. (1976). *The essential Talmud*. New York, NY: Basic Books.

Steinsaltz, A. (2012). *Koren Talmud bavli*. Jerusalem, Israel: Koren Publishers.

Tremblay, R. (1999). L'interprétation a contrario est abusive. *Le Journal du Barrreau du Quebec, 31*(7).

Tufte, E. (1990). *Envisioning information*. Cheshire, CT: Graphics Press.

Ury, I. (2011). *Charting the sea of Talmud*. Jerusalem, Israel: Mosaica Publishing.

ADDITIONAL READING

Carmell, A. (1991). *Aiding Talmud Study*. Nanuet, NY: Feldheim Publishers.

Cohen, Y. (2000) *Kerem Yehoshua – Bring Clarity to Your Learning and Master Shas*, Jerusalem, Israel: self-published

Lopes Cardozo, N. T. (1989). *The Infinite Chain: Torah, Masorah, and Man*. Nanuet, NY: Feldheim Publishers.

Schachter, J. (2005). *The Students' Guide Through the Talmud*. Brooklyn, NY: Yashar Books.

Tufte, E. (1997). *Visual Explanations*. Cheshire, CT: Graphics Press.

Tufte, E. (2001). *The Visual Display of Quantitative Information*. Cheshire, CT: Graphics Press.

Zobin, Z. (1986). *Breakthrough to Learning Gemora*. Jerusalem, Israel: Hed Press.

KEY TERMS AND DEFINITIONS

A Contrario: The argument by which a law known to apply to a first case should not apply to a second case.

A Fortiori: The argument by which a law known to apply to a first case must certainly apply to a second case.

A Pari: The argument by which a law known to apply to a first case should apply to a second case by analogy.

Amah (pl. *Amos*): Cubit – Biblical unit of length.

Gemara: That part of the Talmud that records a lengthy discussion of the Mishnah.

Hermeneutical Principles: The rules by which Jewish Law is derived from passages in the Bible.

Kal Vachomer: Hebrew translation of *a fortiori*.

Kav: Biblical unit of dry measure.

Mishnah: The older part of the Talmud that records the rulings contained in the Oral Law.

Talmud: The written record of classical Jewish Oral Law.

Talmud Diagram: An array of boxes and associated shading pattern used to represent opinions in the Talmud.

Section 2
Visual Representations for Design and Collaboration

Chapter 12
Conceptual Mapping Facilitates Coherence and Critical Thinking in the Science Education System

James Gorman
Northbridge High School, USA

Jane Heinze-Fry
Museum Institute for Teaching Science, USA

EXECUTIVE SUMMARY

In this case, the authors propose a pathway of visual mapping through which the science education system from professional educators who produce representations of national and state standards to curriculum coordinators at the school district level to individual teachers and students in the classroom could be aligned in order to promote meaningful learning of a connected set of concepts. Conceptual mapping is demonstrated to be a tool that promotes critical thinking, cohesion, and meaningful learning in opposition to the learning of arbitrary facts and rote memorization. The authors offer many examples of conceptual maps that have been produced to externalize thinking at each level. This chapter provides a "synthesis case" demonstrating that not only does it require critical thinking to create conceptual maps, but, equally salient, these visual representations of our thinking catalyze further critical thinking and coherence within the science education system.

DOI: 10.4018/978-1-4666-5816-5.ch012

BACKGROUND: CRITICAL THINKING, MEANINGFUL LEARNING, CONCEPTUAL MAPS, AND THE SCIENCE EDUCATION SYSTEM

Critical Thinking and Concept Mapping

A host of researchers have linked constructing concept maps (cmaps) with critical thinking (Jonassen et al., 1998; von der Heidt, 2011; Fonseca & Extremina, 2008.) As the chapters in this book will make abundantly clear, "critical thinking" has been defined different ways by different authors. Further, Krathwohl (2002) recognized the terms 'critical thinking' and 'problem solving' lacked clarity of meaning in popular usage and advised that "one must determine the specific meaning of 'problem solving' and 'critical thinking' from the context in which they are being used." A clear articulation of the relationship between cmapping and critical thinking comes from the field of nursing education. Daley et al. (1999) turned to a Delphi research project of the American Philosophical Association (APA) (1990), which published a consensus definition of 'critical thinking' based on the views of 46 published critical-thinking theorists from numerous disciplines. This definition states: "Critical thinking is the process of purposeful, self-regulatory judgment. This process gives reasoned consideration to evidence, contexts, conceptualizations, methods, and criteria" (APA, 1990, p. 2). She continues with Facione (1995) "Like many other descriptions of higher order thinking, the original Delphi authors conceptualized a simultaneous, metacognitive, self-appraisal of one's thinking process (that is, thinking about and evaluating one's thinking while engaged in the process of purposeful judgment (p.2). Drawing the connections clearly to the cmapping process, Daley concludes: Cmaps. . . link directly to the APA (1990) definition of critical thinking. Cmaps are metacognitive tools that assist learners to develop a self-appraisal of their own individual thinking processes. The maps foster a careful consideration of evidence drawn from clinical practice. Through use of cmaps, learners develop the ability to consider the context of nursing practice in their conceptualization of client problems. Finally, purposeful judgments are made regarding interventions based on how methods and criteria are linked to the conceptualization of the problems." Chabeli (2010) sinks deeper, providing a table correlating core cognitive critical thinking skills, related subskills and affective dispositions with the educational processes of cmapping.

In his literature review pertaining to the use of cmapping techniques and technologies for education and performance support, A. Cañas (2003), listed "to teach critical thinking" along with a variety of uses of cmaps. Novak and Cañas (2008) further explain, that the creation of cmaps clarifies a growing conceptual framework as individuals (or a group) learn a new field of study. This conceptual framework is very significant because it forms one of the filters through which the world is observed and interpreted and forms the basis for problem-solving and decision-making processes. Note that these complex mental processes are undergirded by the higher order thinking processes of analyzing, synthesizing, and evaluating (Anderson & Krathwohl, 2001). Thus, we will restrict our comments to critical thinking as being able to carry out complex problem-solving and decision-making, supported by the foundation of Bloom's higher order thinking, as defined by the American Philosophical Association (APA), and as applied by Daley et al. (APA, 1990; Daley et al, 1999). Further, we make the intellectual leap that strand maps also require critical thinking in their construction. We will demonstrate connections between critical thinking and conceptual mapping at all levels of the science education system. We will articulate some of the critical thinking questions that are asked at each level and we will ask how clarity at each level contributes to the coherence of the system. The salience of this work is highlighted by the addition of "metacognitive knowledge" to the revised Bloom's taxonomy. Regarding knowledge about cognition in general and one's own cognitive knowledge, Krathwohl (2002) stated, "It is of increasing significance as researchers continue to demonstrate the importance of students being made aware of their metacognitive activity, and then using this knowledge to appropriately adapt the ways in which they think and operate." We hope that our work demonstrates the importance of cognitive knowledge for those who work at all levels of the science education system.

Meaningful Learning: Theoretical Underpinnings of Conceptual Maps

The authors will use the term "meaningful learning" as defined by David Ausubel (1978). In its simplest form, meaningful learning requires learners to actively attach new learning to their prior knowledge. Conceptual learning requires the perception of "regularities in objects or events" and labelling them with a term. Meaningful learning requires " 1) that the learner has prior knowledge that is relevant to the new learning to be done; 2) that what is to be learnt is presented in ways that have meaning; and 3) that the learner must choose to learn meaningfully" (Novak, 1998). Meaningful learning, organized in concepts linked in a hierarchical fashion enables long term retention and application of those concepts. Meaningful learning contrasts with rote learning, in which learners memorize arbitrary concepts, do not link them to prior understanding, and consequently do not store them in long term memory nor have access to them for future problem-solving and decision-making. Meaningful learning is characterized by both progressive differentiation and integrative reconciliation. During progressive differentiation, learners over time add subordinate (more specific) concepts to a superordinate (more general) concept. During integrative reconciliation learners restructure conceptual understandings under a new overarching concept.

Conceptual Maps

Conceptual maps are visual representations of knowledge that clarify relationships among multiple concepts. The structure of a topic can be viewed holistically through both strand maps and cmaps. Content presented in either form provides an opportunity to more easily spot patterns of linkages than content presented through traditional bullet points or numbering schemes. While similar in addressing linkages of concepts, strand maps are structurally distinct from cmaps. Strand maps would be helpful in demonstrating the progression of learning over grade spans. The Commonwealth Massachusetts has employed the use of learning progressions to inform the science curriculum review process (Foster & Wiser, 2012).

Strand Maps

Strand maps represent learning progressions, the development of linkages among concepts over the K-12 grade levels. They show the progressive differentiation of big ideas of science over time and the integrative reconciliations that occur going from one grade span to another.

Learning progressions can account for how students think and learn about science from a cognitive perspective. A learning progression, by definition, bridges the scientific version of a big idea to the intuitive ideas children develop about it before formal instruction (Corcorcan et al., 2009; Wiser & Smith, 2009). While learning progressions are research-based, they are hypothetical; they are ideal paths for successful conceptual development about a big idea; they propose how a network of knowledge about a big idea could coherently evolve over long periods of time from young children's ideas if students are exposed to curricula with appropriate consideration given to "concepts, stepping stones, levers, and linchpins." (Wiser & Smith, 2009; Wiser et al., 2009) That is why a learning progression can be so useful; it invites standards developers to design coherent standards that will bring the learning progression about according to cognitively appropriate core ideas.

While strand maps do show conceptual relationships between key concepts, they do not include a variety of linking words that explicate the nature of the relationship between connected concepts; nor are they designed to clarify meaning of particular concepts. Additionally, some standards expressed in strand maps may contain more than one specific concept or skill, depending on how those are written and connected to other standards. We have seen these maps used to clarify representation of learning standards at both the national and state levels. [See Science Literacy Maps at the National Science Digital Library: (http://strandmaps.nsdl.org/) See the Massachusetts Science, Technology and Engineering Framework Strand Maps at: (http://www.doe.mass.edu/omste/maps/default.html).

Concept Maps

Cmaps as defined by Novak (1984) are generally applied at a "finer grain size" than strand maps. These graphical tools for organizing and representing knowledge are characterized by four elements: concepts, propositional linkages, hierarchy, and cross-links.

- **Concepts:** Are defined as perceived regularities in objects (such as "plant") or events (such as "photosynthesis"). Generally, each concept is represented by a one-word label enclosed in a circle or box. (This contrasts with the "standard" composed perhaps of multiple concepts enclosed in a circle or box on a strand map).
- **Propositions:** Are two or more concept labels linked together in a semantic unit. The simplest propositions are composed of only 3 words, such as "grass is green." The more the propositions radiating from a concept label, the richer the meaning of the concept. When a teacher reads a student's cmap, the linking words found on the lines between concept labels clearly indicate *how* the student is making the connections.
- **Hierarchy:** Describes the nature of the organizational layout of the concepts. The most general concept (superordinate) is at the top of the cmap. Progressing to the bottom, the concepts get more and more specific (subordinate). Thus, the map reveals the relationship of the parts to the whole.
- **Cross-Links:** Are particular propositions that connect and integrate different parts of a cmap. One of the strengths of cmaps is that they can actually show this integration, while linear outlines so often used in teaching and learning can *not* perform this function.

Cmaps have been used extensively as a research and "learning-to-learn" tool to clarify and demonstrate how individuals are thinking about a particular concept. In this chapter, we will provide one example in which cmaps were used at the curriculum coordinator level to demonstrate the relationship between a school's program and the state standards. In practice, we have seen these maps used by both teachers and students. We will provide a case study to demonstrate in depth how one of the authors and one of his students exemplify the application of meaningful learning theory to practice through their use of cmaps.

In our view, strand maps and cmaps are valuable visual representations that clarify how individuals serving across the science education system represent the key science concepts. As such, these maps provide "clear thinking," which is the foundation for advanced critical thinking, problem-solving, and decision-making.

Science Education System

The authors present their conceptual mapping experience in a sequential fashion that reflects their thinking about the hierarchy of the U.S. Science Education system from the most broad level, the national level down to the most particular level of the individual student learner. The chapter will link readers to conceptual maps produced at the national level by the AAAS Project 2061; at the state level by the Massachusetts Department of Elementary and Secondary Education by Jacob Foster and the co-authors; at the school district level by the curriculum coordinator of the Lexington Public Schools and co-author Jane Heinze-Fry; at the teacher level by co-author of this chapter James Gorman; and by student teams and an individual student in Gorman's physics classes. The authors will focus on how conceptual maps are produced through critical thinking and how they can provide the foundation for critical thinking questions key to each level of the system. Our hope is that this chapter will catalyze readers to think of conceptual maps as effective tools to enhance critical thinking, meaningful learning. and coherence across the entire science education system. The authors visualize an emerging synergy of the levels of the science education system in which the conceptual maps of each level may serve as advance organizers for each succeeding level of the system.

CONCEPTUAL MAPPING FACILITATES CRITICAL THINKING IN THE SCIENCE EDUCATION SYSTEM

The National Level: U.S. Science Education Reform and the First Strand Maps

Context: Bulleted Standards to Strand Maps

Science education in the United States has been undergoing concerted reform for decades. The first American Association for the Advancement of Science (AAAS) Project 2061 publication, *Science for All Americans* (AAAS, 1989), set out to define science literacy and lay out some principles for effective learning and teaching. This was quickly followed by *Benchmarks for Science Literacy* (AAAS, 1993), specifying how students should progress toward science literacy, recommending what they should know and be able to do by the time they reach grade levels 2, 5, 8, and 12.

The *Atlases of Science Literacy* (AAAS, 2001, 2007) transformed the benchmarks into strand maps that demonstrated how the most important ideas of science fit together and develop across the K-12 grade spans. Each strand map focuses on a topic important for literacy in science, mathematics, and technology and displays the benchmarks across the K-12 span that are most relevant to understanding it. For each benchmark, there is a suggestion of earlier benchmarks upon which it builds and later benchmarks that it supports, thus highlighting the developmental nature of the topic. These maps can be viewed on the Web at http://strandmaps.nsdl.org.

Critical Thinking to Create Strand Maps

Even a brief look at these maps generated by Project 2061 of the AAAS leads one to wonder at the number of critical thinkers who contributed to their construction. It is clear that a considerable amount of higher order analytical, evaluative and synthesis style thinking went into the construction of these maps. They rest on a foundation of knowledge of the content and the processes of science and of the research into student thinking at different grade levels. Of particular note is the use of the Web in making these maps accessible and the linking of these maps to both science education research resources about how students think and instructional resources peer-reviewed for these standards.

Catalyst for More Critical Thinking

Not only, then, did it take critical thinking to construct these strand maps, but they are designed for continued critical thinking to keep them updated with new research and newly created and reviewed resources. Further, curriculum coordinators can use them to guide the development of science curriculum at the school district level and teachers can use them to guide curriculum design at the classroom level. In this process, educators will continue to evaluate and make decisions about the design of instruction at those levels. We see that the construction of the Atlas maps promotes critical thinking by those who constructed them and will be responsible for revising them and for those who use them. What critical thinking questions might these professionals address upon which these maps cast light?

Those who construct the maps might ask: Do these maps reflect our best learning progressions research of science concepts across the K-12 grade spans? Do the strand maps show salient connections across the traditional science disciplines? Do they show important prior knowledge that is prerequisite to learning more complex concepts? Is updated research provided for teachers to understand what students think at each level?

For teachers using the maps: What prior learning should my students have before I start to teach certain concepts? What prior thinking is common about the concepts I teach? What can I tell my students to expect about what they might learn next once their understanding of the concepts at my grade level are understood? What instructional resources are available to teach the concepts for which I am responsible? If I am not satisfied with the progress of my students, are there additional resources I might try in the future? Are there ways to feed back to the map designers if I identify alternative learning pathways in my students?

For those responsible for a state's curriculum framework: Could state standards be represented in strand maps? Would such a representation lead to more coherence in the standards as they are revised? Can the Atlas strand maps offer meaningful connections as standards are revised? How have these strand maps produced by national leaders in science education influenced critical thinking at the state level of the science education system?

The State Level: Creation of Strand Maps for Science, Technology, and Engineering Curriculum Framework Review

Context: The Science Standards Review Process

At the state education governance level, the authors describe how strand maps influenced the critical thinking of the committee responsible for revising the Massachusetts Science, Technology and Engineering Framework (MADESE, 2001/2006) which establishes the state's standards for grades PreK-12. In 2008-2009, the MA Department of Elementary and Secondary Education set out to produce strand maps of the state science standards, modeled on the AAAS *Atlases for Scientific Literacy* (AAAS, 2001, 2007) to facilitate the review and revision of those standards (Heinze-Fry et al., 2010). *CmapTools* was used for the initial production of these state science strand maps.

Strand Maps: Representation of Progressions of Learning

The current Massachusetts science strand maps (available at http://www.doe.mass.edu/omste/maps/) show how students' understanding of ideas and skills that lead to scientific and technological literacy might develop over time from PreK to high school. The *Atlas for Science Literacy* strand maps were used as a model for the Commonwealth's strand maps. All figures in this section are examples taken from the Massachusetts strand maps. Clear text and color-coding can be viewed via Internet. Each cell of the strand map is an actual state science standard. The arrows between cells represent conceptual (not curricular) relationships between concepts.

The strand maps enable educators to see how the knowledge and skills students learn in different grades depend on and support one another. Thus, strand maps represent a progression of learning. For example, Figure 2 presents a portion of the Life Science strand map on the topics of *characteristics of living things* and *evolution and biodiversity.*

Foundations of understanding about evolution and biodiversity are established at the grade 3-5 level. Students are expected to "Give examples of how inherited characteristics may change over time as adaptation to changes in the environment that enable organisms to survive. In grades 6-8, students are expected to develop ideas of evolution further and be able to "recognize that biological evolution accounts for the diversity of species developed through gradual processes over many generations and to give examples of ways in which genetic variation and environmental factors are causes of evolution and the diversity of organisms." By high school, students are expected to construct an even more detailed conception of evolution and be able to "describe species as reproductively distinct groups of organisms; describe the role that geographic isolation can play in speciation; [and]explain that evolution through natural selection can result in changes in biodiversity through increase or decrease of genetic diversity within a population."

As we discuss the strand maps, we will use terminology that is specific to Massachusetts. It is worth taking a moment to define *strand, topic, standard,* and *link.* A *strand* is a science subject or discipline in the state Framework; each strand is represented on its own strand map and assigned a color scheme (Earth and Space Science—blue; Life Science—green; Chemistry—blue-green; Introductory Physics—purple; Technology/ Engineering—yellow-brown). A *topic* is a major subcategory within a strand and is assigned its own color from within the strand color scheme. For example, there are six topics within the Life Science strand: anatomy and physiology; cells and biochemistry; heredity and genetics; characteristics of living things; evolution and biodiversity; and ecology. A *standard* is a particular learning expectation. A standard specifies what students should know and be able to do and explicates the knowledge or skills to be assessed.

A *link* is an arrow that connects standards and represents the conceptual relationship between the two standards. These links are meant to make explicit the concepts that are considered *necessary* in order to learn later concepts, not any *possible* connection between concepts. Links within strands are solid; links across or between strands are dashed. An arrow *leaving* a standard implies that the concept contributes to learning the concept of the next, connected standard. These links are primarily based upon available cognitive research (often limited) specific to a particular idea, general principles of cognitive development (for example, concrete before abstract), logic of the subject matter, and wisdom of practice/ professional judgment.

One additional principle informed the development of these strand maps: simpler is better. The maps aim for as few arrows and crossings as possible. Placement of topics and concepts on the maps is first by "affiliation to a topic" but when needed standards are moved to place them in closer proximity to conceptually connected standards. Figure 1 presents an excerpt highlighting two topics from the Life Science strand map that illustrate each element discussed here. Topics are listed on the left: "Characteristics of Living Things" and "Evolution and Biodiversity." Each cell encloses one standard; each arrow represents a conceptual relationship between standards.

Features Revealed by Strand Maps of the State Science, Technology and Engineering Framework

The strand maps revealed two major features of the current state framework: 1) standards with varying levels of conceptual support across the entire PreK-12 span and 2) recurring patterns of relationships among standards. In particular, the strand maps revealed standards that were not conceptually supported in early grades and "opportunity-to learn-gaps" in which standards for a topic were at early and late grades but without concepts bridging those years, and some standards that were simply isolated from other standards. Patterns of relationships among standards included diverging and converging concepts and cross-linking within and among topics and strands. Readers will recognize the significance of these patterns for their visual representation of Ausubelian learning theory.

Unsupported Standards

Some topics revealed unsupported standards, in which some upper grade-span standards did not have related standards at early grade levels. Sometimes this is quite reasonable given the topic. For example, a number of chemistry concepts are not reasonably considered by elementary or middle school students. Further, not all grade spans must have concepts for each topic. However, this feature is revealed a number of times in each strand. For example, in engineering design, knowledge and skills needed to successfully represent problems and solutions are missing. In particular, analysis of the AAAS Atlases revealed two concepts fundamental to the development of this topic (Figure 2). Thus, the current framework targeting the topic of engineering design might benefit from the addition of foundation standards that emphasize student ability to "draw pictures that portray features of a thing being described" (PreK-2) and to make "scale drawings that show shapes and compare locations of things very different in size" (Grades 3-5).

Figure 1. Excerpt from the Life Science strand map showing standards from multiple topics and cross-linking with Earth & Space Science (From "Strand Maps of the 2001/2006 Science and Technology/Engineering Standards" http://www.doe.mass. edu/omste/maps/)

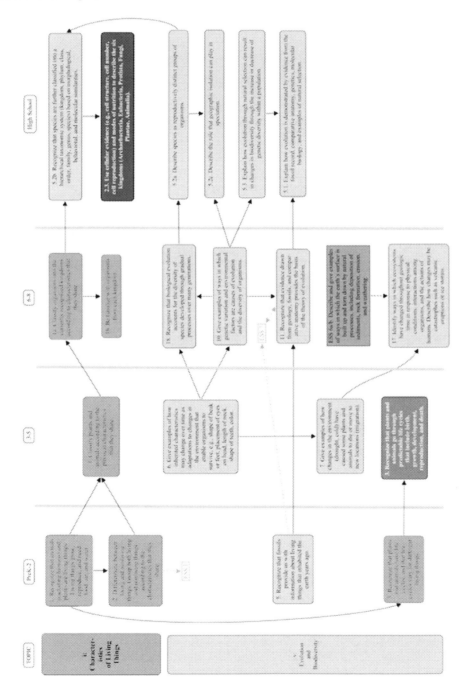

Figure 2. Portion of the Technology/Engineering strand map showing weakly supported standards for representing problems and solutions. Standards from the Atlases of Science Literacy that would better support those begin with "AAAS"(From "Strand Maps of the 2001/2006 Science and Technology/Engineering Standards" http://www.doe.mass.edu/omste/maps/)

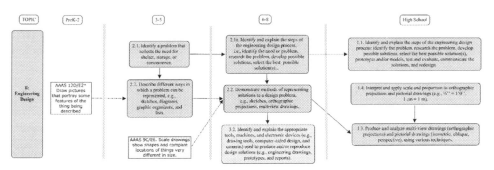

A second type of unsupported standards is represented in an "opportunity-to-learn gap," a break in learning of a topic for a full grade span or more. An example of this is depicted in an excerpt from the Physical Science strand map in Figure 3. The framework stipulates that students begin learning about motion in PreK-2 but then not again until grades 6-8. This presents a large conceptual challenge, as it may be between 4 and 6 years without learning about *force and motion*. How to address this gap, and others like it, is a key issue in the review process. Likely the reviewers will need to reference national documents such as the AAAS Benchmarks to identify appropriate concepts for grades 3-5.

Figure 3. The force and motion topic of the Physical Science strand map showing an opportunity-to-learn gap (grades 3-5) and two isolated concepts (grades PreK-2 and HS) (From "Strand Maps of the 2001/2006 Science and Technology/Engineering Standards" http://www.doe.mass.edu/omste/maps/)

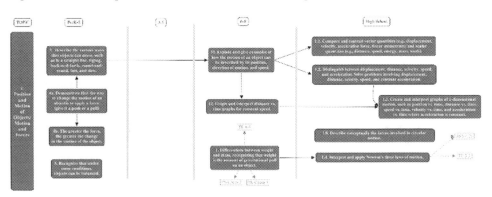

Figure 3 also illustrates a third type of unsupported standard: isolated concepts. At the PreK-2 level, a standard suggesting that students be able to "recognize that under some conditions, objects can be balanced" is not developed further at any grade level; nor is it conceptually related to any other standard. This is also the case for the high school standard suggesting that students "describe conceptually the forces involved in circular motion." Isolated content sends up a "red flag." Research indicates that arbitrary content is learned in a rote manner; i.e., not learned meaningfully, and is, therefore, less likely to be retained and applied in the future (Ausubel, 1978; Novak, 2009).

Patterns of Divergence, Convergence, and Cross-Linking

Three patterns of linkages among standards resonate with Ausubelian learning theory: diverging, converging, and cross-linking standards. Awareness of and emphasis on these linkages increase the opportunities for educators to facilitate meaningful learning by PreK-12 students in the classroom.

Diverging standards reflect what Ausubel would have called "progressive differentiation." Subordinate concepts are linked to or 'subsumed' under superordinate concepts. Learners add details to their general understandings, deepening conceptual structure. Figure 1, for instance visually represents the progressive differentiation of "evolution" over the Grade 3-high school spans.

In a second pattern, simple ideas introduced in early years are synthesized into more complex understandings in later years. None of the relevant concepts are more general than the others. The standards represent the learning of many new linkages among concepts that are non-arbitrary and relate to a broad background of generally relevant content in cognitive structure. Ausubel might have labeled the example in Figure 4 as a "combinatorial relationship." Much construction of knowledge must be carried out in early grades in order for high school students to be able to "provide examples of how the unequal heating of Earth and the Coriolis effect influence global circulation patterns, and show how they impact Massachusetts weather and climate."

A third pattern, cross-linking between topics within a strand and between strands themselves, is also commonly found throughout the standards. For instance, in Figure 4, the PreK-2 standard "understand that air is a mixture of gases that is all around us and that wind is moving air" is an "Earth Processes and Cycles" topic standard that lays a foundation for higher-level "Energy in the Earth System" topic standards. Additionally, in Figure 4, there are two standards from the Physical Science strand (found in sharp-cornered boxes with dashed arrows) that are crucial to the understanding of a Grade 6-8 standard in this excerpt from the Earth and Space Science strand.

Figure 4. Portion of the Earth and Space Science strand map showing converging concepts leading to the high school standard #1.4. Cross-linking between topics and between standards is demonstrated. (From "Strand Maps of the 2001/2006 Science and Technology/Engineering Standards" http://www.doe.mass.edu/omste/maps/)

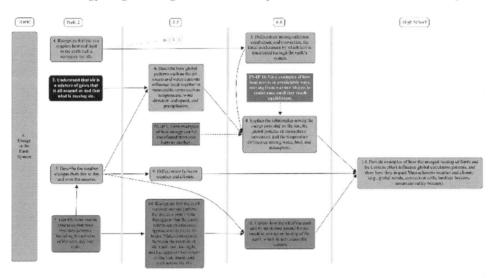

Using Strand Maps and Learning Progression Research to Revise State Standards

While we see the great value and potential of learning progressions on standards development, it is important to note that a full standards development process based on learning progressions is not possible at this time due to the early state of learning progression research. As such, the best we can do at this time is to revise our current standards to include what cognitive insights are now available. Using strand maps to visualize the progressions of standards is key to this process. For the present, our revision process will use what research is available, as well as collective wisdom of those teaching students, to appropriately address the features or patterns identified in the strand maps that may hinder student learning of science. Strand maps will help us enhance the relationships and progressions of standards to better support student learning of science.

Critical Thinking and Strand Maps

It certainly took a considerable amount of critical thinking to produce these maps (note the transformation of an outline style to a learning progressions style with linkages among concepts). In addition, a considerable amount of judgment went into the creation of linkages among the science silos (cross-links). In addition, positioning of concepts to reduce confusion from crossed lines, thus meeting the "keep it simple" criteria, was required. Also, a considerable amount of effort went into filling in potential gaps with input from the AAAS Atlas maps.

The strand maps enabled the committee to question the relevance of some learning standards and to question the strength of learning progressions of the big ideas of science over the K-12 grade spans. Understanding these features is key to revising state standards to enhance progressions of learning across grade spans to make explicit conceptual relationships across grade spans. State standards revised into strand maps offer a foundation to integrate efforts across the educational community that target meaningful learning.

It is important that these maps offer visual representations that were distributed to each member of the review committee to reflect on and offer feedback in groups. As groups, they worked to review and update the standards. They struggled with many critical thinking questions: Do these maps represent what the Commonwealth of Massachusetts expects its students to know and do over the preK-High School experience? Are the learning standards linked in clear learning progressions over the grade spans? Do the citizens of the Commonwealth support the learning standards inclusion of science content and science and engineering practices? Which concepts need more support? How can those gaps be filled? Which concepts should be eliminated?

The School District Level: Coherence with State Standards

Strand maps take a big step toward demonstrating the Pre-K-12 grades connectivity among the Massachusetts standards. Standards connected to prior standards imply that curriculum, teacher's instruction, and student's learning will be targeted toward connectivity and greater coherence. Such an approach foregrounds meaningful learning over rote learning.

Context: Concept Maps to Align Local Curriculum with State Standards

In 2006, the elementary science curriculum coordinator at the Lexington Public Schools worked with Heinze-Fry to investigate how the local life science curriculum benchmarks and the interdisciplinary Big Backyard Program aligned with state standards. Cmaps facilitated this process. (Note that this investigation preceded the development of the state strand maps.) *CmapTools* was used to create a template cmap of the MA Life Science Framework. (Today, either strand or cmaps could be used for this comparison.) The Science, Technology, Engineering Framework is available in pdf format at http://www.doe.mass.edu/frameworks/scitech/2001/0501.pdf.

Individual school districts, as is the case with the Lexington Public Schools, often operate from local curriculum guidelines. The Lexington Elementary Science Benchmarks described the overall goals and objectives of the entire science program. These goals included conceptual content from the life sciences, earth sciences, and physical sciences, as well as inquiry skills. (The original document used in this study has been updated. The current Lexington Public Schools K-5 Science and Technology/Engineering Curriculum is available at http://lps.lexingtonma.org//site/Default.aspx?PageID=1614 .)

A color-coding system was used to compare life science concepts from the Lexington Elementary Life Science Benchmarks with the state template map. Concepts were color-coded to indicate alignment with the state (green in Web version; medium-gray in print version), nonalignment with the state (red in Web version; dark gray in print version), and more depth than the state (yellow in Web version; light gray in print version). The same method was used to examine how the interdisciplinary Lexington Big Backyard program supports the state's life science framework.

This alignment can be viewed in color and with submaps on the Web at: http://cursa.ihmc.us:80/servlet/SBReadResourceServlet?rid=1143727786182_1874593061_6336&partName=htmltext. To view the Lexington Benchmarks concept list, one can click the icon at the bottom of the 'Environment' concept.

The analysis visually represented in Figure 5 is useful in that it offers a clear visual indicator of "fit" between the state framework and local benchmarks. Its utility comes primarily in assuring that the district addresses the state frameworks. This alignment strategy offers insight into recommendations that can easily incorporate "red concepts" into existing instructional activities and objectives. As state science testing becomes more high stakes along with English and mathematics, such alignment methods increase in value. While other alignment strategies exist, cmapping offers a particularly robust decision-making tool for a constructivist-based learning community. In addition to providing a visual framework, the cmaps, by demonstrating connections among concepts, can help teachers develop instructional activities in a cohesive manner.

Potential to Facilitate Critical Thinking and Coherence

Depending upon school policy, the science coordinator could work to increase alignment of the local curriculum to the state framework. Assuming closer alignment is desired, content areas coded 'green' should remain in the local curriculum. In general, educators should consider the green-coded concepts as "core" and strive

Figure 5. 'Core' concept map aligning Lexington Benchmarks with state framework

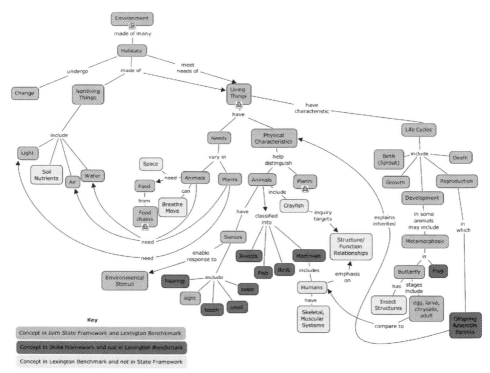

for high performance by all students in attaining them. The curriculum coordinator should work to incorporate content areas coded 'red' into the local benchmarks. The Department of Elementary and Secondary Education [transformed from prior Department of Education (DOE)] might also take note of this analysis. The maps demonstrate areas that the locality considers significant and are areas left unaddressed at the state level. During the review process, participants in the review process consider the importance of those concepts in the larger scheme of the state framework.

Alignment maps could be used in a number of ways by the science coordinator to more fully integrate the educational system. Sharing these alignment maps with teachers and volunteer parents demonstrates how their efforts in individual activities contribute to the development of a larger integrated "whole" for their learners. Individual teachers could create cmaps to align their particular class with local or state curricula to see how their classroom work supports systemic priorities. And they could further link digitized instructional materials to the maps, as demonstrated in the next section, to make the educational system even more coherent.

The Classroom Level: Teacher's Instructional Use of Concept Maps

Guided by state and local standards, teachers through instruction and assessment need to provide an environment that promotes meaningful learning by their students. Foremost in a teacher's mind has to be what order he/she is going to guide students through the established standards which do not prescribe an order but demonstrate a progression of concepts and skills. John Dewey (1910, p. 204) provides insightful advice for teachers:

...[J]ust because the order is logical, it represents the survey of subject matter made by one who already understands it, not the path of progress followed by a mind that is learning. The former may describe a uniform straight-way course; the latter must be a series of tacks, zig-zag movements back and forth.

The most prudent route for teachers is to become familiar with their subject area's pertinent standards described in their state's curriculum framework as well as their district's 'core' cmap if available. This will form the foundation of the curriculum and instruction, addressed in this section. It will also guide assessment of student learning, addressed in the Evaluating Concept Maps For Evidence of Meaningful Learning: the Teacher's Assessment Role section.

Concept Mapping Facilitates Teacher's Critical Thinking and Topic Order

Each teacher comes to the classroom with a personal understanding of the subject area. An expert teacher is one who can move back-and-forth between personal understanding and a sequenced presentation of concepts (Kinchin, 2009). In order to strategically organize the presentation of concepts, teachers must reflect deeply upon their own understanding of the subject. Afamasaga-Fuata'i (2006) has demonstrated the usefulness of cmapping for this purpose. She worked with pre-service teachers to construct concepts maps which represent their understanding of topics they were given. A fascinating observation was that in the process of critically thinking about how two concepts were related, teachers were also drawn to reflect on the relationship between those concepts and ones beyond the scope of their topic.

Gorman has also found this process of reflection to be very effective in his classroom experience. This practice has resulted in the creation of a "course organizer," which is a collection of linked cmaps with student resources attached. The process of constructing a course organizer is laborious because the authors are forced to clarify their own thinking in the process but so worth the investment of time and energy. For his course organizer, Gorman started by establishing the overarching concepts between which he then seeks to establish relationships. (See Figure 6a for an example.) This version is the result of much work and re-working, as new

Figure 6. Example of a course organizer a) Gorman's physics course home page b) 2D motion unit organizer with a partial view of the resources available for the vector addition concept

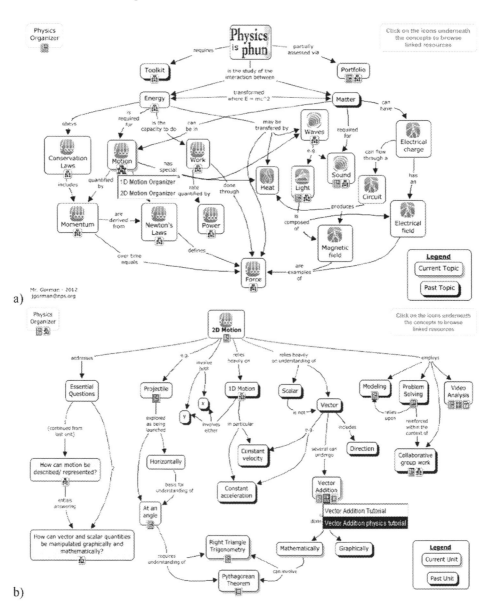

a)

b)

insights change the structure periodically. Part of the beauty cmapping brings to one's understanding is the visualization and construction of a record of how one's understanding changes over time. We will delve more deeply into this idea in the student section below.

Key features of a course organizer are: 1) it is composed of cmaps; 2) resources are attached to concepts; and 3) progress can be visualized. It is crucial that the cmaps have concise concepts since the intent is to break the concepts down for the students. No lengthy statements are allowed. Linkages between concepts must clearly but concisely express the relationship, thereby giving the students some insight into how the two concepts are related. Limiting the number of relationships lends clarity to the overall structure. The purpose here is to create a scaffold for future student work, *not* to do the work for them. Resources should be attached to pertinent concepts (See Figure 6b). Associated resources help students build their own understanding of the concept that they are linked to which can include activity sheets, tutorials, labs, videos, Web pages or any resource in digital format if CmapTools is used. Another important feature is the ability to provide a visualization of progress that not only highlights current concepts but also those already covered. Gorman used different color shadows to differentiate between current and past concepts.

Tracking progress has a couple of pedagogical advantages to the cmap-based course organizer. First, student attention is drawn to the concept at hand and how it relates to previous concepts. Second and more important, the linearity of progress through the concepts covered in class is countered by the cross-links between the different branches on the organizer. The 2D motion unit organizer in Figure 6b demonstrates this point very well. There are three branches evident: 1) unidirectional 1D motion concepts which were studied in the previous unit; 2) vector branch; and 3) the projectile branch. In class, as the students progress down each branch, they can "miss the forest amid the trees." The organizer seeks to remind them of the more complex big picture. Lastly, these organizers help scaffold learning by providing a framework with which students can begin constructing their own understanding (Ausubel, 1968). Prior knowledge is placed into context of the new unit. However, the organizer's author has carefully tried not to provide the students with too much information about the relationships among the concepts. Students are expected to create their own understanding of the topic and not memorize the organizer.

When developing course organizers, physics teachers may wish to consult Hyperphysics (http://hyperphysics.phy-astr.gsu.edu), a Web resource where non-Novakian cmaps are used to help students learn about physics. Conceptual nodes contain links to written tutorials with examples and calculators. Over the years Hyperphysics has continued to develop tutorial resources for chemistry, biology and geophysics. Curriculum developers have also started to provide a cmap overview of their curriculum. For instance, the Boston Museum of Science's acclaimed *Engineering The Future* (ETF) curriculum published unit cmaps in the appendix of their teacher manual (Gorman, 2008). These cmaps are static as it is a print resource so no links can be attached like Gorman's digitally available unit organizers but they provide a cohesive view of the central concepts and the relationships among them. As of the writing of this chapter, Kahn Academy has begun to create "knowledge maps" for their lectures and activities (https://www.khanacademy.org/exercisedashboard). These knowledge maps lack the propositional phrases of Novakian cmaps, but do have links that turn colors according to the user's progress through the activities associated with that particular concept.

Course organizers help clarify the teacher's own understanding and provide a hierarchical view of the topic which can be used in the classroom as a scaffold to facilitate student understanding. An important facet of unit organizers is that prior knowledge is present so that new concepts are shown in relation to them. Cross-linking between branches is a key component as well as showing the progress through a unit. Taking this first step helps teachers break a linear model of teaching (which only promotes a naive, false certainty in students' minds) and bring students to an awareness of more complex understandings.

Concept Mapping Positively Impacts Presentations

Rooted in a strong awareness of their own understanding and the resulting self-confidence, teachers can then begin to construct lesson plans that promote critical thinking. PowerPoint presentations are at the core of many teachers' repertoire and can be a useful tool. However, Kinchin (2007) found that use of linear presentation formats like PowerPoint in an unreflective manner tends to result in short-term learning. They also promote surface learning or rote learning which does not lead to critical thinking or mastery of the material. This is not to say that all linear presentation formats are always bad because in his survey students saw the advantages of bullet-pointed presentations for short-term learning goals. Interestingly, the students were able to recognize the tension between short-term and meaningful learning. This suggests students often adopt a rote learning style to successfully navigate through their school years.

To combat this problem, Kinchin applied cmapping principles to transform the linear PowerPoint format into a more interconnected structure. Students were presented with a cmap which only contained the main concepts of that presentation. Figure 7 is an example of this methodology from Gorman. The slides are numbered in the order they appear in the presentation. This is not meant to be a substitute for taking notes so the bullet-points are not quite readable on the slides. However, the main concepts covered on the slides are more readable. As a cmap, relationships

Figure 7. A cmap view of a lecture slides on MRSA treatment and molecular geometry/bonding. Each slide's position in the linear PowerPoint presentation is noted with a number.

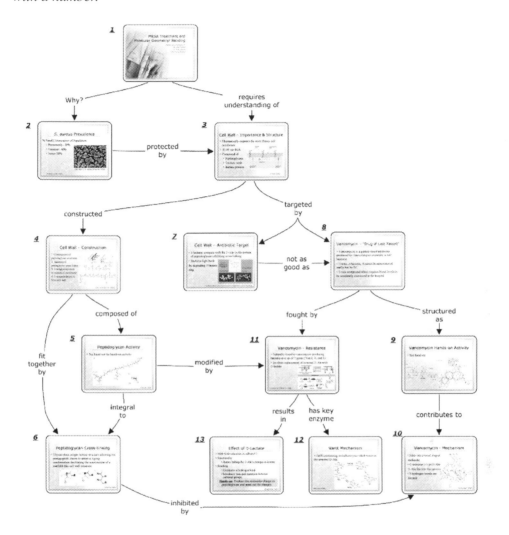

contain linking phrases to move students to think more deeply about the topic. These links not only reveal a hierarchical structure among the concepts, but also provide cross-links between slides which are significantly separated in the linear presentation (e.g., the cross-link between slide 5 and 11 or slide 6 and 10).

Moon *et al.* (2008) followed up on these observations with a quantitative study involving pre- and post-tests. Students were presented with one of four different formats of the same material: journal article in traditional text, a hypertext version of the journal article, a Microsoft PowerPoint presentation, and a set of cmaps with attached resources. When comparing pre- and post-test score, they found that the cmap group showed more learning in comparisons of their pre-test and post-test scores compared to the PowerPoint group. A survey also revealed a compelling preference for cmap format over PowerPoint. Therefore, this study provides positive evidence for a teacher to present material in cmaps as it can promote meaningful learning.

Of significant note is the Concept Mapped Project-based Activity Scaffolding System (CoMPASS) under the direction of Sadhana Puntambekar. CoMPASS is geared toward middle school students and combines a hypertext environment with design challenges. Physics-based units have been developed to facilitate students' visualization of the relationship between concepts and principles. Cmaps are used to supplement the text. In agreement with the previously noted works, Puntambekar et al. (2003, 2007) confirms that when cmaps are used to provide a visual relationship between concepts it promotes meaningful learning and results in significantly improved post-test scores. The significance of this study is that cmapping has been proven to promote critical thinking in grades 6-8. The CoMPASS project can be accessed at http://www.compassproject.net.

The Classroom Level: Student Concept Maps Represent Meaningful Learning

Teaching is more than delivering a presentation or organizing meaningful lessons for students, it is about prompting and facilitating learning in the classroom. A significant shift from focusing on content to the process of learning the content has already been made by teachers who create course organizers and incorporate cmapping into lessons. With the materials in place, now the teachers are ready to engage with the students helping them to create their own understanding of the topic. Teachers must be keenly aware that students' understandings will not be a copy of the their own, but will instead reflect each student's experiences and prior knowledge.

Concept Mapping to Facilitate Personal and Negotiated Meaning

In a meaningful learning environment it is important to start with students' prior knowledge because this is the foundation upon which new knowledge will be constructed. In the teacher section, we reviewed the value and process for reflecting upon their understanding of a topic. For students, however, the process is more in depth as they have little to no knowledge or understanding of the topic. If a student were given the expert cmaps that the teacher created the student could be overwhelmed.

Furthermore, provision of the connections actually blocks the development of the students' own critical thinking skills.

Novak (1984) promotes the use of expert skeleton cmaps (ESCM) which are developed by a teacher from his expert concept maps and can be used as pre-tests to see what knowledge the student has about a particular topic. These pre-tests are not graded. ESCMs also serve as advance organizers to scaffold learning by providing starting points. That is, ESCMs provide an initial hierarchical structure which incorporates prior knowledge and a "parking lot" populated with threshold concepts. "Threshold concepts" are central to the mastery of the subject area (Meyer & Land, 2003). Some main attributes of threshold concepts are transformative (changes the student's view of the subject), troublesome (often are counter-intuitive or alien), irreversible (unlearned only through considerable effort), and integrative (showing the relatedness between two other concepts which were previously hidden) (Meyer & Land, 2005). The utilization of threshold concepts not only focuses the student to critically think about these key concepts but also empowers the teacher to recognize/ assess when students have acquired key understanding and help negotiate a more precise meaning with the students. Through this process, students' assumption of concepts can be concretely visualized over time as the cmaps evolves in complexity to reflect their new understanding.

Novak (1984) found that ESCM help build mapping skills and learner confidence while promoting meaningful learning, as we will point is a manner of promoting critical thinking in the classroom. Additionally, ESCMs reduce the chance of misconceptions being perpetuated and maximize the chance that the knowledge structure will help remove or at the least decrease misconceptions (Novak, 2002). Figure 8a is an example of an ESCM for a physics 1D motion unit. This concept has also been extended to enriched ESCMs by Marée et al. (2012) which like the unit organizers above have resources attached to each concept and found that students' test scores correlated with their cmap scores.

There is one last key component of a ESCM, the focus question which serves to limit the scope of the cmap. Research has demonstrated that phraseology employed in a focus question directs the structure and quality of the resulting cmap. Derbentseva et al. (2004, 2006) studied declarative vs. dynamic focus questions as applied to cmapping and established that dynamic focus questions encouraged the use of richer propositional phrases. Therefore to encourage more critical thinking, dynamic focus questions should be used as much as possible (i.e., "How do the different parts of the plant help to produce food for the plant?" as opposed to "What are the parts of a plant?").

Gorman administers ESCMs as pre-tests not only to get a sense of what students understand, but also to provide students with time to reflect about what they might know or understand about a particular topic. This activity can be eye-opening for

Figure 8. Student example of how his personal understanding has evolved over the unit from a basic spoke structure to the complexity of a network. This example is from a unit on motion with the focus question, "How can motion be described/ represented?"

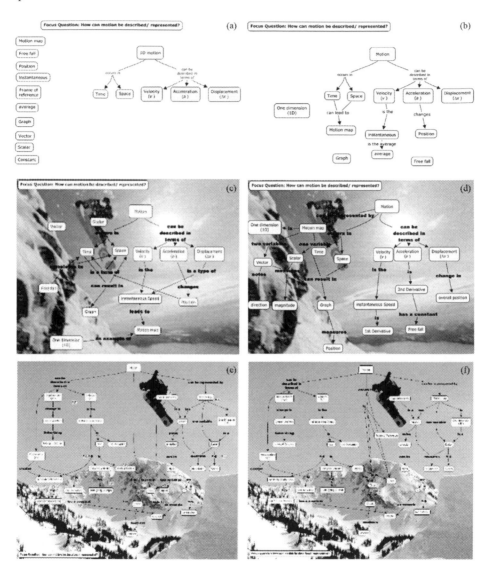

students and helps start the teacher-student conversation. Figure 8b is the result of a student's first attempt to express what he knew using the ESCM. The student only made three connections to the existing structure and was unsure how the other concepts fit in. After some meaningful learning time, the student then revised his cmap,

Figure 8c. Notice that in this cmap, the majority of the concepts are used as well as additional concepts the student has acquired. However, some misconceptions are present. Once the teacher assesses where the students are starting from, he can make adjustments to the lessons to follow. After some instruction, it is important to have students compare their cmaps and negotiate the meaning of the individual concepts.

There are a myriad of different methods to encourage negotiation and group construction of a cmap. Gorman prefers to break students up into groups of three or four and have them negotiate meaning to arrive at a group cmap using 2'x3' whiteboards (Wells et al., 1995) because students can easily erase and redraw their cmap. Sticky notes or index cards would also work well as they can be easily rearranged. As a teacher, this is one of the best times to listen in on student conversations and observe their cmaps. The teacher can quickly identify misconceptions and ask probing questions to make the students critically think about their understanding. Giving them the answer is counterproductive when facilitating critical thinking. When circulating through the classroom and monitoring conversation, the teacher can clearly observe the progressive differentiation (lengthening of chains) and integrative reconciliation (the changing of hierarchical structure and cross-linking). Occasionally, a debate will erupt in a group and the teacher will be brought in to mediate. More often than not, both the students are correct but they think they are at odds with each other because they have been accustomed to thinking that there is only "one correct answer."

Once each group has been given enough time, the groups switch whiteboards and compare their negotiated cmaps, with the opportunity of incorporating any new insights on their own cmap. The rotation continues until the groups are back at their own whiteboard where they review and consider the comments. Their homework is to revise their own personal cmap, the result of which can be seen in Figure 8d. The teacher should be cognizant of the misconceptions and holes in student understanding. After additional meaningful learning time, which seeks to address the persistent misconceptions and elaborate on existing understanding, students revise their cmap to reflect their current understanding. The yellow notes in Figure 8e which was created in CmapTools are the teacher's comments to the student. This version can then be revised in groups and after an additional remediation period a final cmap is constructed, Figure 8f. Comparing the depth and complexity of understanding between the first cmap and last in Figure 8 reveals that this student has significantly improved over the course of the unit. Kern (2008) provides a similar methodology with four cmapping periods each with a different emphasis and role for the teacher.

The knowledge portfolios assigned to Gorman's physics class require the students to make the individual topics of physics relevant to their lives. Thus, the students were challenged to critically think about how the topics they were learning in the classroom applied to their lives. One student's way of demonstrating his connection is demonstrated in Figure 8. The colorful background in the student cmaps were placed there by the student who likes to ski, demonstrating his way of relating to the topic. Steps like this tap into students' emotions (i.e., Bloom's affective domain) by making them realize that these concepts apply to their lives. Making these concepts personal raises student responsiveness and causes them to be active learners, a key component to meaningful learning.

Teachers can focus their critical thinking about teaching methods on a wide array of cmapping activities. Anohina-Naumeca and Graudina (2012) classified cmapping tasks and ranked them from the simplest to the most difficult, Table 1. The simplest tasks involve very little freedom to the student and can be found in many text book chapter review sections. These cmaps. though, require the least amount of critical thinking while the more difficult cmaps offer more freedom to the creator. These are best for a meaningful learning environment as they require the student to critically consider the relationship between concepts and develop the structure of the cmap themselves. There are two cmapping tasks which preclude the use of linking phrases, the 3rd and 5th degrees. The authors strongly advocate for the inclusion of linking phrases because the students are then forced to articulate the relationship between concepts. As Vygotsky (1997, p. 218) states, "Thought is not merely expressed in words; it comes into existence through them." The externalization of student thoughts is a crucial factor to facilitate critical thinking and opens up a space for dialog and negotiated meaning.

Mirzaie et al. (2008) conducted a study with high school chemistry students in which they used cmapping with half of the students and traditional instruction with the other half. Their cmapping methodology was similar to the one described above.

Table 1. Summary of cmap based intelligent knowledge assessment system (IKAS) developed at Riga

Difficulty (Simplest to Most Difficult)	General Task		Cmap Structure		Concepts		Linking Phrases		
	Fill the Blank	Make a Cmap	Given	Student Driven	Some Concepts in Structure	Parking Lot	Not Used	Already in Structure	Parking Lot
1st	X		X		X	X		X	
2nd	X		X			X		X	
3rd	X		X			X	X		
4th	X		X			X			X
5th		X		X		X	X		
6th		X		X		X			X

Technical University, Latvia (table modified from Anohina-Naumeca and Graudina 2012)

The teachers administered pre- and post-tests but the uniqueness of their study is that test questions were designed according to Bloom's taxonomy. The assessments focused on the Bloom's factual and conceptual knowledge dimensions and covered all cognitive process dimensions. In their analysis, Mirzarie et al. found that both groups of students performed similarly on the lower cognitive skills (remember, understand and apply). However, the students who were immersed in a cmapping environment significantly outperformed the traditional classroom students on questions which involved the higher critical thinking skills (analyze, evaluate and create). Cmapping forced the students to break down the information into parts and find evidence to support the generalizations they were making (analyze). The students then had to fit these new insights in relationship with their prior knowledge (create). After reviewing other student cmaps, students needed to "negotiate meaning." (evaluate). Each of these skills are given little emphasis in traditional classrooms so it is little surprise that students who consistently employed cmapping during the learning process would excel with these higher critical thinking skills. This work suggests that instruction in the higher order cognitive processes that address meta-cognition knowledge facilitates learning of the higher order cognitive processes of factual and conceptual knowledge in a science discipline. Furthermore, it is easy to consider that such instruction would also catalyze higher order thinking across all the disciplines, not just the sciences.

Evaluating Concept Maps For Evidence of Meaningful Learning: The Teacher's Assessment Role

Teachers must grade and provide feedback on their students' work to report on their progress. Johnstone and Otis (2006) suggest viewing cmaps as a learning tool rather than an assessment tool. However, even learning tools must be accompanied by some form of assessment. Assessments can be broken into two types: qualitative and quantitative.

Qualitative analysis of cmaps relies heavily on the gross cmap morphology. Kinchin et al. (2000) clearly identify three types of structure with a cmap: spoke, chain and network (Figure 9). A spoke structure is similar to a bulleted list which indicate learner readiness but does not demonstrate an understanding as there are no links present between concepts. Considering Bloom's revised taxonomy, spoke structures can also represent the learner putting factual knowledge on paper without any critical thinking involved. While spoke structures are indicative of novice learners, teachers can guide students to rudimentary understanding that is evident in chain structures which are indicative of goal-oriented learning. Rote learning encourages chain structures which are resistant to change because student are not yet personalizing the concepts. Considering Bloom's revised taxonomy, chain structures

Figure 9. This cmap details knowledge structure variations which can be indicative of types and levels of understanding (modified from Kinchin et al., 2000)

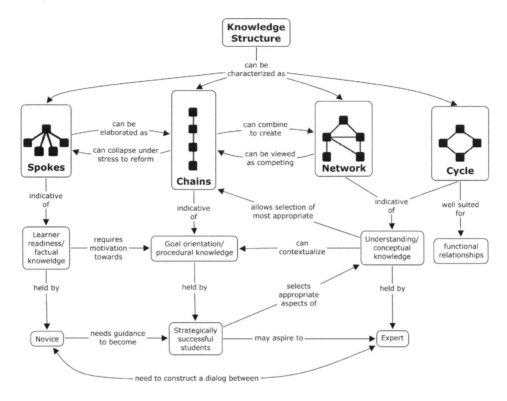

can also be indicative of procedural knowledge. Students who engage in meaningful learning, as seen in the previous section, critically think about the relationship between all the concepts. Thus, they tend to produce network-like cmaps which show a degree of cross-linking between concepts in separate chains. Network structures are evidence that critical thinking is occurring and, as a result, is indicative of student understanding. Since network structures emphasize the link between concepts in different domains it could also be indicative of Bloom's conceptual knowledge dimension which focuses on the interrelationship among concepts. Content experts produce cmaps with a great deal of network structure. Safayeni et al. (2005) identified a fourth morphology called a cycle which is well suited to represent functional or dynamic relationships including mathematical relationships.

The four knowledge structures are not in opposition to each other and often several types can co-exist in a single cmap. Dependent on the focus question, a structure can evolve from spoke to chain to cycles or networks and back again. Where procedural knowledge is asked for, chains become more prevalent, while mathematical relationships favor a cycle structure. While evaluating cmaps, the teacher should be cognizant about these types of structures and how they can give insight into the level of understanding.

It is instructive to apply Kinchin's insights (Figure 9) to analyze the cmap time sequence found in Figure 8. What do the knowledge structures imply about the student's depth of thinking and understanding? At the start of the unit, the student took the skeleton map and was able to relate a couple of concepts in a spoke-like arrangement. By the next snapshot, this student was able to add more concepts and make more connections among them. The cmap has a single cross-link and a chain element demonstrating the fact that the student is beginning to think more critically about the relationship between concepts. In the fourth cmap, there are several chains linked by phrases that are mostly accurate. This is evidence the student has learned at least the definition of each concept but has not yet achieved a cohesive picture of how the concepts relate to one another. The fruit of much critical thinking is clearly evident in the final two cmaps where the student was able to make cross-links between different chains, thus forming a clear network structure typical of an expert.

Knowledge structures present in a cmap provide a key initial impression of the understanding held by a student, but it should not be the only criteria. Hays (2007) suggests qualitative analysis in terms of depth of learning: deep, surface, and non-learning. His methodology takes into consideration knowledge structure and two additional factors: concepts and linkages. A rubric which summarizes Hays' criteria and Kinchin et al.'s (2000) morphologies can be found in Table 2. A cmap demonstrates deep learning when new concepts have been added as well as the linkages are valid and explanatory. These qualitative depth of learning criteria fit well with

Table 2. Rubric for the qualitative analysis of the depth of learning based on cmap analysis

Depth of Learning	Criteria Comparing Final Cmap to the First		
	Concepts	**Linkages**	**Overall Structure**
Deep	• Original concepts remain. • New concepts added	• Valid • Explanatory • Evidence of meaning in the mind of the map author.	• Network and/ or cycles are present. • Well defined organization. • Increased number of cross-links between branches.
Surface	• Significant number of new concepts but not linked with prior knowledge.	• The overall number of linkages has not changed significantly.	• Chain structures are present. • None to few cross-links. • Explanatory power not significantly increased.
Non-Learning	• None to few new concepts added.	• Zero to few new linkages made. • no new cross-linking between concepts.	• No change in knowledge structure or significant reorganization of concepts.

our observations based on the knowledge structure of the student cmaps in Figure 8 while taking into account the concepts & linkages.

From a teacher's perspective, quantitative analysis is often the end result of most activities. However, there are several concerns that need consideration before setting out to "grade" cmaps. First, not all concepts are equal in value or weight. Some concepts are not as crucial to understanding as others (Mintez & Quinn, 2007). Crucial concepts definitely include threshold concepts discussed earlier in reference to ESCMs. Second, the most important concepts are more indicative of student understanding than the overall number of concepts present; bigger is not always better (Clariana & Taricani, 2010). Expert maps tend to have fewer concepts than novice maps as experts are more prudent by selecting the key concepts and linking them with meaningful phrases. Clariana and Taricani (2010) found that a score derived from the 16 most important concepts in cmap correlated well with the performance on a multiple choice test. Third, a student who demonstrates surface learning might understand more than is portrayed because that limited set of propositional phrases might be enough to serve as a memory jog. Any cmap assessment regime must be vigilant to assure that students are accurately representing the full extent of their understanding. Assessment criteria must be made clear and upfront.

A widely used semantic grading rubric was developed for Panama's large-scale *Conéctate al Conocimiento* Project to assess the meaningful learning as evidenced by cmaps. This rubric is content-based and details a set of "six criteria: 1) concept relevance and completeness, 2) correct propositional structure, 3) presence of erroneous propositions (misconceptions), 4) presence of dynamic propositions, 5) number and quality of cross-links, and 6) presence of cycles" (Miller & Cañas, 2008). Even with a rubric, cmap assessment is inherently subjective in nature. However, while testing this rubric over many evaluators, Miller and Cañas (2008) demonstrated a moderate level of consistency between evaluators suggesting that this rubric would have potential for large-scale use. In a classroom where one teacher is assessing all the cmaps, subjectivity between evaluators is negated. A copy of this rubric can be found in the appendix of Miller and Cañas (2008) at http://eprint.ihmc.us/320/1/cmc2008-p253.pdf.

Analysis of large cmaps or large quantities of cmaps can be taxing. In 2010, CmapAnalysis was developed to alleviate some of the pain by automating the collection of key parameters about a set of cmaps (Cañas et al., 2010). This software pulls out data relative to size, quality, and structural properties while remaining flexible so that users may define their own assessment parameters. Output from the software is in the form of an Excel spreadsheet (.xls) for ease of viewing and manipulation.

CmapAnalysis only accepts cmaps in open CXL file format which can be easily exported from CmapTools. This multi-platform software is freely available through the Google Code project at https://code.google.com/p/cmapanalysis/. While this software will not be able to fully automate cmap analysis, it can mitigate some of the more tedious aspects.

Meaningful learning can be assessed using either qualitative or quantitative methods. Qualitative assessments are very well suited for formative evaluations which are extremely important in meaningful learning because it starts a dialog between the students and teachers. Quantitative analysis arrives at a "score" for a cmap but the process can be tedious and requires keeping several caveats in mind.

DISCUSSION

In the recently published book *Surpassing Shanghai: An Agenda for American Education Built on the World's Leading Systems*, editor Marc Tucker summarizes international student performance in science as measured by the PISA assessments, highlights case studies of the five countries who are the top performers, and recommends an action plan for the United States to reassert its efforts in this playing field (Tucker, 2012). Among the top two recommendations is "coherence in the design of the overall education system itself." The authors of this chapter described key levels of the science education system, some of the salient critical thinking questions that must be addressed at each level, and how conceptual maps, as visual representations, can facilitate clear understanding of and communication about the science content at each level. Our hope is that this chapter will catalyze readers to think of conceptual mapping tools in their application to enhance coherence, critical thinking, and meaningful learning across the entire science education system. The authors visualize an emerging synergy of the levels of the science education system in which the conceptual maps of each level may serve as advance organizers for each succeeding level of the system. We can visualize how each lower level in the system can access and use the structure created at the level above, select the most salient parts and add parts particular to its needs, thus benefiting from the work provided, but also adapting it to its own critical thinking questions.

CmapTools is one mechanism which can be used to link all of these efforts together, thus making the system as a whole more coherent. Curriculum coordinators can parse the requisite knowledge into expert cmaps that clearly label the relationship between concepts. The advantage here is that the curriculum coordinator can directly link their school or school system's goals to the standards while fleshing their meaning out for educators. Teachers can also link their instructional efforts to the curriculum coordinators' work. Students, in turn, can demonstrate mastery of subject matter by linking their learning efforts to the teachers' instruction. A demonstration of this vision can be found at http://cmapspublic3.ihmc.us/rid=1HL3HCVNB-8H9KH3-J6J/Vision.cmap. The vision demonstrates that the educational professional and governing institutions can articulate the standards of scientifically literate citizens, and school systems, individual teachers, and students can demonstrate their unique pathways to addressing those standards.

There are many further directions to pursue. The table that articulates the two dimensions of the new Bloom's taxonomy (Krathwohl, 2002) offers a fruitful tool to investigate further the connections between metacognitive instruction and its interaction with instruction targeting different types of knowledge at different levels of cognitive processing. Validity of the cmapping/critical thinking connection still requires work (Daley, 1999). Other mapping strategies, such as vee-mapping (Novak & Gowin, 1984) play a role in problem solving and scientific research. Other metacognitive strategies will surely be developed as mind tools to develop other aspects of both critical and creative thinking.

REFERENCES

Afamasaga-Fuata'i, K. (2006). Innovatively developing a teaching sequence using concept maps. In A. J. Cañas, & J. D. Novak (Eds.), *Concept maps: Theory, methodology, technology: Proceedings of the second international conference on concept mapping*. San José, Costa Rica: Editorial Universidad de Costa Rica.

American Association for the Advancement of Science (AAAS). (1989). *Science for all Americans*. New York: Oxford University Press.

American Association for the Advancement of Science (AAAS). (1993). *Benchmarks for science literacy*. New York: Oxford University Press.

American Association for the Advancement of Science (AAAS). (2001). *Atlas of science literacy* (Vol. 1). American Washington, DC: Association for the Advancement of Science and the National Science Teachers Association.

American Association for the Advancement of Science (AAAS). (2007). *Atlas of science literacy* (Vol. 2). Washington, DC: American Association for the Advancement of Science and the National Science Teachers Association.

American Philosophical Association. (1990). Critical thinking: A statement of expert consensus for purpose of educational assessment and instruction. Columbus, OH: Center on Education and Training for Employment, College of Education, The Ohio State University (ERIC) Document Reproduction No. ED 315-423.

Anderson, L. W., Krathwohl, D. R., Airasian, P. W., Cruikshank, K. A., Mayer, R. E., & Pintrich, P. R. … Wittrock, M.C. (Eds.). (2001). A taxonomy for learning, teaching, and assessing: A revision of Bloom's taxonomy of educational objectives. New York: Longman.

Anohina-Naumeca, A., & Graudina, V. (2012). Diversity of concept mapping tasks: Degree of difficulty, directedness, and task constraints. In A. J. Cañas, J. D. Novak & J. Vanhear (Eds.), *Concept maps: Theory, methodology, technology, proceedings of the fifth international conference on concept mapping.* Valletta, Malta: Academic Press.

Ausubel, D. P. (1968). *Educational psychology: A cognitive view.* New York: Holt, Rinehart & Winston.

Ausubel, D. P., Novak, J. D., & Hanesian, H. (1978). *Educational psychology: A cognitive view* (2nd ed.). New York: Holt, Rinehart, and Winston, Inc.

Cañas, A., Bunch, L., & Priit, R. (2010). Cmapanalysis: An extensible concept map analysis tool. In A. J. Cañas, J. D. Novak & J. Sánchez (Eds.), *Concept maps: Theory, methodology, technology, proceedings of the fourth international conference on concept mapping.* Viña del Mar, Chile: Academic Press.

Cañas, A. J. (2003). *A summary of literature pertaining to the use of concept mapping techniques and technologies or education and performance support.* Pensacola, FL: The Institute for Human and Machine Cognition.

Chabeli, M. (2010). Concept-mapping as a teaching method to facilitate critical thinking in nursing education: A review of the literature. *Health SA Gesondheit, 15*(1).

Clariana, R. B., & Taricani, E. M. (2010). The consequences of increasing the number of terms used to score open-ended concept maps. *International Journal of Instructional Media, 37*(2), 218–226.

Corcoran, T., Mosher, F., & Rogat, A. (2009). *Learning progressions in science: An evidence-based approach to reform.* Philadelphia: Consortium for Policy Research in Education.

Daley, B. J. et al. (1999). Concept maps: A strategy to teach and evaluate critical thinking. *The Journal of Nursing Education, 38*(1). PMID:9921788

Derbentseva, N., Safayeni, F., & Cañas, A. J. (2004). Experiments on the effect of map structure and concept quantification during concept map construction. In A. J. Cañas, J. D. Novak & F. M. González (Eds.), *Concept maps: Theory, methodology, technology, proceedings of the first international conference on concept mapping.* Pamplona, Spain: Universidad Pública de Navarra.

Derbentseva, N., Safayeni, F., & Cañas, A. J. (2006). Two strategies for encouraging functional relationships in concept maps. In A. J. Cañas & J. D. Novak (Eds.), *Concept maps: Theory, methodology, technology: Proceedings of the second international conference on concept mapping.* San Jose, Costa Rica: Universidad de Costa Rica.

Dewey, J. (1910). *How we think.* Boston: DC Heath & Co. doi:10.1037/10903-000

Facione, P. A. (1995). *Critical thinking and clinical judgment: Goals for nursing science.* Paper presented at the Annual Meeting of the Western Institute of Nursing. San Diego, CA.

Fonseca, A. P., & Extremina. (2008). Concept maps as tools for scientific research in microbiology: A case study. In *Proceedings of the Third International Conference on Concept Mapping.* Tallinn, Estonia: Academic Press.

Foster, J., & Wiser, M. (2012). The potential of learning progression research to inform the design of state science standards. In *Learning progressions in science: Current challenges and future directions* (pp. 435–459). Rotterdam, The Netherlands: Sense Publishers. doi:10.1007/978-94-6091-824-7_18

Gorman, J. (2008). Concept map advance organizers. In *Engineering the future: Science, technology, and the design process.* Emeryville, CA: Key Curriculum.

Hays, D. (2007). Using concept maps to measure deep, surface and non-learning outcomes. *Studies in Higher Education, 32*(1), 39–57. doi:10.1080/03075070601099432

Heinze-Fry, J. (2006). CmapTools facilitates alignment of local curriculum with state standards: A case study. In *Concept maps: Theory, methodology, and technology: Proceedings of the second international conference on concept mapping.* San Juan, Costa Rica: Academic Press.

Heinze-Fry, J. Gorman, & Foster. (2010). Conceptual mapping to facilitate review of state science standards. In *Concept maps: Making learning meaningful: Proceedings of the fourth international conference on concept mapping.* San Juan, Costa Rica: Academic Press.

Johnstone, A.H., & Otis. (2006). Concept mapping in problem based learning: A cautionary tale. *Chemistry Education Research and Practice*, *7*(2), 84–95. doi:10.1039/b5rp90017d

Jonassen, D. H., Carr, & Yueh. (1998). Computers as mindtools for engaging learners in critical thinking. *TechTrends*, *43*(2), 24–32. doi:10.1007/BF02818172

Kern, C., & Crippen, K. (2008). Mapping for conceptual change. *Science Teacher (Normal, Ill.)*, *75*(6). PMID:21814296

Kinchin, I. (2007). Using concept mapping principles in PowerPoint. *European Journal of Dental Education*, *11*, 194–199. doi:10.1111/j.1600-0579.2007.00454.x PMID:17935558

Kinchin, I. (2009). A knowledge structures perspective on the scholarship of teaching & learning. *International Journal for the Scholarship of Teaching and Learning*, *3*(2).

Kinchin, I., Hay, D., & Adams, A. (2000). How a qualitative approach to concept map analysis can be used to aid learning by illustrating patterns of conceptual development. *Educational Research*, *42*(1), 43–57. doi:10.1080/001318800363908

Krathwohl, D. R. (2002). A revision of Bloom's taxonomy: An overview. *Theory into Practice*, *41*(4). doi:10.1207/s15430421tip4104_2

Marée, T., van Bruggen, J., & Jochems, G. (2012). Using enriched skeleton concept mapping to support meaningful learning. In A. J. Cañas, J. D. Novak & J. Vanhear (Eds.), *Concept maps: Theory, methodology, technology, proceedings of the fifth international conference on concept mapping*. Valletta, Malta: Academic Press.

Massachusetts Department of Elementary and Secondary Education (MADESE). (2001/2006). *Massachusetts science and technology/engineering curriculum framework*. Retrieved from www.doe.mass.edu/frameworks/current.html

Meyer, J., & Land (2003). *Threshold concepts and troublesome knowledge: Linkages to ways of thinking and practising within the disciplines*. Edinburgh, UK: School of Education, University of Edinburgh Occasional Report 4.

Meyer, J., & Land, R. (2005). Threshold concepts and troublesome knowledge (2), epistemological considerations and a conceptual framework for teaching and learning. *Higher Education*, *49*(3), 373–388. doi:10.1007/s10734-004-6779-5

Miller, N., & Cañas, A. (2008). A semantic scoring rubric for concept maps: Design and reliability. In A. J. Cañas, P. Reiska, M. Åhlberg, & J. D. Novak (Eds.), *Concept maps: Theory, methodology, technology, proceedings of the third international conference on concept mapping.* Tallinn, Estonia: Academic Press. Retrieved from http://cmc.ihmc.us/cmc2008papers/cmc2008-p253.pdf

Mirzaie, R., Abbas, J., & Hatami, J. (2008). Study of concept maps usage effect on meaningful learning frontier in Bloom's taxonomy for atomic structure mental concepts. In A. J. Cañas, P. Reiska, M. Åhlberg, & J. D. Novak (Eds.), *Concept maps: Theory, methodology, technology, proceedings of the third international conference on concept mapping.* Tallinn, Estonia: Academic Press.

Moon, B., Hoffman, R., Shattuck, L., Coffey, J., et al. (2008). Rapid and accurate idea transfer: Evaluating concept maps against other formats for the transfer of complex information. In A. J. Cañas, P. Reiska, M. Åhlberg, & J. D. Novak (Eds.), *Concept maps: Theory, methodology, technology, proceedings of the third international conference on concept mapping.* Tallinn, Estonia: Academic Press.

National Science Digital Library (NSDL). (n.d.). *Literacy maps.* Retrieved from http://strandmaps.nsdl.org/

Novak, J. D. (1998). *Learning, creating, and using knowledge: Concept Maps* ™ *as facilitative tools in schools and corporations.* Mahwah, NJ: Lawrence Erlbaum Associates.

Novak, J. D. (1998). *Learning, creating, and using knowledge: Concept Maps* ™ *as facilitative tools in schools and corporations.* Mahwah, NJ: Lawrence Erlbaum Associates.

Novak, J. D. (2002). Meaningful learning: The essential factor for conceptual change in limited or appropriate propositional hierarchies leading to empowerment of learners. *Science Education, 86*(4), 548–571. doi:10.1002/sce.10032

Novak, J. D. (2009). *Learning, creating, and using knowledge: Concept maps as facilitative tools in schools and corporations* (2nd ed.). New York: Routledge Taylor & Francis Group.

Novak, J. D., & Cañas, A. J. (2008). *The theory underlying concept maps and how to construct them* (Technical Report IHMC CmapTools 2006-01 Rev 01-2008). Retrieved from http://cmap.ihmc.us/publications/researchpapers/theorycmaps/theoryunderlyingconceptmaps.htm

Novak, J. D., & Gowin, D. B. (1984). *Learning how to learn.* Cambridge, UK: Cambridge University Press. doi:10.1017/CBO9781139173469

Puntambekar, S., & Goldstein, J. (2007). Effect of visual representation of the conceptual structure of the domain on science learning and navigation in a hypertext environment. *Journal of Educational Multimedia and Hypermedia, 16*(4), 429–441.

Puntambekar, S., Stylianou, A., & Hübscher, R. (2003). Improving navigation and learning in hypertext environments with navigable concept maps. *Human-Computer Interaction, 18*(4), 395–426. doi:10.1207/S15327051HCI1804_3

Safayeni, F., Derbentseva, N., & Cañas, A. J. (2005). A theoretical note on concepts and the need for cyclic concept maps. *Journal of Research in Science Teaching, 42,* 741–766. doi:10.1002/tea.20074

Tucker, M. S. (Ed.). (2012). *Surpassing Shanghai: An agenda for American education built on the world's leading systems.* Cambridge, MA: Harvard Education Press.

von der Heidt, T. (2011). *Learning with concept maps: A study to measure change in learning in undergraduate Chinese marketing students.* Southern Cross University.

Vygotsky, L. S. (1997). *Thought and language.* Cambridge, MA: MIT.

Wells, M., Hestenes, D., & Swackhamer, G. (1995). A modeling method for high school physics instruction. *American Journal of Physics, 64,* 114–119.

Wiser, M., & Smith, C. (2009). *How does cognitive development inform the choice of core ideas in the physical sciences?* Washington, DC: National Research Council.

Wiser, M., Smith, C. L., Doubler, S., & Asbell-Clarke, J. (2009). *Learning progressions as a tool for curriculum development: Lessons from the inquiry project.* Paper presented at the Learning Progressions in Science (LeaPS) Conference. Iowa City, IA.

KEY TERMS AND DEFINITIONS

Concept: A perceived regularities in objects (such as "plant") or events (such as "photosynthesis"). Generally, each concept is represented by a one-word label enclosed in a circle or box.

Concept Map (Cmap): Guided by a focus question, concept maps are visual representations of the meaningful relationship between concepts. Any relationship between two concept can be read as a precise statement of fact.

Critical Thinking: A higher ordered thinking skill directed toward the purposeful evaluation of evidence, contexts, conceptualizations, methods, and criteria.

Expert Skeleton Concept Map (ESCM): A type of concept map developed by an expert which is composed of a focus question, parking lot of threshold concepts and an initial hierarchical structure which incorporates prior knowledge. ESCMs serve well as advance organizers because they scaffold learning by providing starting points.

Integrative Reconciliation: A metacognitive skill during which the learner restructures their conceptual understanding under a new overarching concept.

Learning Progression: A written description of the road a learner follows to develop mastery of skills or a concept.

Meaningful Learning: In Ausubelian learning theory, meaningful learning describes the active process of incorporating new learning to prior knowledge. This new learning must be presented in ways that are meaningful to the learner who must in turn choose to learn.

Progressive Differentiation: A metacognitive skill where the learner elaborates on an existing, more general concept.

Strand Map: Stand maps represent learning progressions, the development of linkages among concepts over the K-12 grade levels. They show the progressive differentiation of big ideas of science over time and the integrative reconciliations that occur going from one grade span to another.

Threshold Concepts: Concepts which are central to the master of a subject area. Key attributes of threshold concepts are transformative (changes the student's view of the subject), troublesome (often are counter-intuitive or alien), irreversible (unlearned only through considerable effort), and integrative (showing the relatedness between two other concepts which were previously hidden).

Chapter 13
Critical Thinking, Critical Looking:
Key Characteristics of an Educated Person

Richard C. Emanuel
Alabama State University, USA

Siu Challons-Lipton
Queens University of Charlotte, USA

EXECUTIVE SUMMARY

Critical thinking involves the comprehension and expression of the meaning or significance of a wide variety of experiences, situations, data, events, judgments, conventions, beliefs, rules, procedures, and criteria. One important aspect of critical thinking is the analysis, interpretation, and understanding of images. This is generally known as visual literacy. Visual literacy may be initially demonstrated at the basic levels of recognition and understanding – recognizing an image, telling what a symbol means, indicating the name of a painting and/or its artist. As one becomes more skilled at analyzing and interpreting the meaning of visuals, they are maturing toward visual fluency. Studying a cultural artifact provides students an opportunity to put things in context and to practice critical thinking. Two works of art—the Coffee Cup print and The Death of Marat painting—are provided along with example analysis.

DOI: 10.4018/978-1-4666-5816-5.ch013

SETTING THE STAGE

The greatest thing a human soul ever does in this world is to see something, and tell what it saw in a plain way.... To see clearly is poetry, prophecy and religion, all in one. - John Ruskin (1872, p.268)

And then remember...the biggest word of all – LOOK. Everything you need to know is in there somewhere. - Robert Fulghum (1986, p.5)

Critical Thinking

Critical thinking is a liberating force in education and a powerful resource in one's personal and civic life. It involves the comprehension and expression of the meaning or significance of a wide variety of experiences, situations, data, events, judgments, conventions, beliefs, rules, procedures, and criteria. A critical thinker is able to interpret, analyze, evaluate and infer. Strong critical thinkers can also effectively explain what they think and how they arrived at that judgment. They can apply their ability to think critically and thereby advance earlier opinions.

Critical thinkers demonstrate:

- Concern to become and remain well-informed,
- Alertness to opportunities to use critical thinking,
- Trust in the processes of reasoned inquiry,
- Self-confidence in their own abilities to reason,
- Open-mindedness regarding divergent world views,
- Flexibility in considering alternatives and opinions,
- Understanding of the opinions of other people,
- Fair-mindedness in appraising reasoning,
- Honesty in facing their own biases, prejudices, stereotypes, or egocentric tendencies,
- Prudence in suspending, making or altering judgments,
- Willingness to reconsider and revise views when honest reflection suggests warranted change.

Critical thinkers strive to achieve:

- Care in focusing attention on the concern at hand,
- Clarity in stating a question or concern,
- Orderliness in working with complexity,
- Diligence in seeking relevant information,

336

- Reasonableness in selecting and applying criteria,
- Persistence though difficulties are encountered,
- Precision to the degree permitted by the subject and circumstances.

As long as people have deliberate intentions in mind and wish to judge how to accomplish them, as long as people wonder what is true and what is not, what to believe and what to reject, strong critical thinking is implied (Facione,1990). The ability to think critically is almost always listed as one of the desirable outcomes of an undergraduate education (Facione et al., 2000; Halpern, 1998, 1999). Although there is considerable disagreement over who should teach such courses, whether they should be stand-alone generic courses or incorporated into specific content areas, and what sorts of thinking skills students should be learning in these courses, there is virtually no disagreement over the need to help college students improve how they think (Facione et al., 1995; Halpern, 2001; Perkins & Solomon, 1989; Terenzini et al., 1995). There is also virtually no disagreement about the types of learning activities that empower students to think critically. Research consistently identifies student participation, encouragement, and peer-to-peer interaction as being significantly and positively related to critical thinking (Smith, 1977). A study of more than 24,000 college freshmen revealed that writing, interdisciplinary courses, and giving a class presentation are positively correlated with self-reported growth in critical thinking (Tsui, 1999).

In the US, Presidents George H. Bush and Bill Clinton both supported the national education goal for higher education that declared that it was a national priority to enhance critical thinking among college students (*The National Education Goals Report*, 1991). However, this national priority was never funded. In the UK, the now defunct Council for National Academic Awards (CNAA) wrote that higher education courses should foster: "the development of students' intellectual and imaginative powers; their understanding and judgment; their problem-solving skills; their ability to communicate; their ability to see relationships within what they have learned; and to perceive their field of study in a broader perspective" (Gibbs, 1992, p. 1). Despite all the research, policy statements and good intentions, critical thinking remains a relatively elusive academic outcome. One important aspect of critical thinking is the analysis, interpretation and understanding of images. This is generally known as visual literacy.

Critically Thinking about Images: Visual Literacy

The book *Cultural Literacy* (Hirsch, 1987) offers a list of words, phrases and concepts that every American needs to know. The implication is that every American needs to know what the words mean or represent in order to be considered culturally literate. The list of 5,000 items, compiled by three academicians at a university in Virginia, runs the gamut from Hank Aaron to Zurich. There is no suggestion that Americans need to know the origin of the word or phrase or the literary work in which a particular phrase is found; one needs to know only what the word or phrase means. For example, a person might be considered culturally *literate* if he or she knows that Hank Aaron was a baseball player and that Zurich is a city in Switzerland. They might be considered culturally *fluent* if they know that Aaron holds the all-time home run record and that Zurich is the largest city in Switzerland. The list includes some words and phrases that are fairly common and well-known, such as Amazing Grace (song) and Mount Everest. However, there are other words and phrases that are lesser known and more obscure such as "dialectric" and "rheumatic fever." This list "provides a fairly reliable index to the middle-level information that is shared by most literate people but remains largely unfamiliar to most illiterate people" (Hirsch, 1987, p. 136). All the terms collectively comprise an operational definition of cultural literacy. The point is that while Hirsch may reasonably claim that culturally literate Americans need to have a working knowledge of every word or phrase in the list, one's cultural literacy falls somewhere on a continuum. For example, someone may recognize ninety percent of the terms but be able to explain only eighty percent of them in a cursory fashion and sixty percent at a deep level. Further, the terms may be reasonably grouped based on how prominent, mainstream or well-known they are with the most mainstream terms referred to as primary terms. Lesser-known terms would be considered secondary terms. People possess some degree of literacy for each group – primary and secondary. One may be familiar with most or all of the primary terms while being familiar with only some of the secondary terms. Within a level and overall, people are more or less culturally literate.

Visual literacy is much like cultural literacy in that there are more and less prominent, mainstream, well-known images. Regardless of image prominence, one's understanding of the meaning of an image ranges from basic recognition to deep analysis and evaluation. This conceptualization of visual literacy is consistent with Bloom's taxonomy of learning (Anderson & Krathwohl, 2001). Bloom provides a progression of increasingly sophisticated strata of engagement: recognizing, understanding, applying, analyzing, evaluating and creating. So it is with visual literacy. One's visual literacy can be described as occurring on a continuum from basic literacy to sophisticated fluency within and across levels of learning or aesthetic development for each group of images, primary and secondary. It is much like learning a foreign language. One begins by learning the letters and their sounds and progresses to basic grammar and vocabulary. At this point the person may be considered literate in their new language. As they continue to expand their vocabulary, hone their pronunciation, grasp colloquialisms, and master the rhythm and other nuances of the new language, they may be considered fluent (Table 1).

Table 1. Visual proficiency continuum

Level of Learning (Bloom)	Aesthetic Development (Housen)	Primary Images	Secondary Images
Creating	Re-creative	Fluent	Fluent
Evaluating	Interpretive	↑	↑
Analyzing	Classifying	↑	↑
Applying	Constructive	↑	↑
Understanding		↑	↑
Remembering (recognizing)	Accountive	Literate	Literate

While visual literacy focuses on the skills of decoding images, visual creation and design is the other side of the visual coin. It is the encoding or output aspect of one's visual proficiency. These two spheres–visual literacy or "reading" images and visual creation or "writing" images–are held together by visual thinking. And all three call upon a visual vocabulary which enables image readers and writers to express to others what they see (Figure 1).

Historically, images have played an important role in developing consciousness and the relationship of self to its surroundings. We learn who we are by seeing ourselves reflected in images, and we learn who we can become by transporting ourselves into images (Hill & Helmers, 2004). Images have been influencing people for millennia. Images and the pictorial world are powerful communicators and creators of culture. Literate societies have been surrounded by visual rhetoric, overt or subliminal, since before the dawn of the "optical age." Most people are overwhelmed by the flood of images in this digital world. And the often quoted phrase is true: a picture is worth a thousand words. Leonhard Nelson stated: "the processes of reception and interpretation cannot be separated, they are completely interdependent" (Geissner, 2008, p. 28). This view agrees with that of Ed Black (1979) who, speaking from the perspective of rhetorical criticism, said: "Beyond

Figure 1. Components of visual proficiency

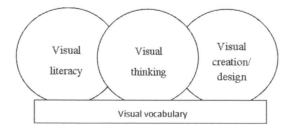

perception is appraisal; beyond seeing a thing is attaching value to it. These two acts–perception and evaluation– …are generally experienced as inseparable phases of the same process" (p. 5). If art is an expedition to the truth, then critical analysis and communication provide the path, and it would be both frustrating and frivolous to approach art without the necessary training and intellectual equipment.

In 1935, Mohoy-Nagy said, "the illiterate of the future will be ignorant of pen and camera alike" (Dondis, 1973, p. xi). Restated, the illiterate of the future will be ignorant of both text and images. "More and more of our young people don't know things we used to assume they knew" (Hirsch, 1987, p. 5). Brumberger (2011) echoes this sentiment when she stated that "students who currently populate our classrooms do not possess a high degree of visual literacy" (p. 44). And this is not entirely their fault. Most undergraduate curricula do little or nothing to enrich students' visual literacy. According to Alejandro (1977), this ability to make meaning from an image, this interpretation, is an ability that all students need to develop. "Students need to learn how to see, to interpret…the canvas and the page" (p. 795).

Daniel Pink, author of *A Whole New Mind* (2005) and *Drive* (2009), is at the forefront of a movement that promotes the importance of an arts education in forming a well-rounded, competitive job-force: "The future belongs to a very different kind of person with a very different kind of mind–creators and empathizers, pattern recognizers and meaning makers. These people… artists, inventors, designers, storytellers, caregivers, consolers… will now reap society's richest rewards and share its greatest joys" (Pink, 2005, p. 2).

Our culture is so bombarded with visual images from the television to the Internetthat there is a tendency to develop lazy looking. Careful visual examination must include formal and contextual analysis. Formal analysis includes the visual and physical aspects of a work. Formal elements include: color, line, space/mass, scale, and composition. Contextual analysis involves going outside the work and includes the writings and experiences of the artist. It involves understanding a work of art in a particular cultural moment. To get at the content or meanings of a work we need to interpret the following:

- Subject matter,
- Material and form (size, shape, texture, color),
- Socio-historic context (including our own),
- Artist's intentions (if known).

Research by Housen (1983) has shown that, regardless of socioeconomic background, those who view art gain an understanding in predictable patterns or stages. By looking at and talking about a carefully sequenced series of art works, viewers' visual literacy skills evolve in predictable ways (Housen, 1983, 1992, 2000, 2001,

2001-2002; Housen & Yenawine, 2001; Yenawine, 1997). This evolution occurs in stages of aesthetic development. In Stage I, Accountive, viewers make simple, concrete observations about the image; they tell a story. In Stage 2, Constructive, the viewer compares the image to what they know from their own experiences, beliefs and values. They begin to consider the artist's intentions. Stage 3, Classifying, is characterized by an exploration and understanding of the artist's life and work so as to place the artwork in a context of time and style. The viewer adopts the analytical and critical approach of the art historian. By properly classifying the artwork the viewer is better able to explain and rationalize its meaning. In Stage 4, Interpretive, the viewer steps back for a more holistic view. Formal subtleties are noticed and feelings and intuitions take precedence allowing the meaning of the work – its symbols – to emerge. The result is an interactive and spontaneous encounter with the image. Stage 5, Re-Creative, is characterized by a combining of personal contemplation with views that broadly encompass and reflect universal concerns. The viewer suspends belief and, with childlike openness, sees the work as having a life of its own (Housen, 2007).

Robert Fulghum, in his book *All I Really Need to Know I Learned in Kindergarten*, reminded a generation of the importance of the word "look." "Everything you need to know is in there somewhere" (Fulgham, 2003, p. 2). Looking indicates a curious inquisitive mind and some degree of attentiveness, but understanding requires a grasp of the context.

The Importance of Context

Context enlarges our view by looking at the social, political, spiritual and economic significance of a work. As artist Eliel Saarinen stated: "Always design a thing by considering it in its context – a chair in a room, a room in a house, a house in an environment, an environment in a city plan" (Ashton, 1985, p. 123).

The context of any communicative act affects all other aspects of the process: who the potential participants might be, the nature of the messages, the available channels, and so on. Meanings occur in context. For example, a red light in and of itself holds little or no meaning. But a red light at a traffic intersection communicates a clear message. A red light flashing in a fire station has a different meaning and a red light atop a buoy in a river channel has yet a different meaning. The red light takes on meaning depending on its context. Thus, an adequate understanding of context is essential to extract accurate meaning in a communicative situation. It provides what the late radio news commentator Paul Harvey used to call "the rest of the story."

Art history is an important key to understanding context. Many undergraduate students take art history to fulfill a general education requirement, others to become more cultivated, but more importantly art history teaches us to think differently, to ask interesting questions, to reject standard answers, to see the nuances of things. It is in Belgian painter René Magritte's (1898-1967) words, "the art of thinking" (Geissner, 2008). It gives us access to our past through an emotional and intellectual experience that helps us develop a visual language. In 20th Century artist Jean Dubuffet's words: "Art is a language, an instrument of knowledge, an instrument of communication" (Roth & Roth, 1998, p. 14).

An Interdisciplinary Approach

With an ever-increasing vocational emphasis in higher education and declining enrollments in liberal arts programs, faculty in the arts and humanities are showing renewed interest in interdisciplinary approaches to teaching. The contours of the disciplines themselves are changing. Out of academic necessity, new investigative links are being drawn and old ones re-drawn. Scholars at all levels are seeking to strengthen the connections between diverse disciplines. Collaboration among disciplines is not only the key to academic viability; it effectively communicates the connectedness of things which is foundational to learning. With repeated exposure to interdisciplinary thought, learners develop enhanced critical thinking ability and metacognitive skills, and an understanding of the relations among perspectives derived from different disciplines (Ivanitskaya, Clark, & Primeau, 2002; Smith & McCann, 2001).

Nearly seven decades ago, Mark Van Doren wrote in *Liberal Education*: "The connectedness of things is what the educator contemplates to the limit of his capacity…The student who can begin early in life to think of things as connected, even if he revises his view with every succeeding year, has begun the life of learning" (Van Doren, 1943, p. 115). These shifts represent an important change in the way we think about the way we think.

CASE DESCRIPTION

Generating Questions

Studying a cultural artifact provides students an opportunity to put things in context and to practice critical thinking. For example, students are assigned the challenge of analyzing a work of art. The instructor chooses the art and asks students to begin their own detailed study of it by brainstorming questions about it. Students then meet in class to discuss their questions in Socratic circles. Once a relatively exhaustive list of questions has been generated, students embark on group and individual research and discussion aimed at addressing the questions.

Typically, Socratic circles consist of two concentric circles of students — one circle focusing on exploring the meaning expressed in the artifact, and a second circle observing the conversation (Copeland, 2005, p.9). In the case of visual criticism, the inner circle begins by posing questions about the artifact. The outer circle observes. After about ten minutes the students switch circles. The new inner circle then adds to, deletes, and/or refines the questions provided by the previous inner circle. The circles continue to alternate as they take turns posing and then answering questions (Copeland, 2005; Foss, 1989, 1992, 2009). Some example questions might be:

- Who is the artist?
- Who is/are the intended audience(s)?
- What is the artist trying to communicate?
- What do I need to know in order to better understand how this was created and what it might mean?
- What assumptions can I (or do I) make about this (message) image?
- What does the artist want me to think/feel?
- What cultural values are being communicated here?
- What other shapes/objects could have been used?
- When was this created?
- Where was this created?
- How did the artist decide on this subject?
- How might others see this same (message) image differently?

The purpose is not simply generating questions and seeking answers, but rather the judging of whether there *is* an answer and, if so, whether or not it is relevant (Faigley et al., 2004). The process is one of exploration. After all, the mark of an educated person is not that they have all the answers, but that they pose important questions. There is not a right or wrong analysis, but there may be a more or less informed one. Two works of art are provided, *Coffee Cup*, a contemporary print, and *The Death of Marat*, a historical 19th Century oil painting, along with a sample analysis of each. These two works well exemplify the importance of context in understanding and appreciating each.

Coffee Cup

To demonstrate how this might play out, an art print – *Coffee Cup* – is used as the artifact (Figure 2). *Coffee Cup* is a commercial print created in 2008 as a local (Charlotte, NC) collaboration between African/Jewish photographer Wayne St. John

Figure 2. The Coffee Cup

and Jewish attorney Mark Farbman. Formal analysis begins by noting the bright colors of Pop Art that first arrest the viewer's attention. The print is rendered in a garish pink to an optimistic blue and edgy orange. Then the analysis evolves to a contextual question. Why coffee cups? Is this print another Pop Art image, an icon of our obsessive coffee culture, a Warhol copy, a mass produced print from another Factory? Why anonymous coffee cups and not Starbucks – the commensurate embodiment of our hectic lives resting on moments of escapism in coffee? On closer observation, these cups have more texture than Warhol's Coke bottles or soup cans. In some ways, they are less polished, more expressive – their texture appears somewhat tarnished, damaged by age. The lettering is personal, almost hand-written. There is history implied. The formal and contextual analyses merge to disclose that these vivid yet textured coffee cups are not icons of the present, but reminders of the past. The Coffee Cup print has a link to and is symbolic of a historic landmark.

The Coffee Cup Soda Grill was built and opened in 1948 on the corner of South Clarkson and Dunbar Streets in Charlotte, North Carolina. This food stand (vs. fast-food restaurant), featuring traditional Southern style African American cooking, catered to workers in the surrounding industrial and warehouse district ("Survey," 2006). In its early years, White patrons could dine in while Black patrons were allowed to order and pick up meals at the pick-up window, but had to sit on the curb or at a picnic table to eat. It was one of the first Charlotte businesses to embrace diversity by welcoming Black patrons to dine in. By 1980 an African American former waitress at the Coffee Cup was its co-owner. The Coffee Cup was the sole surviving example in Charlotte's central business district of a roadside food stand that appeared in cities throughout the United States in the 1940s with the advent of the automobile age and the onset of widespread industrialization. The building also served as part of the city's architectural history as an example of the Art Moderne style. This architectural style, popular immediately before and after World War II, featured a sleek cube-like or rectangular shape building with smooth white walls, little ornamentation, and a flat roof. The Coffee Cup was a street level, one-story, masonry building on a treeless lot with a gravel parking area. Its most distinctive features were the three octagonal windows, two on the right side of the building and one on the front. Above the windowless front door was a sign shaped like a coffee cup which read "COFFEE CUP." The cup was colored a light earth tone brown or mocha and the lettering was rust red. The coffee in the cup was black.

The Coffee Cup Soda Grill became an icon of racial equality, diversity, and harmony in Charlotte and a symbol of African American cuisine. The building was appraised at $3,000 and the 1.17 acres of land on which it sat was appraised at $814,800 ("Survey," 2006). In 2005 Atlanta developer Beazer Homes, Inc. bought the property. That same year the Coffee Cup was recommended for designation as a historic landmark, which it received. The Coffee Cup closed some time in 2007. In May 2008, Beazer Homes petitioned to demolish the Coffee Cup. On or about June 4, 2008 the Coffee Cup sign was stolen. And, despite community opposition and petitions, the Coffee Cup Soda Grill was demolished on September 24, 2009.

The *Coffee Cup* print recalls the history of the Coffee Cup Soda Grill, an African American business that was closed under controversy – a local landmark torn down. *Coffee Cup* now becomes symbolic of that building, a place of community lost, yet not forgotten. In the bright colors and clear simplistic imagery of Pop Art, this print celebrates the Coffee Cup food stand, which has become a poignant icon of the past.

A critique of *Coffee Cup* involves art, history, economics, politics, critical thinking and research. The process provides a conduit for connecting students with the struggle for civil rights. Awakened by the role one restaurant played in promoting racial harmony, they are less likely to take for granted, and more likely to appreciate, civil rights landmarks that have been preserved in their own community. They have, through one brief academic exercise, explored and uncovered the often hidden messages and meanings of symbols. Their understanding of and appreciation for *Coffee Cup* has been enriched and deepened. And they have not only connected with a piece of history, but they have engaged themselves in the process of critical thinking.

The Death of Marat

Analysis of a historically famous artwork – *The Death of Marat* – involves the same process of visualization, from literacy to fluency. *The Death of Marat* (*Marat assassiné*) is a 5'5" x 4'2" oil painting on canvas, executed by the French master, Jacques-Louis David (1748-1825) in 1793 (Figure 3). Formal analysis begins by noting the realistic portrayal of a dying man in what appears to be a bath. The eye follows the polished rendition of brush strokes detailing the man, a quill in one hand and a letter in the other, the knife on the floor, and the signature "À Marat" ("To Marat") with the artist's name, David. The painting is rendered in monochrome tones, with a darkened background and a bright spotlight on the figure of Marat,

Figure 3. The Death of Marat

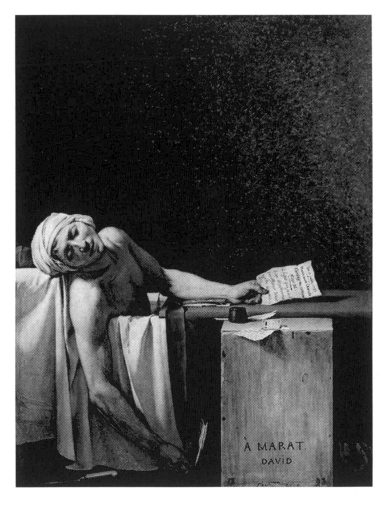

the letter, the quill and the knife. Then the analysis evolves to a contextual question. Who is Marat? Is he dead or dying? Why does he appear so peaceful in death? Did David know him? What does the letter read? Why did David paint him? On closer inspection, Marat is dying, his eyelids droop, his head lies on his shoulder. The cloth enveloping him is blood stained from a wound to the chest as is the bath water he lies in. The bloodied knife lies on the floor-a murder implied. Marat's arm is heavy with death in this moment, the letter in his left hand points to the accused-Charlotte Corday and the date of the murder-July 13, 1793. She is not visible in the painting. The formal and contextual analyses merge revealing the moment of a political assassination.

Jean-Paul Marat (1743-1793) was the French revolutionary Montagnard leader, the radical faction of the Reign of Terror, friend of Robespierre, Jacobin deputy to the Convention, and editor-in-chief of *L'Ami du Peuple*. He voted for the death of King Louis XVI and Marie-Antoinette, as well as thousands of others. A fiery orator and radical journalist, he was a violent man, quick to take offense. Charlotte Corday was a Girondin from a minor aristocratic family and a political enemy of Marat who blamed him for mob massacres. On July 13, 1793, she entered Marat's apartment and stabbed him to death. Marat, who suffered from a skin ailment, was killed in his bath. Charlotte Corday did not attempt to escape and was later executed.

Jacques-Louis David (1748-1825), the leading French painter of his era, was a Montagnard and a Jacobin with Marat and Robespierre, who voted for the death of the king and queen. David was the painter of the French Revolution and this was one of the most famous images of the Revolution. His heroic, historical works were hailed as artistic demands for political action. The day after Marat's murder, David was asked by the Convention to arrange the funeral ceremony and to paint his portrait. David promised the National Convention that he would depict Marat writing for the good of the people, though in reality he was probably signing death warrants.

Painted in a Neoclassical style that revived the art of ancient Greece and Rome, David saw in Marat a model of antique virtue and stoic resolve. Despite the disfiguring skin disease from which Marat suffered, David idealized him in the manner of antique sculptures, painting a healthy young man. His face implies suffering, but is also gentle and peaceful. David transferred the sacred qualities affiliated with the monarchy and the Church to the new French Republic. He painted Marat as martyr of the Revolution. In a style reminiscent of a Christian martyr, his face and body are bathed in a soft, glowing light in the manner of Michelangelo's *Pietà* and Caravaggio's *Entombment*. David surrounded Marat with a number of harsh realistic details, painted with smooth brushstrokes, including the knife and Charlotte Corday's petition, and details drawn from his visit to Marat's residence the day before the assassination-the tub, the mended sheet, the green rug, the makeshift writing desk, the wooden packing case, the papers, and the pen of the journalist. Through these simple objects, David suggested the "noble simplicity and quiet grandeur" of the victim (Winckelmann). It is ultimately with the warm and clear light of Caravaggio, wedded to the pathos of Michelangelo, that David pulls the viewer into the image, and for a moment, as Marat takes his last breath, we are one with him. The background, heavy with impasto paint, falls into shadow and emptiness. We encounter the compassion and outrage David felt before the victim, David's personal hero.

The painting was presented to the Convention on November 15, 1793. Widely admired, several copies were made. The original was returned to David in 1795, himself prosecuted for his involvement in the Terror. From 1795 to David's death, the painting lay in obscurity. It was rediscovered by critics in the mid-19th century, especially by Charles Baudelaire, who in *The Divine Marat* in 1846 summarized the painting with the following:

The divine Marat, one arm hanging out of the bath, its hand still loosely holding on to its last quill, and his chest pierced by the sacrilegious wound, has just breathed his last. On the green desk in front of him, his other hand still holds the treacherous letter: "Citizen, it is enough that I am really miserable to have a right to your benevolence." The bath water is red with blood, the paper is blood-stained; on the ground lies a large kitchen knife soaked in blood; on a wretched packing case, which constituted the working furniture for the tireless journalist we read: "À Marat, David".... There is in this work something both tender and poignant, a soul hovers in the chilled air of this room, on these cold walls, around the cold and funereal bath.... This painting was a gift to a tearful nation, and our own tears are not dangerous (Art in Paris, 1981, pp. 34-35).

In the 20th century, the work inspired several painters, including Picasso and Munch, who delivered their own versions. The original painting is currently on display at the Royal Museum of Fine Arts in Brussels, donated in 1886 by his descendants, to the city in which David died in exile.

A critique of *The Death of Marat*, like *The Coffee Cup,* involves art, history, economics, politics, critical thinking and research. The experience connects students with the French Revolution and the history of art, particularly the 19th century and Neoclassicism. Moved by the work of one artist, they are more likely to stop and reflect on what they see. They have explored and uncovered the often hidden messages and meanings of symbols as reflected in the formal elements of artistic style. Their understanding of and appreciation for *The Death of Marat* has been enriched and deepened through the process of critical thinking. As poet Robert Frost suggested, they have taken the road less traveled by, and that has made (and will continue to make) all the difference.

SOLUTIONS AND RECOMMENDATIONS

With today's overreliance on course texts, memorization, credits, attendance, grades, course outlines and general "spoon feeding," critical thinking is essential. If the goal of college-level general education is to prepare students for generative and productive civic, personal, and professional lives, then few things could be more crucial to a successful college curriculum than the cultivation of critical thinking. Facione et al. (1995), in their study of students' disposition toward critical thinking, found that students "are not inclined toward focus, diligence, and persistence in inquiry" (p.14).

As educators assess their own teaching and student learning, emphasis must be placed on the experience, not just on the result. Interdisciplinary classes focusing on critical thinking must be reinforced to foster independent thought. Students must be challenged and allowed to take risks, make mistakes, to fail, to realize their full potential. Educators must challenge students to take responsibility for their own education. Central to this process is providing students with experiences in critical thinking so that they can develop and mature.

REFERENCES

Alejandro, A. (1997). Like happy dreams: Integrating visual arts, writing and reading. In J. Flood, S. B. Heath, & D. Lapp (Eds.), *Handbook of research on teaching literacy through the communicative and visual arts*. New York: Simon & Schuster Macmillan.

Anderson, L. W., & Krathwohl, D. R. (Eds.). (2001). A taxonomy for learning, teaching and assessing: A revision of Bloom's taxonomy of educational objectives: Complete Ed. New York: Longman.

Ashton, D. (1985). *Twentieth century artists on art*. New York: Pantheon Books.

Black, E. (1979). *Rhetorical criticism: A study in method*. Madison, WI: University of Wisconsin Press.

Brumberger, E. (2011). Visual literacy and the digital native: An examination of the millennial learner. *Journal of Visual Literacy, 30*(1), 19–46.

Copeland, M. (2005). *Socratic circles: Fostering critical and creative thinking*. Portland, MN: Stenhouse Publishers.

Delécluze, E.-J. (1983). *Louis David, son école et son temps*. Paris: Didier.

Dondis, D. A. (1973). *A primer of visual literacy*. Cambridge, MA: MIT Press.

Facione, P. A. (1990). *Critical thinking: A statement of expert consensus for purposes of educational assessment and instruction.* Millbrae, CA: The California Academic Press.

Facione, P. A., Facione, N. C., & Giancarlo, C. (2000). The disposition toward critical thinking: Its character, measurement, and relationship to critical thinking skills. *Journal of Informal Logic, 20*(1), 61–84.

Facione, P. A., Sánchez, C. A., Facione, N. C., & Gainen, J. (1995). The disposition toward critical thinking. *The Journal of General Education, 44*(1), 1–25.

Faigley, L., George, D., Palchik, A., & Selfe, C. (2004). *Some questions for analyzing images in picturing texts.* New York: W. W. Norton & Co.

Foss, S. K. (1989). Rhetorical criticism as the asking of questions. *Communication Education, 38*(3), 191–196. doi:10.1080/03634528909378755

Foss, S. K. (1992). Visual imagery as communication. *Text and Performance Quarterly, 12*(1), 85–90. doi:10.1080/10462939209359638

Foss, S. K. (2009). A rhetorical schema for the evaluation of visual imagery. *Communication Studies, 45*(3-4), 213–224. doi:10.1080/10510979409368425

Fulghum, R. (1986). *All I really need to know I learned in kindergarten.* New York: Ballantine Books.

Geissner, H. K. (2008). René Magritte: Thought pictures of rhetorical communication. In *Applied communication in organizational and international contexts.* St.Ingbert, Germany: Röhrig Universitätsverlag.

Gibbs, G. (1992). *Improving the quality of student learning: Based on the improving student learning project funded by the CNAA.* Oxford, UK: Technical & Education Services Limited.

Gretton, T. (2000). *The death of Marat.* New York: Cambridge University Press.

Halliday, T. (2000). *David's Maratas posthumous portrait.* New York: Cambridge University Press.

Halpern, D. F. (1998). Teaching critical thinking for transfer across domains: Disposition, skills, structure training, and metacognitive monitoring. *The American Psychologist, 53*, 449–455. doi:10.1037/0003-066X.53.4.449 PMID:9572008

Halpern, D. F. (1999). Teaching for critical thinking: Helping college students develop the skills and dispositions of a critical thinker. *New Directions for Teaching and Learning, 80*, 69–74. doi:10.1002/tl.8005

Halpern, D. F. (2001). Assessing the effectiveness of critical thinking Instruction. *The Journal of General Education, 50*(4), 270–286. doi:10.1353/jge.2001.0024

Hill, C. A., & Helmers, M. H. (Eds.). (2004). *Defining visual rhetorics*. Mahwah, NJ: Lawrence Erlbaum Associates, Inc.

Hirsch, E. D. (1987). *Cultural literacy*. Boston: Houghton Mifflin Company.

Housen, A. (1983). *The eye of the beholder: Measuring aesthetic development*. (Ed.D. Thesis). Harvard University Graduate School of Education. Cambridge, MA.

Housen, A. (1992). Validating a measure of aesthetic development for museums and schools. *ILVS Review: A Journal of Visitor Behavior, 2* (2), 1-19.

Housen, A. (2000). *Eye of the beholder: Research, theory and practice*. Retrieved April 20, 2012, from http://www.vtshome.org/system/resources/0000/0006/Eye_of_the_Beholder.pdf

Housen, A. (2001). Voice of viewers: Iterative research, theory and practice. *Arts and Learning Research Journal, 17*(1), 2–12.

Housen, A. (2001-2002). Aesthetic thought: Assessment, growth, and transfer. *Arts and Learning Research Journal, 18*(1), 99–131.

Housen, A. (2007). *Art viewing and aesthetic development: Designing for the viewer*. Retrieved April 20, 2012, from http://www.vtshome.org/system/resources/0000/0015/HousenArtViewing.pdf

Housen, A., & Yenawine, P. (2001). *Visual thinking strategies: Understanding the basics*. Retrieved April 20, 2012 from http://www.vtshome.org/system/resources/0000/0039/VTS_Understanding_the_basic.pdf

Ivanitskaya, L., Clark, D., Montgomery, G., & Primeau, R. (2002). Interdisciplinary learning: Process and outcomes. *Innovative Higher Education, 27*(2), 95–111. doi:10.1023/A:1021105309984

Mayne, J. (Ed.). (1981). *Art in Paris 1845-1862: Salons and other exhibitions reviewed by Charles Baudelaire*. Oxford, UK: Phaidon.

Perkins, D. N., & Salomon, G. (1989). Are cognitive skills context bound? *Educational Researcher, 18*, 16–25. doi:10.3102/0013189X018001016

Pink, D. (2005). *A whole new mind: Why right-brainers will rule the future*. New York: Riverhead Books.

Pink, D. (2009). *Drive, the surprising truth about what motivates us*. New York: Riverhead Books.

Roth, R., & Roth, S. K. (1998). *Beauty is nowhere: Ethical issues in art and design*. Amsterdam: The Gordon and Breach Publishing Group.

Ruskin, J. (1872). *Modern painters* (Vol. 3). London: Smith, Elder and Company.

Schama, S. (2006). *The power of art*. New York: HarperCollins Publishers.

Smith, B. L., & McCann, J. (2001). *Reinventing ourselves: Interdisciplinary education, collaborative learning, and experimentation in higher education*. Bolton, MA: Anker Publishing.

Smith, D. (1977). College classroom interactions and critical thinking. *Journal of Educational Psychology, 69*(2), 180–190. doi:10.1037/0022-0663.69.2.180

Survey and Research Report on the Coffee Cup Soda Grill. (2006). Retrieved August 24, 2011 from http://www.cmhpf.org/surveys&rcoffeecup.htm

Terenzini, P. T., Springer, L., Pascarella, E. T., & Nora, A. (1995). Influences affecting the development of students' critical thinking skills. *Research in Higher Education, 36*(1), 29–39. doi:10.1007/BF02207765

(1991). *The national education goals report: Building a nation of learners*. Washington, DC: U.S. Printing Office.

Tsui, L. (1999). Courses and instruction affecting critical thinking. *Research in Higher Education, 40*(2), 185–200. doi:10.1023/A:1018734630124

Van Doren, M. (1943). *Liberal education*. New York: Henry Holt.

Vaughan, W. (2000). *Terror and the tabula rasa*. New York: Cambridge University Press.

Vaughan, W., Weston, H., Gretton, T., & Halliday, T. (2000). *David's the death of Marat*. New York: Cambridge University Press.

Weston, H. (2000). *The Corday Marat affair*. New York: Cambridge University Press.

Winckelmann, J. J. (1756). *Gedanken über die nachahmung der griechischen werke in der malerei und bildhauerkunst* (2nd ed.). Academic Press.

Yenawine, P. (2008). *Writing for adult museum visitors*. Retrieved April 22, 2012, from http://www.museum-ed.org/index.php?option=com_content& view= article &id=80:writing-for-adult-museum-visitors&catid=37:current-practice-interpretation &Itemid=86

KEY TERMS AND DEFINITIONS

Contextual Analysis: Understanding a work of art in a particular cultural moment; it includes an understanding of the writings and experience of the artist.

Critical Thinking: The comprehension and expression of the meaning or significance of a wide variety of experiences, situations, data, events, judgments, conventions, beliefs, rules, procedures, and criteria.

Formal Analysis: Recognizing and understanding the significance of the visual and physical aspects of a work including but not limited to color, line, space/mass, scale, and composition.

Interpretation: Ability to make meaning from a work, especially an image.

Primary: A class of works that are prominent, pervasive, and popular.

Secondary: A class of works that are not as prominent, pervasive or popular as primary works.

Visual Fluency: Skilled at analyzing and interpreting the meaning of visuals. These skills coincide with Bloom's analyzing and evaluating levels of learning and Housen's interpretive and re-creative levels of aesthetic development.

Visual Literacy: Basic ability to decode images. This ability coincides with Bloom's recognizing level of learning and Housen's accountive level of aesthetic development.

Visual Proficiency: The ability to effectively and thoroughly understand, think about, discuss and create images.

Chapter 14
Mind Mapping for Critical Thinking

Roxanne M. O'Connell
Roger Williams University, USA

EXECUTIVE SUMMARY

Mind mapping is a visual technique that exploits the way we actually think—through synaptic connections and non-linear associations. Because mind mapping gives practitioners, be they professional or student, access to subconscious observations and connections, it is a powerful thinking tool, useful in a variety of situations in business and in education. This chapter focuses on how mind mapping fosters the kind of flexible and organic thinking vital to critical thinking and the creative problem-solving process. It explains what is at work in the brain as we create new knowledge and how mind mapping exploits these processes to gain intuitive and concrete understanding in situations requiring critical thinking. A step-by-step outline of how to mind map in both individual and group settings is followed by examples of mind maps from both business and education.

INTRODUCTION

Critical thinking, as defined by Scriven and Paul at the 8th Annual International Conference on Critical Thinking and Education Reform, is the "intellectually disciplined process of actively and skillfully conceptualizing, applying, analyzing, synthesizing, and/or evaluating information gathered from, or generated by, observation, experience, reflection, reasoning, or communication, as a guide to belief and action" (1987, n.p.). We also recognize these activities as those articulated in

DOI: 10.4018/978-1-4666-5816-5.ch014

Benjamin Bloom's taxonomy of learning, in the cognitive domain, as knowledge, comprehension, application, analysis, synthesis and evaluation (1984, p. 18). One can conceive that "critical thinking" is "learning" and, as such, can benefit from the many modes and techniques that facilitate the reasoning and connecting so important to learning, thinking and the emergence of new ideas—not just those of others but also those of our own.

The most important steps in learning and critical thinking are the collecting and connecting of information to create knowledge that can then be analyzed, evaluated and remembered. In critical thinking, this is achieved by a process of questioning and probing. While free-writing and note-taking are common verbal tools for doing this, increasingly, attention is being given to visual modes that involve imagery and spatial displays. The graphic nature of visual symbols and displays helps speed up the processes of information absorption, recall and retention as they exploit the brain's ability to rapidly parallel process sensory information like color, shape, size, orientation, and texture. We are, in essence pattern-seekers that use the visual to link mental and emotional associations that arrange information into patterns we can use (Caine & Caine, 1994; Ware, 2008; Kosslyn, Thompson, & Ganis, 2006; Kosslyn, 1988). Hyerle writes, "These visual-spatial-verbal displays of understanding support all learners in *transforming static information into active knowledge*, thus offering a complementary representational system to more traditional literacies grounded in speaking, writing, and numerating" (2009, p. xix). Mind mapping, developed by learning expert, Tony Buzan in the early 1970s, is one visual technique that excels in helping the learner/thinker to collect and connect information, focus on key points, explore alternatives "at one view"[1] and "see" the patterns that turn information into knowledge that is more easily retained and recalled. In addition, sustained practice in mind mapping fosters a habit of thinking that exploits the brain's "almost unlimited capacity for images" (Wolfe & Sorgen, 1990, p. 8).

Buzan observed that the linear process for note-taking and analysis practiced in organizations, both educational and professional, was ineffectual at helping people gather, absorb and retain information. Moreover, the linear outline method crippled thinking for discovery, for creating and exploring new ideas, for finding breakthrough solutions to complex problems (1974). While maps and diagrams have been used for millennia to graphically illustrate the relationships between concrete things, mind mapping is a visual technique for capturing concepts and ideas that exploits the way we actually think—through synaptic connections and non-linear associations. To mind map a problem or an idea, we start with a central focus: a word or image placed in the middle of the workspace. We then create lines radiating out with words or images on them, branching out with each association until we fill the workspace with connections to all aspects related to the central focus. A mind map looks quite similar to a real brain cell (neuron) with its synaptic connections (see

Figure 1). The use of color, images, doodling and shading further emphasize possibilities. Although various mind mapping computer applications exist, the haptic and synaesthetic qualities of doing mind maps by hand with paper and colored markers are what make this technique so effective as a method for creative and critical thinking. The uses of both manual and computer methods for mind mapping will be discussed briefly at the end of this chapter.

Because mind mapping gives practitioners, be they student, teacher or professional, access to conscious and subconscious observations and connections, it is a powerful brainstorming tool. Hyerle describes mind maps as brainstorming Webs, "natural bridges between the neural networking of the brain and the conscious mapping by the mind" (2009, p. 52). Mind mapping uses the way the brain works to capture existing information, make connections and create new perceptions, relationships and multiple possibilities. Visual thinking elements such as associative memory, imagery, and Gestalt principles are exploited in the mind mapping session and reflect one's internal thought structure and processes. A further advantage is that mind mapping can be done in teams or groups as well as by individuals. Because the process for building a mind map is organic and non-hierarchical, it tends to discourage cognitive narrowing and premature closure in the information gathering and idea connecting process. Because brainstorming with mind mapping is non-judgmental, it helps build consensus, and often leads to breakthrough ideas and solutions (Table 1).

Figure 1. A neuron with synapses. Courtesy of Dr. Gerry Shaw.

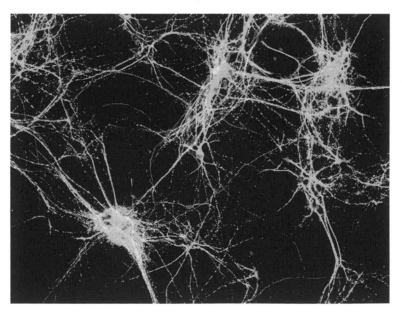

Table 1. Mind mapping for discovery and critical thinking

Areas/Applications:	Contexts:
• Collaboration and teamwork • Self-expression • Elaboration of ideas • Critical thinking	• Business • Education • International/intercultural • One-on-one

This chapter will:

- Establish the relationship between mind mapping and critical thinking.
- Explain how and why mind mapping works as a cognitive process.
- Outline the process of doing a mind map.
- Provide examples (cases) in both education and business contexts for using mind mapping.
- Provide mind mapping activities and assignments for both aspects of critical thinking:
  - **Analysis:** Organization, writing and studying and
  - **Discovery:** Problem solving.

BACKGROUND

One of the basic assumptions about us as human beings is that we are differentiated from the other creatures on this earth by virtue of our ability to engage in higher orders of thinking. While there are other creatures that take in new information, remember it, and even communicate it—such as whales, dolphins, even crows—we appear to have the unique ability to synthesize abstract concepts and project ourselves into an imagined future. We can combine disparate items of data, recognize their relationships, and create new knowledge. Benjamin Bloom (1956), an educational psychologist investigating the theory of mastery-learning, articulated a hierarchy of learning and thinking that has since become known as Bloom's Taxonomy. He discovered that learning happens through three domains: the cognitive (knowing), the affective (feeling), and the psychomotor (doing).

Accepting as the basic premise for this chapter that all knowledge creation, critical thinking and problem-solving are part of a learning process, we can use Bloom's cognitive domain to identify key elements in learning that result in the creation of new knowledge: remembering, understanding, applying, analyzing, synthesizing, and evaluating. The affective domain exploits the power of the brain's synaptic associations to take that new knowledge and connect it to other memories anchored in our values and attitudes. When we create a new synaptic connection by learning something new or experiencing a moment of insight, our brain rewards us by producing endorphins that give us pleasure and a feeling of well-being. When new learning and a feeling of well-being are combined with skillful "doing"—the use of motor skills to articulate and create visible patterns—we hit the learning trifecta. As a tool for fostering creative and critical thinking, mind mapping uses all three learning domains *at the same time.*

We also find key elements from the cognitive domain in theories about critical thinking. According to Richard Paul and Linda Elder (2009), true critical thinking must be cultivated. It does not come naturally. They define critical thinking as an intellectual process in terms similar to Bloom's taxonomy. In addition, they maintain that, "In its exemplary form, it is based on universal intellectual values that transcend subject matter divisions: clarity, accuracy, precision, consistency, relevance, sound evidence, good reasons, depth, breadth, and fairness" (criticalthinking.org). Paul and Elder, in their writings and in the Critical Thinking Community Website, outline critical thinking as a series of questions that probe an idea or subject, examining all of its facets in order to arrive at a clear understanding of the idea, what it means and what it offers us. Critical thinking is the goal of Socratic questioning—a process by which:

We can question goals and purposes. We can probe into the nature of the question, problem, or issue that is on the floor. We can inquire into whether or not we have relevant data and information. We can consider alternative interpretations of the data and information. We can analyze key concepts and ideas. We can question assumptions being made. We can ask students to trace out the implications and consequences of what they are saying. We can consider alternative points of view. (criticalthinking.org)

Most approaches to this kind of analysis and evaluation rely on linear thinking, weighing the known with the known, dealing with conscious observations. Reflection with this approach tends to also be linear, bound in time, space and causality. Being a questioner is essential to thinking critically. However, the linear approach to thinking, critical or otherwise, has inherent limitations and sometimes privileges Cartesian analysis over other forms of knowing.

Mind mapping or building intuitive maps of what we know—and what we don't yet know we know—is not necessarily more easily achieved than the more linear approaches to critical thinking. However it does benefit from exploiting the way the brain works and, in so doing, helps intuitive reflection and subconscious pattern recognition become part of the critical thinking milieu. Where mind mapping helps is in unearthing and *making visible* that which we need to *think about*. It helps us by getting us out of linear thinking into a kind of thought more natural to our brain in structure.

Mind mapping uses the way the brain works to create new perceptions, relationships and multiple possibilities. All the elements of visual thinking are exercised. Associative memory, visual memory, imagery, synaesthesia, and the Gestalt principles are exploited in the mind mapping process and, according to Buzan (1993), "reflect (one's) internal structure and processes" (p. 31).

Getting beyond the "linear" means unfettering our minds and moving beyond traditional mental structures to what our unconscious mind has observed or synaptically connected. This is not "undisciplined thinking"—it takes as much discipline and focus to allow one's inner thoughts to rise to consciousness, to keep distractions and doubts at bay. But we are rewarded by the flashes of insight and meaningful associations that letting go of linear thought make possible. As creative problem-solving expert Edward DeBono (1985) writes:

The brain is designed as a 'recognition machine.' The brain is designed to set up patterns, to use them and to condemn anything that does not 'fit' these patterns. Most thinkers like to be right. Creativity involves provocation, exploration and risk taking. Creativity involves 'thought experiments.' You cannot tell in advance how the experiment is going to turn out (p.137).

Mind mapping, because it is a non-linear reflective approach, helps us break out of unconscious pattern matching and leap into intentional exploration and risk taking. It helps us see the mosaic of the problem beyond the bits and pieces of information, and this, in turn, helps us create new knowledge for analysis, synthesis and evaluation.

HOW THE MIND WORKS

What happens when someone is engaged in thinking? How does the "Aha!" of the mind relate to what is going on between the neurons in the brain? If thinking is logical and ordered, why is it not so for everyone? If thinking is creative, is everyone creative? Does creativity belong only to the few—the artists and inventors? Is logical thinking a strictly linear process? Can one be logical and creative at the same time? Buzan maintains that we can and that the brain's two hemispheres—the pattern, big-picture oriented right side and the linear, logical left side—actually work together through the corpus callosum, an area of the brain with neural pathways to right and left lobes (1974).

First, it is helpful to distinguish between the millions of unconscious decisions your brain makes every day and the kind of thinking and problem-solving we are discussing here. When we are learning a new skill, such as driving a car, or working with an abstract idea, the basal ganglion—the area of our brain where patterns and habits, both motor and behavioral, are formed—lights up with all sorts of activity (Duhigg, 2012). Later, when we are comfortable with these patterns and habits, that part of the brain is quiet while other parts of the brain show activity. While both the left and right lobes of the brain work together through the corpus callosum, the left side is generally concerned with words and speech and behaves much like a computer's serial processor. The right side of the brain, in contrast, is concerned with sensory patterns—the "whole cloth" of our experiences in that moment and how it connects to all our other experienced moments (Bolte Taylor, 2006).

Medical journalist Rita Carter (1998) tells us, "Brain imaging studies confirm that the two hemispheres really do have quite specific skills that are 'hard-wired' to the extent that, in normal circumstances, certain skills will always develop on a particular side" (p. 35). The split-brain theory (Sperry, 1967), as it was first posited, is only half the story. Carter continues, "You can see this happen in a brain scan—the side that is 'in charge' of a particular task will light up while the matching area on the other side will glow far more dully" (p. 38). Moreover, the two sides of the brain seem to be communicating with each other and performing synergistically. "They each process their 'halves' of the big picture, and then pool their information by sending signals back and forth via the corpus callosum" (p. 39).

These two sides of our brain, and their preferred processing schemes, are available to all of us, unless there has been some damage to a particular area of the brain. However, we are more than our biology. Our cultural norms and patterns also influence how we think. Western culture often privileges serial, linear left-brain thinking over intuitive "big picture" right-brain thinking. Consequently, we might spend our thinking lives out of connection with our more intuitive and creative selves. Those who cultivate right-brain thinking are often perceived as being creative, artistic and inventive. However, that could be all of us. The trick is to use both sides of our brain together.

Mind mapping helps us do that. It accesses memories, patterns and associations, while at the same time, it uses words and emergent, organic organization. It is a conscious, semi-structured activity that helps us explore sub-conscious knowledge and insight while using both sides of our brain. This section explores, in more depth, those aspects of our thinking that we rely on using mind mapping for critical and creative thinking: associative memory, visual memory, imagery, synaesthesia, and the Gestalt principles of perception.

Associative Memory

Everything stored in our brain in long term memory is there for as long as we breath. However, our access to those memories depends on the synapses that connect them to each other in neural strings or pathways of associations. When we look at a brain scan, we see lit up areas caused by neuronal activity—biochemical/electromagnetic pathways created or used in the brain when a stimulus sends a message to the brain or a person has a thought (Buzan, 1993, p. 29). This is the basis for associative memory. Neuroscientist Joseph LeDoux (2002) writes:

In order for two stimuli to be bound together in the mind, to be associated, the neural representations of the two events have to meet up in the brain. This means that there has to be some neuron (or a set of neurons) that receives information about both stimuli. Then, and only then, can the stimuli be linked together and an association be formed between them (p. 135).

In the process of making a mind map, one starts with a central word or image and then radiates associated words and images off this central focus, "growing" more connections to those associations. Often a new association is perceived between two unrelated ideas or images and a new neuronal connection, or synapse, is created. As Sidney Parnes describes it in his essay, "Aha!" in *Perspectives in Creativity*, "The typical 'aha' experience may be considered to be the result of the new connection of elements residing inside our mind and/or within our perceptual field" (1975, p. 226-227).

In mind mapping, the number and variety of associations matters a great deal. As a mind map builds, as we add more information and then connect that information to other pieces of information or other parts of the mind map, we are creating a picture of the idea or problem we want to examine, analyze and evaluate. We are making visible the pieces of the information our questioning process collects, and mapping out the associations and relationships between these pieces of information. Pushing the envelope is a necessary act in the process. As the number of associations on the mind map grows, the number of possible ideas or outcomes for us to think about multiply. "The sheer number of answers to the initial question provides a measure of ideational fluency, their rarity is used to assess originality, and the number of shifts from one category to another measures flexibility" (Tyler, 1985, p. 187).

Visual Memory

Thinking takes place in working memory. The synaptic connections generated by making associations between pieces of information are most active in the prefrontal cortex where working memory tasks take place. LeDoux describes the prefrontal cortex as a *convergence zone*. It integrates all the information it gathers, receiving and establishing connections from other parts of the brain like "the hippocampus and other cortical areas involved in long-term explicit memory, allowing it to retrieve stored information relevant to the task at hand" (2002, p. 180). In mind mapping one takes advantage of two different working memory systems, the linguistic system via short, associated words, and sensory imagery, via the radiants of the map, colors and shading, and the pictures one draws to illustrate the concepts and engage visual perception (Paivio, 2001; Kosslyn, 1988). The two systems work together (right and left brain theory) because they "are closely connected and, in a sense, appear to have a common semantic 'grammar,' a set of rules whereby things are interrelated and organized" (Baddeley, 1976, p. 227).

As we see the words and images begin to organize along the radiants in the mind map, we start to see ideas and concepts "organize themselves," showing us a picture of what we are thinking about. LeDoux writes, "Our conscious awareness of who we are depends on our linguistic interpretation (labeling, categorizing, explaining) of our experiences as we go through life" (p. 199). Categorization and hierarchy are essential to the power of a mind map. Without some form of classification of ideas, the associations don't exist and the map is just a bunch of random words and images.

Imagery

The use of images in mind maps is, at the one time, the most enjoyable and the most intimidating aspect of the process. People seem to be concerned that they are not "artistic enough" to create images on their maps and often limit themselves to words. However, Stanford behavioral psychologist Stephen Kosslyn points out in his book, *Ghosts in the Mind's Machine*, that, "Images can be used to establish non-arbitrary associations with objects in the world and can be linked with words (or propositions) to represent classes" (1983, p. 208). Kosslyn sees imagery "as a vehicle for reasoning, a kind of internal representation that is operated on within an information processing system" (1988, p. 247). A single image can convey more meaning than several words or paragraphs of words. That meaning can produce many more rich associations. According to Buzan (1993), "Images are therefore more evocative than words, more precise and potent in triggering a wide range of associations, thereby enhancing creative thinking and memory" (p. 73).

However, for those that are strongly intimidated by the notion of creating pictures, the benefits of imagery can still be made active by using color and shading on words and on the lines in the map to indicate emphasis or distinction. Even the shapes of the letters used in the map can convey more than the meaning of the word itself, as anyone familiar with the art and science of typography will point out. The idea is to allow your mind to create visual emphasis wherever necessary to flesh out the ideas.

Synaesthesia

The clinical definition of synaesthesia is a rare condition in which stimuli are perceived by senses other than that of the root stimulus. For someone with synaesthesia, colors have smells, sounds have colors or both smells and colors. It is a condition of sensory mapping to multiple processing centers in the brain.[2]

In mind mapping we want to synaesthetically stimulate the brain by linking the physical senses (Buzan, 1993). The hand touches the paper and holds the pens and markers, the nose smells the markers, the eye perceives the color, and speaking words out loud while writing stimulates hearing. When the mind mapper consciously involves as many senses as possible, more neuronal activity is created. Artist and lecturer, Lorraine Gill cites the "mind-to-hand-transcribing sensations" as an essential aspect of creativity in her own mind maps (Buzan, 1993, pp. 158-159).

Gestalt Phenomena: Principles of Perception

The Gestalt principles are a set of natural rules that explain why we perceive certain objects to be grouped or not grouped. They include proximity, common fate, similarity, continuity and transparency, closure, the "good Gestalt," and the figure/ground articulation. We encounter, and unconsciously use, the effects of these principles everyday. For instance, in reading this book, we use the principle of *proximity*, which "describes the tendency of individual elements to be associated more strongly with nearby elements than with those that are farther away" (Mullet & Sano, 1995, p. 91). Those letters that are located closely together are perceived as "words," those words that are spatially organized into blocks of text are perceived as "paragraphs." Objects that are close together are perceived as grouped because of their proximity to each other.

Connectivity is perceived because of the Gestalt principle of *continuance*. We see things as connected when joined by a line, regardless of whether that line is suggested with dashes or dots or continuous. In addition, according to Dejan Todorović (2008), "The principle applies in the same way for elements arranged along lines as well as for patterns built from corresponding lines themselves" (n.p.). It is an essential practice in mind mapping to place the key words or key images being used on the lines radiating out from the central focus.

Perhaps the most powerful of the Gestalt principles is that of *closure*. It is the principle which allows us to see the whole from a mere suggestion of the parts and is the reason symbolic icons, like those we use in computer applications or see on international airport signs, work. The mind "leaps" to closure by completing the pattern suggested by what is visible, essentially seeing what is not actually there.

A more subtle principle is the perception of figure versus ground. Certain shapes and contrasts will cause us to perceive certain objects as the central focus (figure), relegating the rest to the background (ground). Todorović explains:

The two components are perceived as two segments of the visual field differing not only in color, but in some other phenomenal characteristics as well. The figure has an object-like character, whereas the ground has less perceptual saliency and appears as 'mere' background. The areas of the figure and the ground usually do not appear juxtaposed in a common plane, as in a mosaic, but rather as stratified in depth: there is a tendency to see the figure as positioned in front, and the ground at a further depth plane and continuing to extend behind the figure, as if occluded by it (figure-ground articulation).

The figure/ground dialectic applies to both visual and abstract thought. The mental trick of instructing someone to "try not to think of a pink elephant" essentially establishes the "image" of a pink elephant as the figure in our thinking, forcing other thoughts to the background. There is a significant benefit to cultivating the flexibility to shift thoughts from figure to ground to figure. Flexible thinkers have access to a broader array of creative possible solutions largely because they can consciously execute these shifts in perception.

The technique of mind mapping uses several of these Gestalt principles for organizing information according to the way the mind works. The two most prominent principles visible in any mind map are continuance/connectivity and proximity. A mind map uses lines radiating out from a central word or image. These radiants have branches that work outward and the lines that connect them help us perceive these as linked or associated. In addition to the radiants upon which the image or word associations are placed, a mapper can draw arrows from one branch of associations to another to symbolize a new relationship.

The Gestalt principle of closure is exploited when a mapper has run out of ideas or feels blocked. By drawing an empty line the mapper tricks the mind into reaching into the subconscious to fill in the blank. Because of the mind's "tendency to interpret visual stimuli as complete, closed figures, even when some of the necessary contour information is absent," it will leap to closure by providing a word or image to fill in the gap, pushing past the mental "censor" that was blocking it (Mullet & Sano, 1995, p. 92).

Patterns are the basis for the underlying structure of any mind map and a good way to perceive the underlying Gestalts is to pull away from the map, much as one does with an impressionist painting. Like the dots on a Seurat painting, if we are too close, all we see are the dots—we need to move back, either in time or by using another's detachment, to see the "big picture." For both the painting and the map, distance helps reinforce the impressions of proximity and connectivity between objects that help meta-patterns emerge. The flexibility of going from the detail to the "big picture" and back to the detail again, is a figure/ground articulation that stimulates both critical thinking and creative problem solving.

So far, we have examined what is at work when the brain is "thinking," whether it is engaged in a conscious or unconscious process. All humans have these capacities as they are biologically based. However, our cultural practices and attitudes privilege some kinds of thinking over others. Mind mapping as a critical thinking approach leverages "whole-mind" thinking by exploiting our brains natural processes and perceptual tendencies, leading to an organic, emergent discovery process and flexible problem solving. We now turn to the specific techniques of mind mapping and how these support the collecting, connecting and evaluating steps in critical thinking.

MIND MAPPING AND CRITICAL THINKING

Critical thinking is all about questions. In this section we look at how mind mapping fosters and supports the processes involved in critical thinking. Critical thinking is based in asking questions that probe and explore an idea or topic, anchored in the Socratic probes, "What do I know? How do I know it? How will I use what I know?" In the *Critical Thinking* pocket guide, Paul and Elder outline a series of questions the critical thinker asks. Many of these questions overlap with the conscious and unconscious exploration undertaken in doing a mind map. The first questions a critical thinker asks are purpose driven: What am I trying to accomplish? What is my central aim? My purpose? Is it to understand an idea? To solve a problem? To organize one's thoughts? Once that purpose is established, the critical thinker can begin mind mapping by asking: What is the main idea here? What word or image should I use as my central focus?

A critical thinker expands the map by probing with questions: What issue am I raising? What question am I addressing? Am I considering the complexities in the questions? The mapper exploits the associative power of the brain using key words that act as both question and answer. Joyce Wycoff writes that, "key words are nouns and verbs which carry a lot of meaning" (p. 47). The benefit to using keywords is their brevity. They are anchored thoughts about the central focus, but they are expressed as only *one word per line* in order to allow for as many associations as come to mind.

A critical thinker asks: What information do I need to settle the question? What information am I using in coming to that conclusion? What experience have I had to support this claim? In mind mapping, these questions ebb and flow as layers of meaning are constructed by the interplay between key words, associations, images, color, lines and shading.

The critical thinker then examines and ponders the map by probing with questions such as, Is there another way to interpret this information? What am I taking for granted? What am I implying? From what point of view am I looking at this issue? Is there another point of view I should consider? Both critical thinking and mind mapping processes require reflection and introspection as well as observation and analysis. In this way mind mapping fosters and supports the critical thinking process by making it visible in both a concrete and symbolic way.

Doing a mind map is often best executed within the flow of a reflective process that involves preparation, incubation, reflection, illumination and iteration. The first iteration of the map is generally the preparation stage. I often recommend that people map for 20 minutes and then take a break. Anything from an hour to 24 hours. That break is the incubation stage where you allow your subconscious mind to do the heavy lifting. Returning to the mind map after incubation often allows one to see even more associations or new patterns. Sometimes this happens immediately, sometimes it happens when the mapper adds images and color—emphasis and embellishment. As Wycoff explains, "Mindmapping helps us pull information together in such a way that it can bounce around and make new connections. It concentrates our thoughts and information quickly and intensely" (p. 29).

Many people feel that they are not creative enough to mind map. While it may be necessary to possess some aesthetic quality or perception to be *artistic*, creativity and creative thinking are innate to everyone. Parnes (1975) draws a distinction between "intelligence" and "creativity" when he writes:

The 'intelligent' person observes and stores relationships that are brought to his attention; he understands them and appreciates their value, and he calls them into play constantly in meeting his problems and his challenges. The 'creative' person does all of this, but goes the next step – that of extending these relationships through the generation of new and more encompassing ones for every initial relationship that is brought to his attention (p. 229).

However, the challenge for researchers is proving this assertion because each person's creativity appears to be unique. Psychologist Leona Tyler (1985) explains the inherent paradox in *Thinking Creatively: A New Approach to Psychology and Individual Lives*:

The diversity and flexibility that comes from the possession of repertoires of cognitive structures is one meaning of creativity. Mainstream psychology, with its goal of predicting and controlling behavior, has never known just what to do with research on creativity. The more creative a person is, the harder he or she is to predict with any precision. And if what is created were predictable, it could no longer be described as creative (p. 200).

When we participate in creative activities, we get connected to a deeper, intuitive sense of meaning "that binds our perceptions into a seamless whole and makes sense of our existence" (Carter, 1998, p. 197). This produces in us a state of *mania* or wellbeing. Conversely, areas of the brain that are most active during these periods of wellbeing are absent of any activity in periods of depression. It could be argued that solving a problem, no matter how great or small, is an act of creativity based on the resulting brain activity. Carter describes people in this state as being "in a state of high creativity—the connections they see between things, which are often invisible or overlooked by others, are often used by them to make new concepts" (p. 197).

HOW TO MIND MAP

How is mind mapping a tool for critical thinking? While other forms of mapping—note-taking, review, concept-mapping—are concerned with capturing and retaining existing knowledge, mind mapping for critical thinking is concerned with either uncovering hidden relationships or creating new associations and ideas. As such, the process is more reliant on the exploration and non-linear thinking required for creative problem solving. This is particularly relevant to critical thinking in that this approach to mind mapping allows the practitioner to question and probe the subject visually.

DeBono (1985) tell us, "The mapmaking type of thinking requires a certain detachment. The walking-talking-breathing type of thinking does not" (p.13). While the mind mapping process requires commitment, it is hampered when the mapper needs to be right. Suspending the evaluative self, or "inner critic" is essential. The commitment is to being open and to pushing through to deeper levels of associative thought. This too is a hallmark of critical thinking and Socratic questioning—breaking away from bias and certainty to embrace the value in the question.

In many cases, the thinking process will require not one mind map, but several. Every idea that comes to mind should radiate from a stimulating central focus, bypassing the inner mental censor who will try to evaluate your choices and look for linear relationships. "In the exercise of creative thinking, it may be necessary to put forward as provocations ideas that are deliberately illogical" (DeBono, p.

136). Sometimes ideas that appear illogical on the surface are perceived so because of hidden biases that, upon reflection and examination, become new and different perspectives. Short breaks and new iterations of a map serve to process and generate more associations. Buzan (1993) recommends using emphasis and linking to reveal "a new mental framework, leading to the flash of insight that occurs when old facts are seen from a new perspective" (p. 157).

Short periods of incubation, when the thinker/mapper rests and relaxes, are necessary between the iterations of the map to allow the mental processing of new information and the generation of new insights. Groups can participate in the enrichment of a mind map by viewing and commenting on themes and relationships that the members of the team perceive. Anecdotal evidence suggests that we often overlook or miss associations our subconscious mind has placed on the map. Another "pair of eyes" will notice these associations, perhaps because they have a level of detachment. Distance, both physical and emotional, helps us create new perceptions.

Getting Started

To create a mind map, start with the biggest piece of paper you can find. I, personally, find using a large sketchpad in landscape orientation (wider than tall) works best as I tend to branch side to side, avoiding top/bottom branching at first. Perhaps that is because, in western culture, we tend to write from left to right. Regardless, it is important to pay attention to where and how we tend to feel comfortable writing and doodling as discomfort will hamper our efforts. When we mind map as a group in class, I use large flip chart paper or, better still but less portable, a white board and colored dry erase markers.

Step One: Establishing the Central Focus

The figure/ground articulation suggests that where we focus our attention creates the path our thoughts will follow. Placing the word, image or graphic representation of the problem in center of the page pulls our attention to those associations that will frame our search for information and ideas. As the central focus is critical, it may be useful to draft a list of possible words or two-word phrases that describe the central focus in order to find the most effective starting point. Alternatively, one can doodle until a central image emerges. I have occasionally started with a central image of a question mark because the "right" word or image has temporarily eluded me. Either way, positioning the central focus in the middle of the page both physically and symbolically establishes the path of thinking.

The shape of the image is a matter of personal preference. Illustrated in Figure 2 are three different forms. My preference is the cloud shape as I find the indenta-

Figure 2. Drawing the central focus

tions natural places to start a radiant. However, the only requirement is that the word or image be clearly in the center of your map and sized so as to indicate its prominence and emphasis.

Step Two: Place Key Words on Radiants

On lines radiating out from the central focus, write single key words that come to mind (Figure 3). There are two "rules" for writing key words. First, use only one word per line. Place the root word first and use branch lines for clarifying, associating and amplifying words. This technique gives the maximum opportunity for exploring the widest range of possibilities associated with the root word.

Second, print using block letters. Letter case suggests hierarchy. Those letters in lowercase are pre-attentively processed as having minor status while letters in uppercase have a higher status. Mixed case will result in some words being elevated in status when capitalized. It's a subtle but powerful influence. Block lettering insures that all words are treated equally by the brain. Words on the radiants closest to the central focus can be larger than keywords on radiants linked further away from the center. The relative size, when used organically, suggests something about the nature of the association and provides additional visual information.

Figure 3. Adding the radiants for keywords

Let your ideas flow freely. If a word seems silly or ridiculous, it doesn't matter. Simply put it on a radiant line. Suspend judgment. We are letting our subconscious mind tap into all kinds of associations and we have no idea, at the outset, which word or idea will be key to a breakthrough understanding or solution.

Step Three: Expand and Fill In

As you keep branching out to fill the page, you may find that you are slowing down. There are two techniques to employ here and you can do one or both. The first is to exploit the Gestalt principle of closure by drawing an empty line from one of the existing radiants or off the central focus, allowing the mind to "leap" to fill it in.

The second technique is to leave the map for a while and engage in another activity that does not concern the problem, one that perhaps is rote or automatic in nature, or which is relaxing, like going for a walk or gardening. Upon returning to the map after a short period of time, look with "new eyes" at what is there and begin to expand or fill in.

Put in all your ideas. Each idea is a potential jumping point to another association (Figure 4), another memory, another emergent pattern. Wycoff (1991) reminds us, "If you remember that mindmapping is not an end result, it's just part of the process, then it's easier to remember that whatever you do on your mindmap is OK. *There are no wrong mindmaps*" (p. 49).

Step Four: Embellish with Color and Imagery

In other words, *doodle*. Unfortunately, our word privileging, linear-thinking culture has a fairly low opinion of the doodle and of those who practice doodling. Sunni Brown, in her March 2011 TED talk, said, "I think that our culture is so intensely

Figure 4. Add radiants for associations

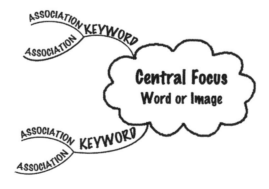

focused on verbal information that we're almost blinded to the value of doodling." Her new definition of doodling is "to make spontaneous marks to help yourself think." In mind mapping, we engage the right side of the brain by using color, shapes, and imagery to help us build focus and participate in deep information processing. Brown claims that there are four ways learners take in information for critical thinking and creative problem solving. "They are visual, auditory, reading and writing, and kinesthetic." She explains that in order for us to process and use information we must use at least two of those learning modalities or couple one of those modalities with an emotional experience—Bloom's affective domain. "The incredible contribution of the doodle is that it engages all four learning modalities simultaneously with the possibility of an emotional experience. That's a pretty solid contribution for a behavior equated with doing nothing."

We process sensory information in the brain immediately. Color, shape, size, the division of space, all contribute information in a manner that are what Wycoff calls "shorthand to the brain" (p. 53) (Figure 5). Mind mapping is a whole brain thinking experience. This last step—embellish—often becomes the most absorbing step as we fully engage the right side of our brain in creating images and symbols. Time after time, when we do mind mapping in class, I find students pulled deep into

Figure 5. Embellish with color, shading and imagery (© 2011, Robert Faustine, use with permission)

another world, one that is more reflective and calming. In their self-observations they invariably note that this is where they experienced their AHA! moment. Things clicked into place, the solution or realization—so elusive at the beginning—pops out and is obvious.

Step Five: Pick a Branch and do Another Map

In some cases, the first mind map only serves to clarify the problem or idea and its many complexities. Often another mind map, using one of the branches as its central focus, is required to get to the optimal solution. The same process is followed, often faster because much of the initial association work has been done.

Alternatively, a second map using the same central focus, might prove useful. This technique will result in a shifting of associations or a reorienting of their relationships. The imagery might take another form with different emphasis. An example of just such a pair of maps on a single theme is included in the case studies which follow.

CASE STUDIES IN MIND MAPPING

In this section, we look at a variety of mind map exercises done in various settings, created by both individuals and in groups. As each map reflects a unique moment in time, it is important to acknowledge that the same problem mapped by other mappers would naturally result in different maps and different solutions. I include with each example excerpted reflections, if available, of the mind mapper so that we can get inside the process.

Mind Mapping as Discussion of Ideas

The most common use of mind mapping to support critical thinking is often done at the whiteboard to review and discuss an assigned reading. Unfortunately these maps are ephemeral, erased from the board once class is over. However, the process is extremely useful, especially when the class size is too large for a seminar-like discussion. Readings for class can often be broken up into chapters or sections and groups of three to four students each assigned to take part of the whiteboard and mind map the readings, putting the central thesis of the chapter/section in the center and then radiating out the arguments, evidence, and critical points. Often the compressed timeframe helps students overcome shyness and self-editing. From there I do one of two exercises depending on the amount of time available.

1.   If we can assume that all of the students read the same assigned chapters, my preferred next step is to have the groups rotate through the maps, having members of the other groups add something to each map, exploring what is there and expanding and building on it. This way everyone participates in a visual discussion of all the material. The instructor is able to drop into the group discussions and facilitate by asking probing questions.
2.   The alternative next step is to have each group present what they mapped and engage their peers in a dialog.

Not surprisingly, the former method generates a much more animated exchange.

Mind Mapping as Review

Another common application of mind mapping in the classroom is to use it to review material in preparation for an exam or paper. Again, this is done in groups of three or four, leveraging the power of many minds for recall and generating associations.

1.   Students mind map for 5-10 minutes, without the benefit of books or notes, plotting and mapping everything they can recall concerning the central topic.
2.   After 10 minutes, they are allowed to use their notes and texts. They are often amazed at the amount of material they were able to map without their notes.
3.   After 5 minutes of this, they must put away their notes and embellish with imagery and shading, exercising the visual parts of their brains.
4.   If there is time, we post the maps on the walls of the classroom and the groups move through the mind maps, for one to two minutes each, to add to the other groups' maps. By the time they are done, each group will have viewed the material five to six times over. Requiring them to each add at least one thing to each map focuses their attention and creates many more synapses for every neuron.

Examples

While mind mapping for discussion and review are more ephemeral, mind maps that explore a problem often take longer and are usually kept as important notes for the problem solving process. For the purpose of this chapter, the following maps are meant illustrate the *visual process* of mind mapping. I have selected examples from both the business world and the higher education settings, done by both individuals and groups.

The first set of maps was done by an individual with a business problem: creating a new consulting practice. In this example, two maps were created using the same central focus. She reflects:

Background: *The subject of this mind map was [evaluating] a new business concept. The central image is the name of the new company, The Learning Muse, a process consulting practice. The first map was intended to capture what were the elements that needed to be put in place to get the business moving.*

Map 1: *The first level of radiants seems to flow according to plan. Typical business elements emerged: income, practice, learning, Web site, core (for core competencies or needs.) After 20 minutes I stopped and took a short break. I decided this first map was ready for another iteration.*

See Figure 6 for mind map 1.

Figure 6. Mind map 1: Business context, single mapper

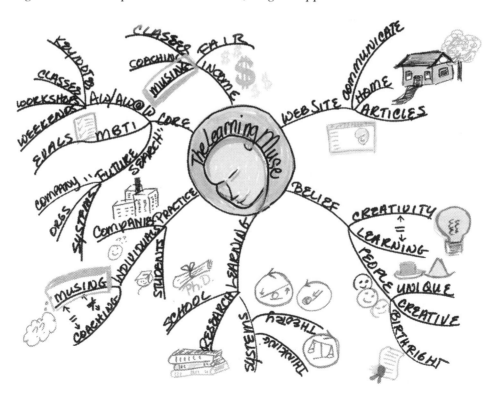

AHA!s: In the scanned image, the words were a little too small to read clearly but I was able to look at the overall imagery I had created doodling around the map. The central image caught my eye—it looked womb-like and the face had the same orientation as an embryo (think 2001: A Space Odyssey, last scene.) It dawned on me that this business that I thought was ready for setting up is still embryonic!

Map 2: I kept the central image – it was so powerful and anchored the theme for the map. I proceeded to focus on "The Practice." If this was waiting to be born, I wanted to find out what it needed to have ready for its coming into the world. Again, I quickly radiated the first words that came to mind: Clients, Needs, Wants, Have, Skills, and, again, Core, which this time radiated to core beliefs and core competencies. I continued to embellish and doodle around the words and finally drew a boundary around the clusters. For some reason I filled in some clusters but others were left "incomplete?"

See Figure 7 for mind map 2.

Figure 7. Mind map 2: Business context, single mapper continued

AHA!s: I thought I would find most of the emphasis around clients or core competencies and beliefs but instead I found the vertical axis had the most emphasis. It appears I feel grounded in my skills and seek balance.

Conclusion: I discovered much more than I expected... primarily that this is a project with more than a few unknowns. It needs more incubation and development before beginning the Web site. However the concept is well grounded in my current skills.

The second set of maps were done individually by students who were given free rein in choosing their topic with the caveat that the map had to be about analyzing and solving a real problem. Certain map patterns emerged with graduating seniors focussing quite naturally on issues of graduation and what they would be doing with their lives. This set of maps used the Sample Mind Mapping Assignment outlined in the next section of this chapter.

Background: As a graduating senior, one of the largest problems that I have encountered is that I am somewhere between a college student and a professional, so I have chosen a main theme of 'transition,' as I am neither here nor there.

Map 1: In doing this mind map, I not only was able to realize that I have a lot of life ahead of me but I also have some unfinished business to take care of as a student. This mind map also helped me realized how fearful and unsure of the future I am.

See Figure 8 for mind map 1.

Map 2: For my second mind map I decided to focus on my future employment. The second mind map allowed me to realize all the different employment options I have ahead of me. One thing that I found particularly tricky while making the mind maps was figuring out how to think more abstractly since I am a very linear thinker, however once I got rolling I found that the ideas began flowing onto the paper....I also had trouble figuring out what to draw and illustrate within my mind map since I am not a very good doodler—I ended up finding that I do enjoy doodling once I get going.

See Figure 9 for mind map 2.

AHA!: One last thing that I would've done differently with more time and resources is to make this mind map bigger on a piece of poster board because I found that the bigger the map was, the more I was able to really see every single association and illustration, which brought the map to life for me. In the future when I study for

Figure 8. Mind map 1: Education context, single mapper

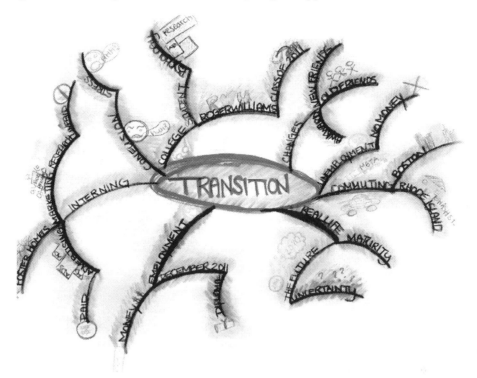

tests and quizzes or prepare to write an essay, I hope to use this mind mapping strategy as it has certainly helped me to open up my mind.

The third set of maps were done by students in groups of three or four working on the problem of Voter Information. The map itself was intended to be a brainstorming tool to discover what would be needed for an information graphic to be used to help voters new to their neighborhood. The maps would not be the final graphic but instead were used to help the team think critically about what they would need to include in an information graphic that would help people learn what they needed to know to be informed, make a decision and be eligible to vote.

Prior to the mind mapping session, students were reminded of the need to keep loading the map up with the broadest number of ideas and that these should include, not only the kinds of information they would need to include in the finished graphic but also formats that would best display the information. Instructions for the team mind map session are included in the Assignment section (Figure 10 and Figure 11).

Additional caption "Students had 15-20 minutes to brainstorm what they would need to create an information graphic on Voting in a New Neighborhood."

Figure 9. Mind map 2: Subset of first mind map

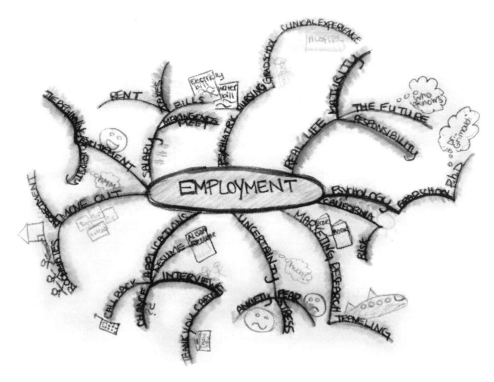

What follows are two sample assignment outlines that can be used in either a classroom or business setting to teach mind mapping techniques to others.

Sample Mind Mapping Assignment: Solo Mind Mapper

This assignment for a solo mind mapper is designed to work in all environments. While the instructions below are written for a university classroom, they are essentially the same as those used in the training delivered at Digital Equipment Corporation in team building and creative problem solving sessions when I was a teamwork consultant there.

- **Task:** Create (by hand in your sketchbook or on a large piece of unlined paper) a Mind Map on a topic or central theme of your choice. It is best to pick a real problem that needs solving.
- **Process:**
  - Mind map for 20 minutes then take a break. (See Mind Map Steps below.)

Figure 10. Group mind maps: Education setting

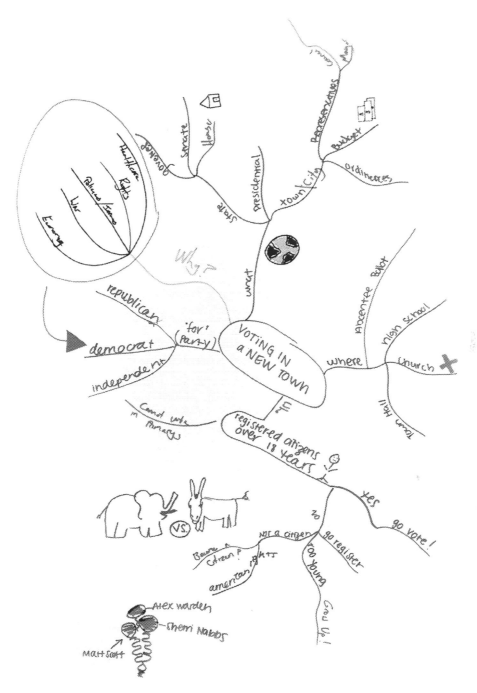

Figure 11. Group mind maps: Education setting

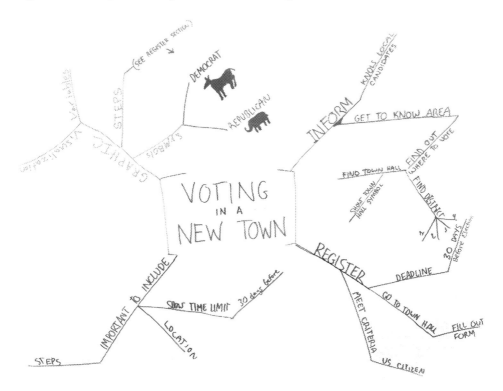

- ○ After an hour come back to your mind map and fill in more items – embellish, color, doodle. Let your mind be drawn to various areas of the map. If you run out of ideas, simply draw another radiant. Your mind will leapt to fill it in (the Gestalt principle of *closure*).
- ○ 24 hours later, create a second Mind Map *exploring a section of the first Mind Map*. Repeat the same process of taking a break and coming back.
- ○ Bring both maps to class. We will discuss the process.
- ○ Take photos of your two Mind Maps and post them in your Blog. Reflecting on the process outlined above, describe the experience of mapping each mind map in your blog. Where did you encounter your inner editor? How did you overcome your mental blocks? What patterns emerged? What were the AHA! moments?
- **Mind Map Instructions:**
  - ○ Place central focus image or graphic representation of problem in center of page.
  - ○ Allow ideas to flow *FREELY*, without judgment.

- Use key words to represent ideas.
- One key word PRINTED per line.
- Connect key word ideas to central image with lines.
- Use color, shading, embellishments, to highlight and emphasize ideas.
- Use images and symbols to highlight ideas and stimulate connections.

Sample Mind Mapping Assignment: Group Mind Mapping Session

The following instructions were given for a group brainstorming session. The individual requirements of the assignment can be changed. The questions in *italics* are standard critical thinking questions and instructions.

- **Task:** Brainstorm what you think you need for this graphic:

  - Subject "Voting in a New Town"
  - *What is the problem?*
  - *What information do you need?* What does a voter need to do to be informed, make a decision and be eligible to vote.
  - *What form should it take?* Use an organizing scheme - Steps, a journey, a clock, a calendar, timeline
  - *Is there another way to look at this? What other perspectives should I consider?*
  - What can you code pre-attentively? TIME is important and the order in which things happen—deadlines, issues, decision points, etc.

Use the power of many minds to generate the many things that should go into the graphic.

Think critically and creatively.

The map is intended as a brainstorming exercise prior to incubation.

BY HAND OR BY COMPUTER

In all of the above examples, the mind maps were created by hand with paper and markers, or on a whiteboard with colored dry erase markers. There are several good reasons for this. First, these examples are using mind mapping to support *thinking*. The tactile, sensory nature of mapping with real materials reinforces the synaesthetic synaptic activity necessary for visual thinking. The working environment is free of computer generated distractions like the beeps and dings of one's email account or browser. If one has completed a mind map and wishes to share a cleaned up, more organized version of it with others, then moving to a digital mind mapping tool is appropriate because one has moved from *visual thinking* to *visual communication*.

The other reason why I discourage using digital tools for mind mapping as thinking is that, by being on the computer, the map is now mediated. Working on the computer introduces navigating the mind map *application* as well as navigating the *map*. One's consciousness is divided between the computer application and the product. Subconscious compulsions for perfection take over, nudging that radiant over a little so that it is symmetrical, or having to group things because our mental aesthetic editor is engaged. This robs us of the opportunity for serendipity and spontaneity in our mapping. I find it interesting that when I first learned mind mapping *by hand* I was working for the second largest computer company in the world. Others may argue differently, but it is my contention that, if you are mind mapping for critical thinking and idea exploration, by hand is still the most effective way.

CONCLUSION

I had been using mind-mapping for over ten years as an organizational consultant, and later as a usability engineer, before I became a teacher. In 2003, when I moved from the business world to academia, I started using mind-mapping, along with other forms of mapping, in the classroom to help students explore, think, review, and organize ideas and arguments. Many of my students have used these skills in other coursework and in their post-baccalaureate academic and professional lives. Many report that they no longer use a linear, hierarchical outlining method for their papers and course notes but, instead, mind map them, often discovering more depth and nuance in their chosen paper topic. In my "Introduction to Visual Communication" course, students have coined and adopted the mantra, "When in doubt, map it out!"

Mind maps work because they mimic the way the mind itself works. By capitalizing on the principles of Gestalt, the multi-sensory effect of synaesthesia, the power of imagery to represent complex concepts, and the electro-chemical processes of associative and visual memory, mind mapping opens the portal to a series of connections. Neurons connect, a new synapse is born, endorphins are released, and the mind says, "Aha!"

Below are some reflections from students posted in their course portfolios regarding mind mapping:

Before I started the mind mapping process, my predictions were that I would run out of ideas before reaching five minutes. However, after twenty minutes of mind mapping the various options, I thought my hand was going to fall off. To my surprise, twenty minutes was not enough time.... Using this technique to solve a problem helped me visualize the pros and cons of each option (S. Deegan).

The mind map not only turned out to be educational in pushing my thoughts and ideas further with each association, but it also turned out to be a rather aesthetically pleasing design.... It is amazing to see how much each concept could build and grow outwards so much (O. Hamilton).

I soon found myself drawing radii without any real thought as to where I was going with my ideas, and yet a structure materialized in my mind map.... The process was in essence my mind getting out of the way of itself, like an unconscious filter being removed unconsciously (S. Wroblewski).

I am deeply appreciative of all of the knowledge and opportunities this class has provided me. I have admittedly used the mind map and the decision tree models to organize and focus my thinking. What I love about this is that it is immediately clear how these concepts can apply to real life (C. Muir).

It is my sincere hope that mind mapping becomes part of the reader's approach to critical thinking and creative problem-solving. Using one's whole mind is so superior and satisfying an experience that it should be second nature for us to reach for paper and colored pencil or marker whenever we are engaged in problem-solving and deep information processing. To paraphrase Sunni Brown, my friends, the mind map has never been the nemesis of critical thinking. In reality, it is one of its greatest allies.

REFERENCES

Baddeley, A. D. (1976). *The psychology of memory*. New York: Basic Books, Inc.

Bloom, B. S., Engelhart, M. D., Furst, E. J., Hill, W. H., & Krathwohl, D. R. (1956). *Taxonomy of educational objectives: The classification of educational goals, handbook I: Cognitive domain*. New York: Longmans, Green.

Bolte Taylor, J. (2006). *My stroke of insight: A brain scientist's personal journey*. New York: Plume.

Brown, S. (2011, March). *Sunni Brown: Doodlers unite!* [Video file]. Retrieved September 30, 2011 from http://www.ted.com/talks/sunni_brown.html

Buzan, T. (1974). *Use both sides of your brain*. New York: E. P. Dutton.

Buzan, T., & Buzan, B. (1993). *The mind map book: How to use radiant thinking to maximize your brain's untapped potential.* New York: Plume Books.

Caine, R. N., & Caine, G. (1994). *Making connections: Teaching and the human brain.* Menlo Park, CA: Addison-Wesley Publishers Co.

Carter, R. (1998). *Mapping the mind.* Berkeley, CA: University of California Press.

DeBono, E. (1985). *Six thinking hats.* Boston: Little Brown and Company.

Duhigg, C. (2012). *The power of habit: Why we do what we do in life and business.* New York: Random House.

Hyerle, D. (2009). *Visual tools for transforming information into knowledge.* Thousand Oaks, CA: Corwin Press.

Kosslyn, S. M. (1983). *Ghosts in the mind's machine: Creating and using images in the brain.* New York: W. W. Norton & Company.

Kosslyn, S. M. (1988). Imagery in learning. In *Perspectives in memory* (pp. 245–273). Cambridge, MA: MIT Press.

LeDoux, J. (2002). *Synaptic self: How our brains become who we are.* New York: Viking.

Mullet, K., & Sano, D. (1995). *Designing visual interfaces: Communication oriented techniques.* Upper Saddle River, NJ: Prentice Hall PTR.

Parnes, S. J. (1975). AHA! In I. A. Taylor, & J. W. Gretz (Eds.), *Perspectives in creativity* (pp. 224–248). Chicago: Aldine Publishing Company.

Paul, R., & Elder, L. (2009). Critical thinking: Where to begin. *The Critical Thinking Community.* Retrieved September 4, 2012, from http://www.criticalthinking.org/pages/critical-thinking-where-to-begin/796

Sadoski, M., Paivio, A., & Andrews, R. (2001). *Imagery and text – A dual coding theory of reading and writing.* Hillsdale, NJ: Lawrence Erlbaum Associates.

Scriven, M., & Paul, R. (1987). *Defining critical thinking.* Paper presented at the 8th Annual International Conference on Critical Thinking and Education Reform, Summer 1987. Retrieved 22 June 2012 from http://www.criticalthinking.org/pages/defining-critical-thinking/766

Sperry, R. W. (1967). Split-brain approach to learning problems. In G. Quarton, F. Schmitt, & T. Melnechuk (Eds.), *The neurosciences: A study program* (pp. 714–722). New York: Rockefeller University Press.

Todorović, D. (2008). Gestalt principles. *Scholarpedia*, *3*(12), 5345. doi:10.4249/scholarpedia.5345

Tyler, L. E. (1983). *Thinking creatively*. San Francisco: Jossey-Bass Publishers.

Wolfe, P., & Sorgen, M. (1990). *Mind, memory and learning*. Napa, CA: Authors.

Wycoff, J. (1991). *Mindmapping: Your personal guide to exploring creativity and problem-solving*. New York: Berkley Books.

KEY TERMS AND DEFINITIONS

Collaboration: The act of working together with others to create something.

Concept Maps: A graphic tool for organizing and representing knowledge.

Critical Thinking: Intellectually disciplined process of actively and skillfully conceptualizing, applying, analyzing, synthesizing, and/or evaluating information gathered from, or generated by, observation, experience, reflection, reasoning, or communication, as a guide to belief and action.

Group Problem Solving: The collaborative effort of people working together to solve a problem.

Mind Mapping: A visual technique for capturing concepts and ideas that exploits the way we actually think—through synaptic connections and non-linear associations.

Mind Maps: A graphic tool for creating webs of interconnections of information, ideas and concepts that lead to new perceptions and possibilities.

Radiant Thinking: A term used to describe the thinking process supported by mind mapping.

Teamwork: Work done by people working together as a team to accomplish something.

ENDNOTES

[1] "At one view" is a phrase used by William Playfair (1759–1823) to describe his new "invention," a method of graphically presenting statistical information we have come to know as multivariate line and bar graphs. He writes, "As knowledge increases amongst mankind, and transactions multiply, it becomes more and more desirable to *abbreviate* and *facilitate* the modes of conveying information from one person to another, and from one individual to the many" (2005, p. 4).

2   For an excellent video on experiencing synaesthesia see artist Carol Steen's YouTube "Introduction to Synaesthesia": http://www.youtube.com/watch?v=Vj5KFhLVbUg

Chapter 15
Concept Maps, VoiceThread, and Visual Images:
Helping Educators Spawn Divergent Thinking and Dialogic Learning

Kristen M. Snyder
Mid Sweden University, Sweden

EXECUTIVE SUMMARY

The context of this chapter has its roots in an educational movement that recognizes the importance of preparing youth for living and working in a global community. Central to this is a belief in 1) engaging students in collaborative learning, 2) developing cultural sensitivity, 3) using digital media for communication and creativity, and 4) transforming pedagogical practice to foster reflection, divergent thinking, and creativity. The question addressed in this chapter is how teachers can use digital media and visual images to spawn divergent thinking and dialogue in a global learning context. This chapter presents a case analysis to examine evidence of inquiry-based collaborative learning and three-dimensional thinking among students when using digital images and collaborative software in a global partnership project.

DOI: 10.4018/978-1-4666-5816-5.ch015

INTRODUCTION

Story!, Design!, Creativity!, Divergent Thinking!, Complexity!, Exploration!, Curiosity!, Empathy! These are just some of the 21st century skills that business and international educational policy leaders suggest are essential for learning and working in a globally connected society. Already many of us, in particular children and youth, have experienced this transition from left-brain dominated communication (text-based) to right-brain communication (visual and spatial) through the Internet and other social media. The growing use of images and video on the Net, for example, is shaping a new way of thinking and communicating that is more divergent and creative. Through social media we are learning to collaborate, expanding our perspectives and stimulating new questions about life, society, and each other. Researchers have found exciting benefits from this networked, visual communication culture that supports the development of 21st century skills and creativity (Nilson & Nocon, 2005; Offir et al., 2008; Schlais & Davis, 2001). Despite this, other international studies (Jerald, 2009) have found little evidence of pedagogical innovation taking place at the classroom level that reflects the above skills and attributes. In general, the majority of schools remain on the outside of this media equation (Snyder, 2007). The dominant learning model is most suited to left-brain analytical thought, while the workforce calls for greater right-brain activity (Pink, 2005; Silverman, 2004). Many now recognize the need to explore pedagogical opportunities that today's media affords innovation in learning.

One of the questions worth asking then is "what can educators do differently to develop learning environments that support holistic learning stemming from inquiry, exploration, creation, and collaboration through the use of digital media? While technology has been used in many classrooms around the world for the past decade or more, many teachers still report that they lack the skills and knowledge to think differently about the use of digital media to support pedagogical innovation (Snyder, 2010). We need to provide teachers with examples of how digital media can be applied pedagogically to stimulate, among other things creativity, diversity of thought, exploration and collaboration. Visual literacy and divergent thinking tools, such as concept maps, can be a helpful step in that direction (Wegerif, 2007). Studies are now reporting the dynamic changes that occur in learning when social software and images are used as part of the curriculum and tools for learning (Beaudry & Wilson, 2010; Stokes, 2001).

In 2010, The Gulf Oil Spill Crisis pilot (GOSP) was developed to support cross-cultural collaboration and pedagogical innovation in 14 schools in Nanshen China and Florida USA. The pilot emerged in response to research findings from the Global Partnership Project (Snyder, 2010). Little evidence was found in student online exchanges that reflected exploration, collaborative learning, and divergent thinking when communication took place predominantly through a text-based learning platform. To support pedagogical innovation, the GOSP pilot introduced the use of digital storytelling (Lambert, 2006) with concept maps (Beaudry & Wilson, 2010; Niesyto et al., 2003) and VoiceThread in an online learning community (Harasim, 1989; Sorensen, 2002). This model was guided by a transformative pedagogical approach that shifted the focus from teacher-driven to student-driven learning (Mezirow, 1997). The intent was to help teachers and students explore the use of collaborative learning media to promote reflective and dialogic learning (Abbey, 2008), as well as divergent thinking through visual literacy. This chapter presents a comparative analysis between the two projects periods examining differences in student exchange and the nature of inquiry when using concept maps and visual images as compared to text-based communication. The purpose is to contribute perspectives on how teachers can use digital media in their classrooms to support 21st century learning skills and help promote critical thinking, creativity and collaboration.

BACKGROUND

In 2007, The EU Commission on education identified eight key competencies that support program development within education, of which digital competence, global awareness, and social skills are included (European Commission on Education, 2007). The call stretches the focus from technology as a mere tool, to technology as a context for interacting and learning. The Commission (2007) states that, "ICT skills comprise the use of multi-media technology to retrieve, assess, store, produce, present and exchange information, and communicate and participate in networks via the Internet" (p. 22). Similarly, U.S. educational programming is guided at the present by an umbrella initiative called Framework for 21st Century Learning (2009), which promotes an integrated model of core subjects, digital media and technology skills, life and career skills, and with learning skills such as communication, creativity, collaboration and critical thinking. These two educational agendas and others alike around the world recognize the importance for schools to redesign their educational programming in ways that integrate pedagogy, technology, and workforce preparation. They suggest it no longer is sufficient to focus solely on core subjects, for social skills, digital literacy and visual literacy are essential for preparing youth for the kind of divergent, inter-connected, networking, and creative work that is demanded of business for the future workforce.

Messages from the business community echo these educational agendas as well, and at the same time caution us about the gap between need and reality. Jerald (2009) reported in a study examining 21st century business skills that creativity, communication, divergent thinking, and collaboration are essential and need to be more fully developed in school curricula. Unfortunately, they report, the dominant educational model is overloaded with a focus on well-structured problems; students are not prepared to meet the real world of complex problems that require new ways of seeing and thinking. Moreover, reports Jerald (ibid), students are exhibiting difficulty presenting their thoughts and ideas, and lack a sense of passion and focus in their thinking. This would suggest that it is time for educators to take stock in the research on learning styles, brain based learning, and arts and education to understand more fully what teachers can do to integrate right-brain learning activities in the classroom and spawn divergent thinking, curiosity, creativity, and dialogic learning among students. And further, learn how visual images can be used to facilitate communication and learning across cultures where spoken and written language are often barriers.

The time has come, according to Pink (2005), to take advantage of the arts, and in particular visual thinking, to inform pedagogical development and programming in schools to open space for imagination and divergent thought. He claims that society is engaged in a paradigm shift from a left-brain dominated focus to a focus on the whole new mind, in which the left and right brain work in partnership with each other. The heavy emphasis on productivity and effectiveness in the industrial age, he suggests, is being replaced by a need among humans to have greater social connections, spirituality and creativity. He, and others (Snyder, et al., 2008) propose that the jobs of the future will be more focused on artistry, empathy, emotion, design, invention, counseling, ethnography, networking, and global. These jobs incorporate right brain activities, including, design, story, symphony, empathy, play and meaning (Pink, 2005). According to Silverman (2004),

Visual-spatial learners are individuals who think in pictures rather than in words… They are non-sequential, which means that they do not learn in the step-by-step manner in which most teachers teach. They arrive at correct solutions without taking steps, so "show your work" may be impossible for them. They may have difficulty with easy tasks, but show amazing ability with difficult, complex tasks. They are systems thinkers who can orchestrate large amounts of information from different domains, but they often miss the details. They tend to be organizationally impaired and unconscious about time. They are often gifted creatively, artistically, technologically, mathematically or emotionally (p. 2).

Unfortunately, as research shows, schools have difficulty addressing the needs of right-brain visual learners because they are designed from a left-brain dominant model (Cochrane, 1999; Silverman, 2004). According to Silverman (ibid), "the school curriculum is sequential, the textbooks are sequential, the workbooks are sequential, the teaching methods are sequential, and most teachers learn sequentially". What is important is for educators to seek ways to build learning environments that embrace both the left and right brain and also encourage dialog and collaboration. Building brain-friendly learning environments engages both brains and is stimulated by challenge and feedback, as well as artistic expression (Galyean, 1983; Pink, 2005; Respress & Lufti, 2006).

Advances in Web 2.0 technology create possibilities for educators to develop classroom practices that promote 21st century skills including creativity, critical thinking, collaboration, empathy, and reflection. Needed is a pedagogical framework that helps teachers utilize the technology in ways that stimulate creativity and divergent thinking through discovery and inquiry. Traditional classrooms that reflect the left-brain dominated learning environment are guided by a pedagogical approach that assumes the teacher as knowledge bearer (ISTE, 2000); Knowledge is expert driven and in order to obtain knowledge one needs to learn from those who have it. Transformative learning (Mezirow, 1997) environments are guided by the pedagogical principles of among others, Dewey (1938, 1998), Vygotsky (1978), and Kolb (1984) who suggest learning occurs best when it is social, interactive, reflective, multisensory, collaborative and designed around a student's own questions. Such learning environments promote a balance between left-brain and right-brain activities as learners utilize a variety of media and art forms to explore phenomena as well as learn the basics in the core subjects.

A missing link for educators in the age of technology and social networking, I would suggest, is the use of visual images and representation that naturally invite open and creative thinking, as well as collaborative media that calls for students to work together on shared questions. Studies suggest (Snyder, 2010) that it is not enough to put students in learning groups and ask them to find information about problems or issues. This approach is limited in its linear orientation and is not sufficient to help students master the kinds of right-brain skills and competencies that are being called for by business today (Pink, 2005; Silverman, 2004). Whole brain learning requires a stimulus that invites thinking, exploration and curiosity (Dewey, 1998) and a forum for representing ideas as they grow. Visual thinking is a key ingredient in opening new doors for such learning to occur. It creates possibilities to incorporate both left-brain linear, logical thinking, and right-brain spatial and divergent thinking, while representing complex relationships in a variety of mediums.

The Arts, Visual Literacy and Creativity

Proponents of arts education have for years been seeking to help educators and politicians understand the significant role of the arts for holistic learning (Eisner, 2002; Greene, 1995; Rabkin & Redmond, 2004). According to Respress and Lufti (2006) "the arts pay off most expansively in basic reading skills, language development, and writing skills. Increases in general academic skills also show up and appear to reinforce these specific literacy-related developments. These skills emphasize focus and concentration, skills in expression, persistence, imagination, creativity and inclinations to tackle problems" (p. 26). Dickinson (2002) demonstrated interesting relationships between different art forms and thinking and reasoning. For example, music has a strong correlation to spatial reasoning, which is used in mathematics, while drama helps stimulate problem solving, concentration and analytical reasoning. And dance increases self-confidence, tolerance and appreciation for others.

Eisner (2002) and Greene (1988, 1995) focus on the use of the arts to stimulate imagination. Eisner (ibid) contends the arts "provide not only permission but also encouragement to use one's imagination as a source of content. Unlike in the sciences, where imagination is also of fundamental importance, in the arts there is a tradition that does not hold the artist responsible for 'telling it like it is'" (p. 82). Working with imagery can help foster a kind of divergent thinking that is essential for creativity and imagination. It is in this role that visual literacy becomes significant for helping bridge the gap between business needs and student preparation for 21st century work. While the arts have remained external to the core curriculum and pedagogical practice in most educational systems, the growing use of images for communication on the Internet is causing us to take a second look and rethink the importance of visual literacy for 21st century living and work.

"A picture is worth a thousand words" is an old saying that can be heard around the world in a variety of languages. It reminds us that there is power in images that cannot be captured in words. Visual communication is a language of its own, and it is universal, like music. Moreover, and more significantly, interpreting images allows for divergent thought for there is no single right answer to the meaning of an image (Eisner, 2002). Images are everywhere, in our landscape, in museums, on TV, books, and on the Internet, and it is now becoming clearer that visual literacy needs to be developed in order to participate in knowledge sharing and development in the 21st century (Stokes, 2001). Visual literacy is the ability to read and interpret messages conveyed through visual images, as well as producing images for an audience (Bamford, 2003; Yenawine, 1997). It provides for a deep and reflective understanding of a topic or concept in a way that text-based representation does not invite in particular because reading and communicating with images involves critical thinking and multi-modal learning that stimulate deep learning.

Housen (2002) states that aesthetic thought strongly correlates with critical thinking and creativity and new cognitive growth as students observe, speculate and reason on the basis of evidence. Her work has led to the development of Visual Thinking Strategies (VUE, 2001), which she describes as a discovery process in which questions about images serves as the basis for dialogue. She states, "Discussions are initiated by questions phrased to provoke many thoughtful responses to what is seen in the images. Responding leads to active and extended involvement. The questions students ask become reflective —the basis for thinking critically" (VUE, 2001, p. 2). Starting with visual images, students begin to explore by asking, "what's going on in this picture," which serves as the basis for opening dialog for learning. Further exploration leads to the next level of questioning, "what do you see that makes you say that" and then finally, "what more can we find." These open, exploratory questions lead students into a reflective dialogue that stimulates divergent thought and creativity.

Within the context of cross-cultural sharing and learning, the arts, and in particular visual communication, can play a significant role in both communication and development of cultural sensitivity as youth explore common questions from different perspectives using a shared language of visual representation. Bamford (2009) suggests that the arts can serve as a cultural agent, helping students to develop an understanding of human experience and cultural identity and explore issues in a dialogic space that stimulate creative solutions. Working with imagery provides students a focal point for generating questions that are more divergent in nature, and foster exploration rather than argumentation and proof. Such questions invite dialogic learning (Shor & Freire, 1987) in which youth explore questions and perspectives in collaboration with one another, rather than arguing a particular point of view. It is through reflection, critical thinking and dialogue that creativity and knowledge transfer are supported (Frijters et al., 2008).

Collaborative Learning Software

Collaborating and working with diverse perspectives in an exploratory manner is not easy and automatic for all students. Often students need help finding ways to represent their ideas, communicate their thoughts, or organize information to see relationship between concepts or perspectives. Moreover, students need tools to help them develop collaborative inquiry. Two useful tools that are analyzed in this chapter are VoiceThread and Concept mapping. VoiceThread is a collaborative multimedia tool in the form of a slideshow that allows users to interact with the context via text, voice, audio and video. As a pedagogical tool, VoiceThread creates conditions for student introduction, reviews of literature, reflection, brainstorming and digital storytelling. Its use in education is growing, and in particular it offers a multi-modal option for youth to explore, communication and collaborate around ideas. Brunvand and Byrd (2011) suggest that, "interface and feature set are well-suited for promoting student engagement and motivation, as well as helping students develop as independent learners" (p. 30). They promote the tool based on its flexibility to offer both synchronous and asynchronous learning, as well as a storage facility of ideas that can be accessed at a later date. Its intended use makes VoiceThread a useful tool for both collaboration and peer learning. Gillis et al. (2012) applied VoiceThread with young children to support language development, and found that it supported expressive language through storytelling, receptive language through listening to stories, comprehension through story retelling, and inferencing. They conclude VoiceThread to be a significant technology for its multimodal interactive ability including, voice, photo, and text, that engage students in active learning and expression.

Burden and Atkinson (2008) state that while VoiceThread was not originally designed for education, its application for learning is significant in relation to 21st century skill building. In particular they highlight strengths of VoiceThread as a social software for supporting 1) "connectivity and social rapport," 2) "collaborative information discovery and sharing," 3) "content creation," and 4) knowledge and information aggregation and content modification" (p.122). They point out, however, that it is not the software itself that stimulates a collaborative inquiry based learning, but rather it affords teachers the opportunity to support students in engagement. Benefiting from VoiceThread, among other social software, requires careful planning and stimulation on the part of the teacher to facilitate students' use of the software´.

Concept mapping is a higher-order thinking tool that has been used as a graphic organizer to help reflect and represent relationships between concepts (Novak & Canas, 2008). Nesbit and Adesope (2006) report that they were initially used as "advanced organizers, priming students for learning by activating prior knowledge and illustrating relationships with new concepts" (p. 413). Since then, the application of concept maps in education has developed in a variety of directions and is often used to support both collaboration (Gaines et. al., 1995) and divergent thinking. For students who have difficulty communicating their ideas in text-form, concept maps function as a spatial learning tool and offer visual learners possibilities to both explore the relationship between thoughts and represent them on paper, albeit in another form than pure text.

Research on concepts maps and learning demonstrate significant gains in retention and transfer. Nesbit and Adesope (2006) state that

In comparisons with activities such as reading text passages, attending lectures, and participating in class discussions, concept mapping activities are more effective for attaining knowledge retention and transfer. Concept mapping was found to benefit learners across a broad range of educational levels, subject areas, and settings. Much of this benefit was due to greater learner engagement, occasioned by concept mapping in comparison with reading and listening, rather than the properties of the concept map as an information medium (p. 434).

Clearly stated here is the possibility that concept maps afford student engagement that is different from typical student involvement in class discussions. In part, the key lies in the construction of information and ideas students generate through the concept maps, unlike when they engage in a verbal dialogue. Beaudry and Wilson (2010) provide further evidence of the use of concept maps for student engagement. In their study of the use of concept maps and formative assessment, they reported that students experienced a progressive mapping model, including collaborative learning phases, to be a strong factor in their learning. They claim that concept maps "are products that facilitate interactions of multiple forms of literacy, bringing thinking, writing, visualizing together with listening and speaking" (p. 7). Their argument supports the use of concept mapping and visual representation to stimulate a dialogic learning model that can promote critical thinking skills, questioning skills and deep reflective learning.

Findings from those who have worked with and studied the use of concept mapping, voice thread and visual images paint a picture for educators that demonstrates possibilities for creating learner-centered environments that spawn divergent thinking and creativity through the use of arts and technology. The next section of this chapter presents an analysis of data on the Gulf Oil Spill Project (GOSP) to explore the evidence of changes in student engagement, thinking and learning comparing the use of concept maps and voice threads with text-based exchange in Moodle.

THE GLOBAL PARTNERSHIP PROJECT

In 2009 the Global Partnership Project (GPP) formed to support international school partnership in China, USA, and Sweden. The GPP's mission was to help advance education through cross-cultural learning and collaboration for the development of global citizenship and pedagogical innovation (Snyder et al., 2010). Twenty-two school teams participated during the first two years (N=36 schools) from China, Sweden and the U.S. engaged during which educators were encouraged to build cross-cultural learning groups with their students through the support of communication technology (Moodle, ooVoo and Skype) to address global issues. The GPP was designed around an entire academic year with the fall term focused on helping students get acquainted using both Moodle and Skype. The curriculum was designed by the teachers in the three countries to support learning about global issues within the context of the curriculum focus in the partnering schools. The general framework began with a unit on "getting acquainted" in which students were asked to present themselves to each other in Moodle. The next unit focused on a community presentation by each school sharing something unique about their school or community and everyday life. The third unit was designed to stimulate global collaborative learning around a selected global theme, including water, the environment, or recycling. Research on this project (Snyder, 2010) showed that while student awareness for global issues increased and curiosity for different cultures expanded, little collaboration took place between students, in large part due to the text-based, linear nature of Moodle in which teachers were the main communicators.

In response to these findings, The Gulf Oil Spill Project was designed to advance pedagogical development in the GPP introducing visual images and collaborative tools including concept maps and voice threads (Beaudry et al., 2011). The pilot project title was conceived from the content, context and process of the intended learning model: *Gulf Oil Spill Project: Cross-cultural Digital Story-telling (GOSP)* and eight project goals that were identified. The project was designed to support collaborative learning in cross-cultural learning communities. The pedagogical framework that underpinned the project was drawn from transformative learning theory (Mezirow, 1997), visual thinking (Niesyto et al., 2003), intercultural competence development (Deardorff, 2004) and online collaborative learning (Sorensen, 2002). Three primary tools were introduced including a visual image data repository, VoiceThread and Webspiration, which is a collaborative concept mapping tool. The tools were designed for use in a discovery model designed (Beaudry et al., 2011) that reflected four stages of learning for transformation: investigate through photos and information, create (digital stories), share (on concept maps and voice thread), and evaluate the information collaborative for knowledge transfer. The model is illustrated in Figure 1.

METHODOLOGY

This chapter examines how communication exhibited by students in a global learning context differs when using concept maps and visual images as compared to

Figure 1. Digital work flow model (copyright Beaudry, Burden, Keuchel, Snyder, 2011)

text-based responses, and explores any differences that are visible in the dialogic nature of the inquiry that ensued. Articulating a specific method that was used in this analysis is not a clear-cut process, for the focus of this chapter lies in between two worlds. On the one hand the study is a phenomenological exploration of changes in classroom-based learning that takes place in a cross-cultural learning context with different uses of digital media and concept mapping. At the same, it is not a pure phenomenological (Lancy, 1993) study in the classic sense, given that the focus is on patterns of change in the kinds of questions and communication that students engage in using digital technology, rather than on their experience with the technology. At best it can be described as a comparative collective instrumental case study (Stake, 1995), borrowing from Stake (ibid) and from Denzin and Lincoln (1994). Stake (ibid) defines an instrumental case study as a method to examine a particular question by studying a particular case. The case itself is not the object of study, but rather the vehicle through which a researcher can understand a situation, phenomenon, etc. to answer a question. When several cases are used as study objects to examine a question, the case becomes collective. I have chosen to include the use of the term "comparative" since this particular study examined differences in the types of questions and cross-cultural communication that occurred between students who participated in a global partnership project over a three-year period.

Data for purposes of this analysis were selected from student communication during the two project periods. In total 12 school partnerships were represented in the first project phase (GPP) with a total of 3 schools in each partnership team from China, USA, and Sweden (N=36 schools). Seven school partnerships participated in the pilot project (GOSP) with a total of 14 schools arranged in seven teams. Due to several logistical factors related to language and technology, the cross-cultural exchange dimension was not developed. Data were not available from the schools in China, and of the participating American schools, data were available from four schools out of seven. Data were then selected from the remaining schools that had demonstrated student work relevant to the purpose of this chapter, which included three middle partnerships from the first project phase, represented by schools in both the USA and China, and three schools in the USA from the pilot phase: one middle school and two elementary schools.

Selected data used in this analysis included: Seventeen concept maps from one seventh grade class in the USA (GOSP 7), seven VoiceThreads from two middle school classes in the USA, and text-based dialogue exchange in Moodle from a three middle school partnership in both USA and China. Individual interviews with 7 teachers in the U.S. were conducted via Skype and one focus group with all participating teachers in Florida (N=12) was conducted via Flashmeeting. Due to language barriers, communication with the teachers in China was limited and did not permit for a focus group or online survey.

Data were analyzed using a semantic approach to examine the content of communication as well as the form and structure, and social interaction of images, ideas and text. Erikson's (2007) Thinking Classroom model was applied to identify questions as either two-dimensional, reflecting fact-based knowledge, or three-dimensional questions that are conceptual and provocative. Two-dimensional questions relate to convergent, non-dialogic learning, and three-dimensional questions relate to divergent and critical thinking. The Digital Work Flow model was applied to explore the ways in which student communication showed evidence of inquiry-based dialogic learning using digital media.

FINDINGS

Findings are presented with respect to the two project phases of GPP and GOSP. The first analysis explores student inquiry and collaboration within the context of a teacher-driven curriculum that was carried out in a predominantly text-based communication platform (Moodle). The second analysis explored student inquiry and exchange in a student-driven model in which visual literacy tools (concept maps and voice thread) dominated the form and structure for communication. Following these findings, an analysis is provided that compares differences in student learning and explores potential reasons for the differences that can help to answer the question posed in this chapter: "what can educators do differently to develop learning environments that support holistic learning stemming from inquiry, exploration, creation, and collaboration through the use of digital media?

Moodle Discussion Forums and Text-Based Exchange

Examining text-based data from the first phase of the project, it is clear that when students engaged in learning by responding to teacher questions in a discussion forum, the communication was limited to fact-based responses for personal beliefs. Little to no dialogue occurred between students, and when it did, it was limited to one or two sentences. Rarely did students ask any questions of each other more than, "what do you think"? and, "tell me what it is like in your country."

The first example, found in Figure 2, depicts the type of questions that teachers asked as organizers for learning. Here we see that the question asks for facts and does not invite any particular kind of inquiry. The phrasing, "describe what it would be like if that system was no longer functioning properly" does not necessarily elicit inquiry from students. Moreover, the Moodle discussion forum was organized so that each student had a separate discussion forum in which to post. This required each student to open the individual discussions and post to each one, as opposed

Figure 2. Screenshot of Moodle online discussion forum

to seeing the entire discussion thread as a dialogic space. This one-to-one communication structure appeared to affect the type of exchange between students, as evidenced by the little to no commenting on the different threads.

In another example, teachers identified two project themes: Earth and Carbon Emission, and asked students to generate questions that they could then work on together. The Moodle environment was identical to that depicted in Figure 2 above. One student responded to the question about Earth with a simple comment, "I think more people should recycle and maybe we would have less earth related issues!" Another group prepared a power point slide that focused on "how to reduce your footstep" using data from different Internet sources that point to the need to use energy saving features in your home, for example, use cleaner transport or choose sustainable building materials. No exchange or dialogue followed the posting of this power point in Moodle.

Following this activity, teachers then chose to post a new question on Moodle: "What do you recycle at home"? and "how do you recycle at home"? The stated objectives from the teachers were for "learners to give examples of renewable and non-renewable resources and explain the differences between the two categories of resources, 2) generate a list of non-traditional uses for a given object or material, and 3) address problems that come with a nations prosperity and growth." Students began to post in a common discussion forum their responses to the questions. What is evident from the postings, as highlighted in Figure 3, is that students merely answered the question, rather than engaging in an exploratory dialogue together. Furthermore, the content of their postings does not reflect deep learning. Rather it was descriptive of what they already do at home to recycle.

Figure 3. Online text-communication in Moodle between two students

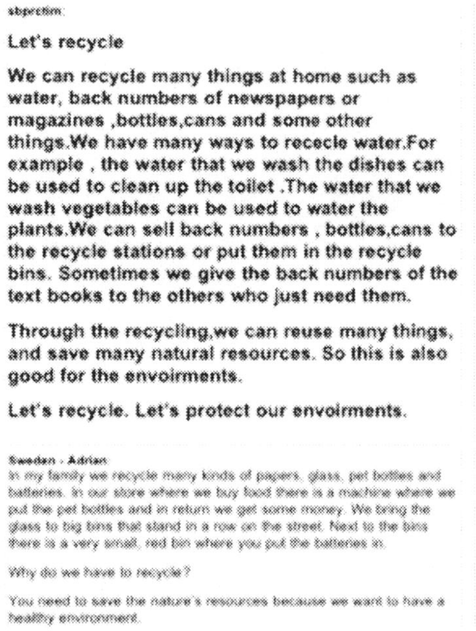

subrotim

Let's recycle

We can recycle many things at home such as water, back numbers of newspapers or magazines ,bottles,cans and some other things.We have many ways to rececle water.For example , the water that we wash the dishes can be used to clean up the toilet .The water that we wash vegetables can be used to water the plants.We can sell back numbers , bottles,cans to the recycle stations or put them in the recycle bins. Sometimes we give the back numbers of the text books to the others who just need them.

Through the recycling,we can reuse many things, and save many natural resources. So this is also good for the envoirments.

Let's recycle. Let's protect our envoirments.

Sweden - Adrian

In my family we recycle many kinds of papers, glass, pet bottles and batteries. In our store where we buy food there is a machine where we put the pet bottles and in return we get some money. We bring the glass to big bins that stand in a row on the street. Next to the bins there is a very small, red bin where you put the batteries in.

Why do we have to recycle?

You need to save the nature's resources because we want to have a healthy environment.

In another school partnership, students used word documents to communicate their thoughts and ideas about an environmental issue in response to a teacher-initiated question posted in Moodle: "What kind of global issues can we explore together? Post a question or comments about an issue and let's talk about it." Following this question, teachers had identified two thematic areas in which they intended for students to respond to the initial question. The themes included the environment and water resource management. The theme of environment generated dialogue between six students representing the schools in Sweden and the U.S. In one of the postings, a student asked questions of their partners:

What do you think we should do about the environmental problems of the world?

How do you think the world will look like in 20-30 years?

Do you think there will be new and dangerous diseases that may lead to thousands of people dying due to the rise in temperatures?

Some people think that they do not care about the environment and that everyone takes it too seriously. What should we do to change that kind of person and get them to understand the importance of global warming?

Responses by other students to these questions included, 1) "I think you are right. We need to help out the earth. I do not think we residents have a choice about fossil fuels, but we can walk and other things that will help"; 2) "what I think we should do about the environment crisis is we should pay attention to the small things like riding your bike to the store instead of driving a car. We could trade our old light bulbs for environmental friendly ones. I think that if we start paying attention to the small things now, later on our world will start to mend itself back together, but the Earth cannot mend itself on its own, so let's start going green!"

In this online exchange, the initial questions asked by one student indicated three-dimensional thinking in that they suggested an awareness of implications for the future based on the current environmental issues, for example: "do you think there will be new and dangerous diseases that may lead to thousands of people dying due to rising temperatures?" The relationship identified the connection between rising temperatures, disease and death. It appears from the responses that the format for communication did not invite exploration or dialogue, as none of the responses were in direct relation to the questions. They reflected a collegial perspective, but no collaboration, dialogue, or reflection that was stimulated by the posting.

Another student in the same partnership posted their comments individually in a word document, asking questions of their school partners at the end of the letter. They wrote the following:

The environmental problems are something that I think we should start thinking more about. Before when I was younger I didn't care so much about it so much but now I can't avoid it. Something that our country can do is to stop produce so much environment pollutions things. I don't think that I as a private person can do so much to change the environment problems and not my parents either. Now some questions to you.

Do you care much about the environment problems?

Do you try to do something to change the problems?

How much does your country care about the problems?

How much do your parents care about the problems?

Have you noticed some different about the climate now and for some years ago?

The types of questions raised in this posting reflect mostly convergent thought and two-dimensional thinking focusing on facts and skills for how to care for the environment. The affective nature of the questions suggests potentially divergent thinking, but this is not evident since there is no dialogue to follow or follow-up. It is conceivable that if these students had another forum for connecting, and were encouraged to dialogue, their questions could support creative inquiry. However, in the text-based forum the questions became mostly rhetorical.

These examples suggest that while students may possess skills in inquiry, using them to facilitate deep learning requires more than just posting thoughts. It requires a forum, process or method that invites exchange and exploration, as well as testing concepts. In relation to the first set of questions posed by the teachers on Earth and Carbon Emission, only one student responded in the U.S. to the question about Earth, and one class in China to the question about Carbon emissions. In a separate question to the same schools about recycling, only seven students responded representing two different schools. This would suggest that the discussion forum model in combination with a teacher driven curriculum framework, was not enough to evoke dialogic learning, curiosity and divergent thinking among students.

Concept Maps and Visual Images

In contrast to the first phase of the project, the second phase (GOSP) employed a transformative pedagogical approach grounded in student-inquiry in which teachers served as facilitators. The concept maps, VoiceThreads and visual images were used as stimuli and platforms for communication for student inquiry and collaboration. To begin, students were asked by their teachers to choose between one and 3 photos from a photo bank of 12 photos, each from the Gulf Oil Spill and the Yushu Earthquake. Using a Visual Thinking Strategy model they then asked students the question, "What do you think is happening in this photo?" followed by a series of questions that began with "Why?" The purpose according to the teachers was to help students engage in a deeper learning process using the photos as a stimulus. According to one teacher, the photos, helped students "to generate emotion, talk about personal experience, including such questions as how the gulf oil spill affected our sea life and seafood prices." The teacher further shared that 'The pictures brought emotion. We asked students to look at the photo without saying anything and then asked, 'what are you feeling'. This helped them to generate questions that then became a part of their investigation.

Following exploration of the photos, students collaborated in groups of three from each school working with concept maps to explore further the initial questions that had emerged from the photos. They received help from the teachers to generate a question that could help them start their inquiry. In the concept maps that were generated, there was evidence of three-dimensional thinking represented by the different types of questions asked that illustrate an understanding of the relationship between concepts. In the first concept map, the collaborating students asked the main question, "What happened to the sea animals during the oil spill?" Their inquiry included sub questions, such as "did the animals get cleaned after the oil spill? In which they explored information about the cleaning process. As well they learned that the particular timing of the oil spill had an impact on sea life in a larger sense, as many of them had begun the spawning and nesting period. According to the teacher, the photos helped the students to make different kinds of connections to additional questions so that their inquiry was not just fact based; it also included affect, which is linked to divergent thinking. They guided:, "as you type in the concept map, you enter data in different boxes. As the boxes develop, you see how questions become sub-sets of questions, and how concepts relate."

In one concept map in Figure 4, elements of affect are displayed in the questions, as well as deeper exploration of what can be done to help China in the cleanup. Rather than asking only fact-based questions, students were curious about how

Figure 4. Concept map from a seventh grade team

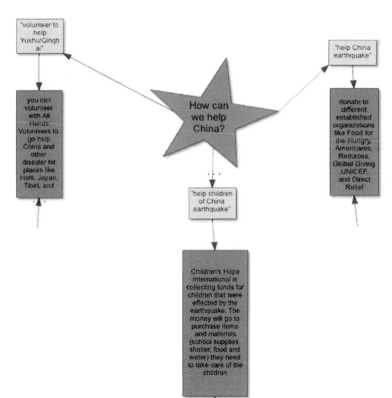

to engage in the issue, which is considered an important characteristic of critical thinking and creative learning.

In another concept map, presented in Figure 5, we see again evidence of the kinds of sub-questions that emerged in the student's inquiry that were generated from one major question: what happed to China's major cities. This question is reflective of an "essential question" which fosters divergent thinking. The question itself can be answered from a variety of points of view both fact-based and affect-based. The sub-questions that were generated during the inquiry indicate an awareness of the complexity of the event and its impact on china.

In the concept maps there is also evidence of collaboration. Students who worked in groups of three began with a common question and then generated a series of sub-questions, which they explored individually to begin with. Students collaborated on the concept map, filling in their information and then dialoging about its implications. During the interview with the technology teacher in one of the schools, they shared that the concept map was significant in stimulating collaboration: "When students researched their questions, they could collaborate on one document in Webspiration (a concept mapping software). Students were asked to find a different

Figure 5. Concept map from a seventh grade team

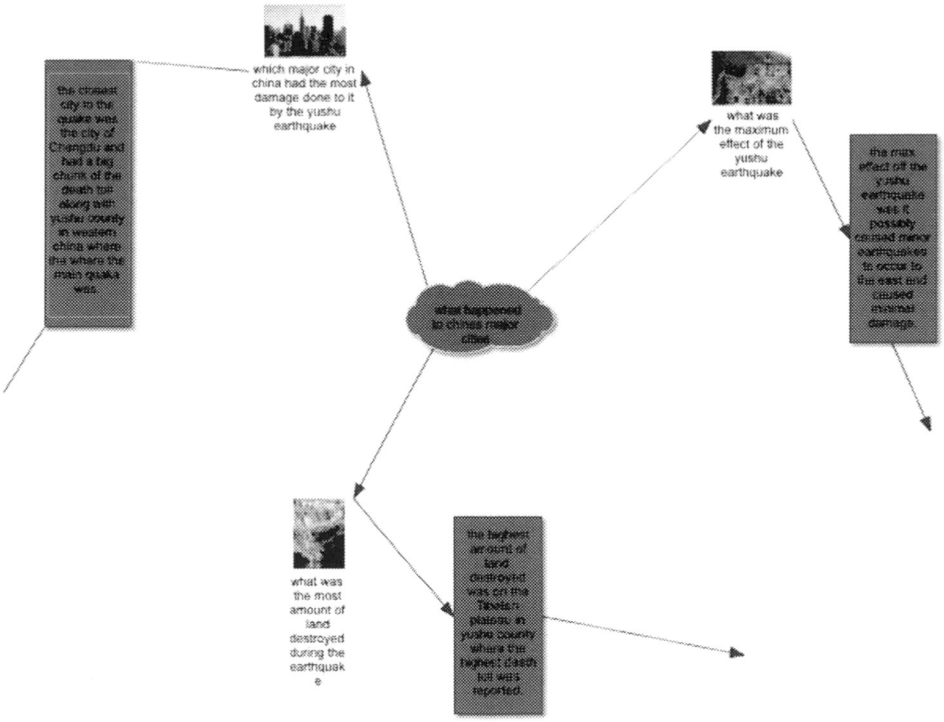

photo to support their question. Then they uploaded them to the concept map. Then they had to research and enter their info. Ask questions about the picture and then research. They then saw that student A's question could relate to student B and C based on their pictures. We found that this stimulated students' curiosity and interest." What was not evident in second phases on the GPP project was cross-cultural collaboration. According to the teachers, the project was implemented too late during the spring term and did not allow time for cross-cultural sharing. However, according to teachers, the photos helped students develop a sense of curiosity about the respective countries and sense of empathy for the experience of both natural disasters for its citizens.

VoiceThread

In another class, students began to study the photos as a stimulus for dialogue. Instead of concept mapping, they used VoiceThread as the medium for communication, both to present their knowledge of the Gulf Oil Spill and Yushu Earthquake, as well as to present their experiment with how to clean up an oil spill using a simulated project model. In the first VoiceThread as depicted in Figure 6, two students presented information about the Gulf Oil Spill. A transcription of their postings showed that students incorporated facts they presented in narrative form. They used imagery in their words to paint a picture of the human element, rather than just reporting facts. For example, one student shared, "When the gulf oil spill happened they were a mile underground and there were eleven workers onboard who died because of the

Figure 6. VoiceThread from an elementary school team

explosion and that's because there were a few glitches with the machine." Another student shared the following, "The gulf oil spill was terrible. It killed a lot of marine life. Mostly sea turtles, but it spread for a 100 miles and it also killed a lot of people." Together, these two different storylines embedded within the same VoiceThread represented collaboration around information about the event. One student focused on the explosion, its cause and impact on workers, while another focused on the impact on marine life. The two different questions, in collaboration with one another illustrate three-dimensional learning that connects facts with emotion and skills for working with visual imagery and digital media.

In the second voice thread, depicted in Figure 7, students shared the simulation they made to learn how to clean oil. They simulated an actual ocean using a variety of materials that functioned similarly to elements found in an ocean. Embedded in the VoiceThread are the voices of two different presenters.

Figure 7. VoiceThread from an elementary school team demonstrating the oil clean up simulation

In an interview with teachers, they shared their observations of students working with VoiceThread and compared this to text-based exchange on Moodle. Students were more engaged with each other when working with the voice thread, and were more creative in their thinking: "when the students see photos they spur ideas, and the VT also stimulated new ideas listening to one another talk about the global events." The teachers also perceived other benefits to voice thread and working with visual images. According to them, "some students are more comfortable talking and have difficulty writing. For them, the options in VoiceThread help them to present their thoughts. Working with images they can also illustrate their ideas differently. In Moodle, it requires that students read everything in order to participate in a dialogue. That takes more time and another kind of skill that not all students are comfortable with."

Analysis

What can we learn from the above findings to help teachers think differently about the use of digital media to engage students in discovery, collaboration and 21st century skill development? Analysis of the findings show that students appeared to be more engaged, inquiry-driven and collaborative when working visually with concept maps and VoiceThread as compared to text-based dominated exchange. Understanding potential reasons for this can be found in other studies about the power of image for stimulating creativity (Bamford, 2009; Eisner 2002), and the interactive nature of learning that takes place with a transformative pedagogical practice (Mezirow, 1997; Sorensen, 2002; Snyder, 2007). In the text-based Moodle environment, which was teacher-driven, students displayed an interest in sharing their thoughts and ideas, however, they did not appear to engage in collaborative or shared learning. Their exchanges were based predominantly on sharing what they do or think and asking of their global partners what they thought. Salmon (2000) would suggest, in this text-based dominated platform the need to build a culture of learning that engages students in higher order thinking over time. She suggests that the text-based model requires a facilitator to help students move from engagement to involvement.

In contrast, the content of the VoiceThreads reflected dialogic inquiry that was evidence of what Pink (2005) refers to as storytelling and empathy, and an understanding of the parts in relation to the whole. In the GOSP project, students worked in groups to select photos from the photo data bank that were then used to spawn questions for collaborative discovery. What was interesting in listening to the postings and reading their text was the narrative nature of their communication. There were elements of story, including scenic description and emotion as well as facts about the oil spill. Unlike the text-based communication in Moodle, the messages in the VoiceThread had a more dynamic dimension as well as storytelling model that are akin to critical thinking, reflective learning, and divergent thinking. The work with VoiceThread also highlighted how students worked following the digital workflow model as they first used the photos to investigate answers to questions that they identified. With the information they began to create a collaborative story that was built by the variety of postings, told often in narrative form. In so doing, they developed a dialogic dimension in their learning through which student's individual knowledge, curiosity and understanding about the Gulf Oil Spill and Yushu earthquake was deepened and contribute to a collaborative knowledge transformation.

There was also evidence from the analysis that the role of the teacher and the pedagogical approach were significant for fostering divergent thinking and collaborative learning. In the GOSP project, in which concept maps and voice thread was used, teachers worked with questions to help probe students to explore and reflect on ideas and information. The use of photos transformed the concept map into a dynamic collaborative exploratory. By taking time to select photos and explore the potential significance of them, students arrived at deeper questions for their collaborative inquiry. This process reflected transformative learning (Burden & Atkinson, 2008; Mezirow, 1997) depicted in the digital workflow model: investigate, create, share, and evaluate (Snyder et al., 2010).

Solutions and Recommendations

Asking questions stimulates curiosity and the desire to discover. The types of questions we ask have profound implications for the type of learning that can ensue (Erikson 2007; Wilson, 1997). Children in their early years reflect a natural, innate behavior, for divergent thinking and curiosity that somehow reduces with the years. It is often suggested that the left-brain dominated, prove it to me, model of schooling and educational politics has killed this wonder (Eisner, 2002; Silverman, 2004). Educators like Dewey and Vygotsky remind us of the need to keep the wonder alive by creating learning environments for youth that invite and stimulate curiosity and secure the notion that the process and experience of learning is just as important, if not more important than the outcome.

The standardized testing movement has challenged teachers to find ways to embrace discovery learning amidst the demands to prepare students for selected aptitudes that are tested on national and international tests. This paradoxical condition between proof of educational success and natural learning through discovery and social interaction has created a condition in which teachers themselves often do not take the risks to be creative. Their visions, albeit worthy, are often limited to the confines of the testing culture (Snyder et. al., 2008). This was evident in the Global Partnership Project in which carefully articulated lesson plans reflected the traditions of testing, in the form of stated objectives that sought proof of student knowledge acquisition. Despite the group context for learning, there was little to no evidence of teachers facilitating a dialogic, discovery based learning in Moodle that encouraged students to develop their sense of curiosity and investigation.

Dewey (1938; 1998) speaks of the importance of experience for learning and the need for teachers to create learning environments that invite curiosity, investigation and sharing. He states,

In a word, we live from birth to death in a world of persons and things, which in large measure is what it is because of what had been done and transmitted from previous human activity. When this fact is ignored, experience is treated as it if were something which goes on exclusively inside an individual's body and mind. It ought not be necessary to say that experience does not occur in a vacuum. There are sources outside an individual which give rise to experience. It is constantly fed from these springs. A primary responsibility of educators is that they not only be aware of the general principle of the shaping of actual experience by environing conditions, but that they also recognize in the concrete what surroundings are conducive to having experiences that lead to growth (pp.34-35).

The context of the Global Partnership Project (GPP), one could argue, was well thought through from the start, with a base in contemporary research on learning and school development (Snyder, et al, 2010). The approach was holistic from a whole school perspective rather than classroom-based. The leadership and teaching staff planned together what was needed to foster learning in a cross-cultural context. Technology specialists were on hand to assist teachers with the development of Moodle and connections in Skype and ooVoo. These measures are certainly commendable as research from this project phases indicated many positive outcomes for students and teachers regarding global awareness and the use of technology (Snyder, 2010). What was missing, I would contend, was an understanding of the need to create an environment that supported discovery and dialogue in order to fulfill the dream. The limitations could be understood from a variety of perspectives that emerged during the initial research, including language barrier, technological challenges, and schedule conflicts between countries which created a dynamic in which students did not have access to work together on a regular basis using face-to-face technologies. However, the analysis presented in this chapter suggests that perhaps something more fundamental was at play: the type of technology and the pedagogical model needed to invite student-driven participation and inquiry in order to stimulate creativity and divergent thinking

The GOSP pilot project, regardless of its introduction of concept mapping, visual images, and VoiceThreads, suffered from similar technological challenges as participating schools had difficulty accessing some of the software (despite prior testing of the tools). This limited the cross-cultural dimension of the learning space. Despite this, there is still evidence of a different kind of learning between and among students in local groups working with concept maps and VoiceThread, which is represented in the storytelling nature of their communication, as well as the reflective nature of their presentations.

There are two aspects, I suggest, that are important to consider from this analysis to understand what teachers can do differently to spawn divergent thinking with the use of digital media. The first is to consider the digital media that is chosen and the degree to which the interface invites discovery and sharing. The second is to understand the implications for teachers to create a learning environment that invites experience. The interface in Moodle was more linear and it was designed around individual postings, rather than group discussion threads. The dominant form of sharing was text-based, and didn't invite collaboration. Compare this with concept mapping and VoiceThreads in which the interface was both multi-modal, and the documents were shared among the students in each group inviting collaboration and dialogue around the content.

Another important factor is for teachers to understand how they can incorporate digital media to support discovery and experience. In the first project the curriculum framework was strict and evidence-based with an emphasis on sharing findings across cultures. In the second pilot project, the focus was on helping students explore two major events by reflecting on a set of photos from the Gulf Oil Spill and the Yushu Earthquake. The set-up of the learning activity from the teachers was experience-based both in exploring meaning behind photos, as well as experimenting with how to clean up an oil spill. In many of the dialogues students explored the meaning of the natural disasters for themselves, trying to understand, for example, what the students in the Yushu Earthquake must have experienced and what that would have been like for them, or the availability of seafood after so many marine life died in the Gulf Oil Spill. The more students explored their own questions together, the less they were interested in the teachers input. For the teachers, watching their students engage with eagerness stimulated new responses in their own teaching as facilitators of discovery and creativity.

FUTURE RESEARCH DIRECTIONS

This chapter has been developed in relation to a broader question spawned by the editors: "Can students improve their critical thinking, their understanding and production of arguments by being given practice in mapping?" The analysis was based on a comparison of the same schools over a two-year period that applied two different models and digital technology to support learning in a global context. The findings help to provide insights to answer the editors' question, suggesting there is strength in the use of concept mapping to stimulate divergent thinking, exploration and inquiry, as well as collaboration, which are linked to critical thinking and deep learning.

The chapter also pointed to gaps in the knowledge among educators about how to connect pedagogical models that support inquiry and social learning with digital media. One significant element that is supported by both brain-based learning and arts education is the need for teachers to work with multi-sensory learning and allow these tools and approaches to support a new kind of learning environment. Considering future directions of both research and practice, it seems necessary to begin connecting knowledge from different fields into a holistic understanding for teaching and learning. For example, the research on arts education tends to remain on the periphery of pedagogical practice, yet there is strong evidence to suggest the arts should be central to informing pedagogy. In research on technology and learning, there is a strong knowledge base developed about the strengths of media to support collaborative learning. And the theories of Dewey and Vygotsky related to social and experience-based learning have found a home in the practice of creation that is afforded by social collaborative technology such as concept mapping. Educational policies such as Framework for 21st century learning (2009) provide a natural context in which schools can begin to embrace the diversity of research to inform practice. Yet, the standardized test model of education seems to dominate. Perhaps this is the area that we need to be focusing on: how to rethink testing and accountability so that educators are supported by an environment in which they can offer students possibilities for developing 21st century skills that integrate knowledge and experience from a variety of disciplines including technology, the arts, communication, and social learning theory.

CONCLUSION

Helping teachers understand what they can do in their classrooms to spawn divergent thinking with the use of digital media has been the focus of this chapter. A review of research on future workforce skills for the 21st century presented in the beginning of this chapter suggests the need for continued exploration as too many schools continue to develop in an arena fixated on productivity and outcomes at the expense of preparing youth for a future workforce. Dewey's theory of learning is not new, but it is fundamental and paramount for today's educational agenda to help schools prepare youth with 21st century skills. The focus on experience and discovery is more than just social learning in which students work in groups. It is about creating possibilities for students to actively engage in a process of reflection, inquiry, investigation, sharing, and discovery to be prepared with skills to engage in storytelling, divergent thinking, empathy, and networking that are sought after by businesses. With the continued development of technology and digital media since Web 2.0, teachers have at their disposals a myriad of tools with which they can help spawn a stimulating and transformative learning environment for students. It requires, however, that teachers not only select software that supports such learning, but that they also match a learning model that opens doors for investigation, exploration, discovery and creation.

REFERENCES

Abbey, N. (2008). *Developing 21ˢᵗ century teaching and learning: Dialogic literacy.* New Horizons for Learning. Retrieved October 10, from http://www.nvit.bc.ca/docs/developing%2021st%20century%20teaching%20and%20learning%20dialogic%20literacy.pdf

Bamford, A. (2003). *Visual literacy white paper.* Retrieved December 17, 2011, from http://wwwimages.adobe.com/www.adobe.com/content/dam/Adobe/en/education/pdfs/visual-literacy-wp.pdf

Bamford, A. (2009). *The wow factor: Global research compendium on the impact of the arts in education.* New York: Waxman Munster.

Beaudry, J., Burden, K., Keuchel, T., & Snyder, K. (2011). *Cross-cultural digital storytelling: Implications for pedagogical innovation in schools.* Paper presentation at the DIVERSE Conference. Dublin, Ireland.

Beaudry, J. S., & Wilson, P. (Eds.). (2010). *Handbook of research on collaborative learning using concept mapping.* Hershey, PA: IGI.

Brunvand, S., & Byrd, S. (2011). Using VoiceThread to promote learning engagement and success for all students. *Teaching Exceptional Children, 1*(3), 28–37.

Burden, K., & Atkinson, S. (2008). Evaluating pedagogical affordances of media sharing web 2.0 technologies: A case study. In *Proceedings Ascilite.* Melbourne: Ascilite.

Cochrane, P. (1999). *CapeUK-creativity matters: Are we really serious about creativity? In all our futures: Creativity, culture, and education.* Retrieved from www.qca.org.uk

Deardorff, D. K. (2004). *The identification and assessment of intercultural competence as a student outcome of internationalization at institutions of higher education in the United States.* (Doctoral Dissertation). North Carolina State University.

Denzin, N., & Lincoln, Y. (1994). *Handbook of qualitative research.* Thousand Oaks, CA: Sage Publications.

Dewey, J. (1998). Experience and education: The 60th anniversary Ed. West Lafayett, IN: Kappa Delta Pi.

Dickinson, D. (2002). Learning through the arts. *New Horizons for Learning.* Retrieved from http://derryasd.schoolwires.com/725493911205726/lib/725493911205726/Learning_Through_the_Arts.pdf

Eisner, E. (2002). *The arts and the creation of mind.* New Haven, CT: Yale Unversity Press.

Erikson, L. H. (2007). *Concept-based curriculum and instruction for the thinking classroom.* Thousand Oaks, CA: Corwin Press.

European Commission on Education. (2007). *Key competencies for lifelong learning: A European framework.* Retrieved April 12, 2010, from http://ec.europa.eu/dgs/education_culture/publ/pdf/ll-learning/keycomp_en.pdf

Framework for 21st Century Skills. (2009). *A product of partnership for 21st century skills.* Retrieved October 10, 2012, from http://www.p21.org/storage/documents/P21_Framework.pdf

Frijters, S., Geert, T. D., & Rijlaarsdam, G. (2008). Effects of dialogic learning on value-loaded critical thinking. *Learning and Instruction, 18,* 66–82. doi:10.1016/j.learninstruc.2006.11.001

Gaines, B. R., Mildred, L., & Shaw, G. (1995). Collaboration through concept maps. In *Proceedings of CSCL, '95.* Retrieved, September 15, 2012, from http://pages.cpsc.ucalgary.ca/~gaines/reports/LW/CSCL95CM/CSCL95CM.pdf

Galyean, B. C. (1983). *Mind sight: Learning through Imagining.* Long Beach, CA: Center for Integrative Learning.

Gillis, A., Luthin, K., Parette, H. P., & Blum, C. (2012). Using VoiceThread to create meaningful receptive and expressive learning activities for young children. *Early Childhood Education Journal, 40,* 203–211. doi:10.1007/s10643-012-0521-1

Greene, M. (1988). *The dialectic of freedom.* New York: Teachers College Press.

Greene, M. (1995). *Releasing the imagination: Essays on education, the arts and social change*. San Francisco: Jossey-Bass.

Harasim, L. M. (1989). Online education: A new domain. In *Mindwave, communication, computers and distance education*. Oxford, UK: Pergamon Press.

Housen, A. (2002). Aestethic thought, critical thinking, and transfer. *Arts and Learning Research Journal, 18*(1).

International Society for Technology in Education. (2000). *Establishing new learning environments*. Retrieved March 7 2004, from http://www.iste.org/docs/pdfs/nets-t-standards.pdf?sfvrsn=2

Jerald, C. D. (2009). Defining a 21st century education: Competencies, literacy, and knowledge. *The Center for Public Education*. Retrieved October 10, 2012, from http://www.centerforpubliceducation.org/Learn-About/21st-Century/Defining-a-21st-Century-Education-Full-Report-PDF.pdf

Kolb, D. A. (1984). *Experiential learning: Experience as the source of learning and development*. Upper Saddle River, NJ: Prentice-Hall.

Lambert, J. (2006). *Digital storytelling cookbook*. Digital Diner Press.

Lancy, D. F. (1993). *Qualitative research in education: An introduction to the major traditions*. New York: Longman.

Mezirow, J. (1997). Transformative learning theory. *New Directions for Adult and Continuing Education*, 74.

Nesbit, J. C., & Adesope, O. O. (2006). Learning with concept and knowledge maps: A meta-analysis. *Review of Educational Research, 76*(3), 413–448. doi:10.3102/00346543076003413

Niesyto, H., Buckingham, D., & Fisherkeller, J. (2003). Video culture: Crossing borders with young people's video productions. *Television and Media, 4* (4).

Nilson, M., & Nocon, H. (2005). *School of tomorrow: Teaching and technology in local and global communities*. Bern, Switzerland: Peter Lang.

Novak, J. D., & Canas, A. J. (2008). *The theory underlying concept maps and how to construct and use them* (Technical Report IHMC Cmap). Retrieved September 3, 2012, from http://cmap.ihmc.us/Publications/ResearchPapers/TheoryUnderlyingConceptMapsHQ.pdf

Offir, B., Yossi, L., & Bezalel, R. (2008). Surface and deep learning processes in distance education: Synchronous versus asynchronous systems. *Computers & Education, 51*, 1172–1183. doi:10.1016/j.compedu.2007.10.009

Pink, D. H. (2005). *A whole new mind: Why right brain learners will rule the future.* New York: The Berkely Publishing Group.

Rabkin, N., & Redmon, R. (2004). *Putting the arts in the picture: Reframing education in the 21st century.* Chicago, IL: Columbia College Chicago.

Respress, T., & Lufti, G. (2006). Whole brain learning: The fine arts with students at risk. *Reclaiming Children and Youth, 15*(1), 24–31.

Salmon, G. (2000). e Moderating: The key to teaching and learning online. London: Kogan Page.

Schlais, D., & Davis, R. (2001). Distance learning through educational networks: The global view experience. In *Teaching and learning online: Pedagogies for new technologies.* London: Kogan Page Limited.

Shor, I., & Freire, P. (1987). What is the dialogic method of teaching? *Journal of Education, 169*(3), 11–31.

Silverman, L. K. (2004). *At-risk youth and the creative process.* Paper presented at the Alternatives for At-Risk Youth Conference. Colorado Springs, CO.

Snyder, K. J., Acker-Hocever, M., & Snyder, K. M. (2008). *Living on the edge of chaos: Leading schools into the global age.* Milwaukee, WI: ASQ A Quality Press.

Snyder, K. J., Mann, J., Johnson, E., & Xing, M. (2010, Fall). Connecting students across cultures: The global partnership project. *Innovation (Abingdon).*

Snyder, K. M. (2007). The digital culture and peda-socio transformation. *Seminar. net: Media, Technology and Lifelong Learning, 3*(1).

Snyder, K. M. (2010). *Breaking ground across cultures: How visual communication is used to support peer- to-peer learning in an international project.* Paper presentation at the DIVERSE Annual Conference. Portland, ME.

Sorensen, E. K. (2002). Designing for collaborative knowledge building in online communities of practice. In H. Hansson (Ed.), *Eight contributions on quality and flexible learning. Härnösand: DISTUM.*

Stake, R. (1995). *The art of case study research.* Thousand Oaks, CA: Sage Publications.

Stokes, S. (2001). Visual literacy in teaching and learning: A literature perspective. *Electronic Journal for the Integration of Technology in Education, 1*(1), 10–19.

VUE. (2001). *Visual thinking strategies: Understanding the basics.* Retrieved from www.vue.org

Vygotsky, L. (1978). *Mind in society: The development of higher psychological processes.* Cambridge, MA: Harvard University Press.

Wegerif, R. (2007). *Dialogic education and technology: Expanding the space of learning.* New York: Springer Science. doi:10.1007/978-0-387-71142-3

Wilson, L. O. (1997). *Newer views of learning: Types of questions.* Retrieved September 3, 2012, from http://www4.uwsp.edu/Education/lwilson/learning/quest2.htm

Yenawine, P. (1997). Thoughts on visual literacy. In *Handbook of research on teaching literacy through the communicative and visual arts.* New York: Macmillan Library Reference.

KEY TERMS AND DEFINITIONS

Collaborative Learning: A concept that suggests learning occurs best when the participants themselves determine the focus of learning, the question to explore and the ways in which they will explore the focus of interest. Compared to cooperative learning in which a framework or structure is externally determined, collaborative learning engages participants in the creation of their own structures and determinants of learning.

Concept Mapping: A higher-order thinking tool that has been used as a graphic organizer to help reflect and represent relationships between concepts.

Creativity: Seeing relationships between unrelated ideas, objects, or concepts and combining them to make something new.

Digital Media: Used to indicate a variety of software programs that are used to communicate and represent information. The media can be visual and or auditory.

Transformative Pedagogy: A philosophical orientation to learning in which students engage in shaping the curriculum through their own questions and curiosity. The role of the teacher is to facilitate conditions for students to arrive at their own answers, rather than to provide the students with answers. One of the main intentions is to transfer the learning from the classroom to the real world.

Visual Literacy: The ability to represent and interpret ideas using graphical models and pictures. In the context of learning it is related to right-brain higher order thinking skills and it leads to cognitive growth in observing, speculating and reasoning based on evidence.

Whole-Brain Learning: Pedagogical praxis that engages both left-brain logical, analytic reasoning with right-brain creativity and higher order thinking.

Chapter 16
Learning Argumentation Practices in School with a Graphical Synchronous Discussion Tool

Amnon Glassner
The Kaye Academic College of Education, Israel

Baruch B. Schwarz
The Hebrew University of Jerusalem, Israel

EXECUTIVE SUMMARY

Several computerized representation tools have been developed to enhance collective argumentation in schools. The authors describe Digalo[1], a graphical synchronous e-discussion tool (Schwarz & Glassner, 2007). They focus on how Digalo was used in a program (the Kishurim program) dedicated to foster dialogic and dialectic thinking among students in lessons centered on scientific and social issues. The studies undertaken on the use of Digalo suggest important lessons that moderators of e-discussions should keep in mind while designing, moderating, and evaluating small-group e-discussions.

DOI: 10.4018/978-1-4666-5816-5.ch016

INTRODUCTION

Construction of Knowledge through Visual Representation of Arguments and Argumentation

Collaborative settings in which small groups of students argue with each other have been shown to be powerful tools for knowledge construction (Kuhn, Felton, & Shaw, 1997; Pontecorvo & Girardet, 1993; Andriessen and Schwarz 2009). However, students seldom argue with each other on scientific issues (e. g., De Vries, Lund & Baker, 2002). Andriessen and Schwarz (2009) identified design principles for insuring maintenance of argumentation towards eventual construction of knowledge. Among those design principles: pairing peers with different initial cognitions (Glachan & Light, 1982), providing hypothesis testing devices (Howe, Tolmie, Duchak-Tanner, & Rattay, 2000; Schwarz & Linchevski, 2007) and providing tasks that have the potentiality to engender diverse explanations (van Bruggen & Kirschner, 2003; Schwarz, Neuman, & Biezuner, 2000).

Other design principles concern structuring dialogue in verbal interaction. It has been recognized that this structuring is ineffective unless being practiced intensively (Webb, 2009). Consequently, long run programs were implemented according to different approaches: invoking ground rules for peer-to-peer talk (Mercer, Wegerif, & Dawes, 1999; Schwarz & De Groot, 2007), explicitly teaching basic elements of argumentation (Kuhn et al., 1997; Reznitskaya, Anderson, & Kuo, 2007), or developing communication skill to improve dialogue practices (Gillies & Khan, 2009; Resnick, Michaels, & O'Connor, 2010; Wells, 2007).

These design principles are sometimes successful but they demand economical and pedagogical resources for training and technological infrastructure. Another design effort has been invested to remedy this weakness: the elaboration of technological tools that structure student's representation of their own reasoning/argumentation.

The most productive educational setting will be operated among junior high school students. The school should have an adequate technological infrastructure, a culture of collaboration and practices of learning in small groups. The teachers should be available and motivated to learn and instruct with technology.

Technological Tools for Argument Representation

Bell (1997) has recognized two different types of representations of argumentation: a. representation of argumentation structures; b. representation of argumentative processes. The first type, *knowledge representation tools*, supports the construction of argumentation whose structure and content correspond to a *valid argument*. Examples of such environments are SenseMaker (Bell, 1997) and Belvedere

(Suthers & Weiner, 1995). The ontology of the representations generally displays viewpoints, reasons, and data or backing, according to Toulminian terminology of argumentation. Suthers (2003) notes that environments such as Belvedere provide representational guidance as a set of constraints that initiate negotiation of meaning and provide foundation for shared awareness.

The second type, *discussion-based tools,* consists of graphical representations of *argumentative moves* of participants within discussions. The CSILE environment (Scardamalia & Bereiter, 1994) is a well-known discussion-based tool, whose representations are extremely simple (one box for each intervention and arrows to refer to previous interventions). When discussing an issue, students are required to enter notes with identified types of content: "My Theory," "I need to understand,""Comment." Each CSCL argumentative environment is designed to enable a new discussion space, new ways of negotiating and co-constructing meanings. As is the case for knowledge representation tools, choices must be made concerning the ontologies available, the ways to communicate among participants (the modalities), tools available to evaluate, or the role of the teacher.

Although from a theoretical point of view the distinction between the two types is worthwhile, it is not always a clear cut distinction and tools representing structures as well as processes are used. Particularly fruitful 'hybrid' tools have been designed in science education. These tools provide general structures for the articulation of arguments (Bell & Linn, 2000; Suthers & Weiner, 1995) or building models (Jackson, Stratford, Krajcik, & Soloway, 1994). Sandoval (2003) constructed a tool, the Explanation Constructor, which provides explanation guides. Explanation guides are an epistemic form, a particular knowledge representation that affords particular epistemic games, reasoning strategies and manipulations of the representations that allow particular forms of knowledge construction. Sandoval proved that the epistemic form of explanation guides help students to play the epistemic game of constructing coherent, well-supported causal explanations.

The use of visual representations of argumentation has been shown as successful at mediating critical thinking during construction of knowledge while discussing moral issues (Schwarz, Neuman, Gil, & Ilya, 2003), and scientific issues (Sandoval, 2003; Schwarz & Perret-Clermont, 2008). The reasons for these successes are diverse, some of them referring to visual representation of argumentation as computer mediated communication (CMC) tools in general. First, the possibility to reread and revise contributions and increased time to consider response encourages reflection (Guiller, Durndell, & Ross, 2008). Second, whereas in face-to-face (F2F) conversation verbal cues can be used to assess social status, in CMC these verbal cues are absent, thus allowing for more democratic and less inhibited participation (Herring, 2004).

Third, the possibility to post messages simultaneously may promote egalitarian participation, especially of more reserved or silent (as oppose to active) students (Asterhan & Eisenmann, 2009). Fourth, the lack of nonverbal cues may force discussants to become more explicit and clear to provide more reasoned arguments (Kim, Anderson, Nguyen-Jahiel, & Archodidou, 2007). Finally, visual representations of co-actors' actions may support awareness of important features of collaboration (Suthers, 2003).

Many scaffolds have been developed to support collaborative reasoning in CMC environments. One possibility is to provide sentence openers. Results on their effectiveness are mixed (Jeong & Joung, 2007), depending on the design of the activity. Diagram-based interfaces are another tool for promoting knowledge building (Scardamalia, 2004) or argumentation (Andriessen, Baker, & Suthers, 2003). The Knowledge Forum environment (Scardamalia, 2004; Zhang et al., 2009) provides a shared space in which students' ideas can be arranged in diagrams with several layers and hence shared, examined, improved, synthesized, and used as thinking devices. Other environments regard argumentation as an activity that aims at both progressive elaboration and construction of knowledge, as well as critical reasoning (Asterhan & Schwarz, 2009). Belvedere interface (Suthers, 2003), for example, supports argumentation by providing categories of argumentative moves and sentence openers in a shared graphical space.

The Digalo tool was designed to integrate both knowledge representation with discussion-based tools, and CMC with F2F types of communication. It was developed as an effort of the Kishurim research and development group to promote collaborative reasoning in schools (Schwarz & De Groot, 2007). Teachers in the group aim to instill ground rules for participation, commitment to argumentation, and commitment to dialogic discourse norms.

THE DIGALO TOOL

Digalo is a graphic-based software tool for supporting collaborative argumentation and structured discussion. It has been developed in the framework of the DUNES project (FP5 IST-2001-34153) of the Europe Union. As a standalone application, Digalo works in two modes: Single-user ("Local") and multi-user ("synchronous") mode. In local mode, a single user may operate on a map stored in a local file. In synchronous mode, multiple users, usually, 3-5 students in a group are working on a shared map, stored and coordinated through a shared Digalo server. Digalo uses multiple communication techniques to overcome different technical networking obstacles such as firewalls.

Digalo enable co-creating maps built of written notes inside different cards (represented by diverse geometrical shapes), as well as using different arrows to represent various types of connections between the cards or contributions (see Figure 1). These 'cards' and 'arrows' represent the ontology or the "grammar" of the discussion, which constrains but also facilitates and promotes the discourse by guiding learners to use specific speech acts and raising their awareness to the role of each discursive contribution, thus encouraging a certain type of discussion, such as critical dialogue. In Figure 1 the discussants discussed the advantages and drawbacks of uniform clothing at school.

During the collaborative argumentation and structured critical discussion students are naturally encouraged to raise and reveal different aspects and points of view about specific content, concept, issue, question or problem. They are exposed to different arguments of their classmates which support or attack different claims or premises about specific contents. This is how they expand and create their conceptual knowledge about specific issues, recognizing various parts of different arguments, questions, conclusions, premises and assumptions. The students learn how

Figure 1. An example of Digalo argumentative map

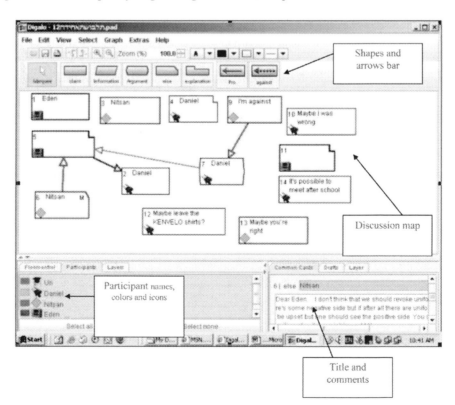

to argue. They exercise their argumentative skills by training how to convince others, strengthen their arguments with explanations and evidence, challenge others' counter arguments and also retreat from their own positions or change them when needed. Sequential F2F discussions with the teacher as moderator may use the electronic discussion map as a learning tool in order to reflect, assess and discuss the quality of the arguments and the whole process of knowledge creation.

User Participation

Users participate in discussion first by choosing and adding a geometrical shape from a shapes bar (e.g., rectangle, pentagon, hexagon or others-see Figure 1). Each shape represents different argumentative component (e.g., claims, evidence, explanation, reason, etc.), but the teacher or moderator may design a different specific ontology for each specific discussion (e.g. roles, aspects, or points or view). The ontology can convey the discursive role of each contribution within the discussion. In the second step, users inscribe the title of their contribution in the title slot within the shape (visible at all times), then possibly type their contribution text into the shapes. Users may choose shapes to write contributions (title and text) as expressions and/or as a reaction to others previous contributions. Typically, a user would type a short text as the title of the shape, and then elaborate further in the "comment" slot. The "comment" slot is visible when shape is clicked open or via a tool tip when the mouse hovers over the shape. Each card contribution is marked with an icon, which represents the contributing user, and a number, which represents the contribution sequential discussion order. Users can choose their identifying icon. Users may also link shapes to other shapes, using arrows of different types (support, opposition, or a neutral link). They may locate their contributions wherever on the screen and change the location of previous shapes.

Moderator Design: Ontology Creation

The teacher (also called moderator to point at the special kind of guidance he/she carries out) designs and prepares the Digalo discussion space for discussion, decides on the ontology – categories of talk, to be used in discussions. The categories are embodied by different shapes and arrows. The decision on the ontology is naturally content-sensitive: possible ontologies for scientific critical reasoning would not be adequate for discussions in social or historical domains. For example, a literature teacher may decide that each shape can use the ontology to represent different characters of specific story. In this case, discussant may choose in which character or voice he/she wishes to speak in specific turn. Figure 2 displays default ontology (claim, information, argument, question comment, idea). It can be easily changed.

Figure 2. The creation of ontology in Digalo

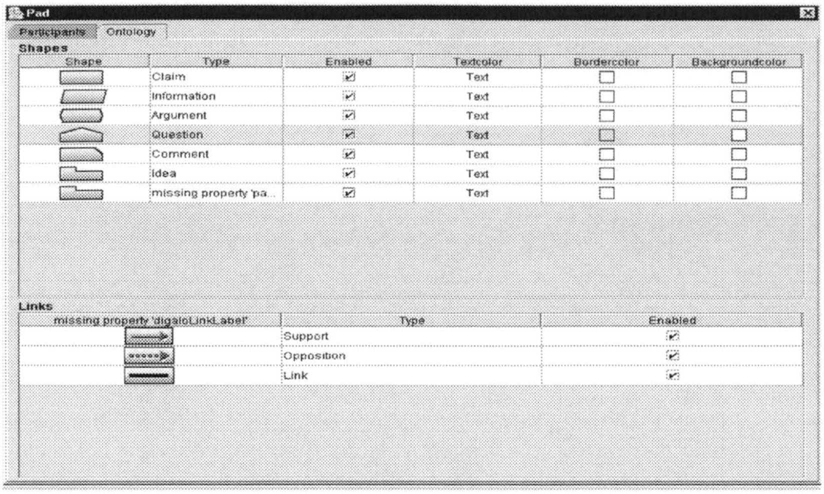

Moderator Design: Synchronicity

Digalo enables two types of synchronicity: (a) synchronous e-discussions with floor control (FC): When FC is activated, only one participant can work on the board (add shapes and text in a shape). The first to request FC by clicking the FC sign will receive it automatically immediately, and others can enter a line for receiving FC. As soon as the participant finishes writing his/her contribution, s/he releases FC (by clicking on the "Release floor" button) and by doing so, allows another participant who requested FC, to add contributions; turn is taken by the student who asked it first. There is an option for the teacher or moderator to decide whether one participant will receive FC before others or vice versa or can take FC from a student if s/he thinks this is necessary. Such action allows collaboration even when some discussants are dominant. (b) Synchronous discussions without floor control: all participants can work simultaneously, without taking turns.

EXPERIMENTAL STUDIES WITH DIGALO

Digalo has been used in many classrooms. Students participating in synchronous discussions with or without FC (Floor control), generally sit in the same room, each participant with his/her personal computer. The teacher or the students form groups of discussants beforehand. In each discussion group, all participants see the actions of their discussion group only as they happen synchronously. Generally, several discussion groups operate in parallel. Groups may interact orally, and/or through Digalo.

Although Digalo was designed to be integrated both in distance-learning settings and face-to-face settings, our experience in schools revealed that teachers and moderators prefer using it in face-to-face collaborative learning settings. Teachers use Digalo in three main ways: a. running an "opening discussion" as a first step of an inquiry process (e.g., brain storming, formulating and communicating opinions); b. Co-constructing argumentative maps in any stage of the learning process; c. summarizing discussions (e.g. making group decisions, graphically presenting the structure of a problem/solution).

In other words, Digalo supports various types of face-to-face collaborative learning activities during the learning process. We also learned that it is of great importance to integrate Digalo activities in face-to-face collaborative learning settings, where the lesson design is as follows:

1. Face-to-face preparation activity (either teacher-led or small groups work);
2. Digalo activity;
3. Face-to-face summarizing activity (teacher led and/or small groups work).

This design has proved to be most effective in terms of students' learning and structuring a whole inquiry process into one lesson unit. The oral face-to-face activities in A and C were found to contribute significantly to this learning.

The first experimental studies we undertook focused on the effectiveness of synchronicity. In a primary study of using Digalo (Schwarz & Glassner, 2007) we examined the effects of ontology and synchronicity on the e- discussion of Fifty-four Grade 7 students from two classes that engage intuitively, without training. The effects of using an argumentative ontology and control over turn taking on the average number of claims and arguments relevant to the issue at stake, the average number of productive references to peers, and on the number of chat expressions (nicknames, swear words, etc.) were tested.

The findings indicated that when providing both, an argumentative ontology and control over turn taking, students express less chat expressions and fewer irrelevant claims or arguments. These findings suggest the immediate beneficial role of integrating the use of argumentative ontology with the operating of control over turn taking, during co-elaboration of knowledge.

We identified the type of ontology and the type of synchronicity as characteristics of argumentative tools whose influence is decisive for the co-elaboration of knowledge.

Students used the argumentative ontology without any prior preparation since they have an intuitive knowledge about the use of language for reasoning. In face-to-face conversations, this intuitive knowledge is implicit. The presence of argumentative ontology demands explicitness: Students need to think and to decide on the function of their intervention in discussions. This decision invites students to reflect on categories that are understood to characterize co-elaboration of knowledge and yields the explicit elaboration of more relevant claims and arguments. The congruence between the choice of ontology and the content was often questionable, but students used the shapes categories to elaborate their own ideas in front of the ideas of their peers or to co-elaborate ideas. The explicitness enables deeper cognitive processing, involving meta-argumentative considerations. The fact that students very often referred to their peers points to another reason for the success of discussions with argumentative tools providing argumentative ontology. When typing their intervention in a map, students can see written accounts of the whole discussion held so far and can take them into account in their moves. Developmental psychologists such as Felton and Kuhn (2001) have shown that in face-to-face conversations, youngsters rarely refer to non-adjacent turns, as opposed to adults. Argumentative maps palliate this shortcoming, since all previous non-adjacent turns are visible to the discussant that easily can refer to them.

Concerning the FC variable it seems that enabling FC afforded the elaboration of more references that make more ideas explicit. Using FC and following others' contributions, each student has more time to think again about his/her contribution and prepare it by writing a draft and copying it to the card he/her chose in his/her turn (there is such possibility in Digalo). Nevertheless, we have to express some doubt from the motivation point of view, since it is not easy for people to be patient or to suspend their reaction during discussion. And indeed students reported that they preferred unconstrained synchronicity to controlled turn taking in further activities because remaining idle during a discussion was often unbearable for them.

Without floor control – when each participant can write his/her contribution in any time, exchanges are often interleaved, and turn adjacency is often disrupted both with and without floor control, floor control confers an orderly character to discussions. When having the floor one has the opportunity to react to all interventions expressed before. It seems reasonable that for learning specific knowledge, floor control is preferable, but for learning to collaborate for example, floor control may be detrimental in the long run because this is not the natural dynamic of negotiation.

And indeed, in spite of these findings that showed the superiority of floor control, students declared that they prefer not being constrained. We then allowed them to use Digalo without floor control but with specific ontology.

In a second phase of our experimental exploration, we checked whether Digalo allow the acquisition of specific knowledge. We checked the acquisition of scientific knowledge.

The Promotion of the Concept of Day/Night with Digalo

New practices utilizing Digalo were prompted by Schwarz, Schur, Pensso and Tayer (2011) to foster collaboration and critical reasoning in science classrooms. Thirty two grade eight students from three different classes in two integrative middle-schools participated in the experiment. These practices were presentation of pictures representing different perspectives (see Figure 3), small group synchronous argumentation, and moderation of synchronous argumentation. It lasted three 90 minute long sessions. The findings indicated that using these practices, the participants were able to successfully learn the complex concept of day/night cycle, as all measures of learning improved. For some students, these practices even led to radical conceptual change.

The study has shown that combining mediated perspective taking and synchronous argumentation may lead to conceptual change for a scientific concept as the day/night cycle. The design was based on three elements: a. the students were explicitly scripted to participate in collaborative reasoning; b. Digalo was used to facilitate collaborative reasoning; c. students were provided with new perspectives materialized by different pictures taken from the moon (see Figure 3).

Thirteen of 32 students were able to explain properly the day/night cycle although none of them could explain it before the experiment. Progression on the different aspects of this change (in mental model, elaboration, simplicity, and integration to

Figure 3. Two pictures used to trigger Digalo discussions on the Day and Night cycle

universality of the day and night conception) was found. The overall deep progress is surprising. The students had to understand that the same scientific principle can be used to explain different phenomena.

The students that could explain the day-night cycle on earth had difficulties in understanding that the same principle governs what happens on the moon. Explaining the day-night cycle on the moon through an eclipse of the earth was frequent at the beginning of discussions (7 out the 32 students). This tendency to stick to one familiar context naturally led to the second obstacle in learning the day and night cycle, geo-centricity. Twenty five students thought that the day-night cycle exists only on earth. Some said that the moon is always dark, because "it appears only at night." Others said that there is no day-night cycle on Mars and on the moon because they are "outside of the earth's range." At the end of the experiment, most of these explanations were replaced by normative ones.

The design of the task, the pictures, the stories, and the instructions were crucial for learning the Day and Night Cycle. In particular, the design was set to trigger conflicts and to solve them.

Without this design, the engagement of the students would not have been so high, especially in unguided collective argumentation, where disengagement is so frequent. Students would not have been able to concentrate throughout the task. The use of different sub-tasks for teaching a single concept would not have been accumulated by the students in repetitive experiences towards the uncovering of critical details from the pictures. Without this design, combining unguided discussions with interpretation of pictures might have remained as unproductive as unexciting.

The quantitative results of the study suggest that the pictures from the moon helped in integrating different contexts, leading to the elaboration of the scientific principle that stands behind the day-night cycle.

The importance of the design is central in this study. However it is well known that individuals are generally reluctant to change mental models when just presented with challenging evidence (Chinn & Brewer 1998). The qualitative analyses of discussions suggest the special contribution of Digalo. Students who were invited to engage in argumentation while confronted with pictures representing new perspectives brought forward different opinions and intertwined their different views with the different pictures in a graphical format. The students were then confronted with a double set of perspectives, the astronomical/pictorial, and the inter-personal. The interpersonal perspective helped turn the astronomical perspective as relevant in the discussion space. With the help of the arrows, discussants referred to previous contributions even when non contiguous.

In conclusion, the ideas of critical reasoning and of collaboration were embedded in the design of the Day/Night Cycle activity. Digalo mediated collective argumentation and perspective taking through the use of pictures, were two main fostering practices.

Pictures are just one example to learning objects for triggering new perspectives, questions and thinking. For the same purposes, teachers may choose video clips, games, texts, comics, stories, cases, or micro-worlds (white book) which stimulate and maintain learning by e-discussion.

Although Digalo greatly contributed to conceptual learning (Schwarz, Schur, Pensso, & Tayer, 2011),, it is surprising that no effect of moderation during discussions was found. This is indeed surprising in the light of the knowledge about the crucial role of mediation in learning scientific concepts. The analyzing of two discussions in Schwarz et al.'s (2011) study contrasted between good and bad moderation. The good moderator could reflect on the discussion and refer to previous intervention to instigate progress. He refuted arguments, challenged explanations, and took into consideration all the opinions given in order to strengthen some of the arguments and challenge others, leading the students themselves to co-construct a scientific explanation of the Day on the moon. Schwarz and his colleagues concluded that good moderators demonstrate flexibility, a quick understanding of students' needs and skills for responding to them. When flexibility is missing, and the moderator responds mostly to one student, the discussion risks getting stuck. Consensus between students may also become problematic and the moderator should help with elaborating understanding by challenging the collective. In case of disagreement, challenging each student separately is a possible mediation. Still, cooperation and discussion between students is a precious asset, and the teacher/moderator should try to support mutual questions and challenges. Moderation of synchronous discussions is a difficult endeavor whose productivity depends on the teachers' mastery of different strategies, and on her flexibility and sensitiveness to students' needs here and now.

Beyond the necessity of human facilitation during synchronous discussions, the role of the teacher in the Day and Night task was varied: orchestration of brainstorming and of summing up discussions. Without those activities, the students would probably not have progressed in their understanding of the day and night cycle.

This study showed that the teacher is necessary in learning tasks with Digalo, but that many teachers fail in moderating activities. We then decided to study more conditions for productive moderation.

Types of Moderation

Schwarz and Asterhan (2011) identified a common set of three basic criteria as indications for good moderation: (a) active and egalitarian participation in discussions, (b) reasoning and argumentation (i.e., providing justifications, arguments, challenges, and so forth toward the development of ideas), and (c) interactive co-construction (i.e., referring to and building others' contributions in a civil manner). Asterhan (2011) distinguished between the following different types of moderation moves in e- discussions: Pedagogical scaffolding, interaction support, managerial support, involved participation, moving forward. In general, teachers believe that good e-moderation moves are essentially organizational and guiding.

When teachers have to enact moderation activities they are challenged since conflicting forces are operating. On the one hand, teachers in classrooms often see themselves at the center. They make their own decisions, initiate questions, evaluate answers, and reformulate or re-voice them. Usually, they summarize discussions in classes. On the other hand, the Digalo tool encourages autonomy of discussants through interaction with peers.

Digalo is a networked-computerized tool for learning in a co-located environment where written-electronic interaction and spoken-oral interaction, take place at the same time. This means a heavier cognitive-load for the teacher or moderator to follow both modes of interaction between students and within groups. Apparently, it seems very difficult to moderate students' activity while monitoring both modes of interaction and at the same time trying to fulfill the entire teacher expected roles. And indeed, a study by Gil, Asterhan, and Schwarz (2007) showed that moderators adopt less desirable moderation styles (authoritative and observing). Moderators often distanced themselves from the flow of ideas that developed. They orchestrated the discussion superficially, they observed, they participated as regular discussants, or they adopted an authoritative but detached style. However, they did not fully endorse their role of moderator to consider the set of all ideas as a whole for helping in their advancement. Such behaviors resemble the findings of previous research (e.g., Chiu, 2004). Gil, Asterhan, and Schwarz concluded that the Digalo map created simultaneously by several participants presented an overload both for the students and the moderator. Such a situation requires high concentration from the participants in order to follow the flow of written contributions. It discourages some moderators from guiding and accompanying discussions.

The Students Point of View about Moderation

In an additional study on the students' point of view, Asterhan, Gil, and Schwarz (2008) found that students expect a good moderator to scaffold their reasoning and knowledge construction and to keep the discussion focused. Other aspects of pedagogical support, such as providing expert advice and feedback were not mentioned or explicitly called undesirable. Among junior high school students, more than half of the boys, but almost none of the girls, clearly indicated that they did not want teacher moderation. The majority of the reasons mentioned for this resistance alluded to student autonomy. Students also frequently mentioned aspects of social support, such as the importance of a good moderator to maintain a supportive relation with the discussants, be objective and create a pleasant atmosphere. These findings seem to emphasize the importance of teacher/tutor impartiality and objectivity. According to students' reports, moderators of synchronous argumentation should scaffold reasoning, without revealing or imposing any personal opinions on the discussion.

In another study, Asterhan and Schwarz (2010) considered relationships between characteristics of moderator interventions, discussant responsiveness, and discussants' subsequent evaluations. They found that discussants expected active involvement of the moderator and did not appreciate when moderator adopted a detached "guide-on-the-side" style of moderation. Students did not appreciate when the moderator used generic prompts (such as "Why do you think that?" or "Can you think of another reason?") to scaffold their reasoning. Content-specific prompts (such as paraphrasing the contribution of a discussant and elaborating on it) were more effective at eliciting responses and were appreciated by discussants. Discussants appreciated and were most responsive to moderators when there was a blend of involved and content specific scaffolding.

The Scalability of Digalo

The use of Digalo has become more widespread in recent years, currently at several schools and universities in Israel, France, Colombia, the Netherlands, Switzerland and the UK (Schwarz & Perret-Clermont, 2008). The Digalo tool can be adapted for use in education and training activities by "translating" existing courses into the Digalo format or by providing the institutions with "cases" which are background instructions and material for discussion and related guidelines for Dunes applications. Indeed, several in-service teacher courses in which Digalo was integrated were developed (Schwarz & de Groot, 2010). These courses were developed in schools – by such following the PDS trend (Professional Development in Schools) according to which teachers develop when the programs proposed are implemented in the natural context of their profession rather than in universities. A team including teachers, researchers, and designers met weekly to design activities and to reflect on the implementation of activities involving dialogic technologies (like Digalo) in classes. Some teachers gained from these meetings and autonomously designed and delivered new courses (for an example in history, see Schwarz and Shachar, in press).

In spite of these successes, we already reported on the fact that teachers had considerable difficulties in following the hectic rhythm of interventions with Digalo, and in providing reasonable help (Asterhan, Schwarz, & Gil, 2012). Additional

431

tools were necessary to help the teacher in facilitating moderation. The Kishurim group became more and more aware of the necessity of the presence of the teacher or moderator in the implementation of the tool.

THE ARGUNAUT PROJECT TOOLS FOR ADVANCED MODERATION AND EVALUATION

Following the aforementioned studies, the Kishurim group instigated the ARGUNAUT project[2] to develop a system that enhances the Digalo tool to enable moderation practices by providing moderators with awareness indicators and alerts, a remote control intervention panel, and classifications of important dialogue features (De Groot et al., 2007). These aids were envisioned to help moderators monitor, evaluate, and guide discussion without disrupting the flow of the argumentation. The design of the tools was based on a participatory, user-centered approach. Teachers experienced in conducting or moderating Digalo discussions in classrooms were asked to evaluate screenshots of different awareness displays (Schwarz & Asterhan, 2011). Teachers were also asked to evaluate discussion maps to identify critical moments during which they would like to intervene.

Most teachers focused on tracking the performance and development of individual students within the group discussion (e.g., they assessed whether individual students provided adequate reasons for their claims, responded to their classmates, and demonstrated improved reasoning over the course of the discussion).

The Argunaut system designed as a result of the participatory study is a platform that combines two graphical discussion environments, Digalo (Schwarz & Glassner, 2007) and FreeStyler (Hoppe & Gaßner, 2002), a separate moderation environment and a module for user and session moderators. In Moderator's Interface (MI), teachers or moderator can monitor discussions and intervene when necessary. The MI is a multipurpose tool that can be used for real-time moderation of ongoing discussions as well as offline analysis of completed discussions. Despite these multiple uses, the main design goal was to generate a user interface for real-time moderation. The MI is capable of supporting simultaneous moderation of parallel discussions. It was designed in a collaborative, iterative design process involving pedagogical experts, technological experts, and teachers from five different countries (Hoppe, De Groot, & Hever, 2009). The main user interface is a single window with a predefined layout. A typical view is shown in Figure 4 when discussants argued about the topic of the cloning issue. The window contains four main components: the session and user list (left column), the main focus view (center), the remote control panel (bottom center, collapsed to a button), and aggregated miniature views (right column).

Figure 4. Main window of the moderator's interface

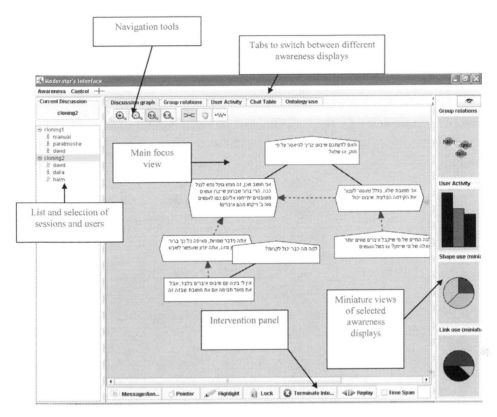

This list includes tools for monitoring presence and for selecting groups or individuals within groups to be shown in the main focus view. Switching between different group discussions is executed through this list. This list also alerts users of important events occurring in other groups' sessions (Hever et al., 2007).

The alerting options that the MI offers range from the detection of superficial discussion features (based on keywords, inactivity, participation, responsiveness, etc.) to alerts based on content-related dialogue analyses (e.g., patterns of reasoning, of interaction) implemented by Artificial Intelligence (McLaren et al., 2007). Because the alerting features were not operated in this study, we do not report any further on them here.

The focus view shows detailed information on the selected discussion with the help of a range of awareness displays. The displays concern participation, argumentation, and references to the other actors. They are designed to provide quick and accurate updates on group and individual processes. By default it shows the session's discussion graph, which is almost identical to the discussants' Digalo interface. Navigation through the main discussion graph enables the moderator to read the content of contribution (tooltip) and see how it is arranged. The moderator can resize and rearrange maps to follow the discussion as well as make patterns in the discussion appear clearer, all without affecting the discussants' environment. Because it is difficult to rely exclusively on the discussion graph to get a quick but detailed idea of what is going on in discussions, the moderator may choose from an array of different awareness displays that highlight different aspects of the interaction. A switch bar at the top of the focus view is used to select the display. These displays provide a broad range of visualizations with detailed information that are continuously updated in real time. We briefly describe the four main Awareness Display tabs.

The Group Relations tab (see Figure 5) shows a Social Network diagram, which describe the relationships or linking patterns between users. The moderator can use this tab to assess the extent to which discussants referred to each other and to easily locate ignored users, focal users, or subgroups.

Figure 5. Awareness display tab: Group relations. Each node represents a different discussant; the width of links represents the frequency with which two discussants created links between each others' contributions (the exact number is visible with tooltips)

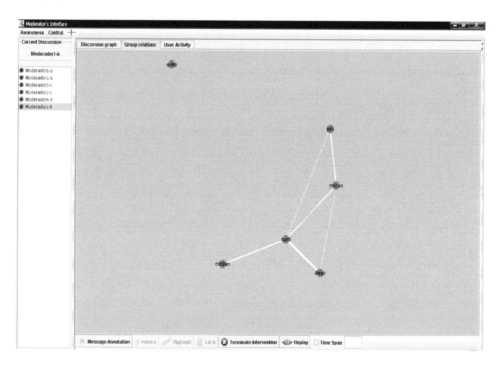

The User Activity tab (see Figure 6) displays a histogram-based representation that reflects the frequency of different discussion operations (e.g., posting/deleting contribution, creating links) by group or by individual. This tab allows the moderator to get a general idea of the participation level among online discussants, easily identifying users who either are not participating enough or are overly dominating the discussion.

The Ontology Use tab (see Figure 7) contains two pie charts. One pie chart describes the relative distribution of the different dialogue shapes used in a Digalo discussion (e.g., argument, question, or clarification), and the other pie chart describes the distribution of the use of different types of links (e.g., opposition, support, or neutral). These provide the moderator with information such as, whether students use all different dialogue shapes, or whether the extent of agreement or disagreement is consistent with the expectations of acceptable group reasoning.

The Chat Table (see Figure 8) gives a textual, chronological representation of the contributions of each discussant in a separate column and can be used to track the course of the discussion over time as well as the development of each participant's reasoning over the course of the discussion. It also allows the moderator to quickly read the most recent contributions. Each Awareness Display tab may be configured by the moderator (e.g., display by group or by individual).

Figure 6. Awareness display tab: User activity. The x-axis shows the number of activities; the y-axis shows the names of participants, and different bar colors represent different type of activities (e.g., create/delete/modify shape/link).

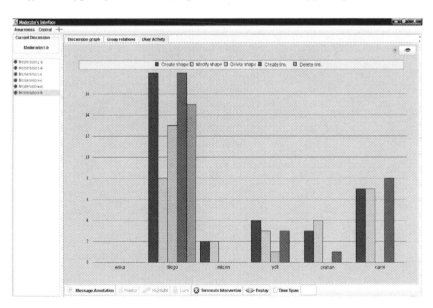

435

Figure 7. Awareness display tab: Ontology use. Pie charts show the relative frequency of the use of different shape types (e.g., argument, question, explanation, claim; left chart) and different link types (e.g., neutral, opposing, and supporting; right chart) in the discussion graph.

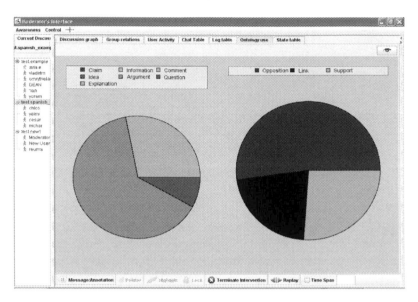

Figure 8. Awareness display tab: Chat table. Contributions are vertically organized per discussant according to chronological order, and deletions or modifications are marked with the help of strike-through font and font colors.

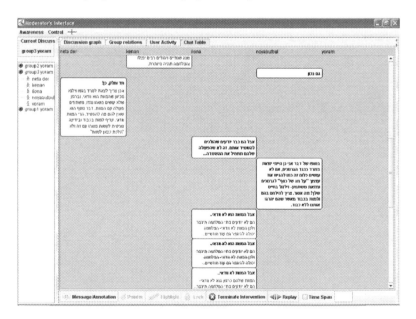

The remote control panel enables real-time moderation of discussions by intervention. It offers a collection of tools for intervening in the discussion without actually being defined as one of the map's discussants and without acting from within the discussion map. The moderator can choose to send these interventions to all groups, selected groups, or selected individuals. This enables both private and public communication, because the interventions are shown on the screens of selected users only.

There are three particularly relevant interventions. First, the moderator can send pop-up messages with graphical or textual content to selected users. Popup windows do not disappear from the discussant's screen until the discussant clicks the OK button. Second, the moderator may also attach annotated notes to one or more selected contribution shapes so that selected students will see the notes on their own discussion maps (see Figure 9 for an example). In Figure 9 in the gray card with the red border line the moderator wrote in Hebrew (our translation): "It's good you justified your point here. Can you explain why do you think it will lead to slavery?" . Through this intervention, the moderator asks for more explanations and for more clarifications. The notes are visually distinguishable from the discussants contributions. The moderator may highlight shapes in order to draw the attention of discussants to a specific shape or group of shapes in the discussion environment.

Figure 9. Moderator message as perceived from the recipient's discussion environment: a textual annotation linked to a selected shape. The moderator's message is linked to a specific shape within the graph and cannot be clicked away by the recipient(s).

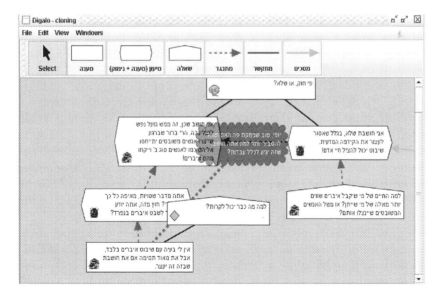

Experiments with Argunaut

In a study on the use of MI, Schwarz and Asterhan (2011) observed two different cases in which one moderator simultaneously moderated synchronous group discussions (2-4 groups of university students). From one more experienced moderator reporting, it appears that e-moderation of parallel synchronous discussions is feasible. This moderator was able to move between discussions and to function as a moderator who guided and cared for the discussion groups and their members without being too intrusive. The use of the MI conveys the fact that the design helped the moderator facilitate collaborative reasoning. For example, reference to peers was fostered through the use of the Ontology tab, which afforded the facilitation of collaborative reasoning as it assisted the moderator in identifying deficiencies in reference to peer contributions. Also, the moderator identifies deficiencies in dialectical argumentation through the Link Pie Chart in which she noticed that only (green) arrows of agreement had been used. This identification led her to open new perspectives in students with the help of generic prompts.

The moderator moderates four simultaneous discussions, but the strategies she enacted were quite similar. She first observed how discussions developed without interventions; then the teacher put public focus on specific issues and checked how her actions were effective. Instead of putting efforts on inclusion, she toned down and tempered heated and emotional contributions.

Schwarz and Asterhan (2011) showed that it is possible to enact sophisticated strategies of moderation in multiple discussions with the help of tools that provide awareness of several crucial features of discussions. They concluded that teachers will be able to work with up to 8 groups of 3–4 students and that e-moderation will be partly triggered by alerts such as "X has not been active for 5 min," "Discussants seem not to challenge each other," or "The discussion is off topic."

With Digalo and MI different tools for observing the development of ideas (e.g., with the Discussion Graph or the Chat Table) or the quality of discussion (e.g., with the Group Relations or the Ontology Use tabs), a moderator can manage his interventions with a careful evaluation of the discussion that has developed so far.

MI allows teachers to attain an approximate form of attunement. They may not be able to attain the perfect attunement that is possible in one-on-one interactions, but they can accompany students in the development of their ideas. They can observe, wait, ponder whether to be explicit, ponder whether and when to help and ponder whether to turn to a whole group, to a subgroup, or to one discussant.

MI provides a new space for supporting classroom group work in which the flexibility in using both private and public communication channels enables instructors to avoid the potential pitfalls of each and to gain from their respective advantages. The experienced moderator helped boost the commitment of the individual to the collective through the private channel. She also turns to the collective for the selection of particular individual contributions because they included worthy ideas.

The study showed that a new practice was born – the moderation of multiple synchronous e-discussions. The most stunning result was that the teacher lost her centrality in many discussions. In some discussions, some students claimed that there was no moderation at all although some of their peers received advice (but others did not know about this private channel of communication). Moderation with Argunaut was characterized by care and at the same time by minimal intrusion. Following this successful study, the Kishurim group decided to use extensively Argunaut in classrooms with non-expert teachers. From informal reports of the teachers, it seems that moderation is effective with two small groups (3-5 students), but not with more groups, because of the complexity of the task. With Argunaut, teachers can inspect the argumentative quality of critical discussions: they can see very quickly whether the discussion is animated enough (with challenges and oppositions) and whether it is reasoned. They can also observe the convergence of the discussion. These achievements show that dedicated tools can revolutionize the use of classroom talk/discussions for learning new ideas.

REFERENCES

Andriessen, J. E. B., Baker, M. J., & Suthers, D. (2003). *Arguing to learn: Confronting cognitions in computer-supported collaborative learning environments.* Dordrecht, The Netherlands: Kluwer Academic. doi:10.1007/978-94-017-0781-7

Andriessen, J. E. B., & Schwarz, B. B. (2009). Argumentative design. In N. Muller Mirza, & A.-N. Perret Clermont (Eds.), *Argumentation and education: Theoretical foundations and practices* (pp. 145–176). Dordrecht, The Netherlands: Springer. doi:10.1007/978-0-387-98125-3_6

Asterhan, C. S. C. (2011). Assessing e-moderation behavior from synchronous discussion protocols with a multi-dimensional methodology. *Computers in Human Behavior, 27*, 449–458. doi:10.1016/j.chb.2010.09.008

Asterhan, C. S. C., & Eisenmann, T. (2009). Online and face-to-face discussions in the classroom: A study on the experiences of active and silent students. In C. O'Malley, D. Suthers, P. Reimann, & A. Dimitracopoulou (Eds.), *Computer supported collaborative learning practices: CSCL2009 conference proceedings* (pp. 132–136). Rhodes, Greece: CSCL.

Asterhan, C. S. C., Gil, J., & Schwarz, B. B. (2008). Students' perspectives on e-moderation of synchronous argumentation. In Y. Eshet-Alkalai, A. Caspi, & N. Geri (Eds.), *Proceedings of the 2008 Chais Conference on Instructional Technologies Research: Learning in the Technological Era* (pp. 102-103). Raanana: Open University Press.

Asterhan, C. S. C., & Schwarz, B. B. (2009). Transformation of robust misconceptions through peer argumentation. In B. B. Schwarz, T. Dreyfus, & R. Hershkowitz (Eds.), *Transformation of knowledge through classroom interaction* (pp. 159–172). New York, NY: Routledge.

Asterhan, C. S. C., & Schwarz, B. B. (2010). On-line moderation of small group discussions. *International Journal of Computer-Supported Collaborative Learning, 5*, 259–282. doi:10.1007/s11412-010-9088-2

Asterhan, C. S. C., Schwarz, B. B., & Gil, J. (2012). Small-group, computer-mediated argumentation in middle-school classrooms: The effects of gender and different types of online teacher guidance. *The British Journal of Educational Psychology, 82*(3), 375–397. doi:10.1111/j.2044-8279.2011.02030.x PMID:22881045

Bell, P. (1997). Using argument representations to make thinking visible for individuals and groups. In R. Hall, N. Miyake, & N. Enyedy (Eds.), *Proceedings of CSCL '97: The Second International Conference on Computer Support for Collaborative Learning* (pp. 10-19). Toronto: University of Toronto Press.

Bell, P., & Linn, M. (2000). Scientific arguments as learning artifacts: Designing for learning from the web with KIE. *International Journal of Science Education, 22*, 797–817. doi:10.1080/095006900412284

Chinn, C. A., & Brewer, W. F. (1998). An empirical test of a taxonomy of responses to anomalous data in science. *Journal of Research in Science Teaching, 35*(6), 623–654. doi:10.1002/(SICI)1098-2736(199808)35:6<623::AID-TEA3>3.0.CO;2-O

Chiu, M. M. (2004). Adapting teacher interventions to student needs during cooperative learning: How to improve student problem solving and time on-task. *American Educational Research Journal, 41*, 365–399. doi:10.3102/00028312041002365

De Groot, R., Drachman, R., Hever, R., Schwarz, B. B., Hoppe, U., Harrer, A., & Baurens, B. (2007). Computer supported moderation of e-discussions: The ARGU-NAUT approach. In C. A. Chinn, G. Erkens, & S. Puntambekar (Eds.), *Mice, minds, and society: Proceedings of the 2007 computer supported collaborative learning (CSCL) conference* (pp. 165–167). New Brunswick, NJ: Rutgers University.

De Vries, E., Lund, C., & Baker, M. (2002). Computer-mediated epistemic dialogue: Explanation and argumentation as vehicles for understanding scientific notions. *Journal of the Learning Sciences, 11*(1), 63–103. doi:10.1207/S15327809JLS1101_3

Felton, M., & Kuhn, D. (2001). The development of discourse skills. *Discourse Processes, 32*(2-3). doi:10.1080/0163853X.2001.9651595

Gil, J., Schwarz, B. B., & Asterhan, C. S. C. (2007). Intuitive moderation styles and beliefs of teachers in CSCL-based argumentation. In C. A. Chinn, G. Erkens, & S. Puntambekar (Eds.), *Mice, minds, and society: Proceedings of the 2007 computer supported collaborative learning (CSCL) conference* (pp. 219–229). New Brunswick, NJ: Rutgers University.

Gillies, R. M., & Khan, A. (2009). Promoting reasoned argumentation, problem-solving and learning during small-group work. *Cambridge Journal of Education, 39*, 7–27. doi:10.1080/03057640802701945

Glachan, M., & Light, P. (1982). Peer interaction and learning: Can two wrongs make a right? In G. Butterworth, & P. Light (Eds.), *Social cognition: Studies in the development of understanding* (pp. 238–262). Chicago: University of Chicago Press.

Guiller, J., Durndell, A., & Ross, A. (2008). Peer interaction and critical thinking: Face-to-face or online discussion. *Learning and Instruction, 18*, 187–200. doi:10.1016/j.learninstruc.2007.03.001

Herring, S. C. (2004). Computer-mediated discourse analysis: An approach to researching online behavior. In S. A. Barab, R. Kling, & J. H. Gray (Eds.), *Designing for virtual communities in the service of learning* (pp. 338–376). New York, NY: Cambridge University Press. doi:10.1017/CBO9780511805080.016

Hever, R., De Groot, R., De Laat, M., Harrer, A., Hoppe, U., McLaren, B. M., & Scheuer, O. (2007). Combining structural, process-oriented and textual elements to generate alerts for graphical e-discussions. In C. A. Chinn, G. Erkens, & S. Puntambekar (Eds.), *Mice, minds, and society: Proceedings of the 2007 the 2007 computer supported collaborative learning (CSCL) conference* (pp. 286–288). New Brunswick, NJ: Rutgers University.

Hoppe, H. U., De Groot, R., & Hever, R. (2009). Implementing technology-facilitated collaboration and awareness in the classroom: Roles for teachers, educational and technology researchers. In B. B. Schwarz, T. Dreyfus, & R. Hershkowitz (Eds.), *Transformation of knowledge through classroom interaction: New perspectives in learning and instruction* (pp. 130–142). New York, NY: Routledge.

Hoppe, H. U., & Gaßner, K. (2002). Integrating collaborative concept mapping tools with group memory and retrieval functions. In G. Stahl (Ed.), *Proceedings of the CSCL Conference: Foundations for a CSCL Community* (pp. 716–725). Boulder, CO: Erlbaum.

Howe, C., Tolmie, A., Duchak-Tanner, V., & Rattay, C. (2000). Hypothesis-testing in science: Group consensus and the acquisition of conceptual and procedural knowledge. *Learning and Instruction, 10*, 361–391. doi:10.1016/S0959-4752(00)00004-9

Jackson, S. L., Stratford, S. J., Krajcik, J., & Soloway, E. (1994). Making dynamic modeling accessible to precollege science students. *Interactive Learning Environments, 3*, 233–257. doi:10.1080/1049482940040305

Jeong, A., & Joung, S. (2007). Scaffolding collaborative argumentation in asynchronous discussions with message constraints and message labels. *Computers & Education, 48*, 427–445. doi:10.1016/j.compedu.2005.02.002

Kim, I.-H., Anderson, R. C., Nguyen-Jahiel, K., & Archodidou, A. (2007). Discourse patterns during children's collaborative online discussions. *Journal of the Learning Sciences, 16*, 333–370. doi:10.1080/10508400701413419

Kuhn, D., Shaw, V., & Felton, M. (1997). Effects of dyadic interaction on argumentative reasoning. *Cognition and Instruction, 15*, 287–315. doi:10.1207/s1532690xci1503_1

McLaren, B. M., Scheuer, O., De Laat, M., Hever, R., De Groot, R., & Rosé, C. P. (2007). Using machine learning techniques to analyze and support mediation of student e-discussions. In R. Luckin, K. R. Koedinger, & J. Greer (Eds.), *Proceedings of the 13th International Conference on Artificial Intelligence in Education (AIED-07), Artificial Intelligence in Education: Building Technology Rich Learning Contexts That Work* (pp. 331–338). Amsterdam, The Netherlands: IOS Press.

Mercer, N., Wegerif, R., & Dawes, L. (1999). Children's talk and the development of reasoning in the classroom. *British Educational Research Journal, 25*(1), 95–111. doi:10.1080/0141192990250107

Pontecorvo, C., & Girardet, H. (1993). Arguing and reasoning in understanding historical topics. *Cognition and Instruction, 11*(3-4), 365–395. doi:10.1080/0737 0008.1993.9649030

Resnick, L. B., Michaels, S., & O'Connor, C. (2010). How (well structured) talk builds the mind. In D. Preiss, & R. Sternberg (Eds.), *Innovations in educational psychology: Perspectives on learning, teaching and human development* (pp. 163–194). New York, NY: Springer.

Reznitskaya, A., Anderson, R. C., & Kuo, L.-J. (2007). Teaching and learning argumentation. *The Elementary School Journal*, *107*, 449–472. doi:10.1086/518623

Sandoval, W. (2003). Conceptual and epistemic aspects of students' scientific explanations. *Journal of the Learning Sciences*, *12*(1), 5–51. doi:10.1207/S15327809JLS1201_2

Scardamalia, M. (2004). CSILE/knowledge forum. In A. Kovalchick, & K. Dawson (Eds.), *Education and technology: An encyclopedia* (pp. 183–192). Santa Barbara, CA: ABC-CLIO.

Scardamalia, M., & Bereiter, C. (1994). Computer support for knowledge building communities. *Journal of the Learning Sciences*, *3*(3), 265–283. doi:10.1207/s15327809jls0303_3

Schwarz, B., & Perret-Clermont, A.-N. (Eds.). (2008). *ESCALATE's white book on argumentation and enquiry-based science learning*. Retrieved August, 29 from www.escalate.org.il/Multimedia/upl_doc/D5_1_White_book_v4.pdf

Schwarz, B. B., & Asterhan, C. S. C. (2011). E-moderation of synchronous discussions in educational settings: A nascent practice. *Journal of the Learning Sciences*, *20*(3), 395–442. doi:10.1080/10508406.2011.553257

Schwarz, B. B., & De Groot, R. (2007). Argumentation in a changing world. *Computer-Supported Collaborative Learning*, *2*(2-3), 297–313. doi:10.1007/s11412-007-9020-6

Schwarz, B. B., & De Groot, R. (2010). Breakdowns between teachers, educators and designers in elaborating new technologies as precursors of change in education to dialogic thinking. In S. Ludvigsen, A. Lund, & R. Säljö (Eds.), *Learning across sites: New tools, infrastructures and practices* (pp. 261–277). New York: Routledge.

Schwarz, B. B., & Glassner, A. (2003). The blind and the paralytic: fostering argumentation in everyday and scientific issues. In J. Andriessen, M. Baker, & D. Suthers (Eds.), *Arguing to learn: Confronting cognitions in computer-supported collaborative learning environments* (pp. 227–260). Dordrecht, The Netherlands: Kluwer Academic Publishers. doi:10.1007/978-94-017-0781-7_9

Schwarz, B. B., & Glassner, A. (2007). The role of floor control and of ontology in argumentative activities with discussion-based tools. *Computer Supported Collaborative Learning*, *3*(4), 449–478. doi:10.1007/s11412-007-9024-2

Schwarz, B. B., & Linchevski, L. (2007). The role of task design and of argumentation in cognitive development during peer interaction: The case of proportional reasoning. *Learning and Instruction*, *17*(5), 510–531. doi:10.1016/j.learninstruc.2007.09.009

Schwarz, B. B., Neuman, Y., & Biezuner, S. (2000). Two wrongs may make a right… If they argue together! *Cognition and Instruction*, *18*(4), 461–494. doi:10.1207/S1532690XCI1804_2

Schwarz, B. B., Neuman, Y., Gil, J., & Ilya, M. (2003). Construction of collective and individual knowledge in argumentative activity: An empirical study. *Journal of the Learning Sciences*, *12*(2), 221–258. doi:10.1207/S15327809JLS1202_3

Schwarz, B. B., Schur, Y., Pensso, H., & Tayer, N. (2011). Perspective taking and synchronous argumentation for learning the day/night cycle. *Computer-Supported Collaborative Learning*, *6*, 113–138. doi:10.1007/s11412-010-9100-x

Schwarz, B. B., & Shahar, N. (in press). Combining the dialogic and the dialectic: Putting argumentation into practice for classroom talk. *Cognition and Instruction*.

Suthers, D., & Hundhausen, C. (2003). An empirical study of the effects of representational guidance on collaborative learning. *Journal of the Learning Sciences*, *12*(2), 183–219. doi:10.1207/S15327809JLS1202_2

Suthers, D. D. (2003). Representational guidance for collaborative inquiry. In J. Andriessen, M. Baker, & D. Suthers (Eds.), *Arguing to learn: Confronting cognitions in computer-supported collaborative learning environments* (pp. 27–46). Dordrecht, The Netherlands: Kluwer Academic Publishers. doi:10.1007/978-94-017-0781-7_2

Suthers, D. D., & Weiner, A. (1995). *Groupware for developing critical discussion skills*. Paper presented in the 1st International Conference on Computer Support for Cooperative Learning. Bloomington, IN.

van Bruggen, J. M., & Kirschner, P. A. (2003). Designing external representations to support solving wicked problems. In J. Andriessen, M. Baker, & D. Suthers (Eds.), *Arguing to learn: Confronting cognitions in computer-supported collaborative learning environments* (pp. 177–204). Dordrecht, The Netherlands: Kluwer Academic Publishers. doi:10.1007/978-94-017-0781-7_7

Wells, G. (2007). Semiotic mediation, dialogue and the construction of knowledge. *Human Development*, *50*, 244–274. doi:10.1159/000106414

Zhang, J., Scardamalia, M., Reeve, M., & Messina, R. (2009). Designs for collective cognitive responsibility in knowledge-building communities. *Journal of the Learning Sciences*, *18*, 7–44. doi:10.1080/10508400802581676

KEY TERMS AND DEFINITIONS

Argumentation: A discussion involving differing arguments and counter arguments.

Discussion-Based Tools: Discussion-based tools, consists of graphical representations of argumentative moves of participants within discussions.

E- Discussion: An Internet synchronous or a-synchronous discussion such as forum, mail or chat.

Knowledge Representation Tools: Knowledge representation tools, supports the construction of argumentation whose structure and content correspond to a valid argument.

Visual Representation: A visual or graphical representation presents an idea, concept or process in visual way to have its meaning or symbolism.

ENDNOTES

[1]   This tool was developed within the framework of the EC-funded DUNES project (IST 2001-341653, http://www.dunes.gr/).

[2]   IST-2005-027728 - EC the 6th Framework Program, http://www.argunaut.org

Chapter 17
Mapping the Doctorate:
A Longitudinal Study of PhD Students and their Supervisors

Camille B. Kandiko Howson
King's College London, UK

Ian Kinchin
University of Surrey, UK

EXECUTIVE SUMMARY

This chapter reports on the results of a four-year longitudinal study of PhD students and their supervisors, from which the evidence gained suggests that the students tend to focus on the PhD in terms of a product to be completed (in terms of writing a thesis and peer-reviewed journals), whilst the supervisors tend to concentrate more on the process of learning and scientific development, placing the student's contribution into the wider disciplinary discourse. The structural observations from the concept maps generated within this research are that the students perceive the PhD as a linear structure, whereas the supervisors are more likely to generate a cyclic structure to illustrate the dynamic, iterative processes of research more generally. Further structural elements emerge from the analysis of the maps, indicating the need for holistic understanding of the content, structure, and meanings in concept maps and their relationship with safe spaces for the development of critical thinking.

DOI: 10.4018/978-1-4666-5816-5.ch017

INTRODUCTION

Doctoral education pedagogy has been a traditionally understudied area (Pearson, 1999; Pearson & Brew, 2002; Walker et al., 2008). Building on research of the visualisation of learning (Kinchin, Hay, & Adams, 2000), the graphical depiction of the components of the underlying conceptual structure can be seen as a natural feature of the doctoral thesis. However, most theses tend to be less visual and more textual in their representations, and so the uncovering of the underlying framework may be more problematic. This study used concept mapping (Novak, 2010) to explore how students and supervisors represented their underlying conceptual frameworks in a visual manner, and how this developed and changed over time. The subsequent question that emerged was whether common features developed and if there were sufficient recognisable attributes to describe 'conceptual structures' within doctoral studies. This would allow for the development of a generic visualisation of conceptual structures to be used as a tool in the supervisory relationship of doctoral studies.

This chapter reports on the results of a four-year longitudinal study of PhD students and their supervisors. The students were all registered in lab-based PhDs at a research-intensive university within the UK. Sequential concept map-mediated interviews were used to gain insight to the students' and supervisors' perspectives on the purpose, content and the process of gaining a doctorate. Part of a larger study, this chapter specifically focuses on changes in underlying conceptual structures, and this may, or may not, coincide with notions of advanced critical and independent thinking, and how mapping the understanding of the content and purpose of a PhD can support the development of critical thinking.

DOCTORAL PEDAGOGY

Research into doctoral education is often government policy-oriented (e.g., HEFCE, 2005, 2001; HEFCW, 2000a, 2000b) on issues such as completion rates, doctorates granted in strategic fields and international recruitment. Another major body of research is designed as advice-focused handbooks for students and supervisors (Phillips & Pugh 2005; Trafford & Lesham, 2008; Whisker, 2004). In terms of education, much research and practice in the UK, and other countries, focuses more on the fitness of purpose of the doctoral qualification across disciplines and fields (Bourner, Bowden, & Laing, 2001; Costley & Lester, 2011; Denicolo & Park, 2010; Park, 2005; Roberts Report, 2002) to guide program development and structures.

However, recent scholarship has begun to emerge around the notion of doctoral pedagogy, but sometimes with a focus on what it could do rather than offering empirical studies. This includes linking it to the modern knowledge economy through an interdisciplinary lens (Manathunga et al., 2006), using it as the basis of designing a PhD (Danby & Lee, 2012) or rethinking the structure of the supervisory system (Olson & Clark, 2009). In this chapter, we have focused on exploring what happens within the supervisory relationship, and attempting to develop a method to visualise the change and development of understanding over time.

CONCEPT MAPPING

Concept maps have been widely used to interrogate the quality of understanding held by students at all levels of education (Novak, 2010; Turner, 2011). The qualitative analysis of concept maps has revealed relationships between the structures produced and the nature of the understanding displayed (Kinchin et al., 2000). The spokes, chains and networks described by Kinchin *et al.* (2000) have been augmented with cyclic maps identified by Safayeni, Derbentseva, and Cañas (2005), in which concepts are viewed as continuously changing and influencing each other in a loop. Such cyclic representations are seen to be more dynamic than other structures, such as chains and spokes, which seem to represent more static relationships (see Figure 1).

Clariana (2010: 119) considers that the tasks involved in the creation of a concept map leave markers described as 'cognitive residue' within the map. These include the selection and grouping of concepts; identifying propositions and adding linking phrases to show the meaning of the proposition and finally revising the map to

Figure 1. Map of chain, spoke and cyclical maps (redrawn afterPopova-Gonci & Lamb, 2012)

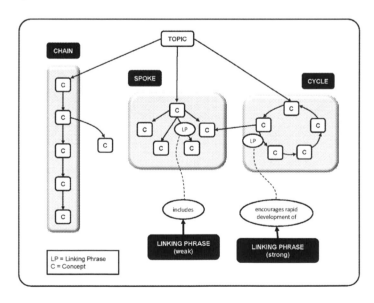

reflect both the structure of [the learner's] knowledge and an internalized graphic grammar. The key is to get the right balance between the idiosyncratic nature of personalized knowledge construction in the form of an agreed visual grammar that is intelligible to others, which is a particular challenge at the higher education level.

Several studies have explored the role of concept mapping in developing and measuring critical thinking in higher education, particularly in the field of nursing. This began with work by King (2002) and Wheeler (2003), who used maps to evaluate how nursing students developed critical thinking in clinical settings. This research has been furthered by Wilgis and McConnell (2008) in the hospital setting and by Taylor and Littleton-Kearney (2011) as an educational approach. Using concept maps versus traditional teaching methods to develop critical thinking in the field of nursing was recently studied by Chen et al. (2011), who found concept mapping was an effective tool for developing critical thinking in students. Whilst these studies add to the field of teaching and learning in nursing, they have not heavily influenced the discourse in other fields, particularly for more advanced research-orientated higher education studies.

METHODOLOGY

In this longitudinal study (Kandiko & Kinchin, 2009, 2010, 2012, 2013), PhD students and their supervisors were interviewed in order to gain a picture of how each viewed the content of the PhD and the nature of doctoral study more generally. The interviews were mediated by the production of concept maps (Kinchin et al., 2010) that were then the main artefacts for analysis, augmented by transcripts from the interviews. The concept maps were developed by each participant around the two main areas of research: one on the topic of the student's PhD and the other on what is a PhD. The interviews were conducted separately with students and supervisors to avoid any interference of the supervisory relationship.

During the first interview, the interviewee developed maps for each of the questions using large sheets of paper and post-it notes to allow easy repositioning of concepts on the page during construction to avoid continually having to redraw the map (Weisenberg, 1997). Once the interviewee was happy with the structure of the map they were then made into electronic versions, with feedback from the interviewee. The interviews were repeated every three to four months with students and with supervisors throughout the life of the PhD, during which the participants were invited to develop the ideas presented in their initial maps (Figure 2).

Study participants included five supervisory pairs (although one student had two supervisors, giving a total of eleven participants). All of the students successfully

Figure 2. Overview of the research method

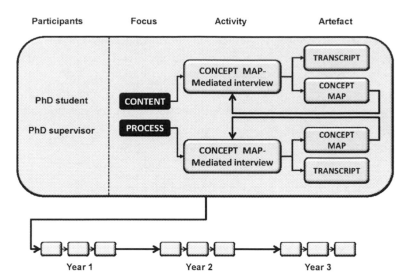

completed their doctoral degrees. The pairs came from humanities fields, clinical sciences and biomedical sciences. This process has generated a large volume of data over four years, although space permits the representation of only four concept maps from the total of 123 unique maps, collected over 88 interviews during the four years of the study.

The goal of this research approach is to provide rich descriptions of the beliefs and understanding of the participants in a particular context. This is to be expressed in participants' own language, representing their world view rather than a research-er's conceptualisation of participants' personal constructs. This is not intended to contribute to the bureaucratisation of the supervisor-student relationship (Cribb & Gewirtz, 2006), but as a tool to help supervisors to engage with the conceptual framework for the thesis.

The Concept Map-Mediated Interview

An aspect of the method adopted in this research project that requires elaboration is the nature of the concept map-mediated interview. The standard interview set-up requires the interviewer to present questions to the interviewee in order to gain access to the interviewee's individual insights and personal perspective. This is achieved by engaging in dialogue (verbal or textual) that is by its very nature linear in structure. Within that linear narrative, it is then up to the researcher-interviewer to determine the underlying structure within that dialogue to construct an interpretation of the interviewee's understanding. In essence, the interviewer has to interrogate the interviewee's invisible knowledge structure.

Within the concept map-mediated interview, that dynamic is changed in a subtle, but important way (see Figure 3). Here it is the interviewee that exposes his/her knowledge structure through the emerging concept map. The interviewer's job is then to prompt the interviewee with questions that encourage him/her to interrogate his/her own knowledge structure. This means that the interviewer no longer has to impose a structure on the linear narrative, but rather interpret the structure that has emerged from the dialogue. This process makes it less likely that the interviewer imposes an inappropriate knowledge structure based on his/her prior conceptions.

Analysis

The concept maps and accompanying interview transcripts were analysed throughout the project. Comparisons were made mainly within each supervisory group (the student and supervisor maps), but also across the student participants and supervisors. Data were explored in terms of content, process, development and knowledge structures. The transcripts were used to clarify terms and provide a record of the discussions surrounding the creation and modification of the maps. Findings from the project include the analysis of product versus process orientation of students and supervisors (Kandiko & Kinchin, 2012), competing discourses of understanding in the supervisory relationship (Kandiko & Kinchin, 2013), the idea of PhD supervision as intellectual courtship (2009) and challenges in cross-cultural supervision (Kandiko, 2012). In this chapter we are exploring the structures of the maps, in particular how the links, cross-links and directionality show different conceptualisations of the purpose and process of doctoral education.

Figure 3. The concept-map-mediated interview

Results

The concept maps revealed that the supervisors and students held different perceptions of both the content of the PhD and the process of doctoral study (Kandiko &
Kinchin, 2012). The supervisors saw each student's PhD as part of a bigger picture,
both in relation to their own work and to the specific area of study. The supervisors
tended to view doctoral study as a process rather than as development of a product.
The students were more focused on their own studies than on the discipline as a
whole, and were very product (thesis) oriented – represented as a linear pathway
that has an observable end point. An example is seen in a Humanities student's map
of the process of a PhD (see Figure 4).

In Figure 4, although the approach is direct (need a PhD to get a job), the skills
and developments in the spoke-like structure, seen in the left-hand column of the
map, relate mainly to learning. However, these concepts, such as 'ability to assess
and judge own work' and 'build identity as "legitimate researcher"' are not connected to the outcome of the PhD. These are placed as isolated concepts, not linked
to each other or developed through a process.

The accompanying supervisor's map (see Figure 5) is dominated by a linear
structure. However, a cycle is displayed through the relationship of the concepts:
methodology → first draft → upgrade (similar to a proposal defence) → more drafts
→ methodology. For the supervisor, this process is repeated throughout the PhD,
and is fundamental to development of an academic career. The role of the supervi-

Figure 4. Student A map of PhD process

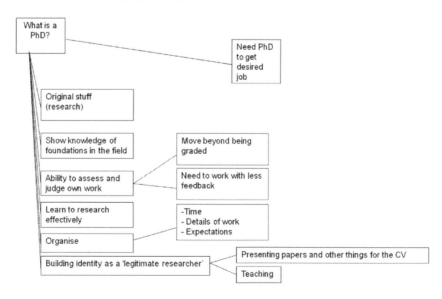

Figure 5. Supervisor A map of PhD process

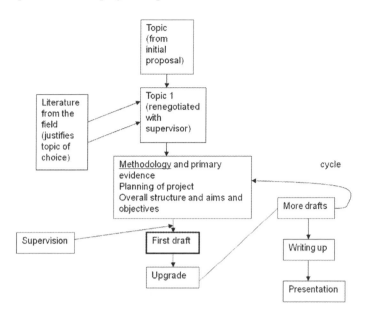

sor is focused on commenting on and steering drafts of chapters and the thesis, not on directing the research itself. The cycle is not repeated in a linear sense, rather the student's understanding is developed throughout the process, providing the opportunity for developing new approaches to problems and seeing challenges from new directions. This repeated cycle, almost a liminal space, is the place where supervisors give students the opportunity to develop their critical thinking and problem solving abilities.

A contrast is seen in a different supervisor's map about the process of a PhD, from the lab-based sciences (see Figure 6). This map takes on a 'matrix' structure, which differs from the linear, spoke and cyclic models. The four sets of concepts that run horizontally are structured roughly as a chain, but interrelate with the other concepts. There is also a nascent cycle connecting the fourth concept back to the first one. The four concepts that run vertically are concepts that represent actions and learning that a student 'should' do. The matrix design in the middle of the map is specific, meaning that not all concepts link to one another, although there is generic use of linking words ('in order to' and 'feed into'). The matrix map does not represent a traditional concept map hierarchy. There is no sense of differing importance amongst the concepts, particularly the four that run vertically along the left of the map. Overall the matrix functions as more than a combined linear set of chains, but does not fully describe cycles of learning and development.

Figure 6. Supervisor B map of PhD process

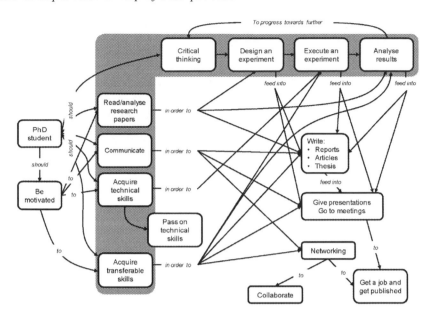

A third supervisor's map on the process of a PhD, from the clinical sciences, (see Figure 7) is further indication that in the complex environment of doctoral education there can be many 'sets' of conceptual frameworks or understandings. Moving from the upper left-hand side diagonally into the centre of the map is a rough chain of concepts. This leads to the 'cyclic' structure in the bottom right, which the supervisor saw the student being 'stuck in' for some time. This then led into another cycle, seen in the bottom left of the map. This indicates a 'bottleneck' where the student feels like the experiments have reached a dead-end and that her thesis is ruined. Similar patterns of behaviour often emerged for students a few months after the mid-point of the PhD, when suddenly the final thesis deadline seems to be looming. This cycle (in grey) leads to the third cycle, seen in the upper right. Together these cycles represent combinations of trial and error, the development and refinement of the scientific process and progression within a complex learning environment.

Static and Linear Structures

The supervision of the PhD might be expected to exhibit a close relationship between teaching and research in a way that allows the structure of the discipline to dominate proceedings. However, when viewed through a Bernsteinian lens, this study suggests evidence of considerable interference of the development of disciplinary knowledge

Figure 7. Supervisor C map of PhD process

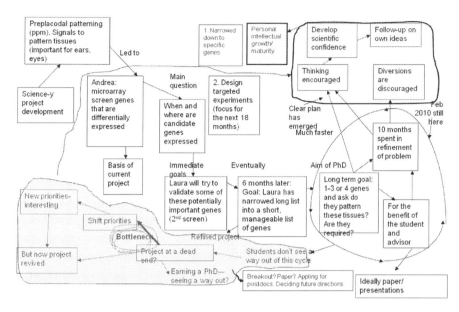

structure and its accompanying discourse. Bernstein considers a linear/horizontal structure to describe local, segmentally arranged and context-specific discourse (Bernstein, 1990, 2000). In the setting of the PhD, much of this discourse can be seen in the sequential content development of the thesis, but this then gets confused with the linear mechanisms of supervision and assessment that concentrate on developing drafts of thesis chapters; preparing for upgrade committees, submissions and vivas (dissertation defences) - issues that are often foremost in the minds of the student. This can overshadow the vertical/hierarchical discourse concerned with the integration of knowledge at the level of meanings rather than contexts, where the systematically principled structure of the discipline takes shape.

The typical linear structure of concept maps on the PhD process produced by students, and seen in supervisor maps as well, is suggestive of a 'pedagogised' version of the PhD (*sensu* Singh 2002), in which the discourse of 'passing' trumps any notion of contributing to the wider discipline. The students' focus on the linear/ horizontal would seem to embody Bernstein's view of pedagogy that "dislocates a discourse from its substantive practice" and relocates it "according to its own principle of selective reordering and focusing" (Bernstein 1990 p. 184). This pedagogic discourse may be a more understandable feature of the undergraduate curriculum, where the curriculum is arbitrarily reframed into teaching segments (such as 'module 1', 'module 2' etc). The appearance of a similar masking of disciplinary structure by a pedagogical structure within doctoral studies may be a concern if doctoral candidates are not only required to appreciate disciplinary knowledge structures, but are also expected to be in a position to contribute to their evolution (*sensu* Keiny, 2002). This research suggests that the contribution of doctoral candidates to their disciplinary knowledge structures may reflect their student experience, and so may over-emphasise a linear structure.

Maps with predominately linear and spoke structures seem to show a separation of content and process. The development of content is focused on acquiring facts, collecting data and writing up findings. The PhD is structured as an isolated project to be completed, rather than as one integrating with developments in the field, as seen in Figure 4. Supervision is 'pedagogised', meaning that there is a separation between the supervisor's research process and interactions with students. The process of gaining a PhD is seen as a short term, product-focused endeavour. The context is narrow, often closely related to the supervisor's own work. In this static view, administrative aspects of supervision are seen as hurdles, and work is done to meet the minimum standards at each check point.

Over time static maps tend to change in the details of the content, often in the accumulation of additional concepts, but rarely in their integration. Similarly, the process is developed through new methodologies or techniques, but is unrelated to changes in content. A linear map can only be 'followed' once, there is a beginning and an end. Once the PhD is completed, the map has no use. A successful PhD can be completed with a static approach, but students often fail to develop their own ideas and critical thinking skills; supervisors often see these PhDs as a time burden rather a contribution of new knowledge to the field.

Dynamic Structures and Critical Thinking

In contrast to the learning associated with static and linear structures, dynamic structures create the opportunity for critical thinking to develop, through repeated approaches to problems and the working through of new solutions. Dynamic structures include cycles, networks and matrices. Maps can be dynamic and have linear elements (as seen in Figure 5); in fact maps without any static structures can lack entry points and necessary guideposts. The resulting consequence of dynamic maps is the merging of content and process development in the conception of the PhD. Such maps are dynamic because they constantly renegotiate the relationship between what is content and what is process. Over time, such maps often have to be rewritten as the central idea changes, or the problem is addressed from a new perspective.

The dynamic nature of the maps, with intersections, 'bottlenecks', repeated cycles and complex networks, is a consequence of seeing the content and the process as being inseparable. This structure for conceptualising the PhD allows the capacity for change and the development of critical thinking, through repeated approaches to a problem (as seen in Figure 7), a lack of roadblocks and a 'safe' space to develop new learning pathways. Ideas are integrated and linked with developments in the discipline. The approach is longer term and in a wider context. In dynamic maps, administrative and bureaucratic hurdles still exist, but can be seen as natural gateways to next steps. Unlike the 'single-use, disposable nature' of static maps, dynamic maps are 'reusable', in that elements can change, but the structure, the underlying patterns for learning and development, could be repeated throughout a research-oriented career.

Cañas *et al*, (2012) consider the impact that a framing question or starting perspective will have on the final structure of a student's concept map. A framing question that refers to dynamic processes (i.e. educational change) should be predictive of a more integrated structure than occurs with a less dynamic starting point (i.e. education). However, when we are explicitly encouraging mappers to describe processes in the PhD, students still come out with a 'linear/static' map structure. It seems that the processes are seen only as a means to the end, and that an 'end point' is best represented as a linear chain. Where more dynamic cyclic or network structures are produced, the focus is on the process rather than the end point. This may be understandable as the PhD student's commitment is often to the PhD (i.e. a short-term contract with an evident end-point) rather than to the wider discipline.

DISCUSSION

It is claimed by Maton (2013 p. 8) that researchers typically aim to generate ideas that have utility or appeal beyond the specifications of their originating contexts, and that "almost everyone in education shares a desire for cumulative knowledge building." This cumulative knowledge should be indicated by the development of non-linear knowledge structures (Kinchin, 2012). However, as we have shown, this is not always evident in the knowledge structures described by emergent researchers – PhD students. The messiness of some of the maps, particularly the dynamic structures, may be taken as an indication that the map is acting as a 'trading ground for ideas' or an 'arena for rehearsal of understanding' rather than a record of learning that has been completed. Johnstone and Otis (2006) have noted that students can be wrestling with the construction of new understanding whilst also 'testing' the grammar of the concept map, such that what may appear to be a mess to an observer, may actually be a powerful learning tool for the student constructing the map. Consideration of the concept maps produced in this context further reinforces the notion that supervisors focus more on the PhD as a process of learning, compared with the student concentration on the product (Kandiko & Kinchin, 2012). In the maps presented, it may be the case that students are trying to 'make sense' and use the maps as an organising tool, whereas the supervisors have the big picture of the research in their minds and can use the maps to 'trace the journey' on how to get there. The arrows for the static maps point to the 'end goal' of the completed thesis, whereas the arrows in the dynamic structures show the cyclical and multiple pathways that are an inherent part of the research process.

Students may also be copying the structure of much of the research they read about, in neat and orderly written journal articles and papers. In such publications, research is described in a linear fashion and data are presented and conclusions drawn. The messiness of the supervisors' maps may in part be an indication of the research process itself, which is cyclical, full of dead-ends and requires multiple approaches to problems, and often the redefinition of research questions and the path to answer them.

The multiple conceptual structures that exist within the maps can make them difficult to understand (as seen in Figure 5 and 7), particularly without the wider context of the PhD topic and research field. However, following the arrows within the structures presented can be seen as indications of learning pathways. The importance of the arrows can be seen within the linear and hierarchical structures; linear chains may be seen as irreversible (one-way) systems, unlike network and cyclical structures. So for example, in dentistry, the clinical procedure (linear chain) may be seen as irreversible; e.g. once a hole has been drilled in a tooth, it cannot be "undrilled." Similarly in teaching, once a classroom activity has occurred, it cannot "un-occur." Whereas the network of understanding in dynamic structures has multiple routes through the concepts which can be revisited and revised in such a way that it does not have such an evident pre-conceived end point.

What we can see emerging are 'knowledge structures', or learning activities, which make up the conception of the process of the PhD. Three of these have been developed in the work of Kinchin et al. (2000). Building on the work of Safayeni et al. (2005) and Kinchin (2011), we have also added the cyclic model, describing the notion that the concepts develop and influence one another (see Figure 8). We are further adding the matrix structure (E), which is characterised by the supervisor map in Figure 6. This structure contains elements from the other four structures described, but appears to function in a different way.

A key difference between spokes and chains on one side and networks, cycles and matrices on the other is the notion of reversibility. In the former, once a step has been taken, there is no 'revisiting' the learning process. The student must carry on to the next step, or the supervisor must move on to the next point. In the case of the latter, cycles and repetitions develop dynamically, allowing for concepts and

Figure 8. An expanded typology of conceptual structures, a. spoke; b. chain; c. network; d. cyclical; e. matrix

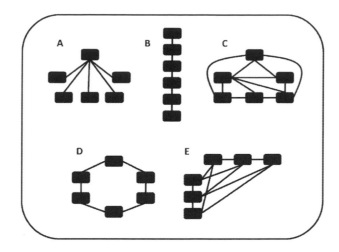

processes to be revisited. This is where the direction of the arrows is important, which allows one to follow a chain, enter into a network or cycle, or become enmeshed in a matrix. These can be revisited a number of times, in similar or changing pathways.

We argue that the major matrix intersections and cyclical formations are indications of thresholds, either of concepts or processes. These cycles, or interstices, represent continuous, but developing, learning processes and 'safe' spaces to develop new approaches that lead to critical thinking. This follows in the tradition of the Hegelian dialectic, often depicted as an upward spiral of cycles of thesis, antithesis, synthesis and thesis again. This notion is depicted in Figure 9, which shows a conceptual structure, which through repeated cycles of rehearsal leads to greater conceptual development and sublation of previous understanding. These developments extend the traditional notions of traditional concept mapping when using it in higher level learning. This reiterates the need for the holistic assessment of concept maps in higher education settings (Kandiko, Hay, & Weller, 2013).

For advanced higher education, postgraduate education and research-based work, it is not only the development of concepts or the links between them, but also the broader knowledge structures that are formed. Although the participants in the study were briefed on concept mapping, many of the maps that developed strayed from traditional Novakian concept maps; this can be seen particularly in Figure 6. The structure and style of the maps may in fact more closely relate to the 'messy' and developing nature of the thesis and the process which eventually leads to the final

Figure 9. Repeated cycles of conceptual development

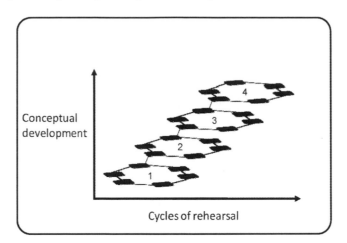

product. Although a final map of the thesis, reflecting back from the position of the final product, may resemble a traditional concept map, the maps represented here reflect the dynamic process of learning and development within the setting of advanced doctoral education

SUMMARY

In this study, concept mapping revealed more than interviews and transcripts alone. The content and the structure of the maps produced were indicative of the divide in understanding through different approaches to the PhD, often between supervisors and students, even when they appear to be talking about the same topic and using the same terms. Dynamic-oriented map production is seen as a useful addition to the doctoral supervision process. The cyclic processes indicate their appreciation of the changing nature of understanding and the necessity for repeated interaction with the material being studied. The cycles of learning that are described can be used as a tool within the supervisory process, which often represent the dominant method of learning, development and discovery in the discipline. In concept maps from the humanities, the cycles described are referenced to drafts, feedback, edits, and redrafts of essays and chapters.

Concept maps can be used by students and supervisors as pedagogical tools, as points of departure for conversation and dialogue, and as physical representations of conceptual understandings. Such maps can also function as synopses of a student's developing thesis, which can be useful when sharing the work outside of the supervisory relationship, at a conference or with a lab-group, for example. Supervisors can investigate common 'threshold areas' and develop strategies to help students progress, particularly for when students are stuck in the 'bottlenecks' and may not see the process as one of repeated cycles of rehearsal, advancing conceptual development and enhancing critical thinking.

REFERENCES

Bernstein, B. (1990). Class, codes and control: Vol. IV. *The structuring of pedagogic discourse*. London: Routledge. doi:10.4324/9780203011263

Bernstein, B. (2000). *Pedagogy, symbolic control and identity*. Lanham, MD: Rowman & Littlefield.

Cañas, A. J., Novak, J. D., & Reiska, P. (2012). Freedom vs. restriction of content and structure during concept mapping – Possibilities and limitations for construction and assessment. In *Concept maps: Theory, methodology, technology: Proceedings of the fifth international conference on concept mapping*. Valletta, Malta: Academic Press.

Chen, S. L., Liang, T., Lee, M. L., & Liao, I. C. (2011). Effects of concept map teaching on students' critical thinking and approach to learning and studying. *The Journal of Nursing Education*, *50*(8), 466–469. doi:10.3928/01484834-20110415-06 PMID:21524017

Clariana, R. B. (2010). Deriving individual and group knowledge structure from network diagrams and from essays. In Computer-based diagnostics and systematic analysis of knowledge (pp. 117 – 130). Berlin: Springer Science + Business Media.

Cribb, A., & Gewirtz, S. (2006). Doctoral student supervision in a managerial climate. *International Studies in Sociology of Education*, *16*(3), 223–236. doi:10.1080/09620210601037787

Danby, S. J., & Lee, A. (2012). Framing doctoral pedagogy as design and action. In *Reshaping doctoral education: International approaches and pedagogies*. London: Routledge.

HEFCE. (2001). *Review of research*. England: Higher Education Funding Council.

HEFCE. (2005). *PhD research degrees: Entry and completion*. Retrieved from http://www.hefce.ac.uk/pubs/hefce/2005/05_02/05_02.pdf

HEFCW. (2000a). *Review of research policy*. Wales: Higher Education Funding Council for Wales.

HEFCW. (2000b). *Review subsequent consultation: Review of research policy and funding method*. Higher Education Funding Council for Wales.

Johnstone, A. H., & Otis, K. H. (2006). Concept mapping in problem-based learning: A cautionary tale. *Chemistry Education Research and Practice*, *7*(2), 84–95. doi:10.1039/b5rp90017d

Kandiko, C. B., Hay, D. B., & Weller, S. (2013). Concept mapping in the humanities to facilitate reflection: Externalising the relationship between public and personal learning. *Arts and Humanities in Higher Education*, *12*(1), 70–87. doi:10.1177/1474022211399381

Kandiko, C. B., & Kinchin, I. M. (2009). *PhD supervision as intellectual courtship*. Paper presented at the Society for Research into Higher Education (SRHE) Annual Conference. Newport, UK.

Kandiko, C. B., & Kinchin, I. M. (2010). What is a PhD? Process versus product in PhD supervision. In J. Sánchez, A. J. Cañas, & J. D. Novak (Eds.), *Concept maps: Making learning meaningful, proceedings of the fourth international conference on concept mapping*. Viña del Mar, Chile: Universidad de Chile.

Kandiko, C. B., & Kinchin, I. M. (2012). What is a doctorate? A concept-mapped analysis of process versus product in the supervision of lab-based PhDs. *Educational Research*, *54*(1), 3–16. doi:10.1080/00131881.2012.658196

Kandiko, C. B., & Kinchin, I. M. (2013). Developing discourses of knowledge and understanding: Longitudinal studies of PhD supervision. *London Review of Education*, *11*(1), 46–58. doi:10.1080/14748460.2012.761819

Keiny, S. (2002). *Ecological thinking: A new approach to educational change*. Lanham, MD: University of America Press.

Kinchin, I. M. (2011). Relating knowledge structures to learning styles and university teaching. In *Style differences in cognition, learning, and management* (pp. 129–142). London: Routledge.

Kinchin, I. M. (2012). Visualising knowledge structures of university teaching to relate pedagogic theory and academic practice. In *Handbook of college and university teaching: A global perspective* (pp. 314–332). Thousand Oaks, CA: Sage. doi:10.4135/9781412996891.n21

Kinchin, I. M., Hay, D. B., & Adams, A. (2000). How a qualitative approach to concept map analysis can be used to aid learning by illustrating patterns of conceptual development. *Educational Research*, *42*, 43–57. doi:10.1080/001318800363908

Kinchin, I. M., Streatfield, D., & Hay, D. B. (2010). Using concept mapping to en-hance the research interview. *International Journal of Qualitative Methods*, *9*, 52–68.

King, M. (2002). Teaching and evaluating critical thinking with concept maps. *Nurse Educator*, *27*(5), 214–216. doi:10.1097/00006223-200209000-00008 PMID:12355046

Manathunga, C., Lant, P., & Mellick, G. (2006). Imagining an interdisci-plinary doctoral pedagogy. *Teaching in Higher Education*, *11*(3), 365–379. doi:10.1080/13562510600680954

Maton, K. (2013). Making semantic waves: A key to cumulative knowledge-building. *Linguistics and Education*, *24*, 8–22. doi:10.1016/j.linged.2012.11.005

Novak, J. D. (2010). *Learning, creating, and using knowledge: Concept maps as facilitative tools in schools and corporations* (2nd ed.). Oxford, UK: Routledge.

Olson, K., & Clark, C. M. (2009). A signature pedagogy in doctoral educa-tion: The leader-scholar community. *Educational Researcher*, *38*(3), 216–221. doi:10.3102/0013189X09334207

Pearson, M. (1999). The changing environment for doctoral education in Australia: Implications for quality management, improvement and innovation. *Higher Educa-tion Research & Development*, *18*(3), 269–287. doi:10.1080/0729436990180301

Pearson, M., & Brew, A. (2002). Research training and supervision development. *Studies in Higher Education*, *27*(2), 135–150. doi:10.1080/03075070220119986c

Phillips, E. M., & Pugh, D. S. (2005). How to get a PhD: A handbook for students and their supervisors (4thed.). Berkshire, UK: Open University Press.

Popova-Gonci, V., & Lamb, M. C. (2012). Assessment of integrated learning: Sug-gested application of concept mapping to prior learning assessment practices. *The Journal of Continuing Higher Education*, *60*, 186–191. doi:10.1080/07377363.2 012.726175

Safayeni, F., Derbentseva, N., & Cañas, A. J. (2005). A theoretical note on concepts and the need for cyclic concept maps. *Journal of Research in Science Teaching*, *42*, 741–766. doi:10.1002/tea.20074

Senita, J. (2011). The use of concept maps to evaluate critical thinking in the clinical setting. *Teaching and Learning in Nursing*, *3*(1), 6–10. doi:10.1016/j.teln.2007.08.002

Singh, P. (2002). Pedagogising knowledge: Bernstein's theory of the pedagogic device. *British Journal of Sociology of Education*, *23*(4), 571–582. doi:10.1080/0142569022000038422

Taylor, L. A., & Littleton-Kearney, M. (2011). Concept mapping: A distinctive educational approach to foster critical thinking. *Nurse Educator*, *36*(2), 84–88. doi:10.1097/NNE.0b013e31820b5308 PMID:21330901

Trafford, V. N., & Leshem, S. (2008). *Stepping stones to achieving your doctorate*. Maidenhead, UK: Open University Press.

Turner, S. (2011). Evaluating learning through the use of concept maps. In *Proceedings of the 3rd Annual Conference on Higher Education Pedagogy* (pp. 21 – 22). Blacksburg, VA: Virginia Tech.

Walker, G. E., Golde, C. M., Jones, L., Bueschel, A. C., & Hutchings, P. (2008). *The formation of scholars: Rethinking doctoral education for the twenty-first century*. San Francisco: Jossey-Bass.

Weisenberg, R. C. (1997). Appropriate technology for the classroom - Using 'Post-It Notes©' as an active learning tool. *Journal of College Science Teaching*, *26*(5), 339–344.

Wheeler, L. A. (2003). The influence of concept mapping on critical thinking in baccalaureate nursing students. *Journal of Professional Nursing*, *19*(6), 339–346. doi:10.1016/S8755-7223(03)00134-0 PMID:14689390

Whisker, G. (2004). *The good supervisor*. London: Macmillan Palgrave.

Wilgis, M., & McConnell, J. (2008). Concept mapping: An educational strategy to improve graduate nurses' critical thinking skills during a hospital orientation program. *Continuing Education in Nursing*, *39*(3), 119–126. doi:10.3928/00220124-20080301-12 PMID:18386699

KEY TERMS AND DEFINITIONS

Chains: A sequential series with a clear start and end.

Clinical Education: Education that takes place in a clinical environment (for doctors, nurses, dentists and allied health professionals).

Concept Map-Mediated Interview: An interview in which the construction of a concept map is the focus for discussion and in which the concept map is the main artefact of record.

Concept Mapping: A graphical tool to visualize connections between ideas that is used to demonstrate the quality of learning.

Conceptual Development: Moving from simple representations of complex ideas, to more sophisticated representations.

Conceptual Structures: The ways in which ideas are linked together (often to form chains or networks of understanding).

Content Knowledge: The facts that make up the elements of a conceptual structure.

Cycles of Rehearsal: Iterations of learning episodes in which the conceptual structure is likely to develop through a process of conceptual development.

Cyclical: A series which repeats; having no clear end point (with possible development at each turn of the cycle).

Development: Moving from the simple to the more complex.

Doctoral Education: Study leading to the award of a doctorate (usually PhD, DPhil or EdD).

Doctoral Student: A student studying for a PhD or equivalent research degree.

Doctoral Supervisor: An academic who guides and supports a doctoral student.

Education Research: Research into any aspect of the learning process (from single case studies of teachers to global analyses of policy).

Matrix: A grid.

Networks: Structures exhibiting multiple links and multiple routes from one side of the structure to the other.

Novak: Joseph Novak – credited with the development of concept mapping at Cornell University in the 1970s.

Pedagogy: The factors that underpin teaching (including the values, beliefs and theories that influence teachers).

PhD Supervision: The act of guiding a PhD student (usually on a one-to-one basis).

Spokes: A structure in which all subsidiary elements link directly to a central element.

Supervisory Relationship: The professional relationship between the PhD supervisor and the PhD student.

Typology: The exhibition of different types or forms.

Chapter 18

Mapping Out Scientists' Messages:
Models that Support Collaborative Critical Thinking

Annette deCharon
University of Maine, USA

EXECUTIVE SUMMARY

Funded by the Centers for Ocean Sciences Education Excellence (COSEE) program of the National Science Foundation (NSF), COSEE-Ocean Systems (OS) has employed concept mapping to facilitate collaboration and communication between ocean scientists and educators. Based on iterative feedback from and interaction with its participants, COSEE-OS has developed online concept mapping software linked to an ever-growing database with thousands of scientist-vetted resources, known as the Concept Linked Integrated Media Builder (CLIMB; cosee.umaine. edu/climb). Concomitant with the evolution of its CLIMB software functionality, COSEE-OS has transitioned from exclusively holding in-person concept mapping workshops to predominantly preparing for and delivering concept map-based webinar events, featuring ocean science researchers. This transition to webinars has greatly increased the number of participants and expanded the geographic reach from local to global. This chapter focuses on three key areas in which COSEE-OS has supported critical thinking: (1) the collaborative process of making meaningful learning by creating, analyzing, and improving concept maps with others; (2) facilitating subject-matter experts in the formulation of concept map-based presentations,

DOI: 10.4018/978-1-4666-5816-5.ch018

which audiences can use to evaluate the validity of their connections and conclusions; and (3) the training of scientists to use concept mapping as a technique to more clearly delineate and explain how their research is tied to societally relevant issues. Three case descriptions on how COSEE-OS concept mapping facilitation and infrastructure have been applied to ocean sciences education efforts—both within the COSEE Network and beyond to the National Aeronautics and Space Administration (NASA)—are also presented.

BACKGROUND

COSEE-OS Support of Critical Thinking

The COSEE program was born out of a workshop report (McManus et al., 2000), which recommended that the NSF play a leadership role in forming a mechanism through which exemplary practices in ocean sciences education be organized into distributed centers. A subsequent NSF-appointed COSEE Implementation Steering Committee reviewed the workshop report and recommended that NSF and other funding agencies proceed with establishing COSEE (Walker et al., 2001). They noted that, "The overarching goal is to increase and enhance collaboration and communications among ocean scientists, educators, and the general public." From these initial steps, a national Network of 10 COSEE Centers and a Central Coordinating Office were funded.

In fall 2005, Ocean Systems joined the COSEE Network with the objective of fostering substantive dialogue between scientists, educators, and the public through concept mapping. COSEE-OS developed, tested and iterated models of applied collaborative concept mapping and a related suite of interactive multimedia tools that focus on ocean and climate core concepts. These online tools are designed to graphically display how scientists see relationships among the concepts in their field.

Through its workshops and webinars, COSEE-OS has developed innovative methods to help scientists break down their research into core components and use creative thinking to make new connections for nonscientist audiences (deCharon et al., 2009; Bailin, 2002; Ennis, 1985; Paul & Elder, 2006). Having trained over 275 faculty- and graduate-level scientists, COSEE-OS has also supported several other types of critical thinking as defined by the California Critical Thinking Skills Test (CCTST; Insight Assessment, 2013) including analysis, evaluation and explanation. Facione (2000) designed the CCTST as a general test of critical thinking rather than one embedded within the context of a specific domain. Yet in 1990, he also noted the importance of domain-specific knowledge in the application of critical thinking skills and abilities. By focusing on concept mapping of ocean and climate sciences, COSEE-OS is able to test how domain-specific knowledge is translated into explanations, evaluations and evidence, providing some examples of the value of background knowledge to critical thinking (Ennis, 1985; McPeck, 1990; Bailin et al., 1999). Participant feedback shows that COSEE-OS applications of concept mapping are effective methods to help scientists work collaboratively with others to analyze their collective understanding of relationships among concepts. As a result, their concept maps have been used successfully to both evaluate and explain how these scientists' research is related to broader domains.

Critical Thinking Area #1: Collaborative Analysis to Make Meaningful Learning

- Sharing your science with someone who cares but doesn't know the topic
  - Concept mapping can help to… *UNDERSTAND YOUR RESEARCH*

The "Analysis" scale of the CCTST is described as follows: "Analytical reasoning skills enable people to identify assumptions, reasons and claims, and to examine how they interact in the formation of arguments. We use analysis to gather information from charts, graphs, diagrams, spoken language, and documents. People with strong analytical skills attend to patterns and to details. They identify the elements of a situation and determine how those parts interact. Strong interpretation skills can support high quality analysis by providing insights into the significance of what a person is saying or what something means." For its early workshops, COSEE-OS recruited scientists to illustrate the analytical constructs of their research via concept mapping. Given that the vast majority of ocean scientists had no training in – or even familiarity with – this technique, these content experts were teamed with educators well versed in "deconstructing" scientific knowledge for nonscientists (e.g., pre-college students).

Prior to the arrival of the educators, workshop facilitators worked one-on-one with scientists to create draft concept maps of their research. These draft maps were subsequently analyzed and reworked in small teams of one scientist with three or four educators to create concept map-based presentations for specific audiences (e.g., eighth grade students in an Earth Sciences course). These collaborative concept-mapping efforts gave science experts the chance to identify essential components of their research and receive feedback on their depictions and explanations of how concepts are interlinked. Education experts analyzed and identified how well the content tied to student understanding and motivation, as well as science education standards.

Evaluation data from participating educators demonstrates that the COSEE-OS collaborative concept mapping process supported analytical critical thinking. Over

80% of participating educators (n=162) agreed that concept mapping helped them "think through the topics" presented by scientists during the workshop (Figure 1). Open-ended responses from educators repeatedly mentioned the value in discussing visual representations of the scientists' understandings as a way to analyze their own depth and breath of content knowledge. For example, one educator commented that collaborative concept mapping was "a great way to explore and test your own understanding of a topic. It allows you to reframe concepts in a way that makes the links between ideas more obvious, and consequently more meaningful."

Collaborative concept mapping also provided a mutually beneficial process to foster analytical discussions between two groups that, in traditional workshops, do not work together as peers. Post-event evaluations posed two questions that addressed the quality of scientist-education interactions during the workshops (red and blue data on Figure 1), both of which received overwhelmingly positive responses. Participating educators' comments addressed the reciprocal benefits of concept mapping with scientists including, "Scientists were great about allowing us to incorporate their extensive content knowledge with what we know about how students learn and what students know and are able to do" and "This was a learning process for all partners - the teams seemed to meet in the middle somewhere, and all appeared to

Figure 1. Graphs show participant feedback data from several Scientist-Educator Collaborative (SEC) workshops. Green data show strong agreement with concept mapping as a way to help educators and scientists think through topics during workshop events. Red and blue data show results from two questions posed at a subset of SEC workshops, which addressed communication and peer-based interaction.

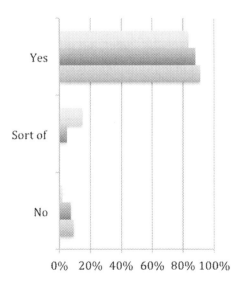

enjoy the result of these energetic conversations." Interviews with scientists revealed that analyzing and reworking their concept maps during COSEE-OS workshops helped the scientists to communicate their research more clearly and logically (deCharon et al., 2009).

In addition to collecting data on the efficacy of the workshop model, COSEE-OS also relied on these events to gather requirements for the development of concept-mapping software. The earliest COSEE-OS workshops employed paper, pencils and sticky notes for concept mapping. The focus on ocean and climate topics resulted in participants quickly identifying the need for interactive, online concept maps directly linked to scientist-vetted charts, graphs, diagrams and movies. In addition, organization of the content often entailed grouping concepts into categories using colors (e.g., blue sticky notes for biological concepts, green for geological concepts, etc.). This resulted in the request to toggle groups of concepts on/off by color (see "Technology Use" section). In addition, the participants requested the functionality of linking concept maps together.

Critical Thinking Area #2: Creating Concept-Map Presentations for External Evaluation

- Defending your science to someone who cares and knows about the topic
  - Concept maps can help to… *VALIDATE YOUR RESEARCH*

The "Evaluation" scale of the CCTST is described as follows: "Evaluative reasoning skills enable us to assess the credibility of sources of information and the claims they make. And, we use these skills to determine the strength or weakness of arguments. Applying evaluation skills we can judge the quality of analyses, interpretations, explanations, inferences, options, opinions, beliefs, ideas, proposals, and decisions. Strong explanation skills can support high quality evaluation by providing the evidence, reasons, methods, criteria, or assumptions behind the claims made and the conclusions reached." Based on recommendations by university faculty members who worked with educators during collaborative concept-mapping workshops, COSEE-OS led a multi-institution effort to design and implement concept map-based trainings for graduate students in ocean and climate sciences. One objective was improving graduate students' ability to evaluate and articulate connections within a research topic outside their own discipline (i.e., that of the faculty member with whom they were assigned to work). In addition, graduate student teams delivered concept map-based presentations to nonscientists (e.g., undergraduates), practicing the skill of making valid connections to issues of societal importance. This approach is consistent with the transferability of critical thinking skills into new domains, given that the graduate students had opportunities to practice in multiple contexts (Kennedy et al., 1991). It also demonstrates the value of transferring critical thinking skills and abilities to real-world contexts (McPeck, 1990).

Prior to the arrival of the graduate students, faculty-level scientists worked with facilitators to create concept maps for that workshop's designated target audience (Table 1). Faculty scientists and graduate students were placed in small teams, typically one faculty member per three or four students. Together, each team: (i) evaluated and adjusted the faculty member's preliminary concept map for the designated target audience; and (ii) created digital interactive copies of their concept maps using COSEE-OS software, attaching images and videos from the online database. In teams, graduate students presented their modified interactive concept maps directly to target audiences and other graduate students (the latter providing peer-level feedback to their fellow graduate students).

Table 1. Overview of "Faculty-Graduate Student Collaborative" concept mapping workshops conducted at four COSEE Centers (Ocean Systems, West, Networked Ocean World, California). From February 2010 to October 2011, four workshops were held at University of Maine, University of Southern California (USC), Rutgers University and Scripps Institution of Oceanography. Seventy-three graduate students and post-docs from these institutions, Bigelow Laboratory for Ocean Sciences, University of California at Los Angeles (UCLA) and two California State Universities (Long Beach and Fullerton) created concept map-based presentations with 20 faculty members for designated target audiences of high school students, undergraduate students and experts in informal education.

	Ocean Systems (OS)	West	Networked Ocean World (NOW)	California
Month/Year	February 2010	April 2011	May 2011	October 2011
Participants' Home Institutions	University of Maine; Bigelow Laboratory for Ocean Sciences	USC; UCLA; Cal State Long Beach; Cal State Fullerton	Rutgers University	Scripps Institution of Oceanography
Number of Graduate Student Participants	17	20	20	16
Number of Faculty Scientist Participants	5	5	5	5
Designated Target Audience	High School Students	High School Students	Informal Education Experts	Undergraduate Students

471

Survey data were collected at the end of each workshop and 85% (n=71) of graduate students agreed that concept mapping helped them "think through topics" while preparing presentation materials with faculty members. This evidence supports that the workshop series successfully met one of its key objectives: to train graduate students to view concept mapping as an effective method to deconstruct and analyze complex science (deCharon et al., 2013). Responses to open-ended survey questions revealed graduate students' recognition of the potential for concept mapping to help them validate scientific connections within their research. In addition, they saw concept maps as effective aids for evaluation of their thesis work by scientific peers and advisors. When asked how they might use concept mapping in the future, organization and/or communication of their research were most frequently mentioned by graduate students, for example: "(Concept mapping) will help to explain my line of thinking to peers/faculty mentors, which will result in helping me to better organize my thoughts" and "It will definitely help me think about my research in a way that will translate better when I'm talking with people in other disciplines."

In late January 2012, a follow-up survey was administered to all graduate students who participated in the workshop series to determine longer-term impacts. In terms of applying content or skills learned during the workshops to their scientific research, the most frequently selected uses of concept mapping were to "organize thinking about an existing research/dissertation topic" (56%; n=48), "develop research/dissertation topic" (44%; n=48), and "explain research to my colleagues and/or peers" (43%; n=48). Nearly all (92%; n=47) of the graduate students indicated that they had already or were planning to add concept mapping to their tools for organizing their research (deCharon et al., 2013). Graduate student comments support concept mapping as an evaluative critical thinking skill, "I included concept maps in my dissertation work, in lectures and presentations, in organizing thoughts instead of taking regular notes, and last but not least, in designing new algorithms e.g., in testing new data analysis tools" and "I used a concept map to explain my research to a group of scientist peers whose specialty is outside my own field. I was working to synthesize several different research projects into a single dissertation, and the concept map helped me to both organize my thoughts and share the information with them."

COSEE-OS also gathered data from graduate students to improve the concept-mapping software itself. The timing of this workshop series (Table 1) allowed participants to use the CLIMB, which merged COSEE-OS's Concept Map Builder and Concept Map Viewer functionalities (see "Technology Use" section). The integration of these previously separate tools also added the ability to search for and link items from the COSEE-OS database in "build" mode with seamless presentation of maps in "viewer" mode. During this workshop series, each team built, iterated and presented at least two concept maps over the course of two days. The high degree of collaboration among team members revealed the need for sharing among individual users (i.e., with separately registered profiles) and management of concept maps within a group profile. The COSEE Network-wide feedback from this workshop series also resulted in a request for making "public maps," i.e., viewable online by users who had not previously registered to use CLIMB.

All 40 concept maps created during the COSEE Faculty-Graduate Student Collaborative workshops can be viewed online at: *cosee.umaine.edu/coseeos/workshops/fgsc.htm.*

Critical Thinking Area #3: Explaining Broadly Relevant Connections Using Concept Maps

- Explaining your science to someone who doesn't know your topic and likely doesn't care
  - Concept maps can help… *OTHERS TO CARE ABOUT YOUR RESEARCH*

The "Explanation" scale of the CCTST is described as follows: "Explanatory reasoning skills, when exercised prior to making a final decision about what to believe or what to do, enable us to describe the evidence, reasons, methods, assumptions, standards or rationale for those decisions, opinions, beliefs and conclusions. Strong explanatory skills enable people to discover, to test and to articulate the reasons for beliefs, events, actions and decisions." *Science* Executive Publisher Alan Leshner (2007) called upon scientists to engage in "a genuine dialogue with our fellow citizens about how we can approach their concerns and what specific scientific findings mean." However, scientists are seldom given the tools to properly carry out this mission and thus are often unable to explain how their research connects to broadly relevant issues such as climate change. COSEE-OS's work with faculty-level scientists – in collaborative workshops with both educators and graduate students – revealed the value of concept mapping for "deconstructing" the complex connections that naturally exist within ocean and climate sciences.

To help faculty-level scientists understand how their research might fit in the context of public understanding, COSEE facilitators turned to the *Ocean* and *Climate Literacy Essential Principles* (National Geographic Society et al., 2005; NOAA et al., 2008), a set of community-developed documents that capture "ideas scientists and educators agree everyone should understand." In advance of each workshop, facilitators used these documents to formulate two to three "Focus Question" options per participating scientist. After providing an overview of public literacy efforts, COSEE staff worked with scientists to make their draft – and, in most cases, first-ever – concept maps, addressing their preferred "Focus Question." Each scientist, in turn, modified his or her map in collaboration with a small team of educators or graduate students.

Faculty were administered a five-question survey to elicit open-ended responses on the workshop experience, concept-mapping process, and applications of concept mapping to their primary work. The value of receiving feedback on the simplification of their science and reduction of jargon was repeatedly mentioned as valuable aspects of the workshop. Two representative comments: "I thought specifically about simplifying the number of concepts included in the base map and the language used both in the (concepts) and linking phrases. I also intentionally used examples and key concepts that were sure to be tangible and familiar to members of the target audience" and "(This) mapping tool will help share my ideas and state a comprehensive image to my students, funding agency, and colleagues. (It) is great in the sense that it can serve as a self-reflecting tool... if your map is not clear to others, that means your ideas are not clearly organized in your head!" Scientists were also specifically asked about how their initial concept maps were modified for the target audience of nonscientists. A common response was the addition of concepts that addressed impacts on humankind (Table 2).

Faculty-level scientists who participated in COSEE-OS workshops presented unique technical recommendations for COSEE-OS software development. For example, they expressed the desire to upload their personal resources (e.g., images, graphs, etc.) to the CLIMB database. In addition, some scientists wanted to embed working versions of their concept maps on their university faculty or laboratory webpages (see "Technology Use" section).

Table 2. Example comments from scientists about modifying their concept maps

We decided to take one of the sections and make a concept diagram at another "human" level.
I went from a linear map to a "top-down" map that had branches. Also, I ended up with three main themes, and a component about the people making some of the initial scientific discoveries. It was a very interesting approach provided by the teachers.
Some links were labeled more clearly and a mitigation (concept) was added to link impacts (and) problem solving.
Motivate problem by making explicit link to pollution issues. Make flow simpler and put in terms of what, where, when, why (and) how.
Using a case study to work through the concepts rather than using a generalized schema.

TECHNOLOGY USE

COSEE-OS has developed and evolved a suite of multimedia tools designed to promote ocean and climate literacy. These tools are rooted in COSEE-OS's earliest online user interface, the "Ocean-Climate Interactive" (OCI) Flash-based interactive, which emphasized key connections between the ocean and climate systems (Figure 2). The OCI design was based on paper concept maps co-developed by scientists and COSEE-OS facilitators. Although navigation among OCI concepts was interactive, the maps themselves were hard coded (i.e., not editable by external users). Clicking on an OCI concept (e.g., "Climate Change," Figure 2, left) revealed an overview of that topic, along with tabs to view scientist-vetted "assets" from the COSEE-OS database. Categories of assets included images, videos, news items, and resources for teaching (see tabs on Figure 2 right).

After the OCI was publicly released in 2007, educators responded favorably to the use of interactive concept maps that aided in the navigation through scientist-vetted assets. Scientists consistently recommended that COSEE-OS expand the breadth of assets in its database, usually citing specific examples to add. All agreed, however, that COSEE-OS should expand its concept-mapping functionality for direct use by others. Simply put, both educators and scientists wanted the OCI to evolve into a publicly accessible, cost-free online concept map builder and viewer.

Figure 2. Left: Entry page for the "Ocean-Climate Interactive" (OCI), which illustrates connections between concepts from the perspective of the solar system (top), earth system (middle), and ocean-land system (bottom). Right: "Image" detail page for the "Climate Change" concept. Images are selected using the horizontal scroll bar at bottom (e.g., this example shows "North Atlantic – Spring" selected in the zoom view).

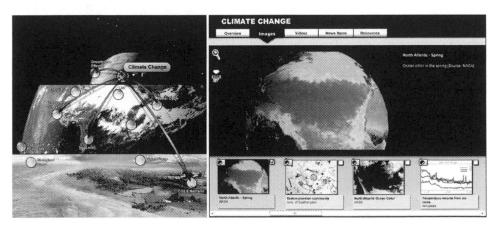

Given that concept-mapping software designed for educators had been available since the 1990s, COSEE-OS focused its early efforts on gathering software requirements from members of the ocean and climate sciences communities. Figure 3 shows an example of one ocean scientist's hand-drawn draft map for a 40-minute "Oceanography 101" presentation during a 2008 COSEE-OS educator workshop.

Several levels of complexity are evident such as branches from central to detailed ideas, numbering and color-coding of "main concepts," and annotation with specific graphical representations, chemical formulas, and tables. Several key software

Figure 3. Scientist's original hand-drawn map outlining concepts to be covered in a 40-minute presentation during a 2008 COSEE-OS educator workshop at the University of New Hampshire

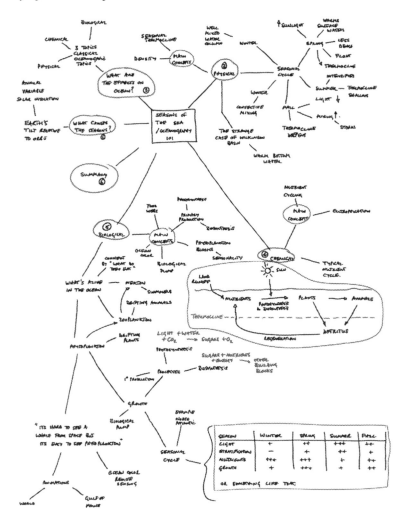

requirements are contained within this example including clicking from main concepts (e.g., "Biological Pump" at bottom of Figure 4) to reveal detailed assets (e.g., example shown in Figure 5), as well as categorizing and ordering concepts by color.

Over time, scientists' reliance on using particular graphical aids to "tell their stories" in concept-mapping workshops and webinars has been a very effective way to expand the COSEE-OS database of assets. Figure 6 (left) shows the cumulative numbers of four categories of database assets; note the significant increase in images and news items, both of which are tied to recommendations from over 100 faculty-level scientists who have received concept map training from COSEE-OS.

Figure 4. Concept map created using beta COSEE-OS software, based on the hand-drawn map in Figure 3

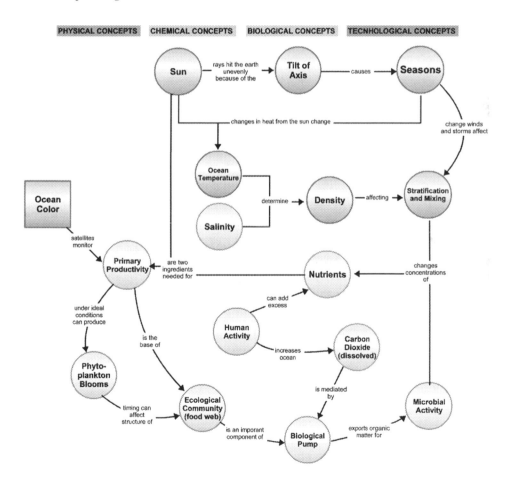

Figure 5. Scientist-recommended example "asset" from the COSEE-OS database used to illustrate the concept of "Biological Pump," a general model of how carbon is moved from the atmosphere to the deep sea via marine food web processes

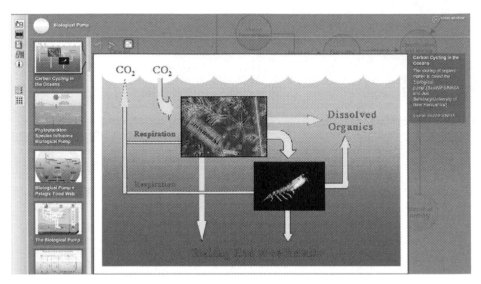

Not only has the inventory of database assets expanded over time, the numbers of registered users and maps created have grown significantly since 2009 (Figure 6, right).

Iterative and ongoing cycles of development, testing and user feedback have allowed COSEE-OS software tools to keep pace with the evolving needs of scientists and educators. Their suggestions for further improvements have been periodically reviewed to determine the direction of subsequent software development. For example, beta testing within 2007 COSEE-OS workshops led to the development of the prototype Concept Map Builder (CMB), released in January 2008. Six months later, version 1.2 of the CMB allowed registered users to create their own interactive concept maps, which could be printed, downloaded, shared via email, and displayed in the Concept Map Viewer (CMV) presentation window.

Over the following three years, 52 scientists and 68 educators conducted targeted field tests of the CMB and CMV during collaborative concept-mapping workshops. During this same period, free-choice users of the CMB and CMV provided comments through online (e.g., post-webinar) surveys and by email. Feedback from all of these users resulted in periodic releases of new software versions with additional features or enhancements. Version 1.5, released in January 2010, allowed users to search the resource database and save a "library" of assets that could be linked to concepts, connect maps together with hyperlinks, preview assets attached to concepts and more easily edit concept attributes (e.g., font size and type).

Figure 6. Left: Cumulative assets in COSEE-OS database from 2007 through mid-October 2013. The four categories of assets are images, videos, news items, and resources for teaching (e.g., lessons, activities). Right: Cumulative user-registered profiles (blue) and concept maps created (orange) from 2007 through mid-October 2013.

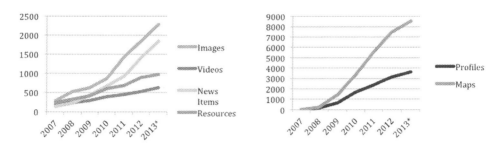

The CMB and CMV were fully integrated into CLIMB in 2011. This software version (2.0) allows users to preview maps in a list, create folders to organize concept maps, view maps full screen, and dynamically zoom in/out of concepts based on their color. This release of CLIMB also significantly improved the sharing of maps, both privately and publicly. Users can share maps by email, into other registered users' accounts, or submit their maps for review by COSEE-OS staff for inclusion in its searchable, sortable public database. The initial availability of CLIMB coincided with an exceptionally busy year for COSEE-OS including 6 concept-mapping workshops for 26 faculty-level scientists, 69 educators and 73 graduate students. During 2011, COSEE-OS also conducted 12 concept map-based webinars featuring 15 researchers, reaching 278 participants in 27 U.S. states, Canada, Germany, and Iceland.

Software functionality enhancement has continued since the 2011 release of CLIMB, with a focus on fulfilling users' requests to: (1) add concept maps to their own webpages; and (2) add their own assets to concept maps. The former, known as the "Embed Widget," provides a few lines of code so users can insert fully interactive versions of any CLIMB concept map on external webpages. The latter recommendation has resulted in a new type of database administrator known as a "Contributor." After receiving brief database management training from COSEE-OS staff members, including instructions on copyright issues, contributors are able to upload their own assets to the database. Currently, COSEE-OS is also developing the ability for registered users to add images to the CLIMB database for their own private use. The evolution of COSEE-OS software over time is summarized as a concept map in Figure 7.

Figure 7. Concept map, created in CLIMB, shows the evolution of COSEE-OS software functionality from 2007 through mid-October 2013

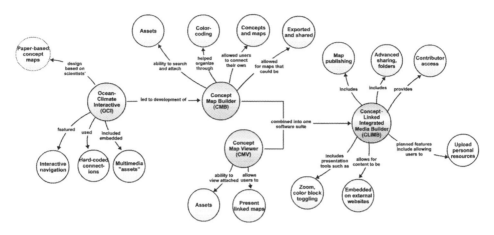

CASE DESCRIPTION

This section covers the evolution from primarily in-person COSEE workshops (i.e., local or regional) to NASA webinars (i.e., international). Each case briefly describes the rationale behind a specific application of concept mapping and the connections to critical thinking.

Scientists and Educators Working Together to Make Meaningful Connections

Tested and refined during the first four years of COSEE-OS, the "Scientist-Educator Collaborative" (SEC) workshop model established the validity of using concept mapping to foster critical thinking of scientists and educators. These workshops engaged over 100 ocean scientists and educators to collaborate on creating concept maps for classrooms or informal education venues. This workshop model aligns with a collaborative approach recommended by several critical thinking researchers (e.g., Nelson, 1994; Paul, 1992; Thayer-Bacon, 2000). The workshop model may be of particular interest to those who argue that critical thinking involves the ability to respond constructively to others during group discussion, such as encouraging and respecting the contributions of others (Bailin et al., 1999).

In traditional scientist-educator interactions, the scientist is considered to be the expert while the educator is primarily considered to be a recipient of science content. The educators, in this scenario, are assumed to have little to contribute to the scientist's knowledge base. In the SEC model, on the other hand, scientists and educators are considered to be on level ground with each participant being an expert in his or her field. It was key that both groups believed they had something to learn from each other, leading to mutually beneficial collaboration. Scientists contributed rigorous content knowledge resulting from their background training and educators likewise contributed rigorous pedagogical expertise about the needs of different audiences. For many scientists, SEC workshops provided an opportunity to receive immediate constructive feedback on the efficacy of their communication to nonscientist audiences. Below are examples of scientists' concept maps "before" and "after" educator interventions during SEC workshops.

Figure 8 shows a pair of scientist concept maps about Persistent Organic Pollutants (POPs), developed before and after collaboration with educators. The "before" map, at left, contains examples of scientific jargon such as "biodegradation" and "photodegradation." Rather than creating a map outlining conceptual ideas, the scientist initially opted to create a graphical depiction of a natural system similar to those found in science textbooks or journals (e.g., atmosphere at top and ocean at the bottom). Working as a team for about three hours, the scientist and educators created the "after" map (Figure 8, right). The team collaboratively analyzed how to revise the map to engage nonscientists, including color-coding concepts by issues related to health, living systems, environmental pathways, and sources of POPs. Although time limitations prevented the team from defining all linking phrases, the

Figure 8. Pair of "before" and "after" concept maps created during an SEC workshop. Left: Scientist's initial map focused on how Persistent Organic Pollutants (POPs) behave and move through the atmosphere, ocean and the biosphere. Right: With educators, the map was refocused to help students and teachers understand where POPs come from in society, how POPs travel through the coastal environment, and how humans and wildlife are affected by the consumption of POPs.

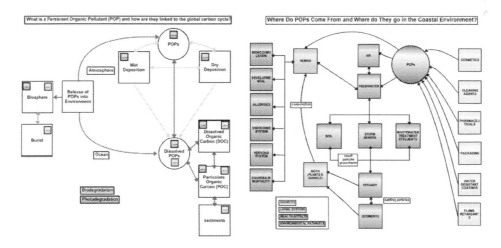

team was pleased with how their consensus map captured the essence of the scientist's original map while explaining broadly relevant connections to nonscientists.

Figure 9 shows a pair of scientist concept maps about toxic algae (i.e., phytoplankton), developed before and after intervention by educators during a workshop. Similar to the previous scientist's original concept map (Figure 8), the map at left graphically depicts how toxins cycle through nature including plankton, shellfish, fish, whales, seabirds and humans. Analysis of the original map with educators elicited ideas on how to make the topic more broadly relevant – for example, by emphasizing human and ecosystem effects – while making its connections more linear (Figure 9, right). According to the scientist: "In my original concept map, I showed the cycle of feedback loops that may occur. Because this is very current research, some of the arrows are hypothetical and not yet proven - that is what I study. The relationships between different parts of the ecosystem itself can change the whole picture. When working with our team of educators, they suggested an alternative arrangement for my concept map, showing the different paths that could be taken. The linear approach was something that helped my point to be more clear, and the educators helped me to see why feedback loops could be a confusing concept for their audiences."

Faculty and Graduate Students Communicating About Science Linkages Using Concept Maps

Implemented based on the recommendations of scientists who had participated in SEC workshops, the "Faculty-Graduate Student Collaborative" (FGSC) workshop series established the validity of emergent scientists using concept map-based pre-

Figure 9. Pair of "before" and "after" concept maps created during an SEC workshop. Left: Scientist's initial map focused on the feedback loops and marine ecosystem impacts of toxic algae. Right: With educators, map connections were more linear and human impacts more clearly defined.

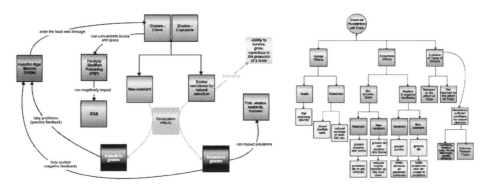

sentations to help others evaluate their scientific connections and conclusions. These workshops engaged 20 faculty-level ocean scientists to help 73 graduate students depict complex scientific ideas using concept maps. All workshop participants (i.e., faculty members and graduate students), as well as members of designated target audiences (Table 1), used a simple rubric worksheet to provide feedback on concept map-based presentations. Presenters were rated on their use of jargon, organization of their concept map(s), and the clarity of their "take-home message." Having a defined rubric is consistent with Paul (1992) who recommends being explicit about the intellectual standards used for evaluating student work. Similarly, Bailin et al. (1999) and Case (2005) include knowledge of criteria for judging the quality of thinking as a resource students need to think critically.

Upon arrival at each workshop, all graduate students rated individual faculty members' presentations. At the conclusion of each workshop, audience members rated graduate student team presentations, including fellow graduate students who provided peer-level feedback. Thus graduate students quickly transitioned from being "reviewers" to being "reviewed" to help them grasp how concept maps can be used to explain scientific concepts. Figure 10 shows average feedback ratings on graduate student teams' concept map-based presentations on a 5-point Likert scale. Feedback from fellow graduate students is shown in blue, while red corresponds to feedback from target audiences (i.e., high school and undergraduate students, informal education experts).

Peers and target audiences gave nearly identical high ratings (4.4 out of a maximum 5.0) in terms of the graduate students' use of jargon. In addition, peers and target audiences gave high marks for the clarity of concept maps presented by the graduate students. Thus it appears that analyzing and revising faculty members' original concept maps helped graduate students to use jargon appropriately and create well-organized concept maps for their own presentations. "Take-home Message" is the evaluation category that showed the most disparity between graduate student peers (4.37; n=278, each responder rated several presentations) and target audiences (4.10; n=256). One plausible explanation is that fellow graduate students were better equipped to decipher their peers' intended "take-home messages" than the target audiences of nonscientists.

In addition to receiving audience feedback on their presentations, post-workshop interviews and/or written surveys were given to graduate- and faculty-level scientists. Both groups mentioned concept mapping's value in representing not only what they know but also how they *think* about science. This indicates that concept mapping has great potential as a tool for scientists at various career stages to analyze, evaluate and explain concepts related to their research. In a journal article summarizing this workshop series, deCharon et al. (2013) concluded that scientist engagement in

Figure 10. Chart shows audience feedback on graduate students' concept map-based presentations in the areas of jargon, concept map clarity, and effectiveness of take-home message. Blue data are averages based on ratings by graduate student peers. Red data are averages based on ratings by target audiences. Lower values (i.e., 1 or 2) correspond to less effective delivery and higher values (i.e., 4 or 5) correspond to more effective delivery in each presentation category. Standard error bars are also shown.

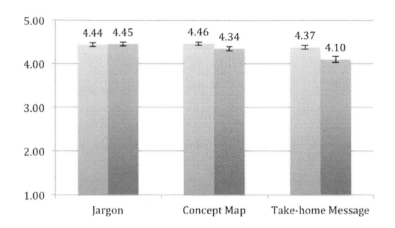

concept mapping "can stimulate creative and analytical spheres of thinking for all parties involved." Furthermore, learning how to better represent and communicate complex science through concept mapping can offer scientists "new perspectives on (their) research while contributing to the scientific literacy of society." Furthermore, by training scientists to use concept maps to make accurate and concrete connections between their research and society, they may be better equipped to frame their work as compelling personal stories while also fulfilling the audience's need to "seek patterns" in their science (Van Gelder, 2005).

Scientists Using Concept Map-Based Webinars to Broaden Their Impact

CLIMB software is being used to deliver authentic science content by the communication and public engagement teams for two NASA ocean research projects: the Aquarius satellite instrument that measures global salinity (aquarius.nasa.gov) and the Salinity Processes in the Upper-ocean Regional Study (SPURS; cosee.umaine. edu/coseeos/spurs). Concept map-based webinars have helped scientists and engineers to clearly delineate and explain how their research is tied to problem-solving and broadly relevant societal issues. Employing concept maps to communicate about

NASA science and engineering allows members of the public to follow experts' paths of critical thinking, including "the mental processes, strategies, and representations (they) use to solve problems, (and) make decisions" (Sternberg, 1986).

Webinars begin with featured presenters verbally describing their content while clicking through CLIMB interactive concept maps and attached assets. These online events conclude with presenters fielding audience-submitted questions in real time, which demonstrates critical thinking by clarification, defining terms, identifying assumptions, interpreting, explaining, reasoning verbally, and, in some cases, predicting potential impacts of ocean or climate change (Ennis, 1985; Paul, 1992; Facione, 1990; Halpern, 1998). Videos of the webinar presentations, embedded interactive concept maps, and transcripts of "question and answer sessions" are archived online, along with selected educational resources (Figure 11).

Since May 2011, Aquarius and SPURS webinars, including Spanish-language events, have engaged 440 participants from 46 U.S. states and 20 non-U.S. countries. Preparing materials for webinars is a synergistic and iterative endeavor, which joins scientists and engineers with experienced educators (i.e., NASA-funded communication and public engagement staff) to produce content that is appropriate for nonscientists. Like the workshop models described earlier, these webinars are designed to be beneficial for all involved: participants, presenters, and facilitators each derive benefit from the experience. In addition, these webinars have allowed those traditionally not represented in science, technology, engineering and math (STEM) to gain better access to high-quality NASA materials.

Post-webinar online evaluation surveys employed the same rubric that was field tested in the COSEE-OS Faculty-Graduate Student Collaborative workshop series. Comparing Figure 12 with Figure 10 shows that the webinar presenters had equivalent success in using jargon appropriately (4.5 out of a maximum 5.0). Ratings of the clarity of the concept maps presented during webinars are on par with those presented during in-person workshops (i.e., 4.3 out of a maximum of 5.0). Ratings on the webinar presenters' "take-home Messages" are equivalent with the ratings given by the workshops' target audiences (i.e., Figure 10, red data; 4.1 out of a maximum 5.0). These results are encouraging in terms of significantly increasing the size and geographic breadth of audience without sacrificing the efficacy of content delivery. In addition, online archives of Aquarius webinars, which have been viewed over 11,000 times since early 2012, provide an efficient way to provide long-term access to scientist- and engineer-vetted NASA materials.

Figure 11. Screen grab shows an example of an online archive from a Spanish-language NASA Aquarius webinar. Video of the presentation is embedded at the top of the webpage. In this example, interactive versions of the four linked concept maps are also available.

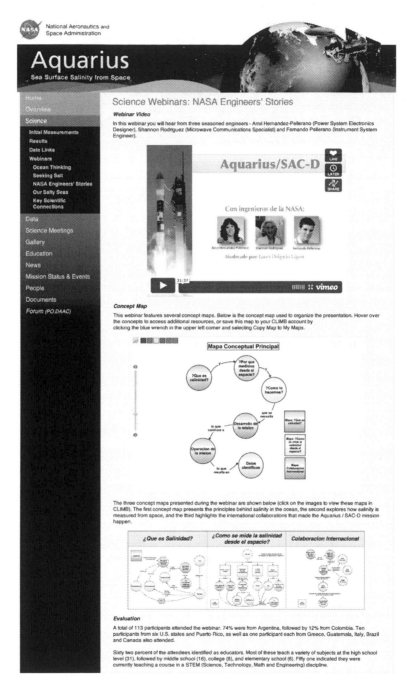

Figure 12. Chart shows audience feedback on concept map-based presentations during NASA webinars (n=98). Presenters were rated in the areas of jargon, concept map clarity, and effectiveness of take-home message. Lower values (i.e., 1 or 2) correspond to less effective delivery and higher values (i.e., 4 or 5) correspond to more effective delivery in each presentation category. Standard error bars are also shown.

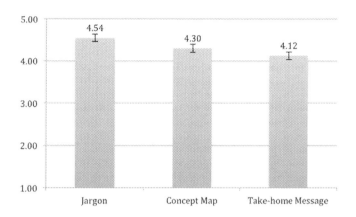

CURRENT CHALLENGES

The accomplishments of COSEE-OS have been achievable in large part due to support from NSF's COSEE Program (i.e., awards OCE-0528706, OCE-0707385/1038786, and OCE-0943448,). The recent cessation of the COSEE program puts enhancement of CLIMB functionality at risk beyond 2014. The use by NASA projects such as Aquarius will nominally help support maintenance of CLIMB during 2015 and beyond.

Several CLIMB functionalities are being integrated into the Education and Public Engagement component of the Ocean Observatories Initiative (OOI; oceanobservatories.org), including the visualization of ontologies (i.e., formally structured representation of knowledge as a set of concepts within a domain) and the ability to view concept maps on mobile devices (e.g., iPads). These features are scheduled for completion before 2015.

The authors are actively seeking new opportunities to foster critical thinking by scientists, graduate students, and educators through collaborative concept-mapping workshops or webinars. Likewise, ideas on how to expand the use of CLIMB to other domains are welcome.

QUESTIONS FOR DISCUSSION

In her 2011 review of critical thinking literature, Emily Lai writes:

Instructors are urged to provide explicit instruction in critical thinking, to teach how to transfer to new contexts, and to use cooperative or collaborative learning methods and constructivist approaches that place students at the center of the learning process. In constructing assessments of critical thinking, educators should use open-ended tasks, real world or 'authentic' problem contexts, and ill-structured problems that require students to go beyond recalling or restating previously learned information. Such tasks should have more than one defensible solution and embed adequate collateral materials to support multiple perspectives. Finally, such assessment tasks should make student reasoning visible by requiring students to provide evidence or logical arguments in support of judgments, choices, claims, or assertions.

Is this a reasonable description of the COSEE-OS workshop model with faculty- and graduate-level scientists as the "students" and CLIMB as a source of "collateral materials"? Why or why not?

Most educators would likely classify ocean and climate research scientists as strong critical thinkers. However, many post-workshop evaluation comments indicated a degree of surprise at scientists' critical thinking dispositions including open-mindedness (Bailin et al., 1999; Ennis, 1985; Facione 1990, 2000; Halpern, 1998), flexibility (Facione, 1990; Halpern, 1998), and willingness to entertain others' viewpoints (Bailin et al., 1999; Facione, 1990). Why would educators expect scientists to not have dispositions that welcome critical thinking?

Although COSEE-OS's application of concept mapping has been shown to be effective in reducing jargon and making societally relevant connections for nonscientists, how might it be used to help improve scientists' "take-home messages"? Or are the critical thinking skills used during collaborative concept mapping inconsistent with those honed during media training (i.e., developing and practicing memorable "sound bites" that are repeated over and over)?

How else might CLIMB be used in the formal training of emergent scientists to improve and communicate their critical thinking skills (e.g., in domains other than ocean and climate sciences)?

How might CLIMB be used in science instruction to improve K-12 student critical thinking skills (e.g., to support the Next Generation Science Standards)?

REFERENCES

Bailin, S., Case, Coombs, & Daniels. (1999). Conceptualizing critical thinking. *Journal of Curriculum Studies*, *31*(3), 285–302. doi:10.1080/002202799183133

Bailin, S. (2002). Critical thinking and science education. *Science & Education*, *11*(4), 361–375. doi:10.1023/A:1016042608621

Case, R. (2005). Moving critical thinking to the main stage. *Education Canada*, *45*(2), 45–49.

deCharon, A., Albright, Herren, Cline, & Repa. (2009). Online tools help get scientists and educators on the same page. *Eos, Transactions, American Geophysical Union*, *90*(34), 289–290. doi:10.1029/2009EO340002

deCharon, A., Duguay, McDonnell, Peach, Companion, Herren, … Whitley. (2013). Concept mapping workshops: Helping ocean scientists represent and communicate science. *Oceanography (Washington, D.C.)*, *26*(1), 98–105. doi:10.5670/oceanog.2013.08

Ennis, R. H. (1985). A logical basis for measuring critical thinking skills. *Educational Leadership*, *43*(2), 44–48.

Facione, P. A. (1990). *Critical thinking: A statement of expert consensus for purposes of educational assessment and instruction: Research findings and recommendations (The Delphi Report)*. Millbrae, CA: The California Academic Press.

Facione, P. A. (2000). The disposition toward critical thinking: Its character, measurement, and relation to crtitical thinking skill. *Informal Logic*, *20*(1), 61–84.

Halpern, D. F. (1998). Teaching critical thinking for transfer across domains: Dispositions, skills, structure training, and metacognitive monitoring. *The American Psychologist*, *53*(4), 449–455. doi:10.1037/0003-066X.53.4.449 PMID:9572008

Insight Assessment. (2013). *California critical thinking skills test*. California Academic Press. Retrieved from http://www.insightassessment.com/Products/Products-Summary/Critical-Thinking-Skills-Tests/California-Critical-Thinking-Skills-Test-CCTST

Kennedy, M. Fisher, & Ennis. (1991). Critical thinking: Literature review and needed research. In L. Idol & B.F. Jones (Eds.), Educational values and cognitive instruction: Implications for reform (pp. 11-40). Hillsdale, NJ: Lawrence Erlbaum & Associates.

Lai, E. (2011). *Critical thinking: A literature review.* Retrieved from http://www. pearsonassessments.com/hai/images/tmrs/criticalthinkingreviewfinal.pdf

Leshner, A. (2007). Outreach training needed. [Editorial]. *Science, 315*(5809), 161. doi:10.1126/science.1138712 PMID:17218495

McManus, D. Walker, Cuker, Goodnight, Humphris, Keener-Chavis,.... Schubel. (2000). *Center for ocean sciences education excellence.* Workshop Report. Retrieved from http://www.ocean.washington.edu/cosee/Text/index.html

McPeck, J. E. (1990). Critical thinking and subject specificity: A reply to Ennis. *Educational Researcher, 19*(4), 10–12. doi:10.3102/0013189X019004010

National Geographic Society. (2005). *Ocean literacy: The essential principles of ocean sciences grades K–12.* Retrieved from http://www.coexploration.org/ocean-literacy/documents/OceanLitChart.pdf

National Oceanic and Atmospheric Administration. (2008). *Climate literacy: The essential principles of climate science Grades K-12.* Brochure. Retrieved from http://www.climate.noaa.gov/education/pdfs/climate_literacy_poster-final.pdf

Nelson, C. E. (1994). Critical thinking and collaborative learning. *New Directions for Teaching and Learning,* (59): 45–58. doi:10.1002/tl.37219945907

Paul, R. W. (1992). Critical thinking: What, why, and how? *New Directions for Community Colleges, 77,* 3–24. doi:10.1002/cc.36819927703

Paul, R.W., & Elder. (2006). Critical thinking: The nature of critical and creative thought. *Journal of Developmental Education, 30*(2), 34–35.

Sternberg, R. J. (1986). *Critical thinking: Its nature, measurement, and improvement.* Washington, DC: National Institute of Education.

Thayer-Bacon, B. J. (2000). *Transforming critical thinking: Thinking constructively.* New York, NY: Teachers College Press.

Van Gelder, T. (2005). Teaching critical thinking: Some lessons from cognitive science. *College Teaching, 53*(1), 41–48. doi:10.3200/CTCH.53.1.41-48

Walker, S., Day, Matsumoto, Elthon, Prager, Keener-Chavis, … McDonnell. (n.d.). Centers for ocean sciences education excellence implementation steering committee report. *The Journal of Marine Education, 17*(2), 5-8.

KEY TERMS AND DEFINITIONS

Analytical: Separating something into component parts or constituent elements.

Archive: An online collection of videos, interactive concept maps, images, documents and contextual information that collectively provides information about a webinar or workshop event.

Asset: A scientist-vetted image, video, document (PDF) or webpage link that is accessible from the Concept Linked Integrated Media Builder (CLIMB) database.

Biodegradation: The chemical dissolution of materials by bacteria or other biological means.

Climate: The weather conditions prevailing in an area in general or over a long period.

Database: A structured set of information held in a computer that is accessible in various ways.

Deconstruct: To break down into constituent parts; dissect; dismantle.

Dissertation: A long essay on a particular subject, especially one written as a requirement for the Doctor of Philosophy degree.

Domain: A sphere of knowledge, influence, or activity.

Ecosystem: A biological community of interacting organisms and their physical environment.

Embed: Computer code that allows a widget (e.g., interactive concept map) to be added to a webpage.

Facilitator: Someone who helps a group of people understand their common objectives and assists them to plan to achieve them without taking a particular position in the discussion.

Faculty: The group of teachers in a school or college.

Feedback (Evaluation): Information about reactions to a product, a person's performance of a task, etc., used as a basis for improvement.

Feedback Loop: The path by which some of the output of a system is returned to the input.

Free-Choice (Users): Individuals who had the option to use Concept Linked Integrated Media Builder (CLIMB) software without being assigned specific tasks.

Interactive: Obtaining data or commands and giving immediate results or updated information.

Jargon: Special words or expressions that are used by a particular profession or group and are difficult for others to understand.

Likert Scale: A fixed choice response format (usually five- or seven- point range) designed by Likert, which is used to allow an individual to express how much s/he agrees or disagrees with a particular statement.

Link (or Hyperlink): A connection from a document to another location or file, typically activated by clicking on a highlighted word or image on a computer screen.

Literacy: A person's knowledge of a particular subject or field (e.g., ocean or climate science).

Multimedia: Using several file types such as images, videos, documents (PDF) and links to webpages to convey information.

Ontologies: Structured vocabularies that define the concepts and relationships used to describe and represent an area of concern.

Open-Ended: Questions where there are no specified answer choices.

Pedagogy: The art, science, or profession of teaching.

Peer: One who is of equal standing with another, especially one belonging to the same group based on age, educational background, or status.

Profile: For the Concept Linked Integrated Media Builder (CLIMB) software, a record of information (e.g., user name, email address, concept maps) tied to an individual's registration data.

Photodegradation: Decomposition of a chemical substance by prolonged exposure to light.

Rubric: A guide listing specific criteria for grading or scoring products (e.g., concept maps).

Salinity: The dissolved salt content of a body of water (e.g., the NASA Aquarius instrument measures the surface *salinity* of Earth's oceans).

Science: Intellectual and practical activity encompassing the systematic study of the structure and behavior of the physical and natural world through observation and experiment.

Scientist: A person who is trained in a science and whose job involves doing scientific research or solving scientific problems.

Scientist-Vetted: Checked for accuracy, authenticity, and validity by a scientist.

Software Requirement: A condition or capability needed by a user to solve a problem or achieve an objective.

System: A set of connected things or parts forming a complex whole (e.g., by exchanging heat, water and carbon, the ocean and climate are a connected *system*).

Take-Home Message: The intended point of an explanation or presentation that listeners can easily digest and remember.

Target Audience: The intended group for which something is performed; the specific group to which an activity is directed.

Thesis: A dissertation involving personal research, written by a candidate for a college degree.

Toxin: A poisonous substance that is a specific product of the metabolic activities of a living organism.

USC: University of Southern California.

UCLA: University of California, Los Angeles.

Webinar: A seminar or other presentation that takes place on the Internet, allowing participants in different locations to see and hear the presenter, ask questions, and answer polls.

Workshop: A meeting at which a group of people engage in intensive discussion and activity on a particular subject or project.

Chapter 19
Concept Maps and the Systematization of Knowledge

Patrícia Lupion Torres
Pontifical Catholic University of Paraná (PUCPr), Brazil

Marcus Vinicius Santos Kucharski
Federal University of Technology – Paraná (UTFPr), Brazil

Rita de Cássia Veiga Marriott
Federal University of Technology – Paraná (UTFPr), Brazil

EXECUTIVE SUMMARY

The act of doing research, reviewing recent literature, checking data, and articulating results and meanings are important but not enough when working with scientific publications in graduate schools. A vital part of the work is authoring an informative text that can be clear enough as to communicate findings of the study and, at the same time, reinforce chosen arguments. This chapter focuses on an experiment at a renowned Brazilian graduate school of education, which uses concept mapping and collective assessment of such maps as fundamental pre-writing stages to guide the authorship of well-thought, well-knit scientific/argumentative texts. Results indicate that the experiment was successful in making students negotiate meanings, clarify ideas and purposes, and write in an academically acceptable style. All this was conducted from a methodological standpoint that makes meaningful knowledge, collective construction, and the reflective, critical work of the author (from the first draft to the final collectively written version given), the foundations to perform a better job at communicating the processes and results of the investigative work.

DOI: 10.4018/978-1-4666-5816-5.ch019

INTRODUCTION

There are many challenges in the construction of knowledge. Some are more theoretical or rhetorical, such as the definition of what knowledge effectively means; others are from a more practical view point, such as its representation in diverse forms: written, graphical, multimedia, etc. From all of the possible challenges, it is on the systematisation of knowledge in the preparation phase that we will concentrate our attention in this chapter.

The main reason for focusing our attention on this area is the constant complaint from teachers, at all levels in the profession, that students do not have a demonstrable ability/capacity to organise and articulate knowledge in a cohesive, coherent and contributive form. Apart from noticing a near incapacity to understand relations and levels of articulation about which they learn, we perceive a much bigger problem than a simple difficulty with the representation of proper knowledge - although it encompasses it – which is the issue of attributing questions to the diverse niches of educational investigation: from teaching theories to learning process, from methodology to didactics, from educational biology / psychology / sociology / anthropology / philosophy / history to educational technology, nearly claiming that a metatheory to propose solutions to the problem that affects all levels of schooling be created.

However, the creation of this metatheory is not a task exclusive to Education or to any one of the contributing sciences and it needs to be undertaken in the confrontation and negotiation of the concepts developed by the diverse areas of educational research, each one applying its speciality to weave the network in its entirety. To be able to properly contribute to the overall discussion, it is necessary to define from where we speak stating clearly what should or should not be considered and to be careful not to exhaust the subject but to explore its facets. In the case of this article, the contribution will come from the exploration of the systematisation of knowledge, which occurs after the end of the exploratory stage and immediately before the creation of the summary of what has been learned, not taking into account the type of document/article/paper it becomes. This is a moment of reflection and individual or group summary, revision, negotiation and planning in the sense of knowledge exchange. In this area of action and reflection, concept maps can fulfil a privileged role in the reduction or elimination of the difficulties of critical and informed systematisation of knowledge, as we have systematically seen in our students. For this, we need to establish a path that clarifies the presuppositions of our stance; this path needs to start from the definition of the main object of the educational process.

THE NATURE OF MEANINGFUL KNOWLEDGE

The understanding of knowledge that underpins our proposal is the one put forward by Ausubel (1963), according to which it is meaningful knowledge that effectively contributes to the personal/social development of the individual. Broadly speaking, in this type of knowledge, new knowledge is incorporated via the assimilation of new concepts and, fundamentally, of new meaningful conceptual relations established with our previous knowledge repertoire. This incorporation – meaningful knowledge as such – happens by the mediation of language[1], provided three basic conditions are met:

(1) The material to be learned must be conceptually clear and presented with language and example relatable to the learner's prior knowledge. (2) The learner must possess relevant prior knowledge. (3) The learner must choose to learn meaningfully (Moreira, 2007, p. 2; Novak & Cañas, 2007, p. 30, italics from original).

In the conditions presented above there are two important implications to clarify: the first one is that the learner's "relevant previous knowledge" forms a network of inter-related concepts and mental models that can be recovered and put into action at the very moment something new needs to be understood or solved. This network system is open, i.e., it is always ready to receive additions that modify it (we do not want to say "better it" as we do not mean that every addition to the system "improves it"); what is important is to see it as a system which is open to modifications and that these will be more meaningful and lasting as more conceptual connexions are established with those pre-existing ones. It is unlikely – although it is not impossible! – that this network of concepts and models be formed based on information assimilated by mechanically memorised concepts, such as ill contextualised formulas that are "learnt" for taking tests, for example. Relevant previous knowledge is meaningful exactly for being able to adjust itself and survive life's continuous/ ongoing daily tests and troubles, overcoming the limits of utilitarianism due to its reapplicability and adaptability to situations that are similar – or not – involving more than skills but concepts and more abstract and encompassing principles.

The second implication that needs clarification is that 'the learner has to choose to learn meaningfully'. Learning meaningfully is not a passive process; it demands an active attitude from the learner in order to focus and *apprehend* new relevant concepts/meanings. The possibility of learning meaningfully by insight cannot be discarded but even so it will only be meaningful if the learner is open to the transformative influence of the recently acquired concept on the pre-existing meaningful structure. Moreira (2007) contributes with our understanding when he introduces his "critical (subversive, anthropologic) vision of learning," according to which

(...) in today's society it is not enough to acquire new knowledge in a meaningful way, it is necessary to acquire it in a critical way too. At the same time that we need to live and integrate in this society, it is also necessary to be its critic (p. 11).

Because

(...) meaning is in people, not in words. The learning-teaching process involves presenting, receiving, negotiating and meaning sharing, in which language is essential and, being so, it is necessary to be always aware that meanings are contextually bound, they are arbitrarily given to objects and events by people who also give idiosyncratic meaning to the world's state of things. Meaningful learning requires sharing of meanings, but it also implies personal meanings (p. 13).

Therefore, there is a balance between social forces (interaction and meaning negotiation) and personal disposition for meaningful learning to take place, in a dialectic process of giving meaning to the world (=apprehend). The essence of *moto perpetuo* in the dialectic process, and its greatest beauty, is the balance which, far from favoring acritical crystallizations of knowledge, it values its multifaceted state: there can be as many understandings and forms of learning as there are learners.

Paulo Freire (2002) always insisted that the meaningful learning-teaching process puts "(...) to the teacher or, more broadly, to the school, the duty not only to respect the learners' knowledge (...) and how they acquired it (...), but also, as I have been suggesting for more than 30 years, discuss with them the reason why some of them have the knowledge they have, if we consider the content that has been taught" (p. 15). According to Freire, actual knowledge construction is only possible if the content, which is achieved socially, is already internalised by the students in a tangible way (i.e., meaningfully).

Freire also asserted – following this line of thought - that the pedagogical work must be dialogical and critical, and that this criticism arises from the possibilities of exploring the subject matter with a rigorousness that arises from the exercise of sharing democratically, overcoming and rebuilding the vision that one has of it.

To me, there is no breach but an overcoming in the difference and distance between naïveness and criticism, between knowledge by experience and knowledge by rigorous methods. The overcoming, and not the breach, occurs when naive curiosity becomes a critical statement. When it becomes critical, it becomes, and I repeat, epistemological curiosity, methodologically rigorous when approaching the subject matter, giving greater precision to the findings (Freire, 2002, p. 16, own translation).

In concept mapping, tangible systematization of pre-existing knowledge, as well as its critical reconstruction and complement, is a valuable resource for its construction. This quality of the pre-existing knowledge occurs not only for its path and possibilities to be drawn more clearly before the author, but also in order to promote even more the clarification of the concepts being used, possibly leading, as Paulo Freire would have said, to "(...) a critical consciousness and, finally, (...) [to] a transforming action" (Loyola & Borges, 2010, p. 316).

Moreover, there is also the easiness of construction sharing, the (re)negotiation of meanings and the pursuit of a creative consensus in an experience of collective intelligence (Lévy, 2012).

THE SYSTEMATISATION OF KNOWLEDGE WITH CONCEPT MAPS

Novak and Cañas (2007, p. 33) claim that there is a growing consensus amongst philosophers and epistemologists that the construction of new knowledge occurs in a constructive process that involves previous knowledge and the drive to create new meanings. As a process of social construction, it finds support in Vygotsky's socio-interactionist theory that was adopted specially by Novak and Gowin (1996) in meaningful learning.

As a process of negotiation of senses, meaningful learning cannot do without ways of representing knowledge, as they regulate both restatement and positive redundancy (*positive* only used for redundancy, not for both redundancy and restatement) of what has been learnt up to the argumentative / persuasive level: well-represented knowledge can be better understood in its relations and implications and thus be considered relevant by those who are in contact, as well as its representations.

The representation of knowledge can come in various ways such as text, image, documents, or digital material, taking into account where it is going to be used and the objectives that one wants to reach when discussing knowledge.

In academia, written scientific and argumentative pieces of text are historically the most valued form of knowledge representation and, for too many different reasons to be able to discuss at the moment, they are the most difficult ones for students to construct – and not say, for many teachers as well!. We highlight a couple of reasons for this occurrence: **a)** a consolidation of linguistic patterns that do not match current genre and text types in the current process of knowledge construction (which includes various forms of graphic representation and writing styles and structures such as the ones used in blogs, discussion lists, wikis, short papers for publication on the Internet – except publications in highly controlled environments such as journals); **b)** and a historical difficulty, possibly inherited from our education system as a whole, to construct textual knowledge representations which fully respect the minimum criteria of textuality.

As much as they are continually developing, scientific writing cannot be purely abandoned in the name of new genre and text types that still lack the representational and argumentative rigour that can be reached by professional writing. Because of this, the main problem to tackle is the preparation for academic writing; being more specific, what needs to be done is to prepare the student for critical writing – and, for this, concept maps represent an unparallel opportunity for visualisation and (re) organisation of concepts from the reconstruction of relationships that occur at the ideological-semantic level. Richter (2000) says: "There would be a lot to gain in activities of text production if they involved the manipulation of the parts in relationship to meanings to express or textual coherence to keep" (p. 87, own translation).

When planning the writing of a text by concept mapping, the student/author can visualise and enrich both sequence and text coherence in such a way as to produce a much more elaborate piece of text as regards the criteria applied to scientific text production. Based on Beaugrande and Dressler, Koch (2001) discusses textual criteria, listing the following ones: *informativity* (what does the text complement to the reader's own knowledge?[2]), *situationality* (is the chosen genre and text type the best for the communicative situation?) *intertextuality* (which connections does the text make with other similar pieces of text, in terms of theme/subject, and what does this demand from the reader's knowledge repertoire?), *intentionality* (is the informative/argumentative intention clear in the text? Does it respect its objectives without committing unwanted ambiguities?[3]), *acceptability* (is the text written in a way as to facilitate understanding by the reader?[4]).

Koch and Travaglia (1999) add other four categories that, although they may seem partially redundant as regards the previous ones, they bring some new perspectives: *contextualization* (does the text reveal its content without treating knowledge as a collection of isolated data?), *focalization* (does the text present its content in such a way as to create a common ground for dialogue with the reader?[5]), *consistency* (is textual construction consistent, with a clear meaning, when considered as a whole in its arguments and images?) and *relevancy* (is there a relevant central subject guiding text construction?) (pp. 76-101, own translation).

It is not difficult to conclude that the above principles can guide the construction of any knowledge representation, even if it is only imaginary – such as a work of art – for image is *language* and if it is used to represent formal knowledge it cannot leave behind any of them. There are principles which focus on the reader's perception, others which focus on the objective of text creation and those which concentrate their interest in intra-textual processes and structures, combining the classic form and content: what?, for whom?, how? This is valid for all knowledge representation, however, our focus will be on the preparation for textual representation.

The process of pre-writing usually concentrates on summaries, topic structure, free association and flowcharts, and each one of them, irrespective of their intrinsic value, presents one or another trap that catches those who are not very careful.

Summaries, even if well-made, are not innovative scientific productions. Starting from summaries help beginners in scientific writing organise content, but it does not prioritise topic discussion, needed for the construction of new knowledge.

Topical structures and flowcharts, although they are a good guide for writing texts, they do not ensure fluency between one topic and another, exactly where the author's contribution can be observed best. When the contribution occurs in the articulation of concepts generated from a central concept, the fluency of the articulations or linkages reflect the author's mastery of the subject and concepts, and not only that s/he is well informed about them (Novak & Cañas, 2007, p. 31).

Free-association is maybe the most dangerous of all the forms of preparation for writing. As the result of a brainstorming activity, they are usually a disorganised list of "n" terms that are related to each other such as *water, sun, food, rest, feelings* and *growth,* and all have some relationship to the umbrella concept of "life." The same way as putting them all together in the same text would hardly result in an objective, coherent and comprehensive production, the same can happen as the result of a flowchart exercise on any other concept; if we do not proceed to level the conceptual field as to establish focus (clear intentionality), we cannot guarantee that the resulting text will be sufficiently contributive, meaningful.

A contributive scientific text works with the articulation of concepts, not only with the mere listing of data – even if it is a detailed listing – suggesting new interpretations and new possibilities that may broaden our understanding about them (informativity). In this chapter, we understand 'concept' as Novak and Cañas's (2007) intend it to mean: "concepts are general linguistic terms that articulate to explain, to a greater or lesser degree of detail, the facts from the world around us" (p. 30). These articulations suffer daily update throughout life, as an open system that is usually linguistically constructed, becoming more abstract and reflecting relations such as cause and effect, dependency, co-existence and exclusion. The more meaningful articulations a concept takes part in, the more relevant the concept will be, especially to form new concepts.

Concept maps are a way of representing, in a graphic and summarised way, the inter-relationships amongst the several concepts and the propositions they form within a specific area of knowledge. Working on the level of concept articulation, concept mapping is more than just a list of topics or suggestions of key words – it is a valuable way of systematization of previous knowledge in formal writing. Developed by Novak's research group at Cornell University in 1972, concept maps were originally used as a visual representation of children's level of knowledge as they deepen their understanding about a particular science topic over a specific period of time. The constant reconstruction of the maps revealed the progress of the conceptual relations and the richness of their experience on the subject matter with the passing of time, proving to be much more effective than the long subjective interviews with participants who found it difficult to express themselves properly and lacked a complete grasp of a more complex verbal explanation.

Generally speaking, concept maps are built from a more abstract and general concept (the theme or subject discussed in general terms) placed at the top of the page which is then, in turn, linked up to other more specific concepts making propositions. Figure 1 illustrates a concept map about Assessment demonstrating the fluidity of a well-built concept map.

The map in Figure 1, which establishes several relationships amongst diagnostic and formative assessment concepts, can be considered both a good systematic initial study of these types of assessment and a starting-point of discussion on what these types of assessment entail.

After careful observation, it is possible to see that the map could have been expanded nearly indefinitely; one could add, for instance, historical data about the development of these types of assessments, as well as their uses and potential in all education sectors. However, this "incompleteness" of the map is directly related to the purpose of its construction: to present, with a good level of detail, what these two types of assessment involve. To achieve this, relevant concepts were chosen considering its goal and audience. The expansion of any of the concepts used would

Figure 1. Concept map about assessment. Created by Rita Marriott © 2013. Used with permission.

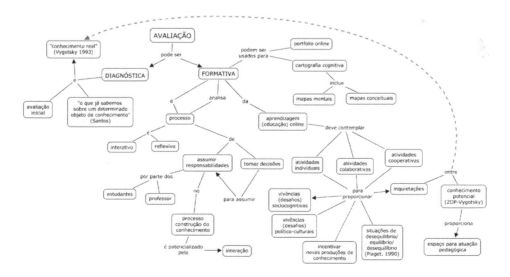

make this into a new map, forming a new network of meaning, illustrating what we mean by meaningful learning.

Considering the concept of a network of meanings, more sophisticated concept mapping software allow the possibility of synchronous and asynchronous collaborative work. There is an important gain in the development of critical thought which stems from the different possibilities of understanding and participants' contribution in the various research channels and discussion threads. Exploring the development of critical thinking and the efficacy of collaborative online groups created for solving complex problems, Mason and Watts (2012) observe that these work groups had a significantly higher performance on problem solving than independent researchers; they have also noted that exploitation usually leads to some level of individual success, but is anticorrelated with collective success. These findings are extremely interesting to pedagogy, particularly to those interested in forming knowledgeable teachers with critical thinking who are ready for a transformative action originated from a collectively solved problem.

As the relationships between concepts on a map are shown in relation to (1) a more encompassing concept; (2) the mapper or mappers' knowledge on the subject; and (3) the purpose of its construction, there will not be two identical concept maps about a specific subject, even if they originate from the same piece of text. The reason for this is, as we said before, that there are no two identical individual or group understandings about a specific subject, because different people and groups assign different values to similar concepts, and these suffer modification with time and the mapper's (mappers') experience. This is what we have repeatedly experienced with our students and in our research into the process of learning/teaching with critical thinking.

PEDAGOGICAL EXPERIMENTS WITH CONCEPT MAPPING AT PUCPR

Since 2006 we have been actively developing teaching/learning and research activities at the Graduate School of Education (at Ed.MA, Ed.D and Ed.PhD levels) at the Catholic University of Parana (PUCPR) using concept mapping as a pre-writing knowledge systematization procedure, investigating the influence such activity would present over the final writings produced once the maps had been drawn and peer-reviewed.

Our investigations present even greater significance for taking place in an environment specifically dedicated to teacher development. Most Graduate Schools of Education throughout Brazil, and at PUCPR in particular, have been known to be guided by critical discussion and questioning activities about both theoretical and methodological aspects of teacher development.

An essential part of these programs, attended by both pedagogy students and lecturers from a wide range of courses, is the scientific writing of pieces of text which are submitted to the rigorous scrutiny of the academic community. However, difficulties related to formal written production are not exclusively to Brazilian scholars and other professionals. We believed, from the beginning of our research efforts, that the possibility of bringing the support of a new technology (a concept mapping software) into a collaborative knowledge systematization and (re)building process could significantly lessen the discomforts caused by the pressure of planning a coherent, cohesive and contributive scientific text in a way that would diminish foreseeable mistakes and inconsistencies brought to light by a metaphoric representation of conceptual interrelations and dependences (Kagan & Kagan, 2008). Moreover, we cherished the possibility of bringing written scientific production even closer to the influence of a critical epistemology of practice – as addressed by Nóvoa (1995), one in which careful reflection stems *from* and is pointed *towards* practical events which elicit an environment of collaborative, democratic and dynamic development: "The exchange of experiences and the sharing of knowledge consolidate mutual formative spaces in which every participant is required to play, simultaneously, the roles of teacher and student" (Nóvoa, 1995, p. 26). As for the dynamics of forming more competent, reflective and critical teachers, Évelyne Charlier (Charlier, 2001) characterizes the teaching profession as one that combines, develops and activates, whenever necessary, schemes that allow them to "Reflect and Perform during Action":

(...) we define (Donnay and Charlier, 1990) the professional teacher as an educator who, in light of an explicit formative project:

- *Deliberately takes into account the greatest number of possible parameters of a given formative scenario;*
- *Articulates them in a critical manner (with the help of personally or collectively accepted theories);*
- *Ponders over one or various possibilities of conduct and makes planning decisions regarding his/her actions;*
- *Puts his/her decisions into practice in concrete situations, resourcing to routines that can assure the efficacy of his actions;*
- *Adjusts his/her actions immediately whenever s/he perceives it as necessary (reflection in action);*
- *Learns from his practice (reflection about action).*

(...) This definition combines two approaches. It defines planning as the stage of decision-making and rational treatment of information, whereas the interactive phase is understood as the consequence of the triggering of action and reflection in action schemes (Charlier, 2001, pp. 88-89, italics in original).

Our research project stood, according to the paraphrases made by Marcelo-García (Marcelo-Garcia, 2005, pp. 19-20) on Debesse's work, in the threshold between hetero and inter-formation. It is hetero-formative because its main objectives, contents and pedagogical sequence were inspired, developed and offered from phenomena external to the setting which congregated its participants – problems that arise daily during teaching practice in the most diverse levels. It is inter-formative in the sense that its explanatory theoretical-methodological bases propose and value collaboration as the most valuable tool for symbolic exchanges that enable constant (re)building of knowledge and competences. The working conditions of PUCPR's Graduate School of Education, where we worked and researched, combined with a collaborative, autonomous, critical and reflective pedagogical approach (which is facilitated by the use of concept maps) created a positive environment where the voices of teachers in continuous formation programs could take precedence over those or their advisors, allowing different views of the study topics to arise under considerably less practical and ideological pressures which are so commonplace in the more pre-structured and submissive ones of the schools where they worked individually (Schön, 1983).

Let us, now, proceed to the description of the working steps we proposed to our students.

There was a pre-research interview in which the participants' basic personal computing skills (especially in dealing with text processing and presentation building software) were questioned. All respondents assured us that they felt comfortable with such tools. As for the utilization of the Internet for professional and personal interests, all respondents said that they accessed the Internet on a daily basis. Therefore, we could affirm that the data we planned to collect would come from a satisfactorily homogeneous population in terms of professional profile and level of technological literacy.

The participants were then introduced to concept maps and soon after that to concept mapping with the use of the CMapTools software[6]. It was asked that all readings requested for the modules "Theory and Practice in Distance Education" and "Thesis Seminar I" (this one exclusive for doctoral students) were systematized as concept maps, first individually and then in groups, representing conceptual relations present in those articles. Figures 2 and 3 illustrate some examples of individual concept maps created by two students in the group.

Figure 2. Concept map about meaningful learning. Created by Marcus Kucharski © 2013. Used with permission.

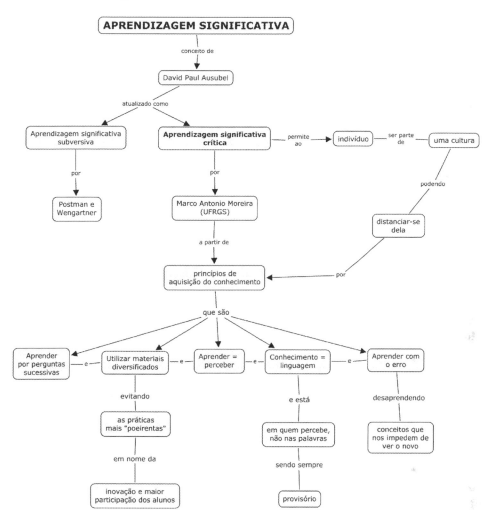

Later on, the collectively created concept maps were exchanged with other groups for peer-review and for an exercise of exchange and negotiation of ideas for implementation (or not) of the map. The newly implemented map would be a new more encompassing collective, critical concept map which would warrant the building of competing concept maps that would enrich further discussions.

The next step was to ask students to transform both individually (first phase) and collectively (last phase) built concept maps into written texts of scientific orientation (especially essays), which were submitted to their lecturers as part of their ongoing evaluation process.

Figure 3. Concept map about concept maps. Created by Lilia Siqueira © 2013. Used with permission.

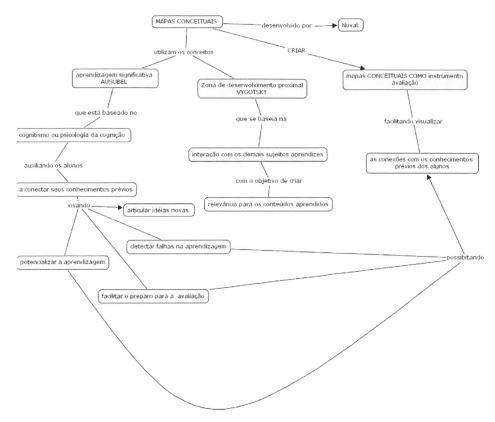

The collectively built pieces of text were also e-mailed to all participants of the other groups and published in the online portfolio of PUCPR's virtual learning environment (Eureka). This virtual portfolio granted free access to everyone's work and promoted the possibility of direct and critical comparative analyses of the progress made, reflecting changes in their perception and knowledge throughout the course, as can be seen in Figures 4 and Figure 5.

Concerning this, Leite and Fernandes (2002) define the construction of portfolios as a pedagogical tool that favors active learning and the development of cognitive, social and affective competences, highlighting students' awareness of their responsibilities over their own learning process as well as over those of their peers – bringing about conscious, contextualized, critical and socially-aware learning.

Stemming from the analysis of our students' portfolios, they were interviewed (in writing) about their perceptions of the relations between the maps they built and the final texts they constructed. A self-evaluation exercise was carried out in which

Figure 4. The virtual portfolio in the Eureka VLE, screen 1

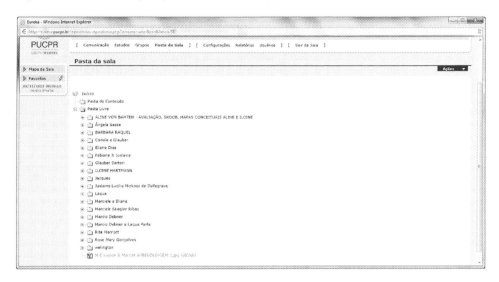

Figure 5. The virtual portfolio in the Eureka VLE, screen 2

they were asked to consider the process they had just undergone in terms of the contributions it might have made (or not) towards their scientific, critical reading and writing competences, as well as to comment on any difficulties they might have experienced during the process. Some of the students' thoughts are expressed next.

In relationship to the use of Concept Maps as an evaluation tool in the course, students highlighted the easiness to summarize and systematise content, as can be observed in the following comments:

It is an intelligent way to summarise content, organise ideas and construct knowledge

By using Concept Maps we can organize the way we study, systematizing content in a clear and precise way.

Students also acknowledge that the Concept Maps aid in the production of texts:

Concept Maps help in the summary of the content covered in the course, moreover, it helps in the production of texts.

It was much easier to write the text after we have built the maps

The maps not only helped me to revise the texts discussed in the course but also made it easier to assimilate the authors' ideas and to write my own text

They also noted how positively the maps contributed to the course:

It is a very interesting tool. It helped summarizing content and enhanced content assimilation in the long-term memory which was very useful. I have already used it with my undergraduate students.

I loved working with Concept Maps! I thought it was great how I was able to assimilate content better with the use of this tool. I could summarize what was studied in a dynamic way, highlighting the most relevant aspects and making connections.

As regards the downside of using Concept Maps in these courses, students did not signal that they have encountered any disadvantage with this technique, although some of them have mentioned some initial difficulty to use *CMapTools*. They said that:

I do not see any disadvantage. I had the experience to use them with my students in the university where I work and I can say that it really works.

There are disadvantages only while we are learning how to use the tool, after we start mastering CMapTools the relationship between concepts and the synthesis become clearer.

Students reported that they felt an improvement in their learning-teaching process with Concept Mapping, as can be read below:

The choosing of the linking word and the concepts demand sharpness and objectiveness. An extraordinary summary exercise. The act of "thinking" has improved.

There was an improvement in my learning-teaching process, mainly when hierarchizing the content.

I felt my learning has improved. The maps enhance comprehension and autonomy in relation to the content covered; it also helps with self-discipline.

The use of Concept Maps enhanced my learning when I realized I could structure content in a meaningful and summarized way. With a single key word it was possible to pinpoint what was the most relevant in the text discussed.

Students who believed that the methodology used produced better knowledge acquisition thought that this happened due to research and knowledge production:

It encouraged us to do research and take a critical stand as regards the literature read.

It made us research more in order to exchange ideas with our colleagues, mainly during collaborative work, more interaction and knowledge dissemination.

The development of research and the building of maps to underpin discussions in class and text production has undoubtedly given us a deeper level of knowledge.

We've built knowledge together and this enabled us, as a group, to reach a critical stand as regards the themes discussed.

Their answers to the questionnaire clearly confirmed a positive evaluation of the process, especially as it was said to have stimulated greater commitment to the collaborative proposal developed in the participating courses. According to the students, peer interaction and collaboration facilitated learning and developed concurring skills and competences such as accountability and autonomy. Interaction also seemed to provide for better performance in research, analytical work, symbolic exchange and negotiation as well as in scientific writing and knowledge production. Students also assured that the use of concept maps as tools for meaningful learning demanded maturing awareness of their roles in the teaching/learning process. The fact of working as actual researchers and becoming authors of their own knowledge as well as important part-takers in similar processes of their peers was also positively observed by the students.

Most respondents considered that the use of concept maps aided their comprehension of the texts whose reading was requested by their lecturers or by their own peers, as well as improved their skills and competences for organizing ideas, structuring analytical assessments, systematizing concepts, organizing their study habits and, especially, prepared them to be authors (both in the sense of becoming responsible for their own learning and as feeling more confident as writers). For them, the concept maps made the whole process more dynamic, creative and interactive, facilitating learning, concentration, motivation and the assessment of their own performances.

FINAL CONSIDERATIONS ABOUT THE RESEARCH

Our research demonstrated the relevance of the utilization of concept maps as a tool to assist in the identification, systematization and distribution of concepts pertaining to the content covered in the two post-graduate courses, as well as for the improvement of students' written scientific production competences.

The research also attended to the assimilation of what was discussed in a meaningful way, having led, on the one hand, the group of teachers in continuing professional development to critical reflection and analysis, and on the other hand, having successfully assisted us in our theoretical-methodological choices for teacher development in our institution.

Our research does not come to an end here, but it will continue in new settings, incorporating different proposals and developments, seeking further validation of our findings and exploring other possibilities of including concept mapping activities into other areas of professional development.

REFERENCES

Ausubel, D. P. (1963). *The psychology of meaningful verbal learning*. New York: Grune and Stratton.

Charlier, É. (2001). Formar professores profissionais para uma formação contínua articulada à prática. In P. Perrenoud, L. Paquay, M. Altet, & É. Charlier (Eds.), *Formando professores profissionais: Quais estratégias? Quais Competências?* (2nd ed., pp. 85–102). Porto Alegre: Artmed.

Freire, P. (2002). *Pedagogia da autonomia: Saberes necessários à prática educativa* (25th ed.). São Paulo: Paz e Terra.

Kagan, S., & Kagan, M. (2008). *Kagan cooperative learning*. San Clemente, CA: Kagan Publishing.

Koch, I. G. V. (2001). Lingüística textual. *Quo vadis? Revista D.E.L.T.A.* -. *Documentação de Estudos em Lingüística Teórica Aplicada, 17*, 11–23. doi:10.1590/S0102-44502001000300002

Koch, I. G. V., & Travaglia, L. C. (1999). *Texto e coerência* (6th ed.). São Paulo: Cortez.

Leite, C., & Fernandes, P. (2002). *A avaliação da aprendizagem: novos contextos, novas práticas*. Porto: ASA.

Lévy, P. (2012). Cibercultura (3rd ed.). São Paulo: Editora 34.

Loyola, F. A., & Borges, C. (2010). A pedagogia de Paulo Freire ou quando a educação se torna um ato político. In C. Gauthier, & M. Tardif (Eds.), *A pedagogia: Teorias e práticas da antiguidade aos nossos dias*. Petrópolis: Vozes.

Marcelo-Garcia, C. (2005). *Formação de professores: Para uma mudança educativa*. Porto: Porto Editora.

Mason, W., & Watts, D. (2012). *Collaborative learning in networks*. Paper presented at the National Academy of Sciences of the United States of America. Retrieved from http://www.pnas.org/content/109/3/764.full.pdf+html

Moreira, M. A. (2007). *Aprendizagem significativa: Da visão clássica à visão crítica*. Paper presented at the Encuentro Nacional sobre Enseñanza de la Matemática. Tandil, Argentina. Retrieved from http://www.if.ufrgs.br/~moreira/visaoclasicavisaocritica.pdf

Novak, J. D., & Cañas, A. J. (2007). Theoretical origins of concept maps, how to construct them and uses in education. *Reflecting Education, 3*(1), 29–42.

Novak, J. D., & Gowin, D. B. (1996). *Aprender a aprender*. Lisboa: Plátano Edições Técnicas.

Nóvoa, A. (1995). *Os professores e sua formação*. Lisbon: Dom Quixote.

Richter, M. G. (2000). *Ensino do Português e interatividade*. Santa Maria: UFSM.

Schön, D. (1983). *The reflective practitioner*. New York: Basic Books, Inc.

ADDITIONAL READING

Cañas. Alberto J. et al. (2003). *A summary of literature pertaining to the use of concept mapping techniques and technologies for education and performance support*. The Institute for Human and Machine Cognition, July 2003. Available at: http://www.ihmc.us/users/acanas/Publications/ConceptMapLitReview/IHMC%20 Literature%20Review%20on%20Concept%20Mapping.pdf. Access on 06 Apr 2010.

Kucharski, M. V. S. (2013). Concept maps as pre-writing, argument-building systematization tools: an experiment with undergraduate students. In M. Carmo (Ed.) *International Conference on Education and New Developments – END 2013* (pp.209-213)

Marriott, R. de C. V. Torres, P. L. (Eds.). (2009). Handbook of research on collaborative learning using concept mapping. Hershey, PA: IGI Global Publishing.

Novak, J. D. (2013). Meaningful learning is the foundation for creativity. In *Qurriculum: revista de teoría, investigación y práctica educativa*. n.26. Universidad de La Laguna. Santa Cruz de Tenerife, Canárias, España. (pp.27-38) Available at http://publica.Webs.ull.es/upload/REV%20QURRICULUM/26%20-%202013/Qurriculum%2026-2013(1).pdf#page=28. Access on 03 Nov 2013.

Novak, J. D., & Cañas, A. (2007) Theoretical origins of concept maps, how to construct them, and uses in Education. In *Reflecting education*. v.3, n.1, Nov. 2007 (pp.29-42). Available at http://www.reflectingeducation.net/index.php/reflecting/article/view/41/43. Access on 03 Nov 2013.

Torres, P. L., & Kucharski, M. V. S. (2012). The utilization of concept maps as knowledge-systematization and text-authoring tools in collaboration-based educational processes: the LOLA experiment. In *H. Hao-Yang, S.C. Yuen. Handbook of research on practices and outcomes in virtual worlds and environments* (Vol. I, pp. 570–586). Hershey, PA: IGI Global Publishing. doi:10.4018/978-1-4666-0011-9. ch311

Tripto, J., & Assaraf, O. B. Amit, Miriam. (2013). Mapping what they know: concept maps as an effective tool for assessing students' systems thinking. In *American Journal of Operations Research*. n.3. January 2013. Available at www.scirp.org/journal/ajor. Access on 03 Nov 2013.

KEY TERMS AND DEFINITIONS

Dialectic Process: An un-ending process in which concepts battle opposing points of view and, from this struggle, new syntheses are constructed – which, in their turn, will face opposing views and bring about new syntheses.

Dialogical: Based on dialogue, the free exchange of ideas – a fundamental part of the dialectic process.

Epistemologists: Those who dedicate themselves to the study of the nature, extent and validity of knowledge.

Genre: A specific category of artistic creations whence its products share common style, form or content.

Intra-Textual Processes: Meanings and arguments that are created within the boundaries of the written text.

Mental Models: Already incorporated schema that explain and articulate the meanings of our own worldly experiences.

Metatheory: A broader, interdisciplinary theory devised to analyze and discuss implications of other individual theories and their complementary sub-theories.

Vygotsky´s Socio-Interactionist Theory: Theoretical proposition that states that learning and development come from the interaction with more experienced peers, broadening both our scope and potential to develop new meaningful knowledge.

ENDNOTES

[1]   The term *language* is used in its broad sense, i.e., indicating human competence to abstract and translate symbolic concepts and their relationship with the world around us. Even if for the majority of people this process is mediated by spoken and written language, it surpasses this variety, including, for example, imaging and synesthetic representations.

[2]   A piece of text whose content is not very informative (i.e., which adds little or nothing to what the reader already knows about the theme/subject) can easily become a boring reading activity and end up being abandoned by the reader. On the other hand, when nearly all the text brings new content to the reader, reading can become inaccessible and can be either underutilised or even abandoned by the reader for the opposite reason: the reader is simply not able to assimilate the conceptual relations introduced because s/he lacks a previous framework with openings ready for additions supplied by the new text.

[3]   The author leaves "purposeful" ambiguities and gaps in the text in order to raise feelings such as curiosity, indignation, discovery and reflexion in the reader.

[4]   Does the author make use of suitable audience-oriented linguistic and stylistic resources, improving the possibility of productive dialogue via the text?

[5]   "According to Grosz, speaker and listener, in a dialogue, focus their attention on a small part of what they know and believe, and emphasise it. Therefore, some entities (objects and relations) are central to the dialogue and not only this, they are also used and seen through perspectives that affect what the speaker says as much as how the listener interprets it." (own translation, KOCH and TRAVAGLIA, 1999, p.82) The text and its construction, especially if we consider its construction and the author's intention, are the materialization of the critical reconstruction of a dialogical and dialectical knowledge.

[6]   Freeware developed by Novak and Cañas' team, to facilitate building concept maps that can combine text, image, audio or any other kind of relevant documentation – individually or in groups, synchronically or not. Available at http://cmap.ihmc.us

Compilation of References

(1991). *The national education goals report: Building a nation of learners*. Washington, DC: U.S. Printing Office.

Abbey, N. (2008). *Developing 21ˢᵗ century teaching and learning: Dialogic literacy*. New Horizons for Learning. Retrieved October 10, from http://www.nvit.bc.ca/docs/developing%2021st%20century%20teaching%20and%20learning%20dialogic%20literacy.pdf

Abel, W. M., & Freeze, M. (2006). Evaluation of concept mapping in an associate degree nursing program. *The Journal of Nursing Education*, *45*(9), 356–365. PMID:17002082

Abrami, P. C., Bernard, R. M., Borokhovski, E., Wade, A., Surkes, M. A., Tamim, R., & Zhang, D. (2008). Instructional interventions affecting critical thinking skills and dispositions: A stage 1 meta-analysis. *Review of Educational Research*, *78*(4), 1102–1134. doi:10.3102/0034654308326084

Adams, M. (1990). *Beginning to read: Thinking and learning about print*. New York: Bradford Books.

Afamasaga-Fuata'i, K. (2006). Innovatively developing a teaching sequence using concept maps. In A. J. Cañas, & J. D. Novak (Eds.), *Concept maps: Theory, methodology, technology: Proceedings of the second international conference on concept mapping*. San José, Costa Rica: Editorial Universidad de Costa Rica.

Ainsworth, L., & Viegut, D. (2006). *Common formative assessments: How to connect ctandards-based instruction and assessment*. Thousand Oaks, CA: Sage.

Akbari, R. (2008). Transforming lives: Introducing critical pedagogy into ELT classroom. *ELT Journal*, *62*(3), 276–283. doi:10.1093/elt/ccn025

Alejandro, A. (1997). Like happy dreams: Integrating visual arts, writing and reading. In J. Flood, S. B. Heath, & D. Lapp (Eds.), *Handbook of research on teaching literacy through the communicative and visual arts*. New York: Simon & Schuster Macmillan.

All, A. C., & Havens, R. L. (1997). Cognitive/concept mapping: A teaching strategy for nursing. *Journal of Advanced Nursing*, *25*, 1210–1219. doi:10.1046/j.1365-2648.1997.19970251210.x PMID:9181419

All, A. C., Huycke, L. I., & Fisher, M. J. (2003). Instructional tools for nursing education: Concept maps. *Nursing Education Perspectives*, *24*(6), 311–317. PMID:14705401

Ambrose, S. A., Bridges, M. W., DiPietro, M., Lovett, C., & Norman, M. (2010). *How learning works: Seven research-based principles for smart teaching*. San Francisco, CA: Josey-Bass.

American Association for the Advancement of Science (AAAS). (1989). *Science for all Americans*. New York: Oxford University Press.

American Association for the Advancement of Science (AAAS). (1993). *Benchmarks for science literacy*. New York: Oxford University Press.

American Association for the Advancement of Science (AAAS). (2001). *Atlas of science literacy* (Vol. 1). American Washington, DC: Association for the Advancement of Science and the National Science Teachers Association.

American Philosophical Association. (1990). Critical thinking: A statement of expert consensus for purpose of educational assessment and instruction. Columbus, OH: Center on Education and Training for Employment, College of Education, The Ohio State University (ERIC) Document Reproduction No. ED 315-423.

Anderson, L. W., & Krathwohl, D. R. (Eds.). (2001). A taxonomy for learning, teaching and assessing: A revision of Bloom's taxonomy of educational objectives: Complete Ed. New York: Longman.

Anderson, M. (2007). What about Bob? *MedEdPORTAL*. Retrieved from http://services.aamc.org/30/mededportal/servlet/s/segment/mededportal/?subid=684

Anderson, M. (2008). Fred and Wilma's lucky day. *MedEdPORTAL*. Retrieved from http://services.aamc.org/30/mededportal/servlet/s/segment/mededportal/?subid=1675

Anderson, M. (2009). Rachel Jacobson's painful hip. *MedEdPORTAL*. Retrieved from http://services.aamc.org/30/mededportal/servlet/s/segment/mededportal/?subid=7702

Anderson, M., & Kirkish, M. (2007). Sophie Claiborne's upset stomach - An ornithine transcarbamolyase deficiency problem-based learning case. *MedEdPORTAL*. Retrieved from http://services.aamc.org/30/mededportal/servlet/s/segment/mededportal/?subid=642

Anderson, L. W., & Krathwohl, D. R. (Eds.). (2001). *A taxonomy for learning, teaching, and assessing: A revision of Bloom's taxonomy of educational objectives*. New York: Longman.

Andriessen, J. E. B., Baker, M. J., & Suthers, D. (2003). *Arguing to learn: Confronting cognitions in computer-supported collaborative learning environments*. Dordrecht, The Netherlands: Kluwer Academic. doi:10.1007/978-94-017-0781-7

Andriessen, J. E. B., & Schwarz, B. B. (2009). Argumentative design. In N. Muller Mirza, & A.-N. Perret Clermont (Eds.), *Argumentation and education: Theoretical foundations and practices* (pp. 145–176). Dordrecht, The Netherlands: Springer. doi:10.1007/978-0-387-98125-3_6

Anning, A. (2003). Pathways to the graphicacy club: The crossroad of home and pre-school. *Journal of Early Childhood Literacy*, 4(1), 109–128.

Anohina-Naumeca, A., & Graudina, V. (2012). Diversity of concept mapping tasks: Degree of difficulty, directedness, and task constraints. In A. J. Cañas, J. D. Novak & J. Vanhear (Eds.), *Concept maps: Theory, methodology, technology, proceedings of the fifth international conference on concept mapping*. Valletta, Malta: Academic Press.

Antonetti, J. (2008). *Using writing as a measure and model of thinking*. Phoenix, AZ: Flying Monkeys Press.

Compilation of References

Arum, R., & Roksa, J. (2011). *Academically adrift: Limited learning on college campuses.* Chicago: University of Chicago Press.

Ashton, D. (1985). *Twentieth century artists on art.* New York: Pantheon Books.

Asterhan, C. S. C., & Eisenmann, T. (2009). Online and face-to-face discussions in the classroom: A study on the experiences of active and silent students. In C. O'Malley, D. Suthers, P. Reimann, & A. Dimitracopoulou (Eds.), *Computer supported collaborative learning practices: CSCL2009 conference proceedings* (pp. 132–136). Rhodes, Greece: CSCL.

Asterhan, C. S. C., Gil, J., & Schwarz, B. B. (2008). Students' perspectives on e-moderation of synchronous argumentation. In Y. Eshet-Alkalai, A. Caspi, & N. Geri (Eds.), *Proceedings of the 2008 Chais Conference on Instructional Technologies Research: Learning in the Technological Era* (pp. 102-103). Raanana: Open University Press.

Asterhan, C. S. C. (2011). Assessing e-moderation behavior from synchronous discussion protocols with a multi-dimensional methodology. *Computers in Human Behavior, 27,* 449–458. doi:10.1016/j.chb.2010.09.008

Asterhan, C. S. C., & Schwarz, B. B. (2009). Transformation of robust misconceptions through peer argumentation. In B. B. Schwarz, T. Dreyfus, & R. Hershkowitz (Eds.), *Transformation of knowledge through classroom interaction* (pp. 159–172). New York, NY: Routledge.

Asterhan, C. S. C., & Schwarz, B. B. (2010). On-line moderation of small group discussions. *International Journal of Computer-Supported Collaborative Learning, 5,* 259–282. doi:10.1007/s11412-010-9088-2

Asterhan, C. S. C., Schwarz, B. B., & Gil, J. (2012). Small-group, computer-mediated argumentation in middle-school classrooms: The effects of gender and different types of online teacher guidance. *The British Journal of Educational Psychology, 82*(3), 375–397. doi:10.1111/j.2044-8279.2011.02030.x PMID:22881045

Atkinson, D. (1997). A critical approach to critical thinking in TESOL. *TESOL Quarterly, 31*(1), 71–94. doi:10.2307/3587975

Ausubel, D. P. (1963). *The psychology of meaningful verbal learning.* New York: Grune & Stratton.

Ausubel, D. P. (2000). *The acquisition and retention of knowledge.* Dordrecht, The Netherlands: Kluwer. doi:10.1007/978-94-015-9454-7

Ausubel, D. P., Novak, J. D., & Hanesian, H. (1978). *Educational psychology: A cognitive view.* New York: Holt, Rinehart, & Winston.

Azila, N. M., Tan, N. H., & Tan, C. P. L. (2006). Inducing curricular change: Initial evaluation of outcomes. *Medical Education, 40,* 123–1147. doi:10.1111/j.1365-2929.2006.02574.x PMID:17054624

Baddeley, A. D. (1976). *The psychology of memory.* New York: Basic Books, Inc.

Baddeley, A. D. (2007). *Working memory, thought and action.* Oxford, UK: Oxford University Press. doi:10.1093/acprof:oso/9780198528012.001.0001

Bailin, S. (2002). Critical thinking and science education. *Science & Education, 11*(4), 361–375. doi:10.1023/A:1016042608621

Bailin, S., Case, Coombs, & Daniels. (1999). Conceptualizing critical thinking. *Journal of Curriculum Studies, 31*(3), 285–302. doi:10.1080/002202799183133

Bamford, A. (2003). *Visual literacy white paper*. Retrieved December 17, 2011, from http://wwwimages.adobe.com/www.adobe.com/content/dam/Adobe/en/education/pdfs/visual-literacy-wp.pdf

Bamford, A. (2009). *The wow factor: Global research compendium on the impact of the arts in education*. New York: Waxman Munster.

Barr, R. B., & Tagg, J. (1995). From teaching to learning: A new paradigm for undergraduate education. *Change, 27*(6), 13–25. doi:10.1080/00091383.1995.10544672

Baugh, N., & Mellott, K. (1998). Clinical concept mapping as preparation for student nurses' clinical experiences. *The Journal of Nursing Education, 37*, 253–256. PMID:9749811

Bazerman, C., Little, J., Bethel, L., Chavkin, T., Fouquette, D., & Garfus, J. (2005). *Reference guide to writing across the curriculum (WAC)*. West Lafayette, IN: Parlor Press and WAC Clearinghouse.

Bean, J. (2011). *Engaging ideas: The professor's guide to integrating writing, critical thinking, and active learning in the classroom*. San Francisco, CA: Jossey Bass.

Beaudry, J., & Wilson, P. (2009). *Concept mapping and formative assessment: Elements supporting literacy and learning*. Retrieved from https://blackboard.une.edu/Webct/RelativeResourceManager/Template/Session5/ConceptMappingandFormativeAssessment.pdf

Beaudry, J., Burden, K., Keuchel, T., & Snyder, K. (2011). *Cross-cultural digital storytelling: Implications for pedagogical innovation in schools*. Paper presentation at the DIVERSE Conference. Dublin, Ireland.

Beaudry, J., & Wilson, P. (2010). Concept mapping and formative assessment: Elements supporting literacy and learning. In *Handbook of research on collaborative learning using concept mapping*. Hershey, PA: IGI Publishing.

Beitz, J. M. (1998). Concept mapping: Navigating the learning process. *Nurse Educator, 23*(5), 35–41. doi:10.1097/00006223-199809000-00015 PMID:9866562

Bell, P. (1997). Using argument representations to make thinking visible for individuals and groups. In R. Hall, N. Miyake, & N. Enyedy (Eds.), *Proceedings of CSCL '97: The Second International Conference on Computer Support for Collaborative Learning* (pp. 10-19). Toronto: University of Toronto Press.

Bell, P., & Linn, M. (2000). Scientific arguments as learning artifacts: Designing for learning from the web with KIE. *International Journal of Science Education, 22*, 797–817. doi:10.1080/095006900412284

Benesch, S. (1993). Critical thinking: A learning process for democracy. *TESOL Quarterly, 27*(3), 545–548. doi:10.2307/3587485

Benesch, S. (1999). Thinking critically, thinking dialogically. *TESOL Quarterly, 33*(3), 573–580. doi:10.2307/3587682

Berge, Z. L. (1997). Characteristics of online teaching in post-secondary, formal education. *Educational Technology, 37*(3), 35–47.

Bernstein, B. (1990). Class, codes and control: Vol. IV. *The structuring of pedagogic discourse*. London: Routledge. doi:10.4324/9780203011263

Bernstein, B. (2000). *Pedagogy, symbolic control and identity*. Lanham, MD: Rowman & Littlefield.

Compilation of References

Beşoluk, Ş., & Önder, İ. (2010). Investigation of teacher candidates' learning approaches, learning styles and critical thinking dispositions. *Elementary Education Online, 9*(2), 679–693.

Bierer, S. B., Dannefer, E. F., Taylor, C., Hall, P., & Hull, A. (2008). Methods to assess students' acquisition, application and integration of basic science knowledge in an innovative competency-based curriculum. *Medical Teacher, 30*(7), e171–e177. doi:10.1080/01421590802139740 PMID:18777415

Black, E. (1979). *Rhetorical criticism: A study in method.* Madison, WI: University of Wisconsin Press.

Bloom, B. S., Engelhart, M. D., Furst, E. J., Hill, W. H., & Krathwohl, D. R. (1956). *Taxonomy of educational objectives: The classification of educational goals, handbook I: Cognitive domain.* New York: Longmans, Green.

Bloxham, S. (2009). Marking and moderation in the UK: False assumptions and wasted resources. *Assessment & Evaluation in Higher Education, 34*(2), 209–220. doi:10.1080/02602930801955978

Boghossian, P. (2012). Critical thinking and constructivism: Mambo dog fish to the banana patch. *Journal of Philosophy of Education, 46*(1), 73–84. doi:10.1111/j.1467-9752.2011.00832.x

Bok, D. (2006). *Our underachieving colleges: A candid look at how much students learn and why they should be learning more.* Princeton, NJ: Princeton University Press.

Bolte Taylor, J. (2006). *My stroke of insight: A brain scientist's personal journey.* New York: Plume.

Boudreau, J. D., Jagosh, J., Slee, R., Macdonald, M. E., & Steinert, Y. (2008). Patients' perspectives on physicians' roles: Implications for curricular reform. *Academic Medicine, 83*(8), 744–753. doi:10.1097/ACM.0b013e31817eb4c0 PMID:18667888

Bowen, J. L. (2006). Medical education: Educational strategies to promote clinical diagnostic reasoning. *The New England Journal of Medicine, 355,* 2217–2225. doi:10.1056/NEJMra054782 PMID:17124019

Brookfield, S. (1995). *Becoming a critically reflective teacher.* San Francisco, CA: Jossey Bass.

Brookfield, S. D. (2012). *Teaching for critical thinking: Tools and techniques to help students question their assumptions.* San Francisco, CA: Jossey-Bass.

Brookfield, S., & Preskill, S. (2005). *Discussion as a way of teaching: Tools and techniques for democratic classrooms* (2nd ed.). San Francisco, CA: Josey Bass.

Brown, S. (2011, March). *Sunni Brown: Doodlers unite!* [Video file]. Retrieved September 30, 2011 from http://www.ted.com/talks/sunni_brown.html

Brown, M. N., & Kelley, S. M. (1986). *Asking the right questions: A guide to critical thinking* (7th ed.). Englewood Cliffs, NJ: Prentice Hall.

Brumberger, E. (2011). Visual literacy and the digital native: An examination of the millennial learner. *Journal of Visual Literacy, 30*(1), 19–46.

Brunvand, S., & Byrd, S. (2011). Using VoiceThread to promote learning engagement and success for all students. *Teaching Exceptional Children, 1*(3), 28–37.

Burbules, N. C., & Berk, R. (1999). Critical thinking and critical pedagogy: Relations, differences, and limits. In T. S. Popkewitz, & L. Fendler (Eds.), *Critical theories in education*. New York: Routledge.

Burden, K., & Atkinson, S. (2008). Evaluating pedagogical affordances of media sharing web 2.0 technologies: A case study. In *Proceedings Ascilite*. Melbourne: Ascilite.

Burmark, L. (2002). *Visual literacy: Learn to see, see to learn*. Alexandria, VA: Association for Supervision and Curriculum Development.

Buzan, T. (1974). *Use both sides of your brain*. New York: E. P. Dutton.

Buzan, T. (1996). *The mind map book, How to use radiant thinking to maximize your brain's untapped potential*. New York, NY: Penguin Books.

Buzan, T., & Buzan, B. (2006). *The mind map book: How to use radiant thinking to maximize your brain's untapped potential*. Upper Saddle River, NJ: Pearson Education.

Caduto, M. J. (1985). *Pond and brook*. Englewood Cliffs, NJ: Prentice-Hall, Inc.

Caine, R., & Caine, G. (1991). *Making connections: Teaching and the human brain*. Association for Supervision and Curriculum Development.

Calkins, L. (1994). *The art of teaching writing*. Portsmouth, NH: Heinemann.

Calkins, L. (2011). *A curricular plan for the writing workshop grade 3*. Portsmouth, NH: Heinemann.

Calkins, L., Ehrenworth, M., & Lehman, C. (2012). *Pathways to the common core: Accelerating achievement*. Portsmouth, NH: Heinemann.

Callahan, D. (1998). Medical education and the goals of medicine. *Medical Teacher, 20*, 85–86. doi:10.1080/01421599881147

Cañas, A. J., & Novak, J. D. (Eds.). (2006). Concept maps: Theory, methodology, technology. In *Proceedings from the Second International Conference on Concept Mapping*. San José, Costa Rica: Universidad de Costa Rica.

Cañas, A. J., Hill, G., Carff, R., Suri, N., Lott, J., Eskridge, T., & Carvajal, R. (2004). CmapTools: A knowledge modeling and sharing environment. In A. J. Cañas, J. D. Novak & F. M. González (Eds.), *Proceedings of the First International Conference on Concept Mapping* (Vol. 1, pp. 125-133). Multibaja, Spain: Novatext.

Cañas, A. J., Novak, J. D., & González, F. M. (Eds.). (2004). Concept maps: Theory, methodology, technology. In *Proceedings from the First International Conference on Concept Mapping*. Multibaja, Spain: Novatext.

Cañas, A. J., Novak, J. D., & Reiska, P. (2012). Freedom vs. restriction of content and structure during concept mapping – Possibilities and limitations for construction and assessment. In *Concept maps: Theory, methodology, technology: Proceedings of the fifth international conference on concept mapping*. Valletta, Malta: Academic Press.

Cañas, A., Bunch, L., & Priit, R. (2010). Cmapanalysis: An extensible concept map analysis tool. In A. J. Cañas, J. D. Novak & J. Sánchez (Eds.), *Concept maps: Theory, methodology, technology, proceedings of the fourth international conference on concept mapping.* Viña del Mar, Chile: Academic Press.

Cañas, A. J. (2003). *A summary of literature pertaining to the use of concept mapping techniques and technologies or education and performance support.* Pensacola, FL: The Institute for Human and Machine Cognition.

Cappelle, G., Crippin, G., & Lundgren, U. (2010). *Emerging global dimensions in education.* London, UK: CiCe Network Working Group.

Carey, S., & Smith, C. (1993). On understanding the nature of scientific knowledge. *Educational Psychologist, 28*(3), 235–251. doi:10.1207/s15326985ep2803_4

Carney, E. (2011). *Cats vs. dogs.* Washington, DC: National Geographic Society.

Carraccio, C. L., Benson, B. J., Nixon, L. J., & Derstine, P. L. (2008). From the educational bench to the clinical bedside: Translating the Dreyfus developmental model to the learning of clinical skills. *Academic Medicine, 83*(8), 761–767. doi:10.1097/ACM.0b013e31817eb632 PMID:18667892

Carter, R. (1998). *Mapping the mind.* Berkeley, CA: University of California Press.

Case, R. (2005). Moving critical thinking to the main stage. *Education Canada, 45*(2), 45–49.

Chabeli, M. (2010). Concept-mapping as a teaching method to facilitate critical thinking in nursing education: A review of the literature. *Health SA Gesondheit, 15*(1).

Chan, C. (2009). *Assessment: Concept map, assessment resources@HKU.* University of Hong Kong. Retrieved from http://ar.cetl.hku.hk

Chang, S., & Chang, Y. (2008). Using online concept mapping with peer learning to enhance concept application. *Quarterly Review of Distance Education, 9*(1), 17–27.

Charlier, É. (2001). Formar professores profissionais para uma formação contínua articulada à prática. In P. Perrenoud, L. Paquay, M. Altet, & É. Charlier (Eds.), *Formando professores profissionais: Quais estratégias? Quais Competências?* (2nd ed., pp. 85–102). Porto Alegre: Artmed.

Chen, S. L., Liang, T., Lee, M. L., & Liao, I. C. (2011). Effects of concept map teaching on students' critical thinking and approach to learning and studying. *The Journal of Nursing Education, 50*(8), 466–469. doi:10.3928/01484834-20110415-06 PMID:21524017

Chinn, C. A., & Brewer, W. F. (1998). An empirical test of a taxonomy of responses to anomalous data in science. *Journal of Research in Science Teaching, 35*(6), 623–654. doi:10.1002/(SICI)1098-2736(199808)35:6<623::AID-TEA3>3.0.CO;2-O

Chiu, M. M. (2004). Adapting teacher interventions to student needs during cooperative learning: How to improve student problem solving and time on-task. *American Educational Research Journal, 41*, 365–399. doi:10.3102/00028312041002365

Clariana, R. B. (2010). Deriving individual and group knowledge structure from network diagrams and from essays. In Computer-based diagnostics and systematic analysis of knowledge (pp. 117–130). Berlin: Springer Science + Business Media.

Clariana, R. B., & Taricani, E. M. (2010). The consequences of increasing the number of terms used to score open-ended concept maps. *International Journal of Instructional Media*, *37*(2), 218–226.

Clayton, L. H. (2006). Concept mapping: An effective teaching-learning method. *Nursing Education Perspectives*, *27*(4), 197–203. PMID:16921805

Cochrane, P. (1999). *CapeUK-creativity matters: Are we really serious about creativity? In all our futures: Creativity, culture, and education*. Retrieved from www.qca.org.uk

Coffey, J. W., Carnot, M. J., Feltovich, P. J., Feltovich, J., Hoffman, R. R., Cañas, A. J., & Novak, J. D. (2003). A summary of literature pertaining to the use of concept mapping techniques and technologies for education and performance support (Technical Report for the Chief of Naval Education and Training). Pensacola, FL: IHMC - Institute for Human and Machine Cognition. Retrieved from http://www.ihmc.us/users/acanas/Publications/ConceptMapLitReview/IHMC Literature Review on Concept Mapping.pdf

Cohen, A. M. (2006). *Untangling the knot*. Southfield, MI: Targum Press.

Condon, W., & Kelly-Riley, D. (2004). Assessing and teaching what we value: The relationship between college level writing and critical thinking abilities. *Assessing Writing*, *9*, 56–75. doi:10.1016/j.asw.2004.01.003

Cooter, B., & Perkins, H. (2011). Much done, much yet to do. *The Reading Teacher*, *64*(8), 563–566.

Copeland, M. (2005). *Socratic circles: Fostering critical and creative thinking*. Portland, MN: Stenhouse Publishers.

Corcoran, T., Mosher, F., & Rogat, A. (2009). *Learning progressions in science: An evidence-based approach to reform*. Philadelphia: Consortium for Policy Research in Education.

Cottrell, S. (2005). *Critical thinking skills: Developing effective analysis and argument*. London: Palgrave Macmillan.

Cribb, A., & Gewirtz, S. (2006). Doctoral student supervision in a managerial climate. *International Studies in Sociology of Education*, *16*(3), 223–236. doi:10.1080/09620210601037787

Çubukcu, Z. (2006). Critical thinking dispositions of the Turkish teacher candidates. *The Turkish Online Journal of Educational Technology*, *5*(4), 22–36.

Daley, B., Torre, D., Stark-Schweitzer, T., Siddartha, S., Ziebert, M., & Petkova, J. (2006). Advancing teaching and learning in medical education through the use of concept maps. In A. J. Cañas & J. D. Novak (Eds.), *Proceedings of the Second International Conference on Concept Mapping*. San José, Costa Rica: Universidad de Costa Rica.

Daley, B. J. et al. (1999). Concept maps: A strategy to teach and evaluate critical thinking. *The Journal of Nursing Education*, *38*(1). PMID:9921788

Daley, B. J., & Torre, D. M. (2010). Concept maps in medical education: An analytical literature review. *Medical Education*, *44*(5), 440–448. doi:10.1111/j.1365-2923.2010.03628.x PMID:20374475

Danby, S. J., & Lee, A. (2012). Framing doctoral pedagogy as design and action. In *Reshaping doctoral education: International approaches and pedagogies*. London: Routledge.

Daniels, H. (1996). *An introduction to Vygotsky*. New York: Routledge.

Daniels, H. A. (1990). Developing a sense of audience. In T. Shanahan (Ed.), *Reading and writing together: New per-spectives for the classroom* (pp. 99–125). Norwood, MA: Christopher-Gordon.

Davies, M. (2010). Concept mapping, mind mapping and argument mapping: What are the differences and do they matter? *Higher Education*, *62*(3), 279–301. doi:10.1007/s10734-010-9387-6

Davies, M. (2011). Introduction to the special issue on critical thinking in higher education. *Higher Education Research & Development*, *30*(3), 255–260. doi:10.1080/07294360.2011.562145

De Groot, R., Drachman, R., Hever, R., Schwarz, B. B., Hoppe, U., Harrer, A., & Baurens, B. (2007). Computer supported moderation of e-discussions: The ARGU-NAUT approach. In C. A. Chinn, G. Erkens, & S. Puntambekar (Eds.), *Mice, minds, and society: Proceedings of the 2007 computer supported collaborative learning (CSCL) conference* (pp. 165–167). New Brunswick, NJ: Rutgers University.

De Vries, E., Lund, C., & Baker, M. (2002). Computer-mediated epistemic dialogue: Explanation and argumentation as vehicles for understanding scientific notions. *Journal of the Learning Sciences*, *11*(1), 63–103. doi:10.1207/S15327809JLS1101_3

Deardorff, D. K. (2004). *The identification and assessment of intercultural competence as a student outcome of internationalization at institutions of higher education in the United States.* (Doctoral Dissertation). North Carolina State University.

DeBono, E. (1985). *Six thinking hats.* Boston: Little Brown and Company.

deCharon, A., Albright, Herren, Cline, & Repa. (2009). Online tools help get scientists and educators on the same page. *Eos, Transactions, American Geophysical Union*, *90*(34), 289–290. doi:10.1029/2009EO340002

deCharon, A., Duguay, McDonnell, Peach, Companion, Herren, … Whitley. (2013). Concept mapping workshops: Helping ocean scientists represent and communicate science. *Oceanography (Washington, D.C.)*, *26*(1), 98–105. doi:10.5670/oceanog.2013.08

Delécluze, E.-J. (1983). *Louis David, son école et son temps*. Paris: Didier.

Demirhan, E., Beşoluk, Ş., & Önder, İ. (2011). The change in academic achievement and critical thinking disposition scores of pre-service science teachers over time. *Western Anatolia Journal of Educational Science*, 403-406.

Denzin, N., & Lincoln, Y. (1994). *Handbook of qualitative research*. Thousand Oaks, CA: Sage Publications.

Derbentseva, N., Safayeni, F., & Cañas, A. J. (2004). Experiments on the effect of map structure and concept quantification during concept map construction. In A. J. Cañas, J. D. Novak & F. M. González (Eds.), *Concept maps: Theory, methodology, technology, proceedings of the first international conference on concept mapping*. Pamplona, Spain: Universidad Pública de Navarra.

Derbentseva, N., Safayeni, F., & Cañas, A. J. (2006). Two strategies for encouraging functional relationships in concept maps. In A. J. Cañas & J. D. Novak (Eds.), *Concept maps: Theory, methodology, technology: Proceedings of the second international conference on concept mapping*. San Jose, Costa Rica: Universidad de Costa Rica.

Dewey, J. (1998). Experience and education: The 60th anniversary Ed. West Lafayett, IN: Kappa Delta Pi.

Dewey, J. (1910). *How we think*. Boston: DC Heath & Co. doi:10.1037/10903-000

Dexter, D. D., & Hughes, C. A. (2011). Graphic organizers and students with learning disabilities: A meta-analysis. *Learning Disability Quarterly*, *34*(1), 51–72.

Dickinson, D. (2002). Learning through the arts. *New Horizons for Learning*. Retrieved from http://derryasd.schoolwires.com/725493911205726/lib/725493911205726/Learning_Through_the_Arts.pdf

Dochy, F. J. R. C. (1992). *Assessment of prior knowledge or expertise as a determinant for future learning: The use of prior knowledge state tests and knowledge profiles*. London: Jessica Kingsley.

Donaldson, G. (2007). What do teachers bring to leadership? *Educational Leadership*, *65*(1), 26–29.

Dondis, D. A. (1973). *A primer of visual literacy*. Cambridge, MA: MIT Press.

Donovan, C., & Smolkin, L. (2011). Supporting informational writing in the elementary grades. *The Reading Teacher*, 406–416. doi:10.1598/RT.64.6.2

Dorfman, L., & Cappelli, R. (2009). *Mentor texts: Teaching informational writing through children's literature K-8*. Portland, ME: Stenhouse.

Dubowski, C. (2009). *Shark attack*. New York, NY: DK Publishing.

Duhigg, C. (2012). *The power of habit: Why we do what we do in life and business*. New York: Random House.

Duke, N., & Bennett-Armistead, S. (2003). *Reading and writing informational text in the primary grades*. New York: Scholastic.

Dunlap, J. C., & Grabinger, R. S. (1996). Rich environments for active learning in the higher education classroom. In B. G. Wilson (Ed.), *Constructivist learning environments: Case studies in instructional design* (pp. 65–82). Englewood Cliffs, NJ: Educational Technology Publications.

Dunleavy, J., & Milton, P. (2009). *What did you do in school today? Exploring the concept of student engagement and its implications for teaching and learning in Canada*. Toronto, Canada: Canadian Education Association.

Dweck, C. S. (2007/2008). The secret to raising smart kids. *Scientific American Mind*, *18*(6), 36–43. doi:10.1038/scientificamericanmind1207-36

Dyson, A. (1989). *Multiple worlds of childwriters: Friends learning to write*. New York: Teachers College Press.

Edwards, A. (2001). Qualitative designs and analysis. In G. MacNaughton, S. A. Rolfe, & I. Siraj-Blatchford (Eds.), *Doing early childhood research: International perspectives on theory and practice* (pp. 117–135). Crows Nest, Australia: Alen & Unwin.

Eisner, E. (2002). *The arts and the creation of mind*. New Haven, CT: Yale Unversity Press.

Eitel, F., & Steiner, S. (1999). Evidence-based learning. *Medical Teacher*, *25*(5), 506–513.

Ennis, R. H. (1985). A logical basis for measuring critical thinking skills. *Educational Leadership*, *43*(2), 44–48.

Ennis, R. H. (1989). Critical thinking and subject specificity: Clarification and needed research. *Educational Researcher*, *18*(3), 4–10. doi:10.3102/0013189X018003004

Compilation of References

Epstein, A. (2003). Me, you, us: Social-emotional learning in preschool. *Young Children*, *58*(5), 28–36.

Erikson, L. H. (2007). *Concept-based curriculum and instruction for the thinking classroom*. Thousand Oaks, CA: Corwin Press.

European Commission on Education. (2007). *Key competencies for lifelong learning: A European framework*. Retrieved April 12, 2010, from http://ec.europa.eu/dgs/education_culture/publ/pdf/ll-learning/keycomp_en.pdf

Facione, P. A. (1995). *Critical thinking and clinical judgment: Goals for nursing science*. Paper presented at the Annual Meeting of the Western Institute of Nursing. San Diego, CA.

Facione, P. W. (1990). *Critical thinking: A statement of expert consensus for purposes of educational assessment and instruction, executive summary*. Millbrae, CA: California Academic Press. Retrieved from http://assessment.aas.duke.edu/documents/Delphi_Report.pdf

Facione, P. A. (2000). The disposition toward critical thinking: Its character, measurement, and relation to crtitical thinking skill. *Informal Logic*, *20*(1), 61–84.

Faigley, L., George, D., Palchik, A., & Selfe, C. (2004). *Some questions for analyzing images in picturing texts*. New York: W. W. Norton & Co.

Felton, M., & Kuhn, D. (2001). The development of discourse skills. *Discourse Processes*, *32*(2-3). doi:10.1080/0163853X.2001.9651595

Filiz, M., Trumpower, D. L., & Atas, S. (2012). Analysis of how well a concept mapping website conforms to principles of effective assessment for learning. In A. J. Cañas, J. D. Novak & J. Vanhear (Eds.), *Proceedings of the Fifth International Conference on Concept Mapping* (Vol. 2). Malta: Veritas Press.

Fisher, A. (2001). *Critical thinking: An introduction*. Cambridge, UK: Cambridge University Press.

Floyd, C. B. (2011). Critical thinking in a second language. *Higher Education Research & Development*, *30*(3), 289–302. doi:10.1080/07294360.2010.501076

Flynt, E., & Brozo, W. (2011). It's all about the teacher. *The Reading Teacher*, *62*(6), 536–538. doi: doi:10.1598/RT.62.6

Flyvbjerg, B. (2006). Five misunderstandings about case-study research. *Qualitative Inquiry*, *12*(2), 219–245. doi:10.1177/1077800405284363

Fonseca, A. P., & Extremina. (2008). Concept maps as tools for scientific research in microbiology: A case study. In *Proceedings of the Third International Conference on Concept Mapping*. Tallinn, Estonia: Academic Press.

Forstd, N., & Taylor, R. (2001). Patterns of change in the university: The impact of "lifelong learning" and the "world of work". *Studies in the Education of Adults*, *33*(1), 49–60.

Foss, S. K. (1989). Rhetorical criticism as the asking of questions. *Communication Education*, *38*(3), 191–196. doi:10.1080/03634528909378755

Foss, S. K. (1992). Visual imagery as communication. *Text and Performance Quarterly, 12*(1), 85–90. doi:10.1080/10462939209359638

Foss, S. K. (2009). A rhetorical schema for the evaluation of visual imagery. *Communication Studies, 45*(3-4), 213–224. doi:10.1080/10510979409368425

Foster, J., & Wiser, M. (2012). The potential of learning progression research to inform the design of state science standards. In *Learning progressions in science: Current challenges and future directions* (pp. 435–459). Rotterdam, The Netherlands: Sense Publishers. doi:10.1007/978-94-6091-824-7_18

Framework for 21st Century Skills. (2009). *A product of partnership for 21st century skills.* Retrieved October 10, 2012, from http://www.p21.org/storage/documents/P21_Framework.pdf

Freire, P. (2002). *Pedagogia da autonomia: Saberes necessários à prática educativa* (25th ed.). São Paulo: Paz e Terra.

Frijters, S., Geert, T. D., & Rijlaarsdam, G. (2008). Effects of dialogic learning on value-loaded critical thinking. *Learning and Instruction, 18*, 66–82. doi:10.1016/j.learninstruc.2006.11.001

Fulghum, R. (1986). *All I really need to know I learned in kindergarten.* New York: Ballantine Books.

Gage, N. L., & Berliner, D. C. (1992). *Educational psychology* (5th ed.). Boston, MA: Houghton Mifflin Company.

Gaines, B. R., Mildred, L., & Shaw, G. (1995). Collaboration through concept maps. In *Proceedings of CSCL, '95.* Retrieved, September 15, 2012, from http://pages.cpsc.ucalgary.ca/~gaines/reports/LW/CSCL95CM/CSCL95CM.pdf

Galyean, B. C. (1983). *Mind sight: Learning through Imagining.* Long Beach, CA: Center for Integrative Learning.

Garmon, M. A. (2001, Fall). The benefits of dialogue journals: What prospective teachers say. *Teacher Education Quarterly,* 37–50.

Garrison, D. R., Anderson, T., & Archer, W. (2001). Critical thinking, cognitive presence, and computer conferencing in distance education. *American Journal of Distance Education, 15*(1), 7–23. doi:10.1080/08923640109527071

Garside, C. (1996). Look who's talking: A comparison of lecture and group discussion teaching strategies in developing critical thinking skills. *Communication Education, 45,* 212–227. doi:10.1080/03634529609379050

Geissner, H. K. (2008). René Magritte: Thought pictures of rhetorical communication. In *Applied communication in organizational and international contexts.* St.Ingbert, Germany: Röhrig Universitätsverlag.

Gibbs, G. (1981, December). *Twenty terrible reasons for lecturing* (SCEDSIP Occasional Paper No.8). Birmingham, UK: SCED Publications.

Gibbs, G. (1992). *Improving the quality of student learning: Based on the improving student learning project funded by the CNAA.* Oxford, UK: Technical & Education Services Limited.

Gil, J., Schwarz, B. B., & Asterhan, C. S. C. (2007). Intuitive moderation styles and beliefs of teachers in CSCL-based argumentation. In C. A. Chinn, G. Erkens, & S. Puntambekar (Eds.), *Mice, minds, and society: Proceedings of the 2007 computer supported collaborative learning (CSCL) conference* (pp. 219–229). New Brunswick, NJ: Rutgers University.

Gillies, R. M., & Khan, A. (2009). Promoting reasoned argumentation, problem-solving and learning during small-group work. *Cambridge Journal of Education, 39*, 7–27. doi:10.1080/03057640802701945

Gillis, A., Luthin, K., Parette, H. P., & Blum, C. (2012). Using VoiceThread to create meaningful receptive and expressive learning activities for young children. *Early Childhood Education Journal, 40*, 203–211. doi:10.1007/s10643-012-0521-1

Glachan, M., & Light, P. (1982). Peer interaction and learning: Can two wrongs make a right? In G. Butterworth, & P. Light (Eds.), *Social cognition: Studies in the development of understanding* (pp. 238–262). Chicago: University of Chicago Press.

Glynn, S. M., & Duit, R. (1995). Learning science meaningfully: Constructing conceptual models. In S. Glynn, & R. Duit (Eds.), *Learning science in the schools: Research reforming practice* (pp. 3–33). Mahwah, NJ: Lawrence Erlbaum Associates.

Goltzberg, S. (2012). *Théorie bidimensionnelle de l'argumentation: Présomption et argument a fortiori*. Brussels: Bruylant.

Gomez, G. (2008). *Use of concept maps for student assessment in an aviation medicine graduate programme (Research Report for the CALT Grant Committee)*. New Zealand: University of Otago.

Gonzalez-Acquaro, K., & Preskill, S. (2011). Using the four lenses of critical reflection to promote collaboration and support creative adaptations of web 2.0 tools in an online environment. In F. Pozzi, & D. Persico (Eds.), *Techniques for fostering collaboration in online learning communities: Theoretical and practical perspectives*. Hershey, PA: IGI Global.

Gonzalez, K., Frumkin, R., & Lauria, J. (2012). Study groups and service learning: A framework for discussion to engage preservice teachers. In T. Murphy, & J. Tan (Eds.), *Service learning and educating in challenging contexts: International perspectives. Location*. Continuum Publishers.

Gorman, J. (2008). Concept map advance organizers. In *Engineering the future: Science, technology, and the design process*. Emeryville, CA: Key Curriculum.

Grabau, L. J. (2007). Effective teaching and learning strategies for critical thinking to foster cognitive development and transformational learning. *Kentucky Journal for Excellence in College Teaching and Learning, 5*, 123–156.

Greene, M. (1988). *The dialectic of freedom*. New York: Teachers College Press.

Greene, M. (1995). *Releasing the imagination: Essays on education, the arts and social change*. San Francisco: Jossey-Bass.

Gretton, T. (2000). *The death of Marat*. New York: Cambridge University Press.

Gudykunst, W. B. (2004). *Bridging differences: Effective intergroup communication* (4th ed.). Thousand Oaks, CA: Sage Publications.

Gudykunst, W. B., & Kim, Y. Y. (1997). *Communicating with strangers* (3rd ed.). New York: McGraw-Hill.

Guiller, J., Durndell, A., & Ross, A. (2008). Peer interaction and critical thinking: Face-to-face or online discussion. *Learning and Instruction, 18*, 187–200. doi:10.1016/j.learninstruc.2007.03.001

Gurlitt, J., & Renkl, A. (2008). Are high-coherent concept maps better for prior knowledge activation? Differential effects of concept mapping tasks on high school vs. university students. *Journal of Computer Assisted Learning*, 24(5), 407–419. doi:10.1111/j.1365-2729.2008.00277.x

Haist, S. A., Swanson, D. B., Holtzman, K. Z., & Grande, J. P. (2010). *The scientific foundations of medicine: Going beyond the first two years of medical school*. Paper presented at the Fourteenth Annual Meeting of the International Association of Medical Science Educators. New Orleans, LA. Retrieved from http://iamse.org/conf/conf14/3fs5.html

Halford, G. S. (1993). *Children's understanding: The development of mental models*. Hillsdale, NJ: Lawrence Erlbaum Associates.

Halliday, T. (2000). *David's Maratas posthumous portrait*. New York: Cambridge University Press.

Halpern, D. F. (1998). Teaching critical thinking for transfer across domains: Dispositions, skills, structure training, and metacognitive monitoring. *The American Psychologist*, 53(4), 449–455. doi:10.1037/0003-066X.53.4.449 PMID:9572008

Halpern, D. F. (1999). Teaching for critical thinking: Helping college students develop the skills and dispositions of a critical thinker. *New Directions for Teaching and Learning*, 80, 69–74. doi:10.1002/tl.8005

Halpern, D. F. (2001). Assessing the effectiveness of critical thinking Instruction. *The Journal of General Education*, 50(4), 270–286. doi:10.1353/jge.2001.0024

Halpern, D. F., & Hakel, M. D. (2003). Applying the science of learning to the university and beyond. *Change*, 35(4), 36–41. doi:10.1080/00091380309604109

Halx, M. D., & Reybold, L. E. (2005). A pedagogy of force: Faculty perspectives of critical thinking capacity in undergraduate students. *The Journal of General Education*, 54(4), 293–315. doi:10.1353/jge.2006.0009

Hamilton, J. D. (1999). Outcomes in medical education must be wide, long and deep. *Medical Teacher*, 21, 125–126. doi:10.1080/01421599979725 PMID:21275724

Hammerich, P. (1998). Confronting students' conceptions of the nature of science with cooperative controversy. In *The nature of science in science education rationales and strategies* (pp. 127–136). Dordrecht, The Netherlands: Kluwer Academic Publishers.

Harasim, L. M. (1989). Online education: A new domain. In *Mindwave, communication, computers and distance education*. Oxford, UK: Pergamon Press.

Harden, R. M., Crosby, J. R., Davis, M. H., & Friedman, M. (1999). AMEE guide no.14: Outcome-based education: Part 5--from competency to meta-competency: A model for the specification of learning outcomes. *Medical Teacher*, 21(6), 546–553. doi:10.1080/01421599978951 PMID:21281173

Hardie, J. C. (2009). *New opportunities or difficult challenges? Self-regulation of learning of chinese students in a western university setting*. (Doctoral Dissertation). University of Canterbury, New Zealand. Retrieved from http://hdl.handle.net/10092/3392

Compilation of References

Harrell, M. (2008). *No computer program required: Even pencil-and-paper argument mapping improves critical thinking skills.* Department of Philosophy, Paper 350. Retrieved May 15, 2012 from http://repository.cmu.edu/philosophy/350

Harrell, M. (2011). Argument diagramming and critical thinking in introductory philosophy. *Higher Education Research & Development, 30*(3), 371–385. doi:10.1080/07294360.2010.502559

Hawke, G. (2002). *Keeping curriculum relevant in a changing world.* Paper presented at the SENAI International Seminar. Belo Horizante, Brasil.

Hay, D. B. (2007). Using concept mapping to measure deep, surface and non-learning outcomes. *Studies in Higher Education, 32*(1), 39–57. doi:10.1080/03075070601099432

Hay, D., & Kinchin, I. (2008). Using concept mapping to measure learning quality. *Education + Training, 50,* 167–182. doi:10.1108/00400910810862146

Hay, D., Kinchin, I., & Lygo-Baker, S. (2008). Making learning visible: The role of concept mapping in higher education. *Studies in Higher Education, 33,* 295–311. doi:10.1080/03075070802049251

Haynes, T., & Bailey, G. (2003). Are you and your basic business students asking the right questions? *Business Education Forum, 57*(3), 33–37.

HEFCE. (2001). *Review of research.* England: Higher Education Funding Council.

HEFCE. (2005). *PhD research degrees: Entry and completion.* Retrieved from http://www.hefce.ac.uk/pubs/hefce/2005/05_02/05_02.pdf

HEFCW. (2000). *Review of research policy.* Wales: Higher Education Funding Council for Wales.

HEFCW. (2000). *Review subsequent consultation: Review of research policy and funding method.* Higher Education Funding Council for Wales.

Heinrich, E., Milne, J., Ramsay, A., & Morrison, D. (2009). Recommendations for the use of e-tools for improvements around assignment marking quality. *Assessment & Evaluation in Higher Education, 34*(4), 469–479. doi:10.1080/02602930802071122

Heinze-Fry, J. (2006). CmapTools facilitates alignment of local curriculum with state standards: A case study. In *Concept maps: Theory, methodology, and technology: Proceedings of the second international conference on concept mapping.* San Juan, Costa Rica: Academic Press.

Heinze-Fry, J. Gorman, & Foster. (2010). Conceptual mapping to facilitate review of state science standards. In *Concept maps: Making learning meaningful: Proceedings of the fourth international conference on concept mapping.* San Juan, Costa Rica: Academic Press.

Hemming, H. E. (2000). Encouraging critical thinking: But...what does that mean? *Journal of Education, 35*(2), 173–186.

Herring, S. C. (2004). Computer-mediated discourse analysis: An approach to researching online behavior. In S. A. Barab, R. Kling, & J. H. Gray (Eds.), *Designing for virtual communities in the service of learning* (pp. 338–376). New York, NY: Cambridge University Press. doi:10.1017/CBO9780511805080.016

Hever, R., De Groot, R., De Laat, M., Harrer, A., Hoppe, U., McLaren, B. M., & Scheuer, O. (2007). Combining structural, process-oriented and textual elements to generate alerts for graphical e-discussions. In C. A. Chinn, G. Erkens, & S. Puntambekar (Eds.), *Mice, minds, and society: Proceedings of the 2007 the 2007 computer supported collaborative learning (CSCL) conference* (pp. 286–288). New Brunswick, NJ: Rutgers University.

Hicks-Moore, S. L. (2005). Clinical concept maps in nursing education: An effective way to link theory and practice. *Nurse Education in Practice*, *5*(6), 348–352. doi:10.1016/j.nepr.2005.05.003 PMID:19040844

Hilbert, T., & Renkl, A. (2006). *Concept mapping as a follow-up strategy to learning from texts: What characterizes good and poor mappers*. Freiburg, Germany: Department of Psychology, University of Freiburg.

Hill, L. H. (2006). Using visual concept mapping to communicate medication information to patients with low health literacy: A preliminary study In *Proceedings of the Second International Conference on Concept Mapping* (Vol. 1, pp. 621-628). San Jose, Costa Rica: Universidad de Costa Rica.

Hill, C. A., & Helmers, M. H. (Eds.). (2004). *Defining visual rhetorics*. Mahwah, NJ: Lawrence Erlbaum Associates, Inc.

Hill, C. M. (2006). Integrating clinical experiences into the concept mapping process. *Nurse Educator*, *31*(1), 36–39. doi:10.1097/00006223-200601000-00010 PMID:16601605

Hinck, S. M., Webb, P., Sims-Giddens, S., Helton, C., Hope, K. L., Utley, R., & Yarbrough, S. (2006). Student learning with concept mapping of care plans in community-based education. *Journal of Professional Nursing*, *22*(1), 23–29. doi:10.1016/j.profnurs.2005.12.004 PMID:16459286

Hirsch, E. D. (1987). *Cultural literacy*. Boston: Houghton Mifflin Company.

Holliday, A. (2005). *The struggle to teach English as an international language*. Oxford, UK: Oxford University Press.

Hoover, L. A. (1994). Reflective writing as a window on preservice teachers' thought processes. *Teaching and Teacher Education*, *10*(1), 83–93. doi:10.1016/0742-051X(94)90042-6

Hoppe, H. U., & Gaßner, K. (2002). Integrating collaborative concept mapping tools with group memory and retrieval functions. In G. Stahl (Ed.), *Proceedings of the CSCL Conference: Foundations for a CSCL Community* (pp. 716–725). Boulder, CO: Erlbaum.

Hoppe, H. U., De Groot, R., & Hever, R. (2009). Implementing technology-facilitated collaboration and awareness in the classroom: Roles for teachers, educational and technology researchers. In B. B. Schwarz, T. Dreyfus, & R. Hershkowitz (Eds.), *Transformation of knowledge through classroom interaction: New perspectives in learning and instruction* (pp. 130–142). New York, NY: Routledge.

Horton, P. B., McConney, A. A., Gallo, M., Woods, A. L., Senn, G. J., & Hamelin, D. (1993). An investigation of the effectiveness of concept mapping as an instructional tool. *Science Education*, *77*, 95–111. doi:10.1002/sce.3730770107

Compilation of References

Housen, A. (1983). *The eye of the beholder: Measuring aesthetic development.* (Ed.D. Thesis). Harvard University Graduate School of Education. Cambridge, MA.

Housen, A. (1992). Validating a measure of aesthetic development for museums and schools. *ILVS Review: A Journal of Visitor Behavior, 2* (2), 1-19.

Housen, A. (2000). *Eye of the beholder: Research, theory and practice.* Retrieved April 20, 2012, from http://www.vtshome. org/system/resources/0000/0006/Eye_of_ the_Beholder.pdf

Housen, A. (2002). Aestethic thought, critical thinking, and transfer. *Arts and Learning Research Journal, 18*(1).

Housen, A. (2007). *Art viewing and aesthetic development: Designing for the viewer.* Retrieved April 20, 2012, from http://www. vtshome.org/system/resources/0000/ 0015/ HousenArtViewing.pdf

Housen, A., & Yenawine, P. (2001). *Visual thinking strategies: Understanding the basics.* Retrieved April 20, 2012 from http://www. vtshome.org/system/resources/0000/0039/ VTS_Understanding_the_basic.pdf

Housen, A. (2001). Voice of viewers: Iterative research, theory and practice. *Arts and Learning Research Journal, 17*(1), 2–12.

Housen, A. (2001-2002). Aesthetic thought: Assessment, growth, and transfer. *Arts and Learning Research Journal, 18*(1), 99–131.

Howard, J. R., & Baird, R. (2000). The consolidation of responsibility and students' definitions of the college classroom. *The Journal of Higher Education, 71,* 700–721. doi:10.2307/2649159

Howe, C., Tolmie, A., Duchak-Tanner, V., & Rattay, C. (2000). Hypothesis-testing in science: Group consensus and the acquisition of conceptual and procedural knowledge. *Learning and Instruction, 10,* 361–391. doi:10.1016/S0959-4752(00)00004-9

Hsu, L., & Hsieh, S. I. (2005). Concept maps as an assessment tool in a nursing course. *Journal of Professional Nursing, 21*(3), 141–149. doi:10.1016/j.profnurs.2005.04.006 PMID:16021557

Hunt, S., Simonds, C., & Simonds, B. (2007, November). Uniquely qualified, distinctively competent: Delivering 21st century skills in the basic course. In *Proceedings of 93rd Annual Convention.* National Communication Association.

Hyerle, D., & Williams, K. (2010). Bifocal assessment in the cognitive age: Thinking maps for assessing content learning and cognitive processes. *The New Hampshire Journal of Education,* 32-38. Retrieved from http:// thinkingfoundation.org/research/journal_articles/journal_articles.html

Hyerle, D. (1996). *Visual tools for constructing knowledge.* Alexandria, VA: Association for Supervision and Curriculum Development.

Hyerle, D. (2008). Thinking maps: Visual tools for activating habits of mind. In *Learning and leading with habits of mind: 16 essential characteristics for success* (pp. 149–176). Academic Press.

Hyerle, D. (2009). *Visual tools for transforming information into knowledge* (2nd ed.). Thousand Oaks, CA: Sage.

Insight Assessment. (2013). *California critical thinking skills test*. California Academic Press. Retrieved from http://www.insightassessment.com/Products/Products-Summary/Critical-Thinking-Skills-Tests/California-Critical-Thinking-Skills-Test-CCTST

Institute for Human and Machine Cognition. (2007). *Hybrid concept map/procedure on building a concept map*. Retrieved September 1, 2007, from http://cmapskm.ihmc.us/servlet/SBReadResourceServlet?rid=1064009710027_279131382_27088&partName=htmltext

Institute for Human and Machine Cognition. (2008). *Publications*. Retrieved April 27, 2008, from http://cmap.ihmc.us/Publications/

International Society for Technology in Education. (2000). *Establishing new learning environments*. Retrieved March 7 2004, from http://www.iste.org/docs/pdfs/nets-t-standards.pdf?sfvrsn=2

Irvine, L. C. (1995). Can concept mapping be used to promote meaningful learning in nurse education? *Journal of Advanced Nursing*, *21*(6), 1175–1179. doi:10.1046/j.1365-2648.1995.21061175.x PMID:7665784

Israel, L. (2005). *Get ahead and ace your grades*. [DVD]. London, UK: Aulis Publishers.

Ivanitskaya, L., Clark, D., Montgomery, G., & Primeau, R. (2002). Interdisciplinary learning: Process and outcomes. *Innovative Higher Education*, *27*(2), 95–111. doi:10.1023/A:1021105309984

Jackson, S. L., Stratford, S. J., Krajcik, J., & Soloway, E. (1994). Making dynamic modeling accessible to precollege science students. *Interactive Learning Environments*, *3*, 233–257. doi:10.1080/1049482940040305

Jenson, J. D. (2011). Promoting self-regulation and critical reflection through writing students' use of electronic portfolio. *International Journal of ePortfolio, 1* (1), 49-60.

Jeong, A., & Joung, S. (2007). Scaffolding collaborative argumentation in asynchronous discussions with message constraints and message labels. *Computers & Education*, *48*, 427–445. doi:10.1016/j.compedu.2005.02.002

Jerald, C. D. (2009). Defining a 21st century education: Competencies, literacy, and knowledge. *The Center for Public Education*. Retrieved October 10, 2012, from http://www.centerforpubliceducation.org/Learn-About/21st-Century/Defining-a-21st-Century-Education-Full-Report-PDF.pdf

Johnson-Laird, P. N. (1983). *Mental models*. Cambridge, MA: Harvard University Press.

Johnstone, A.H., & Otis. (2006). Concept mapping in problem based learning: A cautionary tale. *Chemistry Education Research and Practice*, *7*(2), 84–95. doi:10.1039/b5rp90017d

Jonassen, D. H. (1996). *Computers in the classroom: Mindtools for critical thinking*. Columbus, OH: Merrill/Prentice-Hall.

Jonassen, D. H. (2000). Toward a design theory of problem solving. *Educational Technology Research and Development*, *48*(4), 63–63. doi:10.1007/BF02300500

Jonassen, D. H., Carr, & Yueh. (1998). Computers as mindtools for engaging learners in critical thinking. *TechTrends*, *43*(2), 24–32. doi:10.1007/BF02818172

Jonassen, D. H., Howland, J., Marra, R. M., & Crismond, D. (1999). *Meaningful learning with technology* (3rd ed.). Columbus, OH: Pearson.

Compilation of References

Jonassen, D. H., Reeves, T. C., Hong, N., Harvey, D., & Peters, K. (1997). Concept mapping as cognitive learning and assessment tools. *Journal of Interactive Learning Research, 8*, 289–308.

Joyce, B., Calhoun, E., & Hopkins, D. (2000). *Models of learning, Tools for teaching.* Berkshire, UK: McGraw-Hill Education.

Kagan, S., & Kagan, M. (2008). *Kagan cooperative learning.* San Clemente, CA: Kagan Publishing.

Kandiko, C. B., & Kinchin, I. M. (2009). *PhD supervision as intellectual courtship.* Paper presented at the Society for Research into Higher Education (SRHE) Annual Conference. Newport, UK.

Kandiko, C. B., & Kinchin, I. M. (2010). What is a PhD? Process versus product in PhD supervision. In J. Sánchez, A. J. Cañas, & J. D. Novak (Eds.), *Concept maps: Making learning meaningful, proceedings of the fourth international conference on concept mapping.* Viña del Mar, Chile: Universidad de Chile.

Kandiko, C. B., Hay, D. B., & Weller, S. (2013). Concept mapping in the humanities to facilitate reflection: Externalising the relationship between public and personal learning. *Arts and Humanities in Higher Education, 12*(1), 70–87. doi:10.1177/1474022211399381

Kandiko, C. B., & Kinchin, I. M. (2012). What is a doctorate? A concept-mapped analysis of process versus product in the supervision of lab-based PhDs. *Educational Research, 54*(1), 3–16. doi:10.1080/00131881.2012.658196

Kandiko, C. B., & Kinchin, I. M. (2013). Developing discourses of knowledge and understanding: Longitudinal studies of PhD supervision. *London Review of Education, 11*(1), 46–58. doi:10.1080/14748460.2012.761819

Kane, F. (1982). Thinking, drawing-writing, reading. *Childhood Education, 58*(5), 292–297. doi:10.1080/00094056.1982.10520534

Keiny, S. (2002). *Ecological thinking: A new approach to educational change.* Lanham, MD: University of America Press.

Kelly-Riley, D., Brown, G., Condon, B., & Law, R. (2007). *Washington State University critical thinking project.* Retrieved April 27, 2007 from http://wsuctproject.ctlt.wsu.edu/ctm.htm

Kendrick, M., & McKay, R. (2004). Drawings as an alternative way of understanding young children's constructions of literacy. *Journal of Early Childhood Literacy, 4*(1), 109–128. doi:10.1177/1468798404041458

Kennedy, M., Fisher, M. B., & Ennis, R. H. (1991). Critical thinking: Literature review and needed research. In L. Idol, & B. F. Jones (Eds.), *Educational values and cognitive instruction: Implications for reform* (pp. 11–40). Hillsdale, NJ: Lawrence Erlbaum & Associates.

Kern, C., & Crippen, K. (2008). Mapping for conceptual change. *Science Teacher (Normal, Ill.), 75*(6). PMID:21814296

Kesteren, M. T. R., & Fernández, G. (2011). Stress-related noradrenergic activity prompts large-scale neural network reconfiguration. *Science, 334*, 1151–1153. doi:10.1126/science.1209603 PMID:22116887

Khodadady, E., & Ghanizadeh, A. (2011). The impact of concept mapping on EFL learners' critical thinking ability. *English Language Teaching*, *4*(4), 49–60. doi:10.5539/elt.v4n4p49

Kim, I.-H., Anderson, R. C., Nguyen-Jahiel, K., & Archodidou, A. (2007). Discourse patterns during children's collaborative online discussions. *Journal of the Learning Sciences*, *16*, 333–370. doi:10.1080/10508400701413419

Kim, Y. Y. (2005). Adapting to a new culture: An integrative communication theory. In W. B. Gudykunst (Ed.), *Theorizing about intercultural communication* (pp. 375–400). Thousand Oaks, CA: Sage Publications.

Kinchin, I. (2007). Using concept mapping principles in PowerPoint. *European Journal of Dental Education*, *11*, 194–199. doi:10.1111/j.1600-0579.2007.00454.x PMID:17935558

Kinchin, I. (2009). A knowledge structures perspective on the scholarship of teaching & learning. *International Journal for the Scholarship of Teaching and Learning*, *3*(2).

Kinchin, I. M. (2000). Using concept maps to reveal understanding: A two-tier analysis. *The School Science Review*, *81*, 41–46.

Kinchin, I. M. (2011). Relating knowledge structures to learning styles and university teaching. In *Style differences in cognition, learning, and management* (pp. 129–142). London: Routledge.

Kinchin, I. M. (2012). Visualising knowledge structures of university teaching to relate pedagogic theory and academic practice. In *Handbook of college and university teaching: A global perspective* (pp. 314–332). Thousand Oaks, CA: Sage. doi:10.4135/9781412996891.n21

Kinchin, I. M., Lygo-Baker, & Hay. (2008). Universities as centers of non-learning. *Studies in Higher Education*, *33*(1), 89–103. doi:10.1080/03075070701794858

Kinchin, I. M., Streatfield, D., & Hay, D. B. (2010). Using concept mapping to enhance the research interview. *International Journal of Qualitative Methods*, *9*, 52–68.

Kinchin, I., & Hay, D. (2000). How a qualitative approach to concept map analysis can be used to aid learning by illustrating patterns of conceptual development. *Educational Research*, *42*(1), 43–57. doi:10.1080/001318800363908

King, A. (1993). From sage on the stage to guide on the side. *College Teaching*, *41*(1), 30–35. doi:10.1080/87567555.1993.9926781

King, M. (2002). Teaching and evaluating critical thinking with concept maps. *Nurse Educator*, *27*(5), 214–216. doi:10.1097/00006223-200209000-00008 PMID:12355046

Kletzien, S. B., & Dreher, M. J. (2004). *Informational text in K-3 classrooms: Helping children read and write*. Newark, DE: International Reading Association.

Koch, I. G. V. (2001). Lingüística textual. *Quo vadis? Revista D.E.L.T.A. -. Documentação de Estudos em Lingüística Teórica Aplicada*, *17*, 11–23. doi:10.1590/S0102-44502001000300002

Koch, I. G. V., & Travaglia, L. C. (1999). *Texto e coerência* (6th ed.). São Paulo: Cortez.

Koç, Y., Isiksal, M., & Bulut, S. (2007). Elementary school curriculum reform in Turkey. *International Education Journal*, *8*(1), 30–39.

Kolb, D. A. (1984). *Experiential learning: Experience as the source of learning and development*. Upper Saddle River, NJ: Prentice-Hall.

Korb, K., & van Gelder, T. (2010). Editorial and interview with Tim van Gelder. *The Reasoner*, *4*(2), 18–21.

Kosslyn, S. M. (1983). *Ghosts in the mind's machine: Creating and using images in the brain*. New York: W. W. Norton & Company.

Kosslyn, S. M. (1988). Imagery in learning. In *Perspectives in memory* (pp. 245–273). Cambridge, MA: MIT Press.

Kostovich, C. T., Poradzisz, M., Wood, K., & O'Brien, K. L. (2007). Learning style preference and student aptitude for concept maps. *The Journal of Nursing Education*, *46*(5), 225–231. PMID:17547346

Krathwohl, D. R. (2002). A revision of Bloom's taxonomy: An overview. *Theory into Practice*, *41*(4). doi:10.1207/s15430421tip4104_2

Kress, G. (1997). *Before writing: Rethinking the paths to literacy*. London: Routledge.

Kristo, J., & Bamford, R. (2004). *Non-fiction in focus: A comprehensive framework for helping students become independent readers and writers of non-fiction*. New York: Scholastic.

Kuhn, D., Shaw, V., & Felton, M. (1997). Effects of dyadic interaction on argumentative reasoning. *Cognition and Instruction*, *15*, 287–315. doi:10.1207/s1532690xci1503_1

Lai, E. (2011). *Critical thinking: A literature review*. Retrieved from http://www.pearson-assessments.com/hai/images/tmrs/criticalthinkingreviewfinal.pdf

Laight, D. W. (2006). Attitudes to concept maps as a teaching/learning activity in undergraduate health professional education: Influence of preferred approach to learning. *Medical Teacher*, *28*(2), e64–e67. doi:10.1080/01421590600617574 PMID:16707287

Lambert, J. (2006). *Digital storytelling cookbook*. Digital Diner Press.

Lancy, D. F. (1993). *Qualitative research in education: An introduction to the major traditions*. New York: Longman.

Larson, D. P., Butler, A. C., & Roediger, H. L. (2009). Repeated testing improves long-term retention relative to repeated study: A randomised controlled trial. *Medical Education*, *43*(12), 1174–1181. doi:10.1111/j.1365-2923.2009.03518.x PMID:19930508

Lau, S., Liem, A. D., & Nie, Y. (2008). Task- and self-related pathways to deep learning: The mediating role of achievement goals, classroom attentiveness, and group participation. *The British Journal of Educational Psychology*, *78*, 639–662. doi:10.1348/000709907X270261 PMID:18166143

Lederman, N., Lederman, J., & Bell, R. (2004). *Constructing science in elementary classrooms*. Boston: Pearson.

LeDoux, J. (2002). *Synaptic self: How our brains become who we are*. New York: Viking.

Lee, I. (2004, Summer). Using dialogue journals as a multi-purpose tool for preservice teacher preparation: How effective is it? *Teacher Education Quarterly*, 73–97.

Leite, C., & Fernandes, P. (2002). *A avaliação da aprendizagem: novos contextos, novas práticas*. Porto: ASA.

Leshner, A. (2007). Outreach training needed.[Editorial]. *Science*, *315*(5809), 161. doi:10.1126/science.1138712 PMID:17218495

Lévy, P. (2012). Cibercultura (3rd ed.). São Paulo: Editora 34.

Lewis, A., & Smith, D. (1993). Defining higher order thinking. *Theory into Practice*, *32*(3), 131–137. doi:10.1080/00405849309543588

Lewis, H. (2006). *Excellence without a soul: How a great university forgot education*. New York, NY: Public Affairs.

Litzelman, D. K., & Cottingham, A. H. (2007). The new formal competency-based curriculum and informal curriculum at Indiana University School of Medicine: Overview and five-year analysis. *Academic Medicine*, *82*(4), 410–421. doi:10.1097/ACM.0b013e31803327f3 PMID:17414200

London, H., & Draper, M. (2008). The silent revolution in higher education. *Academic Questions*, *21*(2), 221–225. doi:10.1007/s12129-008-9052-z

Loyola, F. A., & Borges, C. (2010). A pedagogia de Paulo Freire ou quando a educação se torna um ato político. In C. Gauthier, & M. Tardif (Eds.), *A pedagogia: Teorias e práticas da antiguidade aos nossos dias*. *Petrópolis: Vozes*.

Luckie, D. B., Harrison, S. H., & Ebert-May, D. (2004). Introduction to c-tools: Concept mapping tools for online learning. In *Proceedings of the First International Conference on Concept Mapping* (Vol. 2, pp. 211-214). Multibaja, Spain: Novatext.

Lustig, M. W., & Koester, J. (2010). *Intercultural competence: Interpersonal communication across cultures* (6th ed.). New York: Allyn & Bacon.

Malinowitz, C., et al. (Eds.). (2006). Schottenstein ed. of Talmud Yerushalmi. New York, NY: Mesorah Publications.

Manathunga, C., Lant, P., & Mellick, G. (2006). Imagining an interdisciplinary doctoral pedagogy. *Teaching in Higher Education*, *11*(3), 365–379. doi:10.1080/13562510600680954

Maneval, R., Filburn, M., Deringer, S., & Lum, G. (2011). Concept mapping: Does it improve critical thinking ability in practical nursing students? *Nursing Education Perspectives*, *32*(4), 229–233. doi:10.5480/1536-5026-32.4.229 PMID:21923002

Marcelo-Garcia, C. (2005). *Formação de professores: Para uma mudança educativa*. Porto: Porto Editora.

Marée, T., van Bruggen, J., & Jochems, G. (2012). Using enriched skeleton concept mapping to support meaningful learning. In A. J. Cañas, J. D. Novak & J. Vanhear (Eds.), *Concept maps: Theory, methodology, technology, proceedings of the fifth international conference on concept mapping*. Valletta, Malta: Academic Press.

Marinova-Todd, S. H., Marshall, D. B., & Snow, C. E. (2000). Three misconceptions about age and L2 learning. *TESOL Quarterly*, *34*(1), 9–34. doi:10.2307/3588095

Marton, F., & Ramsden, P. (1988). What does it take to improve learning? In P. Ramsden (Ed.), *Improving learning: New perspectives* (pp. 268–286). London: Kogan Page.

Mason, W., & Watts, D. (2012). *Collaborative learning in networks*. Paper presented at the National Academy of Sciences of the United States of America. Retrieved from http://www.pnas.org/content/109/3/764.full.pdf+html

Mason, M. (2008). Critical thinking and learning. In M. Mason (Ed.), *Critical thinking and learning*. Malden, MA: Blackwell Publishing. doi:10.1002/9781444306774.ch1

Massachusetts Department of Elementary and Secondary Education (MADESE). (2001/2006). *Massachusetts science and technology/engineering curriculum framework.* Retrieved from www.doe.mass.edu/frameworks/current.html

Maton, K. (2013). Making semantic waves: A key to cumulative knowledge-building. *Linguistics and Education, 24,* 8–22. doi:10.1016/j.linged.2012.11.005

Mayer, R. E., & Moreno, R. (2003). Nine ways to reduce cognitive load in multimedia learning. *Educational Psychologist, 38*(1), 43–52. doi:10.1207/S15326985EP3801_6

Mayne, J. (Ed.). (1981). *Art in Paris 1845-1862: Salons and other exhibitions reviewed by Charles Baudelaire.* Oxford, UK: Phaidon.

McAleese, R. (1994). A theoretical view on concept mapping. *Research in Learning Technology, 2* (1).

McCloud, C. (2007). *Enhance comprehension in the science classroom.* Comments from CRISS.

McGregor, J. H. (1994). Information seeking and use, students and their mental models. *Journal of Youth Services in Libraries, 8*(1), 69–76.

McKeachie, W., Pintrich, P., Lin, Y., & Smith, D. (1986). *Teaching and learning in the college classroom: A review of the research literature.* Ann Arbor, MI: University of Michigan, National Center for Research to Improve Post-Secondary Teaching and Learning.

McLaren, B. M., Scheuer, O., De Laat, M., Hever, R., De Groot, R., & Rosé, C. P. (2007). Using machine learning techniques to analyze and support mediation of student e-discussions. In R. Luckin, K. R. Koedinger, & J. Greer (Eds.), *Proceedings of the 13th International Conference on Artificial Intelligence in Education (AIED-07), Artificial Intelligence in Education: Building Technology Rich Learning Contexts That Work* (pp. 331–338). Amsterdam, The Netherlands: IOS Press.

McManus, D. Walker, Cuker, Goodnight, Humphris, Keener-Chavis,.... Schubel. (2000). *Center for ocean sciences education excellence.* Workshop Report. Retrieved from http://www.ocean.washington.edu/cosee/Text/index.html

McMillan, J. H. (1987). Enhancing college students' critical thinking: A review of studies. *Research in Higher Education, 26*(1), 3–29. doi:10.1007/BF00991931

McPeck, J. E. (1990). Critical thinking and subject specificity: A reply to Ennis. *Educational Researcher, 19*(4), 10–12. doi:10.3102/0013189X019004010

McTighe, J., & O'Connor, K. (2005). Seven practices for effective learning. *Educational Leadership, 63,* 10–17.

McTigue, E., & Flowers, A. (2011). Science visual literacy: Learners' perceptions and knowledge of diagrams. *The Reading Teacher, 64*(8), 578–589. doi:10.1598/RT.64.8.3

Mercer, N., Wegerif, R., & Dawes, L. (1999). Children's talk and the development of reasoning in the classroom. *British Educational Research Journal, 25*(1), 95–111. doi:10.1080/0141192990250107

Meyer, J., & Land (2003). *Threshold concepts and troublesome knowledge: Linkages to ways of thinking and practising within the disciplines*. Edinburgh, UK: School of Education, University of Edinburgh Occasional Report 4.

Meyer, K. (2003). Face-to-face versus threaded discussion: The role of time and higher-order thinking. *JALN, 7*(3), 55–65.

Meyers, N. M., & Nulty, D. D. (2009). How to use (five) curriculum design principles to align authentic learning environments, assessment, students' approaches to thinking and learning outcomes. *Assessment & Evaluation in Higher Education, 34*(5), 565–577. doi:10.1080/02602930802226502

Mezirow, J. (1997). Transformation theory: Theory to practice. *New Directions for Adult and Continuing Education, 74*, 5-12.

Mezirow, J. (1997). Transformative learning theory. *New Directions for Adult and Continuing Education, 74*.

Mezirow, J. (2000). Learning to think like an adult. In *Learning as transformation: Critical perspectives on a theory in progress* (pp. 3–33). San Francisco, CA: Jossey-Bass Publishers.

Mezirow, J. (2000). *Learning as transformation: Critical perspectives on a theory in progress*. San Francisco, CA: Jossey-Bass Publishers.

Mezirow, J. (2003). Transforming learning as discourse. *Journal of Transformative Education, 1*(1), 58–63. doi:10.1177/1541344603252172

Miller, N., & Cañas, A. (2008). A semantic scoring rubric for concept maps: Design and reliability. In A. J. Cañas, P. Reiska, M. Åhlberg, & J. D. Novak (Eds.), *Concept maps: Theory, methodology, technology, proceedings of the third international conference on concept mapping*. Tallinn, Estonia: Academic Press. Retrieved from http://cmc.ihmc.us/cmc2008papers/cmc2008-p253.pdf

Miller, K. J. (2009). Concept mappping as a research tool to evaluate conceptual change related to instructional methods. *Teacher Education and Special Education: The Journal of the Teacher Education Division of the Council for Exceptional Children, 32*(4), 365–378. doi:10.1177/0888406409346149

Miller, M., & Veatch, N. (2010). Teaching literacy in context: Choosing and using instructional strategies. *The Reading Teacher, 64*(3), 154–165. doi:10.1598/RT.64.3.1

Ministry of National Education. (2006). *Support to basic education project teacher training component: Generic teacher competencies*. Ankara, Turkey: Author.

Mintzes, J. J., Wandersee, J. H., & Novak, J. D. (Eds.). (2005). *Teaching sciences for understanding: A human constructivist view*. New York: Elsevier Academic Press.

Mirzaie, R., Abbas, J., & Hatami, J. (2008). Study of concept maps usage effect on meaningful learning frontier in Bloom's taxonomy for atomic structure mental concepts. In A. J. Cañas, P. Reiska, M. Åhlberg, & J. D. Novak (Eds.), *Concept maps: Theory, methodology, technology, proceedings of the third international conference on concept mapping*. Tallinn, Estonia: Academic Press.

Compilation of References

Montgomery, J. M., & Ritchey, T. (2010). *The answer model: A new path to healing.* Santa Monica, CA: TAM Books.

Montgomery, J., & Ritchey, T. (2008). *The answer model theory.* Santa Monica, CA: TAM Books.

Moon, B., Hoffman, R., Shattuck, L., Coffey, J., et al. (2008). Rapid and accurate idea transfer: Evaluating concept maps against other formats for the transfer of complex information. In A. J. Cañas, P. Reiska, M. Åhlberg, & J. D. Novak (Eds.), *Concept maps: Theory, methodology, technology, proceedings of the third international conference on concept mapping.* Tallinn, Estonia: Academic Press.

Moon, J. (2005). *We seek it here...a new perspective on the elusive activity of critical thinking: A theoretical and practical approach.* ESCalate Discussion Series. Retrieved November 29, 2012 from http://escalate.ac.uk/downloads/2041.pdf

Moreira, M. A. (2007). *Aprendizagem significativa: Da visão clássica à visão crítica.* Paper presented at the Encuentro Nacional sobre Enseñanza de la Matemática. Tandil, Argentina. Retrieved from http://www.if.ufrgs.br/~moreira/visaoclasicavisaocritica.pdf

Moss, B. (2005). Making a case and a place for effective content area literacy instruction in the elementary grades. *The Reading Teacher, 59*(1), 46–55. doi:10.1598/RT.59.1.5

Mukerjea, D. (2004). *Unleashing genius: With the world's most powerful learning systems.* Singapore: The Brainware Press.

Mullet, K., & Sano, D. (1995). *Designing visual interfaces: Communication oriented techniques.* Upper Saddle River, NJ: Prentice Hall PTR.

Muukkonen, H., & Lakkala, M. (2009). Exploring metaskills of knowledge-creating inquiry in higher education. *International Journal of Computer-Supported Collaborative Learning, 4*(2), 187–211. doi:10.1007/s11412-009-9063-y

Nast, J. (2006). *Idea mapping, How to access your hidden brain power, learn faster, remember more and achieve success in business.* Hoboken, NJ: John Wiley & Sons, Inc.

National Geographic Society. (2005). *Ocean literacy: The essential principles of ocean sciences grades K–12.* Retrieved from http://www.coexploration.org/oceanliteracy/documents/OceanLitChart.pdf

National Oceanic and Atmospheric Administration. (2008). *Climate literacy: The essential principles of climate science Grades K-12.* Brochure. Retrieved from http://www.climate.noaa.gov/education/pdfs/climate_literacy_poster-final.pdf

National Research Council. (2007). *Taking science to school: Learning and teaching science in grades K - 8.* Washington, DC: National Academies Press.

National Science Digital Library (NSDL). (n.d.). *Literacy maps.* Retrieved from http://strandmaps.nsdl.org/

Nelson Laird, T. F., & Garver, A. K. (2010). The effect of teaching general education courses on deep approaches to learning: How disciplinary context matters. *Research in Higher Education, 51*(3), 248–265. doi:10.1007/s11162-009-9154-7

Nelson, C. E. (1994). Critical thinking and collaborative learning. *New Directions for Teaching and Learning,* (59): 45–58. doi:10.1002/tl.37219945907

Nesbit, J. C., & Adesope, O. O. (2006). Learning with concept and knowledge maps: A meta-analysis. *Review of Educational Research*, *76*(3), 413–448. doi:10.3102/00346543076003413

Newman, F., Couturier, L., & Scurry, J. (2004). *The future of higher education: Rhetoric, reality the risks of the market*. San Francisco, CA: Jossey-Bass.

Niesyto, H., Buckingham, D., & Fisherkeller, J. (2003). Video culture: Crossing borders with young people's video productions. *Television and Media, 4* (4).

Nilson, M., & Nocon, H. (2005). *School of tomorrow: Teaching and technology in local and global communities*. Bern, Switzerland: Peter Lang.

Nishida, H. (2005). Cultural schema theory. In W. B. Gudykunst (Ed.), *Theorizing about intercultural communication* (pp. 401–418). Thousand Oaks, CA: Sage Publications.

Novak, J. D. (1990). Concept mapping: A useful tool for science education. *Journal of Research in Science Teaching*, *27*, 937–949. doi:10.1002/tea.3660271003

Novak, J. D. (1990). Concept maps and Vee diagrams: Two metacognitive tools to facilitate meaningful learning. *Instructional Science*, *19*(1), 29–52. doi:10.1007/BF00377984

Novak, J. D. (2002). Meaningful learning: The essential factor for conceptual change in limited or inappropriate propositional hierarchies leading to empowerment of learners. *Science Education*, *86*, 548–571. doi:10.1002/sce.10032

Novak, J. D. (2005). Results and implications of a 12-year longitudinal study of science concept learning. *Research in Science Education*, *35*(1), 23–40. doi:10.1007/s11165-004-3431-4

Novak, J. D. (2010). *Learning, creating and using knowledge: Concept maps as facilitative tools in schools and corporations* (2nd ed.). New York, NY: Routledge.

Novak, J. D., & Cañas, A. J. (2006). The origins of the concept mapping tool and the continuing evolution of the tool. *Information Visualization*, *5*(3), 175–175. doi:10.1057/palgrave.ivs.9500126

Novak, J. D., & Cañas, A. J. (2006). *The theory underlying concept maps and how to construct them (Technical Report IHMC CmapTools 2006-01 Rev 01-2008)*. Florida Institute for Human and Machine Cognition.

Novak, J. D., & Cañas, A. J. (2007). Theoretical origins of concept maps, how to construct them and uses in education. *Reflecting Education*, *3*(1), 29–42.

Novak, J. D., & Gowin, D. B. (1984). *Learning how to learn* (21st ed.). New York: Cambridge University Press. doi:10.1017/CBO9781139173469

Novak, J. D., & Gowin, D. B. (1996). *Aprender a aprender*. Lisboa: Plátano Edições Técnicas.

Novak, J. D., & Musonda, D. (1991). A twelve-year longitudinal study of science concept learning. *American Educational Research Journal*, *28*, 117–153. doi:10.3102/00028312028001117

Novak, J. D., & Wandersee, J. (1990). Perspectives on concept mapping [Special issue]. *Journal of Research in Science Teaching*, *27*(10), 921–1074.

Compilation of References

Nóvoa, A. (1995). *Os professores e sua formação*. Lisbon: Dom Quixote.

Nummedal, S., & Halpern, D. (1995). Making the case for psychologists teach critical thinking. *Teaching of Psychology, 22*(1), 4–5.

O'Neil, H. F., & Klein, D. C. D. (1997). *Feasibility of machine scoring of concept maps* (CSE Technical Report 460). Los Angeles, CA: National Center for Research on Evaluation, Standards, and Student Testing.

Offir, B., Yossi, L., & Bezalel, R. (2008). Surface and deep learning processes in distance education: Synchronous versus asynchronous systems. *Computers & Education, 51*, 1172–1183. doi:10.1016/j.compedu.2007.10.009

Ogle, D. (1986). A teaching model that develops active reading of expository text. *The Reading Teacher, 39*(6), 564–570. doi:10.1598/RT.39.6.11

Ogle, D. (2009). Creating contexts for inquiry: From KWL to PRC2. *Knowedge Quest, 38*(1), 57–61.

Okebukola, P. A. (1992). Concept mapping with a cooperative learning flavor. *The American Biology Teacher*, 218–221.

Oliver, K., & Hannafin, M. (2001). Developing and refining mental models in open-ended learning environments: A case study. *Educational Technology Research and Development, 49*(4), 5–32. doi:10.1007/BF02504945

Olson, K., & Clark, C. M. (2009). A signature pedagogy in doctoral education: The leader-scholar community. *Educational Researcher, 38*(3), 216–221. doi:10.3102/0013189X09334207

Otterman, S. (2012, August 1). Orthodox Jews celebrate cycle of Talmudic study. *The New York Times*. Retrieved from http://www.nytimes.com

Pantaleo, S. (2005). Reading young children's visual texts. *Early Childhood Research and Practice, 7*(1). doi: http://ecrp.uiuc.edu/v7n1/pantaleo.html

Parnes, S. J. (1975). AHA! In I. A. Taylor, & J. W. Gretz (Eds.), *Perspectives in creativity* (pp. 224–248). Chicago: Aldine Publishing Company.

Passmore, G. G., Owen, M. A., & Prabakaran, K. (2011). Empirical evidence of the effectiveness of concept mapping as a learning intervention for nuclear medicine technology students in a distance learning raditation protection and biology course. *Journal of Nuclear Medicine Technology, 39*(4), 284–289. doi:10.2967/jnmt.111.093062 PMID:22080436

Patterson, F. (2007). *Provoking students into thinking*. Retrieved from http://images.austhink.com/pdf/Compak_Critical_Thinking_in_Legal_Studies_March_07.pdf

Paul, R. (1982). Teaching critical thinking in the 'strong sense': A focus on self-deception, world views, and a dialectical mode of analysis. *Informal Logic Newsletter, 4*(2).

Paul, R., & Elder, L. (2009). Critical thinking: Where to begin. *The Critical Thinking Community*. Retrieved September 4, 2012, from http://www.criticalthinking.org/pages/critical-thinking-where-to-begin/796

Paul, R. W. (1992). Critical thinking: What, why, and how? *New Directions for Community Colleges*, (77): 3–24. doi:10.1002/cc.36819927703

Paul, R., & Elder, L. (2008). *Critical thinking*. Dillon Beach, CA: Foundation for Critical Thinking.

Paul, R. W., & Elder. (2006). Critical thinking: The nature of critical and creative thought. *Journal of Developmental Education, 30*(2), 34–35.

Pearson, M. (1999). The changing environment for doctoral education in Australia: Implications for quality management, improvement and innovation. *Higher Education Research & Development, 18*(3), 269–287. doi:10.1080/0729436990180301

Pearson, M., & Brew, A. (2002). Research training and supervision development. *Studies in Higher Education, 27*(2), 135–150. doi:10.1080/03075070220119986c

Pennycook, A. (2001). *Critical applied linguistics: A critical introduction*. Mahwah, NJ: Erlbaum Associates.

Perkins, D. N., & Salomon, G. (1989). Are cognitive skills context bound? *Educational Researcher, 18*, 16–25. doi:10.3102/0013189X018001016

Phillips, E. M., & Pugh, D. S. (2005). How to get a PhD: A handbook for students and their supervisors (4thed.). Berkshire, UK: Open University Press.

Phye, G. D. (1997). *Handbook of classroom assessment: Learning, achievement, and adjustment*. San Diego, CA: Academic Press.

Pink, D. (2009). *Drive, the surprising truth about what motivates us*. New York: Riverhead Books.

Pink, D. H. (2005). *A whole new mind: Why right brain learners will rule the future*. New York: The Berkely Publishing Group.

Pintrich, P. R., Smith, D. A. F., Garcia, T., & McKeachie, W. J. (1991). *A manual for the use of the motivated strategies for learning questionnaire (MSLQ)* (Technical Report No. 91-B-004). Ann Arbor, MI: National Center for Research to Improve Postsecondary Teaching and Learning.

Plotnick, E. (2001). A graphical system for understanding the relationship between concepts. *Teacher Librarian, 28*(4), 42–45.

Pontecorvo, C., & Girardet, H. (1993). Arguing and reasoning in understanding historical topics. *Cognition and Instruction, 11*(3-4), 365–395. doi:10.1080/07370008.1993.9649030

Popova-Gonci, V., & Lamb, M. C. (2012). Assessment of integrated learning: Suggested application of concept mapping to prior learning assessment practices. *The Journal of Continuing Higher Education, 60*, 186–191. doi:10.1080/07377363.2012.726175

Puntambekar, S., & Goldstein, J. (2007). Effect of visual representation of the conceptual structure of the domain on science learning and navigation in a hypertext environment. *Journal of Educational Multimedia and Hypermedia, 16*(4), 429–441.

Puntambekar, S., Stylianou, A., & Hübscher, R. (2003). Improving navigation and learning in hypertext environments with navigable concept maps. *Human-Computer Interaction, 18*(4), 395–426. doi:10.1207/S15327051HCI1804_3

Rabkin, N., & Redmon, R. (2004). *Putting the arts in the picture: Reframing education in the 21st century*. Chicago, IL: Columbia College Chicago.

Compilation of References

Read, S. (2005). First and second graders writing informational text. *The Reading Teacher*, 36–44. doi:10.1598/RT.59.1.4

Reece, G. (2002). *Critical thinking and transferability: A review of the literature*. American University Library. Retrieved May 15, 2012 from http://www.library.american.edu/Help/research/lit_review/critical_thinking.pdf

Rendas, A. B., Fonseca, M., & Pinto, P. R. (2006). Toward meaningful learning in undergraduate medical education using concept maps in a PBL pathophysiology course. *Advances in Physiology Education*, *30*(1), 23–29. doi:10.1152/advan.00036.2005 PMID:16481605

Resnick, L. B., Michaels, S., & O'Connor, C. (2010). How (well structured) talk builds the mind. In D. Preiss, & R. Sternberg (Eds.), *Innovations in educational psychology: Perspectives on learning, teaching and human development* (pp. 163–194). New York, NY: Springer.

Respress, T., & Lufti, G. (2006). Whole brain learning: The fine arts with students at risk. *Reclaiming Children and Youth*, *15*(1), 24–31.

Reznitskaya, A., Anderson, R. C., & Kuo, L.-J. (2007). Teaching and learning argumentation. *The Elementary School Journal*, *107*, 449–472. doi:10.1086/518623

Richter, M. G. (2000). *Ensino do Português e interatividade*. Santa Maria: UFSM.

Riding, R., & Raynor, S. (1998). *Cognitive styles and learning strategies*. London: David Fulton Publishers, Ltd.

Robson, S. (2006). *Developing thinking and understanding in young children*. New York, NY: Routledge.

Rogers, E. M., & Steinfatt, T. M. (1999). *Intercultural communication*. Long Grove, IL: Waveland Press.

Rolfe, S. A. (2001). Direct observation. In G. MacNaughton, S. A. Rolfe, & I. Siraj-Blatchford (Eds.), *Doing early childhood research: International perspectives on theory and practice* (pp. 224–239). Crows Nest, Australia: Alen & Unwin.

Roop, K. M. (2002). *Effect of concept mapping as a learning strategy on certificate practical nursing students' academic achievement and critical thinking development*. (Doctoral dissertation). Wilmington College, Wilmington, DE.

Rosenblatt, L. (1978). *The reader, the poem, the text: The transactional theory of the literary work*. Carbondale, IL: Southern Illinois University Press.

Roth, R., & Roth, S. K. (1998). *Beauty is nowhere: Ethical issues in art and design*. Amsterdam: The Gordon and Breach Publishing Group.

Rourke, L., & Kanuka, H. (2007). Computer conferencing and distance learning. In *The handbook of computer networks* (Vol. 3, pp. 831–842). Hoboken, NJ: John Wiley & Sons.

Rushton, A. (2005). Formative assessment: a key to deep learning? *Medical Teacher*, *27*(6), 509–513. doi:10.1080/01421590500129159 PMID:16199357

Ruskin, J. (1872). *Modern painters* (Vol. 3). London: Smith, Elder and Company.

Sadoski, M., Paivio, A., & Andrews, R. (2001). *Imagery and text – A dual coding theory of reading and writing*. Hillsdale, NJ: Lawrence Erlbaum Associates.

Safayeni, F., Derbentseva, N., & Cañas, A. J. (2005). A theoretical note on concepts and the need for cyclic concept maps. *Journal of Research in Science Teaching, 42,* 741–766. doi:10.1002/tea.20074

Salmon, G. (2000). e Moderating: The key to teaching and learning online. London: Kogan Page.

Sandoval, W. (2003). Conceptual and epistemic aspects of students' scientific explanations. *Journal of the Learning Sciences, 12*(1), 5–51. doi:10.1207/S15327809JLS1201_2

Scardamalia, M. (2002). Collective cognitive responsibility for the advancement of knowledge. In B. Smith (Ed.), *Liberal education in a knowledge society* (pp. 67–98). Chicago, IL: Open Court.

Scardamalia, M. (2004). CSILE/knowledge forum. In A. Kovalchick, & K. Dawson (Eds.), *Education and technology: An encyclopedia* (pp. 183–192). Santa Barbara, CA: ABC-CLIO.

Scardamalia, M., & Bereiter, C. (1994). Computer support for knowledge building communities. *Journal of the Learning Sciences, 3*(3), 265–283. doi:10.1207/s15327809jls0303_3

Scardamalia, M., & Bereiter, C. (2006). Knowledge building: Theory, pedagogy and technology. In R. K. Sawyer (Ed.), *The Cambridge handbook of the learning sciences* (pp. 97–118). New York: Cambridge University Press.

Schama, S. (2006). *The power of art.* New York: HarperCollins Publishers.

Schlais, D., & Davis, R. (2001). Distance learning through educational networks: The global view experience. In *Teaching and learning online: Pedagogies for new technologies.* London: Kogan Page Limited.

Schmidt, H. J. (2004). Alternative approaches to concept mapping and implications for medical education: Commentary on reliability, validity and future research directions. *Advances in Health Sciences Education : Theory and Practice, 9*(3), 251–256. doi:10.1023/B:AHSE.0000038309.92212.44 PMID:15316275

Schön, D. (1983). *The reflective practitioner.* New York: Basic Books, Inc.

Schreiber, J. B., Verdi, M. P., Patock-Peckham, J., Johnson, J. T., & Kealy, W. A. (2002). Differing map construction and text organization and their effects on retention. *Journal of Experimental Education, 70*(2), 114–130. doi:10.1080/00220970209599502

Schuster, P. M. (2000). Concept mapping: Reducing clinical care plan paperwork and increasing learning. *Nurse Educator, 25*(2), 76–81. doi:10.1097/00006223-200003000-00009 PMID:11052005

Schwarz, B., & Perret-Clermont, A.-N. (Eds.). (2008). *ESCALATE's white book on argumentation and enquiry-based science learning.* Retrieved August, 29 from www.escalate.org.il/Multimedia/upl_doc/D5_1_White_book_v4.pdf

Schwarz, B. B., & Asterhan, C. S. C. (2011). E-moderation of synchronous discussions in educational settings: A nascent practice. *Journal of the Learning Sciences, 20*(3), 395–442. doi:10.1080/10508406.2011.553257

Schwarz, B. B., & De Groot, R. (2007). Argumentation in a changing world. *Computer-Supported Collaborative Learning, 2*(2-3), 297–313. doi:10.1007/s11412-007-9020-6

Compilation of References

Schwarz, B. B., & De Groot, R. (2010). Breakdowns between teachers, educators and designers in elaborating new technologies as precursors of change in education to dialogic thinking. In S. Ludvigsen, A. Lund, & R. Säljö (Eds.), *Learning across sites: New tools, infrastructures and practices* (pp. 261–277). New York: Routledge.

Schwarz, B. B., & Glassner, A. (2003). The blind and the paralytic: fostering argumentation in everyday and scientific issues. In J. Andriessen, M. Baker, & D. Suthers (Eds.), *Arguing to learn: Confronting cognitions in computer-supported collaborative learning environments* (pp. 227–260). Dordrecht, The Netherlands: Kluwer Academic Publishers. doi:10.1007/978-94-017-0781-7_9

Schwarz, B. B., & Glassner, A. (2007). The role of floor control and of ontology in argumentative activities with discussion-based tools. *Computer Supported Collaborative Learning*, *3*(4), 449–478. doi:10.1007/s11412-007-9024-2

Schwarz, B. B., & Linchevski, L. (2007). The role of task design and of argumentation in cognitive development during peer interaction: The case of proportional reasoning. *Learning and Instruction*, *17*(5), 510–531. doi:10.1016/j.learninstruc.2007.09.009

Schwarz, B. B., Neuman, Y., & Biezuner, S. (2000). Two wrongs may make a right… If they argue together! *Cognition and Instruction*, *18*(4), 461–494. doi:10.1207/S1532690XCI1804_2

Schwarz, B. B., Neuman, Y., Gil, J., & Ilya, M. (2003). Construction of collective and individual knowledge in argumentative activity: An empirical study. *Journal of the Learning Sciences*, *12*(2), 221–258. doi:10.1207/S15327809JLS1202_3

Schwarz, B. B., Schur, Y., Pensso, H., & Tayer, N. (2011). Perspective taking and synchronous argumentation for learning the day/night cycle. *Computer-Supported Collaborative Learning*, *6*, 113–138. doi:10.1007/s11412-010-9100-x

Schwarz, B. B., & Shahar, N. (in press). Combining the dialogic and the dialectic: Putting argumentation into practice for classroom talk. *Cognition and Instruction*.

Scouller, K. (1998). The influence of assessment method on students' learning approaches: Multiple choice question examination versus assignment essay. *Higher Education*, *35*, 453–472. doi:10.1023/A:1003196224280

Scriven, M., & Paul, R. (1987). *Defining critical thinking*. Paper presented at the 8th Annual International Conference on Critical Thinking and Education Reform, Summer 1987. Retrieved 22 June 2012 from http://www.criticalthinking.org/pages/defining-critical-thinking/766

Scriven, M., & Paul, R. (2003). *Defining critical thinking*. Retrieved from http://www.criticalthinking.org/University/univclass/Defining.html

Seabrook Primary School. (2004). *Seabrook report: Mind mapping the learning platform at Seabrook Primary School*. Melbourne, Australia: Seabrook Primary School.

Selwyn, N., & Facer, K. (2007). *Beyond the digital divide: Rethinking digital inclusion for the 21st*. Retrieved from http://www.futurelab.org.uk/resources/documents/opening_education/Digital_Divide.pdf

Senita, J. (2011). The use of concept maps to evaluate critical thinking in the clinical setting. *Teaching and Learning in Nursing*, *3*(1), 6–10. doi:10.1016/j.teln.2007.08.002

Shedletsky, L. (2010). Critical thinking in discussion: Online versus face-to-face. In D. Russell (Ed.), *Cases on collaboration in virtual environments: Processes and interactions*. Hershey, PA: Information Science Reference.

Shedletsky, L. (2010). Does online discussion produce increased interaction and critical thinking? In L. Shedletsky, & J. Aitken (Eds.), *Cases on online discussion and interaction: Experiences and outcomes*. Hershey, PA: IGI Global. doi:10.4018/978-1-61520-863-0.ch001

Shedletsky, L., & Aitken, J. (Eds.). (2010). *Cases on online discussion and interaction: Experiences and outcomes*. Hershey, PA: IGI Global. doi:10.4018/978-1-61520-863-0

Shermis, M. D., & DiVesta, F. J. (2011). *Classroom assessment in action*. Plymouth, UK: Rowman & Littlefield Publishers.

Shor, I., & Freire, P. (1987). What is the dialogic method of teaching? *Journal of Education, 169*(3), 11–31.

Silverman, L. K. (2004). *At-risk youth and the creative process*. Paper presented at the Alternatives for At-Risk Youth Conference. Colorado Springs, CO.

Sinatra, R. (1986). *Visual literacy connections to thinking, reading, and writing*. Springfield, IL: Charles Thomas Press.

Singh, P. (2002). Pedagogising knowledge: Bernstein's theory of the pedagogic device. *British Journal of Sociology of Education, 23*(4), 571–582. doi:10.1080/0142569022000038422

Siraj-Blatchford, I., & Siraj-Blatchford, J. (2001). An ethnographic approach to researching young children's learning. In G. MacNaughton, S. A. Rolfe, & I. Siraj-Blatchford (Eds.), *Doing early childhood research: International perspectives on theory and practice* (pp. 193–207). Crows Nest, Australia: Alen & Unwin.

Smith, A. (2001). *The brain's behind it*. Stafford, UK: Network Educational Press Ltd.

Smith, B. L., & McCann, J. (2001). *Reinventing ourselves: Interdisciplinary education, collaborative learning, and experimentation in higher education*. Bolton, MA: Anker Publishing.

Smith, D. G. (1977). College classroom interactions and critical thinking. *Journal of Educational Psychology, 69*, 180–190. doi:10.1037/0022-0663.69.2.180

Smith, J., diSessa, & Roschelle, J. (1993). Misconceptions reconceived: A constructivist analysis of knowledge in transition. *Journal of the Learning Sciences, 3*, 115–163. doi:10.1207/s15327809jls0302_1

Smith, S. R., & Dollase, R. (1999). An introduction to outcome-based education. *Medical Teacher, 21*(1), 15–22. doi:10.1080/01421599979978

Smith, S. R., Dollase, R. H., & Boss, J. A. (2003). Assessing students' performances in a competency-based curriculum. *Academic Medicine, 78*(1), 97–107. doi:10.1097/00001888-200301000-00019 PMID:12525418

Smolken & Donovan. (2004). Improving science instruction with information books: Understanding multimodal presentations. In E. W. Saul (Ed.), *Crossing borders in literacy and science education: Perspectives on theory and science instruction* (pp. 190–208). Newark, DE: International Reading Association.

Snyder, K. M. (2007). The digital culture and peda-socio transformation. *Seminar.net: Media, Technology and Lifelong Learning, 3*(1).

Snyder, K. M. (2010). *Breaking ground across cultures: How visual communication is used to support peer- to-peer learning in an international project.* Paper presentation at the DIVERSE Annual Conference. Portland, ME.

Snyder, K. J., Acker-Hocever, M., & Snyder, K. M. (2008). *Living on the edge of chaos: Leading schools into the global age.* Milwaukee, WI: ASQ A Quality Press.

Snyder, K. J., Mann, J., Johnson, E., & Xing, M. (2010, Fall). Connecting students across cultures: The global partnership project. *Innovation (Abingdon).*

Snyder, M. J. (2008). Teaching critical thinking and problem solving skills. *Delta Pi Epsilon Journal, 50*(2), 90–99.

Sorensen, E. K. (2002). Designing for collaborative knowledge building in online communities of practice. In H. Hansson (Ed.), *Eight contributions on quality and flexible learning. Härnösand: DISTUM.*

Spanjers, I. E., van Gog, T., & van Merriënboer, J. G. (2010). A theoretical analysis of how segmentation of dynamic visualizations optimizes students' learning. *Educational Psychology Review, 22*(4), 411–423. doi:10.1007/s10648-010-9135-6

Sperry, R. W. (1967). Split-brain approach to learning problems. In G. Quarton, F. Schmitt, & T. Melnechuk (Eds.), *The neurosciences: A study program* (pp. 714–722). New York: Rockefeller University Press.

Stake, R. E. (1995). *The art of case study research.* Thousand Oaks, CA: SAGE Publications, Inc.

Staton, J. (1988). ERIC/RCS report: Dialogue journals. *Language Arts, 65*, 198–201.

Stead, T., & Hoyt, L. (2011). A guide to teaching nonfiction writing, K-2: Explorations in nonfiction writing. Portsmouth, NH: firsthand.

Stead, T. (2000). *Should there be zoos? A persuasive text.* New York, NY: Mondo Publishing.

Stead, T. (2002). *Is that a fact? Teaching nonfiction writing K-3.* Portland, ME: Stenhouse.

Steinsaltz, A. (1976). *The essential Talmud.* New York, NY: Basic Books.

Steinsaltz, A. (2012). *Koren Talmud bavli.* Jerusalem, Israel: Koren Publishers.

Stepans, J. (2003). *Targeting students' science misconceptions.* Tampa, FL: Showboard, Inc.

Sternberg, R. J. (1986). *Critical thinking: Its nature, measurement, and improvement.* National Institute of Education. Retrieved from http://eric.ed.gov/PDFS/ED272882.pdf

Stewart, M. (2011). *Deadliest animals.* Washington, DC: National Geographic Society.

Stokes, S. (2001). Visual literacy in teaching and learning: A literature perspective. *Electronic Journal for the Integration of Technology in Education, 1*(1), 10–19.

Survey and Research Report on the Coffee Cup Soda Grill. (2006). Retrieved August 24, 2011 from http://www.cmhpf.org/surveys&rcoffeecup.htm

Suthers, D. D., & Weiner, A. (1995). *Groupware for developing critical discussion skills*. Paper presented in the 1ˢᵗ International Conference on Computer Support for Cooperative Learning. Bloomington, IN.

Suthers, D. D. (2003). Representational guidance for collaborative inquiry. In J. Andriessen, M. Baker, & D. Suthers (Eds.), *Arguing to learn: Confronting cognitions in computer-supported collaborative learning environments* (pp. 27–46). Dordrecht, The Netherlands: Kluwer Academic Publishers. doi:10.1007/978-94-017-0781-7_2

Suthers, D., & Hundhausen, C. (2003). An empirical study of the effects of representational guidance on collaborative learning. *Journal of the Learning Sciences*, *12*(2), 183–219. doi:10.1207/S15327809JLS1202_2

Swaminatham, N. (2006). Testing improves retention--Even of material not on exam. *Scientific American*, *295*(5).

Sylwester, R. (1995). *A celebration of neurons: An educator's guide to the human brain*. Andrewandria, VA: ASCD.

Tagg, J. (2003). *The learning paradigm college*. San Francisco, CA: Anker Publishing.

Tarman, B. (2010). Global perspectives and challenges on teacher education in Turkey. *International Journal of Arts and Sciences*, *3*(17), 78–96.

Taylor, L. A., & Littleton-Kearney, M. (2011). Concept mapping: A distinctive educational approach to foster critical thinking. *Nurse Educator*, *36*(2), 84–88. doi:10.1097/NNE.0b013e31820b5308 PMID:21330901

Terenzini, P. T., Springer, L., Pascarella, E. T., & Nora, A. (1995). Influences affecting the development of students' critical thinking skills. *Research in Higher Education*, *36*(1), 23–39. doi:10.1007/BF02207765

Thayer-Bacon, B. J. (2000). *Transforming critical thinking: Thinking constructively*. New York, NY: Teachers College Press.

Thompson, C. (2011). Critical thinking across the curriculum. *International Journal of Humanities and Social Sciences*, *1*(9), 1–7.

Thompson, J., Licklider, B., & Jungst, S. (2003). Learner-centered teaching: Postsecondary strategies that promote thinking like a professional. *Theory into Practice*, *42*(2), 133–141.

Thompson, R., & Zamboanga, B. (2004). Academic aptitude and prior knowledge as predictors of student achievement in introduction to psychology. *Journal of Educational Psychology*, *96*, 778–784. doi:10.1037/0022-0663.96.4.778

Thomson, A. (2002). *Critical reasoning: A practical introduction*. London: Routledge.

Thornburg, H. D. (1984). *Introduction to educational psychology*. St. Paul, MN: West Publishing Company.

Todorović, D. (2008). Gestalt principles. *Scholarpedia*, *3*(12), 5345. doi:10.4249/scholarpedia.5345

Torres, P. L., & Marriott, R. C. V. (Eds.). (2010). *Handbook of research on collaborative learning using concept mapping*. Hershey, PA: Information Science Reference.

Toy, E. C., Seifert, W. E., Strobel, H. W., & Harms, K. P. (2005). *Case files biochemistry*. New York: McGraw-Hill, Medical Publishing Division.

Compilation of References

Trafford, V. N., & Leshem, S. (2008). *Stepping stones to achieving your doctorate*. Maidenhead, UK: Open University Press.

Tremblay, R. (1999). L'interprétation a contrario est abusive. *Le Journal du Barrreau du Quebec, 31*(7).

Trowbridge, J. E., & Wandersee, J. E. (2005). Theory-driven graphic organizers. In J. J. Mintzes, J. H. Wandersee, & J. D. Novak (Eds.), *Teaching sciences for understanding: A human constructivist view* (pp. 95–131). New York: Elsevier Academic Press. doi:10.1016/B978-012498360-1/50005-2

Trowbridge, J. E., & Wandersee, J. H. (1998). Theory-driven graphic organizers. In J. J. Mintzes, J. H. Wandersee, & J. D. Novak (Eds.), *Assessing science understanding: A human constructivist view* (pp. 15–40). San Diego, CA: Academic Press.

Trumpower, D. L., & Sarwar, G. S. (2010). Formative structural assessment: Using concept maps as assessment for learning. In J. Sanchez, A. J. Cañas & J. D. Novak (Eds.), *Proceedings of the Fourth International Conference on Concept Mapping* (Vol. 2, pp. 132-136). Santiago de Chile: Lom Ediciones S.A.

Tsui, L. (1999). Courses and instruction affecting critical thinking. *Research in Higher Education, 40*(2), 185–200. doi:10.1023/A:1018734630124

Tsui, L. (2002). Fostering critical thinking through effective pedagogy: Evidence from four institutional case studies. *The Journal of Higher Education, 73*, 740–763. doi:10.1353/jhe.2002.0056

Tucker, M. S. (Ed.). (2012). *Surpassing Shanghai: An agenda for American education built on the world's leading systems*. Cambridge, MA: Harvard Education Press.

Tufte, E. (1990). *Envisioning information*. Cheshire, CT: Graphics Press.

Turner, S. (2011). Evaluating learning through the use of concept maps. In *Proceedings of the 3rd Annual Conference on Higher Education Pedagogy* (pp. 21 – 22). Blacksburg, VA: Virginia Tech.

Twardy, C. R. (2004). Argument maps improve critical thinking. *Teaching Philosophy, 27*(2). doi:10.5840/teachphil200427213

Tyler, L. E. (1983). *Thinking creatively*. San Francisco: Jossey-Bass Publishers.

Ury, I. (2011). *Charting the sea of Talmud*. Jerusalem, Israel: Mosaica Publishing.

van Boxtel, C., van der Linden, J., Roelofs, E., & Erkens, G. (2002). Collaborative concept mapping: Provoking and supporting meaningful discourse. *Theory into Practice, 41*(1), 40–46. doi:10.1207/s15430421tip4101_7

van Bruggen, J. M., & Kirschner, P. A. (2003). Designing external representations to support solving wicked problems. In J. Andriessen, M. Baker, & D. Suthers (Eds.), *Arguing to learn: Confronting cognitions in computer-supported collaborative learning environments* (pp. 177–204). Dordrecht, The Netherlands: Kluwer Academic Publishers. doi:10.1007/978-94-017-0781-7_7

Van Doren, M. (1943). *Liberal education*. New York: Henry Holt.

Van Gelder, T. (n.d.). *What is visual deliberation?* Retrieved from http://timvangelder.com/2010/09/27/what-is-visual-deliberation/

Van Gelder, T. (2003). Enhancing deliberation through computer supported argument visualization. In *Visualizing argumentation: Software tools for collaborative and educational sense-making* (pp. 97–115). Academic Press. doi:10.1007/978-1-4471-0037-9_5 van Gelder, T. J. (2005). Teaching critical thinking: some lessons from cognitive science. *College Teaching, 53*, 41–46. doi:10.3200/CTCH.53.1.41-48

van Gelder, T. J. (2006). Vertical thinking. *Leadership Excellence, 23*(7), 20.

van Gelder, T. J. (2013). Argument mapping. In H. Pashler (Ed.), *Encyclopedia of the mind*. Thousand Oaks, CA: Sage. doi:10.4135/9781452257044.n19

Varner, I., & Beamer, L. (2010). *Intercultural communication in the global workplace* (5th ed.). New York: McGraw-Hill.

Vasquez, V. (2008). *Negotiating critical literacies with young children*. Mahwah, NJ: Lawrence Erlbaum Associates, Inc.

Vaughan, W. (2000). *Terror and the tabula rasa*. New York: Cambridge University Press.

Vaughan, W., Weston, H., Gretton, T., & Halliday, T. (2000). *David's the death of Marat*. New York: Cambridge University Press.

Villalon, J., & Calvo, R. A. (2011). Concept maps as cognitive visualizations of writing assignments. *Journal of Educational Technology & Society, 14*(3), 16–27.

Vogel-Walcutt, J.J., Gebrim, J.B., Bowers, C., & Carper, T.M., & Nicholson. (2011). Cognitive load theory vs. constructivist approaches: Which best leads to efficient, deep learning? *Journal of Computer Assisted Learning, 27*, 133–145. doi:10.1111/j.1365-2729.2010.00381.x

von der Heidt, T. (2011). *Learning with concept maps: A study to measure change in learning in undergraduate Chinese marketing students*. Southern Cross University.

VUE. (2001). *Visual thinking strategies: Understanding the basics*. Retrieved from www.vue.org

Vygotsky, L. (1962). *Thought and language*. Boston, MA: The MIT Press. doi:10.1037/11193-000

Vygotsky, L. (1978). *Mind and society*. Cambridge, MA: Harvard University Press.

Vygotsky, L. (1978). *Mind in society: The development of higher psychological processes*. Cambridge, MA: Harvard University Press.

Walker, S., Day, Matsumoto, Elthon, Prager, Keener-Chavis, … McDonnell. (n.d.). Centers for ocean sciences education excellence implementation steering committee report. *The Journal of Marine Education, 17*(2), 5-8.

Walker, G. E., Golde, C. M., Jones, L., Bueschel, A. C., & Hutchings, P. (2008). *The formation of scholars: Rethinking doctoral education for the twenty-first century*. San Francisco: Jossey-Bass.

Walker, M. (2009). An investigation into written comments on assignments: Do students find them usable? *Assessment & Evaluation in Higher Education, 34*(1), 67–78. doi:10.1080/02602930801895752

Wallace, C. (2003). *Critical reading in language education*. New York: Palgrave Macmillan. doi:10.1057/9780230514447

Walsh, S. (2010). The portal for postgraduates in medicine. In J. Sanchez, A. J. Cañas & J. D. Novak (Eds.), *Proceedings of the Fourth International Conference on Concept Mapping* (Vol. 2, pp. 224-227). Santiago de Chile: Lom Ediciones S.A.

Compilation of References

Wandersee, J. H. (1990). Concept mapping and the cartography of cognition. *Journal of Research in Science Teaching, 27*(10), 923–936. doi:10.1002/tea.3660271002

Wang, M., Peng, J., Cheng, B., Zhou, H., & Liu, J. (2011). Knowledge visualization for self-regulated learning. *Journal of Educational Technology & Society, 14*(3), 28–42.

Watson, G. R. (1998). What is. concept maps? *Medical Teacher, 11*(3-4), 265–269. doi:10.3109/01421598909146411

Wegerif, R. (2007). *Dialogic education and technology: Expanding the space of learning*. New York: Springer Science. doi:10.1007/978-0-387-71142-3

Weimer, M. (2002). *Learner-centered teaching: Five key changes to practice*. San Francisco: Jossey-Bass.

Weisenberg, R. C. (1997). Appropriate technology for the classroom - Using 'Post-It Notes©' as an active learning tool. *Journal of College Science Teaching, 26*(5), 339–344.

Wells, G. (2007). Semiotic mediation, dialogue and the construction of knowledge. *Human Development, 50*, 244–274. doi:10.1159/000106414

Wells, M., Hestenes, D., & Swackhamer, G. (1995). A modeling method for high school physics instruction. *American Journal of Physics, 64*, 114–119.

West, D. C., Park, J. K., Pomeroy, J. R., & Sandoval, J. (2002). Concept mapping assessment in medical education: A comparison of two scoring systems. *Medical Education, 38*, 820–826. doi:10.1046/j.1365-2923.2002.01292.x PMID:12354244

Weston, H. (2000). *The Corday Marat affair*. New York: Cambridge University Press.

Wheeler, L. A., & Collins, S. K. (2003). The influence of concept mapping on critical thinking in baccalaureate nursing students. *Journal of Professional Nursing, 19*(6), 339–346. doi:10.1016/S8755-7223(03)00134-0 PMID:14689390

Whisker, G. (2004). *The good supervisor*. London: Macmillan Palgrave.

Wiggins, G. P., & McTighe, J. (1998). *Understanding by design*. Alexandria, VA: Association for Supervision and Curriculum Development.

Wilgis, M., & McConnell, J. (2008). Concept mapping: An educational strategy to improve graduate nurses' critical thinking skills during a hospital orientation program. *Journal of Continuing Education in Nursing, 39*(3), 119–126. doi:10.3928/00220124-20080301-12 PMID:18386699

Wilkes, L., Cooper, K., Lewin, J., & Batts, J. (1999). Concept mapping: Promoting science learning in BN learners in Australia. *Journal of Continuing Education in Nursing, 30*(1), 37–44. PMID:10036416

Williams, M. (2004). Concept mapping - A strategy for assessment. *Nursing Standard, 19*(9), 33–38. doi:10.7748/ns2004.11.19.9.33.c3754 PMID:15574052

Williams, R. L. (2005). Targeting critical thinking within teacher education: The potential impact on society. *Teacher Educator, 40*(3), 163–187. doi:10.1080/08878730509555359

Willingham, D. T. (2008). Critical thinking: Why is it so hard to teach? *Arts Education Policy Review, 109*(4), 21–32. doi:10.3200/AEPR.109.4.21-32

Wilson, L. O. (1997). *Newer views of learning: Types of questions*. Retrieved September 3, 2012, from http://www4.uwsp.edu/Education/lwilson/learning/quest2.htm

Wilson, B. G. (1996). What is a constructivist learning environment? In B. G. Wilson (Ed.), *Constructivist learning environments: Case studies in instructional design* (pp. 3–8). Englewood Cliffs, NJ: Educational Technology Publications.

Winckelmann, J. J. (1756). *Gedanken über die nachahmung der griechischen werke in der malerei und bildhauerkunst* (2nd ed.). Academic Press.

Windschitl, M. (2002). Framing constructivism in practice as the negotiation of dilemmas: An analysis of the conceptual, pedagogical, cultural and political challenges facing teachers. *Review of Educational Research*, 72(2), 131–175. doi:10.3102/00346543072002131

Wiser, M., Smith, C. L., Doubler, S., & Asbell-Clarke, J. (2009). *Learning progressions as a tool for curriculum development: Lessons from the inquiry project*. Paper presented at the Learning Progressions in Science (LeaPS) Conference. Iowa City, IA.

Wiser, M., & Smith, C. (2009). *How does cognitive development inform the choice of core ideas in the physical sciences?* Washington, DC: National Research Council.

Wolfe, P., & Sorgen, M. (1990). *Mind, memory and learning*. Napa, CA: Authors.

Woods, N. N. (2007). Science is fundamental: The role of biomedical knowledge in clinical reasoning. *Medical Education*, 41(12), 1173–1177. doi:10.1111/j.1365-2923.2007.02911.x PMID:18045369

Woods, N. N., Brooks, L. R., & Norman, G. R. (2007). It all make sense: Biomedical knowledge, causal connections and memory in the novice diagnostician. *Advances in Health Sciences Education: Theory and Practice*, 12, 405–415. doi:10.1007/s10459-006-9055-x PMID:17318360

Woods, N. N., Brooks, L. R., & Norman, G. R. (2007). The role of biomedical knowledge in diagnosis of difficult clinical cases. *Advances in Health Sciences Education: Theory and Practice*, 12(4), 417–426. doi:10.1007/s10459-006-9054-y PMID:17206465

WSU Critical Thinking Project. (n.d.). Retrieved from http://wsuctproject.wsu.edu/

WSU Critical Thinking Rubric. (n.d.). Retrieved from http://wsuctproject.wsu.edu/fa-1.htm

Wycoff, J. (1991). *Mindmapping: Your personal guide to exploring creativity and problem-solving*. New York: Berkley Books.

Yenawine, P. (2008). *Writing for adult museum visitors*. Retrieved April 22, 2012, from http://www.museum-ed.org/index.php?option=com_content&view=article&id=80:writing-for-adult-museum-visitors&catid=37:current-practice-interpretation&Itemid=86

Yenawine, P. (1997). Thoughts on visual literacy. In *Handbook of research on teaching literacy through the communicative and visual arts*. New York: Macmillan Library Reference.

Yenice, N. (2011). Investigating pre-service teachers' critical thinking disposition in terms of different variables. *European Journal of Soil Science*, 20(4), 593–603.

Compilation of References

Young, T., & Moss, B. (2006). Nonfiction in the classroom library: A literacy necessity. *Childhood Education*, *82*(4), 207–212. doi: 10.1080/00094056.2006.10522824

Yücel, A. S. Ö., & Koçak, C. (2010). Determining the critical thinking levels of the student teachers and evaluating through some variables. *International Online Journal of Educational Sciences*, *2*(3), 865–882.

Yuen, E. Y., Wei, J., Liu, W., Zhong, P., Li, X., & Yan, Z. (2012). Repeated stress causes cognitive impairment by suppressing glutamate receptor expression and function in prefrontal cortex. *Neuron*, *73*, 962–977. doi:10.1016/j.neuron.2011.12.033 PMID:22405206

Zhang, J., Scardamalia, M., Reeve, M., & Messina, R. (2009). Designs for collective cognitive responsibility in knowledge-building communities. *Journal of the Learning Sciences*, *18*, 7–44. doi:10.1080/10508400802581676

About the Contributors

Leonard J. Shedletsky, Ph.D., is Professor of Communication at The University of Southern Maine. He is the author of *Meaning and Mind: An Intrapersonal Approach to Human Communication* (1989), co-author of *Human Communication on the Internet*, co-editor of *Intrapersonal Communication Processes* (1995), co-editor in 2010 of *Cases on Online Discussion and Interaction: Experiences and Outcomes*. He wrote the entry, "Cognition," for the *International Encyclopedia of Communication* (2008). He has been teaching since 1974. He teaches a range of courses in communication with cognition, discourse, and meaning as underlying themes. He was awarded recognition for Stellar Scholarship and Teaching, University of Southern Maine (USM) 2003, 2007, and 2011. He was named The Russell Chair, 2009 – 2011. He has recently taught a number of online courses that make heavy use of discussion and mapping.

Jeffrey S. Beaudry, Ph.D., is an Associate Professor, Educational Leadership, at the University of Southern Maine. He aims to explore issues relating to visual learning, formative assessment, authentic learning, and science literacy. His publication of "Concept Mapping and Formative Assessment: Elements Supporting Literacy and Learning" published in the *Handbook for Research on Concept Mapping and Collaborative Research*, and the co-edited a book *Cases on Teaching Critical Thinking through Visual Representation Strategies* builds the argument for visual literacy for teachers from early childhood to graduate level. He has a degree and freelanced as a pre-digital photographer, and his work is published in numerous books and magazines. Dr. Beaudry now teaches courses online and in blended media formats with Webinars and video networks for the USM. He is an active, contributing faculty member to the USM Center for Technology Education and Learning (CTEL), where he collaborates and leads professional development on multimedia, especially concept mapping and customized, interactive, interactive videos.

* * *

Robin M. Bright is a Professor of Education at the University of Lethbridge in Alberta, Canada. She teaches courses to undergraduate and graduate students in the areas of the literacy, writing, writing across the curriculum, multi- and digital-literacies, and gender. Previously, Dr. Bright taught elementary school for ten years. She is the author of several books, most recently, *Write through the Grades: Teaching Writing in the Secondary Grades* (2007) and co-author of the Canadian edition of the textbook, *Language Arts: Content and Teaching Strategies* (2011). Her work has appeared in the *Journal of Reading Education, Canadian Children, The Canadian Journal of English Language Arts, Alberta English, The Writing Teacher, English Quarterly,* and the *Journal of Teacher Education.* Her current research focuses on middle-school youth and their in- and out-of-school literacies and writing instruction.

Siu Challons-Lipton is Chair of the Art Department and Associate Professor of Art History at Queens University of Charlotte. She earned her doctorate degree in 19th Century Art from the University of Oxford and her bachelor's and master's of art degrees in Baroque Art from McGill University. She also trained at Sotheby's, London, in 19th and 20th Century Decorative Arts. She is a member of the Board of Directors of the Mint Museums. Her research interests include 19th Century Academic and Realist Art, Internationalism in late 19th Century Paris, Scandinavian Art of the 19th and 20th Centuries, Black Mountain College of North Carolina, Critical and Creative Thinking, and Visual Literacy. She published a book in 2002 on *The Scandinavian Pupils of the Atelier Bonnat, 1867-1894.* Dr. Challons-Lipton spent her childhood in Africa, Europe, and the South Pacific. She continues to be passionate about travel, culture, languages, and, of course, art.

Annette deCharon is a Senior Marine Education Scientist in the University of Maine's School of Marine Sciences. Her academic background is in earth sciences (B.S. in Geology and M.S. in Oceanography). Her interests in science communication and multimedia began at the Jet Propulsion Laboratory, where she was awarded a NASA Exceptional Service Medal for her work. Recent activities have focused on fostering collaboration between scientists, educators and students to improve understanding of the relevance of ocean research to society.

Kate Dunsmore, Ph.D., is Assistant Professor in Communication Studies at Fairleigh Dickinson University, Madison, NJ. Her areas of research include political communication, international communication, and public discourse. She has published in the areas of political communication and pedagogical research. Her dissertation (2008, University of Washington), titled *Mediating Alliance: The Role* *of the Press in Sustaining Reciprocity in the US-Canada Relationship,* won the 2009 ACSUS Distinguished Dissertation Award. She is also the recipient of the Fairleigh Dickinson University Educational Opportunity Fund 2010 Outstanding Faculty Award, recognizing her work with disadvantaged students. She is currently extending her findings on 20th and 21st century discourses in the Canada-US relationship by exploring the roots of these discourses in the late 18th and early 19th century period.

Richard Emanuel is a Professor of Communication at Alabama State University in Montgomery. He earned his doctorate degree in Communication Theory and Research from Florida State University, a master's degree in Speech Communication from Auburn University, and a bachelor's degree in Speech and Theater from the University of Montevallo. Dr. Emanuel has taught at two-year and four-year public and private colleges. His research has been published in national and international journals and he has made presentations throughout the United States and in Great Britain. His research interests include the health of the communication profession in higher education, communication style, campus sustainability, college student cell phone use, customer service, and visual literacy. He has also compiled, edited, and produced several Readers Theater scripts including *The Montgomery Bus Boycott.* Dr. Emanuel is a certified scuba diver and he enjoys racquetball, movies, music, and travel.

Rhoda Frumkin received her Ed.D. from Rutgers University in New Jersey. She is an Associate Professor of Education at Wagner College focusing on Literacy, Service Learning, and Teacher Training. Dr. Frumkin's scholarly interests include cross-discipline literacy learning and the use of collaborative techniques and tools to facilitate interactive collegial dialogue about classroom practices.

Amnon Glassner was trained as a math teacher and then completed his M.A. and Ph.D. in the center of cognition, instruction, and computers at the Hebrew University in Jerusalem. He participated in some studies about learning and argumentation in the frame of Kishurim Group under the leadership of Prof. Baruch Schwarz. His current educational interest is to lead some new progressive programs of teacher training, such as those who use PBL (Project- or Product-Based Learning) as main direction for learning and instruction. He serves as the head of Education Department, the head of Informal Studies, and a pedagogical guide in Kaye Academic College of Education in Beer-Sheva. His current research directions include infusion of creative and critical thinking during learning of any content, learning with PBL, learning by successes, and moderation of dialogical learning discussion.

Cristine G. Goldberg is currently an adjunct professor at the University of the Cumberlands in the College of Education. She completed her doctorate in Curriculum and Instruction at the University of Sarasota. Other graduate degrees include a specialist (school library media) from the University of West Georgia, and a master's (English education) from the University of Tennessee at Chattanooga, and undergraduate work in liberal arts and teaching from Florida International University. Dr. Goldberg is a retired professor from the University of West Georgia, College of Education, Department of Educational Foundations and Technology. Prior work experiences include 30 years of teaching in the K-12 public school area with an emphasis in English, Gifted, Honors, and School Library Media. Dr. Goldberg has also developed and taught gifted courses and grant writing for Global Classroom. She has conducted professional learning courses in the fine arts, puppetry arts, storytelling, concept mapping, speed-reading, critical thinking skills, and grant writing. She has also conducted courses in concept mapping and speed-reading for corporate clients and private individuals in Brazil.

Gloria Gomez, Ph.D., undertakes applied design research for new product development that enables innovative areas of practices to emerge in the fields of early childhood education, online education, and more recently, government and welfare technology. Her contributions have informed research and development of new concept products for one start-up and several university organizations. Her interests include studies and explorations on how theory informs practice in design, in particular how human-centered design (HCD) methods can be revised so small organizations can effectively apply them during the fuzzy front end (FFE) process of new product development. Gloria is an assistant professor at the University of Southern Denmark. Prior to this appointment, she intermittently worked for the University of Otago in diverse research and professional capacities. Before her Ph.D. studies, she undertook professional design in multidisciplinary software projects such as the award-winning Proyecto Ludomatica and the CmapTools software project. In addition to her university appointment, Gloria is a strategic consultant in the educational and interaction design of OB3 – a Web application for online academic study that is being developed by OceanBrowser Ltd.

Katia Gonzalez received her Ed.D from Columbia University, Teachers College in New York. She is an Associate Professor of Education at Wagner College and the Faculty Scholar for the Center for Teaching, Learning, and Research. Dr. Gonzalez's expertise is in curriculum development and teacher preparation, early childhood, intellectual disabilities, and autism. Research interests include the role of discussion and group dynamics in teacher education, strategies, and techniques to enhance and measure critical thinking and the impact of community and family in inclusive education.

James Gorman holds a Masters Degree in Chemical and Life Sciences from the University of Maryland. With over 10 years of experience, he teaches physics and chemistry at Northbridge High School in Whitinsville, MA, and is an educational consultant who specializes in applying meaningful learning techniques in the classroom. In particular, he emphasizes the use of concept mapping to facilitate the elucidation of student understanding. His work on applications of concept mapping in the classroom has been published and presented at the Massachusetts Computer Using Teachers Conference (MassCUE), National Science Teachers Association (NSTA) conference, and the International Conference on Concept Mapping. James has also collaborated with the Massachusetts Department of Elementary and Secondary Education (MADESE) to create strand maps of the Massachusetts Science and Technology/Engineering Curriculum Framework. His focus was the construction of the physical sciences (chemistry and physics) and technology/engineering strands. James has consulted for the Boston Museum of Science during the development of a full-year course called *Engineering the Future: Science, Technology, and the Design Process*™. The unit concept map he developed was published in the teacher manual.

Robin Griffiths is Director of Occupational and Aviation Medicine, University of Otago Wellington, New Zealand. He heads a "virtual department" of 18 academic staff based in North America, Middle East, Europe, and Australasia, who provide international distance teaching and research supervision to students in every continent (including Antarctica) in aviation medicine, occupational medicine, and aeromedical retrieval and transport. His research interests include creating learning communities in international distance learning and use of technology to overcome barriers to participation.

Jane Heinze-Fry, Ph.D., currently serves as the Special Programs Director at the Museum Institute for Teaching Science (MITS). She is an experienced educational collaborator, presenter, teacher, researcher, and writer. She works with colleagues across Massachusetts to offer professional development institutes in hands-on, minds-on, inquiry-based science to K-12 teachers. Jane has presented extensively at state and national science education conferences. Her teaching experience ranges from courses in teaching methods at the graduate level to life science courses at the middle school, high school, and college levels. In addition to her teaching experience, she consulted with the Massachusetts Department of Elementary and Secondary

Education to develop the life science and earth science strand maps of the science, technology/engineering framework. Jane's writing includes journal articles that address various applications of concept mapping to science education and instructional materials to accompany environmental science textbooks. She earned her Ph.D. in Science and Environmental Education from Cornell University.

Camille B. Kandiko Howson is a Research Fellow at King's College London, working on curriculum and student enhancement initiatives. Her research focuses on international and comparative higher education, with areas of interest in the student experience, student engagement, and the curriculum; interdisciplinarity and creativity; academic motivation and prestige; PhD supervision; and developing the use of concept mapping in higher education. Supporting this research are notions of networks in higher education, the role of student engagement in the student experience and the environment for learning, and intersectionality as a methodological approach to exploring student and academic identities. Camille holds degrees in English and Classics from Cornell University and a Master's in Higher Education Administration from The University of Pennsylvania. She was awarded her PhD by Indiana University. Before taking up her post at the Institute, she was Project Associate at IU working on the National Survey of Student Engagement (NSSE).

Ian Kinchin is Head of the Department of Higher Education at the University of Surrey, UK. His current research is focused on the development of the "expert student" through the application of concept mapping. Ian is the editor of the *Journal of Biological Education*. He is an advisory committee member for the series of International Concept Mapping Conferences (http://cmc.ihmc.us/), a Senior Fellow of the Higher Education Academy, and is a member of the Governing Council of the Society for Research into Higher Education. He is also a Bruce Springsteen fan.

Marcus Vinicius Santos Kucharski is a professor at the Federal University of Technology – Paraná (UTFPr) in Curitiba, Brazil, where he acts as deputy coordinator of the Educational Technology Office, and a researcher in the areas of Educational Technology and Teacher Training. He has dedicated the last 15 years to developing teaching-learning strategies supported by digital technologies and to promoting the effective use of such technologies in regular and distance courses. Given that his academic origins lie in Linguistic Studies, concept maps as a means of knowledge systematization and as a critical pre-writing tool have been a constant target of his interests. Professor Kucharski holds Licentiate degrees in Languages (Portuguese and English), Specialist's degrees in Portuguese Language and Brazilian Literature Teaching, and also Master's and Ph.D. degrees in Education.

Rita de Cassia Veiga Marriott holds a Master's in Education from the Catholic University of Parana (PUC-PR), where she is a PhD candidate in Education. She is currently an English language teacher and was an English language teacher at PUC-PR for 5 years and at the Federal University of Parana (UFPR) for 3 years; she was also a Portuguese language teacher at the University of Birmingham for 6 years (including 2 years as course coordinator). Her areas of interest are teacher training, language teaching, concept mapping, second language acquisition, and distance learning. She has several publications including the co-edited *Handbook of Research on E-Learning Methodologies for Language Acquisition* (2009) and *Handbook of Research on Collaborative Learning using Concept Mapping* (2010) published by the Information Science Reference, USA.

Margaret L. Merrill was born and raised in Cincinnati, Ohio. After moving to Massachusetts, she graduated from Curry College in 1984 with a degree in Early Childhood Education. Dr. Merrill completed her masters in Early Childhood Education at Wheelock College in 1986. For the following 21 years, she taught at the elementary level in private and public schools. In 2005, after being nominated for and winning a Presidential Award for Excellence in Mathematics and Science Teaching, Dr. Merrill left the elementary classroom environment to become an Education Fellow in the offices of Senator Joseph Lieberman on Capitol Hill for one year. At the conclusion of the fellowship, she applied for and was accepted into the University of Maine's College of Education and Human Development graduate program. Dr. Merrill graduated in August 2012 with a Doctorate of Education Degree (Individualized Program) from the University of Maine. Recently, she traveled to Malta to present her research at the 5th International Concept Mapping Conference.

John Montgomery received his Ph.D. in Neuroscience from Caltech in Pasadena, California, and his B.A. in Molecular Genetics from Trinity College in Dublin, Ireland. Currently an Adjunct Professor in the Department of Psychology at the State University of New York at New Paltz, he is the primary author of *The Answer Model Theory and the Answer Model: A New Path to Healing*. He has also written for *The Washington Post*, *The Economist*, and *Psychology Today*.

Pooshan Navathe, MBBS, Dip Occ Med, Dip Aviation Safety Regulation, B Ed, MD, MBA, FAFOEM (RACP), FRACMA, FRAeS, FACAsM, PhD, is the Principal Medical Officer at the Australian Civil Aviation Safety Authority's Office of Aviation Medicine. Dr. Navathe has spent over three decades in aviation medicine, occupational medicine, and medical leadership. Navathe is a thought leader in areas of operational and clinical aviation medicine, with his current interest surrounding aeromedical decision making. While having remained a practitioner throughout his career, he has participated in research, as demonstrated by the preparation of more than 175 articles and scientific presentations to professional societies. He has been a teacher for over two decades, continues to teach clinical aviation medicine, and with his active involvement in research and teaching, continues to be actively involved in the assessment and mentoring of physicians in all areas of his expertise.

Roxanne O'Connell, Ph.D., is associate professor and Chair of the Department of Communication at Roger Williams University teaching visual communication and digital media. Her work has been published in edited books and journals such as *Visualizing the Web* (Peter Lang) and *The Internet Media Review* (now published by Mequoda.com). She is the editor of the two-volume series *Teaching with Multimedia* (Hampton Press) and the editor-in-chief of the *Proceedings for the New York State Communication Association*. Her professional life has fallen into two areas: visual media and music. As a teacher and Web publishing consultant with more than 20 years of experience in design, e-commerce, and marketing, she specializes in information design, audience research, and Website usability. Media research interests include traditional and digital media, particularly blogging and podcasting, perception, and visual rhetoric. A musician since age 12, she has performed with her husband, Robbie O'Connell, on stages large and small, from coffeehouses to international music festivals, in village pubs and on outdoor stages. Before she started teaching at university, she recorded backup vocals on five CDs. She now uses what she knows about media and sound to teach her students how to create multimodal narratives and essays.

Yasemin Oral is an Assistant Professor of English language teaching at Istanbul University, Turkey, where she teaches courses in foreign/second language teaching methodology, critical reading and thinking, and research methods. She received both her MA and doctoral degrees in English language teaching from Istanbul University. Her doctoral research involved an investigation into classroom power relations in an English as a foreign language setting. Her primary research interests include critical pedagogies, cultural aspects of language teaching/learning and identity and language learning. She is currently working on her postdoctoral research on the intersections of issues of identity and English language learning/use.

Amina Sadik is interested in identifying anticarcinogenic compounds in plant extracts as adjuvant therapy for breast cancer, skin cancer and human leukemia and determining the mechanism of action of these compounds. She is also looking into the antioxidative effects of commonly consumed berries and Yerba Maté in human myocardiocytes. She involves medical students and graduate students in all her research projects. Her scholarly activities include conducting workshops, giving presentations at national and international conferences regarding medical education, and publishing peer review papers on quantitative and qualitative research. She works diligently to demonstrate the relevance of the basic sciences in the practice of medicine.

Baruch B. Schwarz began his career as a mathematician and as a researcher in mathematics education. He first focused on the role of computerized environments in conceptual learning. The recognition of the importance of argumentative forms of talk in mathematics classrooms led him to widen his research focus on the study of relationships between argumentation and learning in general. He has led many European R&D projects dedicated to the development of technologies to enhance argumentation and collaborative learning in small groups. His current research directions include argumentation and conceptual change, small group moderation, dialogic teaching, mathematical abstraction, social networks and learning/teaching, and traditional dyadic Yeshiva learning.

Bev Smith has been an elementary school teacher for the past 26 years. She has taught all elementary school grades, but for the majority of her career, she has worked with primary-aged students. Bev obtained her Bachelor of Education degree from the University of Saskatchewan in 1986. She completed her Master of Education degree at the University of Lethbridge in 2012 and focused her research in the area of literacy, particularly the instruction of writing and student engagement. Throughout her career, Bev has strived to continually improve literacy instruction in her classroom. As a result, she has worked with teachers in a variety of regions across Canada. Particularly noteworthy is the work she has done with teachers from remote communities in Nunavut, travelling there twice to collaborate with teachers to improve the literacy instruction for their students. Bev is currently a literacy coach with Palliser School District in Alberta, Canada.

Kristen Snyder is an Associate Professor in Education at Mid Sweden University since 2001. Originally from the U.S., Snyder received her Ph.D. in Educational Research with an emphasis on school and leadership development. Snyder's work is grounded in cultural studies, which she combines with her formal training and experience in the arts as a musician and graphic designer. For more than 20 years, Snyder has been driven by questions about how educators can generate learning environments that are stimulating for students, based on discovery learning and creativity. In more recent years, she has focused on the role of technology and the potential it affords for pedagogical innovation in a global context of learning.

Patricia Lupion Torres has been a lecturer at the Catholic University of Parana (PUC-PR, Brazil) since 1981. She holds a Ph.D. in Production and Knowledge Engineering from the Federal University of Santa Catarina (2002). At PUC-PR, she was the Director of Distance Education (2005-2009), the Director of Education (1995-1999 and 2003-2005); in addition, she was responsible for the Evaluation and Research sector for the Distance Learning Center (2002-2003). She has published books in the Dominican Republic, UK, USA, Colombia, Mexico, Portugal, and Brazil. Her experience is in Education, mainly in the following areas: educational technology, distance learning, professional training, teacher training, higher education. She is currently a tenured professor of the master's and doctorate courses in Education at PUCPr, the Education coordinator for the National Service for Rural Learning (SENAR-PR), and the Director for the Brazilian Distance Learning Association (ABED – Associação Brasileira de Educação a Distância).

Israel Ury received BSc and MSc degrees in Engineering from the University of California at Los Angeles. In 1980, he received a PhD degree in Applied Physics from the California Institute of Technology for work done on semiconductor lasers and optoelectronics. In that same year, he and two colleagues founded Ortel Corporation where he served as Chief Technology Officer for twenty years. Ortel revolutionized and supplied the cable television industry with the technology to replace coaxial cables with high capacity optical fibers. In 2000, Israel founded and became a Director of Maalot Los Angeles, a liberal arts college. He and his wife moved to Israel in 2008, and since then, he has been developing visual methods for teaching and understanding the Talmud. In 2011, he published *Charting the Sea of Talmud*, which introduced the method of Talmud Diagrams.

Chigozirim Utah is a doctoral student studying organizational communication and rhetoric at the University of Nebraska, Lincoln with an emphasis in organizational communication. She studies how macro-level and global discourses affect everyday organizing and identity construction. Most of her research is focused on illuminating possibilities for more effective organizing in the African context. She is also passionate about undergraduate education and seeks to empower her students to make the most of their college experience by taking charge of their own learning. She currently teaches intercultural communication and business and professional communication. Besides academics, she enjoys music, Charles Dickens novels, and copious amounts of tea and chocolate.

Alexis Waters is an interpersonal and family communication scholar with an emphasis in health communication and a doctoral student at the University of Nebraska, Lincoln. She is interested in how people communicate about and make sense of trauma and marginalization in the health sector. In the area of pedagogy, she seeks to discover ways to engage students in the critical thinking process and help them gain knowledge and skills that will be applicable to their everyday lives. Alexis hopes to continue doing research that will help students, trauma victims, and marginalized groups make sense of their experiences.

Index